SAS | SAS Publishing

Personal property
of Dr. Toichoa
2011

SAS/ETS® 9.1

User's Guide
Volume 3

The Power to Know.

The correct bibliographic citation for this manual is as follows: SAS Institute Inc. 2004. *SAS/ETS® 9.1 User's Guide.* Cary, NC: SAS Institute Inc.

SAS/ETS® 9.1 User's Guide

ISBN 1-59047-244-6

SAS Institute Inc., SAS Campus Drive, Cary, North Carolina 27513.

1st printing, January 2004

Contents

Chapter 20
The MODEL Procedure

Chapter Contents

Chapter 20
The MODEL Procedure

Overview

The MODEL procedure analyzes models in which the relationships among the variables comprise a system of one or more nonlinear equations. Primary uses of the MODEL procedure are estimation, simulation, and forecasting of nonlinear simultaneous equation models.

PROC MODEL features include

- SAS programming statements to define simultaneous systems of nonlinear equations
- tools to analyze the structure of the simultaneous equation system
- ARIMA, PDL, and other dynamic modeling capabilities
- tools to specify and estimate the error covariance structure
- tools to estimate and solve ordinary differential equations
- the following methods for parameter estimation:
  - Ordinary Least Squares (OLS)
  - Two-Stage Least Squares (2SLS)
  - Seemingly Unrelated Regression (SUR) and iterative SUR (ITSUR)
  - Three-Stage Least Squares (3SLS) and iterative 3SLS (IT3SLS)
  - Generalized Method of Moments (GMM)
  - Simulated Method of Moments (SMM)
  - Full Information Maximum Likelihood (FIML)
  - General Log-Likelihood maximization
- simulation and forecasting capabilities
- Monte Carlo simulation
- goal seeking solutions

Experimental graphics are now available with the MODEL procedure. For more information, see the "ODS Graphics" section on page 1166.

A system of equations can be nonlinear in the parameters, nonlinear in the observed variables, or nonlinear in both the parameters and the variables. *Nonlinear* in the parameters means that the mathematical relationship between the variables and parameters is not required to have a linear form. (A linear model is a special case of a nonlinear model.) A general nonlinear system of equations can be written as

$$\begin{aligned}
q_1(y_{1,t}, y_{2,t}, \ldots, y_{g,t}, x_{1,t}, x_{2,t}, \ldots, x_{m,t}, \theta_1, \theta_2, \ldots, \theta_p) &= \epsilon_{1,t} \\
q_2(y_{1,t}, y_{2,t}, \ldots, y_{g,t}, x_{1,t}, x_{2,t}, \ldots, x_{m,t}, \theta_1, \theta_2, \ldots, \theta_p) &= \epsilon_{2,t} \\
&\vdots \\
q_g(y_{1,t}, y_{2,t}, \ldots, y_{g,t}, x_{1,t}, x_{2,t}, \ldots, x_{m,t}, \theta_1, \theta_2, \ldots, \theta_p) &= \epsilon_{g,t}
\end{aligned}$$

where $y_{i,t}$ is an endogenous variable, $x_{i,t}$ is an exogenous variable, θ_i is a parameter, and ϵ_i is the unknown error. The subscript t represents time or some index to the data. In econometrics literature, the observed variables are either *endogenous* (dependent) variables or *exogenous* (independent) variables. This system can be written more succinctly in vector form as

$$\mathbf{q}(\mathbf{y}_t, \mathbf{x}_t, \theta) = \epsilon_t$$

This system of equations is in *general form* because the error term is by itself on one side of the equality. Systems can also be written in *normalized form* by placing the endogenous variable on one side of the equality, with each equation defining a predicted value for a unique endogenous variable. A normalized form equation system can be written in vector notation as

$$\mathbf{y}_t = \mathbf{f}(\mathbf{y}_t, \mathbf{x}_t, \theta) + \epsilon_t.$$

PROC MODEL handles equations written in both forms.

Econometric models often explain the current values of the endogenous variables as functions of past values of exogenous and endogenous variables. These past values are referred to as *lagged* values, and the variable x_{t-i} is called lag *i* of the variable x_t. Using lagged variables, you can create a *dynamic*, or time dependent, model. In the preceding model systems, the lagged exogenous and endogenous variables are included as part of the exogenous variables.

If the data are time series, so that *t* indexes time (see Chapter 2, "Working with Time Series Data," for more information on time series), it is possible that ϵ_t depends on ϵ_{t-i} or, more generally, the ϵ_t's are not identically and independently distributed. If the errors of a model system are autocorrelated, the standard error of the estimates of the parameters of the system will be inflated.

Sometimes the ϵ_i's are not identically distributed because the variance of ϵ is not constant. This is known as *heteroscedasticity*. Heteroscedasticity in an estimated model can also inflate the standard error of the estimates of the parameters. Using a weighted estimation can sometimes eliminate this problem. Alternately, a variance model such as GARCH or EGARCH can be estimated to correct for heteroscedasticity. If the proper weighting scheme and the form of the error model is difficult to determine, generalized methods of moments (GMM) estimation can be used to determine parameter estimates with very few assumptions about the form of the error process.

Other problems may also arise when estimating systems of equations. Consider the system of equations:

$$
\begin{aligned}
y_{1,t} &= \theta_1 + (\theta_2 + \theta_3\theta_4^t)^{-1} + \theta_5 y_{2,t} + \epsilon_{1,t} \\
y_{2,t} &= \theta_6 + (\theta_7 + \theta_8\theta_9^t)^{-1} + \theta_{10} y_{1,t} + \epsilon_{2,t}
\end{aligned}
$$

which is nonlinear in its parameters and cannot be estimated with linear regression. This system of equations represents a rudimentary predator-prey process with y_1 as the prey and y_2 as the predator (the second term in both equations is a logistics curve). The two equations must be estimated simultaneously because of the cross dependency of y's. This cross-dependency makes ϵ_1 and ϵ_2 violate the assumption of indpendence. Nonlinear ordinary least-squares estimation of these equations will produce biased and inconsistent parameter estimates. This is called *simultaneous equation bias*.

One method to remove simultaneous equation bias, in the linear case, is to replace the endogenous variables on the right-hand side of the equations with predicted values that are uncorrelated with the error terms. These predicted values can be obtained through a preliminary, or "first stage," *instrumental variable regression. Instrumental variables*, which are uncorrelated with the error term, are used as regressors to model the predicted values. The parameter estimates are obtained by a second regression using the predicted values of the regressors. This process is called *two-stage least squares*.

In the nonlinear case, nonlinear ordinary least-squares estimation is performed iteratively using a linearization of the model with respect to the parameters. The instrumental solution to simultaneous equation bias in the nonlinear case is the same as the linear case except the linearization of the model with respect to the parameters is predicted by the instrumental regression. Nonlinear two-stage least squares is one of several instrumental variables methods available in the MODEL procedure to handle simultaneous equation bias.

When you have a system of several regression equations, the random errors of the equations can be correlated. In this case, the large-sample efficiency of the estimation can be improved by using a joint generalized least-squares method that takes the cross-equation correlations into account. If the equations are not simultaneous (no dependent regressors), then *seemingly unrelated regression* (SUR) can be used. The SUR method requires an estimate of the cross-equation error covariance matrix, Σ. The usual approach is to first fit the equations using OLS, compute an estimate $\hat{\Sigma}$ from the OLS residuals, and then perform the SUR estimation based on $\hat{\Sigma}$. The MODEL procedure estimates Σ by default, or you can supply your own estimate of Σ.

If the equation system is simultaneous, you can combine the 2SLS and SUR methods to take into account both simultaneous equation bias and cross-equation correlation of the errors. This is called *three-stage least squares* or 3SLS.

A different approach to the simultaneous equation bias problem is the full information maximum likelihood, or FIML, estimation method. FIML does not require instrumental variables, but it assumes that the equation errors have a multivariate normal distribution. 2SLS and 3SLS estimation do not assume a particular distribution for the errors.

Other non-normal error distribution models can be estimated as well. The centered t-distribution with estimated degrees of freedom and non-constant variance is an additional built in likelihood function. If the distribution of the equation errors is not normal or t but known, then the log likelihood can be specified using the ERRORMODEL statement.

Once a nonlinear model has been estimated, it can be used to obtain forecasts. If the model is linear in the variables you want to forecast, a simple linear solve can generate the forecasts. If the system is nonlinear, an iterative procedure must be used. The preceding example system is linear in its endogenous variables. The MODEL procedure's SOLVE statement is used to forecast nonlinear models.

One of the main purposes of creating models is to obtain an understanding of the relationship among the variables. There are usually only a few variables in a model you can control (for example, the amount of money spent on advertising). Often you want to determine how to change the variables under your control to obtain some target goal. This process is called *goal seeking*. PROC MODEL allows you to solve for any subset of the variables in a system of equations given values for the remaining variables.

The nonlinearity of a model creates two problems with the forecasts: the forecast errors are not normally distributed with zero mean, and no formula exits to calculate the forecast confidence intervals. PROC MODEL provides Monte Carlo techniques, which, when used with the covariance of the parameters and error covariance matrix, can produce approximate error bounds on the forecasts. The following distributions on the errors are supported for multivariate Monte Carlo simulation:

- Cauchy
- Chi-squared
- Empirical
- F
- Poisson
- t
- Uniform

A transformation technique is used to create a covariance matrix for generating the correct innovations in a Monte Carlo simulation.

Getting Started

This section introduces the MODEL procedure and shows how to use PROC MODEL for several kinds of nonlinear regression analysis and nonlinear systems simulation problems.

Nonlinear Regression Analysis

One of the most important uses of PROC MODEL is to estimate unknown parameters in a nonlinear model. A simple nonlinear model has the form:

$$y = f(\mathbf{x}, \theta) + \epsilon$$

where $\mathbf{x}$ is a vector of exogenous variables. To estimate unknown parameters using PROC MODEL, do the following:

1. Use the DATA= option in a PROC MODEL statement to specify the input SAS data set containing $\mathbf{y}$ and $\mathbf{x}$, the observed values of the variables.
2. Write the equation for the model using SAS programming statements, including all parameters and arithmetic operators but leaving off the unobserved error component, ϵ.
3. Use a FIT statement to fit the model equation to the input data to determine the unknown parameters, θ.

An Example

The SASHELP library contains the data set CITIMON, which contains the variable LHUR, the monthly unemployment figures, and the variable IP, the monthly industrial production index. You suspect that the unemployment rates are inversely proportional to the industrial production index. Assume that these variables are related by the following nonlinear equation:

$$lhur = \frac{1}{a \cdot \mathrm{ip} + b} + c + \epsilon$$

In this equation *a*, *b*, and *c* are unknown coefficients and ϵ is an unobserved random error.

The following statements illustrate how to use PROC MODEL to estimate values for *a*, *b*, and *c* from the data in SASHELP.CITIMON.

```
proc model data=sashelp.citimon;
   lhur = 1/(a * ip + b) + c;
   fit lhur;
run;
```

Notice that the model equation is written as a SAS assignment statement. The variable LHUR is assumed to be the dependent variable because it is named in the FIT statement and is on the left-hand side of the assignment.

PROC MODEL determines that LHUR and IP are observed variables because they are in the input data set. A, B, and C are treated as unknown parameters to be estimated from the data because they are not in the input data set. If the data set contained a variable named A, B, or C, you would need to explicitly declare the parameters with a PARMS statement.

In response to the FIT statement, PROC MODEL estimates values for A, B, and C using nonlinear least squares and prints the results. The first part of the output is a "Model Summary table, shown in Figure 20.1.

```
                 The MODEL Procedure

                    Model Summary

            Model Variables            1
            Parameters                 3
            Equations                  1
            Number of Statements       1


              Model Variables   LHUR
                   Parameters   a b c
                    Equations   LHUR
```

Figure 20.1. Model Summary Report

This table details the size of the model, including the number of programming statements defining the model, and lists the dependent variables (LHUR in this case), the unknown parameters (A, B, and C), and the model equations. In this case the equation is named for the dependent variable, LHUR.

PROC MODEL then prints a summary of the estimation problem, as shown in Figure 20.2.

```
                 The MODEL Procedure

           The Equation to Estimate is

              LHUR =   F(a, b, c(1))
```

Figure 20.2. Estimation Problem Report

The notation used in the summary of the estimation problem indicates that LHUR is a function of A, B, and C, which are to be estimated by fitting the function to the data. If the partial derivative of the equation with respect to a parameter is a simple variable or constant, the derivative is shown in parentheses after the parameter name. In this case, the derivative with respect to the intercept C is 1. The derivatives with respect to A and B are complex expressions and so are not shown.

Next, PROC MODEL prints an estimation summary as shown in Figure 20.3.

```
                  The MODEL Procedure
                OLS Estimation Summary

                   Data Set Options

              DATA=     SASHELP.CITIMON


                 Minimization Summary

        Parameters Estimated              3
        Method                        Gauss
        Iterations                       10


            Final Convergence Criteria

            R                     0.000737
            PPC(b)                0.003943
            RPC(b)                 0.00968
            Object                4.784E-6
            Trace(S)              0.533325
            Objective Value       0.522214


                 Observations Processed

                    Read        145
                    Solved      145
                    Used        144
                    Missing       1
```

Figure 20.3. Estimation Summary Report

The estimation summary provides information on the iterative process used to compute the estimates. The heading "OLS Estimation Summary" indicates that the nonlinear ordinary least-squares (OLS) estimation method is used. This table indicates that all 3 parameters were estimated successfully using 144 nonmissing observations from the data set SASHELP.CITIMON. Calculating the estimates required 10 iterations of the GAUSS method. Various measures of how well the iterative process converged are also shown. For example, the "RPC(B)" value 0.00968 means that on the final iteration the largest relative change in any estimate was for parameter B, which changed by .968 percent. See the section "Convergence Criteria" later in this chapter for details.

PROC MODEL then prints the estimation results. The first part of this table is the summary of residual errors, shown in Figure 20.4.

```
                          The MODEL Procedure

              Nonlinear OLS Summary of Residual Errors

                   DF       DF                                               Adj
Equation        Model    Error          SSE         MSE    R-Square         R-Sq

LHUR                3      141      75.1989      0.5333      0.7472       0.7436
```

Figure 20.4. Summary of Residual Errors Report

This table lists the sum of squared errors (SSE), the mean square error (MSE), the root mean square error (Root MSE), and the R^2 and adjusted R^2 statistics. The R^2 value of .7472 means that the estimated model explains approximately 75 percent more of the variability in LHUR than a mean model explains.

Following the summary of residual errors is the parameter estimates table, shown in Figure 20.5.

```
                          The MODEL Procedure

                  Nonlinear OLS Parameter Estimates

                                     Approx                     Approx
Parameter          Estimate         Std Err     t Value       Pr > |t|

a                  0.009046         0.00343        2.63         0.0094
b                  -0.57059          0.2617       -2.18         0.0309
c                  3.337151          0.7297        4.57         <.0001
```

Figure 20.5. Parameter Estimates

Because the model is nonlinear, the standard error of the estimate, the t value, and its significance level are only approximate. These values are computed using asymptotic formulas that are correct for large sample sizes but only approximately correct for smaller samples. Thus, you should use caution in interpreting these statistics for nonlinear models, especially for small sample sizes. For linear models, these results are exact and are the same as standard linear regression.

The last part of the output produced by the FIT statement is shown in Figure 20.6.

```
                          The MODEL Procedure

        Number of Observations          Statistics for System

        Used                144        Objective           0.5222
        Missing               1        Objective*N        75.1989
```

Figure 20.6. System Summary Statistics

This table lists the objective value for the estimation of the nonlinear system, which is a weighted system mean square error. This statistic can be used for testing cross-equation restrictions in multi-equation regression problems. See the section "Restrictions and Bounds on Parameters" for details. Since there is only a single equation in this case, the objective value is the same as the residual MSE for LHUR except that the objective value does not include a degrees of freedom correction. This can be seen in the fact that "Objective*N" equals the residual SSE, 75.1989. N is 144, the number of observations used.

Convergence and Starting Values

Computing parameter estimates for nonlinear equations requires an iterative process. Starting with an initial guess for the parameter values, PROC MODEL tries different parameter values until the objective function of the estimation method is minimized.

(The objective function of the estimation method is sometimes called the *fitting function.*) This process does not always succeed, and whether it does succeed depends greatly on the starting values used. By default, PROC MODEL uses the starting value .0001 for all parameters.

Consequently, in order to use PROC MODEL to achieve convergence of parameter estimates, you need to know two things: how to recognize convergence failure by interpreting diagnostic output, and how to specify reasonable starting values. The MODEL procedure includes alternate iterative techniques and grid search capabilities to aid in finding estimates. See the section "Troubleshooting Convergence Problems" for more details.

Nonlinear Systems Regression

If a model has more than one endogenous variable, several facts need to be considered in the choice of an estimation method. If the model has endogenous regressors, then an instrumental variables method such as 2SLS or 3SLS can be used to avoid simultaneous equation bias. Instrumental variables must be provided to use these methods. A discussion of possible choices for instrumental variables is provided in the the section "Choice of Instruments" on page 1135 in this chapter.

The following is an example of the use of 2SLS and the INSTRUMENTS statement:

```
proc model data=test2 ;
   exogenous x1 x2;
   parms a1 a2 b2 2.5 c2 55 d1;

   y1 = a1 * y2 + b2 * x1 * x1 + d1;
   y2 = a2 * y1 + b2 * x2 * x2 + c2 / x2 + d1;

   fit y1 y2 / 2sls;
   instruments b2 c2 _exog_;
run;
```

The estimation method selected is added after the slash (/) on the FIT statement. The INSTRUMENTS statement follows the FIT statement and in this case selects all the exogenous variables as instruments with the _EXOG_ keyword. The parameters B2 and C2 on the instruments list request that the derivatives with respect to B2 and C2 be additional instruments.

Full information maximum likelihood (FIML) can also be used to avoid simultaneous equation bias. FIML is computationally more expensive than an instrumental variables method and assumes that the errors are normally distributed. On the other hand, FIML does not require the specification of instruments. FIML is selected with the FIML option on the FIT statement.

The preceding example is estimated with FIML using the following statements:

```
proc model data=test2 ;
   exogenous x1 x2;
   parms a1 a2 b2 2.5 c2 55 d1;

   y1 = a1 * y2 + b2 * x1 * x1 + d1;
   y2 = a2 * y1 + b2 * x2 * x2 + c2 / x2 + d1;

   fit y1 y2 / fiml;
run;
```

General Form Models

The single equation example shown in the preceding section was written in normalized form and specified as an assignment of the regression function to the dependent variable LHUR. However, sometimes it is impossible or inconvenient to write a nonlinear model in normalized form.

To write a general form equation, give the equation a name with the prefix "EQ." . This EQ.-prefixed variable represents the equation error. Write the equation as an assignment to this variable.

For example, suppose you have the following nonlinear model relating the variables x and y:

$$\epsilon = a + b \ln(cy + dx)$$

Naming this equation 'one', you can fit this model with the following statements:

```
proc model data=xydata;
   eq.one = a + b * log( c * y + d * x );
   fit one;
run;
```

The use of the EQ. prefix tells PROC MODEL that the variable is an error term and that it should not expect actual values for the variable ONE in the input data set.

Supply and Demand Models

General form specifications are often useful when you have several equations for the same dependent variable. This is common in supply and demand models, where both the supply equation and the demand equation are written as predictions for quantity as functions of price.

For example, consider the following supply and demand system:

$$\text{(supply)} \qquad \text{quantity} = \alpha_1 + \alpha_2 \,\text{price} + \epsilon_1$$

$$\text{(demand)} \qquad \text{quantity} = \beta_1 + \beta_2\,\text{price} + \beta_3\,\text{income} + \epsilon_2$$

Assume the *quantity* of interest is the amount of energy consumed in the U.S.; the *price* is the price of gasoline, and the *income* variable is the consumer debt. When the market is at equilibrium, these equations determine the market price and the equilibrium quantity. These equations are written in general form as

$$\epsilon_1 = quantity - (\alpha_1 + \alpha_2\, price)$$

$$\epsilon_2 = quantity - (\beta_1 + \beta_2\, price + \beta_3\, income)$$

Note that the endogenous variables *quantity* and *price* depend on two error terms so that OLS should not be used. The following example uses three-stage least-squares estimation.

Data for this model is obtained from the SASHELP.CITIMON data set.

```
title1 'Supply-Demand Model using General-form Equations';
proc model data=sashelp.citimon;
   endogenous eegp eec;
   exogenous exvus cciutc;
   parameters a1 a2 b1 b2 b3 ;
   label eegp   = 'Gasoline Retail Price'
         eec    = 'Energy Consumption'
         cciutc = 'Consumer Debt';

   /* -------- Supply equation ------------- */
   eq.supply = eec - (a1 + a2 * eegp );

   /* -------- Demand equation ------------- */
   eq.demand = eec - (b1 + b2 * eegp + b3 * cciutc);

   /* -------- Instrumental variables -------*/
   lageegp = lag(eegp); lag2eegp=lag2(eegp);

   /* -------- Estimate parameters --------- */
   fit supply demand / n3sls fsrsq;
   instruments _EXOG_ lageegp lag2eegp;
run;
```

The FIT statement specifies the two equations to estimate and the method of estimation, N3SLS. Note that '3SLS' is an alias for N3SLS. The option FSRSQ is selected to get a report of the first stage R^2 to determine the acceptability of the selected instruments.

Since three-stage least squares is an instrumental variables method, instruments are specified with the INSTRUMENTS statement. The instruments selected are all the exogenous variables, selected with the _EXOG_ option, and two lags of the variable EEGP, LAGEEGP and LAG2EEGP.

The data set CITIMON has four observations that generate missing values because values for either EEGP, EEC, or CCIUTC are missing. This is revealed in the "Observations Processed" output shown in Figure 20.7. Missing values are also generated when the equations cannot be computed for a given observation. Missing observations are not used in the estimation.

```
                Supply-Demand Model using General-form Equations

                            The MODEL Procedure
                          3SLS Estimation Summary

                          Observations Processed

                            Read         145
                            Solved       143
                            First          3
                            Last         145
                            Used         139
                            Missing        4
                            Lagged         2
```

Figure 20.7. Supply-Demand Observations Processed

The lags used to create the instruments also reduce the number of observations used. In this case, the first 2 observations were used to fill the lags of EEGP.

The data set has a total of 145 observations, of which 4 generated missing values and 2 were used to fill lags, which left 139 observations for the estimation. In the estimation summary, in Figure 20.8, the total degrees of freedom for the model and error is 139.

```
                 Supply-Demand Model using General-form Equations

                               The MODEL Procedure

                   Nonlinear 3SLS Summary of Residual Errors

                   DF      DF                                                  Adj
Equation        Model   Error        SSE       MSE   Root MSE   R-Square      R-Sq

supply              2     137    43.2677    0.3158     0.5620
demand              3     136    39.5791    0.2910     0.5395


                       Nonlinear 3SLS Parameter Estimates

                                                                               1st
                                     Approx                       Approx      Stage
  Parameter         Estimate        Std Err     t Value    Pr > |t|     R-Square

  a1                 7.30952         0.3799       19.24      <.0001       1.0000
  a2                -0.00853        0.00328       -2.60      0.0103       0.9617
  b1                 6.82196         0.3788       18.01      <.0001       1.0000
  b2                -0.00614        0.00303       -2.02      0.0450       0.9617
  b3                    9E-7       3.165E-7        2.84      0.0051       1.0000
```

Figure 20.8. Supply-Demand Parameter Estimates

One disadvantage of specifying equations in general form is that there are no actual values associated with the equation, so the R^2 statistic cannot be computed.

Solving Simultaneous Nonlinear Equation Systems

You can use a SOLVE statement to solve the nonlinear equation system for some variables when the values of other variables are given.

Consider the demand and supply model shown in the preceding example. The following statement computes equilibrium price (EEGP) and quantity (EEC) values for given observed cost (CCIUTC) values and stores them in the output data set EQUILIB.

```
title1 'Supply-Demand Model using General-form Equations';
proc model data=sashelp.citimon;
   endogenous eegp eec;
   exogenous exvus cciutc;
   parameters a1 a2 a3 b1 b2 ;
   label eegp   = 'Gasoline Retail Price'
         eec    = 'Energy Consumption'
         cciutc = 'Consumer Debt';

   /* -------- Supply equation ------------- */
   eq.supply = eec - (a1 + a2 * eegp + a3 * cciutc);

   /* -------- Demand equation ------------- */
   eq.demand = eec - (b1 + b2 * eegp );

   /* -------- Instrumental variables -------*/
   lageegp = lag(eegp); lag2eegp=lag2(eegp);

   /* -------- Estimate parameters --------- */
   instruments _EXOG_ lageegp lag2eegp;
   fit supply demand / n3sls ;
   solve eegp eec / out=equilib;
run;
```

As a second example, suppose you want to compute points of intersection between the square root function and hyperbolas of the form $a + b/x$. That is, solve the system:

$$\text{(square root)} \qquad y = \sqrt{x}$$

$$\text{(hyperbola)} \qquad y = a + \frac{b}{x}$$

The following statements read parameters for several hyperbolas in the input data set TEST and solve the nonlinear equations. The SOLVEPRINT option on the SOLVE statement prints the solution values. The ID statement is used to include the values of A and B in the output of the SOLVEPRINT option.

```
data test;
  input a b @@;
  datalines;
  0 1   1 1   1 2
;

proc model data=test;
   eq.sqrt      = sqrt(x) - y;
   eq.hyperbola = a + b / x - y;
   solve x y / solveprint;
   id a b;
run;
```

The printed output produced by this example consists of a model summary report, a listing of the solution values for each observation, and a solution summary report. The model summary for this example is shown in Figure 20.9.

```
              Supply-Demand Model using General-form Equations

                          The MODEL Procedure

                            Model Summary

                      Model Variables          2
                      ID Variables             2
                      Equations                2
                      Number of Statements     2


                   Model Variables  x y
                         Equations  sqrt hyperbola
```

Figure 20.9. Model Summary Report

The output produced by the SOLVEPRINT option is shown in Figure 20.10.

```
                          The MODEL Procedure
                        Simultaneous Simulation

Observation   1  a                 0  b       1.0000  eq.hyperbola    0.000000
                 Iterations       17  CC    0.000000


                            Solution Values

                             x                 y

                      1.000000          1.000000


Observation   2  a            1.0000  b       1.0000  eq.hyperbola    0.000000
                 Iterations        5  CC    0.000000


                            Solution Values

                             x                 y

                      2.147899          1.465571


Observation   3  a            1.0000  b       2.0000  eq.hyperbola    0.000000
                 Iterations        4  CC    0.000000


                            Solution Values

                             x                 y

                      2.875130          1.695621
```

Figure 20.10. Solution Values for Each Observation

For each observation, a heading line is printed that lists the values of the ID variables for the observation and information on the iterative process used to compute the solution. Following the heading line for the observation, the solution values are printed.

The heading line shows the solution method used (Newton's method by default), the number of iterations required, and the convergence measure, labeled CC=. This convergence measure indicates the maximum error by which solution values fail to satisfy the equations. When this error is small enough (as determined by the CONVERGE= option), the iterations terminate. The equation with the largest error is indicated in parentheses. For example, for observation 3 the HYPERBOLA equation has an error of 4.42×10^{-13} while the error of the SQRT equation is even smaller.

The last part of the SOLVE statement output is the solution summary report shown in Figure 20.11. This report summarizes the iteration history and the model solved.

```
                 The MODEL Procedure
               Simultaneous Simulation

                  Data Set Options

                  DATA=     TEST


                  Solution Summary

          Variables Solved                 2
          Implicit Equations               2
          Solution Method             NEWTON
          CONVERGE=                     1E-8
          Maximum CC                 9.176E-9
          Maximum Iterations              17
          Total Iterations                26
          Average Iterations        8.666667


               Observations Processed

                    Read       3
                    Solved     3


     Variables Solved For      x y
     Equations Solved          sqrt hyperbola
```

Figure 20.11. Solution Summary Report

Monte Carlo Simulation

The RANDOM= option is used to request Monte Carlo (or stochastic) simulation to generate confidence intervals for a forecast. The confidence intervals are implied by the model's relationship to the the implicit random error term ϵ and the parameters.

The Monte Carlo simulation generates a random set of additive error values, one for each observation and each equation, and computes one set of perturbations of the parameters. These new parameters, along with the additive error terms, are then used to compute a new forecast that satisfies this new simultaneous system. Then a new set of additive error values and parameter perturbations is computed, and the process is repeated the requested number of times.

Consider the following exchange rate model for the U.S. dollar with the German mark and the Japanese yen:

$$rate\_jp = a_1 + b_1 im\_jp + c_1 di\_jp;$$

$$rate\_wg = a_2 + b_2 im\_wg + c_1 di\_wg;$$

where *rate_jp* and *rate_wg* are the exchange rate of the Japanese yen and the German mark versus the U.S. dollar respectively; *im_jp* and *im_wg* are the imports from Japan and Germany in 1984 dollars respectively; and *di_jp* and *di_wg* are the differences in inflation rate of Japan and the U.S., and Germany and the U.S. respectively. The

Monte Carlo capabilities of the MODEL procedure are used to generate error bounds on a forecast using this model.

```
proc model data=exchange;
   endo im_jp im_wg;
   exo di_jp di_wg;
   parms a1 a2 b1 b2 c1 c2;
   label rate_jp = 'Exchange Rate of Yen/$'
         rate_wg = 'Exchange Rate of Gm/$'
         im_jp = 'Imports to US from Japan in 1984 $'
         im_wg = 'Imports to US from WG in 1984 $'
         di_jp = 'Difference in Inflation Rates US-JP'
         di_wg = 'Difference in Inflation Rates US-WG';

   rate_jp = a1 + b1*im_jp + c1*di_jp;
   rate_wg = a2 + b2*im_wg + c2*di_wg;

            /* Fit the EXCHANGE data */
   fit rate_jp rate_wg / sur outest=xch_est outcov outs=s;

            /* Solve using the WHATIF data set */
   solve rate_jp rate_wg / data=whatif estdata=xch_est sdata=s
         random=100 seed=123 out=monte forecast;
   id yr;
   range yr=1986;
run;
```

Data for the EXCHANGE data set was obtained from the Department of Commerce and the yearly "Economic Report of the President."

First, the parameters are estimated using SUR selected by the SUR option on the FIT statement. The OUTEST= option is used to create the XCH_EST data set which contains the estimates of the parameters. The OUTCOV option adds the covariance matrix of the parameters to the XCH_EST data set. The OUTS= option is used to save the covariance of the equation error in the data set S.

Next, Monte Carlo simulation is requested using the RANDOM= option on the SOLVE statement. The data set WHATIF, shown below, is used to drive the forecasts. The ESTDATA= option reads in the XCH_EST data set which contains the parameter estimates and covariance matrix. Because the parameter covariance matrix is included, perturbations of the parameters are performed. The SDATA= option causes the Monte Carlo simulation to use the equation error covariance in the S data set to perturb the equation errors. The SEED= option selects the number 123 as seed value for the random number generator. The output of the Monte Carlo simulation is written to the data set MONTE selected by the OUT= option.

```
/* data for simulation */
data whatif;
   input yr rate_jp rate_wg imn_jp imn_wg emp_us emp_jp
      emp_wg prod_us prod_jp prod_wg cpi_us cpi_jp cpi_wg;
   label cpi_us = 'US CPI 1982-1984 = 100'
```

```
            cpi_jp = 'JP CPI 1982-1984 = 100'
            cpi_wg = 'WG CPI 1982-1984 = 100';
      im_jp = imn_jp/cpi_us;
      im_wg = imn_wg/cpi_us;
      ius = 100*(cpi_us-(lag(cpi_us)))/(lag(cpi_us));
      ijp = 100*(cpi_jp-(lag(cpi_jp)))/(lag(cpi_jp));
      iwg = 100*(cpi_wg-(lag(cpi_wg)))/(lag(cpi_wg));
      di_jp = ius - ijp;
      di_wg = ius - iwg;
   datalines;
   1980 226.63 1.8175 30714 11693 103.3 101.3 100.4 101.7
        125.4 109.8  .824  .909  .868
   1981 220.63 2.2631 35000 11000 102.8 102.2  97.9 104.6
        126.3 112.8  .909  .954  .922
   1982 249.06 2.4280 40000 12000  95.8 101.4  95.0 107.1
        146.8 113.3  .965  .980  .970
   1983 237.55 2.5539 45000 13100  94.4 103.4  91.1 111.6
        152.8 116.8  .996  .999 1.003
   1984 237.45 2.8454 50000 14300  99.0 105.8  90.4 118.5
        152.2 124.7 1.039 1.021 1.027
   1985 238.47 2.9419 55000 15600  98.1 107.6  91.3 124.2
        161.1 128.5 1.076 1.042 1.048
   1986    .      .   60000 17000  96.8 107.3  92.7 128.8
        163.8 130.7 1.096 1.049 1.047
   1987    .      .   65000 18500  97.1 106.1  92.8 132.0
        176.5 129.9 1.136 1.050 1.049
   1988    .      .   70000 20000  99.6 108.8  92.7 136.2
        190.0 135.9 1.183 1.057 1.063
   ;
```

To generate a confidence interval plot for the forecast, use PROC UNIVARIATE to generate percentile bounds and use PROC GPLOT to plot the graph. The following SAS statements produce the graph in Figure 20.12.

```
   proc sort data=monte;
      by yr;
   run;

   proc univariate data=monte noprint;
      by yr;
      var rate_jp rate_wg;
      output out=bounds mean=mean p5=p5 p95=p95;
   run;

   title "Monte Carlo Generated Confidence
               Intervals on a Forecast";
   proc gplot data=bounds;
      plot mean*yr p5*yr p95*yr /overlay;
      symbol1 i=join value=triangle;
      symbol2 i=join value=square l=4;
      symbol3 i=join value=square l=4;
   run;
```

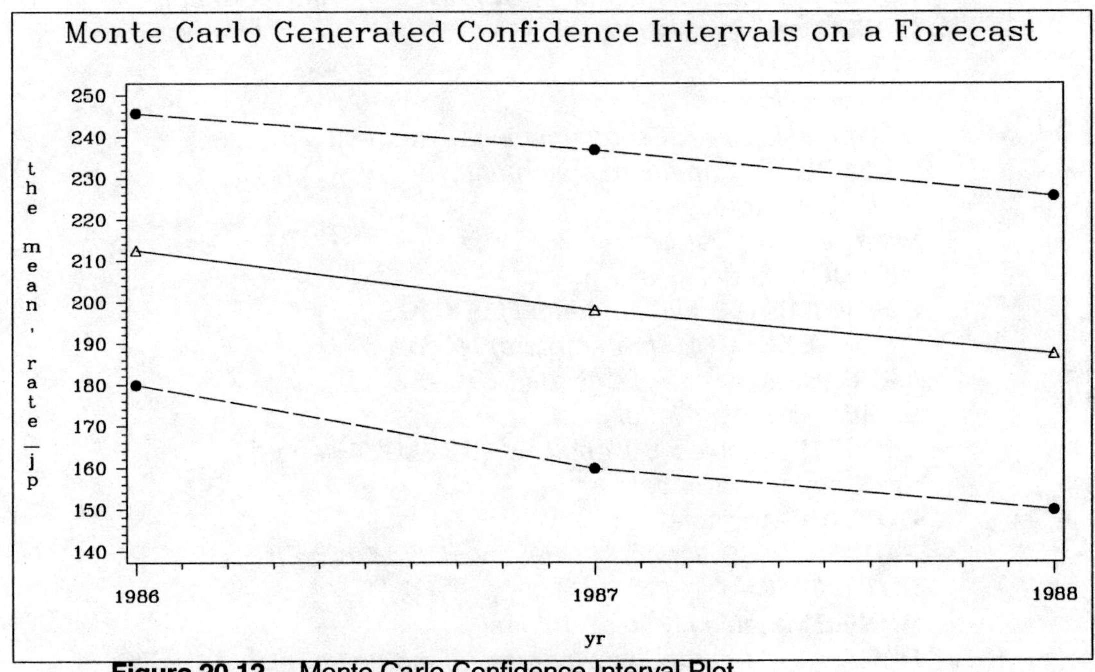

Figure 20.12. Monte Carlo Confidence Interval Plot

Syntax

The following statements can be used with the MODEL procedure:

PROC MODEL *options*;
    ABORT ;
    ARRAY *arrayname variables ...* ;
    ATTRIB *variable-list attribute-list [variable-list attribute-list]*;
    BOUNDS *bound1, bound2 ...* ;
    BY *variables*;
    CALL *name [(expression [, expression ...])]* ;
    CONTROL *variable [value] ...* ;
    DELETE ;
    DO *[variable = expression [TO expression] [BY expression]*
            [, expression **TO** *expression] [* **BY** *expression] ...]*
      [**WHILE** *expression] [* **UNTIL** *expression]* ;
    END ;
    DROP *variable ...* ;
    ENDOGENOUS *variable [initial values] ...* ;
    ERRORMODEL *equation-name ~ distribution*
            [**CDF=(** *CDF(options))]* ;
    ESTIMATE *item [, item ...] [,/ options]* ;
    EXOGENOUS *variable [initial values] ...* ;
    FIT *equations [* **PARMS=** *(parameter values ...)]*
            START= *(parameter values ...)*
            [**DROP=** *(parameters)] [/ options]*;

FORMAT *variables [format] [* **DEFAULT** *= default-format]*;
GOTO *statement_label* ;
ID *variables*;
IF *expression* ;
IF *expression* **THEN** *programming_statement* ;
  ELSE *programming_statement* ;
variable = *expression* ;
variable + *expression* ;
INCLUDE *model files . . .* ;
INSTRUMENTS *[instruments] [*_**EXOG**_ *]*
    *[***EXCLUDE***=(parameters)] [/ options]* ;
KEEP *variable . . .* ;
LABEL *variable ='label' . . .* ;
LENGTH *variables [***$** *] length . . . [***DEFAULT***=length]*;
LINK *statement_label* ;
OUTVARS *variable . . .* ;
PARAMETERS *variable [value] variable [value] . . .* ;
PUT *print_item . . . [@] [@ @]* ;
RANGE *variable [= first] [***TO** *last]*;
RENAME *old-name =new-name . . . [old-name=new-name]*;
RESET *options*;
RESTRICT *restriction1 [, restriction2 . . .]* ;
RETAIN *variables values [variables values. . .]* ;
RETURN ;
SOLVE *variables [***SATISFY***=(equations)] [/ options]* ;
SUBSTR*(variable, index, length) = expression* ;
SELECT *[(expression)]* ;
  OTHERWISE *programming_statement* ;
STOP ;
TEST *["name"] test1 [, test2 . . .] [,/ options]* ;
VAR *variable [initial values] . . .* ;
WEIGHT *variable*;
WHEN *(expression) programming_statement* ;

Functional Summary

The statements and options in the MODEL procedure are summarized in the following table.

Description	Statement	Option
Data Set Options		
specify the input data set for the variables	FIT, SOLVE	DATA=
specify the input data set for parameters	FIT, SOLVE	ESTDATA=
specify the method for handling missing values	FIT	MISSING=

Description	Statement	Option
specify the input data set for parameters	MODEL	PARMSDATA=
specify the output data set for residual, predicted, or actual values	FIT	OUT=
specify the output data set for solution mode results	SOLVE	OUT=
write the actual values to OUT= data set	FIT	OUTACTUAL
select all output options	FIT	OUTALL
write the covariance matrix of the estimates	FIT	OUTCOV
write the parameter estimates to a data set	FIT	OUTEST=
write the parameter estimates to a data set	MODEL	OUTPARMS=
write the observations used to start the lags	SOLVE	OUTLAGS
write the predicted values to the OUT= data set	FIT	OUTPREDICT
write the residual values to the OUT= data set	FIT	OUTRESID
write the covariance matrix of the equation errors to a data set	FIT	OUTS=
write the **S** matrix used in the objective function definition to a data set	FIT	OUTSUSED=
write the estimate of the variance matrix of the moment generating function	FIT	OUTV=
read the covariance matrix of the equation errors	FIT, SOLVE	SDATA=
read the covariance matrix for GMM and ITGMM	FIT	VDATA=
specify the name of the time variable	FIT, SOLVE, MODEL	TIME=
select the estimation type to read	FIT, SOLVE	TYPE=
General ESTIMATE Statement Options		
specify the name of the data set in which the estimate of the functions of the parameters are to be written	ESTIMATE	OUTEST=
write the covariance matrix of the functions of the parameters to the OUTEST= data set	ESTIMATE	OUTCOV
print the covariance matrix of the functions of the parameters	ESTIMATE	COVB
print the correlation matrix of the functions of the parameters	ESTIMATE	CORRB
Printing Options for FIT Tasks		
print the modified Breusch-Pagan test for heteroscedasticity	FIT	BREUSCH
print the Chow test for structural breaks	FIT	CHOW=
print collinearity diagnostics	FIT	COLLIN

Description	Statement	Option
print the correlation matrices	FIT	CORR
print the correlation matrix of the parameters	FIT	CORRB
print the correlation matrix of the residuals	FIT	CORRS
print the covariance matrices	FIT	COV
print the covariance matrix of the parameters	FIT	COVB
print the covariance matrix of the residuals	FIT	COVS
print Durbin-Watson *d* statistics	FIT	DW
print first-stage R^2 statistics	FIT	FSRSQ
print Godfrey's tests for autocorrelated residuals for each equation	FIT	GODFREY
print Hausman's specification test	FIT	HAUSMAN
print tests of normality of the model residuals	FIT	NORMAL
print the predictive Chow test for structural breaks	FIT	PCHOW=
specify all the printing options	FIT	PRINTALL
print White's test for heteroscedasticity	FIT	WHITE
Options to Control FIT Iteration Output		
print the inverse of the crossproducts Jacobian matrix	FIT	I
print a summary iteration listing	FIT	ITPRINT
print a detailed iteration listing	FIT	ITDETAILS
print the crossproduct Jacobian matrix	FIT	XPX
specify all the iteration printing-control options	FIT	ITALL
Options to Control the Minimization Process		
specify the convergence criteria	FIT	CONVERGE=
select the Hessian approximation used for FIML	FIT	HESSIAN=
specifies the local truncation error bound for the integration	FIT, SOLVE, MODEL	LTEBOUND=
specify the maximum number of iterations allowed	FIT	MAXITER=
specify the maximum number of subiterations allowed	FIT	MAXSUBITER=
select the iterative minimization method to use	FIT	METHOD=
specifies the smallest allowed time step to be used in the integration	FIT, SOLVE, MODEL	MINTIMESTEP=
modify the iterations for estimation methods that iterate the **S** matrix or the **V** matrix	FIT	NESTIT
specify the smallest pivot value	MODEL, FIT, SOLVE	SINGULAR

Description	Statement	Option
specify the number of minimization iterations to perform at each grid point	FIT	STARTITER=
specify a weight variable	WEIGHT	
Options to Read and Write Model Files		
read a model from one or more input model files	INCLUDE	MODEL=
suppress the default output of the model file	MODEL, RESET	NOSTORE
specify the name of an output model file	MODEL, RESET	OUTMODEL=
delete the current model	RESET	PURGE
Options to List or Analyze the Structure of the Model		
print a dependency structure of a model	MODEL	BLOCK
print a graph of the dependency structure of a model	MODEL	GRAPH
print the model program and variable lists	MODEL	LIST
print the derivative tables and compiled model program code	MODEL	LISTCODE
print a dependency list	MODEL	LISTDEP
print a table of derivatives	MODEL	LISTDER
print a cross-reference of the variables	MODEL	XREF
General Printing Control Options		
expand parts of the printed output	FIT, SOLVE	DETAILS
print a message for each statement as it is executed	FIT, SOLVE	FLOW
select the maximum number of execution errors that can be printed	FIT, SOLVE	MAXERRORS=
select the number of decimal places shown in the printed output	FIT, SOLVE	NDEC=
suppress the normal printed output	FIT, SOLVE	NOPRINT
specify all the noniteration printing options	FIT, SOLVE	PRINTALL
print the result of each operation as it is executed	FIT, SOLVE	TRACE
request a comprehensive memory usage summary	FIT, SOLVE, MODEL, RESET	MEMORYUSE
turns off the NOPRINT option	RESET	PRINT
Statements that Declare Variables		
associate a name with a list of variables and constants	ARRAY	
declare a variable to have a fixed value	CONTROL	

Description	Statement	Option
declare a variable to be a dependent or endogenous variable	ENDOGENOUS	
declare a variable to be an independent or exogenous variable	EXOGENOUS	
specify identifying variables	ID	
assign a label to a variable	LABEL	
select additional variables to be output	OUTVARS	
declare a variable to be a parameter	PARAMETERS	
force a variable to hold its value from a previous observation	RETAIN	
declare a model variable	VAR	
declare an instrumental variable	INSTRUMENTS	
omit the default intercept term in the instruments list	INSTRUMENTS	NOINT
General FIT Statement Options		
omit parameters from the estimation	FIT	DROP=
associate a *variable* with an initial value as a parameter or a constant	FIT	INITIAL=
bypass OLS to get initial parameter estimates for GMM, ITGMM, or FIML	FIT	NOOLS
bypass 2SLS to get initial parameter estimates for GMM, ITGMM, or FIML	FIT	NO2SLS
specify the parameters to estimate	FIT	PARMS=
request confidence intervals on estimated parameters	FIT	PRL=
select a grid search	FIT	START=
Options to Control the Estimation Method Used		
specify nonlinear ordinary least squares	FIT	OLS
specify iterated nonlinear ordinary least squares	FIT	ITOLS
specify seemingly unrelated regression	FIT	SUR
specify iterated seemingly unrelated regression	FIT	ITSUR
specify two-stage least squares	FIT	2SLS
specify iterated two-stage least squares	FIT	IT2SLS
specify three-stage least squares	FIT	3SLS
specify iterated three-stage least squares	FIT	IT3SLS
specify full information maximum likelihood	FIT	FIML
specify simulated method of moments	FIT	NDRAW
specify number of draws for the V matrix	FIT	NDRAWV

Description	Statement	Option
specify number of initial observations for SMM	FIT	NPREOBS
select the variance-covariance estimator used for FIML	FIT	COVBEST=
specify generalized method of moments	FIT	GMM
specify the kernel for GMM and ITGMM	FIT	KERNEL=
specify iterated generalized method of moments	FIT	ITGMM
specify the type of generalized inverse used for the covariance matrix	FIT	GINV=
specify the denominator for computing variances and covariances	FIT	VARDEF=
specify adding the variance adjustment for SMM	FIT	ADJSMMV
specify variance correction for heteroscedasticity	FIT	HCCME=
specify GMM variance under arbitrary weighting matrix	FIT	GENGMMV
specify GMM variance under optimal weighting matrix	FIT	NOGENGMMV
Solution Mode Options		
select a subset of the model equations	SOLVE	SATISFY=
solve only for missing variables	SOLVE	FORECAST
solve for all solution variables	SOLVE	SIMULATE
Solution Mode Options: Lag Processing		
use solved values in the lag functions	SOLVE	DYNAMIC
use actual values in the lag functions	SOLVE	STATIC
produce successive forecasts to a fixed forecast horizon	SOLVE	NAHEAD=
select the observation to start dynamic solutions	SOLVE	START=
Solution Mode Options: Numerical Methods		
specify the maximum number of iterations allowed	SOLVE	MAXITER=
specify the maximum number of subiterations allowed	SOLVE	MAXSUBITER=
specify the convergence criteria	SOLVE	CONVERGE=
compute a simultaneous solution using a Jacobi-like iteration	SOLVE	JACOBI

Description	Statement	Option
compute a simultaneous solution using a Gauss-Seidel-like iteration	SOLVE	SEIDEL
compute a simultaneous solution using Newton's method	SOLVE	NEWTON
compute a nonsimultaneous solution	SOLVE	SINGLE
Monte Carlo Simulation Options		
specify quasi-random number generator	SOLVE	QUASI=
specify pseudo-random number generator	SOLVE	PSUEDO=
repeat the solution multiple times	SOLVE	RANDOM=
initialize the pseudo-random number generator	SOLVE	SEED=
Solution Mode Printing Options		
print between data points integration values for the DERT. variables and the auxiliary variables	FIT, SOLVE, MODEL	INTGPRINT
print the solution approximation and equation errors	SOLVE	ITPRINT
print the solution values and residuals at each observation	SOLVE	SOLVEPRINT
print various summary statistics	SOLVE	STATS
print tables of Theil inequality coefficients	SOLVE	THEIL
specify all printing control options	SOLVE	PRINTALL
General TEST Statement Options		
specify that a Wald test be computed	TEST	WALD
specify that a Lagrange multiplier test be computed	TEST	LM
specify that a likelihood ratio test be computed	TEST	LR
requests all three types of tests	TEST	ALL
specify the name of an output SAS data set that contains the test results	TEST	OUT=
Miscellaneous Statements		
specify the range of observations to be used	RANGE	
subset the data set with *by* variables	BY	

PROC MODEL Statement

PROC MODEL *options;*

The following options can be specified in the PROC MODEL statement. All of the nonassignment options (the options that do not accept a value after an equal sign) can have NO prefixed to the option name in the RESET statement to turn the option off. The default case is not explicitly indicated in the discussion that follows. Thus, for example, the option DETAILS is documented in the following, but NODETAILS is not documented since it is the default. Also, the NOSTORE option is documented because STORE is the default.

Data Set Options

DATA= *SAS-data-set*

names the input data set. Variables in the model program are looked up in the DATA= data set and, if found, their attributes (type, length, label, format) are set to be the same as those in the input data set (if not previously defined otherwise). The values for the variables in the program are read from the input data set when the model is estimated or simulated by FIT and SOLVE statements.

OUTPARMS= *SAS-data-set*
writes the parameter estimates to a SAS data set. See "Output Data Sets" for details.

PARMSDATA= *SAS-data-set*
names the SAS data set that contains the parameter estimates. See "Input Data Sets" for details.

Options to Read and Write Model Files

MODEL= *model-name*
MODEL= *(model-list)*
reads the model from one or more input model files created by previous PROC MODEL executions. Model files are written by the OUTMODEL= option.

NOSTORE
suppresses the default output of the model file. This option is only applicable when FIT or SOLVE statements are not used, the MODEL= option is not used, and when a model is specified.

OUTMODEL= *model-name*
specifies the name of an output model file to which the model is to be written. Model files are stored as members of a SAS catalog, with the type MODEL.

V5MODEL= *model-name*
reads model files written by Version 5 of SAS/ETS software.

Options to List or Analyze the Structure of the Model

These options produce reports on the structure of the model or list the programming statements defining the models. These options are automatically reset (turned off) after the reports are printed. To turn these options back on after a RUN statement has been entered, use the RESET statement or specify the options on a FIT or SOLVE statement.

BLOCK

prints an analysis of the structure of the model given by the assignments to model variables appearing in the model program. This analysis includes a classification of model variables into endogenous (dependent) and exogenous (independent) groups based on the presence of the variable on the left-hand side of an assignment statement. The endogenous variables are grouped into simultaneously determined blocks. The dependency structure of the simultaneous blocks and exogenous variables is also printed. The BLOCK option cannot analyze dependencies implied by general form equations.

GRAPH

prints the graph of the dependency structure of the model. The GRAPH option also invokes the BLOCK option and produces a graphical display of the information listed by the BLOCK option.

LIST

prints the model program and variable lists, including the statements added by PROC MODEL and macros.

LISTALL

selects the LIST, LISTDEP, LISTDER, and LISTCODE options.

LISTCODE

prints the derivative tables and compiled model program code. LISTCODE is a debugging feature and is not normally needed.

LISTDEP

prints a report that lists for each variable in the model program the variables that depend on it and that it depends on. These lists are given separately for current-period values and for lagged values of the variables.

The information displayed is the same as that used to construct the BLOCK report but differs in that the information is listed for all variables (including parameters, control variables, and program variables), not just the model variables. Classification into endogenous and exogenous groups and analysis of simultaneous structure is not done by the LISTDEP report.

LISTDER

prints a table of derivatives for FIT and SOLVE tasks. (The LISTDER option is only applicable for the default NEWTON method for SOLVE tasks.) The derivatives table shows each nonzero derivative computed for the problem. The derivative listed can be a constant, a variable in the model program, or a special derivative variable created to hold the result of the derivative expression. This option is turned on by the LISTCODE and PRINTALL options.

XREF

prints a cross-reference of the variables in the model program showing where each variable was referenced or given a value. The XREF option is normally used in conjunction with the LIST option. A more detailed description is given in the "Diagnostics and Debugging" section.

General Printing Control Options

DETAILS

specifies the detailed printout. Parts of the printed output are expanded when the DETAILS option is specified. If ODS GRAPHICS=ON is selected the following additional graphs of the residuals are produced: ACF, PACF, IACF, white noise, and QQ plot versus the normal.

FLOW

prints a message for each statement in the model program as it is executed. This debugging option is needed very rarely and produces voluminous output.

MAXERRORS= *n*

specifies the maximum number of execution errors that can be printed. The default is MAXERRORS=50.

NDEC= *n*

specifies the precision of the format that PROC MODEL uses when printing various numbers. The default is NDEC=3, which means that PROC MODEL attempts to print values using the D format but ensures that at least three significant digits are shown. If the NDEC= value is greater than nine, the BEST. format is used. The smallest value allowed is NDEC=2.

The NDEC= option affects the format of most, but not all, of the floating point numbers that PROC MODEL can print. For some values (such as parameter estimates), a precision limit one or two digits greater than the NDEC= value is used. This option does not apply to the precision of the variables in the output data set.

NOPRINT

suppresses the normal printed output but does not suppress error listings. Using any other print option turns the NOPRINT option off. The PRINT option can be used with the RESET statement to turn off NOPRINT.

PRINTALL

turns on all the printing-control options. The options set by PRINTALL are DETAILS; the model information options LIST, LISTDEP, LISTDER, XREF, BLOCK, and GRAPH; the FIT task printing options FSRSQ, COVB, CORRB, COVS, CORRS, DW, and COLLIN; and the SOLVE task printing options STATS, THEIL, SOLVEPRINT, and ITPRINT.

TRACE

prints the result of each operation in each statement in the model program as it is executed, in addition to the information printed by the FLOW option. This debugging option is needed very rarely and produces voluminous output.

MEMORYUSE

prints a report of the memory required for the various parts of the analysis.

FIT Task Options

The following options are used in the FIT statement (parameter estimation) and can also be used in the PROC MODEL statement: COLLIN, CONVERGE=, CORR, CORRB, CORRS, COVB, COVBEST=, COVS, DW, FIML, FSRSQ,

GMM, HESSIAN=, I, INTGPRINT, ITALL, ITDETAILS, ITGMM, ITPRINT, ITOLS, ITSUR, IT2SLS, IT3SLS, KERNEL=, LTEBOUND=, MAXITER=, MAXSUBITER=, METHOD=, MINTIMESTEP=, NESTIT, N2SLS, N3SLS, OLS, OUTPREDICT, OUTRESID, OUTACTUAL, OUTLAGS, OUTERRORS, OUTALL, OUTCOV, SINGULAR=, STARTITER=, SUR, TIME=, VARDEF, and XPX. See "FIT Statement Syntax" later in this chapter for a description of these options.

When used in the PROC MODEL or RESET statement, these are default options for subsequent FIT statements. For example, the statement

```
proc model n2sls ... ;
```

makes two-stage least squares the default parameter estimation method for FIT statements that do not specify an estimation method.

SOLVE Task Options

The following options used in the SOLVE statement can also be used in the PROC MODEL statement: CONVERGE=, DYNAMIC, FORECAST, INTGPRINT, ITPRINT, JACOBI, LTEBOUND=, MAXITER=, MAXSUBITER=, MINTIMESTEP=, NAHEAD=, NEWTON, OUTPREDICT, OUTRESID, OUTACTUAL, OUTLAGS, OUTERRORS, OUTALL, SEED=, SEIDEL, SIMULATE, SINGLE, SINGULAR=, SOLVEPRINT, START=, STATIC, STATS, THEIL, TIME=, and TYPE=. See "SOLVE Statement Syntax" later in this chapter for a description of these options.

When used in the PROC MODEL or RESET statement, these options provide default values for subsequent SOLVE statements.

BOUNDS Statement

BOUNDS *bound1 [, bound2 ...] ;*

The BOUNDS statement imposes simple boundary constraints on the parameter estimates. BOUNDS statement constraints refer to the parameters estimated by the associated FIT statement (that is, to either the preceding FIT statement or, in the absence of a preceding FIT statement, to the following FIT statement). You can specify any number of BOUNDS statements.

Each *bound* is composed of parameters and constants and inequality operators:

item operator item [operator item [operator item . . .]]

Each *item* is a constant, the name of an estimated parameter, or a list of parameter names. Each *operator* is '<', '>', '<=', or '>='.

You can use both the BOUNDS statement and the RESTRICT statement to impose boundary constraints; however, the BOUNDS statement provides a simpler syntax for specifying these kinds of constraints. See the "RESTRICT Statement" section on page 1048 for more information on the computational details of estimation with inequality restrictions.

Lagrange multipliers are reported for all the active boundary constraints. In the printed output and in the OUTEST= data set, the Lagrange multiplier estimates are identified with the names BOUND1, BOUND2, and so forth. The probability of the Lagrange multipliers are computed using a beta distribution (LaMotte 1994). To give the constraints more descriptive names, use the RESTRICT statement instead of the BOUNDS statement.

The following BOUNDS statement constrains the estimates of the parameters A and B and the ten parameters P1 through P10 to be between zero and one. This example illustrates the use of parameter lists to specify boundary constraints.

```
bounds 0 < a b p1-p10 < 1;
```

The following is an example of the use of the BOUNDS statement:

```
title 'Holzman Function (1969), Himmelblau No. 21, N=3';
data zero;
   do i = 1 to 99;
      output;
   end;
run;

proc model data=zero ;
   parms x1= 100 x2= 12.5 x3=  3;
   bounds .1 <= x1 <= 100,
           0 <= x2 <=  25.6,
           0 <= x3 <=    5;

   t = 2 / 3;
   u = 25 + (-50 * log(0.01 * i )) ** t;
   v = (u - x2) ** x3;
   w = exp(-v / x1);
   eq.foo = -.01 * i + w;

   fit foo / method=marquardt;
run;
```

```
                Holzman Function (1969), Himmelblau No. 21, N=3

                            The MODEL Procedure

                      Nonlinear OLS Parameter Estimates

                                        Approx                      Approx
    Parameter          Estimate         Std Err      t Value       Pr > |t|

    x1                 49.99999               0            .              .
    x2                       25               0            .              .
    x3                      1.5               0            .              .


         Number of Observations            Statistics for System

         Used                      99      Objective          5.455E-18
         Missing                    0      Objective*N          5.4E-16
```

Figure 20.13. Output from Bounded Estimation

BY Statement

BY *variables;*

A BY statement is used with the FIT statement to obtain separate estimates for observations in groups defined by the BY variables. Note that if an output model file is written, using the OUTMODEL= option, the parameter values stored are those from the last BY group processed. To save parameter estimates for each BY group, use the OUTEST= option in the FIT statement.

A BY statement is used with the SOLVE statement to obtain solutions for observations in groups defined by the BY variables. If the BY variables are identical in the DATA= data set and the ESTDATA= data set, then the two data sets are synchronized and the simulations are performed using the data and parameters for each BY group. This holds for BY variables in the SDATA= data set as well. If, at some point, the BY variables don't match, BY processing is abandoned in either the ESTDATA= data set or the SDATA= data set, whichever has the missing BY value. If the DATA= data set does not contain BY variables and the ESTDATA= data set or the SDATA= data set does, then BY processing is performed for the ESTDATA= data set and the SDATA= data set by reusing the data in the DATA= data set for each BY group.

CONTROL Statement

CONTROL *variable [value] ... ;*

The CONTROL statement declares control variables and specifies their values. A control variable is like a parameter except that it has a fixed value and is not estimated from the data. You can use control variables for constants in model equations that you may want to change in different solution cases. You can use control variables to vary the program logic. Unlike the retained variables, these values are fixed across iterations.

ENDOGENOUS Statement

ENDOGENOUS *variable [initial-values] ... ;*

The ENDOGENOUS statement declares model variables and identifies them as endogenous. You can declare model variables with an ENDOGENOUS statement instead of with a VAR statement to help document the model or to indicate the default solution variables. The variables declared endogenous are solved when a SOLVE statement does not indicate which variables to solve. Valid abbreviations for the ENDOGENOUS statement are ENDOG and ENDO.

The DEPENDENT statement is equivalent to the ENDOGENOUS statement and is provided for the convenience of non-econometric practitioners.

The ENDOGENOUS statement optionally provides initial values for lagged dependent variables. See "Lag Logic" in the "Functions Across Time" section for more information.

ERRORMODEL Statement

ERRORMODEL *equation-name* ~ *distribution* **[CDF=(** *CDF(options)* **)] ;**

The ERRORMODEL statement is the mechanism for specifying the distribution of the residuals. You must specify the dependent/endogenous variables or general form model name, a tilde (~), and then a distribution with its parameters. The following options are used in the ERRORMODEL statement:

Options to Specify the Distribution

CAUCHY(*<location, scale>* **)**
specifies the Cauchy distribution. This option is only supported for simulation. The arguments correspond to the arguments of the SAS CDF function (ignoring the random variable argument).

CHISQUARED (*df < , nc>* **)**
specifies the χ^2 distribution. This option is only supported for simulation. The arguments correspond to the arguments of the SAS CDF function (ignoring the random variable argument).

GENERAL(*Likelihood, <parm1, parm2, ... parmn>* **)**
specifies minus a general log likelihood function that you construct using SAS programming statements. $parm1, parm2, ...parmn$ are optional parameters for this distribution and are used for documentation purposes only.

F(*ndf, ddf < , nc>* **)**
specifies the F distribution. This option is only supported for simulation. The arguments correspond to the arguments of the SAS CDF function (ignoring the random variable argument).

NORMAL($v_1\ v_2\ \dots\ v_n$ **)**

specifies a multivariate normal (Gaussian) distribution with mean 0 and variances v_1 through v_n.

POISSON(*mean* **)**

specifies the Poisson distribution. This option is only supported for simulation. The arguments correspond to the arguments of the SAS CDF function (ignoring the random variable argument).

T($v_1 v_2 \cdots v_n$, *df* **)**

specifies a multivariate t distribution with noncentrality 0, variance v_1 through v_n, and common degrees of freedom df.

UNIFORM(*<left, right>* **)**

specifies the uniform distribution. This option is only supported for simulation. The arguments correspond to the arguments of the SAS CDF function (ignoring the random variable argument).

Options to Specify the CDF for Simulation

CDF=(*CDF(options)* **)**

specifies the univariate distribution that is used for simulation so that the estimation can be done for one set of distributional assumptions and the simulation for another. The CDF can be any of the distributions from the previous section with the exception of the General Likelihood. In addition, you can specify the empirical distribution of the residuals.

EMPIRICAL= (<TAILS=*(options)*>)

uses the sorted residual data to create an empirical CDF.

TAILS=(*tail options* **)**

specifies how to handle the tails in computing the inverse CDF from an empirical distribution, where *Tail options* are:

NORMAL	specifies the normal distribution to extrapolate the tails.
T(*df*)	specifies the t distribution to extrapolate the tails.
PERCENT= *p*	specifies the percent of the observations to use in constructing each tail. The default for the PERCENT= option is 10. A normal distribution or a t distribution is used to extrapolate the tails to infinity. The variance for the tail distributions is are obtained from the data so that the empirical CDF is continuous.

ESTIMATE Statement

ESTIMATE *item [, item ...] [,/ options] ;*

The ESTIMATE statement computes estimates of functions of the parameters.

The ESTIMATE statement refers to the parameters estimated by the associated FIT statement (that is, to either the preceding FIT statement or, in the absence of a preceding FIT statement, to the following FIT statement). You can use any number of ESTIMATE statements.

If you specify options on the ESTIMATE statement, a comma is required before the "/" character separating the test expressions from the options, since the "/" character can also be used within test expressions to indicate division. Each *item* is written as an optional name followed by an expression,

["name"] expression

where *"name"* is a string used to identify the estimate in the printed output and in the OUTEST= data set.

Expressions can be composed of parameter names, arithmetic operators, functions, and constants. Comparison operators (such as "=" or "<") and logical operators (such as "&") cannot be used in ESTIMATE statement expressions. Parameters named in ESTIMATE expressions must be among the parameters estimated by the associated FIT statement.

You can use the following options in the ESTIMATE statement:

OUTEST=

specifies the name of the data set in which the estimate of the functions of the parameters are to be written. The format for this data set is identical to the OUTEST= data set for the FIT statement.

If you specify a *name* in the ESTIMATE statement, that name is used as the parameter name for the estimate in the OUTEST= data set. If no *name* is provided and the expression is just a symbol, the symbol name is used; otherwise, the string "_Estimate #" is used, where "#" is the variable number in the OUTEST= data set.

OUTCOV

writes the covariance matrix of the functions of the parameters to the OUTEST= data set in addition to the parameter estimates.

COVB

prints the covariance matrix of the functions of the parameters.

CORRB

prints the correlation matrix of the functions of the parameters.

The following is an example of the use of the ESTIMATE statement in a segmented model:

```
data a;
   input y x @@;
   datalines;
   .46 1  .47  2 .57  3 .61  4 .62  5 .68  6 .69  7
   .78 8  .70  9 .74 10 .77 11 .78 12 .74 13 .80 13
   .80 15 .78 16
   ;

title 'Segmented Model -- Quadratic with Plateau';
proc model data=a;
```

```
      x0 = -.5 * b / c;

      if x < x0 then y = a + b*x + c*x*x;
      else           y = a + b*x0 + c*x0*x0;

      fit y start=( a .45 b .5 c -.0025 );

      estimate 'Join point' x0 ,
               'plateau' a + b*x0 + c*x0**2 ;
   run;
```

```
                    Segmented Model -- Quadratic with Plateau

                              The MODEL Procedure

                           Nonlinear OLS  Estimates

                                Approx                   Approx
Term               Estimate    Std Err    t Value    Pr > |t|    Label

Join point          12.7504     1.2785       9.97      <.0001    x0
plateau            0.777516     0.0123      63.10      <.0001    a + b*x0 + c*x0**2
```

Figure 20.14. ESTIMATE Statement Output

EXOGENOUS Statement

EXOGENOUS *variable [initial-values] ... ;*

The EXOGENOUS statement declares model variables and identifies them as exogenous. You can declare model variables with an EXOGENOUS statement instead of with a VAR statement to help document the model or to indicate the default instrumental variables. The variables declared exogenous are used as instruments when an instrumental variables estimation method is requested (such as N2SLS or N3SLS) and an INSTRUMENTS statement is not used. Valid abbreviations for the EXOGENOUS statement are EXOG and EXO.

The INDEPENDENT statement is equivalent to the ENDOGENOUS statement and is provided for the convenience of non-econometric practitioners.

The EXOGENOUS statement optionally provides initial values for lagged exogenous variables. See "Lag Logic" in the "Functions Across Time" section for more information.

FIT Statement

FIT *[equations] [* **PARMS=(** *parameter [values] ...)]*

[**START=(** *parameter values ...)]*
[**DROP=(** *parameter ...)]*
[**INITIAL=(** *variable = [parameter | constant] ...)*
[/ options] **;**

The FIT statement estimates model parameters by fitting the model equations to input data and optionally selects the equations to be fit. If the list of equations is omitted, all model equations containing parameters are fit.

The following options can be used in the FIT statement.

DROP= *(parameters ...)*
specifies that the named parameters not be estimated. All the parameters in the equations fit are estimated except those listed in the DROP= option. The dropped parameters retain their previous values and are not changed by the estimation.

INITIAL= *(variable = [parameter | constant] ...)*
associates a *variable* with an initial value as a *parameter* or a *constant*.

PARMS= *(parameters [values] ...)*
selects a subset of the parameters for estimation. When the PARMS= option is used, only the named parameters are estimated. Any parameters not specified in the PARMS= list retain their previous values and are not changed by the estimation.

PRL= WALD | LR | BOTH
requests confidence intervals on estimated parameters. By default the PRL option produces 95% likelihood ratio confidence limits. The coverage of the confidence interval is controlled by the ALPHA= option in the FIT statement.

START= *(parameter values ...)*
supplies starting values for the parameter estimates. If the START= option specifies more than one starting value for one or more parameters, a grid search is performed over all combinations of the values, and the best combination is used to start the iterations. For more information, see the STARTITER= option.

Options to Control the Estimation Method Used

ADJSMMV
specifies adding the variance adjustment from simulating the moments to the variance-covariance matrix of the parameter estimators. By default no adjustment is made.

COVBEST=GLS | CROSS | FDA
specifies the variance-covariance estimator used for FIML. COVBEST=GLS selects the generalized least-squares estimator. COVBEST=CROSS selects the crossproducts estimator. COVBEST=FDA selects the inverse of the finite difference approximation to the Hessian. The default is COVBEST=CROSS.

FIML
specifies full information maximum likelihood estimation.

GINV=G2 | G4
specifies the type of generalized inverse to be used when computing the covariance matrix. G4 selects the Moore Penrose generalized inverse. The default is GINV=G2.

Rather than deleting linearly related rows and columns of the covariance matrix, the Moore-Penrose generalized inverse averages the variance effects between collinear rows. When the option GINV=G4 is used, the Moore-Penrose generalized inverse is use to calculate standard errors and the covariance matrix of the parameters as well as the change vector for the optimization problem. For singular systems, a normal G2 inverse is used to determine the singular rows so that the parameters can be marked in the Parameter Estimates table. Whether or not you use a G4 inverse, if the covariance matrix is singular, the parameter estimates are not unique. Refer to Noble and Daniel (1977, pp. 337–340) for more details on generalized inverses.

GENGMMV

specify GMM variance under arbitrary weighting matrix. See the "Estimation Methods" section for more details.

The is the default method for GMM estimation.

GMM

specifies generalized method of moments estimation.

HCCME= 0 | 1 | 2 | 3 | NO

specifies the type of heteroscedasticity-consistent covariance matrix estimator to use for OLS, 2SLS, 3SLS, SUR, and the iterated versions of these estimation methods. The number corresponds to the type of covariance matrix estimator to use as

$$
\begin{array}{ll}
HC_0: & \hat{\epsilon}_t^2 \\
HC_1: & \frac{n}{n-df}\hat{\epsilon}_t^2 \\
HC_2: & \hat{\epsilon}_t^2/(1-\hat{h}_t) \\
HC_3: & \hat{\epsilon}_t^2/(1-\hat{h}_t)^2
\end{array}
$$

The default is NO.

ITGMM

specifies iterated generalized method of moments estimation.

ITOLS

specifies iterated ordinary least-squares estimation. This is the same as OLS unless there are cross-equation parameter restrictions.

ITSUR

specifies iterated seemingly unrelated regression estimation

IT2SLS

specifies iterated two-stage least-squares estimation. This is the same as 2SLS unless there are cross-equation parameter restrictions.

IT3SLS

specifies iterated three-stage least-squares estimation.

KERNEL=(PARZEN | BART | QS, ***[c], [e]*** **)**
KERNEL=PARZEN | BART | QS

specifies the kernel to be used for GMM and ITGMM. PARZEN selects the Parzen kernel, BART selects the Bartlett kernel, and QS selects the Quadratic Spectral kernel. $e \geq 0$ and $c \geq 0$ are used to compute the bandwidth parameter. The default is KERNEL=(PARZEN, 1, 0.2). See the "Estimation Methods" section for more details.

N2SLS | 2SLS

specifies nonlinear two-stage least-squares estimation. This is the default when an INSTRUMENTS statement is used.

N3SLS | 3SLS

specifies nonlinear three-stage least-squares estimation.

NDRAW *<=number of draws>*

requests the simulation method for estimation. H is the *number of draws*. If *number of draws* is not specified, the default H is set to 10.

NOOLS
NO2SLS

specifies bypassing OLS or 2SLS to get initial parameter estimates for GMM, ITGMM, or FIML. This is important for certain models that are poorly defined in OLS or 2SLS, or if good initial parameter values are already provided. Note that for GMM, the V matrix is created using the initial values specified and this may not be consistently estimated.

NO3SLS

specifies not to use 3SLS automatically for FIML initial parameter starting values.

NOGENGMMV

specify not to use GMM variance under arbitrary weighting matrix. Use GMM variance under optimal weighting matrix instead. See the "Estimation Methods" section for more details.

NPREOBS *=number of obs to initialize*

specifies the initial number of observations to run the simulation before the simulated values are compared to observed variables. This option is most useful in cases where the program statements involve lag operations. Use this option to avoid the effect of the starting point on the simulation.

NVDRAW *=number of draws for V matrix*

specifies H', the *number of draws for V matrix*. If this option is not specified, the default H' is set to 20.

OLS

specifies ordinary least-squares estimation. This is the default when no INSTRUMENTS statement is used.

SUR

specifies seemingly unrelated regression estimation.

VARDEF=N | WGT | DF | WDF

specifies the denominator to be used in computing variances and covariances. VARDEF=N specifies that the number of nonmissing observations be used. VARDEF=WGT specifies that the sum of the weights be used. VARDEF=DF specifies that the number of nonmissing observations minus the model degrees of freedom (number of parameters) be used. VARDEF=WDF specifies that the sum of the weights minus the model degrees of freedom be used. The default is VARDEF=DF. VARDEF=N is used for FIML estimation.

Data Set Options

DATA= *SAS-data-set*

specifies the input data set. Values for the variables in the program are read from this data set. If the DATA= option is not specified on the FIT statement, the data set specified by the DATA= option on the PROC MODEL statement is used.

ESTDATA= *SAS-data-set*

specifies a data set whose first observation provides initial values for some or all of the parameters.

MISSING= PAIRWISE | DELETE

The option MISSING=PAIRWISE specifies that missing values are tracked on an equation-by-equation basis. The MISSING=DELETE option specifies that the entire observation is omitted from the analysis when any equation has a missing predicted or actual value for the equation. The default is MISSING=DELETE.

OUT= *SAS-data-set*

names the SAS data set to contain the residuals, predicted values, or actual values from each estimation. Only the residuals are output by default.

OUTACTUAL

writes the actual values of the endogenous variables of the estimation to the OUT= data set. This option is applicable only if the OUT= option is specified.

OUTALL

selects the OUTACTUAL, OUTERRORS, OUTLAGS, OUTPREDICT, and OUTRESID options.

OUTCOV
COVOUT

writes the covariance matrix of the estimates to the OUTEST= data set in addition to the parameter estimates. The OUTCOV option is applicable only if the OUTEST= option is also specified.

OUTEST= *SAS-data-set*

names the SAS data set to contain the parameter estimates and optionally the covariance of the estimates.

OUTLAGS

writes the observations used to start the lags to the OUT= data set. This option is applicable only if the OUT= option is specified.

OUTPREDICT

writes the predicted values to the OUT= data set. This option is applicable only if OUT= is specified.

OUTRESID

writes the residual values computed from the parameter estimates to the OUT= data set. The OUTRESID option is the default if neither OUTPREDICT nor OUTACTUAL is specified. This option is applicable only if the OUT= option is specified.

OUTS= *SAS-data-set*

names the SAS data set to contain the estimated covariance matrix of the equation errors. This is the covariance of the residuals computed from the parameter estimates.

OUTSN= *SAS-data-set*

names the SAS data set to contain the estimated normalized covariance matrix of the equation errors. This is valid for multivariate t-distribution estimation.

OUTSUSED= *SAS-data-set*

names the SAS data set to contain the S matrix used in the objective function definition. The OUTSUSED= data set is the same as the OUTS= data set for the methods that iterate the S matrix.

OUTUNWGTRESID

writes the unweighted residual values computed from the parameter estimates to the OUT= data set. These are residuals computed as $actual - predicted$ with no accounting for the WEIGHT statement, the _WEIGHT_ variable, or any variance expressions. This option is applicable only if the OUT= option is specified.

OUTV= *SAS-data-set*

names the SAS data set to contain the estimate of the variance matrix for GMM and ITGMM.

SDATA= *SAS-data-set*

specifies a data set that provides the covariance matrix of the equation errors. The matrix read from the SDATA= data set is used for the equation covariance matrix (S matrix) in the estimation. (The SDATA= S matrix is used to provide only the initial estimate of **S** for the methods that iterate the S matrix.)

TIME= *name*

specifies the name of the time variable. This variable must be in the data set.

TYPE= *name*

specifies the estimation type to read from the SDATA= and ESTDATA= data sets. The name specified in the TYPE= option is compared to the _TYPE_ variable in the ESTDATA= and SDATA= data sets to select observations to use in constructing the covariance matrices. When the TYPE= option is omitted, the last estimation type in the data set is used. Valid values are the estimation methods used in PROC MODEL.

VDATA= *SAS-data-set*

specifies a data set containing a variance matrix for GMM and ITGMM estimation.

Printing Options for FIT Tasks

BREUSCH= *(variable-list)*

specifies the modified Breusch-Pagan test, where *variable-list* is a list of variables used to model the error variance.

CHOW= *obs*
CHOW= *(obs1 obs2 ... obsn)*

prints the Chow test for break points or structural changes in a model. The argument is the number of observations in the first sample or a parenthesized list of first sample sizes. If the size of the one of the two groups in which the sample is partitioned is less than the number of parameters, then a Predictive Chow test is automatically used. See the section "Chow Tests" on page 1131 for details.

COLLIN

prints collinearity diagnostics for the Jacobian crossproducts matrix (XPX) after the parameters have converged. Collinearity diagnostics are also automatically printed if the estimation fails to converge.

CORR

prints the correlation matrices of the residuals and parameters. Using CORR is the same as using both CORRB and CORRS.

CORRB

prints the correlation matrix of the parameter estimates.

CORRS

prints the correlation matrix of the residuals.

COV

prints the covariance matrices of the residuals and parameters. Specifying COV is the same as specifying both COVB and COVS.

COVB

prints the covariance matrix of the parameter estimates.

COVS

prints the covariance matrix of the residuals.

DW <=>

prints Durbin-Watson d statistics, which measure autocorrelation of the residuals. When the residual series is interrupted by missing observations, the Durbin-Watson statistic calculated is d' as suggested by Savin and White (1978). This is the usual Durbin-Watson computed by ignoring the gaps. Savin and White show that it has the same null distribution as the DW with no gaps in the series and can be used to test for autocorrelation using the standard tables. The Durbin-Watson statistic is not valid for models containing lagged endogenous variables.

You can use the DW= option to request higher order Durbin-Watson statistics. Since the ordinary Durbin-Watson statistic tests only for first-order autocorrelation, the Durbin-Watson statistics for higher-order autocorrelation are called *generalized Durbin-Watson* statistics.

DWPROB

Use the DWPROB option to print the significance level (p-values) for the Durbin-Watson tests. Since the Durbin-Watson p-values are computationally expensive, they are not reported by default. In the Durbin-Watson test, the null hypothesis is that there is autocorrelation at a specific lag.

See the section "Generalized Durbin-Watson Tests" in the Autoreg Chapter for limitations of the statistic.

FSRSQ

prints the first-stage R^2 statistics for instrumental estimation methods. These R^2s measure the proportion of the variance retained when the Jacobian columns associated with the parameters are projected through the instruments space.

GODFREY
GODFREY= *n*

performs Godfrey's tests for autocorrelated residuals for each equation, where n is the maximum autoregressive order, and specifies that Godfrey's tests be computed for lags 1 through n. The default number of lags is one.

HAUSMAN

performs Hausman's specification test, or m-statistics.

NORMAL

performs tests of normality of the model residuals.

PCHOW= *obs*
PCHOW= *(obs1 obs2 ... obsn)*

prints the Predictive Chow test for break points or structural changes in a model. The argument is the number of observations in the first sample or a parenthesized list of first sample sizes. See the section "Chow Tests" on page 1131 for details.

PRINTALL

specifies the printing options COLLIN, CORRB, CORRS, COVB, COVS, DETAILS, DW, and FSRSQ.

WHITE

specifies White's test.

Options to control iteration output

Details of the output produced are discussed in the section "Iteration History".

I

prints the inverse of the crossproducts Jacobian matrix at each iteration.

ITALL

specifies all iteration printing-control options (I, ITDETAILS, ITPRINT, and XPX). ITALL also prints the crossproducts matrix (labeled CROSS), the parameter change vector, and the estimate of the cross-equation covariance of residuals matrix at each iteration.

ITDETAILS

prints a detailed iteration listing. This includes the ITPRINT information and additional statistics.

ITPRINT

prints the parameter estimates, objective function value, and convergence criteria at each iteration.

XPX

prints the crossproducts Jacobian matrix at each iteration.

Options to Control the Minimization Process

The following options may be helpful when you experience a convergence problem:

CONVERGE= *value1*

CONVERGE= *(value1, value2)*

specifies the convergence criteria. The convergence measure must be less than *value1* before convergence is assumed. *value2* is the convergence criterion for the **S** and **V** matrices for **S** and **V** iterated methods. *value2* defaults to *value1*. See "The Convergence Criteria" for details. The default value is CONVERGE=.001.

HESSIAN= CROSS | GLS | FDA

specifies the Hessian approximation used for FIML. HESSIAN=CROSS selects the crossproducts approximation to the Hessian, HESSIAN=GLS selects the generalized least-squares approximation to the Hessian, and HESSIAN=FDA selects the finite difference approximation to the Hessian. HESSIAN=GLS is the default.

LTEBOUND= *n*

specifies the local truncation error bound for the integration. This option is ignored if no ODE's are specified.

MAXITER= *n*

specifies the maximum number of iterations allowed. The default is MAXITER=100.

MAXSUBITER= *n*

specifies the maximum number of subiterations allowed for an iteration. For the GAUSS method, the MAXSUBITER= option limits the number of step halvings. For the MARQUARDT method, the MAXSUBITER= option limits the number of times λ can be increased. The default is MAXSUBITER=30. See "Minimization Methods" for details.

METHOD= GAUSS | MARQUARDT

specifies the iterative minimization method to use. METHOD=GAUSS specifies the Gauss-Newton method, and METHOD=MARQUARDT specifies the Marquardt-Levenberg method. The default is METHOD=GAUSS. See "Minimization Methods" for details.

MINTIMESTEP= *n*

specifies the smallest allowed time step to be used in the integration. This option is ignored if no ODE's are specified.

NESTIT

changes the way the iterations are performed for estimation methods that iterate the estimate of the equation covariance (**S** matrix). The NESTIT option is relevant only for the methods that iterate the estimate of the covariance matrix (ITGMM, ITOLS, ITSUR, IT2SLS, IT3SLS). See "Details on the Covariance of Equation Errors" for an explanation of NESTIT.

SINGULAR= *value*

specifies the smallest pivot value allowed. The default 1.0E-12.

STARTITER= *n*

specifies the number of minimization iterations to perform at each grid point. The default is STARTITER=0, which implies that no minimization is performed at the grid points. See "Using the STARTITER option" for more details.

Other Options

Other options that can be used on the FIT statement include the following that list and analyze the model: BLOCK, GRAPH, LIST, LISTCODE, LISTDEP, LISTDER, and XREF. The following printing control options are also available: DETAILS, FLOW, INTGPRINT, MAXERRORS=, NOPRINT, PRINTALL, and TRACE. For complete descriptions of these options, see the discussion of the PROC MODEL statement options earlier in this chapter.

ID Statement

ID *variables;*

The ID statement specifies variables to identify observations in error messages or other listings and in the OUT= data set. The ID variables are normally SAS date or datetime variables. If more than one ID variable is used, the first variable is used to identify the observations; the remaining variables are added to the OUT= data set.

INCLUDE Statement

INCLUDE *model-names ... ;*

The INCLUDE statement reads model files and inserts their contents into the current model. However, instead of replacing the current model as the RESET MODEL= option does, the contents of included model files are inserted into the model program at the position that the INCLUDE statement appears.

INSTRUMENTS Statement

The INSTRUMENTS statement specifies the instrumental variables to be used in the N2SLS, N3SLS, IT2SLS, IT3SLS, GMM, and ITGMM estimation methods. There are three forms of the INSTRUMENTS statement:

INSTRUMENTS *variables [* **_EXOG_** *] ;*

INSTRUMENTS *[instruments] [* **_EXOG_** *]*
[**EXCLUDE=(** *parameters)] [/ options]* **;**

INSTRUMENTS *(equation, variables) (equation, variables) ... ;*

The first form of the INSTRUMENTS statement is used only before a FIT statement and defines the default instruments list. The items specified as instruments can be variables or the special keyword _EXOG_. _EXOG_ indicates that all the model variables declared EXOGENOUS are to be added to the instruments list.

The second form of the INSTRUMENTS statement is used only after the FIT statement and before the next RUN statement. The items specified as instruments for the second form can be variables, names of parameters to be estimated, or the special keyword _EXOG_. If you specify the name of a parameter in the instruments list, the partial derivatives of the equations with respect to the parameter (that is, the columns of the Jacobian matrix associated with the parameter) are used as instruments. The parameter itself is not used as an instrument. These partial derivatives should not depend on any of the parameters to be estimated. Only the names of parameters to be estimated can be specified.

EXCLUDE= *(parameters)*

specifies that the derivatives of the equations with respect to all of the parameters to be estimated, except the parameters listed in the EXCLUDE list, be used as instruments, in addition to the other instruments specified. If you use the EXCLUDE= option, you should be sure that the derivatives with respect to the nonexcluded parameters in the estimation are independent of the endogenous variables and not functions of the parameters estimated.

A third form of the INSTRUMENTS statement is used to specify instruments for each equation. There is no explicit intercept added, parameters cannot be specified to represent instruments, and the _EXOG_ keyword is not allowed. Equations not explicitly assigned instruments will use all the instruments specified for the other equations as well as instruments not assigned specific equations. In the following example, z1, z2, and z3 are instruments used with equation y1, and z2, z3, and z4 are instruments used with equation y2.

```
proc model data=data_sim;
   exogenous x1 x2;
   parms a b c d e f;

   y1 =a*x1**2 + b*x2**2 + c*x1*x2    ;
   y2 =d*x1**2 + e*x2**2 + f*x1*x2**2;

   fit y1 y2 / 3sls ;
   instruments (y1, z1 z2 z3) (y2,z2 z3 z4);
run;
```

The following option is specified on the INSTRUMENTS statement following a slash (/):

NOINTERCEPT
NOINT

excludes the constant of 1.0 (intercept) from the instruments list. An intercept is always included as an instrument unless NOINTERCEPT is specified.

When a FIT statement specifies an instrumental variables estimation method and no INSTRUMENTS statement accompanies the FIT statement, the default instruments are used. If no default instruments list has been specified, all the model variables declared EXOGENOUS are used as instruments. See the section "Choice of Instruments" on page 1135 for more details.

INTONLY

INTONLY

specifies that only the intercept be used as an instrument. This option is used for GMM estimation where the moments have been specified explicitly.

LABEL Statement

LABEL *variable='label' ... ;*

The LABEL statement specifies a label of up to 255 characters for parameters and other variables used in the model program. Labels are used to identify parts of the printout of FIT and SOLVE tasks. The labels will be displayed in the output if the LINESIZE= option is large enough.

MOMENT Statement

In many scenarios, endogenous variables are observed from data. From the models we can simulate these endogenous variables based on a fixed set of parameters. The goal of SMM is to find a set of parameters such that the moments of the simulated data match the moments of the observed variables. If there are many moments to match, the code may be tedious. The following MOMENT statement provides a way to generate some commonly used moments automatically. Multiple MOMENT statements can be used.

MOMENT *variables = moment specification ;*

variables can be one or more endogenous variables.

moment specification can have the following four types:

1. (*number list*) – the endogenous variable is raised to the power specified by each number in *number list.* For example,

```
moment y = (2 3);
```

adds the following two equations to be estimated:

```
eq._moment_1 = y**2 - pred.y**2;
eq._moment_2 = y**3 - pred.y**3;
```

2. ABS(*number list*) – the absolute value of the endogenous variable is raised to the power specified by each number in *number list.* For example,

```
moment y = ABS(3);
```

adds the following equation to be estimated:

```
eq._moment_2 = abs(y)**3 - abs(pred.y)**3;
```

3. LAG*num* (*number list*) – the endogenous variable is multiplied by the *num*th lag of the endogenous variable, and this product is raised to the power specified by each number in *number list*. For example,

```
moment y = LAG4(3);
```

adds the following equation to be estimated:

```
eq._moment_3 = (y*lag4(y))**3 - (pred.y*lag4(pred.y))**3;
```

4. ABS_LAG*num* (*number list*) – the endogenous variable is multiplied by the *num*th lag of the endogenous variable, and the absolute value of this product is raised to the power specified by each number in *number list*. For example,

```
moment y = ABS_LAG4(3);
```

adds the following equation to be estimated:

```
eq._moment_4 = abs(y*lag4(y))**3 - abs(pred.y*lag4(pred.y))**3;
```

The following PROC MODEL code utilizes the MOMENT statement to generate 24 moments and fit these moments using SMM.

```
proc model data=_tmpdata list;
      parms a b .5 s 1;
      instrument _exog_ / intonly;

      u = rannor( 10091 );
      z = rannor( 97631 );

      lsigmasq = xlag(sigmasq,exp(a));

      lnsigmasq = a + b * log(lsigmasq) + s * u;
      sigmasq = exp( lnsigmasq );

      y = sqrt(sigmasq) * z;

      moment y = (2 4) abs(1 3) abs_lag1(1 2) abs_lag2(1 2);
      moment y = abs_lag3(1 2) abs_lag4(1 2)
                 abs_lag5(1 2) abs_lag6(1 2)
                 abs_lag7(1 2) abs_lag8(1 2)
                 abs_lag9(1 2) abs_lag10(1 2);

      fit y  / gmm npreobs=20 ndraw=10;
      bound s > 0, 1>b>0;

run;
```

OUTVARS Statement

OUTVARS *variables;*

The OUTVARS statement specifies additional variables defined in the model program to be output to the OUT= data sets. The OUTVARS statement is not needed unless the variables to be added to the output data set are not referred to by the model, or unless you wish to include parameters or other special variables in the OUT= data set. The OUTVARS statement includes additional variables, whereas the KEEP statement excludes variables.

PARAMETERS Statement

PARAMETERS *variable [value] [variable [value]] ... ;*

The PARAMETERS statement declares the parameters of a model and optionally sets their initial values. Valid abbreviations are PARMS and PARM.

Each parameter has a single value associated with it, which is the same for all observations. Lagging is not relevant for parameters. If a value is not specified in the PARMS statement (or by the PARMS= option of a FIT statement), the value defaults to 0.0001 for FIT tasks and to a missing value for SOLVE tasks.

RANGE Statement

RANGE *variable [= first] [***TO** *last];*

The RANGE statement specifies the range of observations to be read from the DATA= data set. For FIT tasks, the RANGE statement controls the period of fit for the estimation. For SOLVE tasks, the RANGE statement controls the simulation period or forecast horizon.

The RANGE variable must be a numeric variable in the DATA= data set that identifies the observations, and the data set must be sorted by the RANGE variable. The first observation in the range is identified by *first*, and the last observation is identified by *last*.

PROC MODEL uses the first *l* observations prior to *first* to initialize the lags, where *l* is the maximum number of lags needed to evaluate any of the equations to be fit or solved, or the maximum number of lags needed to compute any of the instruments when an instrumental variables estimation method is used. There should be at least *l* observations in the data set before *first*. If *last* is not specified, all the nonmissing observations starting with *first* are used.

If *first* is omitted, the first *l* observations are used to initialize the lags, and the rest of the data, until *last*, is used. If a RANGE statement is used but both *first* and *last* are omitted, the RANGE statement variable is used to report the range of observations processed.

The RANGE variable should be nonmissing for all observations. Observations containing missing RANGE values are deleted.

The following are examples of RANGE statements:

```
range year = 1971 to 1988;                 /* yearly  data  */
range date = '1feb73'd to '1nov82'd;       /* monthly data  */
range time = 60.5;                         /* time in years */
range year to 1977;          /* use all years through 1977 */
range date; /* use values of date to report period-of-fit */
```

RESET Statement

RESET *options;*

All of the options of the PROC MODEL statement can be reset by the RESET statement. In addition, the RESET statement supports one additional option:

PURGE

deletes the current model so that a new model can be defined.

When the MODEL= option is used in the RESET statement, the current model is deleted before the new model is read.

RESTRICT Statement

RESTRICT *restriction1 [, restriction2 ...] ;*

The RESTRICT statement is used to impose linear and nonlinear restrictions on the parameter estimates.

RESTRICT statements refer to the parameters estimated by the associated FIT statement (that is, to either the preceding FIT statement or, in the absence of a preceding FIT statement, to the following FIT statement). You can specify any number of RESTRICT statements.

Each *restriction* is written as an optional name, followed by an expression, followed by an equality operator (=) or an inequality operator (<, >, <=, >=), followed by a second expression:

["name"] expression operator expression

The optional *"name"* is a string used to identify the restriction in the printed output and in the OUTEST= data set. The *operator* can be =, <, >, <= , or >=. The operator and second expression are optional, as in the TEST statement (=0).

Restriction expressions can be composed of parameter names, arithmetic operators, functions, and constants. Comparison operators (such as "=" or "<") and logical operators (such as "&") cannot be used in RESTRICT statement expressions. Parameters named in restriction expressions must be among the parameters estimated by the associated FIT statement. Expressions can refer to variables defined in the program.

The restriction expressions can be linear or nonlinear functions of the parameters.

The following is an example of the use of the RESTRICT statement:

```
proc model data=one;
   endogenous y1 y2;
   exogenous x1 x2;
   parms a b c;
   restrict b*(b+c) <= a;

   eq.one = -y1/c + a/x2 + b * x1**2 + c * x2**2;
   eq.two = -y2 * y1 + b * x2**2 - c/(2 * x1);

   fit one two / fiml;
run;
```

SOLVE Statement

SOLVE *[variables]* [**SATISFY=** *equations]* [**INITIAL=** *(variable=[parameter]]* *[/options];*

The SOLVE statement specifies that the model be simulated or forecast for input data values and, optionally, selects the variables to be solved. If the list of variables is omitted, all of the model variables declared ENDOGENOUS are solved. If no model variables are declared ENDOGENOUS, then all model variables are solved.

The following specification can be used in the SOLVE statement:

SATISFY= *equation*
SATISFY= *(equations)*
specifies a subset of the model equations that the solution values are to satisfy. If the SATISFY= option is not used, the solution is computed to satisfy all the model equations. Note that the number of equations must equal the number of variables solved.

Data Set Options

DATA= *SAS-data-set*
names the input data set. The model is solved for each observation read from the DATA= data set. If the DATA= option is not specified on the SOLVE statement, the data set specified by the DATA= option on the PROC MODEL statement is used.

ESTDATA= *SAS-data-set*
names a data set whose first observation provides values for some or all of the parameters and whose additional observations (if any) give the covariance matrix of the parameter estimates. The covariance matrix read from the ESTDATA= data set is used to generate multivariate normal pseudo-random shocks to the model parameters when the RANDOM= option requests Monte Carlo simulation.

OUT= *SAS-data-set*
outputs the predicted (solution) values, residual values, actual values, or equation errors from the solution to a data set. Only the solution values are output by default.

OUTACTUAL

outputs the actual values of the solved variables read from the input data set to the OUT= data set. This option is applicable only if the OUT= option is specified.

OUTALL

specifies the OUTACTUAL, OUTERRORS, OUTLAGS, OUTPREDICT, and OUTRESID options

OUTERRORS

writes the equation errors to the OUT= data set. These values are normally very close to zero when a simultaneous solution is computed; they can be used to double-check the accuracy of the solution process. It is applicable only if the OUT= option is specified.

OUTLAGS

writes the observations used to start the lags to the OUT= data set. This option is applicable only if the OUT= option is specified.

OUTPREDICT

writes the solution values to the OUT= data set. This option is relevant only if the OUT= option is specified.

The OUTPREDICT option is the default unless one of the other output options is used.

OUTRESID

writes the residual values computed as the difference of the solution values and the values for the solution variables read from the input data set to the OUT= data set. This option is applicable only if the OUT= option is specified.

PARMSDATA= *SAS-data-set*

specifies a data set that contains the parameter estimates. See the "Input Data Sets" section for more details.

RESIDDATA= *sas data-set*

specifies a data set that contains the residuals that are to be used in the empirical distribution. This data set can be created using the OUT= option on the Fit statement.

SDATA= *SAS-data-set*

specifies a data set that provides the covariance matrix of the equation errors. The covariance matrix read from the SDATA= data set is used to generate multivariate normal pseudo-random shocks to the equations when the RANDOM= option requests Monte Carlo simulation.

TYPE= *name*

specifies the estimation type. The name specified in the TYPE= option is compared to the _TYPE_ variable in the ESTDATA= and SDATA= data sets to select observations to use in constructing the covariance matrices. When TYPE= is omitted, the last estimation type in the data set is used.

Solution Mode Options: Lag Processing

DYNAMIC

specifies a dynamic solution. In the dynamic solution mode, solved values are used by the lagging functions. DYNAMIC is the default.

NAHEAD= *n*

specifies a simulation of *n*-period-ahead dynamic forecasting. The NAHEAD= option is used to simulate the process of using the model to produce successive forecasts to a fixed forecast horizon, with each forecast using the historical data available at the time the forecast is made.

Note that NAHEAD=1 produces a static (one-step-ahead) solution. NAHEAD=2 produces a solution using one-step-ahead solutions for the first lag (LAG1 functions return static predicted values) and actual values for longer lags. NAHEAD=3 produces a solution using NAHEAD=2 solutions for the first lags, NAHEAD=1 solutions for the second lags, and actual values for longer lags. In general, NAHEAD=*n* solutions use NAHEAD=*n*-1 solutions for LAG1, NAHEAD=*n*-2 solutions for LAG2, and so forth.

START= *s*

specifies static solutions until the *s*th observation and then changes to dynamic solutions. If the START=*s* option is specified, the first observation in the range in which LAG*n* delivers solved predicted values is *s*+*n*, while LAG*n* returns actual values for earlier observations.

STATIC

specifies a static solution. In static solution mode, actual values of the solved variables from the input data set are used by the lagging functions.

Solution Mode Options: Use of Available Data

FORECAST

specifies that the actual value of a solved variable is used as the solution value (instead of the predicted value from the model equations) whenever nonmissing data are available in the input data set. That is, in FORECAST mode, PROC MODEL solves only for those variables that are missing in the input data set.

SIMULATE

specifies that PROC MODEL always solves for all solution variables as a function of the input values of the other variables, even when actual data for some of the solution variables are available in the input data set. SIMULATE is the default.

Solution Mode Options: Numerical Solution Method

JACOBI

computes a simultaneous solution using a Jacobi iteration.

NEWTON

computes a simultaneous solution using Newton's method. When the NEWTON option is selected, the analytic derivatives of the equation errors with respect to the solution variables are computed and memory-efficient sparse matrix techniques are used for factoring the Jacobian matrix.

The NEWTON option can be used to solve both normalized-form and general-form equations and can compute goal-seeking solutions. NEWTON is the default.

SEIDEL

computes a simultaneous solution using a Gauss-Seidel method.

SINGLE
ONEPASS

specifies a single-equation (nonsimultaneous) solution. The model is executed once to compute predicted values for the variables from the actual values of the other endogenous variables. The SINGLE option can only be used for normalized-form equations and cannot be used for goal-seeking solutions.

For more information on these options, see the "Solution Modes" section later in this chapter.

Monte Carlo Simulation Options

PSEUDO= DEFAULT | TWISTER

specifies which pseudo number generator is too be use in generating draws for Monte Carlo simulation. The two pseudo-random number generators supported by the MODEL procedure are a default congruential generator which has period $2^{31} - 1$ and Mersenne-Twister pseudo-random number generator which has an extraordinarily long period $2^{19937} - 1$.

QUASI= NONE|SOBOL|FAURE

specifies a pseudo or quasi-random number generator. Two Quasi-random number generators supported by the MODEL procedure, the Sobol sequence (QUASI=SOBOL) and the Faure sequence (QUASI=FAURE). The default is QUASI=NONE which is the pseudo random number generator.

RANDOM= *n*

repeats the solution *n* times for each BY group, with different random perturbations of the equation errors if the SDATA= option is used; with different random perturbations of the parameters if the ESTDATA= option is used and the ESTDATA= data set contains a parameter covariance matrix; and with different values returned from the random-number generator functions, if any are used in the model program. If RANDOM=0, the random-number generator functions always return zero. See "Monte Carlo Simulation" for details. The default is RANDOM=0.

SEED= *n*

specifies an integer to use as the seed in generating pseudo-random numbers to shock the parameters and equations when the ESTDATA= or the SDATA= options are specified. If *n* is negative or zero, the time of day from the computer's clock is used as the seed. The SEED= option is only relevant if the RANDOM= option is used. The default is SEED=0.

WISHART= *df*

specifies that a Wishart distribution with degrees of freedom *df* be used in place of the normal error covariance matrix. This option is used to model the variance of the error covariance matrix when Monte Carlo simulation is selected.

Options for Controlling the Numerical Solution Process

The following options are useful when you have difficulty converging to the simultaneous solution.

CONVERGE= *value*

specifies the convergence criterion for the simultaneous solution. Convergence of the solution is judged by comparing the CONVERGE= value to the maximum over the equations of

$$\frac{|\epsilon_i|}{|y_i| + 1E - 6}$$

if it is computable, otherwise

$$|\epsilon_i|$$

where ϵ_i represents the equation error and y_i represents the solution variable corresponding to the ith equation for normalized-form equations. The default is CONVERGE=1E-8.

MAXITER= *n*

specifies the maximum number of iterations allowed for computing the simultaneous solution for any observation. The default is MAXITER=50.

INITIAL= *(variable= [parameter])*

specifies starting values for the parameters

MAXSUBITER= *n*

specifies the maximum number of damping subiterations that are performed in solving a nonlinear system when using the NEWTON solution method. Damping is disabled by setting MAXSUBITER=0. The default is MAXSUBITER=10.

Printing Options

INTGPRINT

prints between data points integration values for the DERT. variables and the auxiliary variables. If you specify the DETAILS option, the integrated derivative variables are printed as well.

ITPRINT

prints the solution approximation and equation errors at each iteration for each observation. This option can produce voluminous output.

PRINTALL

specifies the printing control options DETAILS, ITPRINT, SOLVEPRINT, STATS, and THEIL.

SOLVEPRINT
prints the solution values and residuals at each observation

STATS
prints various summary statistics for the solution values

THEIL
prints tables of Theil inequality coefficients and Theil relative change forecast error measures for the solution values. See "Summary Statistics" in the "Details" section for more information.

Other Options

Other options that can be used on the SOLVE statement include the following that list and analyze the model: BLOCK, GRAPH, LIST, LISTCODE, LISTDEP, LISTDER, and XREF. The LTEBOUND= and MINTIMESTEP= options can be used to control the integration process. The following printing-control options are also available: DETAILS, FLOW, MAXERRORS=, NOPRINT, and TRACE. For complete descriptions of these options, see the PROC MODEL and FIT statement options described earlier in this chapter.

TEST Statement

TEST *["name"] test1 [, test2 ...] [,/ options] ;*

The TEST statement performs tests of nonlinear hypotheses on the model parameters.

The TEST statement applies to the parameters estimated by the associated FIT statement (that is, either the preceding FIT statement or, in the absence of a preceding FIT statement, the following FIT statement). You can specify any number of TEST statements.

If you specify options on the TEST statement, a comma is required before the "/" character separating the test expressions from the options, because the "/" character can also be used within test expressions to indicate division.

Each test is written as an expression optionally followed by an equal sign (=) and a second expression:

[expression] [= expression]

Test expressions can be composed of parameter names, arithmetic operators, functions, and constants. Comparison operators (such as "=") and logical operators (such as "&") cannot be used in TEST statement expressions. Parameters named in test expressions must be among the parameters estimated by the associated FIT statement.

If you specify only one expression in a test, that expression is tested against zero. For example, the following two TEST statements are equivalent:

```
test a + b;

test a + b = 0;
```

When you specify multiple tests on the same TEST statement, a joint test is performed. For example, the following TEST statement tests the joint hypothesis that both A and B are equal to zero.

```
test a, b;
```

To perform separate tests rather than a joint test, use separate TEST statements. For example, the following TEST statements test the two separate hypotheses that A is equal to zero and that B is equal to zero.

```
test a;
test b;
```

You can use the following options in the TEST statement.

WALD
specifies that a Wald test be computed. WALD is the default.

LM
RAO
LAGRANGE
specifies that a Lagrange multiplier test be computed.

LR
LIKE
specifies that a likelihood ratio test be computed.

ALL
requests all three types of tests.

OUT=
specifies the name of an output SAS data set that contains the test results. The format of the OUT= data set produced by the TEST statement is similar to that of the OUTEST= data set produced by the FIT statement.

VAR Statement

VAR *variables [initial_values] ... ;*

The VAR statement declares model variables and optionally provides initial values for the variables' lags. See the "Lag Logic" section for more information.

WEIGHT Statement

WEIGHT *variable;*

The WEIGHT statement specifies a variable to supply weighting values to use for each observation in estimating parameters.

If the weight of an observation is nonpositive, that observation is not used for the estimation. *variable* must be a numeric variable in the input data set.

An alternative weighting method is to use an assignment statement to give values to the special variable _WEIGHT_. The _WEIGHT_ variable must not depend on the parameters being estimated. If both weighting specifications are given, the weights are multiplied together.

Details: Estimation

Estimation Methods

Consider the general nonlinear model:

$$\begin{aligned} \epsilon_t &= \mathbf{q}(\mathbf{y}_t, \mathbf{x}_t, \theta) \\ \mathbf{z}_t &= Z(\mathbf{x}_t) \end{aligned}$$

where $\mathbf{q} \in R^g$ is a real vector valued function, of $\mathbf{y}_t \in R^g$, $\mathbf{x}_t \in R^l$, $\theta \in R^p$, g is the number of equations, l is the number of exogenous variables (lagged endogenous variables are considered exogenous here), p is the number of parameters and t ranges from 1 to n. $\mathbf{z}_t \in R^k$ is a vector of instruments. ϵ_t is an unobservable disturbance vector with the following properties:

$$\begin{aligned} E(\epsilon_t) &= 0 \\ E(\epsilon_t \epsilon_t') &= \Sigma \end{aligned}$$

All of the methods implemented in PROC MODEL aim to minimize an *objective function*. The following table summarizes the objective functions defining the estimators and the corresponding estimator of the covariance of the parameter estimates for each method.

Table 20.1. Summary of PROC MODEL Estimation Methods

Method	Instruments	Objective Function	Covariance of θ
OLS	no	$\mathbf{r}'\mathbf{r}/n$	$(\mathbf{X}'(\text{diag}(\mathbf{S})^{-1}\otimes\mathbf{I})\mathbf{X})^{-1}$
ITOLS	no	$\mathbf{r}'(\text{diag}(\mathbf{S})^{-1}\otimes\mathbf{I})\mathbf{r}/\text{n}$	$(\mathbf{X}'(\text{diag}(\mathbf{S})^{-1}\otimes\mathbf{I})\mathbf{X})^{-1}$
SUR	no	$\mathbf{r}'(\mathbf{S}_{\text{OLS}}^{-1}\otimes\mathbf{I})\mathbf{r}/n$	$(\mathbf{X}'(\mathbf{S}^{-1}\otimes\mathbf{I})\mathbf{X})^{-1}$
ITSUR	no	$\mathbf{r}'(\mathbf{S}^{-1}\otimes\mathbf{I})\mathbf{r}/n$	$(\mathbf{X}'(\mathbf{S}^{-1}\otimes\mathbf{I})\mathbf{X})^{-1}$
N2SLS	yes	$\mathbf{r}'(\mathbf{I}\otimes\mathbf{W})\mathbf{r}/n$	$(\mathbf{X}'(\text{diag}(\mathbf{S})^{-1}\otimes\mathbf{W})\mathbf{X})^{-1}$
IT2SLS	yes	$\mathbf{r}'(\text{diag}(\mathbf{S})^{-1}\otimes\mathbf{W})\mathbf{r}/\text{n}$	$(\mathbf{X}'(\text{diag}(\mathbf{S})^{-1}\otimes\mathbf{W})\mathbf{X})^{-1}$
N3SLS	yes	$\mathbf{r}'(\mathbf{S}_{\text{N2SLS}}^{-1}\otimes\mathbf{W})\mathbf{r}/n$	$(\mathbf{X}'(\mathbf{S}^{-1}\otimes\mathbf{W})\mathbf{X})^{-1}$
IT3SLS	yes	$\mathbf{r}'(\mathbf{S}^{-1}\otimes\mathbf{W})\mathbf{r}/n$	$(\mathbf{X}'(\mathbf{S}^{-1}\otimes\mathbf{W})\mathbf{X})^{-1}$
GMM	yes	$[n\mathbf{m}_n(\theta)]'\hat{\mathbf{V}}_{\text{N2SLS}}^{-1}[n\mathbf{m}_n(\theta)]/n$	$[(\mathbf{YX})'\hat{\mathbf{V}}^{-1}(\mathbf{YX})]^{-1}$
ITGMM	yes	$[n\mathbf{m}_n(\theta)]'\hat{\mathbf{V}}^{-1}[n\mathbf{m}_n(\theta)]/n$	$[(\mathbf{YX})'\hat{\mathbf{V}}^{-1}(\mathbf{YX})]^{-1}$
FIML	no	$constant + \frac{n}{2}\ln(\det(\mathbf{S})) - \sum_1^n \ln\|(\mathbf{J}_t)\|$	$[\hat{\mathbf{Z}}'(\mathbf{S}^{-1}\otimes\mathbf{I})\hat{\mathbf{Z}}]^{-1}$

The column labeled "Instruments" identifies the estimation methods that require instruments. The variables used in this table and the remainder of this chapter are defined as follows:

$n =$ is the number of nonmissing observations.

$g =$ is the number of equations.

$k =$ is the number of instrumental variables.

$\mathbf{r} = \begin{bmatrix} r_1 \\ r_2 \\ \vdots \\ r_g \end{bmatrix}$ is the $ng \times 1$ vector of residuals for the g equations stacked together.

$\mathbf{r}_i = \begin{bmatrix} q_i(\mathbf{y}_1, \mathbf{x}_1, \theta) \\ q_i(\mathbf{y}_2, \mathbf{x}_2, \theta) \\ \vdots \\ q_i(\mathbf{y}_n, \mathbf{x}_n, \theta) \end{bmatrix}$ is the $n \times 1$ column vector of residuals for the ith equation.

S is a $g \times g$ matrix that estimates Σ, the covariances of the errors across equations (referred to as the **S** matrix).

X is an $ng \times p$ matrix of partial derivatives of the residual with respect to the parameters.

W is an $n \times n$ matrix, $\mathbf{Z}(\mathbf{Z}'\mathbf{Z})^{-1}\mathbf{Z}'$.

Z is an $n \times k$ matrix of instruments.

Y is a $gk \times ng$ matrix of instruments. $\mathbf{Y} = \mathbf{I}_g \otimes \mathbf{Z}'$.

$\hat{\mathbf{Z}}$ $\hat{\mathbf{Z}} = (\hat{Z}_1, \hat{Z}_2, \ldots, \hat{Z}_p)$ is an $ng \times p$ matrix. $\hat{Z}_i$ is a $ng \times 1$ column vector obtained from stacking the columns of

$$\mathbf{U}\frac{1}{n}\sum_{t=1}^{n}\left(\frac{\partial \mathbf{q}(\mathbf{y}_t, \mathbf{x}_t, \theta)'}{\partial y_t}\right)^{-1}\frac{\partial^2 \mathbf{q}(\mathbf{y}_t, \mathbf{x}_t, \theta)'}{\partial y_t \partial \theta_i} - \mathbf{Q}_i$$

U is an $n \times g$ matrix of residual errors. $\mathbf{U} = \epsilon_1, \epsilon_2, \ldots, \epsilon_n{}'$

Q is the $n \times g$ matrix $\mathbf{q}(\mathbf{y}_1, \mathbf{x}_1, \theta), \mathbf{q}(\mathbf{y}_2, \mathbf{x}_2, \theta), \ldots, \mathbf{q}(\mathbf{y}_n, n, \theta)$.

$\mathbf{Q}_i$ is an $n \times g$ matrix $\frac{\partial \mathbf{Q}}{\partial \theta_i}$.

I is an $n \times n$ identity matrix.

$\mathbf{J}_t$ is $\frac{\partial \mathbf{q}(\mathbf{y}_t, \mathbf{x}_t, \theta)}{\partial \mathbf{y}_t'}$ which is a $g \times g$ Jacobian matrix.

$\mathbf{m}_n$ is first moment of the crossproduct $\mathbf{q}(\mathbf{y}_t, \mathbf{x}_t, \theta) \otimes \mathbf{z}_t$.

$m_n = \frac{1}{n}\sum_{t=1}^{n} \mathbf{q}(\mathbf{y}_t, \mathbf{x}_t, \theta) \otimes \mathbf{z}_t$

$\mathbf{z}_t$ is a k column vector of instruments for observation t. $\mathbf{z}_t'$ is also the tth row of **Z**.

$\hat{\mathbf{V}}$	is the $gk \times gk$ matrix representing the variance of the moment functions.
k	is the number of instrumental variables used.
constant	is the constant $\frac{ng}{2}(1 + \ln(2\pi))$.
$\otimes$	is the notation for a Kronecker product.

All vectors are column vectors unless otherwise noted. Other estimates of the covariance matrix for FIML are also available.

Dependent Regressors and Two-Stage Least Squares

Ordinary regression analysis is based on several assumptions. A key assumption is that the independent variables are in fact statistically independent of the unobserved error component of the model. If this assumption is not true–if the regressor varies systematically with the error–then ordinary regression produces inconsistent results. The parameter estimates are *biased.*

Regressors might fail to be independent variables because they are dependent variables in a larger simultaneous system. For this reason, the problem of dependent regressors is often called *simultaneous equation bias*. For example, consider the following two-equation system.

$$y_1 = a_1 + b_1 y_2 + c_1 x_1 + \epsilon_1$$

$$y_2 = a_2 + b_2 y_1 + c_2 x_2 + \epsilon_2$$

In the first equation, y_2 is a dependent, or *endogenous*, variable. As shown by the second equation, y_2 is a function of y_1, which by the first equation is a function of ϵ_1, and therefore y_2 depends on ϵ_1. Likewise, y_1 depends on ϵ_2 and is a dependent regressor in the second equation. This is an example of a *simultaneous equation* system; y_1 and y_2 are a function of all the variables in the system.

Using the ordinary least squares (OLS) estimation method to estimate these equations produces biased estimates. One solution to this problem is to replace y_1 and y_2 on the right-hand side of the equations with predicted values, thus changing the regression problem to the following:

$$y_1 = a_1 + b_1 \hat{y}_2 + c_1 x_1 + \epsilon_1$$

$$y_2 = a_2 + b_2 \hat{y}_1 + c_2 x_2 + \epsilon_2$$

This method requires estimating the predicted values $\hat{y}_1$ and $\hat{y}_2$ through a preliminary, or "first stage," *instrumental regression*. An instrumental regression is a regression of the dependent regressors on a set of *instrumental variables*, which can be any independent variables useful for predicting the dependent regressors. In this example, the equations are linear and the exogenous variables for the whole system are known.

Thus, the best choice for instruments (of the variables in the model) are the variables x_1 and x_2.

This method is known as *two-stage least squares* or 2SLS, or more generally as the *instrumental variables method.* The 2SLS method for linear models is discussed in Pindyck (1981, p. 191-192). For nonlinear models this situation is more complex, but the idea is the same. In nonlinear 2SLS, the derivatives of the model with respect to the parameters are replaced with predicted values. See the section "Choice of Instruments" for further discussion of the use of instrumental variables in nonlinear regression.

To perform nonlinear 2SLS estimation with PROC MODEL, specify the instrumental variables with an INSTRUMENTS statement and specify the 2SLS or N2SLS option on the FIT statement. The following statements show how to estimate the first equation in the preceding example with PROC MODEL.

```
proc model data=in;
   y1 = a1 + b1 * y2 + c1 * x1;
   fit y1 / 2sls;
   instruments x1 x2;
run;
```

The 2SLS or instrumental variables estimator can be computed using a first-stage regression on the instrumental variables as described previously. However, PROC MODEL actually uses the equivalent but computationally more appropriate technique of projecting the regression problem into the linear space defined by the instruments. Thus PROC MODEL does not produce any "first stage" results when you use 2SLS. If you specify the FSRSQ option on the FIT statement, PROC MODEL prints "first-stage R^2" statistic for each parameter estimate.

Formally, the $\hat{\theta}$ that minimizes

$$\hat{S}_n = \frac{1}{n}\left(\sum_{t=1}^{n}(\mathbf{q}(\mathbf{y}_t,\mathbf{x}_t,\theta)\otimes\mathbf{z}_t)\right)'\left(\sum_{t=1}^{n}I\otimes\mathbf{z}_t\mathbf{z}_t'\right)^{-1}\left(\sum_{t=1}^{n}(\mathbf{q}(\mathbf{y}_t,\mathbf{x}_t,\theta)\otimes\mathbf{z}_t)\right)$$

is the N2SLS estimator of the parameters. The estimate of Σ at the final iteration is used in the covariance of the parameters given in Table 20.1. Refer to Amemiya (1985, p. 250) for details on the properties of nonlinear two-stage least squares.

Seemingly Unrelated Regression

If the regression equations are not simultaneous, so there are no dependent regressors, *seemingly unrelated regression* (SUR) can be used to estimate systems of equations with correlated random errors. The large-sample efficiency of an estimation can be improved if these cross-equation correlations are taken into account. SUR is also known as *joint generalized least squares* or *Zellner regression*. Formally, the $\hat{\theta}$ that minimizes

$$\hat{S}_n = \frac{1}{n}\sum_{t=1}^{n} \mathbf{q}(\mathbf{y}_t, \mathbf{x}_t, \theta)'\hat{\Sigma}^{-1}\mathbf{q}(\mathbf{y}_t, \mathbf{x}_t, \theta)$$

is the SUR estimator of the parameters.

The SUR method requires an estimate of the cross-equation covariance matrix, Σ. PROC MODEL first performs an OLS estimation, computes an estimate, $\hat{\Sigma}$, from the OLS residuals, and then performs the SUR estimation based on $\hat{\Sigma}$. The OLS results are not printed unless you specify the OLS option in addition to the SUR option.

You can specify the $\hat{\Sigma}$ to use for SUR by storing the matrix in a SAS data set and naming that data set in the SDATA= option. You can also feed the $\hat{\Sigma}$ computed from the SUR residuals back into the SUR estimation process by specifying the ITSUR option. You can print the estimated covariance matrix $\hat{\Sigma}$ using the COVS option on the FIT statement.

The SUR method requires estimation of the Σ matrix, and this increases the sampling variability of the estimator for small sample sizes. The efficiency gain SUR has over OLS is a large sample property, and you must have a reasonable amount of data to realize this gain. For a more detailed discussion of SUR, refer to Pindyck (1981, p. 331-333).

Three-Stage Least-Squares Estimation

If the equation system is simultaneous, you can combine the 2SLS and SUR methods to take into account both dependent regressors and cross-equation correlation of the errors. This is called *three-stage least squares* (3SLS).

Formally, the $\hat{\theta}$ that minimizes

$$\hat{S}_n = \frac{1}{n}\left(\sum_{t=1}^{n}(\mathbf{q}(\mathbf{y}_t, \mathbf{x}_t, \theta)\otimes\mathbf{z}_t)\right)'\left(\sum_{t=1}^{n}(\hat{\Sigma}\otimes\mathbf{z}_t\mathbf{z}_t')\right)^{-1}\left(\sum_{t=1}^{n}(\mathbf{q}(\mathbf{y}_t, \mathbf{x}_t, \theta)\otimes\mathbf{z}_t)\right)$$

is the 3SLS estimator of the parameters. For more details on 3SLS, refer to Gallant (1987, p. 435).

Residuals from the 2SLS method are used to estimate the Σ matrix required for 3SLS. The results of the preliminary 2SLS step are not printed unless the 2SLS option is also specified.

To use the three-stage least-squares method, specify an INSTRUMENTS statement and use the 3SLS or N3SLS option on either the PROC MODEL statement or a FIT statement.

Generalized Method of Moments - GMM

For systems of equations with heteroscedastic errors, generalized method of moments (GMM) can be used to obtain efficient estimates of the parameters. See the "Heteroscedasticity" section for alternatives to GMM.

Consider the nonlinear model

$$\begin{aligned} \epsilon_t &= \mathbf{q}(\mathbf{y}_t, \mathbf{x}_t, \theta) \\ \mathbf{z}_t &= Z(\mathbf{x}_t) \end{aligned}$$

where $\mathbf{z}_t$ is a vector of instruments and ϵ_t is an unobservable disturbance vector that can be serially correlated and nonstationary.

In general, the following orthogonality condition is desired:

$$E(\epsilon_t \otimes \mathbf{z}_t) = 0$$

which states that the expected crossproducts of the unobservable disturbances, ϵ_t, and functions of the observable variables are set to 0. The first moment of the crossproducts is

$$\begin{aligned} \mathbf{m}_n &= \frac{1}{n}\sum_{t=1}^{n} \mathbf{m}(\mathbf{y}_t, \mathbf{x}_t, \theta) \\ \mathbf{m}(\mathbf{y}_t, \mathbf{x}_t, \theta) &= \mathbf{q}(\mathbf{y}_t, \mathbf{x}_t, \theta) \otimes \mathbf{z}_t \end{aligned}$$

where $\mathbf{m}(\mathbf{y}_t, \mathbf{x}_t, \theta) \in R^{gk}$.

The case where $gk > p$ is considered here, where p is the number of parameters.

Estimate the true parameter vector θ^0 by the value of $\hat{\theta}$ that minimizes

$$S(\theta, V) = [n\mathbf{m}_n(\theta)]' V^{-1} [n\mathbf{m}_n(\theta)]/n$$

where

$$V = \mathrm{Cov}\left([\mathbf{nm_n}(\theta^0)], [\mathbf{nm_n}(\theta^0)]'\right)$$

The parameter vector that minimizes this objective function is the GMM estimator. GMM estimation is requested on the FIT statement with the GMM option.

The variance of the moment functions, V, can be expressed as

$$
\begin{aligned}
V &= E\left(\sum_{t=1}^{n} \epsilon_t \otimes \mathbf{z}_t\right)\left(\sum_{s=1}^{n} \epsilon_s \otimes \mathbf{z}_s\right)' \\
&= \sum_{t=1}^{n}\sum_{s=1}^{n} E\left[(\epsilon_t \otimes \mathbf{z}_t)(\epsilon_s \otimes \mathbf{z}_s)'\right] \\
&= nS_n^0
\end{aligned}
$$

where S_n^0 is estimated as

$$
\hat{S}_n = \frac{1}{n}\sum_{t=1}^{n}\sum_{s=1}^{n} (\mathbf{q}(\mathbf{y}_t, \mathbf{x}_t, \theta)\otimes \mathbf{z}_t)(\mathbf{q}(\mathbf{y}_s, \mathbf{x}_s, \theta)\otimes \mathbf{z}_s)'
$$

Note that $\hat{S}_n$ is a $gk \times gk$ matrix. Because Var $(\hat{S}_n)$ will not decrease with increasing n we consider estimators of S_n^0 of the form:

$$
\begin{aligned}
\hat{S}_n(l(n)) &= \sum_{\tau=-n+1}^{n-1} w\left(\frac{\tau}{l(n)}\right) D\hat{S}_{n,\tau} D \\
\hat{S}_{n,\tau} &= \begin{cases} \sum_{t=1+\tau}^{n} [\mathbf{q}(\mathbf{y}_t, \mathbf{x}_t, \theta^{\#})\otimes \mathbf{z}_t][\mathbf{q}(\mathbf{y}_{t-\tau}, \mathbf{x}_{t-\tau}, \theta^{\#})\otimes \mathbf{z}_{t-\tau}]' & \tau \geq 0 \\ (\hat{S}_{n,-\tau})' & \tau < 0 \end{cases}
\end{aligned}
$$

where $l(n)$ is a scalar function that computes the bandwidth parameter, $w(\cdot)$ is a scalar valued kernel, and the diagonal matrix D is used for a small sample degrees of freedom correction (Gallant 1987). The initial $\theta^{\#}$ used for the estimation of $\hat{S}_n$ is obtained from a 2SLS estimation of the system. The degrees of freedom correction is handled by the VARDEF= option as for the **S** matrix estimation.

The following kernels are supported by PROC MODEL. They are listed with their default bandwidth functions.

Bartlett: KERNEL=BART

$$
\begin{aligned}
w(x) &= \begin{cases} 1 - |x| & |x| <= 1 \\ 0 & \text{otherwise} \end{cases} \\
l(n) &= \frac{1}{2} n^{1/3}
\end{aligned}
$$

Parzen: KERNEL=PARZEN

$$
\begin{aligned}
w(x) &= \begin{cases} 1-6|x|^2+6|x|^3 & 0 <= |x| <= \frac{1}{2} \\ 2(1-|x|)^3 & \frac{1}{2} <= |x| <= 1 \\ 0 & \text{otherwise} \end{cases} \\
l(n) &= n^{1/5}
\end{aligned}
$$

Quadratic Spectral: KERNEL=QS

$$
\begin{aligned}
w(x) &= \frac{25}{12\pi^2x^2}\left(\frac{sin(6\pi x/5)}{6\pi x/5} - cos(6\pi x/5)\right) \\
l(n) &= \frac{1}{2}n^{1/5}
\end{aligned}
$$

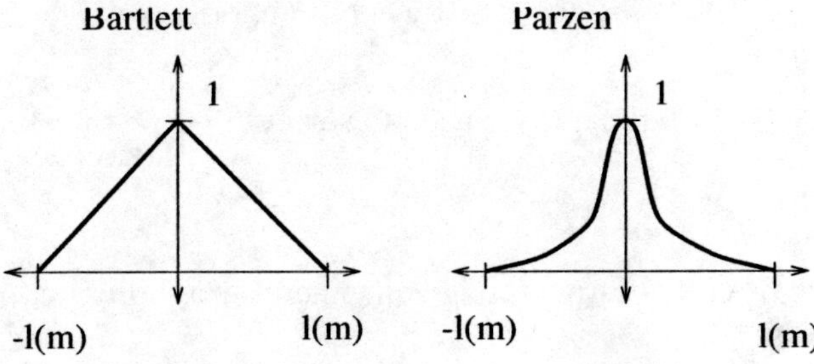

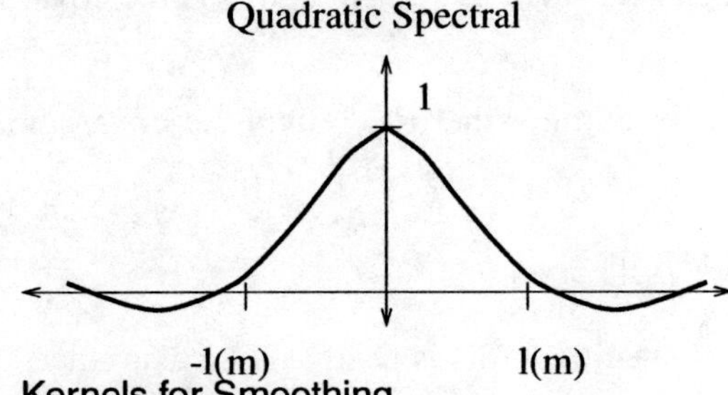

Figure 20.15. Kernels for Smoothing

Details of the properties of these and other kernels are given in Andrews (1991). Kernels are selected with the KERNEL= option; KERNEL=PARZEN is the default. The general form of the KERNEL= option is

```
KERNEL=( PARZEN | QS | BART, c, e )
```

where the $e \geq 0$ and $c \geq 0$ are used to compute the bandwidth parameter as

$$l(n) = cn^e$$

The bias of the standard error estimates increases for large bandwidth parameters. A warning message is produced for bandwidth parameters greater than $n^{\frac{1}{3}}$. For a discussion of the computation of the optimal $l(n)$, refer to Andrews (1991).

The "Newey-West" kernel (Newey (1987)) corresponds to the Bartlett kernel with bandwidth parameter $l(n) = L + 1$. That is, if the "lag length" for the Newey-West kernel is L then the corresponding Model procedure syntax is KERNEL=(bart, L+1, 0).

Andrews (1992) has shown that using prewhitening in combination with GMM can improve confidence interval coverage and reduce over rejection of *t*-statistics at the cost of inflating the variance and MSE of the estimator. Prewhitening can be performed using the %AR macros.

For the special case that the errors are not serially correlated, that is

$$E(e_t \otimes \mathbf{z}_t)(e_s \otimes \mathbf{z}_s) = 0 \qquad t \neq s$$

the estimate for S_n^0 reduces to

$$\hat{S}_n = \frac{1}{n} \sum_{t=1}^{n} [\mathbf{q}(\mathbf{y}_t, \mathbf{x}_t, \theta) \otimes \mathbf{z}_t][\mathbf{q}(\mathbf{y}_t, \mathbf{x}_t, \theta) \otimes \mathbf{z}_t]'$$

The option KERNEL=(*kernel*,0,) is used to select this type of estimation when using GMM.

Covariance of GMM estimators

The Covariance of GMM estimators given general weighting matrix $\mathbf{V}_{\mathrm{G}}^{-1}$ is

$$[(\mathbf{YX})'\mathbf{V}_{\mathrm{G}}^{-1}(\mathbf{YX})]^{-1}(\mathbf{YX})'\mathbf{V}_{\mathrm{G}}^{-1}\hat{\mathbf{V}}\mathbf{V}_{\mathrm{G}}^{-1}(\mathbf{YX})[(\mathbf{YX})'\mathbf{V}_{\mathrm{G}}^{-1}(\mathbf{YX})]^{-1}$$

By default or when GENGMMV is specified, this is the covariance of GMM estimators.

If the weighting matrix is the same as $\hat{\mathbf{V}}$, then the covariance of GMM estimators becomes

$$[(\mathbf{YX})'\hat{\mathbf{V}}^{-1}(\mathbf{YX})]^{-1}$$

If NOGENGMMV is specified, this is used as the covariance estimators.

Testing Over-Identifying Restrictions

Let *r* be the number of unique instruments times the number of equations. The value *r* represents the number of orthogonality conditions imposed by the GMM method. Under the assumptions of the GMM method, $r - p$ linearly independent combinations of the orthogonality should be close to zero. The GMM estimates are computed by setting these combinations to zero. When *r* exceeds the number of parameters to be estimated, the OBJECTIVE*N, reported at the end of the estimation, is an asymptoticly valid statistic to test the null hypothesis that the over-identifying restrictions of the model are valid. The OBJECTIVE*N is distributed as a chi-square with $r - p$ degrees of freedom (Hansen 1982, p. 1049).

Iterated Generalized Method of Moments - ITGMM

Iterated generalized method of moments is similar to the iterated versions of 2SLS, SUR, and 3SLS. The variance matrix for GMM estimation is re-estimated at each iteration with the parameters determined by the GMM estimation. The iteration terminates when the variance matrix for the equation errors change less than the CONVERGE= value. Iterated generalized method of moments is selected by the ITGMM option on the FIT statement. For some indication of the small sample properties of ITGMM, refer to Ferson and Foerster (1993).

Simulated Method of Moments - SMM

The SMM method uses simulation techniques in model inference and estimation. It is appropriate for estimating models in which integrals appear in the objective function and these integrals can be approximated by simulation. There may be various reasons for integrals to appear in an objective function, for example, transformation of a latent model into an observable model, missing data, random coefficients, heterogeneity, etc.

This simulation method can be used with all the estimation methods except Full Information Maximum Likelihood (FIML) in PROC MODEL. SMM, also known as Simulated Generalized Method of Moments (SGMM), is the default estimation method because of its nice properties.

Estimation Details

A general nonlinear model can be described as

$$\epsilon_t = \mathbf{q}(\mathbf{y}_t, \mathbf{x}_t, \theta)$$

where $\mathbf{q} \in R^g$ is a real vector valued function of $\mathbf{y}_t \in R^g$, $\mathbf{x}_t \in R^l$, $\theta \in R^p$, g is the number of equations, l is the number of exogenous variables (lagged endogenous variables are considered exogenous here), p is the number of parameters, and t ranges from 1 to n. ϵ_t is an unobservable disturbance vector with the following properties:

$$\begin{aligned} E(\epsilon_t) &= 0 \\ E(\epsilon_t \epsilon_t^{'}) &= \Sigma \end{aligned}$$

In many cases it is not possible to write $\mathbf{q}(\mathbf{y}_t, \mathbf{x}_t, \theta)$ in a closed form. Instead $\mathbf{q}$ is expressed as an integral of a function $\mathbf{f}$, that is,

$$\mathbf{q}(\mathbf{y}_t, \mathbf{x}_t, \theta) = \int \mathbf{f}(\mathbf{y}_t, \mathbf{x}_t, \theta, \mathbf{u}_t) dP(\mathbf{u})$$

where $\mathbf{f} \in R^g$ is a real vector valued function of $\mathbf{y}_t \in R^g$, $\mathbf{x}_t \in R^l$, $\theta \in R^p$, and $\mathbf{u}_t \in R^m$, m is the number of stochastic variables with a known distribution $P(\mathbf{u})$. Since the distribution of $\mathbf{u}$ is completely known, it is possible to simulate artificial draws from this distribution. Using such independent draws $\mathbf{u}_{ht}$, $h = 1, \ldots, H$, and the strong law of large numbers, $\mathbf{q}$ can be approximated by

$$\frac{1}{H}\sum_{h=1}^{H}\mathbf{f}(\mathbf{y}_t, \mathbf{x}_t, \theta, \mathbf{u}_{ht}).$$

Simulated Generalized Method of Moments - SGMM

Generalized Method of Moments (GMM) is widely used to obtain efficient estimates for general model systems. When the moment conditions are not readily available in closed forms but can be approximated by simulation, Simulated Generalized Method of Moments (SGMM) can be used. The SGMM estimators have the nice property of being asymptotically consistent and normally distributed even if the number of draws H is fixed (see McFadden 1989, Pakes and Pollard 1989).

Consider the nonlinear model

$$\begin{aligned} \epsilon_t &= \mathbf{q}(\mathbf{y}_t, \mathbf{x}_t, \theta) = \frac{1}{H}\sum_{h=1}^{H}\mathbf{f}(\mathbf{y}_t, \mathbf{x}_t, \theta, \mathbf{u}_{ht}) \\ \mathbf{z}_t &= Z(\mathbf{x}_t) \end{aligned}$$

where $\mathbf{z}_t \in R^k$ is a vector of k instruments and ϵ_t is an unobservable disturbance vector that can be serially correlated and nonstationary. In case of no instrumental variables, $\mathbf{z}_t$ is 1. $\mathbf{q}(\mathbf{y}_t, \mathbf{x}_t, \theta)$ is the vector of moment conditions, and it is approximated by simulation.

In general, theory suggests the following orthogonality condition

$$E(\epsilon_t \otimes \mathbf{z}_t) = 0$$

which states that the expected crossproducts of the unobservable disturbances, ϵ_t, and functions of the observable variables are set to 0. The sample means of the crossproducts are

$$\begin{aligned} \mathbf{m}_n &= \frac{1}{n}\sum_{t=1}^{n}\mathbf{m}(\mathbf{y}_t, \mathbf{x}_t, \theta) \\ \mathbf{m}(\mathbf{y}_t, \mathbf{x}_t, \theta) &= \mathbf{q}(\mathbf{y}_t, \mathbf{x}_t, \theta) \otimes \mathbf{z}_t \end{aligned}$$

where $\mathbf{m}(\mathbf{y}_t, \mathbf{x}_t, \theta) \in R^{gk}$. The case where $gk > p$, where p is the number of parameters, is considered here. An estimate of the true parameter vector θ^0 is the value of $\hat{\theta}$ that minimizes

$$S(\theta, V) = [n\mathbf{m}_n(\theta)]' V^{-1} [n\mathbf{m}_n(\theta)]/n$$

where

$$V = \mathrm{Cov}\left(\mathbf{m}(\theta^0), \mathbf{m}(\theta^0)'\right).$$

The steps for SGMM are as follows:

1. Start with a positive definite $\hat{V}$ matrix. This $\hat{V}$ matrix can be estimated from a consistent estimator of θ. If $\hat{\theta}$ is a consistent estimator, then $\mathbf{u}_t$ for $t = 1, ..., n$ can be simulated H' number of times. A consistent estimator of V is obtained as

$$\hat{V} = \frac{1}{n}\sum_{t=1}^{n}[\frac{1}{H'}\sum_{h=1}^{H'}\mathbf{f}(\mathbf{y}_t, \mathbf{x}_t, \hat{\theta}, \mathbf{u}_{ht})\otimes\mathbf{z}_t][\frac{1}{H'}\sum_{h=1}^{H'}\mathbf{f}(\mathbf{y}_t, \mathbf{x}_t, \hat{\theta}, \mathbf{u}_{ht})\otimes\mathbf{z}_t]'$$

H' must be large so that this is an consistent estimator of V.

2. Simulate H number of $\mathbf{u}_t$ for $t = 1, ..., n$. As shown by Gourieroux and Monfort (1993), the number of simulations H does not need to be very large. For $H = 10$, the SGMM estimator achieves 90% of the efficiency of the corresponding GMM estimator. Find $\hat{\theta}$ that minimizes the quadratic product of the moment conditions again with the weight matrix being $\hat{V}^{-1}$.

$$\min_{\theta}\, [n\mathbf{m}_n(\theta)]'\hat{V}^{-1}[n\mathbf{m}_n(\theta)]/n$$

3. The covariance matrix of $\sqrt{n}\theta$ is given as (Gourieroux and Monfont 1993)

$$\Sigma_1^{-1}D\hat{V}^{-1}V(\hat{\theta})\hat{V}^{-1}D'\Sigma_1^{-1} + \frac{1}{H}\Sigma_1^{-1}D\hat{V}^{-1}E[\mathbf{z}\otimes Var(\mathbf{f}|\mathbf{x})\otimes\mathbf{z}]\hat{V}^{-1}D'\Sigma_1^{-1}$$

where $\Sigma_1 = D\hat{V}^{-1}D$, D is the matrix of partial derivatives of the residuals with respect to the parameters, $V(\hat{\theta})$ is the covariance of moments from estimated parameters $\hat{\theta}$, and $Var(\mathbf{f}|\mathbf{x})$ is the covarince of moments for each observation from simulation. The first term is the variance-covariance matrix of the exact GMM estimator, and the second term accounts for the variation contributed by simulating the moments.

Implementation in PROC MODEL

In PROC MODEL, if the user specifies the GMM and NDRAW options on the FIT statement, PROC MODEL first fits the model using N2SLS and computes $\hat{V}$ using the estimates from N2SLS and H' simulation. If NO2SLS is specified on the FIT statement, $\hat{V}$ is read from VDATA= data set. If the user does not provide a $\hat{V}$ matrix, the initial starting value of θ is used as the estimator for computing the $\hat{V}$ matrix in step 1. If ITGMM option is specified instead of GMM, then PROC MODEL iterates from step 1 to step 3 until the V matrix converges.

The consistency of the parameter estimates is not affected by the variance correction shown in the second term in step 3. The correction on the variance of parameter estimates is not computed by default. To add the adjustment, use ADJSMMV option on the FIT statement. This correction is of the order of $\frac{1}{H}$ and is small even for moderate H.

The following example illustrates how to use SMM to estimate a simple regression model. Suppose the model is

$$y = a + bx + u, u \sim iid\, N(0, s^2).$$

First, consider the problem in GMM context. The first two moments of y are easily derived:

$$\begin{aligned} E(y) &= a + bx \\ E(y^2) &= (a + bx)^2 + s^2 \end{aligned}$$

Rewrite the moment conditions in the form similar to the discussion above:

$$\begin{aligned} \epsilon_{1t} &= y_t - (a + bx_t) \\ \epsilon_{2t} &= y_t^2 - (a + bx_t)^2 - s^2 \end{aligned}$$

Then you can estimate this model using GMM with following code:

```
proc model data=a;
  parms a b s;
  instrument x;
  eq.m1 = y-(a+b*x);
  eq.m2 = y*y - (a+b*x)**2 - s*s;
  bound s > 0;
  fit m1 m2 / gmm;
run;
```

Now suppose you do not have the closed form for the moment conditions. Instead you can simulate the moment conditions by generating H number of simulated samples based on the parameters. Then the simulated moment conditions are

$$\begin{aligned} \epsilon_{1t} &= \frac{1}{H}\sum_{h=1}^{H}\{y_t - (a + bx_t + su_{t,h})\} \\ \epsilon_{2t} &= \frac{1}{H}\sum_{h=1}^{H}\{y_t^2 - (a + bx_t + su_{t,h})^2\} \end{aligned}$$

This model can be estimated using SGMM with the following code:

```
proc model data=_tmpdata;
       parms a b s;
       instrument x;
       ysim = (a+b*x) + s * rannor( 98711 );
       eq.m1 = y-ysim;
       eq.m2 = y*y - ysim*ysim;
       bound s > 0;
       fit m1 m2 / gmm ndraw=10;
run;
```

Note that the NDRAW= option tells PROC MODEL that this is a simulation-based estimation. Thus the random number function RANNOR returns random numbers in estimation process. During the simulation, 10 draws of $m1$ and $m2$ are generated for each observation, and the averages enter the objective functions just as the equations specified previously.

Other Estimation Methods

The simulation method can be used not only with GMM and ITGMM, but also with OLS, ITOLS, SUR, ITSUR, N2SLS, IT2SLS, N3SLS, and IT3SLS. These simulation-based methods are similar to the corresponding methods in PROC MODEL; however, the only difference is that the objective functions include the average of the H simulations.

Full Information Maximum Likelihood Estimation - FIML

A different approach to the simultaneous equation bias problem is the full information maximum likelihood (FIML) estimation method (Amemiya 1977).

Compared to the instrumental variables methods (2SLS and 3SLS), the FIML method has these advantages and disadvantages:

- FIML does not require instrumental variables.
- FIML requires that the model include the full equation system, with as many equations as there are endogenous variables. With 2SLS or 3SLS you can estimate some of the equations without specifying the complete system.
- FIML assumes that the equations errors have a multivariate normal distribution. If the errors are not normally distributed, the FIML method may produce poor results. 2SLS and 3SLS do not assume a specific distribution for the errors.
- The FIML method is computationally expensive.

The full information maximum likelihood estimators of θ and σ are the $\hat{\theta}$ and $\hat{\sigma}$ that minimize the negative log likelihood function:

$$
\begin{aligned}
\mathbf{l}_n(\theta,\sigma) = {} & \frac{ng}{2}\ \ln(2\pi) - \sum_{t=1}^{n} \ln\left(\left|\frac{\partial \mathbf{q}(\mathbf{y}_t, \mathbf{x}_t, \theta)}{\partial \mathbf{y}'_t}\right|\right) + \frac{n}{2}\ln\left(|\Sigma(\sigma)|\right) \\
& + \frac{1}{2}\mathrm{tr}\left(\Sigma(\sigma)^{-1}\sum_{\mathrm{t}=1}^{\mathrm{n}} \mathbf{q}(\mathbf{y}_\mathrm{t}, \mathbf{x}_\mathrm{t}, \theta)\mathbf{q}'(\mathbf{y}_\mathrm{t}, \mathbf{x}_\mathrm{t}, \theta)\right)
\end{aligned}
$$

The option FIML requests full information maximum likelihood estimation. If the errors are distributed normally, FIML produces efficient estimators of the parameters. If instrumental variables are not provided the starting values for the estimation are obtained from a SUR estimation. If instrumental variables are provided, then the starting values are obtained from a 3SLS estimation. The negative log likelihood value and the l_2 norm of the gradient of the negative log likelihood function are shown in the estimation summary.

FIML Details

To compute the minimum of $\mathbf{l}_n(\theta, \sigma)$, this function is *concentrated* using the relation

$$\Sigma(\theta) = \frac{1}{n} \sum_{t=1}^{n} \mathbf{q}(\mathbf{y}_t, \mathbf{x}_t, \theta)\mathbf{q}'(\mathbf{y}_t, \mathbf{x}_t, \theta)$$

This results in the concentrated negative log likelihood function:

$$\mathbf{l}_n(\theta) = \frac{ng}{2}(1 + \ln(2\pi)) - \sum_{t=1}^{n} \ln\left|\frac{\partial}{\partial \mathbf{y}_t'}\mathbf{q}(\mathbf{y}_t, \mathbf{x}_t, \theta)\right| + \frac{n}{2}\ln|\Sigma(\theta|)$$

The gradient of the negative log likelihood function is

$$\frac{\partial}{\partial \theta_i}\mathbf{l}_n(\theta) = \sum_{t=1}^{n} \nabla_i(t)$$

$$\begin{aligned}
\nabla_i(t) &= -\mathrm{tr}\left(\left(\frac{\partial \mathbf{q}(\mathbf{y}_t, \mathbf{x}_t, \theta)}{\partial \mathbf{y}_t'}\right)^{-1} \frac{\partial^2 \mathbf{q}(\mathbf{y}_t, \mathbf{x}_t, \theta)}{\partial \mathbf{y}_t' \partial \theta_i}\right) \\
&+ \frac{1}{2}\mathrm{tr}\left(\Sigma(\theta)^{-1}\frac{\partial \Sigma(\theta)}{\partial \theta_i}\right. \\
&\qquad \left[I - \Sigma(\theta)^{-1}\mathbf{q}(\mathbf{y}_t, \mathbf{x}_t, \theta)\mathbf{q}(\mathbf{y}_t, \mathbf{x}_t, \theta)'\right]\Big) \\
&+ \mathbf{q}(\mathbf{y}_t, \mathbf{x}_t, \theta')\Sigma(\theta)^{-1}\frac{\partial \mathbf{q}(\mathbf{y}_t, \mathbf{x}_t, \theta)}{\partial \theta_i}
\end{aligned}$$

where

$$\frac{\partial \Sigma(\theta)}{\partial \theta_i} = \frac{2}{n}\sum_{t=1}^{n} \mathbf{q}(\mathbf{y}_t, \mathbf{x}_t, \theta)\frac{\partial \mathbf{q}(\mathbf{y}_t, \mathbf{x}_t, \theta)'}{\partial \theta_i}$$

The estimator of the variance-covariance of $\hat{\theta}$ (COVB) for FIML can be selected with the COVBEST= option with the following arguments:

CROSS selects the crossproducts estimator of the covariance matrix (default) (Gallant 1987, p. 473):

$$C = \left(\frac{1}{n}\sum_{t=1}^{n} \nabla(t)\nabla'(t)\right)^{-1}$$

where $\nabla(t) = [\nabla_1(t), \nabla_2(t), \ldots, \nabla_p(t)]'$

GLS selects the generalized least-squares estimator of the covariance matrix. This is computed as (Dagenais 1978)

$$C = [\hat{Z}'(\Sigma(\theta)^{-1} \otimes I)\hat{Z}]^{-1}$$

where $\hat{Z} = (\hat{Z}_1, \hat{Z}_2, \ldots, \hat{Z}_p)$ is $ng \times p$ and each $\hat{Z}_i$ column vector is obtained from stacking the columns of

$$U \frac{1}{n} \sum_{t=1}^{n} \left(\frac{\partial \mathbf{q}(\mathbf{y}_t, \mathbf{x}_t, \theta)'}{\partial y} \right)^{-1} \frac{\partial^2 \mathbf{q}(\mathbf{y}_t, \mathbf{x}_t, \theta)'}{\partial \mathbf{y}'_n \partial \theta_i} - Q_i$$

U is an $n \times g$ matrix of residuals and q_i is an $n \times g$ matrix $\frac{\partial \mathbf{Q}}{\partial \theta_i}$.

FDA selects the inverse of concentrated likelihood Hessian as an estimator of the covariance matrix. The Hessian is computed numerically, so for a large problem this is computationally expensive.

The HESSIAN= option controls which approximation to the Hessian is used in the minimization procedure. Alternate approximations are used to improve convergence and execution time. The choices are as follows.

CROSS The crossproducts approximation is used.

GLS The generalized least-squares approximation is used (default).

FDA The Hessian is computed numerically by finite differences.

HESSIAN=GLS has better convergence properties in general, but COVBEST=CROSS produces the most pessimistic standard error bounds. When the HESSIAN= option is used, the default estimator of the variance-covariance of $\hat{\theta}$ is the inverse of the Hessian selected.

Multivariate t-Distribution Estimation

The multivariate *t*-distribution is specified using the ERRORMODEL statement with the T option. Other method specifications (FIML and OLS, for example) are ignored when the ERRORMODEL statement is used for a distribution other than normal.

The probability density function for the multivariate *t*-distribution is

$$P_q = \frac{\Gamma(\frac{df+m}{2})}{(\pi * df)^{\frac{m}{2}} * \Gamma(\frac{df}{2}) \, |\Sigma(\sigma)|^{\frac{1}{2}}} * \left(1 + \frac{\mathbf{q}'(\mathbf{y}_t, \mathbf{x}_t, \theta)\Sigma(\sigma)^{-1}\mathbf{q}(\mathbf{y}_t, \mathbf{x}_t, \theta)}{df}\right)^{-\frac{df+m}{2}}$$

where m is the number of equations and *df* is the degrees of freedom.

The maximum likelihood estimators of θ and σ are the $\hat{\theta}$ and $\hat{\sigma}$ that minimize the negative log-likelihood function:

$$\begin{aligned}
\mathbf{l}_n(\theta,\sigma) &= -\sum_{t=1}^{n} \ln\left(\frac{\Gamma(\frac{df+m}{2})}{(\pi * df)^{\frac{m}{2}} * \Gamma(\frac{df}{2})} * \left(1+\frac{q_t'\Sigma^{-1}q_t}{df}\right)^{-\frac{df+m}{2}}\right) \\
&+\frac{n}{2} * \ln\left(|\Sigma|\right) - \sum_{t=1}^{n} \ln\left(\left|\frac{\partial q_t}{\partial y_t'}\right|\right)
\end{aligned}$$

The ERRORMODEL statement is used to request the *t*-distribution maximum likelihood estimation. An OLS estimation is done to obtain initial parameter estimates and MSE.*var* estimates. Use NOOLS to turn off this initial estimation. If the errors are distributed normally, *t*-distribution estimation will produce results similar to FIML.

The multivariate model has a single shared degrees of freedom parameter, which is estimated. The degrees of freedom parameter can also be set to a fixed value. The negative log-likelihood value and the $\mathbf{l}_2$ norm of the gradient of the negative log-likelihood function are shown in the estimation summary.

t-Distribution Details

Since a variance term is explicitly specified using the ERRORMODEL statement, $\Sigma(\theta)$ is estimated as a correlation matrix and $\mathbf{q}(\mathbf{y}_t, \mathbf{x}_t, \theta)$ is normalized by the variance. The gradient of the negative log-likelihood function with respect to the degrees of freedom is

$$\begin{aligned}
\frac{\partial l_n}{\partial df} &= \frac{nm}{2\, df} - \frac{n}{2}\frac{\Gamma'(\frac{df+m}{2})}{\Gamma(\frac{df+m}{2})} + \frac{n}{2}\frac{\Gamma'(\frac{df}{2})}{\Gamma(\frac{df}{2})} + \\
& 0.5\log(1+\frac{\mathbf{q}'\Sigma^{-1}\mathbf{q}}{df}) - \frac{0.5(df+m)}{(1+\frac{\mathbf{q}'\Sigma^{-1}\mathbf{q}}{df})}\frac{\mathbf{q}'\Sigma^{-1}\mathbf{q}}{df^2}
\end{aligned}$$

The gradient of the negative log-likelihood function with respect to the parameters is

$$\frac{\partial l_n}{\partial \theta_i} = \frac{0.5(df+m)}{(1+\mathbf{q}'\Sigma^{-1}\mathbf{q}/df)}\left[\frac{(2\,\mathbf{q}'\Sigma^{-1}\frac{\partial \mathbf{q}}{\partial \theta_i})}{df} + \mathbf{q}'\Sigma^{-1}\frac{\partial \Sigma}{\partial \theta_i}\Sigma^{-1}\mathbf{q}\right] - \frac{n}{2}\mathrm{trace}(\Sigma^{-1}\frac{\partial \Sigma}{\partial \theta_i})$$

where

$$\frac{\partial \Sigma(\theta)}{\partial \theta_i} = \frac{2}{n}\sum_{t=1}^{n} \mathbf{q}(\mathbf{y}_t, \mathbf{x}_t, \theta)\frac{\partial \mathbf{q}(\mathbf{y}_t, \mathbf{x}_t, \theta)'}{\partial \theta_i}$$

and

$$\mathbf{q}(\mathbf{y}_t, \mathbf{x}_t, \theta) = \frac{\epsilon(\theta)}{\sqrt{h(\theta)}} \in R^{m \times n}$$

The estimator of the variance-covariance of $\hat{\theta}$ (COVB) for the *t*-distribution is the inverse of the likelihood Hessian. The gradient is computed analytically and the Hessian is computed numerically.

Empirical Distribution Estimation and Simulation

The following SAS statements fit a model using least squares as the likelihood function, but represent the distribution of the residuals with an empirical CDF. The plot of the empirical probability distribution is shown in the following output.

```
data t;   /* Sum of two normals   */
   format date monyy.;
   do t=0 to 3 by 0.1;
      date = intnx( 'month', '1jun90'd,(t*10)-1);
      y =   0.1 *  (rannor(123)-10) +
              .5 *(rannor(456)+10);
      output;
   end;
run;

proc model data=t time=t itprint;
   dependent y;
   parm a 5 ;
   y = a;
   obj = resid.y * resid.y;
   errormodel y ~ general( obj )
      cdf=(empirical=( tails=( t(15) percent= 5)));

   fit y / outns=s out=r;
   id  date;
   solve y / data=t(where=(date='1jun95'd ))
      residdata=r sdata=s random=200 seed=6789 out=monte;
run;

    /*--- Generate the pdf ---*/
proc kde data =monte out=density;
   var y;
run;

symbol1 value=none interpol=join;
proc gplot data=density;
   plot density*y;
run;
```

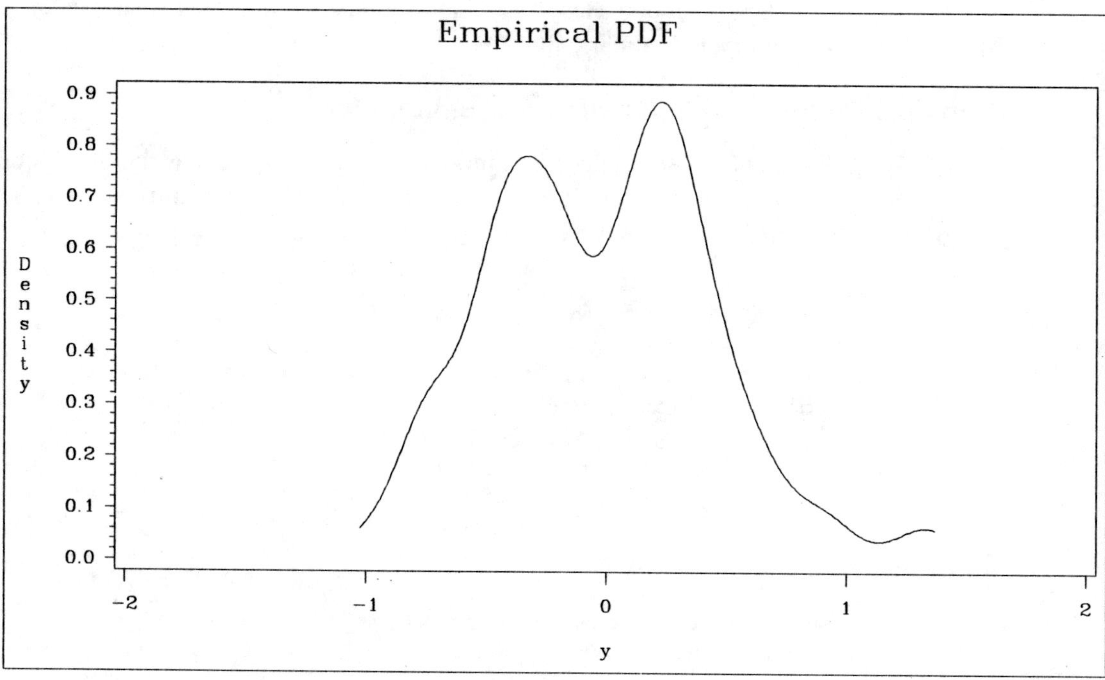

Figure 20.16. Empirical PDF Plot

For simulation, if the CDF for the model is not built in to the procedure, you can use the CDF=EMPIRICAL() option. This uses the sorted residual data to create an empirical CDF. For computing the inverse CDF the program needs to know how to handle the tails. For continuous data, the tail distribution is generally poorly determined. To counter this, the PERCENT= option specifies the percent of the observations to use in constructing each tail. The default for the PERCENT= option is 10.

A normal distribution or a *t*-distribution is used to extrapolate the tails to infinity. The standard errors for this extrapolation are obtained from the data so that the empirical CDF is continuous.

Properties of the Estimates

All of the methods are consistent. Small sample properties may not be good for nonlinear models. The tests and standard errors reported are based on the convergence of the distribution of the estimates to a normal distribution in large samples.

These nonlinear estimation methods reduce to the corresponding linear systems regression methods if the model is linear. If this is the case, PROC MODEL produces the same estimates as PROC SYSLIN.

Except for GMM, the estimation methods assume that the equation errors for each observation are identically and independently distributed with a 0 mean vector and positive definite covariance matrix Σ consistently estimated by **S**. For FIML, the errors need to be normally distributed. There are no other assumptions concerning the distribution of the errors for the other estimation methods.

The consistency of the parameter estimates relies on the assumption that the **S** matrix is a consistent estimate of Σ. These standard error estimates are asymptotically valid, but for nonlinear models they may not be reliable for small samples.

The **S** matrix used for the calculation of the covariance of the parameter estimates is the best estimate available for the estimation method selected. For **S**-iterated methods this is the most recent estimation of Σ. For OLS and 2SLS, an estimate of the **S** matrix is computed from OLS or 2SLS residuals and used for the calculation of the covariance matrix. For a complete list of the **S** matrix used for the calculation of the covariance of the parameter estimates, see Table 20.1.

Missing Values

An observation is excluded from the estimation if any variable used for FIT tasks is missing, if the weight for the observation is not greater than 0 when weights are used, or if a DELETE statement is executed by the model program. Variables used for FIT tasks include the equation errors for each equation, the instruments, if any, and the derivatives of the equation errors with respect to the parameters estimated. Note that variables can become missing as a result of computational errors or calculations with missing values.

The number of usable observations can change when different parameter values are used; some parameter values can be invalid and cause execution errors for some observations. PROC MODEL keeps track of the number of usable and missing observations at each pass through the data, and if the number of missing observations counted during a pass exceeds the number that was obtained using the previous parameter vector, the pass is terminated and the new parameter vector is considered infeasible. PROC MODEL never takes a step that produces more missing observations than the current estimate does.

The values used to compute the Durbin-Watson, R^2, and other statistics of fit are from the observations used in calculating the objective function and do not include any observation for which any needed variable was missing (residuals, derivatives, and instruments).

Details on the Covariance of Equation Errors

There are several **S** matrices that can be involved in the various estimation methods and in forming the estimate of the covariance of parameter estimates. These **S** matrices are estimates of Σ, the true covariance of the equation errors. Apart from the choice of instrumental or noninstrumental methods, many of the methods provided by PROC MODEL differ in the way the various **S** matrices are formed and used.

All of the estimation methods result in a final estimate of Σ, which is included in the output if the COVS option is specified. The final **S** matrix of each method provides the initial **S** matrix for any subsequent estimation.

This estimate of the covariance of equation errors is defined as

$$\mathbf{S} = \mathbf{D}(\mathbf{R}'\mathbf{R})\mathbf{D}$$

where $\mathbf{R} = (\mathbf{r}_1, \ldots, \mathbf{r}_g)$ is composed of the equation residuals computed from the current parameter estimates in an $n \times g$ matrix and $\mathbf{D}$ is a diagonal matrix that depends on the VARDEF= option.

For VARDEF=N, the diagonal elements of $\mathbf{D}$ are $1/\sqrt{n}$, where n is the number of nonmissing observations. For VARDEF=WGT, n is replaced with the sum of the weights. For VARDEF=WDF, n is replaced with the sum of the weights minus the model degrees of freedom. For the default VARDEF=DF, the ith diagonal element of $\mathbf{D}$ is $1/\sqrt{n - df_i}$, where df_i is the degrees of freedom (number of parameters) for the ith equation. Binkley and Nelson (1984) show the importance of using a degrees-of-freedom correction in estimating Σ. Their results indicate that the DF method produces more accurate confidence intervals for N3SLS parameter estimates in the linear case than the alternative approach they tested. VARDEF=N is always used for the computation of the FIML estimates.

For the fixed **S** methods, the OUTSUSED= option writes the **S** matrix used in the estimation to a data set. This **S** matrix is either the estimate of the covariance of equation errors matrix from the preceding estimation, or a prior Σ estimate read in from a data set when the SDATA= option is specified. For the diagonal **S** methods, all of the off-diagonal elements of the **S** matrix are set to 0 for the estimation of the parameters and for the OUTSUSED= data set, but the output data set produced by the OUTS= option will contain the off-diagonal elements. For the OLS and N2SLS methods, there is no previous estimate of the covariance of equation errors matrix, and the option OUTSUSED= will save an identity matrix unless a prior Σ estimate is supplied by the SDATA= option. For FIML the OUTSUSED= data set contains the **S** matrix computed with VARDEF=N. The OUTS= data set contains the **S** matrix computed with the selected VARDEF= option.

If the COVS option is used, the method is not **S**-iterated, and **S** is not an identity, the OUTSUSED= matrix is included in the printed output.

For the methods that iterate the covariance of equation errors matrix, the **S** matrix is iteratively re-estimated from the residuals produced by the current parameter estimates. This **S** matrix estimate iteratively replaces the previous estimate until both the parameter estimates and the estimate of the covariance of equation errors matrix converge. The final OUTS= matrix and OUTSUSED= matrix are thus identical for the **S**-iterated methods.

Nested Iterations

By default, for **S**-iterated methods, the **S** matrix is held constant until the parameters converge once. Then the **S** matrix is re-estimated. One iteration of the parameter estimation algorithm is performed, and the **S** matrix is again re-estimated. This latter process is repeated until convergence of both the parameters and the **S** matrix. Since the objective of the minimization depends on the **S** matrix, this has the effect of chasing a moving target.

When the NESTIT option is specified, iterations are performed to convergence for the structural parameters with a fixed **S** matrix. The **S** matrix is then re-estimated, the parameter iterations are repeated to convergence, and so on until both the parameters and the **S** matrix converge. This has the effect of fixing the objective function for the inner parameter iterations. It is more reliable, but usually more expensive, to nest the iterations.

R^2

For unrestricted linear models with an intercept successfully estimated by OLS, R^2 is always between 0 and 1. However, nonlinear models do not necessarily encompass the dependent mean as a special case and can produce negative R^2 statistics. Negative R^2's can also be produced even for linear models when an estimation method other than OLS is used and no intercept term is in the model.

R^2 is defined for normalized equations as

$$R^2 = 1 - \frac{SSE}{SSA - \bar{y}^2 \times n}$$

where SSA is the sum of the squares of the actual y's and $\bar{y}$ are the actual means. R^2 cannot be computed for models in general form because of the need for an actual Y.

Minimization Methods

PROC MODEL currently supports two methods for minimizing the objective function. These methods are described in the following sections.

GAUSS

The Gauss-Newton parameter-change vector for a system with g equations, n nonmissing observations, and p unknown parameters is

$$\mathbf{\Delta} = (\mathbf{X}'\mathbf{X})^{-1}\mathbf{X}'\mathbf{r}$$

where Δ is the change vector, $\mathbf{X}$ is the stacked $ng \times p$ Jacobian matrix of partial derivatives of the residuals with respect to the parameters, and $\mathbf{r}$ is an $ng \times 1$vector of the stacked residuals. The components of $\mathbf{X}$ and $\mathbf{r}$ are weighted by the $\mathbf{S}^{-1}$ matrix. When instrumental methods are used, $\mathbf{X}$ and $\mathbf{r}$ are the projections of the Jacobian matrix and residuals vector in the instruments space and not the Jacobian and residuals themselves. In the preceding formula, $\mathbf{S}$ and W are suppressed. If instrumental variables are used, then the change vector becomes:

$$\mathbf{\Delta} = (\mathbf{X}'(\mathbf{S}^{-1}\otimes\mathbf{W})\mathbf{X})^{-1}\mathbf{X}'(\mathbf{S}^{-1}\otimes\mathbf{W})\mathbf{r}$$

This vector is computed at the end of each iteration. The objective function is then computed at the changed parameter values at the start of the next iteration. If the objective function is not improved by the change, the Δ vector is reduced by one-half and the objective function is re-evaluated. The change vector will be halved up to MAXSUBITER= times until the objective function is improved.

For FIML the $\mathbf{X}'\mathbf{X}$ matrix is substituted with one of three choices for approximations to the Hessian. See the "FIML Estimation" section in this chapter.

MARQUARDT

The Marquardt-Levenberg parameter change vector is

$$\mathbf{\Delta} = (\mathbf{X}'\mathbf{X} + \lambda \mathrm{diag}(\mathbf{X}'\mathbf{X}))^{-1}\mathbf{X}'\mathbf{r}$$

where Δ is the change vector, and **X** and **r** are the same as for the Gauss-Newton method, described in the preceding section. Before the iterations start, λ is set to a small value (1E-6). At each iteration, the objective function is evaluated at the parameters changed by Δ. If the objective function is not improved, λ is increased to 10λ and the step is tried again. λ can be increased up to MAXSUBITER= times to a maximum of 1E15 (whichever comes first) until the objective function is improved. For the start of the next iteration, λ is reduced to max(λ/10,1E-10).

Convergence Criteria

There are a number of measures that could be used as convergence or stopping criteria. PROC MODEL computes five convergence measures labeled R, S, PPC, RPC, and OBJECT.

When an estimation technique that iterates estimates of Σ is used (that is, IT3SLS), two convergence criteria are used. The termination values can be specified with the CONVERGE=(*p*,*s*) option on the FIT statement. If the second value, *s*, is not specified, it defaults to *p*. The criterion labeled S (given in the following) controls the convergence of the **S** matrix. When S is less than *s*, the **S** matrix has converged. The criterion labeled R is compared to the *p* value to test convergence of the parameters.

The R convergence measure cannot be computed accurately in the special case of singular residuals (when all the residuals are close to 0) or in the case of a 0 objective value. When either the trace of the **S** matrix computed from the current residuals (trace(S)) or the objective value is less than the value of the SINGULAR= option, convergence is assumed.

The various convergence measures are explained in the following:

R is the primary convergence measure for the parameters. It measures the degree to which the residuals are orthogonal to the Jacobian columns, and it approaches 0 as the gradient of the objective function becomes small. R is defined as the square root of

$$\frac{(r'(S^{-1}\otimes W)X(X'(S^{-1}\otimes W)X)^{-1}X'(S^{-1}\otimes W)r)}{(r'(S^{-1}\otimes W)r)}$$

where **X** is the Jacobian matrix and **r** is the residuals vector. R is similar to the relative offset orthogonality convergence criterion proposed by Bates and Watts (1981).

In the univariate case, the R measure has several equivalent interpretations:

- the cosine of the angle between the residuals vector and the column space of the Jacobian matrix. When this cosine is 0, the residuals are orthogonal to the partial derivatives of the predicted values with respect to the parameters, and the gradient of the objective function is 0.
- the square root of the R^2 for the current linear pseudo-model in the residuals.
- a norm of the gradient of the objective function, where the norming matrix is proportional to the current estimate of the covariance of the parameter estimates. Thus, using R, convergence is judged when the gradient becomes small in this norm.
- the prospective relative change in the objective function value expected from the next GAUSS step, assuming that the current linearization of the model is a good local approximation.

In the multivariate case, R is somewhat more complicated but is designed to go to 0 as the gradient of the objective becomes small and can still be given the previous interpretations for the aggregation of the equations weighted by $\mathbf{S}^{-1}$.

PPC

is the prospective parameter change measure. PPC measures the maximum relative change in the parameters implied by the parameter-change vector computed for the next iteration. At the *k*th iteration, PPC is the maximum over the parameters

$$\frac{|\theta_i^{k+1} - \theta_i^k|}{|\theta|_i^k + 1.0e^{-6}}$$

where θ_i^k is the current value of the *i*th parameter and θ_i^{k+1} is the prospective value of this parameter after adding the change vector computed for the next iteration. The parameter with the maximum prospective relative change is printed with the value of PPC, unless the PPC is nearly 0.

RPC

is the retrospective parameter change measure. RPC measures the maximum relative change in the parameters from the previous iteration. At the *k*th iteration, RPC is the maximum over *i* of

$$\frac{|\theta_i^k - \theta_i^{k-1}|}{|\theta_i^{k-1} + 1.0e^{-6}|}$$

where θ_i^k is the current value of the *i*th parameter and θ_i^{k-1} is the previous value of this parameter. The name of the parameter with the maximum retrospective relative change is printed with the value of RPC, unless the RPC is nearly 0.

OBJECT

measures the relative change in the objective function value between iterations:

$$\frac{|(O^k - O^{k-1}|}{|O^{k-1} + 1.0e^{-6}|}$$

where O^{k-1} is the value of the objective function (O^k) from the previous iteration.

S
measures the relative change in the **S** matrix. S is computed as the maximum over *i, j* of

$$\frac{|S_{ij}^{k} - S_{ij}^{k-1}|}{|S_{ij}^{k-1} + 1.0e^{-6}|}$$

where S^{k-1} is the previous **S** matrix. The S measure is relevant only for estimation methods that iterate the **S** matrix.

An example of the convergence criteria output is as follows:

```
                    The MODEL Procedure
                 IT3SLS Estimation Summary

                   Minimization Summary

             Parameters Estimated              5
             Method                        Gauss
             Iterations                       35


                Final Convergence Criteria

                R                      0.000883
                PPC(d1)                0.000644
                RPC(d1)                0.000815
                Object                  0.00004
                Trace(S)               3599.982
                Objective Value        0.435683
                S                      0.000052
```

Figure 20.17. Convergence Criteria Output

This output indicates the total number of iterations required by the Gauss minimization for all the **S** matrices was 35. The "Trace(S)" is the trace (the sum of the diagonal elements) of the **S** matrix computed from the current residuals. This row is labeled MSE if there is only one equation.

Troubleshooting Convergence Problems

As with any nonlinear estimation routine, there is no guarantee that the estimation will be successful for a given model and data. If the equations are linear with respect to the parameters, the parameter estimates always converge in one iteration. The methods that iterate the **S** matrix must iterate further for the **S** matrix to converge. Nonlinear models may not necessarily converge.

Convergence can be expected only with fully identified parameters, adequate data, and starting values sufficiently close to solution estimates.

Convergence and the rate of convergence may depend primarily on the choice of starting values for the estimates. This does not mean that a great deal of effort should be invested in choosing starting values. First, try the default values. If the estimation fails with these starting values, examine the model and data and re-run the estimation using reasonable starting values. It is usually not necessary that the starting values be very good, just that they not be very bad; choose values that seem plausible for the model and data.

An Example of Requiring Starting Values

Suppose you want to regress a variable Y on a variable X assuming that the variables are related by the following nonlinear equation:

$$y = a + bx^c + \epsilon$$

In this equation, Y is linearly related to a power transformation of X. The unknown parameters are *a*, *b*, and *c*. ϵ is an unobserved random error. Some simulated data was generated using the following SAS statements. In this simulation, $a = 10$, $b = 2$, and the use of the SQRT function corresponds to $c = .5$.

```
data test;
  do i = 1 to 20;
     x = 5 * ranuni(1234);
     y = 10 + 2 * sqrt(x) + .5 * rannor(2345);
     output;
     end;
run;
```

The following statements specify the model and give descriptive labels to the model parameters. Then the FIT statement attempts to estimate *a*, *b*, and *c* using the default starting value .0001.

```
proc model data=test;
   y = a + b * x ** c;
   label a = "Intercept"
         b = "Coefficient of Transformed X"
         c = "Power Transformation Parameter";
   fit y;
run;
```

PROC MODEL prints model summary and estimation problem summary reports and then prints the output shown in Figure 20.18.

```
                              The MODEL Procedure
                                OLS Estimation

NOTE: The iteration limit is exceeded for OLS.


        ERROR: The parameter estimates failed to converge for OLS after
        100 iterations using CONVERGE=0.001 as the convergence criteria.



                              The MODEL Procedure
                                OLS Estimation

                                                    N
            Iteration N Obs       R Objective Subit        a          b          c
  OLS             100    20 0.9627     3.9678      2 137.3844 -126.536 -0.00213


                      Gauss Method Parameter Change Vector

                           a                 b                 c

                   -69367.57          69366.51             -1.16
NOTE: The parameter estimation is abandoned. Check your model and data. If the
      model is correct and the input data are appropriate, try rerunning the
      parameter estimation using different starting values for the parameter
      estimates.
PROC MODEL continues as if the parameter estimates had converged.
```

Figure 20.18. Diagnostics for Convergence Failure

By using the default starting values, PROC MODEL was unable to take even the first step in iterating to the solution. The change in the parameters that the Gauss-Newton method computes is very extreme and makes the objective values worse instead of better. Even when this step is shortened by a factor of a million, the objective function is still worse, and PROC MODEL is unable to estimate the model parameters.

The problem is caused by the starting value of C. Using the default starting value C=.0001, the first iteration attempts to compute better values of A and B by what is, in effect, a linear regression of Y on the 10,000th root of X, which is almost the same as the constant 1. Thus the matrix that is inverted to compute the changes is nearly singular and affects the accuracy of the computed parameter changes.

This is also illustrated by the next part of the output, which displays collinearity diagnostics for the crossproducts matrix of the partial derivatives with respect to the parameters, shown in Figure 20.19.

```
                         The MODEL Procedure
                           OLS Estimation

                       Collinearity Diagnostics

                              Condition    -----Proportion of Variation----
Number        Eigenvalue         Number            a            b            c

     1          2.376793         1.0000       0.0000       0.0000       0.0000
     2          0.623207         1.9529       0.0000       0.0000       0.0000
     3      1.684616E-12        1187805       1.0000       1.0000       1.0000
```

Figure 20.19. Collinearity Diagnostics

This output shows that the matrix is singular and that the partials of A, B, and C with respect to the residual are collinear at the point $(0.0001, 0.0001, 0.0001)$ in the parameter space. See the section "Linear Dependencies" for a full explanation of the collinearity diagnostics.

The MODEL procedure next prints the note shown in Figure 20.20, which suggests that you try different starting values.

```
                         The MODEL Procedure
                           OLS Estimation

NOTE: The parameter estimation is abandoned. Check your model and data. If the
      model is correct and the input data are appropriate, try rerunning the
      parameter estimation using different starting values for the parameter
      estimates.
PROC MODEL continues as if the parameter estimates had converged.
```

Figure 20.20. Estimation Failure Note

PROC MODEL then produces the usual printout of results for the nonconverged parameter values. The estimation summary is shown in Figure 20.21. The heading includes the reminder "(Not Converged)."

```
                         The MODEL Procedure
                           OLS Estimation

                       Collinearity Diagnostics

                                 Condition     -----Proportion of Variation----
   Number          Eigenvalue       Number            a            b            c

        1            2.376793       1.0000       0.0000       0.0000       0.0000
        2            0.623207       1.9529       0.0000       0.0000       0.0000
        3        1.684616E-12      1187805       1.0000       1.0000       1.0000


                         The MODEL Procedure
               OLS Estimation Summary (Not Converged)

                        Minimization Summary

                  Parameters Estimated               3
                  Method                         Gauss
                  Iterations                       100
                  Subiterations                    239
                  Average Subiterations           2.39


                     Final Convergence Criteria

                     R                   0.962666
                     PPC(b)              548.1977
                     RPC(b)              540.4224
                     Object              2.633E-6
                     Trace(S)            4.667947
                     Objective Value     3.967755


                       Observations Processed

                            Read       20
                            Solved     20
```

Figure 20.21. Nonconverged Estimation Summary

The nonconverged estimation results are shown in Figure 20.22.

```
                              The MODEL Procedure

                    Nonlinear OLS Summary of Residual Errors
                              (Not Converged)
                        DF      DF                                                  Adj
 Equation            Model   Error         SSE        MSE   Root MSE   R-Square      R-Sq

 y                       3      17     79.3551     4.6679     2.1605    -1.6812   -1.9966


                  Nonlinear OLS Parameter Estimates (Not Converged)

                                    Approx                  Approx
 Parameter          Estimate       Std Err    t Value     Pr > |t|     Label

 a                  137.3844        263342       0.00       0.9996     Intercept
 b                  -126.536        263342      -0.00       0.9996     Coefficient of
                                                                        Transformed X
 c                  -0.00213        4.4371      -0.00       0.9996     Power Transformation
                                                                        Parameter
```

Figure 20.22. Nonconverged Results

Note that the R^2 statistic is negative. An $R^2 < 0$ results when the residual mean square error for the model is larger than the variance of the dependent variable. Negative R^2 statistics may be produced when either the parameter estimates fail to converge correctly, as in this case, or when the correctly estimated model fits the data very poorly.

Controlling Starting Values

To fit the preceding model you must specify a better starting value for C. Avoid starting values of C that are either very large or close to 0. For starting values of A and B, you can either specify values, use the default, or have PROC MODEL fit starting values for them conditional on the starting value for C.

Starting values are specified with the START= option of the FIT statement or on a PARMS statement. For example, the following statements estimate the model parameters using the starting values A=.0001, B=.0001, and C=5.

```
proc model data=test;
   y = a + b * x ** c;
   label a = "Intercept"
         b = "Coefficient of Transformed X"
         c = "Power Transformation Parameter";
   fit y start=(c=5);
run;
```

Using these starting values, the estimates converge in 16 iterations. The results are shown in Figure 20.23. Note that since the START= option explicitly declares parameters, the parameter C is placed first in the table.

```
                          The MODEL Procedure

               Nonlinear OLS Summary of Residual Errors

                 DF      DF                                              Adj
Equation      Model   Error        SSE        MSE   Root MSE  R-Square    R-Sq

y                 3      17     5.7359     0.3374     0.5809    0.8062  0.7834


                  Nonlinear OLS Parameter Estimates

                                Approx                  Approx
Parameter       Estimate       Std Err    t Value     Pr > |t|    Label

c               0.327079        0.2892       1.13       0.2738    Power Transformation
                                                                  Parameter
a               8.384311        3.3775       2.48       0.0238    Intercept
b               3.505391        3.4858       1.01       0.3287    Coefficient of
                                                                  Transformed X
```

Figure 20.23. Converged Results

Using the STARTITER Option

PROC MODEL can compute starting values for some parameters conditional on starting values you specify for the other parameters. You supply starting values for some parameters and specify the STARTITER option on the FIT statement.

For example, the following statements set C to 1 and compute starting values for A and B by estimating these parameters conditional on the fixed value of C. With C=1 this is equivalent to computing A and B by linear regression on X. A PARMS statement is used to declare the parameters in alphabetical order. The ITPRINT option is used to print the parameter values at each iteration.

```
proc model data=test;
   parms a b c;
   y = a + b * x ** c;
   label a = "Intercept"
         b = "Coefficient of Transformed X"
         c = "Power Transformation Parameter";
   fit y start=(c=1) / startiter itprint;
run;
```

With better starting values, the estimates converge in only 5 iterations. Counting the 2 iterations required to compute the starting values for A and B, this is 5 fewer than the 12 iterations required without the STARTITER option. The iteration history listing is shown in Figure 20.24.

```
                              The MODEL Procedure
                                OLS Estimation

                                                      N
            Iteration N Obs        R Objective Subit         a          b          c
GRID                0    20 0.9970       161.9     0   0.00010    0.00010    5.00000
GRID                1    20 0.0000      0.9675     0  12.29508    0.00108    5.00000


                                                      N
            Iteration N Obs        R Objective Subit         a          b          c
OLS                 0    20 0.6551      0.9675     0  12.29508    0.00108    5.00000
OLS                 1    20 0.6882      0.9558     4  12.26426    0.00201    4.44013
OLS                 2    20 0.6960      0.9490     4  12.25554    0.00251    4.28262
OLS                 3    20 0.7058      0.9428     2  12.24487    0.00323    4.09977
OLS                 4    20 0.7177      0.9380     2  12.23186    0.00430    3.89040
OLS                 5    20 0.7317      0.9354     2  12.21610    0.00592    3.65450
OLS                 6    20 0.7376      0.9289     3  12.20663    0.00715    3.52417
OLS                 7    20 0.7445      0.9223     2  12.19502    0.00887    3.37407
OLS                 8    20 0.7524      0.9162     2  12.18085    0.01130    3.20393
OLS                 9    20 0.7613      0.9106     2  12.16366    0.01477    3.01460
OLS                10    20 0.7705      0.9058     2  12.14298    0.01975    2.80839
OLS                11    20 0.7797      0.9015     2  12.11827    0.02690    2.58933
OLS                12    20 0.7880      0.8971     2  12.08900    0.03712    2.36306
OLS                13    20 0.7947      0.8916     2  12.05460    0.05152    2.13650
OLS                14    20 0.7993      0.8835     2  12.01449    0.07139    1.91695
OLS                15    20 0.8015      0.8717     2  11.96803    0.09808    1.71101
OLS                16    20 0.8013      0.8551     2  11.91459    0.13284    1.52361
OLS                17    20 0.7987      0.8335     2  11.85359    0.17666    1.35745
OLS                18    20 0.8026      0.8311     1  11.71551    0.28373    1.06872
OLS                19    20 0.7945      0.7935     2  11.57666    0.40366    0.89662
OLS                20    20 0.7872      0.7607     1  11.29346    0.65999    0.67059
OLS                21    20 0.7632      0.6885     1  10.81372    1.11483    0.48842
OLS                22    20 0.6976      0.5587     0   9.54889    2.34556    0.30461
OLS                23    20 0.0108      0.2868     0   8.44333    3.44826    0.33232
OLS                24    20 0.0008      0.2868     0   8.39438    3.49500    0.32790


      NOTE: At OLS Iteration 24 CONVERGE=0.001 Criteria Met.
```

Figure 20.24. ITPRINT Listing

The results produced in this case are almost the same as the results shown in Figure 20.23, except that the PARMS statement causes the Parameter Estimates table to be ordered A, B, C instead of C, A, B. They are not exactly the same because the different starting values caused the iterations to converge at a slightly different place. This effect is controlled by changing the convergence criterion with the CONVERGE= option.

By default, the STARTITER option performs one iteration to find starting values for the parameters not given values. In this case the model is linear in A and B, so only one iteration is needed. If A or B were nonlinear, you could specify more than one "starting values" iteration by specifying a number for the STARTITER= option.

Finding Starting Values by Grid Search

PROC MODEL can try various combinations of parameter values and use the combination producing the smallest objective function value as starting values. (For OLS the objective function is the residual mean square.) This is known as a preliminary *grid search*. You can combine the STARTITER option with a grid search.

For example, the following statements try 5 different starting values for C: 10, 5, 2.5, -2.5, -5. For each value of C, values for A and B are estimated. The combination of A, B, and C values producing the smallest residual mean square is then used to start the iterative process.

```
proc model data=test;
   parms a b c;
   y = a + b * x ** c;
   label a = "Intercept"
         b = "Coefficient of Transformed X"
         c = "Power Transformation Parameter";
   fit y start=(c=10 5 2.5 -2.5 -5) / startiter itprint;
run;
```

The iteration history listing is shown in Figure 20.25. Using the best starting values found by the grid search, the OLS estimation only requires 2 iterations. However, since the grid search required 10 iterations, the total iterations in this case is 12.

```
                              The MODEL Procedure
                                OLS Estimation

                                                    N
           Iteration N Obs       R Objective Subit        a         b         c
GRID               0    20 1.0000    26815.5     0  0.00010   0.00010 10.00000
GRID               1    20 0.0000     1.2193     0 12.51792   0.00000 10.00000
GRID               0    20 0.6012     1.5151     0 12.51792   0.00000  5.00000
GRID               1    20 0.0000     0.9675     0 12.29508   0.00108  5.00000
GRID               0    20 0.7804     1.6091     0 12.29508   0.00108  2.50000
GRID               1    20 0.0000     0.6290     0 11.87327   0.06372  2.50000
GRID               0    20 0.8779     4.1604     0 11.87327   0.06372 -2.50000
GRID               1    20 0.0000     0.9542     0 12.92455  -0.04700 -2.50000
GRID               0    20 0.9998     2776.1     0 12.92455  -0.04700 -5.00000
GRID               1    20 0.0000     1.0450     0 12.86129  -0.00060 -5.00000


                                                    N
           Iteration N Obs       R Objective Subit        a         b         c
OLS                0    20 0.6685     0.6290     0 11.87327   0.06372  2.50000
OLS                1    20 0.6649     0.5871     3 11.79268   0.10083  2.11710
OLS                2    20 0.6713     0.5740     2 11.71445   0.14901  1.81658
OLS                3    20 0.6726     0.5621     2 11.63772   0.20595  1.58705
OLS                4    20 0.6678     0.5471     2 11.56098   0.26987  1.40903
OLS                5    20 0.6587     0.5295     2 11.48317   0.33953  1.26760
OLS                6    20 0.6605     0.5235     1 11.32436   0.48846  1.03784
OLS                7    20 0.6434     0.4997     2 11.18704   0.62475  0.90793
OLS                8    20 0.6294     0.4805     1 10.93520   0.87965  0.73319
OLS                9    20 0.6031     0.4530     1 10.55670   1.26879  0.57385
OLS               10    20 0.6052     0.4526     0  9.62442   2.23114  0.36146
OLS               11    20 0.1652     0.2948     0  8.56683   3.31774  0.32417
OLS               12    20 0.0008     0.2868     0  8.38015   3.50974  0.32664


     NOTE: At OLS Iteration 12 CONVERGE=0.001 Criteria Met.
```

Figure 20.25. ITPRINT Listing

Because no initial values for A or B were provided in the PARAMETERS statement or were read in with a PARMSDATA= or ESTDATA= option, A and B were given the default value of 0.0001 for the first iteration. At the second grid point, C=5, the values of A and B obtained from the previous iterations are used for the initial iteration. If initial values are provided for parameters, the parameters start at those initial values at each grid point.

Guessing Starting Values from the Logic of the Model

Example 20.1, which uses a logistic growth curve model of the U.S. population, illustrates the need for reasonable starting values. This model can be written

$$pop = \frac{a}{1 + \exp(b - c(t - 1790))}$$

where t is time in years. The model is estimated using decennial census data of the U.S. population in millions. If this simple but highly nonlinear model is estimated using the default starting values, the estimation fails to converge.

To find reasonable starting values, first consider the meaning of a and c. Taking the limit as time increases, a is the limiting or maximum possible population. So, as a starting value for a, several times the most recent population known can be used, for example, one billion (1000 million).

Dividing the time derivative by the function to find the growth rate and taking the limit as t moves into the past, you can determine that c is the initial growth rate. You can examine the data and compute an estimate of the growth rate for the first few decades, or you can pick a number that sounds like a plausible population growth rate figure, such as 2%.

To find a starting value for b, let t equal the base year used, 1790, which causes c to drop out of the formula for that year, and then solve for the value of b that is consistent with the known population in 1790 and with the starting value of a. This yields $b = \ln(a/3.9 - 1)$ or about 5.5, where a is 1000 and 3.9 is roughly the population for 1790 given in the data. The estimates converge using these starting values.

Convergence Problems

When estimating nonlinear models, you may encounter some of the following convergence problems.

Unable to Improve

The optimization algorithm may be unable to find a step that improves the objective function. If this happens in the Gauss-Newton method, the step size is halved to find a change vector for which the objective improves. In the Marquardt method, λ will be increased to find a change vector for which the objective improves. If, after MAXSUBITER= step-size halvings or increases in λ, the change vector still does not produce a better objective value, the iterations are stopped and an error message is printed.

Failure of the algorithm to improve the objective value can be caused by a CONVERGE= value that is too small. Look at the convergence measures reported at the point of failure. If the estimates appear to be approximately converged, you can accept the NOT CONVERGED results reported, or you can try re-running the FIT task with a larger CONVERGE= value.

If the procedure fails to converge because it is unable to find a change vector that improves the objective value, check your model and data to ensure that all parameters are identified and data values are reasonably scaled. Then, re-run the model with different starting values. Also, consider using the Marquardt method if Gauss-Newton fails; the Gauss-Newton method can get into trouble if the Jacobian matrix is nearly singular or ill-conditioned. Keep in mind that a nonlinear model may be well-identified and well-conditioned for parameter values close to the solution values but unidentified or numerically ill-conditioned for other parameter values. The choice of starting values can make a big difference.

Nonconvergence

The estimates may diverge into areas where the program overflows or the estimates may go into areas where function values are illegal or too badly scaled for accurate calculation. The estimation may also take steps that are too small or that make only marginal improvement in the objective function and, thus, fail to converge within the iteration limit.

When the estimates fail to converge, collinearity diagnostics for the Jacobian crossproducts matrix are printed if there are 20 or fewer parameters estimated. See "Linear Dependencies" later in this section for an explanation of these diagnostics.

Inadequate Convergence Criterion

If convergence is obtained, the resulting estimates will only approximate a minimum point of the objective function. The statistical validity of the results is based on the exact minimization of the objective function, and for nonlinear models the quality of the results depends on the accuracy of the approximation of the minimum. This is controlled by the convergence criterion used.

There are many nonlinear functions for which the objective function is quite flat in a large region around the minimum point so that many quite different parameter vectors may satisfy a weak convergence criterion. By using different starting values, different convergence criteria, or different minimization methods, you can produce very different estimates for such models.

You can guard against this by running the estimation with different starting values and different convergence criteria and checking that the estimates produced are essentially the same. If they are not, use a smaller CONVERGE= value.

Local Minimum

You may have converged to a local minimum rather than a global one. This problem is difficult to detect because the procedure will appear to have succeeded. You can guard against this by running the estimation with different starting values or with a different minimization technique. The START= option can be used to automatically perform a grid search to aid in the search for a global minimum.

Discontinuities

The computational methods assume that the model is a continuous and smooth function of the parameters. If this is not the case, the methods may not work.

If the model equations or their derivatives contain discontinuities, the estimation will usually succeed, provided that the final parameter estimates lie in a continuous interval and that the iterations do not produce parameter values at points of discontinuity or parameter values that try to cross asymptotes.

One common case of discontinuities causing estimation failure is that of an asymptotic discontinuity between the final estimates and the initial values. For example, consider the following model, which is basically linear but is written with one parameter in reciprocal form:

```
y = a + b * x1 + x2 / c;
```

By placing the parameter C in the denominator, a singularity is introduced into the parameter space at C=0. This is not necessarily a problem, but if the correct estimate of C is negative while the starting value is positive (or vice versa), the asymptotic discontinuity at 0 will lie between the estimate and the starting value. This means that the iterations have to pass through the singularity to get to the correct estimates. The situation is shown in Figure 20.26.

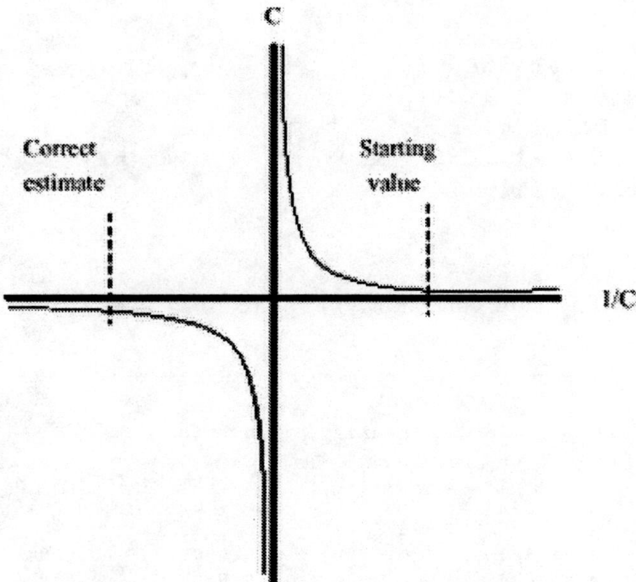

Figure 20.26. Asymptotic Discontinuity

Because of the incorrect sign of the starting value, the C estimate goes off towards positive infinity in a vain effort to get past the asymptote and onto the correct arm of the hyperbola. As the computer is required to work with ever closer approximations to infinity, the numerical calculations break down and an "objective function was not improved" convergence failure message is printed. At this point, the iterations terminate with an extremely large positive value for C. When the sign of the starting value for C is changed, the estimates converge quickly to the correct values.

Linear Dependencies

In some cases, the Jacobian matrix may not be of full rank; parameters may not be fully identified for the current parameter values with the current data. When linear dependencies occur among the derivatives of the model, some parameters appear with a standard error of 0 and with the word BIASED printed in place of the *t* statistic. When this happens, collinearity diagnostics for the Jacobian crossproducts matrix are printed if the DETAILS option is specified and there are twenty or fewer parameters estimated. Collinearity diagnostics are also printed out automatically when a minimization method fails, or when the COLLIN option is specified.

For each parameter, the proportion of the variance of the estimate accounted for by each *principal component* is printed. The principal components are constructed from the eigenvalues and eigenvectors of the correlation matrix (scaled covariance matrix). When collinearity exists, a principal component is associated with proportion of the variance of more than one parameter. The numbers reported are proportions so they will remain between 0 and 1. If two or more parameters have large proportion values associated with the same principle component, then two problems can occur: the computation of the parameter estimates are slow or nonconvergent; and the parameter estimates have inflated variances (Belsley 1980, p. 105-117).

For example, the following cubic model is fit to a quadratic data set:

```
proc model data=test3;
   exogenous x1 ;
   parms b1 a1 c1 ;
   y1 = a1 * x1 + b1 * x1 * x1   + c1 * x1 * x1 *x1;
   fit y1/ collin ;
run;
```

The collinearity diagnostics are shown in Figure 20.27.

The MODEL Procedure

Collinearity Diagnostics

Number	Eigenvalue	Condition Number	-----Proportion of Variation---- b1	a1	c1
1	2.942920	1.0000	0.0001	0.0004	0.0002
2	0.056638	7.2084	0.0001	0.0357	0.0148
3	0.000442	81.5801	0.9999	0.9639	0.9850

Figure 20.27. Collinearity Diagnostics

Notice that the proportions associated with the smallest eigenvalue are almost 1. For this model, removing any of the parameters will decrease the variances of the remaining parameters.

In many models the collinearity might not be clear cut. Collinearity is not necessarily something you remove. A model may need to be reformulated to remove the redundant parameterization or the limitations on the estimatability of the model can be accepted. The GINV=G4 option can be helpful to avoid problems with convergence for models containing collinearities.

Collinearity diagnostics are also useful when an estimation does not converge. The diagnostics provide insight into the numerical problems and can suggest which parameters need better starting values. These diagnostics are based on the approach of Belsley, Kuh, and Welsch (1980).

Iteration History

The options ITPRINT, ITDETAILS, XPX, I, and ITALL specify a detailed listing of each iteration of the minimization process.

ITPRINT Option

The ITPRINT information is selected whenever any iteration information is requested.

The following information is displayed for each iteration:

N	the number of usable observations
Objective	the corrected objective function value
Trace(S)	the trace of the **S** matrix
subit	the number of subiterations required to find a λ or a damping factor that reduces the objective function
R	the R convergence measure

The estimates for the parameters at each iteration are also printed.

ITDETAILS Option

The additional values printed for the ITDETAILS option are:

Theta	is the angle in degrees between Δ, the parameter change vector, and the negative gradient of the objective function.
Phi	is the directional derivative of the objective function in the Δ direction scaled by the objective function.
Stepsize	is the value of the damping factor used to reduce Δ if the Gauss-Newton method is used.
Lambda	is the value of λ if the Marquardt method is used.
Rank(XPX)	If the projected Jacobian crossproducts matrix is singular, the rank of the $\mathbf{X}'\mathbf{X}$ matrix is output.

The definitions of PPC and R are explained in the section "Convergence Criteria." When the values of PPC are large, the parameter associated with the criteria is displayed in parentheses after the value.

XPX and I Options

The XPX and the I options select the printing of the augmented $\mathbf{X'X}$ matrix and the augmented $\mathbf{X'X}$ matrix after a *sweep* operation (Goodnight 1979) has been performed on it. An example of the output from the following statements is shown in Figure 20.28.

```
proc model data=test2 ;
   y1 = a1 * x2 * x2 - exp( d1*x1);
   y2 = a2 * x1 * x1 + b2 * exp( d2*x2);
   fit y1 y2 / XPX I ;
run;
```

The MODEL Procedure
OLS Estimation

Cross Products for System At OLS Iteration 0

	a1	d1	a2	b2	d2	Residual
a1	1839468	-33818.35	0.0	0.00	0.000000	3879959
d1	-33818	1276.45	0.0	0.00	0.000000	-76928
a2	0	0.00	42925.0	1275.15	0.154739	470686
b2	0	0.00	1275.2	50.01	0.003867	16055
d2	0	0.00	0.2	0.00	0.000064	2
Residual	3879959	-76928.14	470686.3	16055.07	2.329718	24576144

XPX Inverse for System At OLS Iteration 0

	a1	d1	a2	b2	d2	Residual
a1	0.000001	0.000028	0.000000	0.0000	0.00	2
d1	0.000028	0.001527	0.000000	0.0000	0.00	-9
a2	0.000000	0.000000	0.000097	-0.0025	-0.08	6
b2	0.000000	0.000000	-0.002455	0.0825	0.95	172
d2	0.000000	0.000000	-0.084915	0.9476	15746.71	11931
Residual	1.952150	-8.546875	5.823969	171.6234	11930.89	10819902

Figure 20.28. XPX and I Options Output

The first matrix, labeled "Cross Products," for OLS estimation is

$$\begin{bmatrix} \mathbf{X'X} & \mathbf{X'r} \\ \mathbf{r'X} & \mathbf{r'r} \end{bmatrix}$$

The column labeled "Residual" in the output is the vector $\mathbf{X'r}$, which is the gradient of the objective function. The diagonal scalar value $\mathbf{r'r}$ is the objective function uncorrected for degrees of freedom. The second matrix, labeled "XPX Inverse," is created through a sweep operation on the augmented $\mathbf{X'X}$ matrix to get:

$$\begin{bmatrix} (\mathbf{X'X})^{-1} & (\mathbf{X'X})^{-1}\mathbf{X'r} \\ (\mathbf{X'r})'(\mathbf{X'X})^{-1} & \mathbf{r'r} - (\mathbf{X'r})'(\mathbf{X'X})^{-1}\mathbf{X'r} \end{bmatrix}$$

Note that the residual column is the change vector used to update the parameter estimates at each iteration. The corner scalar element is used to compute the R convergence criteria.

ITALL Option

The ITALL option, in addition to causing the output of all of the preceding options, outputs the **S** matrix, the inverse of the **S** matrix, the CROSS matrix, and the swept CROSS matrix. An example of a portion of the CROSS matrix for the preceding example is shown in Figure 20.29.

```
                        The MODEL Procedure
                          OLS Estimation

                Crossproducts Matrix  At OLS Iteration 0

                           1      @PRED.y1/@a1      @PRED.y1/@d1      @PRED.y2/@a2

1                      50.00              6409           -239.16            1275.0
@PRED.y1/@a1         6409.08           1839468         -33818.35          187766.1
@PRED.y1/@d1         -239.16            -33818           1276.45           -7253.0
@PRED.y2/@a2         1275.00            187766          -7253.00           42925.0
@PRED.y2/@b2           50.00              6410           -239.19            1275.2
@PRED.y2/@d2            0.00                 1             -0.03               0.2
RESID.y1            14699.97           3879959         -76928.14          420582.9
RESID.y2            16052.76           4065028         -85083.68          470686.3

                Crossproducts Matrix  At OLS Iteration 0

                @PRED.y2/@b2      @PRED.y2/@d2          RESID.y1          RESID.y2

1                      50.00          0.003803             14700             16053
@PRED.y1/@a1         6409.88          0.813934           3879959           4065028
@PRED.y1/@d1         -239.19         -0.026177            -76928            -85084
@PRED.y2/@a2         1275.15          0.154739            420583            470686
@PRED.y2/@b2           50.01          0.003867             14702             16055
@PRED.y2/@d2            0.00          0.000064                 2                 2
RESID.y1            14701.77          1.820356          11827102          12234106
RESID.y2            16055.07          2.329718          12234106          12749042
```

Figure 20.29. ITALL Option Cross-Products Matrix Output

Computer Resource Requirements

If you are estimating large systems, you need to be aware of how PROC MODEL uses computer resources such as memory and the CPU so they can be used most efficiently.

Saving Time with Large Data Sets

If your input data set has many observations, the FIT statement does a large number of model program executions. A pass through the data is made at least once for each iteration and the model program is executed once for each observation in each pass. If you refine the starting estimates by using a smaller data set, the final estimation with the full data set may require fewer iterations.

For example, you could use

```
proc model;
   /* Model goes here */
   fit / data=a(obs=25);
   fit / data=a;
```

where OBS=25 selects the first 25 observations in A. The second FIT statement produces the final estimates using the full data set and starting values from the first run.

Fitting the Model in Sections to Save Space and Time

If you have a very large model (with several hundred parameters, for example), the procedure uses considerable space and time. You may be able to save resources by breaking the estimation process into several steps and estimating the parameters in subsets.

You can use the FIT statement to select for estimation only the parameters for selected equations. Do not break the estimation into too many small steps; the total computer time required is minimized by compromising between the number of FIT statements that are executed and the size of the crossproducts matrices that must be processed.

When the parameters are estimated for selected equations, the entire model program must be executed even though only a part of the model program may be needed to compute the residuals for the equations selected for estimation. If the model itself can be broken into sections for estimation (and later combined for simulation and forecasting), then more resources can be saved.

For example, to estimate the following four equation model in two steps, you could use

```
proc model data=a outmodel=part1;
   parms a0-a2 b0-b2 c0-c3 d0-d3;
   y1 = a0 + a1*y2 + a2*x1;
   y2 = b0 + b1*y1 + b2*x2;
   y3 = c0 + c1*y1 + c2*y4 + c3*x3;
   y4 = d0 + d1*y1 + d2*y3 + d3*x4;
   fit y1 y2;
   fit y3 y4;
   fit y1 y2 y3 y4;
run;
```

You should try estimating the model in pieces to save time only if there are more than 14 parameters; the preceding example takes more time, not less, and the difference in memory required is trivial.

Memory Requirements for Parameter Estimation

PROC MODEL is a large program, and it requires much memory. Memory is also required for the SAS System, various data areas, the model program and associated tables and data vectors, and a few crossproducts matrices. For most models, the memory required for PROC MODEL itself is much larger than that required for the model program, and the memory required for the model program is larger than that required for the crossproducts matrices.

The number of bytes needed for two crossproducts matrices, four **S** matrices, and three parameter covariance matrices is

$$8 \times (2 + k + m + g)^2 + 16 \times g^2 + 12 \times (p + 1)^2$$

plus lower-order terms. *m* is the number of unique nonzero derivatives of each residual with respect to each parameter, *g* is the number of equations, *k* is the number of instruments, and *p* is the number of parameters. This formula is for the memory required for 3SLS. If you are using OLS, a reasonable estimate of the memory required for large problems (greater than 100 parameters) is to divide the value obtained from the formula in half.

Consider the following model program.

```
proc model data=test2 details;
   exogenous x1 x2;
   parms b1 100 a1 a2 b2 2.5 c2 55;
   y1 = a1 * y2 + b1 * x1 * x1;
   y2 = a2 * y1 + b2 * x2 * x2 + c2 / x2;
   fit y1 y2 / n3sls;
   inst b1 b2 c2 x1 ;
run;
```

The DETAILS option prints the storage requirements information shown in Figure 20.30.

```
                     The MODEL Procedure

            Storage Requirements for this Problem

            Order of XPX Matrix                 6
            Order of S Matrix                   2
            Order of Cross Matrix              13
            Total Nonzero Derivatives           5
            Distinct Variable Derivatives       5
            Size of Cross matrix              728
```

Figure 20.30. Storage Requirements Information

The matrix $\mathbf{X'X}$ augmented by the residual vector is called the XPX matrix in the output, and it has the size $m + 1$. The order of the **S** matrix, 2 for this example, is the value of *g*. The CROSS matrix is made up of the *k* unique instruments, a constant column representing the intercept terms, followed by the *m* unique Jacobian variables plus a constant column representing the parameters with constant derivatives, followed by the *g* residuals.

The size of two CROSS matrices in bytes is

$$8 \times (2 + k + m + g)^2 + 2 + k + m + g$$

Note that the CROSS matrix is symmetric, so only the diagonal and the upper triangular part of the matrix is stored. For examples of the CROSS and XPX matrices see "Iteration History" in this section.

The MEMORYUSE Option

The MEMORYUSE option on the FIT, SOLVE, MODEL, or RESET statement may be used to request a comprehensive memory usage summary.

Figure 20.31 shows an example of the output produced by the MEMORYUSE option.

```
                    The MODEL Procedure

              Memory Usage Summary (in bytes)

       Symbols                                  5368
       Strings                                  1057
       Lists                                    1472
       Arrays                                     84
       Statements                                704
       Opcodes                                   800
       Parsing                                   640
       Executable                                220
       Block option                                0
       Cross reference                             0
       Flow analysis                            1024
       Derivatives                              9406
       Data vector                               240
       Cross matrix                              728
       X'X matrix                                392
       S matrix                                   96
       GMM memory                                  0
       Jacobian                                    0
       Work vectors                              692
       Overhead                                 1906
       -----------------------      -------------
       Total                                   24829
```

Figure 20.31. MEMORYUSE Option Output for SOLVE Task

Definitions of the memory components follows:

symbols	memory used to store information about variables in the model
strings	memory used to store the variable names and labels
lists	space used to hold lists of variables
arrays	memory used by ARRAY statements
statements	memory used for the list of programming statements in the model
opcodes	memory used to store the code compiled to evaluate the expression in the model program
parsing	memory used in parsing the SAS statements
executable	the compiled model program size (not correct yet)
block option	memory used by the BLOCK option
cross ref.	memory used by the XREF option
flow analysis	memory used to compute the interdependencies of the variables
derivatives	memory used to compute and store the analytical derivatives
data vector	memory used for the program data vector
cross matrix	memory used for one or more copies of the Cross matrix
$\mathbf{X'X}$ matrix	memory used for one or more copies of the $\mathbf{X'X}$ matrix
S matrix	memory used for the covariance matrix
GMM memory	additional memory used for the GMM and ITGMM methods
Jacobian	memory used for the Jacobian matrix for SOLVE and FIML
work vectors	memory used for miscellaneous work vectors
overhead	other miscellaneous memory

Testing for Normality

The NORMAL option on the FIT statement performs multivariate and univariate tests of normality.

The three multivariate tests provided are Mardia's skewness test and kurtosis test (Mardia 1980) and the Henze-Zirkler $T_{n,\beta}$ test (Henze and Zirkler 1990). The two univariate tests provided are the Shapiro-Wilk W test and the Kolmogorov-Smirnov test. (For details on the univariate tests, refer to "Tests for Normality" in "The UNIVARIATE Procedure" chapter in the *SAS Procedures Guide*.) The null hypothesis for all these tests is that the residuals are normally distributed.

For a random sample $X_1, \ldots, X_n$, $X_i \in \mathrm{R^d}$, where *d* is the dimension of X_i and *n* is the number of observations, a measure of multivariate skewness is

$$b_{1,d} = \frac{1}{n^2} \sum_{i=1}^{n} \sum_{j=1}^{n} [(X_i - \mu)' S^{-1} (X_j - \mu)]^3$$

where **S** is the sample covariance matrix of **X**. For weighted regression, both **S** and $(X_i - \mu)$ are computed using the weights supplied by the WEIGHT statement or the _WEIGHT_ variable.

Mardia showed that under the null hypothesis $\frac{n}{6} b_{1,d}$ is asymptotically distributed as $\chi^2(d(d+1)(d+2)/6)$.

A measure of multivariate kurtosis is given by

$$b_{2,d} = \frac{1}{n} \sum_{i=1}^{n} [(X_i - \mu)' S^{-1} (X_i - \mu)]^2$$

Mardia showed that under the null hypothesis $b_{2,d}$is asymptotically normally distributed with mean $d(d+2)$ and variance $8d(d+2)/n$.

The Henze-Zirkler test is based on a nonnegative functional $D(.,.)$that measures the distance between two distribution functions and has the property that

$$D(\mathrm{N_d}(0, \mathrm{I_d}), \mathrm{Q}) = 0$$

if and only if

$$Q = \mathrm{N_d}(0, \mathrm{I_d})$$

where $\mathrm{N_d}(\mu, \Sigma_\mathrm{d})$ is a d-dimensional normal distribution.

The distance measure $D(.,.)$ can be written as

$$D_\beta(P, Q) = \int_{\mathrm{R^d}} |\hat{P}(t) - \hat{Q}(t)|^2 \varphi_\beta(t) dt$$

where $\hat{P}(t)$ and $\hat{Q}(t)$ are the Fourier transforms of P and Q, and $\varphi_\beta(t)$ is a weight or a kernel function. The density of the normal distribution $\mathrm{N_d}(0, \beta^2 \mathrm{I_d})$ is used as $\varphi_\beta(t)$

$$\varphi_\beta(t) = (2\pi\beta^2)^{\frac{-d}{2}} \exp(\frac{-|\mathrm{t}|^2}{2\beta^2}), \quad \mathrm{t} \in \mathrm{R^d}$$

where $|t| = (t' t)^{0.5}$.

The parameter β depends on n as

$$\beta_d(n) = \frac{1}{\sqrt{2}} (\frac{2d+1}{4})^{1/(d+4)} n^{1/(d+4)}$$

The test statistic computed is called $T_\beta(d)$ and is approximately distributed as a log normal. The log normal distribution is used to compute the null hypothesis probability.

$$T_\beta(d) = \frac{1}{n^2} \sum_{j=1}^{n} \sum_{k=1}^{n} \exp(-\frac{\beta^2}{2} |Y_j - Y_k|^2)$$

$$- \quad 2(1+\beta^2)^{-d/2}\frac{1}{n}\sum_{j=1}^{n}\exp(-\frac{\beta^2}{2(1+\beta^2)}|Y_j|^2) + (1+2\beta^2)^{-d/2}$$

where

$$|Y_j - Y_k|^2 = (X_j - X_k)'S^{-1}(X_j - X_k)$$

$$|Y_j|^2 = (X_j - \bar{X})'S^{-1}(X_j - \bar{X})$$

Monte Carlo simulations suggest that $T_\beta(d)$ has good power against distributions with heavy tails.

The Shapiro-Wilk W test is computed only when the number of observations (*n*) is less than 2000.

The following is an example of the output produced by the NORMAL option.

The MODEL Procedure

Normality Test

Equation	Test Statistic	Value	Prob
y1	Shapiro-Wilk W	0.37	<.0001
y2	Shapiro-Wilk W	0.84	<.0001
System	Mardia Skewness	286.4	<.0001
	Mardia Kurtosis	31.28	<.0001
	Henze-Zirkler T	7.09	<.0001

Figure 20.32. Normality Test Output

Heteroscedasticity

One of the key assumptions of regression is that the variance of the errors is constant across observations. If the errors have constant variance, the errors are called *homoscedastic*. Typically, residuals are plotted to assess this assumption. Standard estimation methods are inefficient when the errors are *heteroscedastic* or have non-constant variance.

Heteroscedasticity Tests

The MODEL procedure provides two tests for heteroscedasticity of the errors: White's test and the modified Breusch-Pagan test.

Both White's test and the Breusch-Pagan are based on the residuals of the fitted model. For systems of equations, these tests are computed separately for the residuals of each equation.

The residuals of an estimation are used to investigate the heteroscedasticity of the true disturbances.

The WHITE option tests the null hypothesis

$$H_0 : \sigma_i^2 = \sigma^2 \quad \text{for all i}$$

White's test is general because it makes no assumptions about the form of the heteroscedasticity (White 1980). Because of its generality, White's test may identify specification errors other than heteroscedasticity (Thursby 1982). Thus White's test may be significant when the errors are homoscedastic but the model is misspecified in other ways.

White's test is equivalent to obtaining the error sum of squares for the regression of the squared residuals on a constant and all the unique variables in $\mathbf{J} \otimes \mathbf{J}$, where the matrix $\mathbf{J}$ is composed of the partial derivatives of the equation residual with respect to the estimated parameters.

Note that White's test in the MODEL procedure is different than White's test in the REG procedure requested by the SPEC option. The SPEC option produces the test from Theorem 2 on page 823 of White (1980). The WHITE option, on the other hand, produces the statistic from Corollary 1 on page 825 of White (1980).

The null hypothesis for the modified Breusch-Pagan test is homosedasticity. The alternate hyposthesis is that the error variance varies with a set of regressors, which are listed in the BREUSCH= option.

Define the matrix Z to be composed of the values of the variables listed in the BREUSCH= option, such that $z_{i,j}$ is the value of the jth variable in the BREUSCH= option for the ith observation. The null hypothesis of the Breusch-Pagan test is

$$\begin{aligned} \sigma_i^2 &= \sigma^2(\alpha_0 + \boldsymbol{\alpha}' \mathbf{z_i}) \\ H_0 : & \quad \boldsymbol{\alpha} = \mathbf{0} \end{aligned}$$

where σ_i^2 is the error variance for the ith observation, and α_0 and $\boldsymbol{\alpha}$ are regression coefficients.

The test statistic for the Breusch-Pagan test is

$$bp = \frac{1}{v}(\mathbf{u} - \bar{u}\mathbf{i})' Z(Z' Z)^{-1} Z' (\mathbf{u} - \bar{u}\mathbf{i})$$

where $\mathbf{u} = (e_1^2, e_2^2, \ldots, e_n^2)$, $\mathbf{i}$ is a $n \times 1$ vector of ones, and

$$v = \frac{1}{n} \sum_{i=1}^{n} (e_i^2 - \frac{\mathbf{e}'\mathbf{e}}{n})^2$$

This is a modified version of the Breusch-Pagan test, which is less sensitive to the assumption of normality than the original test (Greene 1993, p. 395).

The statements in the following example produce the output in Figure 20.33:

```
proc model data=schools;
   parms const inc inc2;

   exp = const + inc * income + inc2 * income * income;
   incsq = income * income;

   fit exp / white breusch=(1 income incsq);
run;
```

```
                              The MODEL Procedure

                            Heteroscedasticity Test
Equation        Test                Statistic    DF  Pr > ChiSq  Variables

exp             White's Test            21.16     4      0.0003  Cross of all vars
                Breusch-Pagan           15.83     2      0.0004  1, income, incsq
```

Figure 20.33. Output for Heteroscedasticity Tests

Correcting for Heteroscedasticity

There are two methods for improving the efficiency of the parameter estimation in the presence of heteroscedastic errors. If the error variance relationships are known, weighted regression can be used or an error model can be estimated. For details on error model estimation see section "Error Covariance Structure Specification". If the error variance relationship is unknown, GMM estimation can be used.

Weighted Regression

The WEIGHT statement can be used to correct for the heteroscedasticity. Consider the following model, which has a heteroscedastic error term:

$$y_t = 250(e^{-0.2t} - e^{-0.8t}) + \sqrt{(9/t)}\epsilon_t$$

The data for this model is generated with the following SAS statements.

```
data test;
   do t=1 to 25;
      y = 250 * (exp( -0.2 * t ) - exp( -0.8 * t )) +
          sqrt( 9 / t ) * rannor(1);
      output;
   end;
run;
```

If this model is estimated with OLS,

```
proc model data=test;
   parms b1 0.1 b2 0.9;
   y = 250 * ( exp( -b1 * t ) - exp( -b2 * t ) );
   fit y;
run;
```

the estimates shown in Figure 20.34 are obtained for the parameters.

The MODEL Procedure

Nonlinear OLS Parameter Estimates

Parameter	Estimate	Approx Std Err	t Value	Approx Pr > |t|
b1	0.200977	0.00101	198.60	<.0001
b2	0.826236	0.00853	96.82	<.0001

Figure 20.34. Unweighted OLS Estimates

If both sides of the model equation are multiplied by $\sqrt{t}$, the model will have a homoscedastic error term. This multiplication or weighting is done through the WEIGHT statement. The WEIGHT statement variable operates on the squared residuals as

$$\epsilon_t^{'}\epsilon_t = weight \times \mathbf{q}_t^{'}\mathbf{q}_t$$

so that the WEIGHT statement variable represents the square of the model multiplier. The following PROC MODEL statements corrects the heteroscedasticity with a WEIGHT statement

```
proc model data=test;
   parms b1 0.1 b2 0.9;
   y = 250 * ( exp( -b1 * t ) - exp( -b2 * t ) );
   fit y;
   weight t;
run;
```

Note that the WEIGHT statement follows the FIT statement. The weighted estimates are shown in Figure 20.35.

The MODEL Procedure

Nonlinear OLS Parameter Estimates

Parameter	Estimate	Approx Std Err	t Value	Approx Pr > |t|
b1	0.200503	0.000844	237.53	<.0001
b2	0.816701	0.0139	58.71	<.0001

Figure 20.35. Weighted OLS Estimates

The weighted OLS estimates are identical to the output produced by the following PROC MODEL example:

```
proc model data=test;
   parms b1 0.1 b2 0.9;
```

```
    y = 250 * ( exp( -b1 * t ) - exp( -b2 * t ) );
    _weight_ = t;
    fit y;
run;
```

If the WEIGHT statement is used in conjunction with the _WEIGHT_ variable, the two values are multiplied together to obtain the weight used.

The WEIGHT statement and the _WEIGHT_ variable operate on all the residuals in a system of equations. If a subset of the equations needs to be weighted, the residuals for each equation can be modified through the RESID. variable for each equation. The following example demonstrates the use of the RESID. variable to make a homoscedastic error term:

```
proc model data=test;
    parms b1 0.1 b2 0.9;
    y = 250 * ( exp( -b1 * t ) - exp( -b2 * t ) );
    resid.y = resid.y * sqrt(t);
    fit y;
run;
```

These statements produce estimates of the parameters and standard errors that are identical to the weighted OLS estimates. The reassignment of the RESID.Y variable must be done after Y is assigned, otherwise it would have no effect. Also, note that the residual (RESID.Y) is multiplied by $\sqrt{t}$. Here the multiplier is acting on the residual before it is squared.

GMM Estimation

If the form of the heteroscedasticity is unknown, generalized method of moments estimation (GMM) can be used. The following PROC MODEL statements use GMM to estimate the example model used in the preceding section:

```
proc model data=test;
    parms b1 0.1 b2 0.9;
    y = 250 * ( exp( -b1 * t ) - exp( -b2 * t ) );
    fit y / gmm;
    instruments b1 b2;
run;
```

GMM is an instrumental method, so instrument variables must be provided.

GMM estimation generates estimates for the parameters shown in Figure 20.36.

The MODEL Procedure

Nonlinear GMM Parameter Estimates

Parameter	Estimate	Approx Std Err	t Value	Approx Pr > |t|
b1	0.200487	0.000807	248.38	<.0001
b2	0.822148	0.0142	57.95	<.0001

Figure 20.36. GMM Estimation for Heteroscedasticity

Heteroscedasticity-Consistent Covariance Matrix Estimation

Homoscedasticity is required for ordinary least-squares regression estimates to be efficient. A nonconstant error variance, heteroscedasticity, causes the OLS estimates to be inefficient, and the usual OLS covariance matrix, $\hat{\Sigma}$, is generally invalid.

$$\hat{\Sigma} = \sigma^2(X'X)^{-1}$$

When the variance of the errors of a classical linear model

$$Y = X\beta + \epsilon$$

is not constant across observations (heteroscedastic), so that $\sigma_i^2 \neq \sigma_j^2$ for some $j > 1$, the OLS estimator

$$\hat{\beta}_{OLS} = (X'X)^{-1}X'Y$$

is unbiased but it is inefficient. Models that take into account the changing variance can make more efficient use of the data. When the variances, σ_t^2, are known, generalized least squares (GLS) can be used and the estimator

$$\hat{\beta}_{GLS} = (X'\Omega X)^{-1}X'\Omega^{-1}Y$$

where

$$\Omega = \begin{bmatrix} \sigma_1^2 & 0 & 0 & 0 \\ 0 & \sigma_2^2 & 0 & 0 \\ 0 & 0 & \ddots & 0 \\ 0 & 0 & 0 & \sigma_T^2 \end{bmatrix}$$

is unbiased and efficient. However, GLS is unavailable when the variances, σ_t^2, are unknown.

To solve this problem White (1980) proposed a heteroscedastic consistent-covariance matrix estimator (HCCME)

$$\hat{\Sigma} = (X'X)^{-1}X'\hat{\Omega}X(X'X)^{-1}$$

that is consistent as well as unbiased, where

$$\hat{\Omega}_0 = \begin{bmatrix} \epsilon_1^2 & 0 & 0 & 0 \\ 0 & \epsilon_2^2 & 0 & 0 \\ 0 & 0 & \ddots & 0 \\ 0 & 0 & 0 & \epsilon_T^2 \end{bmatrix}$$

and $\epsilon_t = Y_t - X_t \hat{\beta_{OLS}}$.

This estimator is considered somewhat unreliable in finite samples. Therefore, Davidson and MacKinnon (1993) propose three different modifications to estimating $\hat{\Omega}$. The first solution is to simply multiply ϵ_t^2 by $\frac{n}{n-df}$, where *n* is the number of observations and *df* is the number of explanatory variables, so that

$$\hat{\Omega}_1 = \begin{bmatrix} \frac{n}{n-df}\,\epsilon_1^2 & 0 & 0 & 0 \\ 0 & \frac{n}{n-df}\,\epsilon_2^2 & 0 & 0 \\ 0 & 0 & \ddots & 0 \\ 0 & 0 & 0 & \frac{n}{n-df}\,\epsilon_n^2 \end{bmatrix}$$

The second solution is to define

$$\hat{\Omega}_2 = \begin{bmatrix} \frac{\epsilon_1^2}{1-\hat{h}_1} & 0 & 0 & 0 \\ 0 & \frac{\epsilon_2^2}{1-\hat{h}_2} & 0 & 0 \\ 0 & 0 & \ddots & 0 \\ 0 & 0 & 0 & \frac{\epsilon_n^2}{1-\hat{h}_n} \end{bmatrix}$$

where $\hat{h}_t = X_t(X'X)^{-1}X_t'$.

The third solution, called the "jackknife," is to define

$$\hat{\Omega}_3 = \begin{bmatrix} \frac{\epsilon_1^2}{(1-\hat{h}_1)^2} & 0 & 0 & 0 \\ 0 & \frac{\epsilon_2^2}{(1-\hat{h}_2)^2} & 0 & 0 \\ 0 & 0 & \ddots & 0 \\ 0 & 0 & 0 & \frac{\epsilon_n^2}{(1-\hat{h}_T)^2} \end{bmatrix}$$

MacKinnon and White (1985) investigated these three modified HCCMEs, including the original HCCME, based on finite-sample performance of pseudo-t statistics. The original HCCME performed the worst. The first modification performed better. The second modification performed even better than the first, and the third modification performed the best. They concluded that the original HCCME should never be used in finite sample estimation, and that the second and third modifications should be used over the first modification if the diagonals of $\hat{\Omega}$ are available.

Seemingly Unrelated Regression HCCME

Extending the discussion to systems of g equations, the HCCME for SUR estimation is

$$(\tilde{X}'\tilde{X})^{-1}\tilde{X}'\hat{\Omega}\tilde{X}(\tilde{X}'\tilde{X})^{-1}$$

where $\tilde{X}$ is a $n\,g \times k$ matrix with the first g rows representing the first observation, the next g rows representing the second observation, and so on. $\hat{\Omega}$ is now a $n\,g \times n\,g$ block diagonal matrix with typical block $g \times g$

$$\hat{\Omega}_i = \begin{bmatrix} \psi_{1,i}\,\psi_{1,i} & \psi_{1,i}\,\psi_{2,i} & \dots & \psi_{1,i}\,\psi_{g,i} \\ \psi_{2,i}\,\psi_{1,i} & \psi_{2,i}\,\psi_{2,i} & \dots & \psi_{2,i}\,\psi_{g,i} \\ \vdots & \vdots & \vdots & \vdots \\ \psi_{g,i}\,\psi_{1,i} & \psi_{g,i}\,\psi_{2,i} & \dots & \psi_{g,i}\,\psi_{g,i} \end{bmatrix}$$

where

$$\psi_{j,i} = \epsilon_{j,i} \quad HC_0$$

or

$$\psi_{j,i} = \sqrt{\frac{n}{n-df}}\epsilon_{j,i} \quad HC_1$$

or

$$\psi_{j,i} = \epsilon_{j,i}/\sqrt{1 - \hat{h}_i} \quad HC_2$$

or

$$\psi_{j,i} = \epsilon_{j,i}/(1 - \hat{h}_i) \quad HC_3$$

Two- and Three-Stage Least Squares HCCME

For two- and three-stage least squares, the HCCME for a g equation system is

$$CovF(\hat{\Omega})Cov$$

where

$$Cov = \left(\frac{1}{n}X'(I \otimes Z(Z'Z)^{-1}Z')X\right)^{-1}$$

is the normal covariance matrix without the S matrix and

$$F(\Omega) = \frac{1}{n}\sum_{i}^{g}\sum_{j}^{g} X_i'Z(Z'Z)^{-1}Z'\hat{\Omega}_{ij}Z(Z'Z)^{-1}Z'X_j$$

where X_j is a $n \times p$ matrix with the jth equations regressors in the appropriate columns and zeros everywhere else.

$$\hat{\Omega}_{ij} = \begin{bmatrix} \psi_{i,1}\psi_{j,1} & 0 & 0 & 0 \\ 0 & \psi_{i,2}\psi_{j,2} & 0 & 0 \\ 0 & 0 & \ddots & 0 \\ 0 & 0 & 0 & \psi_{i,n}\psi_{j,n} \end{bmatrix}$$

For 2SLS $\hat{\Omega}_{ij} = 0$ when $i \neq j$. The ϵ_t used in $\hat{\Omega}$ is computed using the parameter estimates obtained from the instrumental variables estimation.

The leverage value for the ith equation used in the HCCME=2 and HCCME=3 methods is computed as conditional on the first stage as

$$h_{ti} = Z_t(Z'Z)^{-1}X_i(X'(I \otimes Z(Z` * Z)^{-1}Z`)X)^{-1}X_i'Z(Z'Z)^{-1}Z_t'$$

for 2SLS and

$$h_{ti} = Z_t(Z'Z)^{-1}X_i(X'(S^{-1} \otimes Z(Z` * Z)^{-1}Z`)X)^{-1}X_i'Z(Z'Z)^{-1}Z_t'/S_{ii}$$

for 3SLS.

Testing for Autocorrelation

The GODFREY= option on the FIT statement produces the Godfrey Lagrange multiplier test for serially correlated residuals for each equation (Godfrey 1978a and 1978b). n is the maximum autoregressive order, and specifies that Godfrey's tests be computed for lags 1 through n. The default number of lags is four.

The tests are performed separately for each equation estimated by the FIT statement. When a nonlinear model is estimated, the test is computed using a linearized model.

The following is an example of the output produced by the GODFREY=3 option:

```
                      Godfrey Test Output

                     The MODEL Procedure

               Godfrey's Serial Correlation Test

      Equation        Alternative          LM     Pr > LM

      y                         1        6.63      0.0100
                                2        6.89      0.0319
                                3        6.96      0.0732
```

Figure 20.37. Autocorrelation Test Output

The three variations of the test reported by the GODFREY=3 option are designed to have power against different alternative hypothesis. Thus, if the residuals in fact have only first-order autocorrelation, the lag 1 test will have the most power for rejecting the null hypothesis of uncorrelated residuals. If the residuals have second- but not higher-order autocorrelation, the lag 2 test may be more likely to reject; the same is true for third-order autocorrelation and the lag 3 test.

The null hypothesis of Godfrey's tests is that the equation residuals are white noise. However, if the equation includes autoregressive error model of order p (AR(p),) then the lag i test, when considered in terms of the structural error, is for the null hypothesis that the structural errors are from an AR(p) process versus the alternative hypothesis that the errors are from an AR($p+i$) process.

The alternative ARMA(p, i) process is locally equivalent to the alternative AR($p+i$) process with respect to the null model AR(p). Thus, the GODFREY= option results are also a test of AR(p) errors against the alternative hypothesis of ARMA(p, i) errors. Refer to Godfrey (1978a and 1978b) for more detailed information.

Transformation of Error Terms

In PROC MODEL you can control the form of the error term. By default the error term is assumed to be additive. This section demonstrates how to specify nonadditive error terms and discusses the effects of these transformations.

Models with Nonadditive Errors

The estimation methods used by PROC MODEL assume that the error terms of the equations are independently and identically distributed with zero means and finite variances. Furthermore, the methods assume that the RESID.*name* equation variable for normalized form equations or the EQ.*name* equation variable for general form equations contains an estimate of the error term of the true stochastic model whose parameters are being estimated. Details on RESID.*name* and EQ.*name* equation variables are in the section "Model Translations."

To illustrate these points, consider the common loglinear model

$$y = \alpha x^{\beta} \tag{1}$$

$$\ln y = a + b\ln(x) \tag{2}$$

where a=log(α) and b=β. Equation (2) is called the *log form* of the equation in contrast to equation (1), which is called the *level form* of the equation. Using the SYSLIN procedure, you can estimate equation (2) by specifying

```
proc syslin data=in;
   model logy=logx;
run;
```

where LOGY and LOGX are the logs of Y and X computed in a preceding DATA step. The resulting values for INTERCEPT and LOGX correspond to a and b in equation (2).

Using the MODEL procedure, you can try to estimate the parameters in the level form (and avoid the DATA step) by specifying

```
proc model data=in;
   parms alpha beta;
   y = alpha * x ** beta;
   fit y;
run;
```

where ALPHA and BETA are the parameters in equation (1).

Unfortunately, at least one of the preceding is wrong; an ambiguity results because equations (1) and (2) contain no explicit error term. The SYSLIN and MODEL procedures both deal with additive errors; the residual used (the estimate of the error term in the equation) is the difference between the predicted and actual values (of LOGY for PROC SYSLIN and of Y for PROC MODEL in this example). If you perform the regressions discussed previously, PROC SYSLIN estimates equation (3) while PROC MODEL estimates equation (4).

$$\ln y = a + b \ln(x) + \epsilon \tag{3}$$

$$y = \alpha x^{\beta} + \xi \tag{4}$$

These are different statistical models. Equation (3) is the log form of equation (5)

$$y = \alpha x^{\beta} \mu \tag{5}$$

where $\mu = e^{\epsilon}$. Equation (4), on the other hand, cannot be linearized because the error term ξ (different from μ) is additive in the level form.

You must decide whether your model is equation (4) or (5). If the model is equation (4), you should use PROC MODEL. If you linearize equation (1) without considering the error term and apply SYSLIN to MODEL LOGY=LOGX, the results will be wrong. On the other hand, if your model is equation (5) (in practice it usually is), and you want to use PROC MODEL to estimate the parameters in the *level* form, you must do something to account for the multiplicative error.

PROC MODEL estimates parameters by minimizing an objective function. The objective function is computed using either the RESID.-prefixed equation variable or the EQ.-prefixed equation variable. You must make sure that these prefixed equation variables are assigned an appropriate error term. If the model has additive errors that satisfy the assumptions, nothing needs to be done. In the case of equation (5), the error is nonadditive and the equation is in normalized form, so you must alter the value of RESID.Y.

The following assigns a valid estimate of μ to RESID.Y:

```
y = alpha * x ** beta;
resid.y = actual.y / pred.y;
```

However, $\mu = e^{\epsilon}$ and, therefore, μ cannot have a mean of zero and you cannot consistently estimate α and β by minimizing the sum of squares of an estimate of μ. Instead, you use $\epsilon = \ln\mu$.

```
proc model data=in;
   parms alpha beta;
   y = alpha * x ** beta;
   resid.y = log( actual.y / pred.y );
   fit y;
run;
```

If the model was expressed in general form, this transformation becomes

```
proc model data=in;
   parms alpha beta;
   EQ.trans = log( y / (alpha * x ** beta));
   fit trans;
run;
```

Both examples produce estimates of α and β of the level form that match the estimates of a and b of the log form. That is, ALPHA=exp(INTERCEPT) and BETA=LOGX, where INTERCEPT and LOGX are the PROC SYSLIN parameter estimates from the MODEL LOGY=LOGX. The standard error reported for ALPHA is different from that for the INTERCEPT in the log form.

The preceding example is not intended to suggest that loglinear models should be estimated in level form but, rather, to make the following points:

- Nonlinear transformations of equations involve the error term of the equation, and this should be taken into account when transforming models.
- The RESID.-prefixed and the EQ.-prefixed equation variables for models estimated by the MODEL procedure must represent additive errors with zero means.
- You can use assignments to RESID.-prefixed and EQ.-prefixed equation variables to transform error terms.
- Some models do not have additive errors or zero means, and many such models can be estimated using the MODEL procedure. The preceding approach applies not only to multiplicative models but to any model that can be manipulated to isolate the error term.

Predicted Values of Transformed Models

Nonadditive or transformed errors affect the distribution of the predicted values, as well as the estimates. For the preceding loglinear example, the MODEL procedure produces consistent parameter estimates. However, the predicted values for Y computed by PROC MODEL are not unbiased estimates of the expected values of Y, although they do estimate the conditional median Y values.

In general, the predicted values produced for a model with nonadditive errors are not unbiased estimates of the conditional means of the endogenous value. If the model can be transformed to a model with additive errors by using a *monotonic* transformation, the predicted values estimate the conditional medians of the endogenous variable.

For transformed models in which the biasing factor is known, you can use programming statements to correct for the bias in the predicted values as estimates of the endogenous means. In the preceding loglinear case, the predicted values will be biased by the factor exp(σ^2/2). You can produce approximately unbiased predicted values in this case by writing the model as

```
proc model data=in;
   parms alpha beta;
   y=alpha * x ** beta;
   resid.y = log( actual.y / pred.y );

   fit y;
run;
```

Refer to Miller (1984) for a discussion of bias factors for predicted values of transformed models.

Note that models with transformed errors are not appropriate for Monte Carlo simulation using the SDATA= option. PROC MODEL computes the OUTS= matrix from the transformed RESID.-prefixed equation variables, while it uses the SDATA= matrix to generate multivariate normal errors, which are added to the predicted values. This method of computing errors is inconsistent when the equation variables have been transformed.

Error Covariance Structure Specification

One of the key assumptions of regression is that the variance of the errors is constant across observations. Correcting for heteroscedasticity improves the efficiency of the estimates.

Consider the following general form for models:

$$\begin{aligned} \mathbf{q}(\mathbf{y}_t, \mathbf{x}_t, \theta) &= \boldsymbol{\varepsilon}_\mathbf{t} \\ \boldsymbol{\varepsilon}_\mathbf{t} &= H_t * \boldsymbol{\epsilon}_\mathbf{t} \end{aligned}$$

$$H_t = \begin{bmatrix} \sqrt{h_{t,1}} & 0 & \dots & 0 \\ 0 & \sqrt{h_{t,2}} & \dots & 0 \\ & & \ddots & \\ 0 & 0 & \dots & \sqrt{h_{t,g}} \end{bmatrix}$$

$$\mathbf{h_t} = \mathbf{g}(\mathbf{y}_t, \mathbf{x}_t, \phi)$$

where $\epsilon_{\mathbf{t}} \sim N(0, \Sigma)$.

For models that are homoscedastic,

$$h_t = 1$$

If you had a model which was heteroscedastic with known form you can improve the efficiency of the estimates by performing a weighted regression. The weight variable, using this notation, would be $1/\sqrt{h_t}$.

If the errors for a model are heteroscedastic and the functional form of the variance is known, the model for the variance can be estimated along with the regression function.

To specify a functional form for the variance, assign the function to an H.*var* variable where *var* is the equation variable. For example, if you wanted to estimate the scale parameter for the variance of a simple regression model

$$y = a * x + b$$

you can specify

```
proc model data=s;
   y = a * x + b;
   h.y = sigma**2;
fit y;
```

Consider the same model with the following functional form for the variance:

$$h_t = \sigma^2 * x^{2*\alpha}$$

This would be written as

```
proc model data=s;
   y = a * x + b;
   h.y = sigma**2 * x**(2*alpha);
fit y;
```

There are three ways to model the variance in the MODEL procedure; Feasible generalized least squares; Generalized method of moments; and Full information maximum likelihood.

Feasible GLS

A simple approach to estimating a variance function is to estimate the mean parameters θ using some auxiliary method, such as OLS, and then use the residuals of that estimation to estimate the parameters ϕ of the variance function. This scheme is called *feasible GLS*. It is possible to use the residuals from an auxiliary method for the purpose of estimating ϕ because in many cases the residuals consistently estimate the error terms.

For all estimation methods except GMM and FIML, using the H.var syntax specifies that feasible GLS will be used in the estimation. For feasible GLS the mean function is estimated by the usual method. The variance function is then estimated using pseudolikelihood (PL) function of the generated residuals. The objective function for the PL estimation is

$$p_n(\sigma, \theta) = \sum_{i=1}^{n} \left(\frac{(y_i - f(x_i, \hat{\beta}))^2}{\sigma^2 h(z_i, \theta)} + \log[\sigma^2 h(z_i, \theta)] \right)$$

Once the variance function has been estimated the mean function is re-estimated using the variance function as weights. If an S-iterated method is selected, this process is repeated until convergence (iterated feasible GLS).

Note, feasible GLS will not yield consistent estimates when one of the following is true:

- The variance is unbounded.
- There is too much serial dependence in the errors (the dependence does not fade with time).
- A combination of serial dependence and lag dependent variables.

The first two cases are unusual but the third is much more common. Whether iterated feasible GLS avoids consistency problems with the last case is an unanswered research question. For more information see (Davidson and MacKinnon 1993) pages 298-301 or (Gallant 1987) pages 124-125 and (Amemiya 1985) pages 202-203.

One limitation is that parameters can not be shared between the mean equation and the variance equation. This implies that certain GARCH models, cross equation restrictions of parameters, or testing of combinations of parameters in the mean and variance component are not allowed.

Generalized Method of Moments

In GMM, normally the first moment of the mean function is used in the objective function.

$$\begin{aligned} \mathbf{q}(\mathbf{y}_t, \mathbf{x}_t, \theta) &= \epsilon_t \\ \mathbf{E}(\epsilon_t) &= 0 \end{aligned}$$

To add the second moment conditions to the estimation, add the equation

$$\mathbf{E}(\varepsilon_t * \varepsilon_t - h_t) = 0$$

to the model. For example if you wanted to estimate σ for linear example above, you can write

```
proc model data=s;
   y = a * x + b;
   eq.two = resid.y**2 - sigma**2;
fit y two/ gmm;
instruments x;
run;
```

This is a popular way to estimate a continuous-time interest rate processes (see (Chan, et al 1992)). The H.var syntax will automatically generate this system of equations.

To further take advantage of the information obtained about the variance, the moment equations can be modified to

$$\begin{aligned} \mathbf{E}(\varepsilon_t/\sqrt{h_t}) &= 0 \\ \mathbf{E}(\varepsilon_t * \varepsilon_t - h_t) &= 0 \end{aligned}$$

For the above example, this can be written as

```
proc model data=s;
   y = a * x + b;
   eq.two = resid.y**2 - sigma**2;
   resid.y = resid.y / sigma;
fit y two/ gmm;
instruments x;
run;
```

Note that, if the error model is misspecified in this form of the GMM model, the parameter estimates may be inconsistent.

Full Information Maximum Likelihood

For FIML estimation of variance functions, the concentrated likelihood below is used as the objective function. That is, the mean function will be coupled with the variance function and the system will be solved simultaneously.

$$\begin{aligned} l_n(\phi) &= \frac{ng}{2}(1+\ln(2\pi)) - \sum_{t=1}^{n} \ln\left(\left|\frac{\partial \mathbf{q}(\mathbf{y}_t, \mathbf{x}_t, \theta)}{\partial \mathbf{y}_t}\right|\right) \\ &+ \frac{1}{2}\sum_{t=1}^{n}\sum_{i=1}^{g}(\ln(h_{t,i}) + \mathbf{q}_i(\mathbf{y}_t, \mathbf{x}_t, \theta)^2/h_{t,i}) \end{aligned}$$

where g is the number of equations in the system.

The HESSIAN=GLS option is not available for FIML estimation involving variance functions. The matrix used when HESSIAN=CROSS is specified is a cross products matrix which has been enhanced by the dual quasi-newton approximation.

Examples

You can specify a GARCH(1,1) model as follows:

```
proc model data=modloc.usd_jpy;

             /* Mean model --------*/
   jpyret = intercept ;

             /* Variance model ----------------*/
   h.jpyret = arch0 + arch1 * xlag( resid.jpyret ** 2, mse.jpyret  )
                + garch1 * xlag(h.jpyret, mse.jpyret) ;

   bounds arch0 arch1 garch1 >= 0;

fit jpyret/method=marquardt fiml;
run;
```

Note that the BOUNDS statement was used to ensure that the parameters were positive, a requirement for GARCH models.

EGARCH models are used because there is no restrictions on the parameters. You can specify a EGARCH(1,1) model as follows:

```
proc model data=sasuser.usd_dem ;

           /* Mean model ----------*/
   demret = intercept ;

              /* Variance model ----------------*/
   if ( _OBS_ =1 )  then
     h.demret = exp( earch0/ (1. - egarch1)  );
   else
     h.demret = exp( earch0 + earch1 * zlag( g)
                        + egarch1 * log(zlag(h.demret)));
   g = theta * nresid.demret + abs( nresid.demret ) - sqrt(2/3.1415);

                      /* Fit and save the model */
fit demret/method=marquardt fiml  maxiter=100
run;
```

Ordinary Differential Equations

Ordinary differential equations (ODEs) are also called *initial value problems* because a time zero value for each first-order differential equation is needed. The following is an example of a first-order system of ODEs:

$$y' = -0.1y + 2.5z^2$$

$$
\begin{aligned}
z' &= -z \\
y_0 &= 0 \\
z_0 &= 1
\end{aligned}
$$

Note that you must provide an initial value for each ODE.

As a reminder, any n-order differential equation can be modeled as a system of first-order differential equations. For example, consider the differential equation

$$
\begin{aligned}
y'' &= by' + cy \\
y_0 &= 0 \\
y_0' &= 1
\end{aligned}
$$

which can be written as the system of differential equations

$$
\begin{aligned}
y' &= z \\
z' &= by' + cy \\
y_0 &= 0 \\
z_0 &= 1
\end{aligned}
$$

This differential system can be simulated as follows:

```
data t;
   time=0; output;
   time=1; output;
   time=2; output;
run;

proc model data=t ;
   dependent y 0 z 1;
   parm b -2 c -4;
      /* Solve  y''=b y' + c y --------------*/

   dert.y = z;
   dert.z = b * dert.y + c * y;

   solve y z / dynamic solveprint;
run;
```

The preceding statements produce the following output. These statements produce additional output, which is not shown.

```
                              The MODEL Procedure
                            Simultaneous Simulation

           Observation    1    Missing       2    CC      -1.000000
                               Iterations    0


                                Solution Values

                                  y              z

                              0.000000       1.000000


Observation    2    Iterations    0    CC    0.000000    ERROR.y     0.000000

                                Solution Values

                                  y              z

                              0.2096398      -.2687053


Observation    3    Iterations    0    CC    9.464802    ERROR.y    -0.234405

                                Solution Values

                                  y              z

                              -.0247649      -.1035929
```

The differential variables are distinguished by the derivative with respect to time (DERT.) prefix. Once you define the DERT. variable, you can use it on the right-hand side of another equation. The differential equations must be expressed in normal form; implicit differential equations are not allowed, and other terms on the left-hand side are not allowed.

The TIME variable is the *implied with respect to* variable for all DERT. variables. The TIME variable is also the only variable that must be in the input data set.

You can provide initial values for the differential equations in the data set, in the declaration statement (as in the previous example), or in statements in the code. Using the previous example, you can specify the initial values as

```
proc model data=t ;
   dependent y z ;
   parm b -2 c -4;
      /* Solve  y''=b y' + c y --------------*/
   if ( time=0 ) then
      do;
         y=0;
         z=1;
      end;
   else
```

```
            do;
               dert.y = z;
               dert.z = b * dert.y + c * y;
            end;
         end;
         solve y z / dynamic solveprint;
      run;
```

If you do not provide an initial value, 0 is used.

DYNAMIC and STATIC Simulation

Note that, in the previous example, the DYNAMIC option was specified in the SOLVE statement. The DYNAMIC and STATIC options work the same for differential equations as they do for dynamic systems. In the differential equation case, the DYNAMIC option makes the initial value needed at each observation the computed value from the previous iteration. For a static simulation, the data set must contain values for the integrated variables. For example, if DERT.Y and DERT.Z are the differential variables, you must include Y and Z in the input data set in order to do a static simulation of the model.

If the simulation is dynamic, the initial values for the differential equations are obtained from the data set, if they are available. If the variable is not in the data set, you can specify the initial value in a declaration statement. If you do not specify an initial value, the value of 0.0 is used.

A dynamic solution is obtained by solving one initial value problem for all the data. A graph of a simple dynamic simulation is shown in Figure 20.38. If the time variable for the current observation is less than the time variable for the previous observation, the integration is restarted from this point. This allows for multiple samples in one data file.

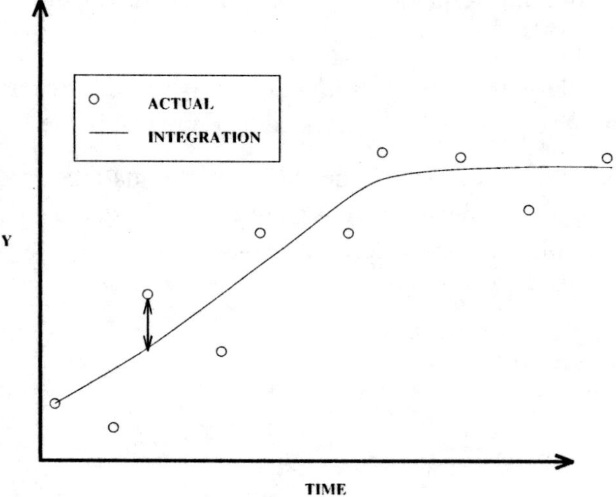

Figure 20.38. Dynamic Solution

In a static solution, n-1 initial value problems are solved using the first n-1 data values as initial values. The equations are integrated using the ith data value as an initial value to the i+1 data value. Figure 20.39 displays a static simulation of noisy data from a simple differential equation. The static solution does not propagate errors in initial values as the dynamic solution does.

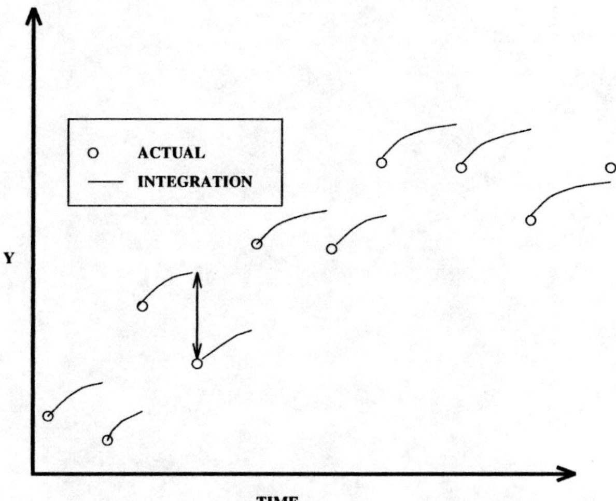

Figure 20.39. Static Solution

For estimation, the DYNAMIC and STATIC options in the FIT statement perform the same functions as they do in the SOLVE statement. Components of differential systems that have missing values or are not in the data set are simulated dynamically. For example, often in multiple compartment kinetic models, only one compartment is monitored. The differential equations describing the unmonitored compartments are simulated dynamically.

For estimation, it is important to have accurate initial values for ODEs that are not in the data set. If an accurate initial value is not known, the initial value can be made an unknown parameter and estimated. This allows for errors in the initial values but increases the number of parameters to estimate by the number of equations.

Estimation of Differential Equations

Consider the kinetic model for the accumulation of mercury (Hg) in mosquito fish (Matis, Miller, and Allen 1991, p. 177). The model for this process is the one-compartment constant infusion model shown in Figure 20.40.

Ku → Fish → Ke

Figure 20.40. One-Compartment Constant Infusion Model

The differential equation that models this process is

$$\begin{aligned} \frac{dconc}{dt} &= k_u - k_e conc \\ conc_0 &= 0 \end{aligned}$$

The analytical solution to the model is

$$conc = (k_u/k_e)(1 - \exp(-k_e t))$$

The data for the model are

```
data fish;
   input day conc;
   datalines;
0.0     0.0
1.0     0.15
2.0     0.2
3.0     0.26
4.0     0.32
6.0     0.33
;
run;
```

To fit this model in differential form, use the following statements:

```
proc model data=fish;
   parm ku ke;

   dert.conc = ku - ke * conc;

   fit conc / time=day;
run;
```

The results from this estimation are shown in Figure 20.41.

The MODEL Procedure

Nonlinear OLS Parameter Estimates

Parameter	Estimate	Approx Std Err	t Value	Approx Pr > |t|
ku	0.180159	0.0312	5.78	0.0044
ke	0.524661	0.1181	4.44	0.0113

Figure 20.41. Static Estimation Results for Fish Model

To perform a dynamic estimation of the differential equation, add the DYNAMIC option to the FIT statement.

```
proc model data=fish;
   parm ku .3 ke .3;

   dert.conc = ku - ke * conc;

   fit conc / time = day dynamic;
run;
```

The equation DERT.CONC is integrated from $conc(0) = 0$. The results from this estimation are shown in Figure 20.42.

```
                         The MODEL Procedure

                 Nonlinear OLS Parameter Estimates

                                   Approx                        Approx
Parameter          Estimate       Std Err     t Value       Pr > |t|

ku                 0.167109        0.0170        9.84         0.0006
ke                 0.469033        0.0731        6.42         0.0030
```

Figure 20.42. Dynamic Estimation Results for Fish Model

To perform a dynamic estimation of the differential equation and estimate the initial value, use the following statements:

```
proc model data=fish;
   parm ku .3 ke .3 conc0 0;

   dert.conc = ku - ke * conc;

   fit conc initial=(conc = conc0) / time = day dynamic;
run;
```

The INITIAL= option in the FIT statement is used to associate the initial value of a differential equation with a parameter. The results from this estimation are shown in Figure 20.43.

```
                         The MODEL Procedure

                 Nonlinear OLS Parameter Estimates

                                   Approx                        Approx
Parameter          Estimate       Std Err     t Value       Pr > |t|

ku                 0.164408        0.0230        7.14         0.0057
ke                  0.45949        0.0943        4.87         0.0165
conc0              0.003798        0.0174        0.22         0.8414
```

Figure 20.43. Dynamic Estimation with Initial Value for Fish Model

Finally, to estimate the fish model using the analytical solution, use the following statements:

```
proc model data=fish;
   parm ku .3   ke .3;

   conc = (ku/ ke)*( 1 -exp(-ke * day));

   fit conc;
run;
```

The results from this estimation are shown in Figure 20.44.

```
                              The MODEL Procedure

                      Nonlinear OLS Parameter Estimates

                                       Approx                        Approx
      Parameter          Estimate     Std Err     t Value     Pr > |t|

      ku                 0.167109      0.0170        9.84       0.0006
      ke                 0.469033      0.0731        6.42       0.0030
```

Figure 20.44. Analytical Estimation Results for Fish Model

A comparison of the results among the four estimations reveals that the two dynamic estimations and the analytical estimation give nearly identical results (identical to the default precision). The two dynamic estimations are identical because the estimated initial value (0.00013071) is very close to the initial value used in the first dynamic estimation (0). Note also that the static model did not require an initial guess for the parameter values. Static estimation, in general, is more forgiving of bad initial values.

The form of the estimation that is preferred depends mostly on the model and data. If a very accurate initial value is known, then a dynamic estimation makes sense. If, additionally, the model can be written analytically, then the analytical estimation is computationally simpler. If only an approximate initial value is known and not modeled as an unknown parameter, the static estimation is less sensitive to errors in the initial value.

The form of the error in the model is also an important factor in choosing the form of the estimation. If the error term is additive and independent of previous error, then the dynamic mode is appropriate. If, on the other hand, the errors are cumulative, a static estimation is more appropriate. See the section "Monte Carlo Simulation" for an example.

Auxiliary Equations

Auxiliary equations can be used with differential equations. These are equations that need to be satisfied with the differential equations at each point between each data value. They are automatically added to the system, so you do not need to specify them in the SOLVE or FIT statement.

Consider the following example.

The Michaelis-Menten Equations describe the kinetics of an enzyme-catalyzed reaction. The enzyme is E, and S is called the *substrate*. The enzyme first reacts with the substrate to form the enzyme-substrate complex ES, which then breaks down in a second step to form enzyme and products P.

The reaction rates are described by the following system of differential equations:

$$\frac{d[ES]}{dt} = k_1([E]-[ES])[S] - k_2[ES] - k_3[ES]$$

$$\frac{d[S]}{dt} = -k_1([E] - [ES])[S] + k_2[ES]$$
$$[E] = [E]_{tot} - [ES]$$

The first equation describes the rate of formation of ES from E + S. The rate of formation of ES from E + P is very small and can be ignored. The enzyme is in either the complexed or the uncomplexed form. So if the total ($[E]_{tot}$) concentration of enzyme and the amount bound to the substrate is known, $[E]$ can be obtained by conservation.

In this example, the conservation equation is an auxiliary equation and is coupled with the differential equations for integration.

Time Variable

You must provide a time variable in the data set. The name of the time variable defaults to TIME. You can use other variables as the time variable by specifying the TIME= option in the FIT or SOLVE statement. The time intervals need not be evenly spaced. If the time variable for the current observation is less than the time variable for the previous observation, the integration is restarted.

Differential Equations and Goal Seeking

Consider the following differential equation

$$y' = a*x$$

and the data set

```
data t2;
   y=0; time=0; output;
   y=2; time=1; output;
   y=3; time=2; output;
run;
```

The problem is to find values for X that satisfy the differential equation and the data in the data set. Problems of this kind are sometimes referred to as *goal seeking problems* because they require you to search for values of X that will satisfy the goal of Y.

This problem is solved with the following statements:

```
proc model data=t2 ;
   dependent x 0;
   independent y;
   parm a 5;
   dert.y = a * x;
   solve x / out=foo;
run;

proc print data=foo; run;
```

The output from the PROC PRINT statement is shown in Figure 20.45.

Obs	_TYPE_	_MODE_	_ERRORS_	x	y	time
1	PREDICT	SIMULATE	0	0.00000	0.00000	0
2	PREDICT	SIMULATE	0	0.80000	2.00000	1
3	PREDICT	SIMULATE	0	-0.40000	3.00000	2

Figure 20.45. Dynamic Solution

Note that an initial value of 0 is provided for the X variable because it is undetermined at TIME = 0.

In the preceding goal seeking example, X is treated as a linear function between each set of data points (see Figure 20.46).

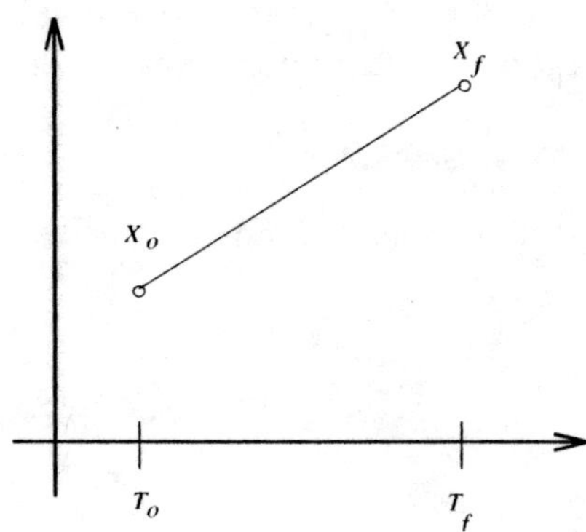

Figure 20.46. Form of X Used for Integration in Goal Seeking

If you integrate $y^{'} = ax$ manually, you have

$$\begin{aligned} x(t) &= \frac{t_f - t}{t_f - t_0} x_0 + \frac{-T_0}{t_f - t_0} x_f \\ y &= \int_{t_o}^{t_f} ax(t)dt \\ &= a\frac{1}{t_f - t_0}(t(t_f x_0 - t_0 x_f) + \frac{1}{2}t^2(x_f - x_0))|_{t_0}^{t_f} \end{aligned}$$

For observation 2, this reduces to

$$y = \frac{1}{2} a{*}x_f$$

$$2 \;=\; 2.5{*}x_f$$

So $x = 0.8$ for this observation.

Goal seeking for the TIME variable is not allowed.

Restrictions and Bounds on Parameters

Using the BOUNDS and RESTRICT statements, PROC MODEL can compute optimal estimates subject to equality or inequality constraints on the parameter estimates.

Equality restrictions can be written as a vector function

$$\mathbf{h}(\theta) = 0$$

Inequality restrictions are either active or inactive. When an inequality restriction is active, it is treated as an equality restriction. All inactive inequality restrictions can be written as a vector function

$$F(\theta) \geq 0$$

Strict inequalities, such as $(f(\theta) > 0)$, are transformed into inequalities as $f(\theta) \times (1 - \epsilon) - \epsilon \geq 0$, where the tolerance ϵ is controlled by the EPSILON= option on the FIT statement and defaults to 10^{-8}. The *i*th inequality restriction becomes active if $F_i < 0$ and remains active until its Lagrange multiplier becomes negative. Lagrange multipliers are computed for all the nonredundant equality restrictions and all the active inequality restrictions.

For the following, assume the vector $\mathbf{h}(\theta)$ contains all the current active restrictions. The constraint matrix A is

$$A(\hat{\theta}) = \frac{\partial \mathbf{h}(\hat{\theta})}{\partial \hat{\theta}}$$

The covariance matrix for the restricted parameter estimates is computed as

$$Z(Z'HZ)^{-1}Z'$$

where H is Hessian or approximation to the Hessian of the objective function $((X'(\mathrm{diag(S)})^{-1}\otimes \mathrm{I})\mathrm{X})$ for OLS), and Z is the last $(np - nc)$ columns of Q. Q is from an LQ factorization of the constraint matrix, *nc* is the number of active constraints, and *np* is the number of parameters. Refer to Gill, Murray, and Wright (1981) for more details on LQ factorization. The covariance column in Table 20.1 summarizes the Hessian approximation used for each estimation method.

The covariance matrix for the Lagrange multipliers is computed as

$$(AH^{-1}A')^{-1}$$

The p-value reported for a restriction is computed from a beta distribution rather than a t-distribution because the numerator and the denominator of the t-ratio for an estimated Lagrange multiplier are not independent.

The Lagrange multipliers for the active restrictions are printed with the parameter estimates. The Lagrange multiplier estimates are computed using the relationship

$$A^{'}\lambda = \mathrm{g}$$

where the dimension of the constraint matrix A is the number of constraints by the number of parameters, λ is the vector of Lagrange multipliers, and g is the gradient of the objective function at the final estimates.

The final gradient includes the effects of the estimated S matrix. For example, for OLS the final gradient would be:

$$\mathrm{g} = X'(\mathrm{diag}(\mathrm{S})^{-1} \otimes \mathrm{I})\mathrm{r}$$

where r is the residual vector. Note that when nonlinear restrictions are imposed, the convergence measure R may have values greater than one for some iterations.

Tests on Parameters

In general, the hypothesis tested can be written as

$$H_0 : \mathbf{h}(\theta) = 0$$

where $\mathbf{h}(\theta)$ is a vector valued function of the parameters θ given by the r expressions specified on the TEST statement.

Let $\hat{V}$ be the estimate of the covariance matrix of $\hat{\theta}$. Let $\hat{\theta}$ be the unconstrained estimate of θ and $\tilde{\theta}$ be the constrained estimate of θ such that $h(\tilde{\theta}) = 0$. Let

$$A(\theta) = \partial h(\theta)/\partial \theta \mid_{\hat{\theta}}$$

Let r be the dimension of $h(\theta)$ and n be the number of observations. Using this notation, the test statistics for the three kinds of tests are computed as follows.

The Wald test statistic is defined as

$$W = h^{'}(\hat{\theta}) \left(A(\hat{\theta})\hat{V}A^{'}(\hat{\theta}) \right)^{-1} h(\hat{\theta})$$

The Wald test is not invariant to reparameterization of the model (Gregory 1985, Gallant 1987, p. 219). For more information on the theoretical properties of the Wald test see Phillips and Park 1988.

The Lagrange multiplier test statistic is

$$R = \lambda' A(\tilde{\theta}) \tilde{V}^{-1} A'(\tilde{\theta}) \lambda$$

where λ is the vector of Lagrange multipliers from the computation of the restricted estimate $\tilde{\theta}$.

The Lagrange multiplier test statistic is equivalent to Rao's efficient score test statistic:

$$R = (\partial L(\tilde{\theta})/\partial \theta)' \tilde{V}^{-1} (\partial L(\tilde{\theta})/\partial \theta)$$

where L is the log likelihood function for the estimation method used. For SUR, 3SLS, GMM, and iterated versions of these methods, the likelihood function is computed as

$$L = Objective \times Nobs/2$$

For OLS and 2SLS the Lagrange multiplier test statistic is computed as:

$$R = [(\partial \hat{S}(\tilde{\theta})/\partial \theta)' \tilde{V}^{-1} (\partial \hat{S}(\tilde{\theta})/\partial \theta)] / \hat{S}(\tilde{\theta})$$

where $\hat{S}(\tilde{\theta})$ is the corresponding objective function value at the constrained estimate.

The likelihood ratio test statistic is

$$T = 2\left(L(\tilde{\theta}) - L(\hat{\theta})\right)$$

where $\tilde{\theta}$ represents the constrained estimate of θ and L is the concentrated log likelihood value.

For OLS and 2SLS, the likelihood ratio test statistic is computed as:

$$T = (n - nparms) \times (\hat{S}(\tilde{\theta}) - \hat{S}(\hat{\theta})) / \hat{S}(\hat{\theta})$$

where *df* is the difference in degrees of freedom for the full and restricted models, and $nparms$ is the number of parameters in the full system.

The Likelihood ratio test is not appropriate for models with nonstationary serially correlated errors (Gallant 1987, p. 139). The likelihood ratio test should not be used for dynamic systems, for systems with lagged dependent variables, or with the FIML estimation method unless certain conditions are met (see Gallant 1987, p. 479).

For each kind of test, under the null hypothesis the test statistic is asymptotically distributed as a χ^2 random variable with r degrees of freedom, where r is the number of expressions on the TEST statement. The p-values reported for the tests are computed from the $\chi^2(r)$ distribution and are only asymptotically valid.

Monte Carlo simulations suggest that the asymptotic distribution of the Wald test is a poorer approximation to its small sample distribution than the other two tests. However, the Wald test has the least computational cost, since it does not require computation of the constrained estimate $\tilde{\theta}$.

The following is an example of using the TEST statement to perform a likelihood ratio test for a compound hypothesis.

```
test a*exp(-k) = 1-k, d = 0 ,/ lr;
```

It is important to keep in mind that although individual t tests for each parameter are printed by default into the parameter estimates table, they are only asymptotically valid for nonlinear models. You should be cautious in drawing any inferences from these t tests for small samples.

Hausman Specification Test

Hausman's specification test, or m-statistic, can be used to test hypotheses in terms of bias or inconsistency of an estimator. This test was also proposed by Wu (1973). Hausman's m-statistic is as follows.

Given two estimators, $\hat{\beta}_0$ and $\hat{\beta}_1$, where under the null hypothesis both estimators are consistent but only $\hat{\beta}_0$ is asymptotically efficient and under the alternative hypothesis only $\hat{\beta}_1$ is consistent, the m-statistic is

$$m = \hat{q}'(\hat{V}_1 - \hat{V}_0)^- \hat{q}$$

where $\hat{V}_1$ and $\hat{V}_0$ represent consistent estimates of the asymptotic covariance matrices of $\hat{\beta}_1$ and $\hat{\beta}_0$, and

$$q = \hat{\beta}_1 - \hat{\beta}_0$$

The m-statistic is then distributed χ^2 with k degrees of freedom, where k is the rank of the matrix $(\hat{V}_1 - \hat{V}_0)$. A generalized inverse is used, as recommended by Hausman (1982).

In the MODEL procedure, Hausman's m-statistic can be used to determine if it is necessary to use an instrumental variables method rather than a more efficient OLS estimation. Hausman's m-statistic can also be used to compare 2SLS with 3SLS for a class of estimators for which 3SLS is asymptotically efficient (similarly for OLS and SUR).

Hausman's m-statistic can also be used, in principle, to test the null hypothesis of normality when comparing 3SLS to FIML. Because of the poor performance of this form of the test, it is not offered in the MODEL procedure. Refer to R.C. Fair (1984, pp. 246-247) for a discussion of why Hausman's test fails for common econometric models.

To perform a Hausman's specification test, specify the HAUSMAN option in the FIT statement. The selected estimation methods are compared using Hausman's *m*-statistic.

In the following example, OLS, SUR, 2SLS, 3SLS, and FIML are used to estimate a model, and Hausman's test is requested.

```
proc model data=one out=fiml2;
   endogenous y1 y2;

   y1 = py2 * y2 + px1 * x1 + interc;
   y2 = py1* y1 + pz1 * z1 + d2;

   fit y1 y2 / ols sur 2sls 3sls fiml hausman;
   instruments x1 z1;
run;
```

The output specified by the HAUSMAN option produces the following results.

The MODEL Procedure

Hausman's Specification Test Results

Comparing	To	DF	Statistic	Pr > ChiSq
SUR	OLS	6	17.77	0.0068
OLS	2SLS	6	13.86	0.0313
3SLS	OLS	6	0.27	0.9996
3SLS	2SLS	6	-0.00	.

Figure 20.47. Hausman's Specification Test Results

Figure 20.47 indicates that 2SLS, a system estimation method, is preferred over OLS. The model needs an IV estimator but not a full error covariance matrix. Note that the FIML estimation results are not compared.

Chow Tests

The Chow test is used to test for break points or structural changes in a model. The problem is posed as a partitioning of the data into two parts of size n_1 and n_2. The null hypothesis to be tested is

$$H_o: \ \beta_1 = \beta_2 = \beta$$

where β_1 is estimated using the first part of the data and β_2 is estimated using the second part.

The test is performed as follows (refer to Davidson and MacKinnon 1993, p. 380).

1. The p parameters of the model are estimated.
2. A second linear regression is performed on the residuals, $\hat{u}$, from the nonlinear estimation in step one.

   $$\hat{u} = \hat{X}b + \text{residuals}$$

   where $\hat{X}$ is Jacobian columns that are evaluated at the parameter estimates. If the estimation is an instrumental variables estimation with matrix of instruments W, then the following regression is performed:

   $$\hat{u} = P_{W^*}\hat{X}b + \text{residuals}$$

   where P_{W^*} is the projection matrix.
3. The restricted SSE (RSSE) from this regression is obtained. An SSE for each subsample is then obtained using the same linear regression.
4. The F statistic is then

   $$f = \frac{(RSSE - SSE_1 - SSE_2)/p}{(SSE_1 + SSE_2)/(n - 2p)}$$

   This test has p and $n - 2p$ degrees of freedom.

Chow's test is not applicable if $\min(n_1, n_2) < p$, since one of the two subsamples does not contain enough data to estimate β. In this instance, the *predictive Chow test* can be used. The predictive Chow test is defined as

$$f = \frac{(RSSE - SSE_1)\times(n_1 - p)}{SSE_1 * n_2}$$

where $n_1 > p$. This test can be derived from the Chow test by noting that the $SSE_2 = 0$ when $n_2 <= p$ and by adjusting the degrees of freedom appropriately.

You can select the Chow test and the predictive Chow test by specifying the CHOW=*arg* and the PCHOW=*arg* options in the FIT statement, where *arg* is either the number of observations in the first sample or a parenthesized list of first sample sizes. If the size of the one of the two groups in which the sample is partitioned is less than the number of parameters, then a Predictive Chow test is automatically used. These tests statistics are not produced for GMM and FIML estimations.

The following is an example of the use of the Chow test.

```
data exp;
   x=0;
   do time=1 to 100;
      if time=50 then x=1;
      y = 35 * exp( 0.01 * time ) + rannor( 123 ) + x * 5;
      output;
   end;
run;
```

```
proc model data=exp;
   parm zo 35 b;
      dert.z = b * z;
      y=z;
   fit y init=(z=zo) / chow =(40 50 60) pchow=90;
run;
```

The data set introduced an artificial structural change into the model (the structural change effects the intercept parameter). The output from the requested Chow tests are shown in Figure 20.48.

The MODEL Procedure

Structural Change Test

Test	Break Point	Num DF	Den DF	F Value	Pr > F
Chow	40	2	96	12.95	<.0001
Chow	50	2	96	101.37	<.0001
Chow	60	2	96	26.43	<.0001
Predictive Chow	90	11	87	1.86	0.0566

Figure 20.48. Chow's Test Results

Profile Likelihood Confidence Intervals

Wald-based and likelihood ratio-based confidence intervals are available in the MODEL procedure for computing a confidence interval on an estimated parameter. A confidence interval on a parameter θ can be constructed by inverting a Wald-based or a likelihood ratio-based test.

The approximate $100(1-\alpha)$ % Wald confidence interval for a parameter θ is

$$\hat{\theta}\pm z_{1-\alpha/2}\hat{\sigma}$$

where z_p is the $100p$th percentile of the standard normal distribution, $\hat{\theta}$ is the maximum likelihood estimate of θ, and $\hat{\sigma}$ is the standard error estimate of $\hat{\theta}$.

A likelihood ratio-based confidence interval is derived from the χ^2 distribution of the generalized likelihood ratio test. The approximate $1-\alpha$ confidence interval for a parameter θ is

$$\theta : 2[l(\hat{\theta}) - l(\theta)]\leq q_{1,1-\alpha} = 2l^{*}$$

where $q_{1,1-\alpha}$ is the $(1-\alpha)$ quantile of the χ^2 with one degree of freedom, and $l(\theta)$ is the log likelihood as a function of one parameter. The endpoints of a confidence interval are the zeros of the function $l(\theta) - l^{*}$. Computing a likelihood ratio-based confidence interval is an iterative process. This process must be performed twice for each parameter, so the computational cost is considerable. Using a modified form of the algorithm recommended by Venzon and Moolgavkar (1988), you can determine that the cost of each endpoint computation is approximately the cost of estimating the original system.

To request confidence intervals on estimated parameters, specify the following option in the FIT statement:

PRL= WALD | LR | BOTH

By default the PRL option produces 95% likelihood ratio confidence limits. The coverage of the confidence interval is controlled by the ALPHA= option in the FIT statement.

The following is an example of the use of the confidence interval options.

```
data exp;
   do time = 1 to 20;
      y = 35 * exp( 0.01 * time ) + 5*rannor( 123 );
   output;
   end;
run;

proc model data=exp;
   parm zo 35 b;
      dert.z = b * z;
      y=z;
   fit y init=(z=zo) / prl=both;
   test zo = 40.475437 ,/lr;
run;
```

The output from the requested confidence intervals and the TEST statement are shown in Figure 20.49

The MODEL Procedure

Nonlinear OLS Parameter Estimates

Parameter	Estimate	Approx Std Err	t Value	Approx Pr > |t|
zo	36.58933	1.9471	18.79	<.0001
b	0.006497	0.00464	1.40	0.1780

Test Results

Test	Type	Statistic	Pr > ChiSq	Label
Test0	L.R.	3.81	0.0509	zo = 40.475437

Parameter Wald 95% Confidence Intervals

Parameter	Value	Lower	Upper
zo	36.5893	32.7730	40.4056
b	0.00650	-0.00259	0.0156

Parameter Likelihood Ratio 95% Confidence Intervals

Parameter	Value	Lower	Upper
zo	36.5893	32.8381	40.4921
b	0.00650	-0.00264	0.0157

Figure 20.49. Confidence Interval Estimation

Note that the likelihood ratio test reported the probability that $zo = 40.47543$ is 5% but $zo = 40.47543$ is the upper bound of a 95% confidence interval. To understand this conundrum, note that the TEST statement is using the likelihood ratio statistic to test the null hypothesis $H_0 : zo = 40.47543$ with the alternate that $H_a : zo \neq 40.47543$. The upper confidence interval can be viewed as a test with the null hypothesis $H_0 : zo <= 40.47543$.

Choice of Instruments

Several of the estimation methods supported by PROC MODEL are instrumental variables methods. There is no standard method for choosing instruments for nonlinear regression. Few econometric textbooks discuss the selection of instruments for nonlinear models. Refer to Bowden, R.J. and Turkington, D.A. (1984, p. 180-182) for more information.

The purpose of the instrumental projection is to purge the regressors of their correlation with the residual. For nonlinear systems, the regressors are the partials of the residuals with respect to the parameters.

Possible instrumental variables include

- any variable in the model that is independent of the errors

- lags of variables in the system
- derivatives with respect to the parameters, if the derivatives are independent of the errors
- low degree polynomials in the exogenous variables
- variables from the data set or functions of variables from the data set.

Selected instruments must not

- depend on any variable endogenous with respect to the equations estimated
- depend on any of the parameters estimated
- be lags of endogenous variables if there is serial correlation of the errors.

If the preceding rules are satisfied and there are enough observations to support the number of instruments used, the results should be consistent and the efficiency loss held to a minimum.

You need at least as many instruments as the maximum number of parameters in any equation, or some of the parameters cannot be estimated. Note that *number of instruments* means linearly independent instruments. If you add an instrument that is a linear combination of other instruments, it has no effect and does not increase the effective number of instruments.

You can, however, use too many instruments. In order to get the benefit of instrumental variables, you must have more observations than instruments. Thus, there is a trade-off; the instrumental variables technique completely eliminates the simultaneous equation bias only in large samples. In finite samples, the larger the excess of observations over instruments, the more the bias is reduced. Adding more instruments may improve the efficiency, but after some point efficiency declines as the excess of observations over instruments becomes smaller and the bias grows.

The instruments used in an estimation are printed out at the beginning of the estimation. For example, the following statements produce the instruments list shown in Figure 20.50.

```
proc model data=test2;
   exogenous x1 x2;
   parms b1 a1 a2 b2 2.5 c2 55;
   y1 = a1 * y2 + b1 * exp(x1);
   y2 = a2 * y1 + b2 * x2 * x2 + c2 / x2;
   fit y1 y2 / n2sls;
   inst b1 b2 c2 x1 ;
run;
```

```
                        The MODEL Procedure

                    The 2 Equations to Estimate

                   y1 =   F(b1, a1(y2))
                   y2 =   F(a2(y1), b2, c2)
           Instruments    1 x1 @y1/@b1 @y2/@b2 @y2/@c2
```

Figure 20.50. Instruments Used Message

This states that an intercept term, the exogenous variable X1, and the partial derivatives of the equations with respect to B1, B2, and C2, were used as instruments for the estimation.

Examples

Suppose that Y1 and Y2 are endogenous variables, that X1 and X2 are exogenous variables, and that A, B, C, D, E, F, and G are parameters. Consider the following model:

```
y1 = a + b * x1 + c * y2 + d * lag(y1);
y2 = e + f * x2 + g * y1;
fit y1 y2;
instruments exclude=(c g);
```

The INSTRUMENTS statement produces X1, X2, LAG(Y1), and an intercept as instruments.

In order to estimate the Y1 equation by itself, it is necessary to include X2 explicitly in the instruments since F, in this case, is not included in the estimation

```
y1 = a + b * x1 + c * y2 + d * lag(y1);
y2 = e + f * x2 + g * y1;
fit y1;
instruments x2 exclude=(c);
```

This produces the same instruments as before. You can list the parameter associated with the lagged variable as an instrument instead of using the EXCLUDE= option. Thus, the following is equivalent to the previous example:

```
y1 = a + b * x1 + c * y2 + d * lag(y1);
y2 = e + f * x2 + g * y1;
fit y1;
instruments x1 x2 d;
```

For an example of declaring instruments when estimating a model involving identities, consider Klein's Model I

```
proc model data=klien;
   endogenous c p w i x wsum k y;
   exogenous  wp g t year;
   parms c0-c3 i0-i3 w0-w3;
   a: c = c0 + c1 * p + c2 * lag(p) + c3 * wsum;
   b: i = i0 + i1 * p + i2 * lag(p) + i3 * lag(k);
   c: w = w0 + w1 * x + w2 * lag(x) + w3 * year;
   x = c + i + g;
   y = c + i + g-t;
   p = x-w-t;
   k = lag(k) + i;
   wsum = w + wp;
```

The three equations to estimate are identified by the labels A, B, and C. The parameters associated with the predetermined terms are C2, I2, I3, W2, and W3 (and the intercepts, which are automatically added to the instruments). In addition, the system includes five identities that contain the predetermined variables G, T, LAG(K), and WP. Thus, the INSTRUMENTS statement can be written as

```
   lagk = lag(k);
   instruments c2 i2 i3 w2 w3 g t wp lagk;
```

where LAGK is a program variable used to hold LAG(K). However, this is more complicated than it needs to be. Except for LAG(K), all the predetermined terms in the identities are exogenous variables, and LAG(K) is already included as the coefficient of I3. There are also more parameters for predetermined terms than for endogenous terms, so you might prefer to use the EXCLUDE= option. Thus, you can specify the same instruments list with the simpler statement

```
   instruments _exog_ exclude=(c1 c3 i1 w1);
```

To illustrate the use of polynomial terms as instrumental variables, consider the following model:

```
   y1 = a + b * exp( c * x1 ) + d * log( x2 ) + e * exp( f * y2 );
```

The parameters are A, B, C, D, E, and F, and the right-hand-side variables are X1, X2, and Y2. Assume that X1 and X2 are exogenous (independent of the error), while Y2 is endogenous. The equation for Y2 is not specified, but assume that it includes the variables X1, X3, and Y1, with X3 exogenous, so the exogenous variables of the full system are X1, X2, and X3. Using as instruments quadratic terms in the exogenous variables, the model is specified to PROC MODEL as follows.

```
proc model;
   parms a b c d e f;
   y1 = a + b * exp( c * x1 ) + d * log( x2 ) + e * exp( f * y2 );
   instruments inst1-inst9;
```

```
      inst1 = x1; inst2 = x2; inst3 = x3;
      inst4 = x1 * x1; inst5 = x1 * x2; inst6 = x1 * x3;
      inst7 = x2 * x2; inst8 = x2 * x3; inst9 = x3 * x3;
      fit y1 / 2sls;
   run;
```

It is not clear what degree polynomial should be used. There is no way to know how good the approximation is for any degree chosen, although the first-stage R^2s may help the assessment.

First-Stage R^2s

When the FSRSQ option is used on the FIT statement, the MODEL procedure prints a column of first-stage R^2 (FSRSQ) statistics along with the parameter estimates. The FSRSQ measures the fraction of the variation of the derivative column associated with the parameter that remains after projection through the instruments.

Ideally, the FSRSQ should be very close to 1.00 for exogenous derivatives. If the FSRSQ is small for an endogenous derivative, it is unclear whether this reflects a poor choice of instruments or a large influence of the errors in the endogenous right-hand-side variables. When the FSRSQ for one or more parameters is small, the standard errors of the parameter estimates are likely to be large.

Note that you can make all the FSRSQs larger (or 1.00) by including more instruments, because of the disadvantage discussed previously. The FSRSQ statistics reported are unadjusted R^2s and do not include a degrees-of-freedom correction.

Autoregressive Moving Average Error Processes

Autoregressive moving average error processes (ARMA errors) and other models involving lags of error terms can be estimated using FIT statements and simulated or forecast using SOLVE statements. ARMA models for the error process are often used for models with autocorrelated residuals. The %AR macro can be used to specify models with autoregressive error processes. The %MA macro can be used to specify models with moving average error processes.

Autoregressive Errors

A model with first-order autoregressive errors, AR(1), has the form

$$y_t = f(x_t, \theta) + \mu_t$$

$$\mu_t = \phi\mu_{t-1} + \epsilon_t$$

while an AR(2) error process has the form

$$\mu_t = \phi_1\mu_{t-1} + \phi_2\mu_{t-2} + \epsilon_t$$

and so forth for higher-order processes. Note that the ϵ_t's are independent and identically distributed and have an expected value of 0.

An example of a model with an AR(2) component is

$$y = \alpha + \beta x_1 + \mu_t$$

$$\mu_t = \phi_1 \mu_{t-1} + \phi_2 \mu_{t-2} + \epsilon_t$$

You would write this model as follows:

```
proc model data=in;
   parms a b p1 p2;
   y = a + b * x1 + p1 * zlag1(y - (a + b * x1)) +
          p2 * zlag2(y - (a + b * x1));
   fit y;
run;
```

or equivalently using the %AR macro as

```
proc model data=in;
   parms a b;
   y = a + b * x1;
   %ar( y, 2 );
   fit y;
run;
```

Moving Average Models

A model with first-order moving average errors, MA(1), has the form

$$y_t = f(x_t) + \mu_t$$

$$\mu_t = \epsilon_t - \theta_1 \epsilon_{t-1}$$

where ϵ_t is identically and independently distributed with mean zero. An MA(2) error process has the form

$$\mu_t = \epsilon_t - \theta_1 \epsilon_{t-1} - \theta_2 \epsilon_{t-2}$$

and so forth for higher-order processes.

For example, you can write a simple linear regression model with MA(2) moving average errors as

```
proc model data=inma2;
   parms a b ma1 ma2;
   y = a + b * x + ma1 * zlag1( resid.y ) +
       ma2 * zlag2( resid.y );
   fit;
run;
```

where MA1 and MA2 are the moving average parameters.

Note that RESID.Y is automatically defined by PROC MODEL as

```
pred.y = a + b * x + ma1 * zlag1( resid.y ) +
         ma2 * zlag2( resid.y );
resid.y = pred.y - actual.y;
```

Note that RESID.Y is ϵ_t.

The ZLAG function must be used for MA models to truncate the recursion of the lags. This ensures that the lagged errors start at zero in the lag-priming phase and do not propagate missing values when lag-priming period variables are missing, and ensures that the future errors are zero rather than missing during simulation or forecasting. For details on the lag functions, see the section "Lag Logic."

This model written using the %MA macro is

```
proc model data=inma2;
   parms a b;
   y =  a + b * x;
   %ma(y, 2);
   fit;
run;
```

General Form for ARMA Models

The general ARMA(*p*,*q*) process has the following form

$$\mu_t = \phi_1\mu_{t-1} + \ldots + \phi_p\mu_{t-p} + \epsilon_t - \theta_1\epsilon_{t-1} - \ldots - \theta_q\epsilon_{t-q}$$

An ARMA(*p*,*q*) model can be specified as follows

```
yhat =  ... compute structural predicted value here ... ;
yarma = ar1 * zlag1( y - yhat ) + ...   /* ar part */
                                + ar(p)  * zlag(p) ( y - yhat )
      + ma1 * zlag1( resid.y )  + ...   /* ma part */
                                + ma(q)  * zlag(q) ( resid.y );
y = yhat + yarma;
```

where AR*i* and MA*j* represent the autoregressive and moving average parameters for the various lags. You can use any names you want for these variables, and there are many equivalent ways that the specification could be written.

Vector ARMA processes can also be estimated with PROC MODEL. For example, a two-variable AR(1) process for the errors of the two endogenous variables Y1 and Y2 can be specified as follows

```
y1hat =  ... compute structural predicted value here ... ;

y1    = y1hat + ar1_1 * zlag1( y1 - y1hat )    /* ar part y1,y1 */
              + ar1_2 * zlag1( y2 - y2hat );   /* ar part y1,y2 */

y21hat =  ... compute structural predicted value here ... ;

y2     = y2hat + ar2_2 * zlag1( y2 - y2hat )    /* ar part y2,y2 */
               + ar2_1 * zlag1( y1 - y1hat );   /* ar part y2,y1 */
```

Convergence Problems with ARMA Models

ARMA models can be difficult to estimate. If the parameter estimates are not within the appropriate range, a moving average model's residual terms will grow exponentially. The calculated residuals for later observations can be very large or can overflow. This can happen either because improper starting values were used or because the iterations moved away from reasonable values.

Care should be used in choosing starting values for ARMA parameters. Starting values of .001 for ARMA parameters usually work if the model fits the data well and the problem is well-conditioned. Note that an MA model can often be approximated by a high order AR model, and vice versa. This may result in high collinearity in mixed ARMA models, which in turn can cause serious ill-conditioning in the calculations and instability of the parameter estimates.

If you have convergence problems while estimating a model with ARMA error processes, try to estimate in steps. First, use a FIT statement to estimate only the structural parameters with the ARMA parameters held to zero (or to reasonable prior estimates if available). Next, use another FIT statement to estimate the ARMA parameters only, using the structural parameter values from the first run. Since the values of the structural parameters are likely to be close to their final estimates, the ARMA parameter estimates may now converge. Finally, use another FIT statement to produce simultaneous estimates of all the parameters. Since the initial values of the parameters are now likely to be quite close to their final joint estimates, the estimates should converge quickly if the model is appropriate for the data.

AR Initial Conditions

The initial lags of the error terms of AR(p) models can be modeled in different ways. The autoregressive error startup methods supported by SAS/ETS procedures are the following:

CLS	conditional least squares (ARIMA and MODEL procedures)
ULS	unconditional least squares (AUTOREG, ARIMA, and MODEL procedures)
ML	maximum likelihood (AUTOREG, ARIMA, and MODEL procedures)
YW	Yule-Walker (AUTOREG procedure only)
HL	Hildreth-Lu, which deletes the first p observations (MODEL procedure only)

See Chapter 12, for an explanation and discussion of the merits of various AR(p) startup methods.

The CLS, ULS, ML, and HL initializations can be performed by PROC MODEL. For AR(1) errors, these initializations can be produced as shown in Table 20.2. These methods are equivalent in large samples.

Table 20.2. Initializations Performed by PROC MODEL: AR(1) ERRORS

Method	Formula
conditional least squares	Y=YHAT+AR1*ZLAG1(Y-YHAT);
unconditional least squares	Y=YHAT+AR1*ZLAG1(Y-YHAT); IF _OBS_=1 THEN RESID.Y=SQRT(1-AR1**2)*RESID.Y;
maximum likelihood	Y=YHAT+AR1*ZLAG1(Y-YHAT); W=(1-AR1**2)**(-1/(2*_NUSED_)); IF _OBS_=1 THEN W=W*SQRT(1-AR1**2); RESID.Y=W*RESID.Y;
Hildreth-Lu	Y=YHAT+AR1*LAG1(Y-YHAT);

MA Initial Conditions

The initial lags of the error terms of MA(q) models can also be modeled in different ways. The following moving average error startup paradigms are supported by the ARIMA and MODEL procedures:

ULS unconditional least squares

CLS conditional least squares

ML maximum likelihood

The conditional least-squares method of estimating moving average error terms is not optimal because it ignores the startup problem. This reduces the efficiency of the estimates, although they remain unbiased. The initial lagged residuals, extending before the start of the data, are assumed to be 0, their unconditional expected value. This introduces a difference between these residuals and the generalized least-squares residuals for the moving average covariance, which, unlike the autoregressive model, persists through the data set. Usually this difference converges quickly to 0, but for nearly noninvertible moving average processes the convergence is quite slow. To minimize this problem, you should have plenty of data, and the moving average parameter estimates should be well within the invertible range.

This problem can be corrected at the expense of writing a more complex program. Unconditional least-squares estimates for the MA(1) process can be produced by specifying the model as follows:

```
yhat =  ... compute structural predicted value here ... ;
if _obs_ = 1 then do;
   h = sqrt( 1 + ma1 ** 2 );
   y = yhat;
```

```
      resid.y = ( y - yhat ) / h;
      end;
   else do;
      g = ma1 / zlag1( h );
      h = sqrt( 1 + ma1 ** 2 - g ** 2 );
      y = yhat + g * zlag1( resid.y );
      resid.y = ( ( y - yhat) - g * zlag1( resid.y ) ) / h;
      end;
```

Moving-average errors can be difficult to estimate. You should consider using an AR(p) approximation to the moving average process. A moving average process can usually be well-approximated by an autoregressive process if the data have not been smoothed or differenced.

The %AR Macro

The SAS macro %AR generates programming statements for PROC MODEL for autoregressive models. The %AR macro is part of SAS/ETS software and no special options need to be set to use the macro. The autoregressive process can be applied to the structural equation errors or to the endogenous series themselves.

The %AR macro can be used for

- univariate autoregression
- unrestricted vector autoregression
- restricted vector autoregression.

Univariate Autoregression

To model the error term of an equation as an autoregressive process, use the following statement after the equation:

```
%ar( varname, nlags )
```

For example, suppose that Y is a linear function of X1 and X2, and an AR(2) error. You would write this model as follows:

```
proc model data=in;
   parms a b c;
   y = a + b * x1 + c * x2;
   %ar( y, 2 )
   fit y / list;
run;
```

The calls to %AR must come *after* all of the equations that the process applies to.

The preceding macro invocation, %AR(y,2), produces the statements shown in the LIST output in Figure 20.51.

```
                         The MODEL Procedure

                    Listing of Compiled Program Code
      Stmt     Line:Col       Statement as Parsed

         1     5738:50        PRED.y = a + b * x1 + c * x2;
         1     5738:50        RESID.y = PRED.y - ACTUAL.y;
         1     5738:50        ERROR.y = PRED.y - y;
         2     7987:23        _PRED__y = PRED.y;
         3     8003:15        #OLD_PRED.y = PRED.y + y_l1
                              * ZLAG1( y - _PRED__y ) + y_l2
                              * ZLAG2( y - _PRED__y );
         3     8003:15        PRED.y = #OLD_PRED.y;
         3     8003:15        RESID.y = PRED.y - ACTUAL.y;
         3     8003:15        ERROR.y = PRED.y - y;
```

Figure 20.51. LIST Option Output for an AR(2) Model

The _PRED__ prefixed variables are temporary program variables used so that the lags of the residuals are the correct residuals and not the ones redefined by this equation. Note that this is equivalent to the statements explicitly written in the "General Form for ARMA Models" earlier in this section.

You can also restrict the autoregressive parameters to zero at selected lags. For example, if you wanted autoregressive parameters at lags 1, 12, and 13, you can use the following statements:

```
proc model data=in;
   parms a b c;
   y = a + b * x1 + c * x2;
   %ar( y, 13, , 1 12 13 )
   fit y / list;
run;
```

These statements generate the output shown in Figure 20.52.

```
                         The MODEL Procedure

                    Listing of Compiled Program Code
      Stmt     Line:Col       Statement as Parsed

         1     8182:50        PRED.y = a + b * x1 + c * x2;
         1     8182:50        RESID.y = PRED.y - ACTUAL.y;
         1     8182:50        ERROR.y = PRED.y - y;
         2     8631:23        _PRED__y = PRED.y;
         3     8647:15        #OLD_PRED.y = PRED.y + y_l1 * ZLAG1( y -
                              _PRED__y ) + y_l12 * ZLAG12( y -
                              _PRED__y ) + y_l13 * ZLAG13(
                              y - _PRED__y );
         3     8647:15        PRED.y = #OLD_PRED.y;
         3     8647:15        RESID.y = PRED.y - ACTUAL.y;
         3     8647:15        ERROR.y = PRED.y - y;
```

Figure 20.52. LIST Option Output for an AR Model with Lags at 1, 12, and 13

There are variations on the conditional least-squares method, depending on whether observations at the start of the series are used to "warm up" the AR process. By default, the %AR conditional least-squares method uses all the observations and assumes zeros for the initial lags of autoregressive terms. By using the M= option, you can request that %AR use the unconditional least-squares (ULS) or maximum-likelihood (ML) method instead. For example,

```
proc model data=in;
   y = a + b * x1 + c * x2;
   %ar( y, 2, m=uls )
   fit y;
run;
```

Discussions of these methods is provided in the "AR Initial Conditions" earlier in this section.

By using the M=CLS*n* option, you can request that the first *n* observations be used to compute estimates of the initial autoregressive lags. In this case, the analysis starts with observation *n*+1. For example:

```
proc model data=in;
   y = a + b * x1 + c * x2;
   %ar( y, 2, m=cls2 )
   fit y;
run;
```

You can use the %AR macro to apply an autoregressive model to the endogenous variable, instead of to the error term, by using the TYPE=V option. For example, if you want to add the five past lags of Y to the equation in the previous example, you could use %AR to generate the parameters and lags using the following statements:

```
proc model data=in;
   parms a b c;
   y = a + b * x1 + c * x2;
   %ar( y, 5, type=v )
   fit y / list;
run;
```

The preceding statements generate the output shown in Figure 20.53.

```
                              The MODEL Procedure

                    Listing of Compiled Program Code
   Stmt      Line:Col         Statement as Parsed

      1      8892:50          PRED.y = a + b * x1 + c * x2;
      1      8892:50          RESID.y = PRED.y - ACTUAL.y;
      1      8892:50          ERROR.y = PRED.y - y;
      2      9301:15          #OLD_PRED.y = PRED.y + y_l1 * ZLAG1( y )
                              + y_l2 * ZLAG2( y ) + y_l3 * ZLAG3( y )
                              + y_l4 * ZLAG4( y ) + y_l5 * ZLAG5( y );
      2      9301:15          PRED.y = #OLD_PRED.y;
      2      9301:15          RESID.y = PRED.y - ACTUAL.y;
      2      9301:15          ERROR.y = PRED.y - y;
```

Figure 20.53. LIST Option Output for an AR model of Y

This model predicts Y as a linear combination of X1, X2, an intercept, and the values of Y in the most recent five periods.

Unrestricted Vector Autoregression

To model the error terms of a set of equations as a vector autoregressive process, use the following form of the %AR macro after the equations:

```
%ar( process_name, nlags, variable_list )
```

The *process_name* value is any name that you supply for %AR to use in making names for the autoregressive parameters. You can use the %AR macro to model several different AR processes for different sets of equations by using different process names for each set. The process name ensures that the variable names used are unique. Use a short *process_name* value for the process if parameter estimates are to be written to an output data set. The %AR macro tries to construct parameter names less than or equal to eight characters, but this is limited by the length of *name*, which is used as a prefix for the AR parameter names.

The *variable_list* value is the list of endogenous variables for the equations.

For example, suppose that errors for equations Y1, Y2, and Y3 are generated by a second-order vector autoregressive process. You can use the following statements:

```
proc model data=in;
   y1 = ... equation for y1 ...;
   y2 = ... equation for y2 ...;
   y3 = ... equation for y3 ...;
   %ar( name, 2, y1 y2 y3 )
   fit y1 y2 y3;
run;
```

which generates the following for Y1 and similar code for Y2 and Y3:

```
y1 = pred.y1 + name1_1_1*zlag1(y1-name_y1) +
     name1_1_2*zlag1(y2-name_y2) +
     name1_1_3*zlag1(y3-name_y3) +
     name2_1_1*zlag2(y1-name_y1) +
     name2_1_2*zlag2(y2-name_y2) +
     name2_1_3*zlag2(y3-name_y3) ;
```

Only the conditional least-squares (M=CLS or M=CLS*n*) method can be used for vector processes.

You can also use the same form with restrictions that the coefficient matrix be 0 at selected lags. For example, the statements

```
proc model data=in;
   y1 = ... equation for y1 ...;
```

```
y2 = ... equation for y2 ...;
y3 = ... equation for y3 ...;
%ar( name, 3, y1 y2 y3, 1 3 )
fit y1 y2 y3;
```

apply a third-order vector process to the equation errors with all the coefficients at lag 2 restricted to 0 and with the coefficients at lags 1 and 3 unrestricted.

You can model the three series Y1-Y3 as a vector autoregressive process in the variables instead of in the errors by using the TYPE=V option. If you want to model Y1-Y3 as a function of past values of Y1-Y3 and some exogenous variables or constants, you can use %AR to generate the statements for the lag terms. Write an equation for each variable for the nonautoregressive part of the model, and then call %AR with the TYPE=V option. For example,

```
proc model data=in;
   parms a1-a3 b1-b3;
   y1 = a1 + b1 * x;
   y2 = a2 + b2 * x;
   y3 = a3 + b3 * x;
   %ar( name, 2, y1 y2 y3, type=v )
   fit y1 y2 y3;
run;
```

The nonautoregressive part of the model can be a function of exogenous variables, or it may be intercept parameters. If there are no exogenous components to the vector autoregression model, including no intercepts, then assign zero to each of the variables. There must be an assignment to each of the variables before %AR is called.

```
proc model data=in;
   y1=0;
   y2=0;
   y3=0;
   %ar( name, 2, y1 y2 y3, type=v )
   fit y1 y2 y3;
```

This example models the vector Y=(Y1 Y2 Y3)′ as a linear function only of its value in the previous two periods and a white noise error vector. The model has 18=(3 × 3 + 3 × 3) parameters.

Syntax of the %AR Macro

There are two cases of the syntax of the %AR macro. The first has the general form

%AR *(name, nlag [,endolist [,laglist]] [,***M=***method] [,***TYPE=***V])*

where

name specifies a prefix for %AR to use in constructing names of variables needed to define the AR process. If the *endolist* is not specified, the endogenous list defaults to *name*, which must be the name of the equation to which the AR error process is to be applied. The *name* value cannot exceed 32 characters.

nlag — is the order of the AR process.

endolist — specifies the list of equations to which the AR process is to be applied. If more than one name is given, an unrestricted vector process is created with the structural residuals of all the equations included as regressors in each of the equations. If not specified, *endolist* defaults to *name*.

laglist — specifies the list of lags at which the AR terms are to be added. The coefficients of the terms at lags not listed are set to 0. All of the listed lags must be less than or equal to *nlag*, and there must be no duplicates. If not specified, the *laglist* defaults to all lags 1 through *nlag*.

M=*method* — specifies the estimation method to implement. Valid values of M= are CLS (conditional least-squares estimates), ULS (unconditional least-squares estimates), and ML (maximum-likelihood estimates). M=CLS is the default. Only M=CLS is allowed when more than one equation is specified. The ULS and ML methods are not supported for vector AR models by %AR.

TYPE=V — specifies that the AR process is to be applied to the endogenous variables themselves instead of to the structural residuals of the equations.

Restricted Vector Autoregression

You can control which parameters are included in the process, restricting those parameters that you do not include to 0. First, use %AR with the DEFER option to declare the variable list and define the dimension of the process. Then, use additional %AR calls to generate terms for selected equations with selected variables at selected lags. For example,

```
proc model data=d;
   y1 = ... equation for y1 ...;
   y2 = ... equation for y2 ...;
   y3 = ... equation for y3 ...;
   %ar( name, 2, y1 y2 y3, defer )
   %ar( name, y1, y1 y2 )
   %ar( name, y2 y3, , 1 )
   fit y1 y2 y3;
run;
```

The error equations produced are

```
y1 = pred.y1 + name1_1_1*zlag1(y1-name_y1) +
     name1_1_2*zlag1(y2-name_y2) + name2_1_1*zlag2(y1-name_y1) +
     name2_1_2*zlag2(y2-name_y2) ;
```

```
y2 = pred.y2 + name1_2_1*zlag1(y1-name_y1) +
     name1_2_2*zlag1(y2-name_y2) + name1_2_3*zlag1(y3-name_y3) ;
y3 = pred.y3 + name1_3_1*zlag1(y1-name_y1) +
     name1_3_2*zlag1(y2-name_y2) + name1_3_3*zlag1(y3-name_y3) ;
```

This model states that the errors for Y1 depend on the errors of both Y1 and Y2 (but not Y3) at both lags 1 and 2, and that the errors for Y2 and Y3 depend on the previous errors for all three variables, but only at lag 1.

%AR Macro Syntax for Restricted Vector AR

An alternative use of %AR is allowed to impose restrictions on a vector AR process by calling %AR several times to specify different AR terms and lags for different equations.

The first call has the general form

%AR(*name, nlag, endolist,* DEFER)

where

name specifies a prefix for %AR to use in constructing names of variables needed to define the vector AR process.

nlag specifies the order of the AR process.

endolist specifies the list of equations to which the AR process is to be applied.

DEFER specifies that %AR is not to generate the AR process but is to wait for further information specified in later %AR calls for the same *name* value.

The subsequent calls have the general form

```
%AR( name, eqlist, varlist, laglist,TYPE= )
```

where

name is the same as in the first call.

eqlist specifies the list of equations to which the specifications in this %AR call are to be applied. Only names specified in the *endolist* value of the first call for the *name* value can appear in the list of equations in *eqlist*.

varlist specifies the list of equations whose lagged structural residuals are to be included as regressors in the equations in *eqlist*. Only names in the *endolist* of the first call for the *name* value can appear in *varlist*. If not specified, *varlist* defaults to *endolist*.

laglist specifies the list of lags at which the AR terms are to be added. The coefficients of the terms at lags not listed are set to 0. All of the listed lags must be less than or equal to the value of *nlag*, and there must be no duplicates. If not specified, *laglist* defaults to all lags 1 through *nlag*.

The %MA Macro

The SAS macro %MA generates programming statements for PROC MODEL for moving average models. The %MA macro is part of SAS/ETS software and no special options are needed to use the macro. The moving average error process can be applied to the structural equation errors. The syntax of the %MA macro is the same as the %AR macro except there is no TYPE= argument.

When you are using the %MA and %AR macros combined, the %MA macro must follow the %AR macro. The following SAS/IML statements produce an ARMA(1, (1 3)) error process and save it in the data set MADAT2.

```
 /* use IML module to simulate a MA process  */
proc iml;
   phi={1 .2};
   theta={ 1 .3 0 .5};
   y=armasim(phi, theta, 0,.1, 200,32565);
   create madat2 from y[colname='y'];
   append to y;
quit;
```

The following PROC MODEL statements are used to estimate the parameters of this model using maximum likelihood error structure:

```
title1 'Maximum Likelihood ARMA(1, (1 3))';
proc model data=madat2;
   y=0;
   %ar(y,1,,  M=ml)
   %ma(y,3,,1 3,  M=ml)   /* %MA always after %AR */
   fit y;
run;
```

The estimates of the parameters produced by this run are shown in Figure 20.54.

```
                    Maximum Likelihood ARMA(1, (1 3))

                           The MODEL Procedure

                 Nonlinear OLS Summary of Residual Errors

                 DF      DF                                                  Adj
Equation      Model   Error        SSE        MSE  Root MSE  R-Square       R-Sq

y                 3     197     2.6383     0.0134    0.1157   -0.0067    -0.0169
RESID.y                 197     1.9957     0.0101    0.1007


                   Nonlinear OLS Parameter Estimates

                                Approx                 Approx
Parameter       Estimate       Std Err    t Value     Pr > |t|   Label

y_l1            -0.10067        0.1187      -0.85       0.3973   AR(y) y lag1
                                                                 parameter
y_m1             -0.1934        0.0939      -2.06       0.0408   MA(y) y lag1
                                                                 parameter
y_m3            -0.59384        0.0601      -9.88       <.0001   MA(y) y lag3
                                                                 parameter
```

Figure 20.54. Estimates from an ARMA(1, (1 3)) Process

Syntax of the %MA Macro

There are two cases of the syntax for the %MA macro. The first has the general form

%MA *(name, nlag [,endolist [,laglist]] [,***M=***method])*

where

name specifies a prefix for %MA to use in constructing names of variables needed to define the MA process and is the default *endolist*.

nlag is the order of the MA process.

endolist specifies the equations to which the MA process is to be applied. If more than one name is given, CLS estimation is used for the vector process.

laglist specifies the lags at which the MA terms are to be added. All of the listed lags must be less than or equal to *nlag*, and there must be no duplicates. If not specified, the *laglist* defaults to all lags 1 through *nlag*.

M=*method* specifies the estimation method to implement. Valid values of M= are CLS (conditional least-squares estimates), ULS (unconditional least-squares estimates), and ML (maximum-likelihood estimates). M=CLS is the default. Only M=CLS is allowed when more than one equation is specified on the *endolist*.

%MA Macro Syntax for Restricted Vector Moving Average

An alternative use of %MA is allowed to impose restrictions on a vector MA process by calling %MA several times to specify different MA terms and lags for different equations.

The first call has the general form

%MA(*name, nlag, endolist,* **DEFER** *)*

where

name	specifies a prefix for %MA to use in constructing names of variables needed to define the vector MA process.
nlag	specifies the order of the MA process.
endolist	specifies the list of equations to which the MA process is to be applied.
DEFER	specifies that %MA is not to generate the MA process but is to wait for further information specified in later %MA calls for the same *name* value.

The subsequent calls have the general form

```
%MA( name, eqlist, varlist, laglist )
```

where

name	is the same as in the first call.
eqlist	specifies the list of equations to which the specifications in this %MA call are to be applied.
varlist	specifies the list of equations whose lagged structural residuals are to be included as regressors in the equations in *eqlist*.
laglist	specifies the list of lags at which the MA terms are to be added.

Distributed Lag Models and the %PDL Macro

In the following example, the variable *y* is modeled as a linear function of *x*, the first lag of *x*, the second lag of *x*, and so forth:

$$y_t = a + b_0 x_t + b_1 x_{t-1} + b_2 x_{t-2} + b_3 x_{t-3} + \ldots + b_n x_{t-l}$$

Models of this sort can introduce a great many parameters for the lags, and there may not be enough data to compute accurate independent estimates for them all. Often, the number of parameters is reduced by assuming that the lag coefficients follow some pattern. One common assumption is that the lag coefficients follow a polynomial in the lag length

$$b_i = \sum_{j=0}^{d} \alpha_j (i)^j$$

where d is the degree of the polynomial used. Models of this kind are called *Almon lag models*, *polynomial distributed lag models*, or *PDLs* for short. For example, Figure 20.55 shows the lag distribution that can be modeled with a low order polynomial. Endpoint restrictions can be imposed on a PDL to require that the lag coefficients be 0 at the 0th lag, or at the final lag, or at both.

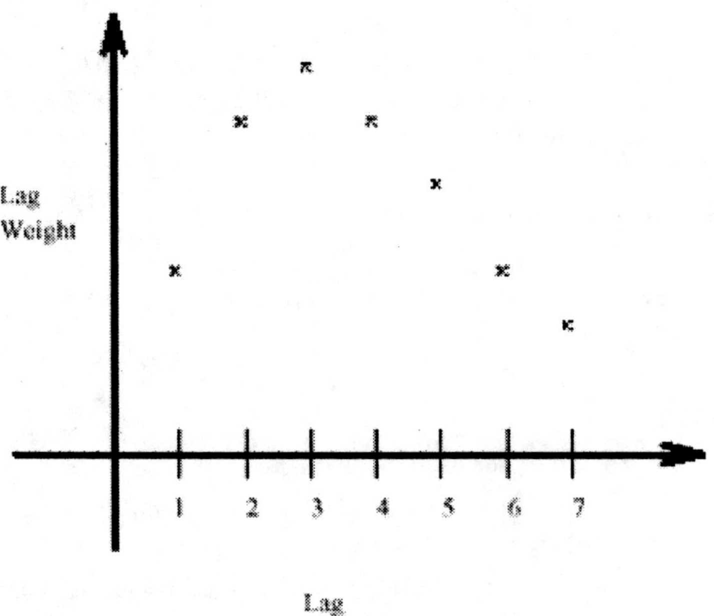

Figure 20.55. Polynomial Distributed Lags

For linear single-equation models, SAS/ETS software includes the PDLREG procedure for estimating PDL models. See Chapter 21, "The PDLREG Procedure," for a more detailed discussion of polynomial distributed lags and an explanation of endpoint restrictions.

Polynomial and other distributed lag models can be estimated and simulated or forecast with PROC MODEL. For polynomial distributed lags, the %PDL macro can generate the needed programming statements automatically.

The %PDL Macro

The SAS macro %PDL generates the programming statements to compute the lag coefficients of polynomial distributed lag models and to apply them to the lags of variables or expressions.

To use the %PDL macro in a model program, you first call it to declare the lag distribution; later, you call it again to apply the PDL to a variable or expression. The first call generates a PARMS statement for the polynomial parameters and assignment statements to compute the lag coefficients. The second call generates an expression that applies the lag coefficients to the lags of the specified variable or expression. A PDL can be declared only once, but it can be used any number of times (that is, the second call can be repeated).

The initial declaratory call has the general form

%PDL *(pdlname, nlags, degree, R=code, OUTEST=dataset)*

where *pdlname* is a name (up to 32 characters) that you give to identify the PDL, *nlags* is the lag length, and *degree* is the degree of the polynomial for the distribution. The R=*code* is optional for endpoint restrictions. The value of *code* can be FIRST (for upper), LAST (for lower), or BOTH (for both upper and lower endpoints). See chapter pdlreg, "The PDLREG Procedure," for a discussion of endpoint restrictions. The option OUTEST=*dataset* creates a data set containing the estimates of the parameters and their covariance matrix.

The later calls to apply the PDL have the general form

```
%PDL( pdlname, expression )
```

where *pdlname* is the name of the PDL and *expression* is the variable or expression to which the PDL is to be applied. The *pdlname* given must be the same as the name used to declare the PDL.

The following statements produce the output in Figure 20.56:

```
proc model data=in list;
   parms int pz;
   %pdl(xpdl,5,2);
   y = int + pz * z + %pdl(xpdl,x);
   %ar(y,2,M=ULS);
   id i;
fit y / out=model1 outresid converge=1e-6;
run;
```

```
                                The MODEL Procedure

                              Nonlinear OLS  Estimates

                                 Approx                    Approx
Term                Estimate    Std Err    t Value     Pr > |t|    Label

XPDL_L0             1.568788     0.0992      15.81       <.0001    PDL(XPDL,5,2)
                                                                   coefficient for lag0
XPDL_L1             0.564917     0.0348      16.24       <.0001    PDL(XPDL,5,2)
                                                                   coefficient for lag1
XPDL_L2             -0.05063     0.0629      -0.80       0.4442    PDL(XPDL,5,2)
                                                                   coefficient for lag2
XPDL_L3             -0.27785     0.0549      -5.06       0.0010    PDL(XPDL,5,2)
                                                                   coefficient for lag3
XPDL_L4             -0.11675     0.0390      -2.99       0.0173    PDL(XPDL,5,2)
                                                                   coefficient for lag4
XPDL_L5              0.43267     0.1445       2.99       0.0172    PDL(XPDL,5,2)
                                                                   coefficient for lag5
```

Figure 20.56. %PDL Macro ESTIMATE Statement Output

This second example models two variables, Y1 and Y2, and uses two PDLs:

```
proc model data=in;
   parms int1 int2;
   %pdl( logxpdl, 5, 3 )
   %pdl( zpdl, 6, 4 )
   y1 = int1 + %pdl( logxpdl, log(x) ) + %pdl( zpdl, z );
   y2 = int2 + %pdl( zpdl, z );
   fit y1 y2;
run;
```

A (5,3) PDL of the log of X is used in the equation for Y1. A (6,4) PDL of Z is used in the equations for both Y1 and Y2. Since the same ZPDL is used in both equations, the lag coefficients for Z are the same for the Y1 and Y2 equations, and the polynomial parameters for ZPDL are shared by the two equations. See Example 20.5 for a complete example and comparison with PDLREG.

Input Data Sets

DATA= Input Data Set

For FIT tasks, the DATA= option specifies which input data set to use in estimating parameters. Variables in the model program are looked up in the DATA= data set and, if found, their attributes (type, length, label, and format) are set to be the same as those in the DATA= data set (if not defined otherwise within PROC MODEL), and values for the variables in the program are read from the data set.

ESTDATA= Input Data Set

The ESTDATA= option specifies an input data set that contains an observation giving values for some or all of the model parameters. The data set can also contain observations giving the rows of a covariance matrix for the parameters.

Parameter values read from the ESTDATA= data set provide initial starting values for parameters estimated. Observations providing covariance values, if any are present in the ESTDATA= data set, are ignored.

The ESTDATA= data set is usually created by the OUTEST= option in a previous FIT statement. You can also create an ESTDATA= data set with a SAS DATA step program. The data set must contain a numeric variable for each parameter to be given a value or covariance column. The name of the variable in the ESTDATA= data set must match the name of the parameter in the model. Parameters with names longer than 32 characters cannot be set from an ESTDATA= data set. The data set must also contain a character variable _NAME_ of length 32. _NAME_ has a blank value for the observation that gives values to the parameters. _NAME_ contains the name of a parameter for observations defining rows of the covariance matrix.

More than one set of parameter estimates and covariances can be stored in the ESTDATA= data set if the observations for the different estimates are identified by the variable _TYPE_. _TYPE_ must be a character variable of length 8. The TYPE= option is used to select for input the part of the ESTDATA= data set for which the _TYPE_ value matches the value of the TYPE= option.

The following SAS statements generate the ESTDATA= data set shown in Figure 20.57. The second FIT statement uses the TYPE= option to select the estimates from the GMM estimation as starting values for the FIML estimation.

```
        /* Generate test data */
data gmm2;
   do t=1 to 50;
      x1 = sqrt(t) ;
      x2 = rannor(10) * 10;
      y1 = -.002 * x2 * x2 - .05 / x2 - 0.001 * x1 * x1;
      y2 = 0.002* y1 + 2 * x2 * x2 + 50 / x2 + 5 * rannor(1);
      y1 = y1 + 5 * rannor(1);
      z1 = 1; z2 = x1 * x1; z3 = x2 * x2; z4 = 1.0/x2;
      output;
   end;
run;

proc model data=gmm2 ;
   exogenous x1 x2;
   parms a1 a2 b1 2.5 b2 c2 55 d1;
   inst b1 b2 c2 x1 x2;
   y1 = a1 * y2 + b1 * x1 * x1 + d1;
   y2 = a2 * y1 + b2 * x2 * x2 + c2 / x2 + d1;

   fit y1 y2 / 3sls gmm kernel=(qs,1,0.2) outest=gmmest;

   fit y1 y2 / fiml type=gmm estdata=gmmest;
run;

proc print data=gmmest;
run;
```

Obs	_NAME_	_TYPE_	_STATUS_		_NUSED_	a1	a2	b1	b2	c2	d1
1		3SLS	0	Converged	50	-.002229607	-1.25002	0.025827	1.99609	49.8119	-0.44533
2		GMM	0	Converged	50	-.002013073	-1.53882	0.014908	1.99419	49.8035	-0.64933

Figure 20.57. ESTDATA= Data Set

MISSING= PAIRWISE | DELETE

When missing values are encountered for any one of the equations in a system of equations, the default action is to drop that observation for all of the equations. The new MISSING=PAIRWISE option on the FIT statement provides a different method of handling missing values that avoids losing data for nonmissing equations for the observation. This is especially useful for SUR estimation on equations with unequal numbers of observations.

The option MISSING=PAIRWISE specifies that missing values are tracked on an equation-by-equation basis. The MISSING=DELETE option specifies that the entire observation is omitted from the analysis when any equation has a missing predicted or actual value for the equation. The default is MISSING=DELETE.

When you specify the MISSING=PAIRWISE option, the S matrix is computed as

$$S = D(R'R)D$$

where D is a diagonal matrix that depends on the VARDEF= option, the matrix R is $(\mathbf{r}_1, \ldots, \mathbf{r}_g)$, and $\mathbf{r}_i$ is the vector of residuals for the *i*th equation with r_{ij} replaced with zero when r_{ij} is missing.

For MISSING=PAIRWISE, the calculation of the diagonal element $d_{i,i}$ of **D** is based on n_i, the number of nonmissing observations for the *i*th equation, instead of on *n* or, for VARDEF=WGT or WDF, on the sum of the weights for the nonmissing observations for the *i*th equation instead of on the sum of the weights for all observations. Refer to the description of the VARDEF= option for the definition of **D**.

The degrees of freedom correction for a shared parameter is computed using the average number of observations used in its estimation.

The MISSING=PAIRWISE option is not valid for the GMM and FIML estimation methods.

For the instrumental variables estimation methods (2SLS, 3SLS), when an instrument is missing for an observation, that observation is dropped for all equations,

regardless of the MISSING= option.

PARMSDATA= Input Data Set

The option PARMSDATA= reads values for all parameters whose names match the names of variables in the PARMSDATA= data set. Values for any or all of the parameters in the model can be reset using the PARMSDATA= option. The PARMSDATA= option goes on the PROC MODEL statement, and the data set is read before any FIT or SOLVE statements are executed.

Together, the OUTPARMS= and PARMSDATA= options allow you to change part of a model and recompile the new model program without the need to reestimate equations that were not changed.

Suppose you have a large model with parameters estimated and you now want to replace one equation, Y, with a new specification. Although the model program must be recompiled with the new equation, you don't need to reestimate all the equations, just the one that changed.

Using the OUTPARMS= and PARMSDATA= options, you could do the following:

```
proc model model=oldmod outparms=temp; run;
proc model outmodel=newmod parmsdata=temp data=in;
   ...  include new model definition with changed y eq. here ...
   fit y;
run;
```

The model file NEWMOD will then contain the new model and its estimated parameters plus the old models with their original parameter values.

SDATA= Input Data Set

The SDATA= option allows a cross-equation covariance matrix to be input from a data set. The **S** matrix read from the SDATA= data set, specified in the FIT statement, is used to define the objective function for the OLS, N2SLS, SUR, and N3SLS estimation methods and is used as the initial **S** for the methods that iterate the **S** matrix.

Most often, the SDATA= data set has been created by the OUTS= or OUTSUSED= option on a previous FIT statement. The OUTS= and OUTSUSED= data sets from a FIT statement can be read back in by a FIT statement in the same PROC MODEL step.

You can create an input SDATA= data set using the DATA step. PROC MODEL expects to find a character variable _NAME_ in the SDATA= data set as well as variables for the equations in the estimation or solution. For each observation with a _NAME_ value matching the name of an equation, PROC MODEL fills the corresponding row of the **S** matrix with the values of the names of equations found in the data set. If a row or column is omitted from the data set, a 1 is placed on the diagonal for the row or column. Missing values are ignored, and since the **S** matrix is symmetric, you can include only a triangular part of the **S** matrix in the SDATA= data set with the omitted part indicated by missing values. If the SDATA= data set contains multiple observations with the same _NAME_, the last values supplied for the _NAME_ are used. The structure of the expected data set is further described in the "OUTS=Data Set" section.

Use the TYPE= option on the PROC MODEL or FIT statement to specify the type of estimation method used to produce the **S** matrix you want to input.

The following SAS statements are used to generate an **S** matrix from a GMM and a 3SLS estimation and to store that estimate in the data set GMMS:

```
proc model data=gmm2 ;
   exogenous x1 x2;
   parms a1 a2 b1 2.5 b2 c2 55 d1;
   inst b1 b2 c2 x1 x2;
   y1 = a1 * y2 + b1 * x1 * x1 + d1;
   y2 = a2 * y1 + b2 * x2 * x2 + c2 / x2 + d1;

   fit y1 y2 / 3sls gmm kernel=(qs,1,0.2) outest=gmmest outs=gmms;
run;
```

The data set GMMS is shown in Figure 20.58.

Obs	_NAME_	_TYPE_	_NUSED_	y1	y2
1	y1	3SLS	50	27.1032	38.1599
2	y2	3SLS	50	38.1599	74.6253
3	y1	GMM	50	27.4205	46.4028
4	y2	GMM	50	46.4028	99.4656

Figure 20.58. SDATA= Data Set

VDATA= Input data set

The VDATA= option allows a variance matrix for GMM estimation to be input from a data set. When the VDATA= option is used on the PROC MODEL or FIT statement, the matrix that is input is used to define the objective function and is used as the initial V for the methods that iterate the V matrix.

Normally the VDATA= matrix is created from the OUTV= option on a previous FIT statement. Alternately an input VDATA= data set can be created using the DATA step. Each row and column of the V matrix is associated with an equation and an instrument. The position of each element in the V matrix can then be indicated by an equation name and an instrument name for the row of the element and an equation name and an instrument name for the column. Each observation in the VDATA= data set is an element in the V matrix. The row and column of the element are indicated by four variables EQ_ROW, INST_ROW, EQ_COL, and INST_COL which contain the equation name or instrument name. The variable name for an element is VALUE. Missing values are set to 0. Because the variance matrix is symmetric, only a triangular part of the matrix needs to be input.

The following SAS statements are used to generate a **V** matrix estimation from GMM and to store that estimate in the data set GMMV:

```
proc model data=gmm2 ;
   exogenous x1 x2;
   parms a1 a2 b2 b1 2.5 c2 55 d1;
   inst b1 b2 c2 x1 x2;
   y1 = a1 * y2 + b1 * x1 * x1 + d1;
   y2 = a2 * y1 + b2 * x2 * x2 + c2 / x2 + d1;

   fit y1 y2 / gmm outv=gmmv;
run;
```

The data set GMM2 was generated by the example in the preceding ESTDATA= section. The **V** matrix stored in GMMV is selected for use in an additional GMM estimation by the following FIT statement:

```
fit y1 y2 / gmm vdata=gmmv;
run;

proc print data=gmmv(obs=15);
run;
```

A partial listing of the GMMV data set is shown in Figure 20.59. There are a total of 78 observations in this data set. The **V** matrix is 12 by 12 for this example.

Obs	_TYPE_	EQ_ROW	EQ_COL	INST_ROW	INST_COL	VALUE
1	GMM	Y1	Y1	1	1	1509.59
2	GMM	Y1	Y1	X1	1	8257.41
3	GMM	Y1	Y1	X1	X1	47956.08
4	GMM	Y1	Y1	X2	1	7136.27
5	GMM	Y1	Y1	X2	X1	44494.70
6	GMM	Y1	Y1	X2	X2	153135.59
7	GMM	Y1	Y1	@PRED.Y1/@B1	1	47957.10
8	GMM	Y1	Y1	@PRED.Y1/@B1	X1	289178.68
9	GMM	Y1	Y1	@PRED.Y1/@B1	X2	275074.36
10	GMM	Y1	Y1	@PRED.Y1/@B1	@PRED.Y1/@B1	1789176.56
11	GMM	Y1	Y1	@PRED.Y2/@B2	1	152885.91
12	GMM	Y1	Y1	@PRED.Y2/@B2	X1	816886.49
13	GMM	Y1	Y1	@PRED.Y2/@B2	X2	1121114.96
14	GMM	Y1	Y1	@PRED.Y2/@B2	@PRED.Y1/@B1	4576643.57
15	GMM	Y1	Y1	@PRED.Y2/@B2	@PRED.Y2/@B2	28818318.24

Figure 20.59. The First 15 Observations in the VDATA= Data Set

Output Data Sets

OUT= Data Set

For normalized form equations, the OUT= data set specified on the FIT statement contains residuals, actuals, and predicted values of the dependent variables computed from the parameter estimates. For general form equations, actual values of the endogenous variables are copied for the residual and predicted values.

The variables in the data set are as follows:

- BY variables
- RANGE variable
- ID variables
- _ESTYPE_, a character variable of length 8 identifying the estimation method: OLS, SUR, N2SLS, N3SLS, ITOLS, ITSUR, IT2SLS, IT3SLS, GMM, ITGMM, or FIML
- _TYPE_, a character variable of length 8 identifying the type of observation: RESIDUAL, PREDICT, or ACTUAL
- _WEIGHT_, the weight of the observation in the estimation. The _WEIGHT_ value is 0 if the observation was not used. It is equal to the product of the _WEIGHT_ model program variable and the variable named in the WEIGHT statement, if any, or 1 if weights were not used.
- the WEIGHT statement variable if used
- the model variables. The dependent variables for the normalized-form equations in the estimation contain residuals, actuals, or predicted values, depending on the _TYPE_ variable, whereas the model variables that are not associated with estimated equations always contain actual values from the input data set.
- any other variables named in the OUTVARS statement. These can be program variables computed by the model program, CONTROL variables, parameters, or special variables in the model program.

The following SAS statements are used to generate and print an OUT= data set:

```
proc model data=gmm2;
   exogenous x1 x2;
   parms a1 a2 b2 b1 2.5 c2 55 d1;
   inst b1 b2 c2 x1 x2;
   y1 = a1 * y2 + b1 * x1 * x1 + d1;
   y2 = a2 * y1 + b2 * x2 * x2 + c2 / x2 + d1;

   fit y1 y2 / 3sls gmm out=resid outall ;
run;

proc print data=resid(obs=20);
run;
```

The data set GMM2 was generated by the example in the preceding ESTDATA= section above. A partial listing of the RESID data set is shown in Figure 20.60.

Obs	_ESTYPE_	_TYPE_	_WEIGHT_	x1	x2	y1	y2
1	3SLS	ACTUAL	1	1.00000	-1.7339	-3.05812	-23.071
2	3SLS	PREDICT	1	1.00000	-1.7339	-0.36806	-19.351
3	3SLS	RESIDUAL	1	1.00000	-1.7339	-2.69006	-3.720
4	3SLS	ACTUAL	1	1.41421	-5.3046	0.59405	43.866
5	3SLS	PREDICT	1	1.41421	-5.3046	-0.49148	45.588
6	3SLS	RESIDUAL	1	1.41421	-5.3046	1.08553	-1.722
7	3SLS	ACTUAL	1	1.73205	-5.2826	3.17651	51.563
8	3SLS	PREDICT	1	1.73205	-5.2826	-0.48281	41.857
9	3SLS	RESIDUAL	1	1.73205	-5.2826	3.65933	9.707
10	3SLS	ACTUAL	1	2.00000	-0.6878	3.66208	-70.011
11	3SLS	PREDICT	1	2.00000	-0.6878	-0.18592	-76.502
12	3SLS	RESIDUAL	1	2.00000	-0.6878	3.84800	6.491
13	3SLS	ACTUAL	1	2.23607	-7.0797	0.29210	99.177
14	3SLS	PREDICT	1	2.23607	-7.0797	-0.53732	92.201
15	3SLS	RESIDUAL	1	2.23607	-7.0797	0.82942	6.976
16	3SLS	ACTUAL	1	2.44949	14.5284	1.86898	423.634
17	3SLS	PREDICT	1	2.44949	14.5284	-1.23490	421.969
18	3SLS	RESIDUAL	1	2.44949	14.5284	3.10388	1.665
19	3SLS	ACTUAL	1	2.64575	-0.6968	-1.03003	-72.214
20	3SLS	PREDICT	1	2.64575	-0.6968	-0.10353	-69.680

Figure 20.60. The OUT= Data Set

OUTEST= Data Set

The OUTEST= data set contains parameter estimates and, if requested, estimates of the covariance of the parameter estimates.

The variables in the data set are as follows:

- BY variables
- _NAME_, a character variable of length 32, blank for observations containing parameter estimates or a parameter name for observations containing covariances
- _TYPE_, a character variable of length 8 identifying the estimation method: OLS, SUR, N2SLS, N3SLS, ITOLS, ITSUR, IT2SLS, IT3SLS, GMM, ITGMM, or FIML
- the parameters estimated.

If the COVOUT option is specified, an additional observation is written for each row of the estimate of the covariance matrix of parameter estimates, with the _NAME_ values containing the parameter names for the rows. Parameter names longer than 32 characters are truncated.

OUTPARMS= Data Set

The option OUTPARMS= writes all the parameter estimates to an output data set. This output data set contains one observation and is similar to the OUTEST= data set, but it contains all the parameters, is not associated with any FIT task, and contains no covariances. The OUTPARMS= option is used on the PROC MODEL statement, and the data set is written at the end, after any FIT or SOLVE steps have been performed.

OUTS= Data Set

The OUTS= SAS data set contains the estimate of the covariance matrix of the residuals across equations. This matrix is formed from the residuals that are computed using the parameter estimates.

The variables in the OUTS= data set are as follows:

- BY variables
- _NAME_, a character variable containing the name of the equation
- _TYPE_, a character variable of length 8 identifying the estimation method: OLS, SUR, N2SLS, N3SLS, ITOLS, ITSUR, IT2SLS, IT3SLS, GMM, ITGMM, or FIML
- variables with the names of the equations in the estimation.

Each observation contains a row of the covariance matrix. The data set is suitable for use with the SDATA= option on a subsequent FIT or SOLVE statement. (See "Tests on Parameters" in this chapter for an example of the SDATA= option.)

OUTSUSED= Data Set

The OUTSUSED= SAS data set contains the covariance matrix of the residuals across equations that is used to define the objective function. The form of the OUTSUSED= data set is the same as that for the OUTS= data set.

Note that OUTSUSED= is the same as OUTS= for the estimation methods that iterate the **S** matrix (ITOLS, IT2SLS, ITSUR, and IT3SLS). If the SDATA= option is specified in the FIT statement, OUTSUSED= is the same as the SDATA= matrix read in for the methods that do not iterate the **S** matrix (OLS, SUR, N2SLS, and N3SLS).

OUTV= Data Set

The OUTV= data set contains the estimate of the variance matrix, V. This matrix is formed from the instruments and the residuals that are computed using the parameter estimates obtained from the initial 2SLS estimation when GMM estimation is selected. If an estimation method other than GMM or ITGMM is requested and OUTV= is specified, a V matrix is created using computed estimates. In the case that a VDATA= data set is used, this becomes the OUTV= data set. For ITGMM, the OUTV= data set is the matrix formed from the instruments and the residuals computed using the final parameter estimates.

ODS Table Names

PROC MODEL assigns a name to each table it creates. You can use these names to reference the table when using the Output Delivery System (ODS) to select tables and create output data sets. These names are listed in the following table. For more information on ODS, see Chapter 8, "Using the Output Delivery System."

Table 20.3. ODS Tables Produced in PROC MODEL

ODS Table Name	Description	Option
	ODS Tables Created by the FIT Statement	
AugGMMCovariance	Cross products matrix	GMM
ChowTest	Structural change test	CHOW=
CollinDiagnostics	Collinearity Diagnostics	
ConfInterval	Profile likelihood Confidence Intervals	PRL=
ConvCrit	Convergence criteria for estimation	default
ConvergenceStatus	Convergence status	default
CorrB	Correlations of parameters	COVB/CORRB
CorrResiduals	Correlations of residuals	CORRS/COVS
CovB	Covariance of parameters	COVB/CORRB
CovResiduals	Covariance of residuals	CORRS/COVS
Crossproducts	Cross products matrix	ITALL/ITPRINT
DatasetOptions	Data sets used	default
DetResidCov	Determinant of the Residuals	DETAILS
DWTest	Durbin Watson Test	DW=
Equations	Listing of equations to estimate	default
EstSummaryMiss	Model Summary Statistics for PAIRWISE	MISSING=
EstSummaryStats	Objective, Objective * N	default
GMMCovariance	Cross products matrix	GMM
Godfrey	Godfrey's Serial Correlation Test	GF=
HausmanTest	Hausman's test table	HAUSMAN
HeteroTest	Heteroscedasticity test tables	BREUSCH/PAGEN
InvXPXMat	X'X inverse for System	I
IterInfo	Iteration printing	ITALL/ITPRINT
LagLength	Model lag length	default
MinSummary	Number of parameters, estimation kind	default
MissingValues	Missing values generated by the program	default
ModSummary	Listing of all categorized variables	default
ModVars	Listing of Model variables and parameters	default
NormalityTest	Normality test table	NORMAL
ObsSummary	Identifies observations with errors	default
ObsUsed	Observations read, used, and missing.	default
ParameterEstimates	Parameter Estimates	default
ParmChange	Parameter Change Vector	
ResidSummary	Summary of the SSE, MSE for the equations	default
SizeInfo	Storage Requirement for estimation	DETAILS
TermEstimates	Nonlinear OLS and ITOLS Estimates	OLS/ITOLS
TestResults	Test statement table	
WgtVar	The name of the weight variable	
XPXMat	X'X for System	XPX

Table 20.3. (continued)

ODS Table Name	Description	Option
ODS Tables Created by the SOLVE Statement		
DatasetOptions	Data sets used	default
DescriptiveStatistics	Descriptive Statistics	STATS
FitStatistics	Fit statistics for simulation	STATS
LagLength	Model lag length	default
ModSummary	Listing of all categorized variables	default
ObsSummary	Simulation trace output	SOLVEPRINT
ObsUsed	Observations read, used, and missing.	default
SimulationSummary	Number of variables solved for	default
SolutionVarList	Solution Variable Lists	default
TheilRelStats	Theil Relative Change Error Statistics	THEIL
TheilStats	Theil Forecast Error Statistics	THEIL
ODS Tables Created by the FIT and SOLVE Statements		
AdjacencyMatrix	Adjacency Graph	GRAPH
BlockAnalysis	Block analysis	BLOCK
BlockStructure	Block structure	BLOCK
CodeDependency	Variable cross reference	LISTDEP
CodeList	Listing of programs statements	LISTCODE
CrossReference	Cross Reference Listing For Program	
DepStructure	Dependency Structure of the System	BLOCK
DerList	Derivative variables	LISTDER
FirstDerivatives	First derivative table	LISTDER
InterIntg	Integration Iteration Output	INTGPRINT
MemUsage	Memory usage statistics	MEMORYUSE
ParmReadIn	Parameter estimates read in	ESTDATA=
ProgList	Listing of Compiled Program Code	
RangeInfo	RANGE statement specification	
SortAdjacencyMatrix	Sorted adjacency Graph	GRAPH
TransitiveClosure	Transitive closure Graph	GRAPH

ODS Graphics (Experimental)

This section describes the use of ODS for creating graphics with the MODEL procedure. These graphics are experimental in this release, meaning that both the graphical results and the syntax for specifying them are subject to change in a future release.

ODS Graph Names

PROC MODEL assigns a name to each graph it creates using ODS. You can use these names to reference the graphs when using ODS. The names are listed in Table 20.4.

To request these graphs, you must specify the ODS GRAPHICS statement. For more information on the ODS GRAPHICS statement, see Chapter 9, "Statistical Graphics Using ODS."

Table 20.4. ODS Graphics Produced by PROC MODEL

ODS Graph Name	Plot Description
ACFPlot	Autocorrelation of residuals
ActualByPredicted	Predicted vs actual plot
CooksD	Cook's *D* plot
IACFPlot	Inverse autocorrelation of residuals
QQPlot	QQ plot of residuals
PACFPlot	Partial autocorrelation of residuals
ResidualHistogram	Histogram of the residuals
StudentResidualPlot	Studentized residual plot

Details: Simulation

The *solution* given the vector **k**, of the following nonlinear system of equations is the vector **u** which satisfies this equation:

$$\mathbf{q}(\mathbf{u}, \mathbf{k}, \theta) = 0$$

A *simulation* is a set of solutions $\mathbf{u}_t$ for a specific sequence of vectors $\mathbf{k}_t$.

Model simulation can be performed to

- check how well the model predicts the actual values over the historical period
- investigate the sensitivity of the solution to changes in the input values or parameters
- examine the dynamic characteristics of the model
- check the stability of the simultaneous solution
- estimate the statistical distribution of the predicted values of the nonlinear model using Monte Carlo methods

By combining the various solution modes with different input data sets, model simulation can answer many different questions about the model. This section presents details of model simulation and solution.

Solution Modes

The following solution modes are commonly used:

- *Dynamic simultaneous forecast* mode is used for forecasting with the model. Collect the historical data on the model variables, the future assumptions of the exogenous variables, and any prior information on the future endogenous values, and combine them in a SAS data set. Use the FORECAST option on the SOLVE statement.
- *Dynamic simultaneous simulation* mode is often called *ex-post simulation, historical simulation*, or *ex-post forecasting*. Use the DYNAMIC option. This mode is the default.
- *Static simultaneous simulation* mode can be used to examine the within-period performance of the model without the complications of previous period errors. Use the STATIC option.
- *NAHEAD=n dynamic simultaneous simulation* mode can be used to see how well *n*-period-ahead forecasting would have performed over the historical period. Use the NAHEAD=*n* option.

The different solution modes are explained in detail in the following sections.

Dynamic and Static Simulations

In model simulation, either solved values or actual values from the data set can be used to supply lagged values of an endogenous variable. A *dynamic* solution refers to a solution obtained by using only solved values for the lagged values. Dynamic mode is used both for forecasting and for simulating the dynamic properties of the model.

A *static* solution refers to a solution obtained by using the actual values when available for the lagged endogenous values. Static mode is used to simulate the behavior of the model without the complication of previous period errors. Dynamic simulation is the default.

If you wish to use static values for lags only for the first *n* observations, and dynamic values thereafter, specify the START=*n* option. For example, if you want a dynamic simulation to start after observation twenty-four, specify START=24 on the SOLVE statement. If the model being simulated had a value lagged for four time periods, then this value would start using dynamic values when the simulation reached observation number 28.

n-Period-Ahead Forecasting

Suppose you want to regularly forecast 12 months ahead and produce a new forecast each month as more data becomes available. *n*-period-ahead forecasting allows you to test how well you would have done over time had you been using your model to forecast 1 year ahead.

To see how well a model predicts *n* time periods in the future, perform an *n*-period-ahead forecast on real data and compare the forecast values with the actual values.

n-period-ahead forecasting refers to using dynamic values for the lagged endogenous variables only for lags *1* through *n-1*. For example, 1-period-ahead forecasting, specified by the NAHEAD=1 option on the SOLVE statement, is the same as if a static solution had been requested. Specifying NAHEAD=2 produces a solution that uses dynamic values for lag one and static, actual, values for longer lags.

The following example is a 2-year-ahead dynamic simulation. The output is shown in Figure 20.61.

```
data yearly;
   input year x1 x2 x3 y1 y2 y3;
   datalines;
84 4 9  0  7  4  5
85 5 6  1  1  27  4
86 3 8  2  5  8  2
87 2 10 3  0  10 10
88 4 7  6  20 60 40
89 5 4  8  40 40 40
90 3 2  10 50 60 60
91 2 5  11 40 50 60
;
run;

proc model data=yearly outmodel=foo;
   endogenous y1 y2 y3;
   exogenous  x1 x2 x3;

   y1 = 2 + 3*x1 - 2*x2 + 4*x3;
   y2 = 4 + lag2( y3 ) + 2*y1 + x1;
   y3 = lag3( y1 ) + y2 - x2;

   solve y1 y2 y3 / nahead=2 out=c;
run;

proc print data=c;run;
```

```
                         The MODEL Procedure
      Dynamic Simultaneous 2-Periods-Ahead Forecasting Simulation

                          Data Set Options

                          DATA=     YEARLY
                          OUT=      C


                         Solution Summary

                 Variables Solved                  3
                 Simulation Lag Length             3
                 Solution Method              NEWTON
                 CONVERGE=                      1E-8
                 Maximum CC                        0
                 Maximum Iterations                1
                 Total Iterations                  8
                 Average Iterations                1


                      Observations Processed

                          Read        20
                          Lagged      12
                          Solved       8
                          First        5
                          Last         8


                 Variables Solved For      y1 y2 y3
```

Figure 20.61. NAHEAD Summary Report

Obs	_TYPE_	_MODE_	_LAG_	_ERRORS_	y1	y2	y3	x1	x2	x3
1	PREDICT	SIMULATE	0	0	0	10	7	2	10	3
2	PREDICT	SIMULATE	1	0	24	58	52	4	7	6
3	PREDICT	SIMULATE	1	0	41	101	102	5	4	8
4	PREDICT	SIMULATE	1	0	47	141	139	3	2	10
5	PREDICT	SIMULATE	1	0	42	130	145	2	5	11

Figure 20.62. C Data Set

The preceding 2-year-ahead simulation can be emulated without using the NAHEAD= option by the following PROC MODEL statements:

```
proc model data=test model=foo;
  range year = 87 to 88;
  solve y1 y2 y3 / dynamic solveprint;
run;

  range year = 88 to 89;
  solve y1 y2 y3 / dynamic solveprint;
run;

  range year = 89 to 90;
  solve y1 y2 y3 / dynamic solveprint;
run;
```

```
range year = 90 to 91;
solve y1 y2 y3 / dynamic solveprint;
```

The totals shown under "Observations Processed" in Figure 20.61 are equal to the sum of the four individual runs.

Simulation and Forecasting

You can perform a simulation of your model or use the model to produce forecasts. *Simulation* refers to the determination of the endogenous or dependent variables as a function of the input values of the other variables, even when actual data for some of the solution variables are available in the input data set. The simulation mode is useful for verifying the fit of the model parameters. Simulation is selected by the SIMULATE option on the SOLVE statement. Simulation mode is the default.

In forecast mode, PROC MODEL solves only for those endogenous variables that are missing in the data set. The actual value of an endogenous variable is used as the solution value whenever nonmissing data for it are available in the input data set. Forecasting is selected by the FORECAST option on the SOLVE statement.

For example, an econometric forecasting model can contain an equation to predict future tax rates, but tax rates are usually set in advance by law. Thus, for the first year or so of the forecast, the predicted tax rate should really be exogenous. Or, you may want to use a prior forecast of a certain variable from a short-run forecasting model to provide the predicted values for the earlier periods of a longer-range forecast of a long-run model. A common situation in forecasting is when historical data needed to fill the initial lags of a dynamic model are available for some of the variables but have not yet been obtained for others. In this case, the forecast must start in the past to supply the missing initial lags. Clearly, you should use the actual data that are available for the lags. In all the preceding cases, the forecast should be produced by running the model in the FORECAST mode; simulating the model over the future periods would not be appropriate.

Monte Carlo Simulation

The accuracy of the forecasts produced by PROC MODEL depends on four sources of error (Pindyck 1981, 405-406):

- The system of equations contains an implicit random error term ϵ

  $$\mathbf{g}(\mathbf{y}, \mathbf{x}, \hat{\theta}) = \epsilon$$

  where $\mathbf{y}$, $\mathbf{x}$, $\mathbf{g}$, $\hat{\theta}$, and ϵ are vector valued.
- The estimated values of the parameters, $\hat{\theta}$, are themselves random variables.
- The exogenous variables may have been forecast themselves and therefore may contain errors.
- The system of equations may be incorrectly specified; the model only approximates the process modeled.

The RANDOM= option is used to request Monte Carlo (or stochastic) simulations to generate confidence intervals for errors arising from the first two sources. The Monte Carlo simulations can be performed with ϵ, θ, or both vectors represented as random variables. The SEED= option is used to control the random number generator for the simulations. SEED=0 forces the random number generator to use the system clock as its seed value.

In Monte Carlo simulations, repeated simulations are performed on the model for random perturbations of the parameters and the additive error term. The random perturbations follow a multivariate normal distribution with expected value of 0 and covariance described by a covariance matrix of the parameter estimates in the case of θ, or a covariance matrix of the equation residuals for the case of ϵ. PROC MODEL can generate both covariance matrices or you can provide them.

The ESTDATA= option specifies a data set containing an estimate of the covariance matrix of the parameter estimates to use for computing perturbations of the parameters. The ESTDATA= data set is usually created by the FIT statement with the OUTEST= and OUTCOV options. When the ESTDATA= option is specified, the matrix read from the ESTDATA= data set is used to compute vectors of random shocks or perturbations for the parameters. These random perturbations are computed at the start of each repetition of the solution and added to the parameter values. The perturbed parameters are fixed throughout the solution range. If the covariance matrix of the parameter estimates is not provided, the parameters are not perturbed.

The SDATA= option specifies a data set containing the covariance matrix of the residuals to use for computing perturbations of the equations. The SDATA= data set is usually created by the FIT statement with the OUTS= option. When SDATA= is specified, the matrix read from the SDATA= data set is used to compute vectors of random shocks or perturbations for the equations. These random perturbations are computed at each observation. The simultaneous solution satisfies the model equations plus the random shocks. That is, the solution is not a perturbation of a simultaneous solution of the structural equations; rather, it is a simultaneous solution of the stochastic equations using the simulated errors. If the SDATA= option is not specified, the random shocks are not used.

The different random solutions are identified by the _REP_ variable in the OUT= data set. An unperturbed solution with _REP_=0 is also computed when the RANDOM= option is used. RANDOM=*n* produces *n*+1 solution observations for each input observation in the solution range. If the RANDOM= option is not specified, the SDATA= and ESTDATA= options are ignored, and no Monte Carlo simulation is performed.

PROC MODEL does not have an automatic way of modeling the exogenous variables as random variables for Monte Carlo simulation. If the exogenous variables have been forecast, the error bounds for these variables should be included in the error bounds generated for the endogenous variables. If the models for the exogenous variables are included in PROC MODEL, then the error bounds created from a Monte Carlo simulation will contain the uncertainty due to the exogenous variables.

Alternatively, if the distribution of the exogenous variables is known, the built-in random number generator functions can be used to perturb these variables appropriately for the Monte Carlo simulation. For example, if you knew the forecast of an exogenous variable, X, had a standard error of 5.2 and the error was normally distributed, then the following statements could be used to generate random values for X:

```
x_new = x + 5.2 * rannor(456);
```

During a Monte Carlo simulation the random number generator functions produce one value at each observation. It is important to use a different seed value for all the random number generator functions in the model program; otherwise, the perturbations will be correlated. For the unperturbed solution, _REP_=0, the random number generator functions return 0.

PROC UNIVARIATE can be used to create confidence intervals for the simulation (see the Monte Carlo simulation example in the "Getting Started" section).

Multivariate t-Distribution Simulation

To perform a Monte Carlo analysis of models that have residuals distributed as a multivariate *t*, use the ERRORMODEL statement with either the $\sim$ t(*variance*, *df*) option or with the CDF=t(*variance*, *df*) option. The CDF= option specifies the distribution that is used for simulation so that the estimation can be done for one set of distributional assumptions and the simulation for another.

The following is an example of estimating and simulating a system of equations with *t*-distributed errors using the ERRORMODEL statement:

```
      /* generate simulation data set */
data five;
set xfrate end=last;
if last then do;
```

```
   todate = date +5;
   do date = date to todate;
      output;
   end;
end;
```

The preceding DATA step generates the data set to request a five-days-ahead forecast. The following statements estimate and forecast the three forward-rate models of the following form.

$$
\begin{aligned}
rate_t &= rate_{t-1} + \mu * rate_{t-1} + \nu \\
\nu &= \sigma * rate_{t-1} * \epsilon \\
\epsilon &\sim \mathrm{N}(0,1)
\end{aligned}
$$

```
Title "Daily Multivariate Geometric Brownian Motion Model "
         "of D-Mark/USDollar Forward Rates";

proc model data=xfrate;

   parms df 15;        /* Give initial value to df */

   demusd1m = lag(demusd1m) + mu1m * lag(demusd1m);
   var_demusd1m = sigma1m ** 2 * lag(demusd1m **2);
   demusd3m = lag(demusd3m) + mu3m * lag(demusd3m);
   var_demusd3m = sigma3m ** 2 * lag(demusd3m ** 2);
   demusd6m = lag(demusd6m) + mu6m * lag(demusd6m);
   var_demusd6m = sigma6m ** 2 * lag(demusd6m ** 2);

      /* Specify the error distribution */
   errormodel demusd1m demusd3m demusd6m
        ~ t( var_demusd1m var_demusd3m var_demusd6m, df );

      /* output normalized S matrix */
   fit demusd1m demusd3m demusd6m / outsn=s;
run;
      /* forecast five days in advance */
   solve demusd1m demusd3m demusd6m /
         data=five sdata=s random=1500 out=monte;
   id date;
run;

   /* select out the last date ---*/
data monte; set monte;
   if date = '10dec95'd then output;
run;

title "Distribution of demusd1m Five Days Ahead";
proc univariate data=monte noprint;
     var demusd1m;
     histogram demusd1m / normal(noprint color=red)
```

```
        kernel(noprint color=blue) cfill=ligr;
run;
```

The Monte Carlo simulation specified in the preceding example draws from a multivariate *t*-distribution with constant degrees of freedom and forecasted variance and computes future states of DEMUSD1M, DEMUSD3M, and DEMUSD6M. The OUTSN= option on the FIT statement is used to specify the data set for the normalized Σ matrix. That is the Σ matrix is created by crossing the normally distributed residuals. The normally distributed residuals are created from the *t*-distributed residuals using the normal inverse CDF and the *t* CDF. This matrix is a correlation matrix.

The distribution of DEMUSD1M on the fifth day is shown in the following output. The two curves overlayed on the graph are a kernel density estimation and a normal distribution fit to the results.

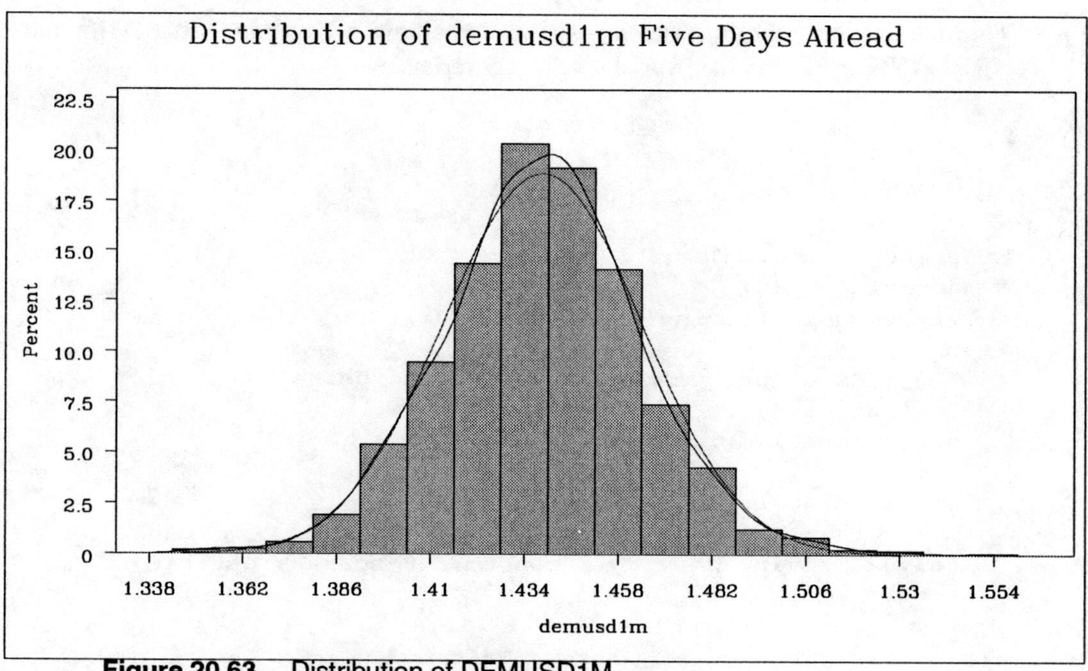

Figure 20.63. Distribution of DEMUSD1M

Alternate Distribution Simulation

As an alternate to the normal distribution, the ERRORMODEL statement can be used in a simulation to specify other distributions. The distributions available for simulation are Cauchy, Chi-squared, *F*, Poisson, *t*, and Uniform. An empirical distribution can also be used if the residuals are specified using the RESIDDATA= option on the SOLVE statement.

Except for the *t*, all of these alternate distributions are univariate but can be used together in a multivariate simulation. The ERRORMODEL statement applies to solved for equations only. That is, the normal form or general form equation referred to by the ERRORMODEL statement must be one of the equations you have selected in the SOLVE statement.

In the following example, two Poisson distributed variables are used to simulate the calls arriving and leaving a call center.

```
data s;     /* Covariance between arriving and leaving */
   arriving = 1; leaving = 0.7; _name_= "arriving";
   output;
   arriving = 0.7; leaving = 1.0; _name_= "leaving";
   output;
run;

data calls;
   date = '20mar2001'd;
   output;
run;
```

The first DATA step generates a data set containing a covariance matrix for the ARRIVING and LEAVING variables. The covariance is

$$\begin{vmatrix} 1 & .7 \\ .7 & 1 \end{vmatrix}$$

```
proc model data=calls;
   arriving = 10;
   errormodel arriving ~ poisson( 10 );

      /* Have four people answering the phone */
   leaving  = 4;
   errormodel leaving ~ poisson( 11 );

   waiting = arriving - leaving;

   solve arriving leaving / random=500 sdata=s out=sim;
run;

title "Distribution of Clients Waiting";
proc univariate data=sim noprint;
     var waiting ;
     histogram waiting / cfill=ligr;
run;
```

The distribution of number of waiting clients is shown in the following output.

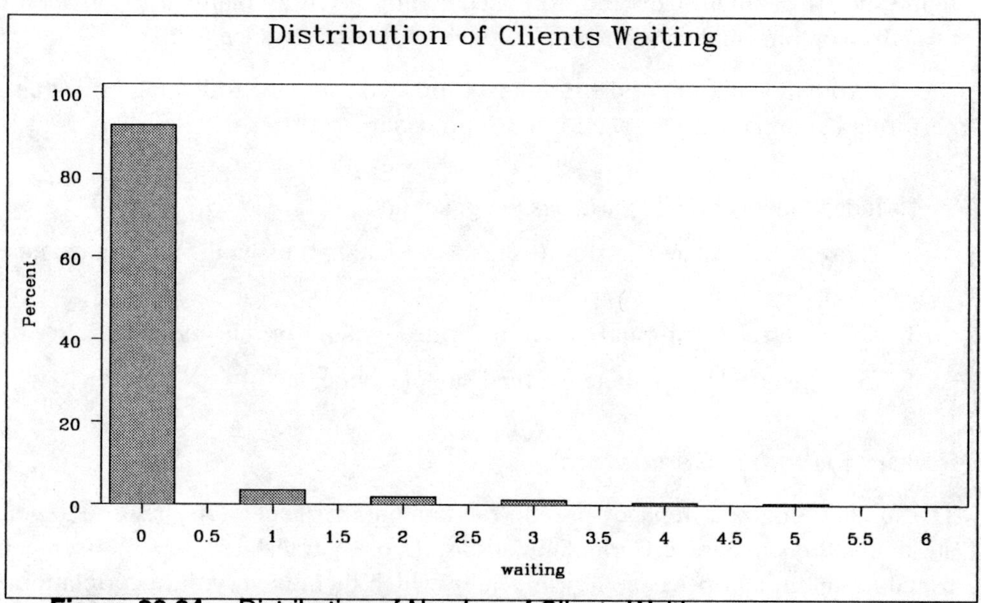

Figure 20.64. Distribution of Number of Clients Waiting

Mixtures of Distributions - Copulas

The theory of copulas is what enables the MODEL procedure to combine and simulate multivariate distributions with different marginals. This section provides a brief overview of copulas.

Modeling a system of variables accurately is a difficult task. The underlying, ideal, distributional assumptions for each variable are usually different from each other. An individual variable may be best modeled as a *t*-distribution or as a Poisson process. The correlation of the various variables are very important to estimate as well. A joint estimation of a set of variables would make it possible to estimate a correlation structure but would restrict the modeling to single, simple multivariate distribution (for example, the norma l). Even with a simple multivariate distribution, the joint estimation would be computationally difficult and would have to deal with issues of missing data.

Using the MODEL procedure ERRORMODEL statement you can combine and simulate from models of different distributions. The covariance matrix for the combined model is constructed using the copula induced by the multivariate normal distribution. A copula is a function that couples joint distributions to their marginal distributions.

The copula used by the model procedure is based on the multivariate normal. This particular multivariate normal has zero mean and covariance matrix R. The user provides R, which can be created using the following steps

1. Each model is estimated separately and their residuals saved.
2. The residuals for each model are converted to a normal distribution using their CDFs, $F_i(.)$, using the relationship $\Phi^{-1}(F(\epsilon_{it}))$.
3. Cross these normal residuals, to create a covariance matrix R.

If the model of interest can be estimated jointly, such as multivariate T, then the OUTSN= option can be used to generate the correct covariance matrix.

A draw from this mixture of distributions is created using the following steps that are performed automatically by the MODEL procedure.

1. Independent $N(0,1)$ variables are generated.
2. These variables are transformed to a correlated set using the covariance matrix R.
3. These correlated normals are transformed to a uniform using $\Phi()$.
4. $F^{-1}()$ is used to compute the final sample value.

Quasi-Random Number Generators

Traditionally high discrepancy pseudo-random number generators are used to generate innovations in Monte Carlo simulations. Loosely translated, a high discrepancy pseudo-random number generator is one in which there is very little correlation between the current number generated and the past numbers generated. This property is ideal if indeed independence of the innovations is required. If, on the other hand, the efficient spanning of a multi-dimensional space is desired, a low discrepancy, quasi-random number generator can be used. A quasi-random number generator produces numbers which have no random component.

A simple one-dimensional quasi-random sequence is the van der Corput sequence. Given a prime number r ($r \geq 2$) any integer has a unique representation in terms of base r. A number in the interval [0,1) can be created by inverting the representation base power by base power. For example, consider r=3 and n=1. 1 in base 3 is

$$1_{10} = 1 \cdot 3^0 = 1_3$$

When the powers of 3 are inverted,

$$\phi(1) = \frac{1}{3}$$

Also 11 in base 3 is

$$11_{10} = 1 \cdot 3^2 + 2 \cdot 3^0 = 102_3$$

When the powers of 3 are inverted,

$$\phi(11) = \frac{1}{9} + 2 \cdot \frac{1}{3} = \frac{7}{9}$$

The first 10 numbers in this sequence $\phi(1) \ldots \phi(10)$ are provided below

$$0, \frac{1}{3}, \frac{2}{3}, \frac{1}{9}, \frac{4}{9}, \frac{7}{9}, \frac{2}{9}, \frac{5}{9}, \frac{8}{9}, \frac{1}{27}$$

As the sequence proceeds it fills in the gaps in a uniform fashion.

Several authors have expanded this idea to many dimensions. Two versions supported by the MODEL procedure are the Sobol sequence (QUASI=SOBOL) and the Faure sequence (QUASI=FAURE). The Sobol sequence is based on binary numbers an is generally computationally faster than the Faure sequence. The Faure sequence uses the dimensionality of the problem to determine the number base to use to generate the sequence. The Faure sequence has better distributional properties than the Sobol sequence for dimensions greater than 8.

As an example of the difference between a pseudo random number and a quasi random number consider simulating a bivariate normal with 100 draws.

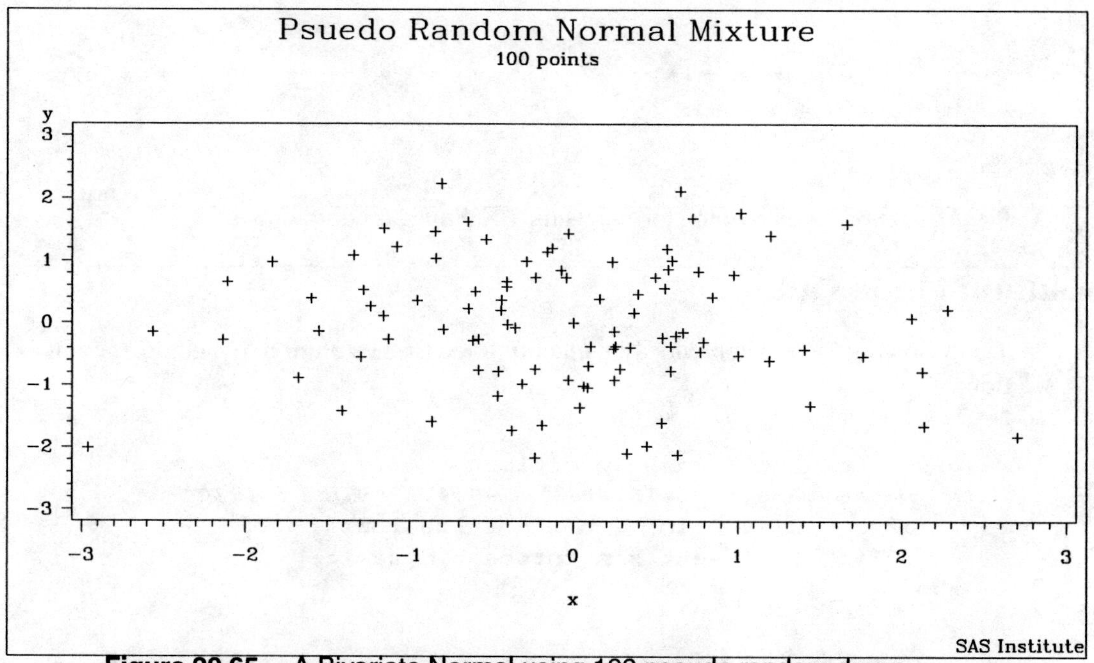

Figure 20.65. A Bivariate Normal using 100 pseudo random draws

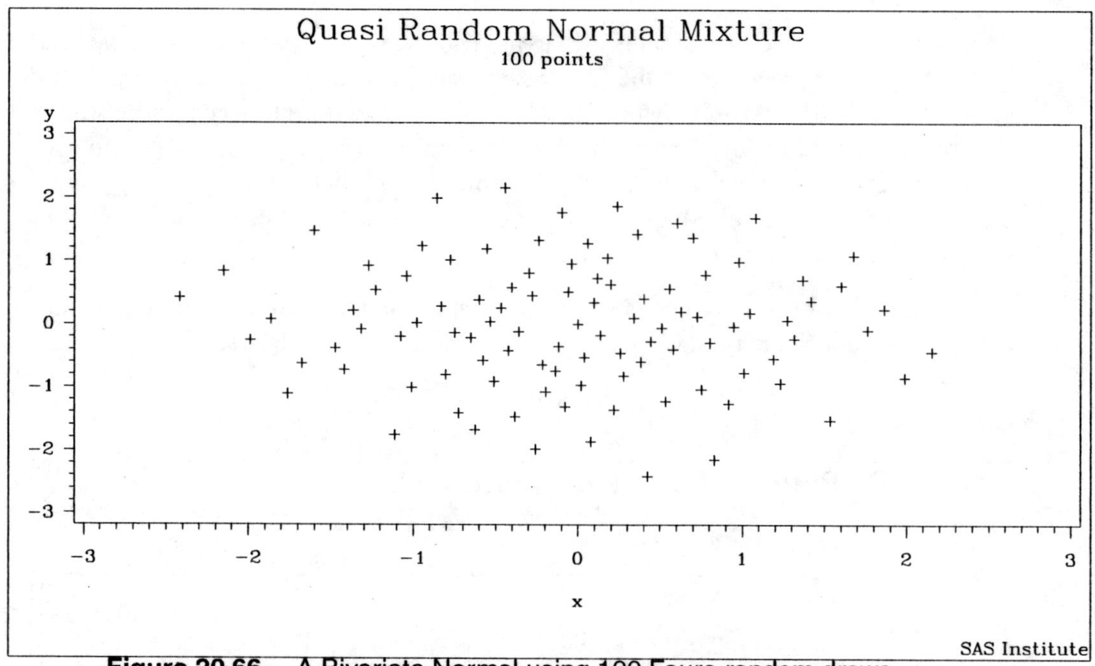

Figure 20.66. A Bivariate Normal using 100 Faure random draws

Solution Mode Output

The following SAS statements dynamically forecast the solution to a nonlinear equation:

```
proc model data=sashelp.citimon;
   parameters a 0.010708  b  -0.478849 c 0.929304;
   lhur = 1/(a * ip) + b + c * lag(lhur);
   solve lhur / out=sim forecast dynamic;
run;
```

The first page of output produced by the SOLVE step is shown in Figure 20.67. This is the summary description of the model. The error message states that the simulation was aborted at observation 144 because of missing input values.

```
                         The MODEL Procedure

                            Model Summary

                   Model Variables           1
                   Parameters                3
                   Equations                 1
                   Number of Statements      1
                   Program Lag Length        1


           Model Variables  LHUR
                Parameters  a(0.010708) b(-0.478849) c(0.929304)
                 Equations  LHUR


                         The MODEL Procedure
                    Dynamic Single-Equation Forecast

ERROR: Solution values are missing because of missing input values for
       observation 144 at NEWTON iteration 0.
NOTE: Additional information on the values of the variables at this
      observation, which may be helpful in determining the cause of the failure
      of the solution process, is printed below.
Iteration Errors - Missing.
NOTE: Simulation aborted.
```

Figure 20.67. Solve Step Summary Output

The second page of output, shown in Figure 20.68, gives more information on the failed observation.

```
                         The MODEL Procedure
                    Dynamic Single-Equation Forecast

ERROR: Solution values are missing because of missing input values for
       observation 144 at NEWTON iteration 0.
NOTE: Additional information on the values of the variables at this
      observation, which may be helpful in determining the cause of the failure
      of the solution process, is printed below.


           Observation      144    Iteration      0    CC     -1.000000
                                   Missing        1
Iteration Errors - Missing.


                    --- Listing of Program Data Vector ---
_N_:                   144    ACTUAL.LHUR:           .    ERROR.LHUR:             .
IP:                      .    LHUR:            7.10000    PRED.LHUR:              .
RESID.LHUR:              .    a:               0.01071    b:               -0.47885
c:                 0.92930

NOTE: Simulation aborted.
```

Figure 20.68. Solve Step Error Message

From the program data vector you can see the variable IP is missing for observation 144. LHUR could not be computed so the simulation aborted.

The solution summary table is shown in Figure 20.69.

```
                    The MODEL Procedure
           Dynamic Single-Equation Forecast

                    Data Set Options

                DATA=      SASHELP.CITIMON
                OUT=       SIM


                    Solution Summary

           Variables Solved                 1
           Forecast Lag Length              1
           Solution Method             NEWTON
           CONVERGE=                     1E-8
           Maximum CC                       0
           Maximum Iterations               1
           Total Iterations               143
           Average Iterations               1


                 Observations Processed

                      Read        145
                      Lagged        1
                      Solved      143
                      First         2
                      Last        145
                      Failed        1


            Variables Solved For      LHUR
```

Figure 20.69. Solution Summary Report

This solution summary table includes the names of the input data set and the output data set followed by a description of the model. The table also indicates the solution method defaulted to Newton's method. The remaining output is defined as follows.

Maximum CC	is the maximum convergence value accepted by the Newton procedure. This number is always less than the value for "CONVERGE=."
Maximum Iterations	is the maximum number of Newton iterations performed at each observation and each replication of Monte Carlo simulations.
Total Iterations	is the sum of the number of iterations required for each observation and each Monte Carlo simulation.
Average Iterations	is the average number of Newton iterations required to solve the system at each step.
Solved	is the number of observations used times the number of random replications selected plus one, for Monte Carlo simulations. The one additional simulation is the original unperturbed solution. For simulations not involving Monte Carlo, this number is the number of observations used.

Summary Statistics

The STATS and THEIL options are used to select goodness of fit statistics. Actual values must be provided in the input data set for these statistics to be printed. When the RANDOM= option is specified, the statistics do not include the unperturbed (_REP_=0) solution.

STATS Option Output

If the STATS and THEIL options are added to the model in the previous section

```
proc model data=sashelp.citimon;
   parameters a 0.010708  b   -0.478849 c 0.929304;
   lhur= 1/(a * ip) + b + c * lag(lhur) ;
   solve lhur / out=sim dynamic stats theil;
   range date to '01nov91'd;
run;
```

the STATS output in Figure 20.70 and the THEIL output in Figure 20.71 are generated.

```
                        The MODEL Procedure
                 Dynamic Single-Equation Simulation

               Solution Range DATE = FEB1980 To NOV1991

                      Descriptive Statistics

                                       Actual              Predicted
Variable      N Obs       N        Mean     Std Dev      Mean     Std Dev

LHUR            142     142      7.0887      1.4509    7.2473      1.1465


                         Statistics of fit

                       Mean     Mean %  Mean Abs  Mean Abs        RMS       RMS %
Variable          N    Error     Error     Error   % Error      Error       Error

LHUR            142   0.1585    3.5289    0.6937   10.0001     0.7854     11.2452

                         Statistics of fit

                Variable      R-Square    Label

                LHUR            0.7049    UNEMPLOYMENT RATE:
                                          ALL WORKERS,
                                          16 YEARS
```

Figure 20.70. STATS Output

The number of observations (Nobs), the number of observations with both predicted and actual values nonmissing (N), and the mean and standard deviation of the actual and predicted values of the determined variables are printed first. The next set of columns in the output are defined as follows.

Mean Error	$\frac{1}{N}\sum_{j=1}^{N}(\hat{y}_j - y_j)$
Mean % Error	$\frac{100}{N}\sum_{j=1}^{N}(\hat{y}_j - y_j)/y_j$
Mean Abs Error	$\frac{1}{N}\sum_{j=1}^{N}\lvert\hat{y}_j - y_j\rvert$
Mean Abs % Error	$\frac{100}{N}\sum_{j=1}^{N}\lvert(\hat{y}_j - y_j)/y_j\rvert$
RMS Error	$\sqrt{\frac{1}{N}\sum_{j=1}^{N}(\hat{y}_j - y_j)^2}$
RMS % Error	$100\sqrt{\frac{1}{N}\sum_{j=1}^{N}((\hat{y}_j - y_j)/y_j)^2}$
R-square	$1 - SSE/CSSA$
SSE	$\sum_{j=1}^{N}(\hat{y}_j - y_j)^2$
SSA	$\sum_{j=1}^{N}(y_j)^2$
$CSSA$	$SSA - \left(\sum_{j=1}^{N} y_j\right)^2$
$\hat{y}$	predicted value
y	actual value

When the RANDOM= option is specified, the statistics do not include the unperturbed (_REP_=0) solution.

THEIL Option Output

The THEIL option specifies that Theil forecast error statistics be computed for the actual and predicted values and for the relative changes from lagged values. Mathematically, the quantities are

$$\hat{yc} = (\hat{y} - lag(y))/lag(y)$$

$$yc = (y - lag(y))/lag(y)$$

where $\hat{yc}$ is the relative change for the predicted value and yc is the relative change for the actual value.

```
                    The MODEL Procedure
             Dynamic Single-Equation Simulation

          Solution Range DATE = FEB1980 To NOV1991

               Theil Forecast Error Statistics

                                       MSE Decomposition Proportions
                                Corr     Bias      Reg     Dist      Var    Covar
Variable        N       MSE      (R)     (UM)     (UR)     (UD)     (US)     (UC)

LHUR        142.0    0.6168     0.85     0.04     0.01     0.95     0.15     0.81

               Theil Forecast Error Statistics

                          Inequality Coef
     Variable                  U1           U      Label

     LHUR                  0.1086      0.0539      UNEMPLOYMENT RATE:
                                                   ALL WORKERS,
                                                   16 YEARS

          Theil Relative Change Forecast Error Statistics

            Relative Change            MSE Decomposition Proportions
                                Corr     Bias      Reg     Dist      Var    Covar
Variable        N       MSE      (R)     (UM)     (UR)     (UD)     (US)     (UC)

LHUR        142.0    0.0126    -0.08     0.09     0.85     0.06     0.43     0.47

          Theil Relative Change Forecast Error Statistics

                          Inequality Coef
     Variable                  U1           U      Label

     LHUR                  4.1226      0.8348      UNEMPLOYMENT RATE:
                                                   ALL WORKERS,
                                                   16 YEARS
```

Figure 20.71. THEIL Output

The columns have the following meaning:

Corr (R)
: is the correlation coefficient, ρ, between the actual and predicted values.

$$\rho = \frac{\mathrm{cov}(y, \hat{y})}{\sigma_a \sigma_p}$$

where σ_p and σ_a are the standard deviations of the predicted and actual values.

Bias (UM)
: is an indication of systematic error and measures the extent to which the average values of the actual and predicted deviate from each other.

$$\frac{(\mathrm{E}(y) - \mathrm{E}(\hat{y}))^2}{\frac{1}{N}\sum_{t=1}^{N}(y_t - \hat{y}_t)^2}$$

Reg (UR) is defined as $(\sigma_p - \rho * \sigma_a)^2 / MSE$. Consider the regression

$$y = \alpha + \beta \hat{y}$$

If $\hat{\beta} = 1$, UR will equal zero.

Dist (UD) is defined as $(1 - \rho^2)\sigma_a \sigma_a / MSE$ and represents the variance of the residuals obtained by regressing yc on $\hat{y}c$.

Var (US) is the variance proportion. US indicates the ability of the model to replicate the degree of variability in the endogenous variable.

$$US = \frac{(\sigma_p - \sigma_a)^2}{MSE}$$

Covar (UC) represents the remaining error after deviations from average values and average variabilities have been accounted for.

$$UC = \frac{2(1 - \rho)\sigma_p \sigma_a}{MSE}$$

U1 is a statistic measuring the accuracy of a forecast.

$$U1 = \frac{\sqrt{MSE}}{\sqrt{\frac{1}{N}\sum_{t=1}^{N}(y_t)^2}}$$

U is the Theil's inequality coefficient defined as follows:

$$U = \frac{\sqrt{MSE}}{\sqrt{\frac{1}{N}\sum_{t=1}^{N}(y_t)^2} + \sqrt{\frac{1}{N}\sum_{t=1}^{N}(\hat{y}_t)^2}}$$

MSE is the mean square error. In the case of the Relative Change Theil statistics, the MSE is computed as follows:

$$MSE = \frac{1}{N}\sum_{t=1}^{N}(\hat{y}c_t - yc_t)^2$$

More information on these statistics can be found in the references Maddala (1977, 344–347) and Pindyck and Rubinfeld (1981, 364–365).

Goal Seeking: Solving for Right-Hand-Side Variables

The process of computing input values needed to produce target results is often called *goal seeking*. To compute a goal-seeking solution, use a SOLVE statement that lists the variables you want to solve for and provide a data set containing values for the remaining variables.

Consider the following demand model for packaged rice

$$quantity\ demanded = \alpha_1 + \alpha_2 price^{2/3} + \alpha_3 income$$

where *price* is the price of the package and *income* is disposable personal income. The only variable the company has control over is the price it charges for rice. This model is estimated using the following simulated data and PROC MODEL statements:

```
data demand;
   do t=1 to 40;
       price = (rannor(10) +5) * 10;
       income = 8000 * t ** (1/8);
       demand = 7200 - 1054 * price ** (2/3) +
                7 * income + 100 * rannor(1);
       output;
   end;
run;

data goal;
    demand = 85000;
    income = 12686;
run;
```

The goal is to find the price the company would have to charge to meet a sales target of 85,000 units. To do this, a data set is created with a DEMAND variable set to 85000 and with an INCOME variable set to 12686, the last income value.

```
proc model data=demand ;
   demand = a1 - a2 * price ** (2/3) + a3 * income;
   fit demand / outest=demest;
run;
```

The desired price is then determined using the following PROC MODEL statement:

```
    solve price / estdata=demest data=goal solveprint;
run;
```

The SOLVEPRINT option prints the solution values, number of iterations, and final residuals at each observation. The SOLVEPRINT output from this solve is shown in Figure 20.72.

```
                         The MODEL Procedure
                     Single-Equation Simulation

Observation    1   Iterations   6   CC     0.000000   ERROR.demand     0.000000

                           Solution Values

                                price

                              33.59016
```

Figure 20.72. Goal Seeking, SOLVEPRINT Output

The output indicates that it took 6 Newton iterations to determine the PRICE of 33.5902, which makes the DEMAND value within 16E-11 of the goal of 85,000 units.

Consider a more ambitious goal of 100,000 units. The output shown in Figure 20.73 indicates that the sales target of 100,000 units is not attainable according to this model.

```
                              The MODEL Procedure
                           Single-Equation Simulation

NOTE: 3 parameter estimates were read from the ESTDATA=DEMEST data set.


                              The MODEL Procedure
                           Single-Equation Simulation

ERROR: Could not reduce norm of residuals in 10 subiterations.

ERROR: The solution failed because 1 equations are missing or have extreme
       values for observation 1 at NEWTON iteration 1.
NOTE: Additional information on the values of the variables at this
      observation, which may be helpful in determining the cause of the failure
      of the solution process, is printed below.


            Observation     1     Iteration     1     CC     -1.000000
                                  Missing       1
Iteration Errors - Missing.


            Observation     1     Iteration     1     CC     -1.000000
                                  Missing       1
ERROR: 2 execution errors for this observation
NOTE: Check for missing input data or uninitialized lags.
      (Note that the LAG and DIF functions return missing values for the
initial lag starting observations. This is a change from the 1982 and earlier
versions of SAS/ETS which returned zero for uninitialized lags.)
NOTE: Simulation aborted.
```

Figure 20.73. Goal Seeking, Convergence Failure

The program data vector indicates that even with PRICE nearly 0 (4.462312E-22) the demand is still 4,164 less than the goal. You may need to reformulate your model or collect more data to more accurately reflect the market response.

Numerical Solution Methods

If the SINGLE option is not used, PROC MODEL computes values that simultaneously satisfy the model equations for the variables named in the SOLVE statement. PROC MODEL provides three iterative methods, Newton, Jacobi, and Seidel, for computing a simultaneous solution of the system of nonlinear equations.

Single-Equation Solution

For normalized-form equation systems, the solution can either simultaneously satisfy all the equations or can be computed for each equation separately, using the actual values of the solution variables in the current period to compute each predicted value.

By default, PROC MODEL computes a simultaneous solution. The SINGLE option on the SOLVE statement selects single-equation solutions.

Single-equation simulations are often made to produce residuals (which estimate the random terms of the stochastic equations) rather than the predicted values themselves. If the input data and range are the same as that used for parameter estimation, a static single-equation simulation will reproduce the residuals of the estimation.

Newton's Method

The NEWTON option on the SOLVE statement requests Newton's method to simultaneously solve the equations for each observation. Newton's method is the default solution method. Newton's method is an iterative scheme that uses the derivatives of the equations with respect to the solution variables, *J*, to compute a change vector as

$$\Delta\mathbf{y}^i = J^{-1}\mathbf{q}(\mathbf{y}^i, \mathbf{x}, \theta)$$

PROC MODEL builds and solves *J* using efficient sparse matrix techniques. The solution variables $\mathbf{y}^i$ at the *i*th iteration are then updated as

$$\mathbf{y}^{i+1} = \mathbf{y}^i + d \times \Delta\mathbf{y}^i$$

d is a damping factor between 0 and 1 chosen iteratively so that

$$\|\mathbf{q}(\mathbf{y}^{i+1}, \mathbf{x}, \theta)\| < \|\mathbf{q}(\mathbf{y}^i, \mathbf{x}, \theta)\|$$

The number of subiterations allowed for finding a suitable *d* is controlled by the MAXSUBITER= option. The number of iterations of Newton's method allowed for each observation is controlled by MAXITER= option. Refer to Ortega and Rheinbolt (1970) for more details.

Jacobi Method

The JACOBI option on the SOLVE statement selects a matrix-free alternative to Newton's method. This method is the traditional nonlinear Jacobi method found in the literature. The Jacobi method as implemented in PROC MODEL substitutes predicted values for the endogenous variables and iterates until a fixed point is reached. Then necessary derivatives are computed only for the diagonal elements of the jacobian, **J**.

If the normalized-form equation is

$$\mathbf{y} = \mathbf{f}(\mathbf{y}, \mathbf{x}, \theta)$$

the Jacobi iteration has the form

$$\mathbf{y}^{i+1} = \mathbf{f}(\mathbf{y}^i, \mathbf{x}, \theta)$$

Seidel Method

The Seidel method is an order-dependent alternative to the Jacobi method. The Seidel method is selected by the SEIDEL option on the SOLVE statement. The Seidel method is like the Jacobi method except that in the Seidel method the model is further edited to substitute the predicted values into the solution variables immediately after they are computed. Seidel thus differs from the other methods in that the values of the solution variables are not fixed within an iteration. With the other methods, the order of the equations in the model program makes no difference, but the Seidel method may work much differently when the equations are specified in a different sequence. Note that this fixed point method is the traditional nonlinear Seidel method found in the literature.

The iteration has the form

$$\mathbf{y}_j^{i+1} = \mathbf{f}(\hat{\mathbf{y}}^i, \mathbf{x}, \theta)$$

where $\mathbf{y}_j^{i+1}$ is the *j*th equation variable at the *i*th iteration and

$$\hat{\mathbf{y}}^i = (y_1^{i+1}, y_2^{i+1}, y_3^{i+1}, \ldots, y_{j-1}^{i+1}, y_j^i, y_{j+1}^i, \ldots, y_g^i)'$$

If the model is recursive, and if the equations are in recursive order, the Seidel method will converge at once. If the model is block-recursive, the Seidel method may converge faster if the equations are grouped by block and the blocks are placed in block-recursive order. The BLOCK option can be used to determine the block-recursive form.

Jacobi and Seidel Methods with General Form Equations

Jacobi and Seidel solution methods support general form equations.

There are two cases where derivatives are (automatically) computed. The first case is for equations with the solution variable on the right-hand side and on the left-hand side of the equation

$$y^i = f(\mathbf{x}, y^i)$$

In this case the derivative of ERROR.y with respect to y is computed, and the new y approximation is computed as

$$y^{i+1} = y^i - \frac{f(\mathbf{x}, y^i) - y^i}{\partial(f(\mathbf{x}, y^i) - y^i)/\partial y}$$

The second case is a system of equations containing one or more EQ.var equations. In this case, a heuristic algorithm is used to make the assignment of a unique solution variable to each general form equation. Use the DETAILS option on the SOLVE statement to print a listing of the assigned variables.

Once the assignment is made, the new y approximation is computed as

$$y^{i+1} = y^i - \frac{f(\mathbf{x}, \mathbf{y}^i) - y^i}{\partial(f(\mathbf{x}, \mathbf{y}^i) - y^i)/\partial y}$$

If k is the number of general form equations, then k derivatives are required.

The convergence properties of the Jacobi and Seidel solution methods remain significantly poorer than the default Newton's method.

Comparison of Methods

Newton's method is the default and should work better than the others for most small- to medium-sized models. The Seidel method is always faster than the Jacobi for recursive models with equations in recursive order. For very large models and some highly nonlinear smaller models, the Jacobi or Seidel methods can sometimes be faster. Newton's method uses more memory than the Jacobi or Seidel methods.

Both the Newton's method and the Jacobi method are order-invariant in the sense that the order in which equations are specified in the model program has no effect on the operation of the iterative solution process. In order-invariant methods, the values of the solution variables are fixed for the entire execution of the model program. Assignments to model variables are automatically changed to assignments to corresponding equation variables. Only after the model program has completed execution are the results used to compute the new solution values for the next iteration.

Troubleshooting Problems

In solving a simultaneous nonlinear dynamic model you may encounter some of the following problems.

Missing Values

For SOLVE tasks, there can be no missing parameter values. If there are missing right-hand-side variables, this will result in a missing left-hand-side variable for that observation.

Unstable Solutions

A solution may exist but be unstable. An unstable system can cause the Jacobi and Seidel methods to diverge.

Explosive Dynamic Systems

A model may have well-behaved solutions at each observation but be dynamically unstable. The solution may oscillate wildly or grow rapidly with time.

Propagation of Errors

During the solution process, solution variables can take on values that cause computational errors. For example, a solution variable that appears in a LOG function may be positive at the solution but may be given a negative value during one of the iterations. When computational errors occur, missing values are generated and propagated, and the solution process may collapse.

Convergence Problems

The following items can cause convergence problems:

- illegal function values (that is $\sqrt{-1}$)
- local minima in the model equation
- no solution exists
- multiple solutions exist
- initial values too far from the solution
- the CONVERGE= value too small.

When PROC MODEL fails to find a solution to the system, the current iteration information and the program data vector are printed. The simulation halts if actual values are not available for the simulation to proceed. Consider the following program:

```
data test1;
   do t=1 to 50;
      x1 = sqrt(t) ;
      y = .;
      output;
   end;

proc model data=test1;
   exogenous x1 ;
   control a1 -1 b1 -29 c1 -4 ;
   y = a1 * sqrt(y) + b1 * x1 * x1 + c1 * lag(x1);
   solve y / out=sim forecast dynamic ;
run;
```

which produces the output shown in Figure 20.74.

```
                          The MODEL Procedure
                    Dynamic Single-Equation Forecast

ERROR: Could not reduce norm of residuals in 10 subiterations.

ERROR: The solution failed because 1 equations are missing or have extreme
       values for observation 1 at NEWTON iteration 1.
NOTE: Additional information on the values of the variables at this
      observation, which may be helpful in determining the cause of the failure
      of the solution process, is printed below.


           Observation     1     Iteration     1     CC     -1.000000
                                 Missing       1
Iteration Errors - Missing.


                    --- Listing of Program Data Vector ---
   _N_:                 12      ACTUAL.x1:      1.41421      ACTUAL.y:              .
   ERROR.y:              .      PRED.y:               .      RESID.y:               .
   a1:                  -1      b1:                 -29      c1:                   -4
   x1:             1.41421      y:             -0.00109
   @PRED.y/@y:            .     @ERROR.y/@y:              .


           Observation     1     Iteration     1     CC     -1.000000
                                 Missing       1
ERROR: 1 execution errors for this observation
NOTE: Check for missing input data or uninitialized lags.
      (Note that the LAG and DIF functions return missing values for the
initial lag starting observations. This is a change from the 1982 and earlier
versions of SAS/ETS which returned zero for uninitialized lags.)
NOTE: Simulation aborted.
```

Figure 20.74. SOLVE Convergence Problems

At the first observation the following equation is attempted to be solved:

$$y = -\sqrt{y} - 62$$

There is no solution to this problem. The iterative solution process got as close as it could to making Y negative while still being able to evaluate the model. This problem can be avoided in this case by altering the equation.

In other models, the problem of missing values can be avoided by either altering the data set to provide better starting values for the solution variables or by altering the equations.

You should be aware that, in general, a nonlinear system can have any number of solutions, and the solution found may not be the one that you want. When multiple solutions exist, the solution that is found is usually determined by the starting values for the iterations. If the value from the input data set for a solution variable is missing, the starting value for it is taken from the solution of the last period (if nonmissing) or else the solution estimate is started at 0.

Iteration Output

The iteration output, produced by the ITPRINT option, is useful in determining the cause of a convergence problem. The ITPRINT option forces the printing of the solution approximation and equation errors at each iteration for each observation. A portion of the ITPRINT output from the following statement is shown in Figure 20.75.

```
proc model data=test1;
   exogenous x1 ;
   control a1 -1 b1 -29 c1 -4 ;
   y = a1 * sqrt(abs(y)) + b1 * x1 * x1 + c1 * lag(x1);
   solve y / out=sim forecast dynamic itprint;
run;
```

For each iteration, the equation with the largest error is listed in parentheses after the Newton convergence criteria measure. From this output you can determine which equation or equations in the system are not converging well.

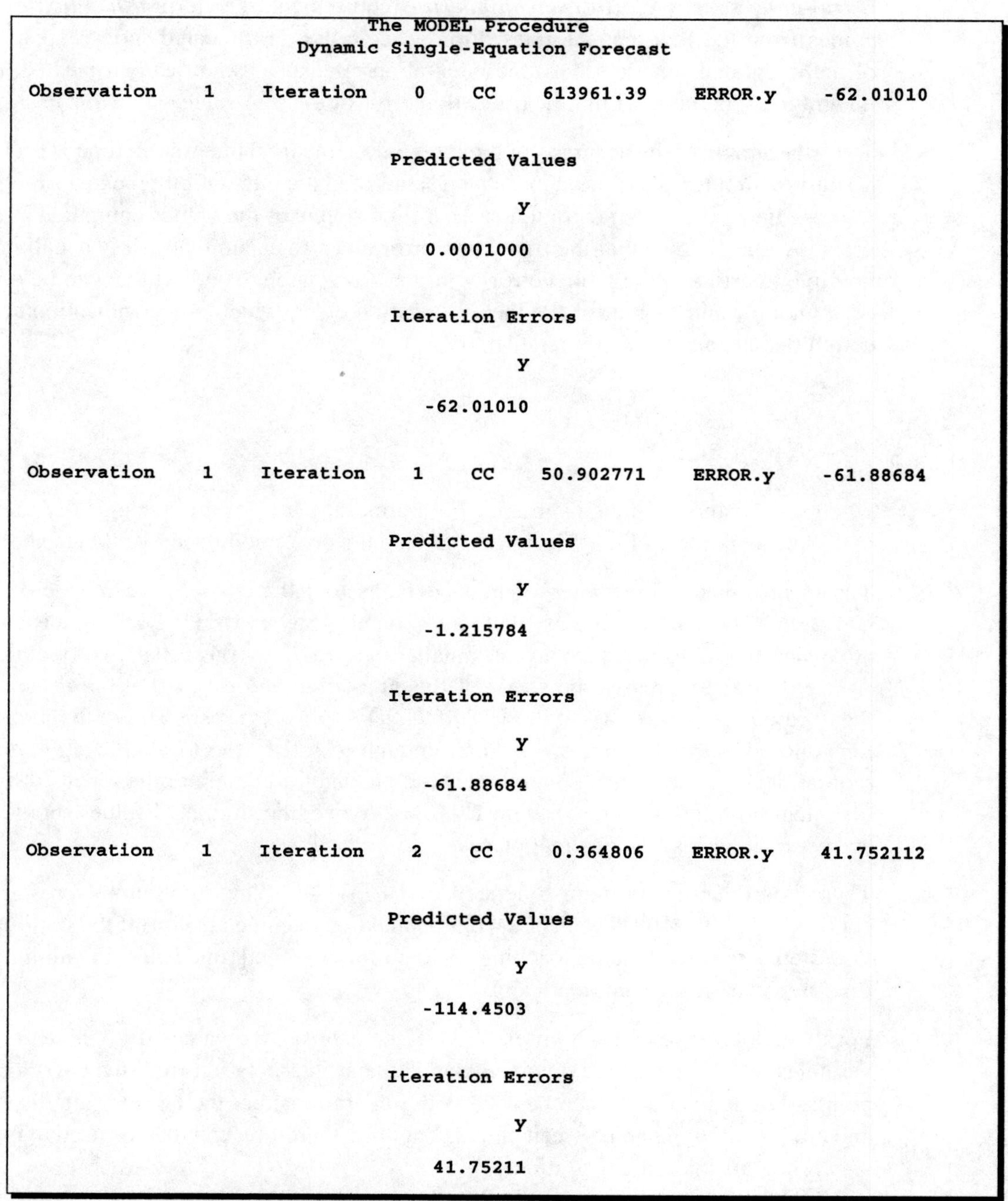

```
                         The MODEL Procedure
                   Dynamic Single-Equation Forecast

Observation    1    Iteration    0    CC    613961.39    ERROR.y    -62.01010

                          Predicted Values

                                 y

                             0.0001000

                          Iteration Errors

                                 y

                             -62.01010

Observation    1    Iteration    1    CC    50.902771    ERROR.y    -61.88684

                          Predicted Values

                                 y

                             -1.215784

                          Iteration Errors

                                 y

                             -61.88684

Observation    1    Iteration    2    CC     0.364806    ERROR.y    41.752112

                          Predicted Values

                                 y

                             -114.4503

                          Iteration Errors

                                 y

                              41.75211
```

Figure 20.75. SOLVE, ITPRINT Output

Numerical Integration

The differential equation system is numerically integrated to obtain a solution for the derivative variables at each data point. The integration is performed by evaluating the provided model at multiple points between each data point. The integration method used is a variable order, variable step-size backward difference scheme; for more detailed information, refer to Aiken (1985) and Byrne (1975). The step size or time step is chosen to satisfy a *local truncation error* requirement. The term *truncation error* comes from the fact that the integration scheme uses a truncated series expansion of the integrated function to do the integration. Because the series is truncated, the integration scheme is within the truncation error of the true value.

To further improve the accuracy of the integration, the total integration time is broken up into small intervals (time steps or step sizes), and the integration scheme is applied to those intervals. The integration at each time step uses the values computed at the previous time step so that the truncation error tends to accumulate. It is usually not possible to estimate the global error with much precision. The best that can be done is to monitor and to control the local truncation error, which is the truncation error committed at each time step relative to

$$d = \max_{0 \leq t \leq T} (\|y(t)\|_{\infty}, 1)$$

where $y(t)$ is the integrated variable. Furthermore, the $y(t)$s are dynamically scaled to within two orders of magnitude one to keep the error monitoring well behaved.

The local truncation error requirement defaults to $1.0E-9$. You can specify the LTEBOUND= option to modify that requirement. The LTEBOUND= option is a relative measure of accuracy, so a value smaller than $1.0E-10$ is usually not practical. A larger bound increases the speed of the simulation and estimation but decreases the accuracy of the results. If the LTEBOUND= option is set too small, the integrator is not able to take time steps small enough to satisfy the local truncation error requirement and still have enough machine precision to compute the results. Since the integrations are scaled to within $1.0E-2$ of one, the simulated values should be correct to at least seven decimal places.

There is a default minimum time step of $1.0E-14$. This minimum time step is controlled by the MINTIMESTEP= option and the machine epsilon. If the minimum time step is smaller than the machine epsilon times the final time value, the minimum time step is increased automatically.

For the points between each observation in the data set, the values for nonintegrated variables in the data set are obtained from a linear interpolation from the two closest points. Lagged variables can be used with integrations, but their values are discrete and are not interpolated between points. Lagging, therefore, can then be used to input step functions into the integration.

The derivatives necessary for estimation (the gradient with respect to the parameters) and goal seeking (the Jacobian) are computed by numerically integrating analytical derivatives. The accuracy of the derivatives is controlled by the same integration techniques mentioned previously.

Limitations

There are limitations to the types of differential equations that can be solved or estimated. One type is an explosive differential equation (finite escape velocity) for which the following differential equation is an example:

$$y' = a \times y, \quad a > 0$$

If this differential equation is integrated too far in time, y exceeds the maximum value allowed on the computer, and the integration terminates.

Likewise, differential systems that are singular cannot be solved or estimated in general. For example, consider the following differential system:

$$\begin{aligned} x' &= -y' + 2x + 4y + \exp(t) \\ y' &= -x' + y + \exp(4{*}t) \end{aligned}$$

This system has an analytical solution, but an accurate numerical solution is very difficult to obtain. The reason is that y' and x' cannot be isolated on the left-hand side of the equation. If the equation is modified slightly to

$$\begin{aligned} x' &= -y' + 2x + 4y + \exp(t) \\ y' &= x' + y + \exp(4t) \end{aligned}$$

the system is nonsingular, but the integration process could still fail or be extremely slow. If the MODEL procedure encounters either system, a warning message is issued.

This system can be rewritten as the following recursive system,

$$\begin{aligned} x' &= 0.5y + 0.5\exp(4t) + x + 1.5y - 0.5\exp(t) \\ y' &= x' + y + \exp(4t) \end{aligned}$$

which can be estimated and simulated successfully with the MODEL procedure.

Petzold (1982) mentions a class of differential algebraic equations that, when integrated numerically, could produce incorrect or misleading results. An example of such a system mentioned in Petzold (1982) is

$$\begin{aligned} y_2'(t) &= y_1(t) + g_1(t) \\ 0 &= y_2(t) + g_2(t) \end{aligned}$$

The analytical solution to this system depends on g and its derivatives at the current time only and not on its initial value or past history. You should avoid systems of this and other similar forms mentioned in Petzold (1982).

SOLVE Data Sets

SDATA= Input Data Set

The SDATA= option reads a cross-equation covariance matrix from a data set. The covariance matrix read from the SDATA= data set specified on the SOLVE statement is used to generate random equation errors when the RANDOM= option specifies Monte Carlo simulation.

Typically, the SDATA= data set is created by the OUTS= on a previous FIT statement. (The OUTS= data set from a FIT statement can be read back in by a SOLVE statement in the same PROC MODEL step.)

You can create an input SDATA= data set using the DATA step. PROC MODEL expects to find a character variable _NAME_ in the SDATA= data set as well as variables for the equations in the estimation or solution. For each observation with a _NAME_ value matching the name of an equation, PROC MODEL fills the corresponding row of the S matrix with the values of the names of equations found in the data set. If a row or column is omitted from the data set, an identity matrix row or column is assumed. Missing values are ignored. Since the S matrix is symmetric, you can include only a triangular part of the S matrix in the SDATA= data set with the omitted part indicated by missing values. If the SDATA= data set contains multiple observations with the same _NAME_, the last values supplied for the _NAME_ variable are used. The "OUTS= Data Set" section contains more details on the format of this data set.

Use the TYPE= option to specify the type of estimation method used to produce the S matrix you want to input.

ESTDATA= Input Data Set

The ESTDATA= option specifies an input data set that contains an observation with values for some or all of the model parameters. It can also contain observations with the rows of a covariance matrix for the parameters.

When the ESTDATA= option is used, parameter values are set from the first observation. If the RANDOM= option is used and the ESTDATA= data set contains a covariance matrix, the covariance matrix of the parameter estimates is read and used to generate pseudo-random shocks to the model parameters for Monte Carlo simulation. These random perturbations have a multivariate normal distribution with the covariance matrix read from the ESTDATA= data set.

The ESTDATA= data set is usually created by the OUTEST= option in a FIT statement. The OUTEST= data set contains the parameter estimates produced by the FIT statement and also contains the estimated covariance of the parameter estimates if the OUTCOV option is used. This OUTEST= data set can be read in by the ESTDATA= option in a SOLVE statement.

You can also create an ESTDATA= data set with a SAS DATA step program. The data set must contain a numeric variable for each parameter to be given a value or covariance column. The name of the variable in the ESTDATA= data set must match the name of the parameter in the model. Parameters with names longer than 32 characters cannot be set from an ESTDATA= data set. The data set must also contain a character variable _NAME_ of length 32. _NAME_ has a blank value for the observation that gives values to the parameters. _NAME_ contains the name of a parameter for observations defining rows of the covariance matrix.

More than one set of parameter estimates and covariances can be stored in the ESTDATA= data set if the observations for the different estimates are identified by the variable _TYPE_. _TYPE_ must be a character variable of length eight. The TYPE= option is used to select for input the part of the ESTDATA= data set for which the value of the _TYPE_ variable matches the value of the TYPE= option.

OUT= Data Set

The OUT= data set contains solution values, residual values, and actual values of the solution variables.

The OUT= data set contains the following variables:

- BY variables
- RANGE variable
- ID variables
- _TYPE_, a character variable of length eight identifying the type of observation. The _TYPE_ variable can be PREDICT, RESIDUAL, ACTUAL, or ERROR.
- _MODE_, a character variable of length eight identifying the solution mode. _MODE_ takes the value FORECAST or SIMULATE.
- if lags are used, a numeric variable, _LAG_, containing the number of dynamic lags that contribute to the solution. The value of _LAG_ is always zero for STATIC mode solutions. _LAG_ is set to a missing value for lag-starting observations.
- _REP_, a numeric variable containing the replication number, if the RANDOM= option is used. For example, if RANDOM=10, each input observation results in eleven output observations with _REP_ values 0 through 10. The observations with _REP_=0 are from the unperturbed solution. (The random-number generator functions are suppressed, and the parameter and endogenous perturbations are zero when _REP_=0.)
- _ERRORS_, a numeric variable containing the number of errors that occurred during the execution of the program for the last iteration for the observation. If the solution failed to converge, this is counted as one error, and the _ERRORS_ variable is made negative.
- solution and other variables. The solution variables contain solution or predicted values for _TYPE_=PREDICT observations, residuals for

TYPE=RESIDUAL observations, or actual values for _TYPE_=ACTUAL observations. The other model variables, and any other variables read from the input data set, are always actual values from the input data set.

- any other variables named in the OUTVARS statement. These can be program variables computed by the model program, CONTROL variables, parameters, or special variables in the model program. Compound variable names longer than 32 characters are truncated in the OUT= data set.

By default only the predicted values are written to the OUT= data set. The OUTRESID, OUTACTUAL, and OUTERROR options are used to add the residual, actual, and ERROR. values to the data set.

For examples of the OUT= data set, see Example 20.6 at the end of this chapter.

DATA= Input Data Set

The input data set should contain all of the exogenous variables and should supply nonmissing values for them for each period to be solved.

Solution variables can be supplied in the input data set and are used as follows:

- to supply initial lags. For example, if the lag length of the model is three, three observations are read in to feed the lags before any solutions are computed.
- to evaluate the goodness of fit. Goodness-of-fit measures are computed based on the difference between the solved values and the actual values supplied from the data set.
- to supply starting values for the iterative solution. If the value from the input data set for a solution variable is missing, the starting value for it is taken from the solution of the last period (if nonmissing) or else the solution estimate is started at zero.
- For STATIC mode solutions, actual values from the data set are used by the lagging functions for the solution variables.
- for FORECAST mode solutions, actual values from the data set are used as the solution values when nonmissing.

Programming Language Overview

Variables in the Model Program

Variable names are alphanumeric but must start with a letter. The length is limited to thirty-two characters.

PROC MODEL uses several classes of variables, and different variable classes are treated differently. Variable class is controlled by *declaration statements*. These are the VAR, ENDOGENOUS, and EXOGENOUS statements for model variables, the PARAMETERS statement for parameters, and the CONTROL statement for control class variables. These declaration statements have several valid abbreviations. Various *internal variables* are also made available to the model program to allow communication between the model program and the procedure. RANGE, ID, and BY variables are also available to the model program. Those variables not declared as any of the preceding classes are *program variables*.

Some classes of variables can be lagged; that is, their value at each observation is remembered, and previous values can be referred to by the lagging functions. Other classes have only a single value and are not affected by lagging functions. For example, parameters have only one value and are not affected by lagging functions; therefore, if P is a parameter, DIF*n*(P) is always 0, and LAG*n*(P) is always the same as P for all values of *n*.

The different variable classes and their roles in the model are described in the following.

Model Variables

Model variables are declared by VAR, ENDOGENOUS, or EXOGENOUS statements, or by FIT and SOLVE statements. The model variables are the variables that the model is intended to explain or predict.

PROC MODEL allows you to use expressions on the left-hand side of the equal sign to define model equations. For example, a log linear model for Y can be written as

```
log( y ) = a + b * x;
```

Previously, only a variable name was allowed on the left-hand side of the equal sign.

The text on the left hand side of the equation serves as the equation name used to identify the equation in printed output, in the OUT= data sets, and in FIT or SOLVE statements. To refer to equations specified using left-hand side expressions (on the FIT statement, for example), place the left-hand side expression in quotes. For example, the following statements fit a log linear model to the dependent variable Y:

```
proc model data=in;
   log( y ) = a + b * x;
   fit "log(y)";
run;
```

The estimation and simulation is performed by transforming the models into general form equations. No actual or predicted value is available for general form equations so no R^2 or adjusted R^2 will be computed.

Equation Variables

An equation variable is one of several special variables used by PROC MODEL to control the evaluation of model equations. An equation variable name consists of one of the prefixes EQ, RESID, ERROR, PRED, or ACTUAL, followed by a period and the name of a model equation.

Equation variable names can appear on parts of the PROC MODEL printed output, and they can be used in the model program. For example, RESID-prefixed variables can be used in LAG functions to define equations with moving-average error terms. See the "Autoregressive Moving-Average Error Processes" section earlier in this chapter for details.

The meaning of these prefixes is detailed in the "Equation Translations" section.

Parameters

Parameters are variables that have the same value for each observation. Parameters can be given values or can be estimated by fitting the model to data. During the SOLVE stage, parameters are treated as constants. If no estimation is performed, the SOLVE stage uses the initial value provided in either the ESTDATA= data set, the MODEL= file, or on the PARAMETER statement, as the value of the parameter.

The PARAMETERS statement declares the parameters of the model. Parameters are not lagged, and they cannot be changed by the model program.

Control Variables

Control variables supply constant values to the model program that can be used to control the model in various ways. The CONTROL statement declares control variables and specifies their values. A control variable is like a parameter except that it has a fixed value and is not estimated from the data.

Control variables are not reinitialized before each pass through the data and can thus be used to retain values between passes. You can use control variables to vary the program logic. Control variables are not affected by lagging functions.

For example, if you have two versions of an equation for a variable Y, you could put both versions in the model and, using a CONTROL statement to select one of them, produce two different solutions to explore the effect the choice of equation has on the model:

```
      select (case);
          when (1) y =  ...first version of equation... ;
          when (2) y =  ...second version of equation... ;
      end;
      control case 1;
      solve / out=case1;
   run;
```

```
    control case 2;
    solve / out=case2;
run;
```

RANGE, ID, and BY Variables

The RANGE statement controls the range of observations in the input data set that is processed by PROC MODEL. The ID statement lists variables in the input data set that are used to identify observations on the printout and in the output data set. The BY statement can be used to make PROC MODEL perform a separate analysis for each BY group. The variable in the RANGE statement, the ID variables, and the BY variables are available for the model program to examine, but their values should not be changed by the program. The BY variables are not affected by lagging functions.

Internal Variables

You can use several internal variables in the model program to communicate with the procedure. For example, if you wanted PROC MODEL to list the values of all the variables when more than 10 iterations are performed and the procedure is past the 20th observation, you can write

```
if _obs_ > 20 then if _iter_ > 10 then _list_ = 1;
```

Internal variables are not affected by lagging functions, and they cannot be changed by the model program except as noted. The following internal variables are available. The variables are all numeric except where noted.

ERRORS a flag that is set to 0 at the start of program execution and is set to a nonzero value whenever an error occurs. The program can also set the _ERRORS_ variable.

ITER the iteration number. For FIT tasks, the value of _ITER_ is negative for preliminary grid-search passes. The iterative phase of the estimation starts with iteration 0. After the estimates have converged, a final pass is made to collect statistics with _ITER_ set to a missing value. Note that at least one pass, and perhaps several subiteration passes as well, is made for each iteration. For SOLVE tasks, _ITER_ counts the iterations used to compute the simultaneous solution of the system.

LAG the number of dynamic lags that contribute to the solution at the current observation. _LAG_ is always 0 for FIT tasks and for STATIC solutions. _LAG_ is set to a missing value during the lag starting phase.

LIST list flag that is set to 0 at the start of program execution. The program can set _LIST_ to a nonzero value to request a listing of the values of all the variables in the program after the program has finished executing.

METHOD is the solution method in use for SOLVE tasks. _METHOD_ is set to a blank value for FIT tasks. _METHOD_ is a character-valued variable. Values are NEWTON, JACOBI, SIEDEL, or ONEPASS.

MODE takes the value ESTIMATE for FIT tasks and the value SIMULATE or FORECAST for SOLVE tasks. _MODE_ is a character-valued variable.

NMISS the number of missing or otherwise unusable observations during the model estimation. For FIT tasks, _NMISS_ is initially set to 0; at the start of each iteration, _NMISS_ is set to the number of unusable observations for the previous iteration. For SOLVE tasks, _NMISS_ is set to a missing value.

NUSED the number of nonmissing observations used in the estimation. For FIT tasks, PROC MODEL initially sets _NUSED_ to the number of parameters; at the start of each iteration, _NUSED_ is reset to the number of observations used in the previous iteration. For SOLVE tasks, _NUSED_ is set to a missing value.

OBS counts the observations being processed. _OBS_ is negative or 0 for observations in the lag starting phase.

REP the replication number for Monte Carlo simulation when the RANDOM= option is specified in the SOLVE statement. _REP_ is 0 when the RANDOM= option is not used and for FIT tasks. When _REP_=0, the random-number generator functions always return 0.

WEIGHT the weight of the observation. For FIT tasks, _WEIGHT_ provides a weight for the observation in the estimation. _WEIGHT_ is initialized to 1.0 at the start of execution for FIT tasks. For SOLVE tasks, _WEIGHT_ is ignored.

Program Variables

Variables not in any of the other classes are called program variables. Program variables are used to hold intermediate results of calculations. Program variables are reinitialized to missing values before each observation is processed. Program variables can be lagged. The RETAIN statement can be used to give program variables initial values and enable them to keep their values between observations.

Character Variables

PROC MODEL supports both numeric and character variables. Character variables are not involved in the model specification but can be used to label observations, to write debugging messages, or for documentation purposes. All variables are numeric unless they are the following.

- character variables in a DATA= SAS data set
- program variables assigned a character value
- declared to be character by a LENGTH or ATTRIB statement.

Equation Translations

Equations written in normalized form are always automatically converted to general form equations. For example, when a normalized-form equation such as

```
y = a + b*x;
```

is encountered, it is translated into the equations

```
PRED.y = a + b*x;
RESID.y = PRED.y - ACTUAL.y;
ERROR.y = PRED.y - y;
```

If the same system is expressed as the following general-form equation, then this equation is used unchanged.

```
EQ.y = y -  a + b*x;
```

This makes it easy to solve for arbitrary variables and to modify the error terms for autoregressive or moving average models.

Use the LIST option to see how this transformation is performed. For example, the following statements produce the listing shown in Figure 20.76.

```
proc model data=line list;
    y = a1 + b1*x1 + c1*x2;
    fit y;
run;
```

```
                         The MODEL Procedure

                    Listing of Compiled Program Code
      Stmt     Line:Col          Statement as Parsed

         1     15820:39          PRED.y = a1 + b1 * x1 + c1 * x2;
         1     15820:39          RESID.y = PRED.y - ACTUAL.y;
         1     15820:39          ERROR.y = PRED.y - y;
```

Figure 20.76. LIST Output

PRED.Y is the predicted value of Y, and ACTUAL.Y is the value of Y in the data set. The predicted value minus the actual value, RESID.Y, is then the error term, ϵ, for the original Y equation. ACTUAL.Y and Y have the same value for parameter estimation. For solve tasks, ACTUAL.Y is still the value of Y in the data set but Y becomes the solved value; the value that satisfies PRED.Y - Y = 0.

The following are the equation variable definitions.

EQ.
: The value of an EQ-prefixed equation variable (normally used to define a general-form equation) represents the failure of the equation to hold. When the EQ.*name* variable is 0, the *name* equation is satisfied.

RESID.
: The RESID.*name* variables represent the stochastic parts of the equations and are used to define the objective function for the estimation process. A RESID.-prefixed equation variable is like an EQ-prefixed variable but makes it possible to use or transform the stochastic part of the equation. The RESID. equation is used in place of the ERROR. equation for model solutions if it has been reassigned or used in the equation.

ERROR.
: An ERROR.*name* variable is like an EQ-prefixed variable, except that it is used only for model solution and does not affect parameter estimation.

PRED.
: For a normalized-form equation (specified by assignment to a model variable), the PRED.*name* equation variable holds the predicted value, where *name* is the name of both the model variable and the corresponding equation. (PRED-prefixed variables are not created for general-form equations.)

ACTUAL.
: For a normalized-form equation (specified by assignment to a model variable), the ACTUAL.*name* equation variable holds the value of the *name* model variable read from the input data set.

DERT.
: The DERT.*name* variable defines a differential equation. Once defined, it may be used on the right-hand side of another equation.

H.
: The H.*name* variable specifies the functional form for the variance of the named equation.

GMM_H.
: This is created for H.*vars* and is the moment equation for the variance for GMM. This variable is used only for GMM.

```
GMM_H.name = RESID.name**2 - H.name;
```

MSE.
: The MSE.*y* variable contains the value of the mean square error for *y* at each iteration. An MSE. variable is created for each dependent/endogenous variable in the model. These variables can be used to specify the missing lagged values in the estimation and simulation of GARCH type models.

```
demret = intercept ;
h.demret = arch0 +
           arch1 * xlag( resid.demret ** 2, mse.demret) +
           garch1 * zlag(h.demret, mse.demret) ;
```

NRESID.
: This is created for H.*vars* and is the normalized residual of the variable <*name*>. The formula is

```
NRESID.name = RESID.name/ sqrt(H.name);
```

The three equation variable prefixes, RESID., ERROR., and EQ. allow for control over the objective function for the FIT, the SOLVE, or both the FIT and the SOLVE stages. For FIT tasks, PROC MODEL looks first for a RESID.*name* variable for each equation. If defined, the RESID-prefixed equation variable is used to define the objective function for the parameter estimation process. Otherwise, PROC MODEL looks for an EQ-prefixed variable for the equation and uses it instead.

For SOLVE tasks, PROC MODEL looks first for an ERROR.*name* variable for each equation. If defined, the ERROR-prefixed equation variable is used for the solution process. Otherwise, PROC MODEL looks for an EQ-prefixed variable for the equation and uses it instead. To solve the simultaneous equation system, PROC MODEL computes values of the solution variables (the model variables being solved for) that make all of the ERROR.name and EQ.*name* variables close to 0.

Derivatives

Nonlinear modeling techniques require the calculation of derivatives of certain variables with respect to other variables. The MODEL procedure includes an analytic differentiator that determines the model derivatives and generates program code to compute these derivatives. When parameters are estimated, the MODEL procedure takes the derivatives of the equation with respect to the parameters. When the model is solved, Newton's method requires the derivatives of the equations with respect to the variables solved for.

PROC MODEL uses exact mathematical formulas for derivatives of non-user-defined functions. For other functions, numerical derivatives are computed and used.

The differentiator differentiates the entire model program, including conditional logic and flow of control statements. Delayed definitions, as when the LAG of a program variable is referred to before the variable is assigned a value, are also differentiated correctly.

The differentiator includes optimization features that produce efficient code for the calculation of derivatives. However, when flow of control statements such as GOTO statements are used, the optimization process is impeded, and less efficient code for derivatives may be produced. Optimization is also reduced by conditional statements, iterative DO loops, and multiple assignments to the same variable.

The table of derivatives is printed with the LISTDER option. The code generated for the computation of the derivatives is printed with the LISTCODE option.

Derivative Variables

When the differentiator needs to generate code to evaluate the expression for the derivative of a variable, the result is stored in a special derivative variable. Derivative variables are not created when the derivative expression reduces to a previously computed result, a variable, or a constant. The names of derivative variables, which may sometimes appear in the printed output, have the form *@obj/@wrt*, where *obj* is the variable whose derivative is being taken and *wrt* is the variable that the differentiation is with respect to. For example, the derivative variable for the derivative of *Y* with respect to *X* is named *@Y/@X*.

The derivative variables cannot be accessed or used as part of the model program.

Mathematical Functions

The following is a brief summary of SAS functions useful for defining models. Additional functions and details are in *SAS Language: Reference.* Information on creating new functions can be found in *SAS/TOOLKIT Software: Usage and Reference*, chapter 15, "Writing a SAS Function or Call Routine."

ABS(x)	the absolute value of x
ARCOS(x)	the arccosine in radians of x. x should be between -1 and 1.
ARSIN(x)	the arcsine in radians of x. x should be between -1 and 1.
ATAN(x)	the arctangent in radians of x
COS(x)	the cosine of x. x is in radians.
COSH(x)	the hyperbolic cosine of x
EXP(x)	e^x
LOG(x)	the natural logarithm of x
LOG10(x)	the log base ten of x
LOG2(x)	the log base two of x
SIN(x)	the sine of x. x is in radians.
SINH(x)	the hyperbolic sine of x
SQRT(x)	the square root of x
TAN(x)	the tangent of x. x is in radians and is not an odd multiple of $\pi/2$.
TANH(x)	the hyperbolic tangent of x

Random-Number Functions

The MODEL procedure provides several functions for generating random numbers for Monte Carlo simulation. These functions use the same generators as the corresponding SAS DATA step functions.

The following random-number functions are supported: RANBIN, RANCAU, RAND, RANEXP, RANGAM, RANNOR, RANPOI, RANTBL, RANTRI, and RANUNI. For more information, refer to *SAS Language: Reference.*

Each reference to a random-number function sets up a separate pseudo-random sequence. Note that this means that two calls to the same random function with the same seed produce identical results. This is different from the behavior of the random-number functions used in the SAS DATA step. For example, the statements

```
x=rannor(123);
y=rannor(123);
z=rannor(567);
q=rand('BETA', 1, 12 );
```

produce identical values for X and Y, but Z is from an independent pseudo-random sequence.

For FIT tasks, all random-number functions always return 0. For SOLVE tasks, when Monte Carlo simulation is requested, a random-number function computes a new random number on the first iteration for an observation (if it is executed on that iteration) and returns that same value for all later iterations of that observation. When Monte Carlo simulation is not requested, random-number functions always return 0.

Functions Across Time

PROC MODEL provides four types of special built-in functions that refer to the values of variables and expressions in previous time periods. These functions have the form

LAG*n*([*i* ,] *x*)	returns the *i*th lag of *x*, where *n* is the maximum lag;
DIF*n*(*x*)	difference of *x* at lag *n*
ZLAG*n*([*i* ,] *x*)	returns the *i*th lag of *x*, where *n* is the maximum lag, with missing lags replaced with zero;
XLAG*n*(*x* , *y*)	returns the *n*th lag of *x* if *x* is nonmissing, or *y* if x is missing;
ZDIF*n*(*x*)	difference with lag length truncated and missing values converted to zero;
MOVAVGn(*x*)	the width of the moving average is *n*, and *x* is the variable or expression to compute the moving average of. Missing values of *x* are omitted in computing the average.

where *n* represents the number of periods, and *x* is any expression. The argument *i* is a variable or expression giving the lag length ($0 <= i <= n$), if the index value *i* is omitted, the maximum lag length *n* is used.

If you do not specify *n*, the number of periods is assumed to be one. For example, LAG(X) is the same as LAG1(X). No more than four digits can be used with a lagging function; that is, LAG9999 is the greatest LAG function, ZDIF9999 is the greatest ZDIF function, and so on.

The LAG functions get values from previous observations and make them available to the program. For example, LAG(X) returns the value of the variable X as it was computed in the execution of the program for the preceding observation. The expression LAG2(X+2*Y) returns the value of the expression X+2*Y, computed using the values of the variables X and Y that were computed by the execution of the program for the observation two periods ago.

The DIF functions return the difference between the current value of a variable or expression and the value of its LAG. For example, DIF2(X) is a short way of writing X-LAG2(X), and DIF15(SQRT(2*Z)) is a short way of writing SQRT(2*Z)-LAG15(SQRT(2*Z)).

The ZLAG and ZDIF functions are like the LAG and DIF functions, but they are not counted in the determination of the program lag length, and they replace missing values with 0s. The ZLAG function returns the lagged value if the lagged value is nonmissing, or 0 if the lagged value is missing. The ZDIF function returns the differenced value if the differenced value is nonmissing, or 0 if the value of the differenced value is missing. The ZLAG function is especially useful for models with ARMA error processes. See "Lag Logic", which follows for details.

Lag Logic

The LAG and DIF lagging functions in the MODEL procedure are different from the queuing functions with the same names in the DATA step. Lags are determined by the final values that are set for the program variables by the execution of the model program for the observation. This can have upsetting consequences for programs that take lags of program variables that are given different values at various places in the program, for example,

```
temp = x + w;
t    = lag( temp );
temp = q - r;
s    = lag( temp );
```

The expression LAG(TEMP) always refers to LAG(Q-R), never to LAG(X+W), since Q-R is the final value assigned to the variable TEMP by the model program. If LAG(X+W) is wanted for T, it should be computed as T=LAG(X+W) and not T=LAG(TEMP), as in the preceding example.

Care should also be exercised in using the DIF functions with program variables that may be reassigned later in the program. For example, the program

```
temp =  x ;
s    = dif( temp );
temp = 3 * y;
```

computes values for S equivalent to

```
s =  x   - lag( 3 * y );
```

Note that in the preceding examples, TEMP is a program variable, *not* a model variable. If it were a model variable, the assignments to it would be changed to assignments to a corresponding equation variable.

Note that whereas LAG1(LAG1(X)) is the same as LAG2(X), DIF1(DIF1(X)) is *not* the same as DIF2(X). The DIF2 function is the difference between the current period value at the point in the program where the function is executed and the final value at the end of execution two periods ago; DIF2 is not the second difference. In contrast, DIF1(DIF1(X)) is equal to DIF1(X)-LAG1(DIF1(X)), which equals X-2*LAG1(X)+LAG2(X), which is the second difference of X.

More information on the differences between PROC MODEL and the DATA step LAG and DIF functions is found in Chapter 2, "Working with Time Series Data." .

Lag Lengths

The lag length of the model program is the number of lags needed for any relevant equation. The program lag length controls the number of observations used to initialize the lags.

PROC MODEL keeps track of the use of lags in the model program and automatically determines the lag length of each equation and of the model as a whole. PROC MODEL sets the program lag length to the maximum number of lags needed to compute any equation to be estimated, solved, or needed to compute any instrument variable used.

In determining the lag length, the ZLAG and ZDIF functions are treated as always having a lag length of 0. For example, if Y is computed as

```
y = lag2( x + zdif3( temp ) );
```

then Y has a lag length of 2 (regardless of how TEMP is defined). If Y is computed as

```
y = zlag2( x + dif3( temp ) );
```

then Y has a lag length of 0.

This is so that ARMA errors can be specified without causing the loss of additional observations to the lag starting phase and so that recursive lag specifications, such as moving-average error terms, can be used. Recursive lags are not permitted unless the ZLAG or ZDIF functions are used to truncate the lag length. For example, the following statement produces an error message:

```
t = a + b * lag( t );
```

The program variable T depends recursively on its own lag, and the lag length of T is therefore undefined.

In the following equation RESID.Y depends on the predicted value for the Y equation but the predicted value for the Y equation depends on the LAG of RESID.Y, and, thus, the predicted value for the Y equation depends recursively on its own lag.

```
y = yhat + ma * lag( resid.y );
```

The lag length is infinite, and PROC MODEL prints an error message and stops. Since this kind of specification is allowed, the recursion must be truncated at some point. The ZLAG and ZDIF functions do this.

The following equation is legal and results in a lag length for the Y equation equal to the lag length of YHAT:

```
y = yhat + ma * zlag( resid.y );
```

Initially, the lags of RESID.Y are missing, and the ZLAG function replaces the missing residuals with 0s, their unconditional expected values.

The ZLAG0 function can be used to zero out the lag length of an expression. ZLAG0(x) returns the current period value of the expression x, if nonmissing, or else returns 0, and prevents the lag length of x from contributing to the lag length of the current statement.

Initializing Lags

At the start of each pass through the data set or BY group, the lag variables are set to missing values and an initialization is performed to fill the lags. During this phase, observations are read from the data set, and the model variables are given values from the data. If necessary, the model is executed to assign values to program variables that are used in lagging functions. The results for variables used in lag functions are saved. These observations are not included in the estimation or solution.

If, during the execution of the program for the lag starting phase, a lag function refers to lags that are missing, the lag function returns missing. Execution errors that occur while starting the lags are not reported unless requested. The modeling system automatically determines whether the program needs to be executed during the lag starting phase.

If L is the maximum lag length of any equation being fit or solved, then the first L observations are used to prime the lags. If a BY statement is used, the first L observations in the BY group are used to prime the lags. If a RANGE statement is used, the first L observations prior to the first observation requested in the RANGE statement are used to prime the lags. Therefore, there should be at least L observations in the data set.

Initial values for the lags of model variables can also be supplied in VAR, ENDOGENOUS, and EXOGENOUS statements. This feature provides initial lags of solution variables for dynamic solution when initial values for the solution variable are not available in the input data set. For example, the statement

```
var x 2 3 y 4 5 z 1;
```

feeds the initial lags exactly like these values in an input data set:

Lag	X	Y	Z
2	3	5	.
1	2	4	1

If initial values for lags are available in the input data set and initial lag values are also given in a declaration statement, the values in the VAR, ENDOGENOUS, or EXOGENOUS statements take priority.

The RANGE statement is used to control the range of observations in the input data set that are processed by PROC MODEL. In the statement

```
range date = '01jan1924'd to '01dec1943'd;
```

'01jan1924' specifies the starting period of the range, and '01dec1943' specifies the ending period. The observations in the data set immediately prior to the start of the range are used to initialize the lags.

Language Differences

For the most part, PROC MODEL programming statements work the same as they do in the DATA step as documented in *SAS Language: Reference*. However, there are several differences that should be noted.

DO Statement Differences

The DO statement in PROC MODEL does not allow a character index variable. Thus, the following DO statement is not valid in PROC MODEL, although it is supported in the DATA step:

```
do i = 'A', 'B', 'C';            /* invalid PROC MODEL code */
```

IF Statement Differences

The IF statement in PROC MODEL does not allow a character-valued condition. For example, the following IF statement is not supported by PROC MODEL:

```
if 'this' then  statement;
```

Comparisons of character values are supported in IF statements, so the following IF statement is acceptable:

```
if 'this' < 'that' then  statement};
```

PROC MODEL allows for embedded conditionals in expressions. For example the following two statements are equivalent:

```
flag = if time = 1 or time = 2 then conc+30/5 + dose*time
            else if time > 5 then (0=1) else (patient * flag);

if time = 1 or time = 2 then flag= conc+30/5 + dose*time;
        else if time > 5 then flag=(0=1); else flag=patient*flag;
```

Note that the ELSE operator only involves the first object or token after it so that the following assignments are not equivalent:

```
total = if sum > 0 then sum else sum + reserve;
total = if sum > 0 then sum else (sum + reserve);
```

The first assignment makes TOTAL always equal to SUM plus RESERVE.

PUT Statement Differences

The PUT statement, mostly used in PROC MODEL for program debugging, only supports some of the features of the DATA step PUT statement. It also has some new features that the DATA step PUT statement does not support.

The PROC MODEL PUT statement does not support line pointers, factored lists, iteration factors, overprinting, the _INFILE_ option, or the colon (:) format modifier.

The PROC MODEL PUT statement does support expressions but an expression must be enclosed in parentheses. For example, the following statement prints the square root of x:

```
put (sqrt(x));
```

Subscripted array names must be enclosed in parentheses. For example, the following statement prints the *i*th element of the array A:

```
put (a i);
```

However, the following statement is an error:

```
put a i;
```

The PROC MODEL PUT statement supports the print item _PDV_ to print a formatted listing of all the variables in the program. For example, the following statement prints a much more readable listing of the variables than does the _ALL_ print item:

```
put _pdv_;
```

To print all the elements of the array A, use the following statement:

```
put a;
```

To print all the elements of A with each value labeled by the name of the element variable, use the statement

```
put a=;
```

ABORT Statement Difference

In the MODEL procedure, the ABORT statement does not allow any arguments.

SELECT/WHEN/OTHERWISE Statement Differences

The WHEN and OTHERWISE statements allow more than one target statement. That is, DO groups are not necessary for multiple statement WHENs. For example in PROC MODEL, the following syntax is valid:

```
select;
   when(exp1)
      stmt1;
      stmt2;
   when(exp2)
      stmt3;
      stmt4;
end;
```

The ARRAY Statement

ARRAY *arrayname [{dimensions}] [$ [length]] [variables and constants];*

The ARRAY statement is used to associate a name with a list of variables and constants. The array name can then be used with subscripts in the model program to refer to the items in the list.

In PROC MODEL, the ARRAY statement does not support all the features of the DATA step ARRAY statement. Implicit indexing cannot be used; all array references must have explicit subscript expressions. Only exact array dimensions are allowed; lower-bound specifications are not supported. A maximum of six dimensions is allowed.

On the other hand, the ARRAY statement supported by PROC MODEL does allow both variables and constants to be used as array elements. You cannot make assignments to constant array elements. Both dimension specification and the list of elements are optional, but at least one must be supplied. When the list of elements is not given or fewer elements than the size of the array are listed, array variables are created by suffixing element numbers to the array name to complete the element list.

The following are valid PROC MODEL array statements:

```
array x[120];              /* array X of length 120         */
array q[2,2];              /* Two dimensional array Q       */
array b[4] va vb vc vd;    /* B[2] = VB, B[4] = VD          */
array x x1-x30;            /* array X of length 30, X[7] = X7  */
array a[5] (1 2 3 4 5);    /* array A initialized to 1,2,3,4,5 */
```

RETAIN Statement

RETAIN *variables initial-values ;*

The RETAIN statement causes a program variable to hold its value from a previous observation until the variable is reassigned. The RETAIN statement can be used to initialize program variables.

The RETAIN statement does not work for model variables, parameters, or control variables because the values of these variables are under the control of PROC MODEL and not programming statements. Use the PARMS and CONTROL statements to initialize parameters and control variables. Use the VAR, ENDOGENOUS, or EXOGENOUS statement to initialize model variables.

Storing Programs in Model Files

Models can be saved and recalled from SAS catalog files. SAS catalogs are special files that can store many kinds of data structures as separate units in one SAS file. Each separate unit is called an entry, and each entry has an entry type that identifies its structure to the SAS system.

In general, to save a model, use the OUTMODEL=*name* option on the PROC MODEL statement, where *name* is specified as *libref.catalog.entry*, *libref.entry*, or *entry*. The *libref*, *catalog*, and *entry* names must be valid SAS names no more than 32 characters long. The *catalog* name is restricted to seven characters on the CMS operating system. If not given, the *catalog* name defaults to MODELS, and the *libref* defaults to WORK. The entry type is always MODEL. Thus, OUTMODEL=X writes the model to the file WORK.MODELS.X.MODEL.

The MODEL= option is used to read in a model. A list of model files can be specified in the MODEL= option, and a range of names with numeric suffixes can be given, as in MODEL=(MODEL1-MODEL10). When more than one model file is given, the list must be placed in parentheses, as in MODEL=(A B C), except in the case of a single name. If more than one model file is specified, the files are combined in the order listed in the MODEL= option.

When the MODEL= option is specified in the PROC MODEL statement and model definition statements are also given later in the PROC MODEL step, the model files are read in first, in the order listed, and the model program specified in the PROC MODEL step is appended after the model program read from the MODEL= files. The class assigned to a variable, when multiple model files are used, is the last declaration of that variable. For example, if Y1 was declared endogenous in the model file M1 and exogenous in the model file M2, the following statement will cause Y1 to be declared exogenous.

```
proc model model=(m1 m2);
```

The INCLUDE statement can be used to append model code to the current model code. In contrast, when the MODEL= option is used on the RESET statement, the current model is deleted before the new model is read.

No model file is output by default if the PROC MODEL step performs any FIT or SOLVE tasks, or if the MODEL= option or the NOSTORE option is used. However, to ensure compatibility with previous versions of SAS/ETS software, when the PROC MODEL step does nothing but compile the model program, no input model file is read, and the NOSTORE option is not used, a model file is written. This model file is the default input file for a later PROC SYSNLIN or PROC SIMNLIN step. The default output model filename in this case is WORK.MODELS._MODEL_.MODEL.

If FIT statements are used to estimate model parameters, the parameter estimates written to the output model file are the estimates from the last estimation performed for each parameter.

Diagnostics and Debugging

PROC MODEL provides several features to aid in finding errors in the model program. These debugging features are not usually needed; most models can be developed without them.

The example model program that follows will be used in the following sections to illustrate the diagnostic and debugging capabilities. This example is the estimation of a segmented model.

```
*---------Fitting a Segmented Model using MODEL----*
|       |                                          |
|   y   | quadratic              plateau           |
|       | y=a+b*x+c*x*x          y=p               |
|       |                       ..................  |
|       |              .        :                  |
|       |          .            :                  |
|       |       .               :                  |
|       |     .                 :                  |
|       |    .                  :                  |
|       +---------------------------------------X  |
|                              x0                  |
|                                                  |
| continuity restriction: p=a+b*x0+c*x0**2         |
| smoothness restriction: 0=b+2*c*x0 so x0=-b/(2*c)|
*--------------------------------------------------*;
title 'QUADRATIC MODEL WITH PLATEAU';
data a;
   input y x @@;
   datalines;
.46 1  .47  2 .57  3 .61  4 .62  5 .68  6 .69  7
.78 8  .70  9 .74 10 .77 11 .78 12 .74 13 .80 13
.80 15 .78 16
;
proc model data=a;
parms a 0.45 b 0.5 c -0.0025;

x0 = -.5*b / c;         /* join point */
if x < x0 then          /* Quadratic part of model */
   y = a + b*x + c*x*x;
else                    /* Plateau part of model */
   y = a + b*x0 + c*x0*x0;

fit y;
run;
```

Program Listing

The LIST option produces a listing of the model program. The statements are printed one per line with the original line number and column position of the statement.

The program listing from the example program is shown in Figure 20.77.

```
                         QUADRATIC MODEL WITH PLATEAU

                              The MODEL Procedure

                        Listing of Compiled Program Code
     Stmt       Line:Col          Statement as Parsed

        1       15888:74          x0 = (-0.5 * b) / c;
        2       15888:96          if x < x0 then
        3       15888:124         PRED.y = a + b * x + c * x * x;
        3       15888:124         RESID.y = PRED.y - ACTUAL.y;
        3       15888:124         ERROR.y = PRED.y - y;
        4       15888:148         else
        5       15888:176         PRED.y = a + b * x0 + c * x0 * x0;
        5       15888:176         RESID.y = PRED.y - ACTUAL.y;
        5       15888:176         ERROR.y = PRED.y - y;
```

Figure 20.77. LIST Output for Segmented Model

The LIST option also shows the model translations that PROC MODEL performs. LIST output is useful for understanding the code generated by the %AR and the %MA macros.

Cross-Reference

The XREF option produces a cross-reference listing of the variables in the model program. The XREF listing is usually used in conjunction with the LIST option. The XREF listing does not include derivative (@-prefixed) variables. The XREF listing does not include generated assignments to equation variables, PRED, RESID, and ERROR-prefixed variables, unless the DETAILS option is used.

The cross-reference from the example program is shown in Figure 20.78.

```
                                The MODEL Procedure

                          Cross Reference Listing For Program
Symbol-----------       Kind       Type       References (statement)/(line):(col)

a                       Var        Num        Used: 3/15913:130 5/15913:182
b                       Var        Num        Used: 1/15913:82 3/15913:133 5/15913:185
c                       Var        Num        Used: 1/15913:85 3/15913:139 5/15913:192
x0                      Var        Num        Assigned: 1/15913:85
                                              Used: 2/15913:103 5/15913:185
                                              5/15913:192 5/15913:195
x                       Var        Num        Used: 2/15913:103 3/15913:133
                                              3/15913:139 3/15913:141
PRED.y                  Var        Num        Assigned: 3/15913:136 5/15913:189
```

Figure 20.78. XREF Output for Segmented Model

Compiler Listing

The LISTCODE option lists the model code and derivatives tables produced by the compiler. This listing is useful only for debugging and should not normally be needed.

LISTCODE prints the operator and operands of each operation generated by the compiler for each model program statement. Many of the operands are temporary variables generated by the compiler and given names such as #temp1. When derivatives are taken, the code listing includes the operations generated for the derivatives calculations. The derivatives tables are also listed.

A LISTCODE option prints the transformed equations from the example shown in Figure 20.79 and Figure 20.80.

```
                          The MODEL Procedure

                    Listing of Compiled Program Code
   Stmt      Line:Col        Statement as Parsed

      1      16459:83        x0 = (-0.5 * b) / c;
      1      16459:83        @x0/@b = -0.5 / c;
      1      16459:83        @x0/@c = (0 - x0) / c;
      2      16459:105       if x < x0 then
      3      16459:133       PRED.y = a + b * x + c * x * x;
      3      16459:133       @PRED.y/@a = 1;
      3      16459:133       @PRED.y/@b = x;
      3      16459:133       @PRED.y/@c = x * x;
      3      16459:133       RESID.y = PRED.y - ACTUAL.y;
      3      16459:133       @RESID.y/@a = @PRED.y/@a;
      3      16459:133       @RESID.y/@b = @PRED.y/@b;
      3      16459:133       @RESID.y/@c = @PRED.y/@c;
      3      16459:133       ERROR.y = PRED.y - y;
      4      16459:157       else
      5      16459:185       PRED.y = a + b * x0 + c * x0 * x0;
      5      16459:185       @PRED.y/@a = 1;
      5      16459:185       @PRED.y/@b = x0 + b * @x0/@b + (c
                             * @x0/@b * x0 + c * x0 * @x0/@b);
      5      16459:185       @PRED.y/@c = b * @x0/@c + ((x0 + c
                             * @x0/@c) * x0 + c * x0 * @x0/@c);
      5      16459:185       RESID.y = PRED.y - ACTUAL.y;
      5      16459:185       @RESID.y/@a = @PRED.y/@a;
      5      16459:185       @RESID.y/@b = @PRED.y/@b;
      5      16459:185       @RESID.y/@c = @PRED.y/@c;
      5      16459:185       ERROR.y = PRED.y - y;
```

Figure 20.79. LISTCODE Output for Segmented Model - Statements as Parsed

```
                        The MODEL Procedure


1 Stmt ASSIGN       line 5619 column
                    83. (1) arg=x0
                    argsave=x0
                    Source Text:            x0 = -.5*b / c;
    Oper *          at 5619:91 (30,0,2).    * : #temp1 <- -0.5 b
    Oper /          at 5619:94 (31,0,2).    / : x0 <- #temp1 c
    Oper eeocf      at 5619:94 (18,0,1).    eeocf : _DER_ <- _DER_
    Oper /          at 5619:94 (31,0,2).    / : @x0/@b <- -0.5 c
    Oper -          at 5619:94 (33,0,2).    - : @1dt1_2 <- 0 x0
    Oper /          at 5619:94 (31,0,2).    / : @x0/@c <- @1dt1_2 c

2 Stmt IF           line 5619 column         ref.st=ASSIGN stmt
                    105. (2) arg=#temp1     number 5 at 5619:185
                    argsave=#temp1
                    Source Text:            if x < x0 then
    Oper <          at 5619:112             < : #temp1 <- x x0
                    (36,0,2).

3 Stmt ASSIGN       line 5619 column
                    133. (1) arg=PRED.y
                    argsave=y
                    Source Text:            y = a + b*x + c*x*x;
    Oper *          at 5619:142             * : #temp1 <- b x
                    (30,0,2).
    Oper +          at 5619:139             + : #temp2 <- a #temp1
                    (32,0,2).
    Oper *          at 5619:148             * : #temp3 <- c x
                    (30,0,2).
    Oper *          at 5619:150             * : #temp4 <- #temp3 x
                    (30,0,2).
    Oper +          at 5619:145             + : PRED.y <- #temp2 #temp4
                    (32,0,2).
    Oper eeocf      at 5619:150             eeocf : _DER_ <- _DER_
                    (18,0,1).
    Oper *          at 5619:150             * : @1dt1_1 <- x x
                    (30,0,2).
    Oper =          at 5619:145 (1,0,1).    = : @PRED.y/@a <- 1
    Oper =          at 5619:145 (1,0,1).    = : @PRED.y/@b <- x
    Oper =          at 5619:145 (1,0,1).    = : @PRED.y/@c <- @1dt1_1

3 Stmt Assign       line 5619 column
                    133. (1) arg=RESID.y
                    argsave=y
    Oper -          at 5619:133             - : RESID.y <- PRED.y ACTUAL.y
                    (33,0,2).
    Oper eeocf      at 5619:133             eeocf : _DER_ <- _DER_
                    (18,0,1).
    Oper =          at 5619:133 (1,0,1).    = : @RESID.y/@a <- @PRED.y/@a
    Oper =          at 5619:133 (1,0,1).    = : @RESID.y/@b <- @PRED.y/@b
    Oper =          at 5619:133 (1,0,1).    = : @RESID.y/@c <- @PRED.y/@c

3 Stmt Assign       line 5619 column
                    133. (1) arg=ERROR.y
                    argsave=y
    Oper -          at 5619:133             - : ERROR.y <- PRED.y y
                    (33,0,2).

4 Stmt ELSE         line 5619 column
                    157. (9)
                    Source Text:            else
```

Figure 20.80. LISTCODE Output for Segmented Model - Compiled Code

Analyzing the Structure of Large Models

PROC MODEL provides several features to aid in analyzing the structure of the model program. These features summarize properties of the model in various forms.

The following Klein's model program is used to introduce the LISTDEP, BLOCK, and GRAPH options.

```
proc model  out=m data=klein listdep graph block;
   endogenous c p w i x wsum k y;
   exogenous  wp g t year;
   parms c0-c3 i0-i3 w0-w3;
   a: c = c0 + c1 * p + c2 * lag(p) + c3 * wsum;
   b: i = i0 + i1 * p + i2 * lag(p) + i3 * lag(k);
   c: w = w0 + w1 * x + w2 * lag(x) + w3 * year;
   x = c + i + g;
   y = c + i + g-t;
   p = x-w-t;
   k = lag(k) + i;
   wsum = w + wp;
   id year;
run;
```

Dependency List

The LISTDEP option produces a dependency list for each variable in the model program. For each variable, a list of variables that depend on it and a list of variables it depends on is given. The dependency list produced by the example program is shown in Figure 20.81.

```
                           The MODEL Procedure

                   Dependency Listing For Program
Symbol-----------          Dependencies

c                          Current values affect: ERROR.c PRED.x
                           RESID.x ERROR.x PRED.y RESID.y ERROR.y
p                          Current values affect: PRED.c RESID.c
                           ERROR.c PRED.i RESID.i ERROR.i ERROR.p
                           Lagged values affect: PRED.c PRED.i
w                          Current values affect: ERROR.w
                           PRED.p RESID.p ERROR.p PRED.wsum
                           RESID.wsum ERROR.wsum
i                          Current values affect: ERROR.i PRED.x
                           RESID.x ERROR.x PRED.y RESID.y
                           ERROR.y PRED.k RESID.k ERROR.k
x                          Current values affect: PRED.w RESID.w
                           ERROR.w ERROR.x PRED.p RESID.p ERROR.p
                           Lagged values affect: PRED.w
wsum                       Current values affect: PRED.c
                           RESID.c ERROR.c ERROR.wsum
k                          Current values affect: ERROR.k
                           Lagged values affect: PRED.i RESID.i
                           ERROR.i PRED.k RESID.k
```

Figure 20.81. A Portion of the LISTDEP Output for Klein's Model

BLOCK Listing

The BLOCK option prints an analysis of the program variables based on the assignments in the model program. The output produced by the example is shown in Figure 20.82.

```
                        The MODEL Procedure
                     Model Structure Analysis
          (Based on Assignments to Endogenous Model Variables)

              Exogenous Variables      wp g t year
              Endogenous Variables     c p w i x wsum k y
NOTE: The System Consists of 2 Recursive Equations and 1 Simultaneous Blocks.


                      Block Structure of the System

                       Block 1     c p w i x wsum


                    Dependency Structure of the System

              Block 1    Depends On All_Exogenous
              k          Depends On Block 1 All_Exogenous
              y          Depends On Block 1 All_Exogenous
```

Figure 20.82. The BLOCK Output for Klein's Model

One use for the block output is to put a model in recursive form. Simulations of the model can be done with the SEIDEL method, which is efficient if the model is recursive and if the equations are in recursive order. By examining the block output, you can determine how to reorder the model equations for the most efficient simulation.

Adjacency Graph

The GRAPH option displays the same information as the BLOCK option with the addition of an adjacency graph. An X in a column in an adjacency graph indicates that the variable associated with the row depends on the variable associated with the column. The output produced by the example is shown in Figure 20.83.

The first and last graphs are straightforward. The middle graph represents the dependencies of the nonexogenous variables after transitive closure has been performed (that is, A depends on B, and B depends on C, so A depends on C). The preceding transitive closure matrix indicates that K and Y do not directly or indirectly depend on each other.

```
                 The MODEL Procedure

         Adjacency Matrix for Graph of System
                                w           y
                                s           e
                                u       w   a
Variable              c p w i x m k y p g t r

                                      * * * *
c                     X X . . . X . . . . . .
p                     . X X . X . . . . . X .
w                     . . X . X . . . . . . X
i                     . X . X . . . . . . . .
x                     X . . X X . . . . X . .
wsum                  . . X . . X . . X . . .
k                     . . . X . . X . . . . .
y                     X . . X . . . X . X X .
wp                  * . . . . . . . . X . . .
g                   * . . . . . . . . . X . .
t                   * . . . . . . . . . . X .
year                * . . . . . . . . . . . X

      (Note: * = Exogenous Variable.)


Transitive Closure Matrix of Sorted System
                                    w
                                    s
                                    u
Block    Variable         c p w i x m k y

    1    c                X X X X X X . .
    1    p                X X X X X X . .
    1    w                X X X X X X . .
    1    i                X X X X X X . .
    1    x                X X X X X X . .
    1    wsum             X X X X X X . .
         k                X X X X X X X .
         y                X X X X X X . X


          Adjacency Matrix for Graph of System
                Including Lagged Impacts
                                    w           y
                                    s           e
                                    u       w   a
Block    Variable         c p w i x m k y p g t r

                                          * * * *
    1    c                X L . . . X . . . . . .
    1    p                . X X . X . . . . . X .
    1    w                . . X . L . . . . . . X
    1    i                . L . X . . L . . . . .
    1    x                X . . X X . . . . X . .
    1    wsum             . . X . . X . . X . . .
         k                . . . X . . L . . . . .
         y                X . . X . . . X . X X .
         wp             * . . . . . . . . X . . .
         g              * . . . . . . . . . X . .
         t              * . . . . . . . . . . X .
         year           * . . . . . . . . . . . X

         (Note: * = Exogenous Variable.)
```

Figure 20.83. The GRAPH Output for Klein's Model

Examples

Example 20.1. OLS Single Nonlinear Equation

This example illustrates the use of the MODEL procedure for nonlinear ordinary least-squares (OLS) regression. The model is a logistic growth curve for the population of the United States. The data is the population in millions recorded at ten year intervals starting in 1790 and ending in 2000. For an explanation of the starting values given by the START= option, see "Troubleshooting Convergence Problems" earlier in this chapter. Portions of the output from the following code are shown in Output 20.1.1 and Output 20.1.2.

```
title 'Logistic Growth Curve Model of U.S. Population';
data uspop;
   input pop :6.3 @@;
   retain year 1780;
   year=year+10;
   label pop='U.S. Population in Millions';
   datalines;
3929  5308  7239   9638  12866  17069  23191  31443  39818 50155
62947 75994 91972 105710 122775 131669 151325 179323 203211
226542 248710
;

proc model data=uspop;
   label a = 'Maximum Population'
         b = 'Location Parameter'
         c = 'Initial Growth Rate';
   pop = a / ( 1 + exp( b - c * (year-1790) ) );
   fit pop start=(a 1000  b 5.5  c .02)/ out=resid outresid;
run;
```

Output 20.1.1. Logistic Growth Curve Model Summary

```
            Logistic Growth Curve Model of U.S. Population

                         The MODEL Procedure

                            Model Summary

                     Model Variables          1
                     Parameters               3
                     Equations                1
                     Number of Statements     1


               Model Variables  pop
                    Parameters  a(1000) b(5.5) c(0.02)
                     Equations  pop
```

```
Logistic Growth Curve Model of U.S. Population

The MODEL Procedure

The Equation to Estimate is

pop =  F(a, b, c)
```

Output 20.1.2. Logistic Growth Curve Estimation Summary

```
Logistic Growth Curve Model of U.S. Population

The MODEL Procedure

Nonlinear OLS Summary of Residual Errors

                     DF      DF                                          Adj
Equation          Model   Error        SSE        MSE   R-Square        R-Sq

pop                   3      18      345.6    19.2020     0.9972      0.9969


Nonlinear OLS Parameter Estimates

                                Approx                  Approx
Parameter       Estimate       Std Err    t Value     Pr > |t|    Label

a               387.9307       30.0404      12.91       <.0001    Maximum Population
b               3.990385        0.0695      57.44       <.0001    Location Parameter
c               0.022703       0.00107      21.22       <.0001    Initial Growth Rate
```

The adjusted R^2 value indicates the model fits the data well. There are only 21 observations and the model is nonlinear, so significance tests on the parameters are only approximate. The significance tests and associated approximate probabilities indicate that all the parameters are significantly different from 0.

The FIT statement included the options OUT=RESID and OUTRESID so that the residuals from the estimation are saved to the data set RESID. The residuals are plotted to check for heteroscedasticity using PROC GPLOT as follows.

```
proc gplot data=resid;
 axis2 label=( a=-90 r=90 'US Pop in Millions' );
 plot pop*year / vref=0 vaxis=axis2
                 haxis=1780 to 2000 by 20;
 title2 "Residual";
 symbol1 v=dot;
run;
```

The plot is shown in Output 20.1.3.

Output 20.1.3. Residual for Population Model (Actual - Predicted)

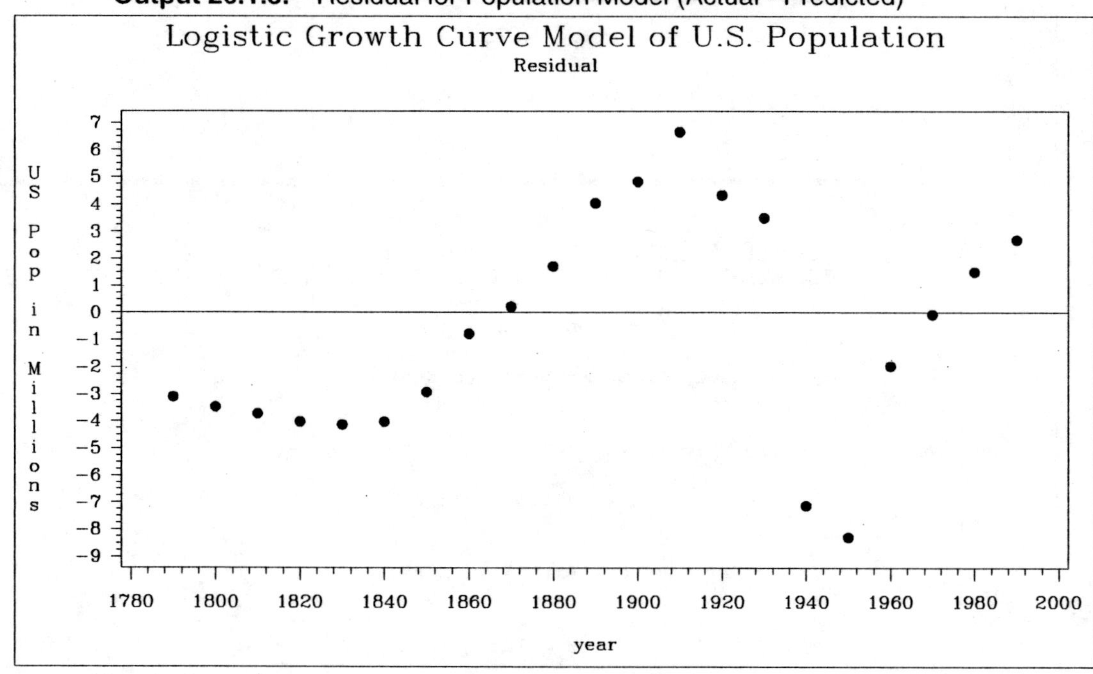

The residuals do not appear to be independent, and the model could be modified to explain the remaining nonrandom errors.

Example 20.2. A Consumer Demand Model

This example shows the estimation of a system of nonlinear consumer demand equations based on the translog functional form using seemingly unrelated regression (SUR). Expenditure shares and corresponding normalized prices are given for three goods.

Since the shares add up to one, the system is singular; therefore, one equation is omitted from the estimation process. The choice of which equation to omit is arbitrary. The nonlinear system is first estimated in unrestricted form.

```
title1 'Consumer Demand--Translog Functional Form';
title2 'Nonsymmetric Model';
proc model data=tlog1;
   endogenous share1 share2;
   parms a1 a2 b11 b12 b13 b21 b22 b23 b31 b32 b33;

   bm1 = b11 + b21 + b31;
   bm2 = b12 + b22 + b32;
   bm3 = b13 + b23 + b33;
   lp1 = log(p1);
   lp2 = log(p2);
   lp3 = log(p3);
   share1 = ( a1 + b11 * lp1 + b12 * lp2 + b13 * lp3 ) /
            ( -1 + bm1 * lp1 + bm2 * lp2 + bm3 * lp3 );
   share2 = ( a2 + b21 * lp1 + b22 * lp2 + b23 * lp3 ) /
            ( -1 + bm1 * lp1 + bm2 * lp2 + bm3 * lp3 );
```

```
    fit share1 share2
         start=( a1 -.14 a2 -.45 b11 .03 b12 .47 b22 .98 b31 .20
                  b32 1.11 b33 .71 ) / outsused = smatrix sur;
run;
```

A portion of the printed output produced in the preceding example is shown in Output 20.2.1.

Output 20.2.1. Estimation Results from the Unrestricted Model

```
                  Consumer Demand--Translog Functional Form
                            Nonsymmetric Model

                            The MODEL Procedure

                               Model Summary

                         Model Variables          5
                         Parameters              11
                         Equations                2
                         Number of Statements     8


Model Variables   share1 share2 p1 p2 p3
     Parameters   a1(-0.14) a2(-0.45) b11(0.03) b12(0.47) b13 b21
                  b22(0.98) b23 b31(0.2) b32(1.11) b33(0.71)
      Equations   share1 share2
```

```
                  Consumer Demand--Translog Functional Form
                            Nonsymmetric Model

                            The MODEL Procedure

                         The 2 Equations to Estimate

      share1 =  F(a1, b11, b12, b13, b21, b22, b23, b31, b32, b33)
      share2 =  F(a2, b11, b12, b13, b21, b22, b23, b31, b32, b33)


    NOTE: At SUR Iteration 2 CONVERGE=0.001 Criteria Met.
```

```
                  Consumer Demand--Translog Functional Form
                              Nonsymmetric Model

                             The MODEL Procedure

                  Nonlinear SUR Summary of Residual Errors

                   DF       DF                                                     Adj
Equation        Model    Error       SSE        MSE   Root MSE   R-Square         R-Sq

share1            5.5     38.5   0.00166   0.000043    0.00656     0.8067       0.7841
share2            5.5     38.5   0.00135   0.000035    0.00592     0.9445       0.9380


                      Nonlinear SUR Parameter Estimates

                                          Approx                      Approx
        Parameter        Estimate        Std Err    t Value         Pr > |t|

        a1               -0.14881        0.00225     -66.08           <.0001
        a2               -0.45776        0.00297    -154.29           <.0001
        b11              0.048382         0.0498       0.97           0.3379
        b12               0.43655         0.0502       8.70           <.0001
        b13              0.248588         0.0516       4.82           <.0001
        b21              0.586326         0.2089       2.81           0.0079
        b22              0.759776         0.2565       2.96           0.0052
        b23              1.303821         0.2328       5.60           <.0001
        b31              0.297808         0.1504       1.98           0.0550
        b32              0.961551         0.1633       5.89           <.0001
        b33                0.8291         0.1556       5.33           <.0001


             Number of Observations        Statistics for System

             Used                  44     Objective          1.7493
             Missing                0     Objective*N       76.9697
```

The model is then estimated under the restriction of symmetry (b_{ij}=b_{ji}).

Hypothesis testing requires that the **S** matrix from the unrestricted model be imposed on the restricted model, as explained in "Tests on Parameters" in this chapter. The **S** matrix saved in the data set SMATRIX is requested by the SDATA= option.

A portion of the printed output produced in the following example is shown in Output 20.2.2.

```
title2 'Symmetric Model';
proc model data=tlog1;
   var share1 share2 p1 p2 p3;
   parms a1 a2 b11 b12 b22 b31 b32 b33;
   bm1 = b11 + b12 + b31;
   bm2 = b12 + b22 + b32;
   bm3 = b31 + b32 + b33;
   lp1 = log(p1);
   lp2 = log(p2);
   lp3 = log(p3);
   share1 = ( a1 + b11 * lp1 + b12 * lp2 + b31 * lp3 ) /
            ( -1 + bm1 * lp1 + bm2 * lp2 + bm3 * lp3 );
   share2 = ( a2 + b12 * lp1 + b22 * lp2 + b32 * lp3 ) /
```

```
                ( -1 + bm1 * lp1 + bm2 * lp2 + bm3 * lp3 );
      fit share1 share2
          start=( a1 -.14 a2 -.45 b11 .03 b12 .47 b22 .98 b31 .20
                  b32 1.11 b33 .71 ) / sdata=smatrix sur;
   run;
```

A chi-square test is used to see if the hypothesis of symmetry is accepted or rejected. (*Oc-Ou*) has a chi-square distribution asymptotically, where *Oc* is the constrained OBJECTIVE*N and *Ou* is the unconstrained OBJECTIVE*N. The degrees of freedom is equal to the difference in the number of free parameters in the two models.

In this example, Ou is 76.9697 and Oc is 78.4097, resulting in a difference of 1.44 with 3 degrees of freedom. You can obtain the probability value by using the following statements:

```
   data _null_;
                     /* reduced-full, nrestrictions */
      p = 1-probchi( 1.44, 3 );
      put p=;
   run;
```

The output from this DATA step run is 'P=0.6961858724'. With this probability you cannot reject the hypothesis of symmetry. This test is asymptotically valid.

Output 20.2.2. Estimation Results from the Restricted Model

```
                  Consumer Demand--Translog Functional Form
                              Symmetric Model

                           The MODEL Procedure

                        The 2 Equations to Estimate

              share1 =   F(a1, b11, b12, b22, b31, b32, b33)
              share2 =   F(a2, b11, b12, b22, b31, b32, b33)
```

```
                    Consumer Demand--Translog Functional Form
                                 Symmetric Model

                               The MODEL Procedure

                    Nonlinear SUR Summary of Residual Errors

                  DF      DF                                                     Adj
Equation       Model   Error        SSE        MSE  Root MSE  R-Square        R-Sq

share1             4      40    0.00166   0.000041   0.00644    0.8066      0.7920
share2             4      40    0.00139   0.000035   0.00590    0.9428      0.9385


                      Nonlinear SUR Parameter Estimates

                                      Approx                      Approx
        Parameter       Estimate     Std Err    t Value     Pr > |t|

        a1              -0.14684     0.00135    -108.99       <.0001
        a2               -0.4597     0.00167    -275.34       <.0001
        b11              0.02886     0.00741       3.89       0.0004
        b12             0.467827      0.0115      40.57       <.0001
        b22             0.970079      0.0177      54.87       <.0001
        b31             0.208143     0.00614      33.88       <.0001
        b32             1.102415      0.0127      86.51       <.0001
        b33             0.694245      0.0168      41.38       <.0001


             Number of Observations       Statistics for System

             Used               44      Objective          1.7820
             Missing             0      Objective*N       78.4097
```

Example 20.3. Vector AR(1) Estimation

This example shows the estimation of a two-variable vector AR(1) error process for the Grunfeld model (Grunfeld 1960) using the %AR macro. First, the full model is estimated. Second, the model is estimated with the restriction that the errors are univariate AR(1) instead of a vector process. The following produces Output 20.3.1 and Output 20.3.2.

```
data grunfeld;
   input year gei gef gec whi whf whc;
   label gei = 'Gross Investment GE'
         gec = 'Capital Stock Lagged GE'
         gef = 'Value of Outstanding Shares GE Lagged'
         whi = 'Gross Investment WH'
         whc = 'Capital Stock Lagged WH'
         whf = 'Value of Outstanding Shares Lagged WH';
   datalines;
1935     33.1      1170.6     97.8      12.93      191.5      1.8
1936     45.0      2015.8     104.4     25.90      516.0      .8
1937     77.2      2803.3     118.0     35.05      729.0      7.4
1938     44.6      2039.7     156.2     22.89      560.4      18.1
1939     48.1      2256.2     172.6     18.84      519.9      23.5
1940     74.4      2132.2     186.6     28.57      628.5      26.5
1941     113.0     1834.1     220.9     48.51      537.1      36.2
1942     91.9      1588.0     287.8     43.34      561.2      60.8
```

```
1943    61.3     1749.4   319.9    37.02    617.2    84.4
1944    56.8     1687.2   321.3    37.81    626.7    91.2
1945    93.6     2007.7   319.6    39.27    737.2    92.4
1946    159.9    2208.3   346.0    53.46    760.5    86.0
1947    147.2    1656.7   456.4    55.56    581.4    111.1
1948    146.3    1604.4   543.4    49.56    662.3    130.6
1949    98.3     1431.8   618.3    32.04    583.8    141.8
1950    93.5     1610.5   647.4    32.24    635.2    136.7
1951    135.2    1819.4   671.3    54.38    723.8    129.7
1952    157.3    2079.7   726.1    71.78    864.1    145.5
1953    179.5    2371.6   800.3    90.08    1193.5   174.8
1954    189.6    2759.9   888.9    68.60    1188.9   213.5
;

title1 'Example of Vector AR(1) Error Process
        Using Grunfeld''s Model';
/* Note: GE stands for General Electric
        and WH for Westinghouse      */

proc model outmodel=grunmod;
   var gei whi gef gec whf whc;
   parms ge_int ge_f ge_c wh_int wh_f wh_c;
   label ge_int = 'GE Intercept'
         ge_f   = 'GE Lagged Share Value Coef'
         ge_c   = 'GE Lagged Capital Stock Coef'
         wh_int = 'WH Intercept'
         wh_f   = 'WH Lagged Share Value Coef'
         wh_c   = 'WH Lagged Capital Stock Coef';
   gei = ge_int + ge_f * gef + ge_c * gec;
   whi = wh_int + wh_f * whf + wh_c * whc;
run;
```

The preceding PROC MODEL step defines the structural model and stores it in the model file named GRUNMOD.

The following PROC MODEL step reads in the model, adds the vector autoregressive terms using %AR, and requests SUR estimation using the FIT statement.

```
title2 'With Unrestricted Vector AR(1) Error Process';
proc model data=grunfeld model=grunmod;
   %ar( ar, 1, gei whi )
   fit gei whi / sur;
run;
```

The final PROC MODEL step estimates the restricted model.

```
title2 'With restricted AR(1) Error Process';
proc model data=grunfeld model=grunmod;
   %ar( gei, 1 )
   %ar( whi, 1)
   fit gei whi / sur;
run;
```

Output 20.3.1. Results for the Unrestricted Model (Partial Output)

```
         Example of Vector AR(1) Error Process Using Grunfeld's Model
                 With Unrestricted Vector AR(1) Error Process

                             The MODEL Procedure

                                Model Summary

                        Model Variables            6
                        Parameters                10
                        Equations                  2
                        Number of Statements       6


Model Variables  gei whi gef gec whf whc
     Parameters  ge_int ge_f ge_c wh_int wh_f wh_c ar_l1_1_1(0)
                 ar_l1_1_2(0) ar_l1_2_1(0) ar_l1_2_2(0)
      Equations  gei whi
```

```
         Example of Vector AR(1) Error Process Using Grunfeld's Model
                 With Unrestricted Vector AR(1) Error Process

                             The MODEL Procedure

                          The 2 Equations to Estimate

    gei =  F(ge_int, ge_f, ge_c, wh_int, wh_f, wh_c, ar_l1_1_1, ar_l1_1_2)
    whi =  F(ge_int, ge_f, ge_c, wh_int, wh_f, wh_c, ar_l1_2_1, ar_l1_2_2)


       NOTE: At SUR Iteration 9 CONVERGE=0.001 Criteria Met.
```

```
      Example of Vector AR(1) Error Process Using Grunfeld's Model
             With Unrestricted Vector AR(1) Error Process

                         The MODEL Procedure

               Nonlinear SUR Summary of Residual Errors

                   DF      DF                                        Adj
 Equation        Model   Error       SSE        MSE   R-Square      R-Sq

 gei                 5      15    9374.5      625.0     0.7910    0.7352
 whi                 5      15    1429.2    95.2807     0.7940    0.7391


                  Nonlinear SUR Parameter Estimates

                             Approx                 Approx
Parameter        Estimate   Std Err    t Value   Pr > |t|   Label

ge_int           -42.2858   30.5284      -1.39     0.1863   GE Intercept
ge_f             0.049894    0.0153       3.27     0.0051   GE Lagged Share
                                                            Value Coef
ge_c             0.123946    0.0458       2.70     0.0163   GE Lagged Capital
                                                            Stock Coef
wh_int           -4.68931    8.9678      -0.52     0.6087   WH Intercept
wh_f             0.068979    0.0182       3.80     0.0018   WH Lagged Share
                                                            Value Coef
wh_c             0.019308    0.0754       0.26     0.8015   WH Lagged Capital
                                                            Stock Coef
ar_l1_1_1        0.990902    0.3923       2.53     0.0233   AR(ar) gei: LAG1
                                                            parameter for gei
ar_l1_1_2        -1.56252    1.0882      -1.44     0.1716   AR(ar) gei: LAG1
                                                            parameter for whi
ar_l1_2_1        0.244161    0.1783       1.37     0.1910   AR(ar) whi: LAG1
                                                            parameter for gei
ar_l1_2_2        -0.23864    0.4957      -0.48     0.6372   AR(ar) whi: LAG1
                                                            parameter for whi
```

Output 20.3.2. Results for the Restricted Model (Partial Output)

```
      Example of Vector AR(1) Error Process Using Grunfeld's Model
                  With Restricted AR(1) Error Process

                         The MODEL Procedure

                            Model Summary

                    Model Variables           6
                    Parameters                8
                    Equations                 2
                    Number of Statements      6


   Model Variables  gei whi gef gec whf whc
        Parameters  ge_int ge_f ge_c wh_int wh_f wh_c gei_l1(0) whi_l1(0)
         Equations  gei whi
```

```
            Example of Vector AR(1) Error Process Using Grunfeld's Model
                        With Restricted AR(1) Error Process

                                The MODEL Procedure

                       Nonlinear SUR Summary of Residual Errors

                  DF      DF                                            Adj
 Equation      Model   Error         SSE         MSE   R-Square        R-Sq

 gei               4      16     10558.8       659.9     0.7646      0.7204
 whi               4      16      1669.8       104.4     0.7594      0.7142


                       Nonlinear SUR Parameter Estimates

                             Approx                  Approx
Parameter       Estimate    Std Err    t Value    Pr > |t|    Label

ge_int          -30.1239    29.7227      -1.01      0.3259    GE Intercept
ge_f            0.043527     0.0149       2.93      0.0099    GE Lagged Share
                                                              Value Coef
ge_c            0.119206     0.0423       2.82      0.0124    GE Lagged Capital
                                                              Stock Coef
wh_int          3.112671     9.2765       0.34      0.7416    WH Intercept
wh_f            0.053932     0.0154       3.50      0.0029    WH Lagged Share
                                                              Value Coef
wh_c            0.038246     0.0805       0.48      0.6410    WH Lagged Capital
                                                              Stock Coef
gei_l1          0.482397     0.2149       2.24      0.0393    AR(gei) gei lag1
                                                              parameter
whi_l1          0.455711     0.2424       1.88      0.0784    AR(whi) whi lag1
                                                              parameter
```

Example 20.4. MA(1) Estimation

This example estimates parameters for an MA(1) error process for the Grunfeld model, using both the unconditional least-squares and the maximum-likelihood methods. The ARIMA procedure estimates for Westinghouse equation are shown for comparison. The output of the following code is summarized in Output 20.4.1:

```
title1 'Example of MA(1) Error Process Using Grunfeld''s Model';
title2 'MA(1) Error Process Using Unconditional Least Squares';
proc model data=grunfeld model=grunmod;
   %ma(gei,1, m=uls);
   %ma(whi,1, m=uls);
   fit whi gei start=( gei_m1 0.8 -0.8) / startiter=2;
run;
```

Output 20.4.1. PROC MODEL Results Using ULS Estimation

```
           Example of MA(1) Error Process Using Grunfeld's Model
           MA(1) Error Process Using Unconditional Least Squares

                          The MODEL Procedure

              Nonlinear OLS Summary of Residual Errors

                  DF      DF                                              Adj
  Equation     Model   Error        SSE        MSE   R-Square            R-Sq

  whi              4      16     1874.0      117.1     0.7299          0.6793
  resid.whi               16     1295.6    80.9754
  gei              4      16    13835.0      864.7     0.6915          0.6337
  resid.gei               16     7646.2      477.9


                 Nonlinear OLS Parameter Estimates

                             Approx                  Approx
Parameter      Estimate     Std Err    t Value     Pr > |t|    Label

ge_int          -26.839     32.0908      -0.84       0.4153    GE Intercept
ge_f           0.038226      0.0150       2.54       0.0217    GE Lagged Share
                                                               Value Coef
ge_c           0.137099      0.0352       3.90       0.0013    GE Lagged Capital
                                                               Stock Coef
wh_int         3.680835      9.5448       0.39       0.7048    WH Intercept
wh_f           0.049156      0.0172       2.85       0.0115    WH Lagged Share
                                                               Value Coef
wh_c           0.067271      0.0708       0.95       0.3559    WH Lagged Capital
                                                               Stock Coef
gei_m1         -0.87615      0.1614      -5.43       <.0001    MA(gei) gei lag1
                                                               parameter
whi_m1         -0.75001      0.2368      -3.17       0.0060    MA(whi) whi lag1
                                                               parameter
```

The estimation summary from the following PROC ARIMA statements is shown in Output 20.4.2.

```
title2 'PROC ARIMA Using Unconditional Least Squares';

proc arima data=grunfeld;
   identify var=whi cross=(whf whc ) noprint;
   estimate q=1 input=(whf whc) method=uls maxiter=40;
run;
```

Output 20.4.2. PROC ARIMA Results Using ULS Estimation

```
              Example of MA(1) Error Process Using Grunfeld's Model
                   PROC ARIMA Using Unconditional Least Squares

                              The ARIMA Procedure

                      Unconditional Least Squares Estimation

                               Approx Std
Parameter      Estimate         Error     t Value   Pr > |t|    Lag  Variable  Shift

MU              3.68608       9.54425        0.39     0.7044      0  whi           0
MA1,1          -0.75005       0.23704       -3.16     0.0060      1  whi           0
NUM1            0.04914       0.01723        2.85     0.0115      0  whf           0
NUM2            0.06731       0.07077        0.95     0.3557      0  whc           0


                         Constant Estimate       3.686077
                         Variance Estimate       80.97535
                         Std Error Estimate      8.998631
                         AIC                     149.0044
                         SBC                     152.9873
                         Number of Residuals           20
```

The model stored in Example 20.3 is read in using the MODEL= option and the moving average terms are added using the %MA macro.

The MA(1) model using maximum likelihood is estimated using the following:

```
title2 'MA(1) Error Process Using Maximum Likelihood ';
proc model data=grunfeld model=grunmod;
   %ma(gei,1, m=ml);
   %ma(whi,1, m=ml);
   fit whi gei;
run;
```

For comparison, the model is estimated using PROC ARIMA as follows:

```
title2 'PROC ARIMA Using Maximum Likelihood ';
proc arima data=grunfeld;
   identify var=whi cross=(whf whc) noprint;
   estimate q=1 input=(whf whc) method=ml;
run;
```

PROC ARIMA does not estimate systems so only one equation is evaluated.

The estimation results are shown in Output 20.4.3 and Output 20.4.4. The small differences in the parameter values between PROC MODEL and PROC ARIMA can be eliminated by tightening the convergence criteria for both procedures.

Output 20.4.3. PROC MODEL Results Using ML Estimation

Example of MA(1) Error Process Using Grunfeld's Model
MA(1) Error Process Using Maximum Likelihood

The MODEL Procedure

Nonlinear OLS Summary of Residual Errors

Equation	DF Model	DF Error	SSE	MSE	R-Square	Adj R-Sq
whi	4	16	1857.5	116.1	0.7323	0.6821
resid.whi		16	1344.0	84.0012		
gei	4	16	13742.5	858.9	0.6936	0.6361
resid.gei		16	8095.3	506.0		

Nonlinear OLS Parameter Estimates

Parameter	Estimate	Approx Std Err	t Value	Approx Pr > |t|	Label
ge_int	-25.002	34.2933	-0.73	0.4765	GE Intercept
ge_f	0.03712	0.0161	2.30	0.0351	GE Lagged Share Value Coef
ge_c	0.137788	0.0380	3.63	0.0023	GE Lagged Capital Stock Coef
wh_int	2.946761	9.5638	0.31	0.7620	WH Intercept
wh_f	0.050395	0.0174	2.89	0.0106	WH Lagged Share Value Coef
wh_c	0.066531	0.0729	0.91	0.3749	WH Lagged Capital Stock Coef
gei_m1	-0.78516	0.1942	-4.04	0.0009	MA(gei) gei lag1 parameter
whi_m1	-0.69389	0.2540	-2.73	0.0148	MA(whi) whi lag1 parameter

Output 20.4.4. PROC ARIMA Results Using ML Estimation

Example of MA(1) Error Process Using Grunfeld's Model
PROC ARIMA Using Maximum Likelihood

The ARIMA Procedure

Maximum Likelihood Estimation

Parameter	Estimate	Approx Std Error	t Value	Pr > |t|	Lag	Variable	Shift
MU	2.95645	9.20752	0.32	0.7481	0	whi	0
MA1,1	-0.69305	0.25307	-2.74	0.0062	1	whi	0
NUM1	0.05036	0.01686	2.99	0.0028	0	whf	0
NUM2	0.06672	0.06939	0.96	0.3363	0	whc	0

Constant Estimate	2.956449
Variance Estimate	81.29645
Std Error Estimate	9.016455
AIC	148.9113
SBC	152.8942
Number of Residuals	20

Example 20.5. Polynomial Distributed Lags Using %PDL

This example shows the use of the %PDL macro for polynomial distributed lag models. Simulated data is generated so that Y is a linear function of six lags of X, with the lag coefficients following a quadratic polynomial. The model is estimated using a fourth-degree polynomial, both with and without endpoint constraints. The example uses simulated data generated from the following model:

$$y_t = 10 + \sum_{z=0}^{6} f(z) x_{t-z} + \epsilon$$

$$f(z) = -5z^2 + 1.5z$$

The LIST option prints the model statements added by the %PDL macro.

```
/*---------------------------------------------------------------*/
/*  Generate Simulated Data for a Linear Model with a PDL on X  */
/*         y = 10 + x(6,2) + e                                  */
/*         pdl(x) = -5.*(lg)**2 + 1.5*(lg) + 0.                 */
/*---------------------------------------------------------------*/
data pdl;
   pdl2=-5.; pdl1=1.5; pdl0=0;
   array zz(i) z0-z6;
   do i=1 to 7;
      z=i-1;
      zz=pdl2*z**2 + pdl1*z + pdl0;
      end;
   do n=-11 to 30;
      x  =10*ranuni(1234567)-5;
      pdl=z0*x + z1*xl1 + z2*xl2 + z3*xl3 + z4*xl4 + z5*xl5 + z6*xl6;
      e  =10*rannor(123);
      y  =10+pdl+e;
      if n>=1 then output;
      xl6=xl5; xl5=xl4; xl4=xl3; xl3=xl2; xl2=xl1; xl1=x;
      end;
run;

title1 'Polynomial Distributed Lag Example';

title3 'Estimation of PDL(6,4) Model-- No Endpoint Restrictions';
proc model data=pdl;
   parms int;                   /* declare the intercept parameter */
   %pdl( xpdl, 6, 4 )           /* declare the lag distribution */
   y = int + %pdl( xpdl, x );   /* define the model equation */
   fit y / list;                /* estimate the parameters */
run;
```

Output 20.5.1. PROC MODEL Listing of Generated Program

```
                    Polynomial Distributed Lag Example

          Estimation of PDL(6,4) Model-- No Endpoint Restrictions

                           The MODEL Procedure

                    Listing of Compiled Program Code
Stmt     Line:Col         Statement as Parsed

   1     25242:14         XPDL_L0 = XPDL_0;
   2     25254:14         XPDL_L1 = XPDL_0 + XPDL_1 +
                          XPDL_2 + XPDL_3 + XPDL_4;
   3     25283:14         XPDL_L2 = XPDL_0 + XPDL_1 *
                          2 + XPDL_2 * 2 ** 2 + XPDL_3
                          * 2 ** 3 + XPDL_4 * 2 ** 4;
   4     25331:14         XPDL_L3 = XPDL_0 + XPDL_1 *
                          3 + XPDL_2 * 3 ** 2 + XPDL_3
                          * 3 ** 3 + XPDL_4 * 3 ** 4;
   5     25379:14         XPDL_L4 = XPDL_0 + XPDL_1 *
                          4 + XPDL_2 * 4 ** 2 + XPDL_3
                          * 4 ** 3 + XPDL_4 * 4 ** 4;
   6     25427:14         XPDL_L5 = XPDL_0 + XPDL_1 *
                          5 + XPDL_2 * 5 ** 2 + XPDL_3
                          * 5 ** 3 + XPDL_4 * 5 ** 4;
   7     25475:14         XPDL_L6 = XPDL_0 + XPDL_1 *
                          6 + XPDL_2 * 6 ** 2 + XPDL_3
                          * 6 ** 3 + XPDL_4 * 6 ** 4;
   8     25121:204        PRED.y = int + XPDL_L0 * x + XPDL_L1 *
                          LAG1( x ) + XPDL_L2 * LAG2( x ) +
                          XPDL_L3 * LAG3( x ) + XPDL_L4
                          * LAG4( x ) + XPDL_L5 * LAG5(
                          x ) + XPDL_L6 * LAG6( x );
   8     25121:204        RESID.y = PRED.y - ACTUAL.y;
   8     25121:204        ERROR.y = PRED.y - y;
   9     25218:15         ESTIMATE XPDL_L0, XPDL_L1, XPDL_L2,
                          XPDL_L3, XPDL_L4, XPDL_L5, XPDL_L6;
  10     25218:15         _est0 = XPDL_L0;
  11     25221:15         _est1 = XPDL_L1;
  12     25224:15         _est2 = XPDL_L2;
  13     25227:15         _est3 = XPDL_L3;
  14     25230:15         _est4 = XPDL_L4;
  15     25233:15         _est5 = XPDL_L5;
  16     25238:14         _est6 = XPDL_L6;
```

Output 20.5.2. PROC MODEL Results Specifying No Endpoint Restrictions

```
                        Polynomial Distributed Lag Example

              Estimation of PDL(6,4) Model-- No Endpoint Restrictions

                              The MODEL Procedure

                     Nonlinear OLS Summary of Residual Errors

                 DF      DF                                                   Adj
 Equation     Model   Error         SSE         MSE  Root MSE  R-Square      R-Sq

 y                6      18      2070.8       115.0   10.7259    0.9998    0.9998


                        Nonlinear OLS Parameter Estimates

                                Approx                   Approx
Parameter       Estimate       Std Err    t Value     Pr > |t|    Label

int             9.621969        2.3238       4.14       0.0006
XPDL_0          0.084374        0.7587       0.11       0.9127    PDL(XPDL,6,4)
                                                                  parameter for (L)**0
XPDL_1          0.749956        2.0936       0.36       0.7244    PDL(XPDL,6,4)
                                                                  parameter for (L)**1
XPDL_2            -4.196        1.6215      -2.59       0.0186    PDL(XPDL,6,4)
                                                                  parameter for (L)**2
XPDL_3          -0.21489        0.4253      -0.51       0.6195    PDL(XPDL,6,4)
                                                                  parameter for (L)**3
XPDL_4          0.016133        0.0353       0.46       0.6528    PDL(XPDL,6,4)
                                                                  parameter for (L)**4
```

The LIST output for the model without endpoint restrictions is shown in Output 20.5.1 and Output 20.5.2. The first seven statements in the generated program are the polynomial expressions for lag parameters XPDL_L0 through XPDL_L6. The estimated parameters are INT, XPDL_0, XPDL_1, XPDL_2, XPDL_3, and XPDL_4.

Portions of the output produced by the following PDL model with endpoints of the model restricted to 0 are presented in Output 20.5.3 and Output 20.5.4.

```
title3 'Estimation of PDL(6,4) Model-- Both Endpoint Restrictions';
proc model data=pdl ;
   parms int;                   /* declare the intercept parameter */
   %pdl( xpdl, 6, 4, r=both )   /* declare the lag distribution */
   y = int + %pdl( xpdl, x );   /* define the model equation */
   fit y /list;                 /* estimate the parameters */
run;
```

Output 20.5.3. PROC MODEL Results Specifying Both Endpoint Restrictions

```
                      Polynomial Distributed Lag Example

          Estimation of PDL(6,4) Model-- Both Endpoint Restrictions

                           The MODEL Procedure

                 Nonlinear OLS Summary of Residual Errors

                   DF      DF                                                Adj
 Equation       Model   Error        SSE        MSE  Root MSE  R-Square    R-Sq

 y                  4      20     449868    22493.4     150.0    0.9596  0.9535


                     Nonlinear OLS Parameter Estimates

                                 Approx                  Approx
Parameter       Estimate        Std Err   t Value     Pr > |t|   Label

int             17.08581        32.4032      0.53       0.6038
XPDL_2          13.88433         5.4361      2.55       0.0189   PDL(XPDL,6,4)
                                                                 parameter for (L)**2
XPDL_3           -9.3535         1.7602     -5.31       <.0001   PDL(XPDL,6,4)
                                                                 parameter for (L)**3
XPDL_4          1.032421         0.1471      7.02       <.0001   PDL(XPDL,6,4)
                                                                 parameter for (L)**4
```

Note that XPDL_0 and XPDL_1 are not shown in the estimate summary. They were used to satisfy the endpoint restrictions analytically by the generated %PDL macro code. Their values can be determined by back substitution.

To estimate the PDL model with one or more of the polynomial terms dropped, specify the largest degree of the polynomial desired with the %PDL macro and use the DROP= option on the FIT statement to remove the unwanted terms. The dropped parameters should be set to 0. The following PROC MODEL code demonstrates estimation with a PDL of degree 2 without the 0th order term.

```
title3 'Estimation of PDL(6,2) Model-- With XPDL_0 Dropped';
proc model data=pdl list;
   parms int;                      /* declare the intercept parameter */
   %pdl( xpdl, 6, 2 )              /* declare the lag distribution */
   y = int + %pdl( xpdl, x );      /* define the model equation */
   xpdl_0 =0;
   fit y drop=xpdl_0;              /* estimate the parameters */
run;
```

The results from this estimation are shown in Output 20.5.4.

Output 20.5.4. PROC MODEL Results Specifying %PDL(XPDL, 6, 2)

```
                    Polynomial Distributed Lag Example

            Estimation of PDL(6,2) Model-- With XPDL_0 Dropped

                          The MODEL Procedure

               Nonlinear OLS Summary of Residual Errors

                 DF      DF                                                  Adj
 Equation      Model   Error       SSE        MSE   Root MSE  R-Square      R-Sq

 y                 3      21    2114.1      100.7    10.0335    0.9998    0.9998


                    Nonlinear OLS Parameter Estimates

                              Approx                  Approx
Parameter      Estimate      Std Err    t Value     Pr > |t|   Label

int            9.536382       2.1685       4.40       0.0003
XPDL_1         1.883315       0.3159       5.96       <.0001   PDL(XPDL,6,2)
                                                               parameter for (L)**1
XPDL_2         -5.08827       0.0656     -77.56       <.0001   PDL(XPDL,6,2)
                                                               parameter for (L)**2
```

Example 20.6. General-Form Equations

Data for this example are generated. General-form equations are estimated and forecast using PROC MODEL. The system is a basic supply-demand model. Portions of the output from the following code is shown in Output 20.6.1 through Output 20.6.4.

```
title1 "General Form Equations for Supply-Demand Model";

proc model;
   var price quantity income unitcost;
   parms d0-d2 s0-s2;
   eq.demand=d0+d1*price+d2*income-quantity;
   eq.supply=s0+s1*price+s2*unitcost-quantity;

/* estimate the model parameters */
   fit supply demand / data=history outest=est n2sls;
   instruments income unitcost year;
run;

/* produce forecasts for income and unitcost assumptions */
   solve price quantity / data=assume out=pq;
run;

/* produce goal-seeking solutions for
     income and quantity assumptions*/
   solve price unitcost / data=goal out=pc;
run;

title2 "Parameter Estimates for the System";
proc print data=est;
run;

title2 "Price Quantity Solution";
```

```
proc print data=pq;
run;

title2 "Price Unitcost Solution";
proc print data=pc;
run;
```

Three data sets were used in this example. The first data set, HISTORY, was used to estimate the parameters of the model. The ASSUME data set was used to produce a forecast of PRICE and QUANTITY. Notice that the ASSUME data set does not have to contain the variables PRICE and QUANTITY.

```
data history;
   input year income unitcost price quantity;
   datalines;
1976     2221.87    3.31220    0.17903    266.714
1977     2254.77    3.61647    0.06757    276.049
1978     2285.16    2.21601    0.82916    285.858
1979     2319.37    3.28257    0.33202    295.034
1980     2369.38    2.84494    0.63564    310.773
1981     2395.26    2.94154    0.62011    319.185
1982     2419.52    2.65301    0.80753    325.970
1983     2475.09    2.41686    1.01017    342.470
1984     2495.09    3.44096    0.52025    348.321
1985     2536.72    2.30601    1.15053    360.750
;

data assume;
   input year income unitcost;
   datalines;
1986     2571.87    2.31220
1987     2609.12    2.45633
1988     2639.77    2.51647
1989     2667.77    1.65617
1990     2705.16    1.01601
;
```

The output produced by the first SOLVE statement is shown in Output 20.6.3.

The third data set, GOAL, is used in a forecast of PRICE and UNITCOST as a function of INCOME and QUANTITY.

```
data goal;
   input year income quantity;
   datalines;
1986     2571.87      371.4
1987     2721.08      416.5
1988     3327.05      597.3
1989     3885.85      764.1
1990     3650.98      694.3
;
```

The output from the final SOLVE statement is shown in Output 20.6.4.

Output 20.6.1. Printed Output from the FIT Statement

```
                 General Form Equations for Supply-Demand Model

                              The MODEL Procedure

                         The 2 Equations to Estimate

                    supply =   F(s0(1), s1(price), s2(unitcost))
                    demand =   F(d0(1), d1(price), d2(income))
                 Instruments   1 income unitcost year
```

```
                 General Form Equations for Supply-Demand Model

                              The MODEL Procedure

                  Nonlinear 2SLS Summary of Residual Errors

                    DF      DF                                                  Adj
Equation         Model   Error        SSE        MSE  Root MSE  R-Square       R-Sq

supply               3       7     3.3240     0.4749    0.6891
demand               3       7     1.0829     0.1547    0.3933


                       Nonlinear 2SLS Parameter Estimates

                                             Approx                    Approx
        Parameter         Estimate          Std Err    t Value       Pr > |t|

        d0                -395.887           4.1841     -94.62         <.0001
        d1                0.717328           0.5673       1.26         0.2466
        d2                0.298061          0.00187     159.65         <.0001
        s0                 -107.62           4.1780     -25.76         <.0001
        s1                201.5711           1.5977     126.16         <.0001
        s2                102.2116           1.1217      91.12         <.0001
```

Output 20.6.2. Listing of OUTEST= Data Set Created in the FIT Statement

```
                 General Form Equations for Supply-Demand Model
                        Parameter Estimates for the System

                _
                S
                T     _
   _  _         A     N
   N  T         T     U
   A  Y         U     S
 O M  P         S     E
 b E  E         _     D      d        d        d        s        s        s
 s _  _         _     _      0        1        2        0        1        2

 1   2SLS 0 Converged 10 -395.887 0.71733 0.29806 -107.620 201.571 102.212
```

Output 20.6.3. Listing of OUT= Data Set Created in the First SOLVE Statement

General Form Equations for Supply-Demand Model
Price Quantity Solution

Obs	_TYPE_	_MODE_	_ERRORS_	price	quantity	income	unitcost	year
1	PREDICT	SIMULATE	0	1.20473	371.552	2571.87	2.31220	1986
2	PREDICT	SIMULATE	0	1.18666	382.642	2609.12	2.45633	1987
3	PREDICT	SIMULATE	0	1.20154	391.788	2639.77	2.51647	1988
4	PREDICT	SIMULATE	0	1.68089	400.478	2667.77	1.65617	1989
5	PREDICT	SIMULATE	0	2.06214	411.896	2705.16	1.01601	1990

Output 20.6.4. Listing of OUT= Data Set Created in the Second SOLVE Statement

General Form Equations for Supply-Demand Model
Price Unitcost Solution

Obs	_TYPE_	_MODE_	_ERRORS_	price	quantity	income	unitcost	year
1	PREDICT	SIMULATE	0	0.99284	371.4	2571.87	2.72857	1986
2	PREDICT	SIMULATE	0	1.86594	416.5	2721.08	1.44798	1987
3	PREDICT	SIMULATE	0	2.12230	597.3	3327.05	2.71130	1988
4	PREDICT	SIMULATE	0	2.46166	764.1	3885.85	3.67395	1989
5	PREDICT	SIMULATE	0	2.74831	694.3	3650.98	2.42576	1990

Example 20.7. Spring and Damper Continuous System

This model simulates the mechanical behavior of a spring and damper system shown in Figure 20.84.

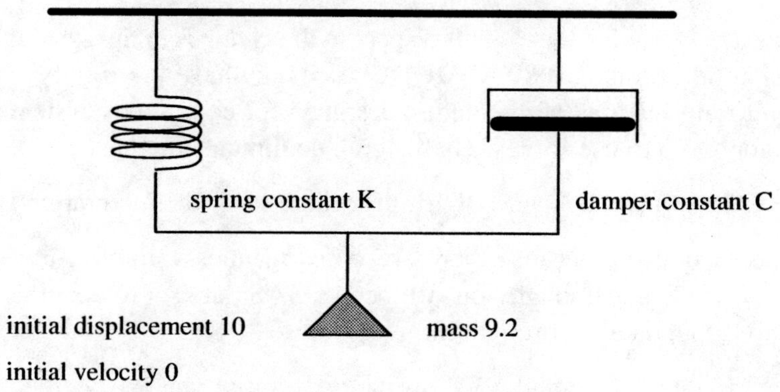

Figure 20.84. Spring and Damper System Model

A mass is hung from a spring with spring constant K. The motion is slowed by a damper with damper constant C. The damping force is proportional to the velocity, while the spring force is proportional to the displacement.

This is actually a continuous system; however, the behavior can be approximated by a discrete time model. We approximate the differential equation

$$\frac{\partial\, disp}{\partial\, time} = velocity$$

with the difference equation

$$\frac{\Delta\, disp}{\Delta\, time} = velocity$$

This is rewritten

$$\frac{disp - \mathrm{LAG(disp)}}{dt} = velocity$$

where *dt* is the time step used. In PROC MODEL, this is expressed with the program statement

```
disp = lag(disp) + vel * dt;
```

or

```
dert.disp = vel;
```

The first statement is simply a computing formula for Euler's approximation for the integral

$$disp = \int velocity\ dt$$

If the time step is small enough with respect to the changes in the system, the approximation is good. Although PROC MODEL does not have the variable step-size and error-monitoring features of simulators designed for continuous systems, the procedure is a good tool to use for less challenging continuous models.

The second form instructs the MODEL procedure to do the integration for you.

This model is unusual because there are no exogenous variables, and endogenous data are not needed. Although you still need a SAS data set to count the simulation periods, no actual data are brought in.

Since the variables DISP and VEL are lagged, initial values specified in the VAR statement determine the starting state of the system. The mass, time step, spring constant, and damper constant are declared and initialized by a CONTROL statement.

```
title1 'Simulation of Spring-Mass-Damper System';

/*- Generate some obs. to drive the simulation time periods ---*/
data one;
   do n=1 to 100;
      output;
   end;
run;
```

```
proc model data=one;
   var      force -200  disp  10  vel  0  accel -20  time 0;
   control  mass   9.2  c    1.5  dt  .1  k        20;
   force = -k * disp -c * vel;
   disp  = lag(disp) + vel * dt;
   vel   = lag(vel) + accel * dt;
   accel = force / mass;
   time  = lag(time) + dt;
```

The displacement scale is zeroed at the point where the force of gravity is offset, so the acceleration of the gravity constant is omitted from the force equation. The control variable C and K represent the damper and the spring constants respectively.

The model is simulated three times, and the simulation results are written to output data sets. The first run uses the original initial conditions specified in the VAR statement. In the second run, the initial displacement is doubled; the results show that the period of the motion is unaffected by the amplitude. In the third run, the DERT. syntax is used to do the integration. Notice that the path of the displacement is close to the old path, indicating that the original time step is short enough to yield an accurate solution. These simulations are performed by the following statements:

```
/*- Simulate the model for the base case -------------------*/
   control run '1';
   solve / out=a;
run;

/*- Simulate the model with twice the initial displacement -*/
   control run '2';
   var disp 20;
   solve / out=c;
run;

/*- Simulate the model with dert. syntax -------------*/
data two;
          do time = 0 to 10 by .2; output;end;
  run;
proc model data=two;
   var      force -200  disp  10  vel  0  accel -20  time 0;
   control  mass   9.2  c    1.5  dt  .1  k        20;
   control run '3' ;
   force = -k * disp -c * vel;
   dert.disp  = vel ;
   dert.vel   = accel;
   accel = force / mass;
   solve / out=b ;
       id time ;
run;
```

The output SAS data sets containing the solution results are merged and the displacement time paths for the three simulations are plotted. The three runs are identified on the plot as 1, 2, and 3. The following code produces Output 20.7.1 through Output 20.7.2.

```
/*- Plot the results ---------------------------------------*/
data p;
   set a b c;
run;

title2 'Overlay Plot of All Three Simulations';
proc gplot data=p;
   plot disp*time=run;
run;
```

Output 20.7.1. Printed Output Produced by PROC MODEL SOLVE Statements

```
                    Simulation of Spring-Mass-Damper System

                              The MODEL Procedure

                                 Model Summary

                           Model Variables          5
                           Control Variables        5
                           Equations                5
                           Number of Statements     5
                           Program Lag Length       1


      Model Variables  force(-200) disp(10) vel(0) accel(-20) time(0)
    Control Variables  mass(9.2) c(1.5) dt(0.1) k(20) run(1)
            Equations  force disp vel accel time
```

```
                 Simulation of Spring-Mass-Damper System

                           The MODEL Procedure
                     Dynamic Simultaneous Simulation

                            Data Set Options

                             DATA=     ONE
                             OUT=      A


                            Solution Summary

                   Variables Solved                 5
                   Simulation Lag Length            1
                   Solution Method             NEWTON
                   CONVERGE=                     1E-8
                   Maximum CC                8.68E-15
                   Maximum Iterations               1
                   Total Iterations                99
                   Average Iterations               1


                         Observations Processed

                            Read      100
                            Lagged      1
                            Solved     99
                            First       2
                            Last      100


          Variables Solved For     force disp vel accel time
```

```
                Simulation of Spring-Mass-Damper System

                          The MODEL Procedure
                    Dynamic Simultaneous Simulation

                           Data Set Options

                           DATA=    ONE
                           OUT=     B


                           Solution Summary

                  Variables Solved                5
                  Simulation Lag Length           1
                  Solution Method            NEWTON
                  CONVERGE=                    1E-8
                  Maximum CC               1.32E-15
                  Maximum Iterations              1
                  Total Iterations               99
                  Average Iterations              1


                        Observations Processed

                            Read      100
                            Lagged      1
                            Solved     99
                            First       2
                            Last      100


          Variables Solved For    force disp vel accel time
```

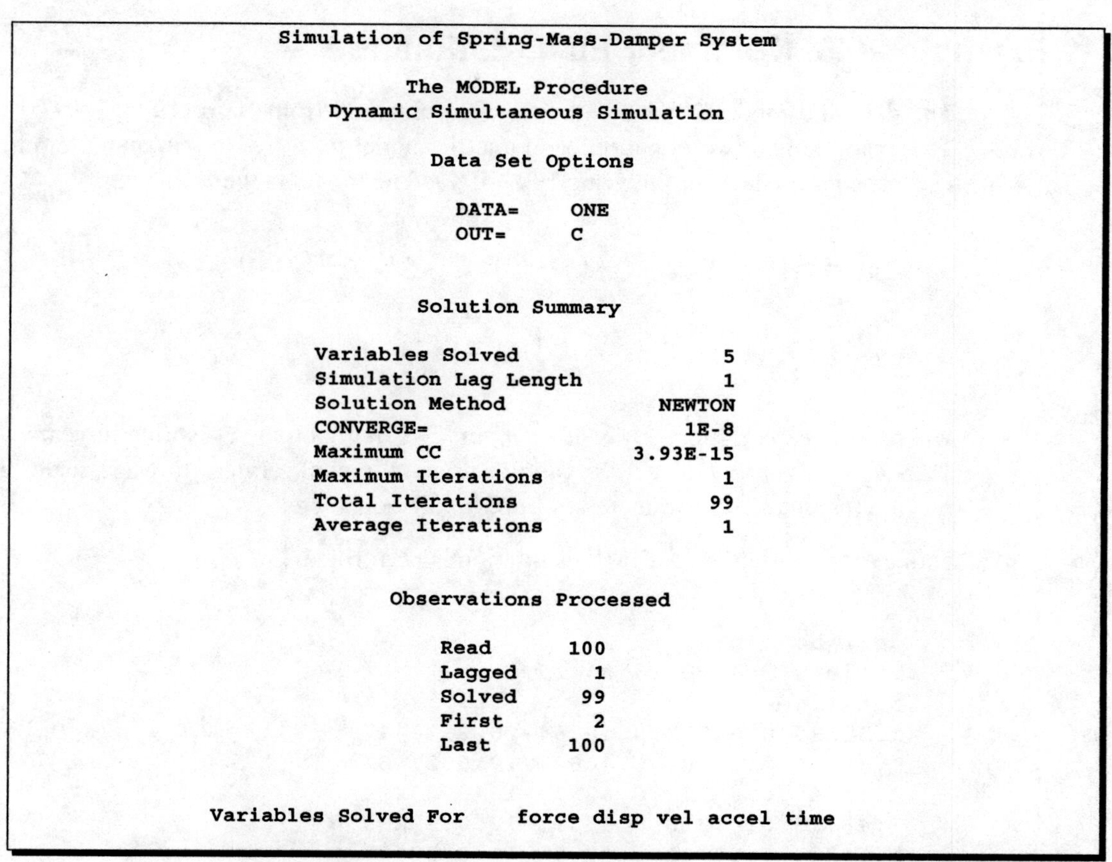

```
                Simulation of Spring-Mass-Damper System

                         The MODEL Procedure
                  Dynamic Simultaneous Simulation

                          Data Set Options

                           DATA=     ONE
                           OUT=      C


                          Solution Summary

                 Variables Solved                  5
                 Simulation Lag Length             1
                 Solution Method              NEWTON
                 CONVERGE=                      1E-8
                 Maximum CC                 3.93E-15
                 Maximum Iterations                1
                 Total Iterations                 99
                 Average Iterations                1


                       Observations Processed

                          Read       100
                          Lagged       1
                          Solved      99
                          First        2
                          Last       100


     Variables Solved For    force disp vel accel time
```

Output 20.7.2. Overlay Plot of all Three Simulations

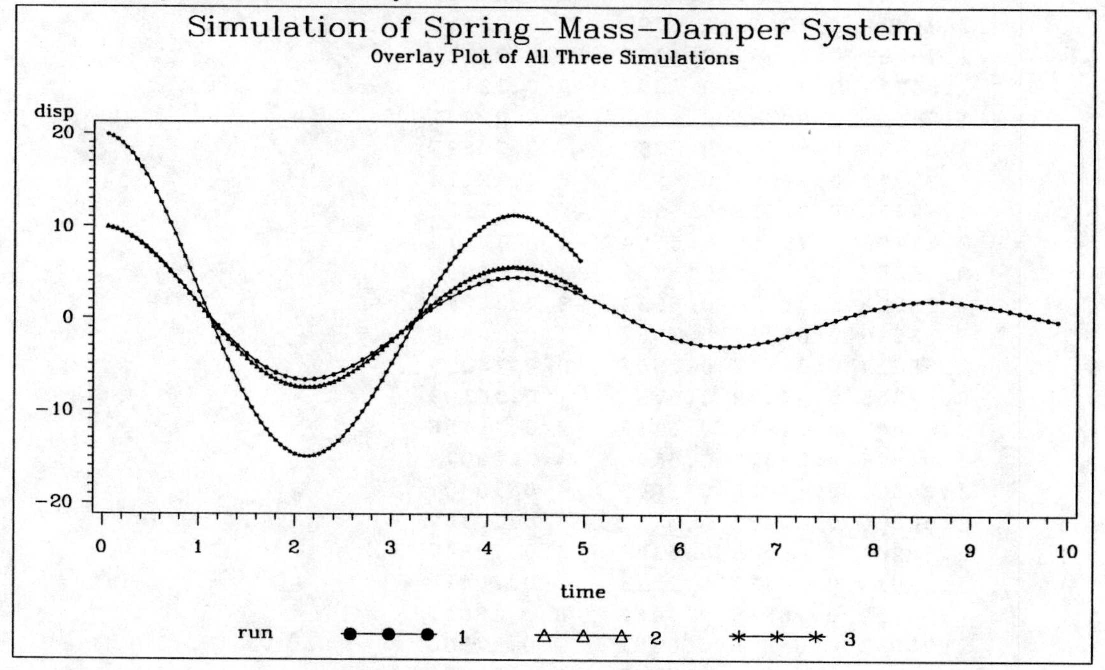

Example 20.8. Nonlinear FIML Estimation

The data and model for this example were obtained from Bard (1974, p.133-138). The example is a two-equation econometric model used by Bodkin and Klein to fit U.S production data for the years 1909-1949. The model is the following:

$$g_1 = c_1 10^{c_2 z_4}(c_5 z_1^{-c_4} + (1 - c_5) z_2^{-c_4})^{-c_3/c_4} - z_3 = 0$$

$$g_2 = [c_5/(1 - c_5)](z_1/z_2)^{(-1-c_4)} - z_5 = 0$$

where z_1 is capital input, z_2 is labor input, z_3 is real output, z_4 is time in years with 1929 as year zero, and z_5 is the ratio of price of capital services to wage scale. The c_i's are the unknown parameters. z_1 and z_2 are considered

endogenous variables. A FIML estimation is performed.

```
data bodkin;
   input z1 z2 z3 z4 z5;
datalines;
1.33135 0.64629 0.4026 -20 0.24447
1.39235 0.66302 0.4084 -19 0.23454
1.41640 0.65272 0.4223 -18 0.23206
1.48773 0.67318 0.4389 -17 0.22291
1.51015 0.67720 0.4605 -16 0.22487
1.43385 0.65175 0.4445 -15 0.21879
1.48188 0.65570 0.4387 -14 0.23203
1.67115 0.71417 0.4999 -13 0.23828
1.71327 0.77524 0.5264 -12 0.26571
1.76412 0.79465 0.5793 -11 0.23410
1.76869 0.71607 0.5492 -10 0.22181
1.80776 0.70068 0.5052  -9 0.18157
1.54947 0.60764 0.4679  -8 0.22931
1.66933 0.67041 0.5283  -7 0.20595
1.93377 0.74091 0.5994  -6 0.19472
1.95460 0.71336 0.5964  -5 0.17981
2.11198 0.75159 0.6554  -4 0.18010
2.26266 0.78838 0.6851  -3 0.16933
2.33228 0.79600 0.6933  -2 0.16279
2.43980 0.80788 0.7061  -1 0.16906
2.58714 0.84547 0.7567   0 0.16239
2.54865 0.77232 0.6796   1 0.16103
2.26042 0.67880 0.6136   2 0.14456
1.91974 0.58529 0.5145   3 0.20079
1.80000 0.58065 0.5046   4 0.18307
1.86020 0.62007 0.5711   5 0.18352
1.88201 0.65575 0.6184   6 0.18847
1.97018 0.72433 0.7113   7 0.20415
2.08232 0.76838 0.7461   8 0.18847
1.94062 0.69806 0.6981   9 0.17800
1.98646 0.74679 0.7722  10 0.19979
2.07987 0.79083 0.8557  11 0.21115
```

```
2.28232 0.88462 0.9925  12 0.23453
2.52779 0.95750 1.0877  13 0.20937
2.62747 1.00285 1.1834  14 0.19843
2.61235 0.99329 1.2565  15 0.18898
2.52320 0.94857 1.2293  16 0.17203
2.44632 0.97853 1.1889  17 0.18140
2.56478 1.02591 1.2249  18 0.19431
2.64588 1.03760 1.2669  19 0.19492
2.69105 0.99669 1.2708  20 0.17912
;

proc model data=bodkin;
   parms c1-c5;
   endogenous z1 z2;
   exogenous z3 z4 z5;

   eq.g1 = c1 * 10 **(c2 * z4) * (c5*z1**(-c4)+
           (1-c5)*z2**(-c4))**(-c3/c4) - z3;
   eq.g2 = (c5/(1-c5))*(z1/z2)**(-1-c4) -z5;

   fit g1 g2 / fiml ;
run;
```

When FIML estimation is selected, the log likelihood of the system is output as the objective value. The results of the estimation are show in Output 20.8.1.

Output 20.8.1. FIML Estimation Results for U.S. Production Data

The MODEL Procedure

Nonlinear FIML Summary of Residual Errors

Equation	DF Model	DF Error	SSE	MSE	Root MSE	R-Square	Adj R-Sq
g1	4	37	0.0529	0.00143	0.0378		
g2	1	40	0.0173	0.000431	0.0208		

Nonlinear FIML Parameter Estimates

Parameter	Estimate	Approx Std Err	t Value	Approx Pr > |t|
c1	0.58395	0.0218	26.76	<.0001
c2	0.005877	0.000673	8.74	<.0001
c3	1.3636	0.1148	11.87	<.0001
c4	0.473688	0.2699	1.75	0.0873
c5	0.446748	0.0596	7.49	<.0001

Number of Observations	
Used	41
Missing	0

Statistics for System	
Log Likelihood	110.7773

Example 20.9. Circuit Estimation

Consider the nonlinear circuit shown in Figure 20.85.

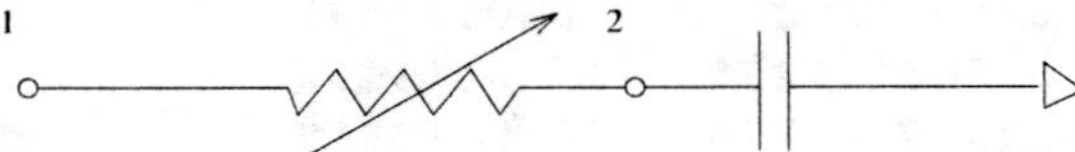

Figure 20.85. Nonlinear Resistor Capacitor Circuit

The theory of electric circuits is governed by Kirchhoff's laws: the sum of the currents flowing to a node is zero, and the net voltage drop around a closed loop is zero. In addition to Kirchhoff's laws, there are relationships between the current I through each element and the voltage drop V across the elements. For the circuit in Figure 20.85, the relationships are

$$C\frac{dV}{dt} = I$$

for the capacitor and

$$V = (R_1 + R_2(1 - \exp(-V)))I$$

for the nonlinear resistor. The following differential equation describes the current at node 2 as a function of time and voltage for this circuit:

label dvdt

$$C\frac{dV_2}{dt} - \frac{V_1 - V_2}{R_1 + R_2(1 - \exp(-V))} = 0$$

This equation can be written in the form

$$\frac{dV_2}{dt} = \frac{V_1 - V_2}{(R_1 + R_2(1 - \exp(-V)))C}$$

Consider the following data.

```
data circ;
   input v2 v1 time@@;
   datalines;
-0.00007 0.0 0.0000000001 0.00912 0.5 0.0000000002
 0.03091 1.0 0.0000000003 0.06419 1.5 0.0000000004
 0.11019 2.0 0.0000000005 0.16398 2.5 0.0000000006
 0.23048 3.0 0.0000000007 0.30529 3.5 0.0000000008
 0.39394 4.0 0.0000000009 0.49121 4.5 0.0000000010
 0.59476 5.0 0.0000000011 0.70285 5.0 0.0000000012
```

```
0.81315 5.0 0.0000000013 0.90929 5.0 0.0000000014
1.01412 5.0 0.0000000015 1.11386 5.0 0.0000000016
1.21106 5.0 0.0000000017 1.30237 5.0 0.0000000018
1.40461 5.0 0.0000000019 1.48624 5.0 0.0000000020
1.57894 5.0 0.0000000021 1.66471 5.0 0.0000000022
;
```

You can estimate the parameters in the previous equation by using the following SAS statements:

```
proc model data=circ mintimestep=1.0e-23;
   parm R2 2000  R1 4000 C 5.0e-13;
   dert.v2 = (v1-v2)/((r1 + r2*(1-exp( -(v1-v2)))) * C);
   fit v2;
run;
```

The results of the estimation are shown in Output 20.9.1.

Output 20.9.1. Circuit Estimation

The MODEL Procedure

Nonlinear OLS Parameter Estimates

Parameter	Estimate	Approx Std Err	t Value	Approx Pr > |t|
R2	3002.465	1556.5	1.93	0.0688
R1	4984.848	1504.9	3.31	0.0037
C	5E-13	1.01E-22	4.941E9	<.0001

Example 20.10. Systems of Differential Equations

The following is a simplified reaction scheme for the competitive inhibitors with recombinant human renin (Morelock et al. 1995).

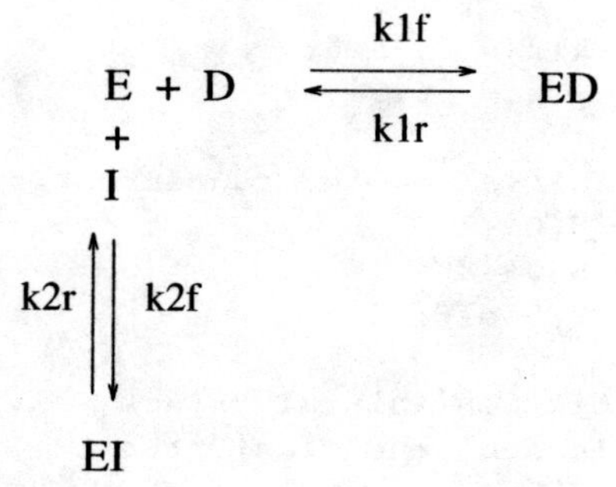

E + D ⇄ ED (k1f forward, k1r reverse)
+
I
⇅ (k2f forward, k2r reverse)
EI

Figure 20.86. Competitive Inhibition of Recombinant Human Renin

In Figure 20.86, *E*= enzyme, *D*= probe, and *I*= inhibitor.

The differential equations describing this reaction scheme are

$$\frac{dD}{dt} = k1r{*}ED - k1f{*}E{*}D$$

$$\frac{dED}{dt} = k1f{*}E{*}D - k1r{*}ED$$

$$\frac{dE}{dt} = k1r{*}ED - k1f{*}E{*}D + k2r{*}EI - k2f{*}E{*}I$$

$$\frac{dEI}{dt} = k2f{*}E{*}I - k2r{*}EI$$

$$\frac{dI}{dt} = k2r{*}EI - k2f{*}E{*}I$$

For this system, the initial values for the concentrations are derived from equilibrium considerations (as a function of parameters) or are provided as known values.

The experiment used to collect the data was carried out in two ways; pre-incubation (type='disassoc') and no pre-incubation (type='assoc'). The data also contain repeated measurements. The data contain values for fluorescence F, which is a function of concentration. Since there are no direct data for the concentrations, all the differential equations are simulated dynamically.

The SAS statements used to fit this model are

```
proc model data=fit;

   parameters qf   = 2.1e8
              qb   = 4.0e9
              k2f  = 1.8e5
              k2r  = 2.1e-3
              l    = 0;

              k1f  = 6.85e6;
              k1r  = 3.43e-4;

      /* Initial values for concentrations */
   control dt 5.0e-7
           et 5.0e-8
           it 8.05e-6;

      /* Association initial values --------------*/
   if type = 'assoc' and time=0 then
      do;
         ed = 0;
            /* solve quadratic equation ----------*/
         a = 1;
         b = -(&it+&et+(k2r/k2f));
         c = &it*&et;
         ei = (-b-(((b**2)-(4*a*c))**.5))/(2*a);
```

```
         d = &dt-ed;
         i = &it-ei;
         e = &et-ed-ei;
      end;

      /* Disassociation initial values ----------*/
   if type = 'disassoc' and time=0 then
      do;
         ei = 0;
         a = 1;
         b = -(&dt+&et+(&k1r/&k1f));
         c = &dt*&et;
         ed = (-b-(((b**2)-(4*a*c))**.5))/(2*a);
         d = &dt-ed;
         i = &it-ei;
         e = &et-ed-ei;
      end;

   if time ne 0 then
      do;
         dert.d = k1r* ed  - k1f *e *d;

         dert.ed = k1f* e *d - k1r*ed;

         dert.e = k1r* ed - k1f* e * d  + k2r * ei - k2f * e *i;

         dert.ei = k2f* e *i - k2r * ei;

         dert.i = k2r * ei - k2f* e *i;

      end;

      /* L - offset between curves  */
   if type = 'disassoc' then
           F = (qf*(d-ed)) + (qb*ed) -L;
   else
           F = (qf*(d-ed)) + (qb*ed);

   Fit F / method=marquardt;
run;
```

This estimation requires the repeated simulation of a system of 42 differential equations (5 base differential equations and 36 differential equations to compute the partials with respect to the parameters).

The results of the estimation are shown in Output 20.10.1.

Output 20.10.1. Kinetics Estimation

```
                              The MODEL Procedure

                    Nonlinear OLS Summary of Residual Errors

                    DF      DF                                                   Adj
Equation         Model   Error        SSE        MSE   Root MSE  R-Square       R-Sq

f                    5     797     2525.0     3.1681     1.7799    0.9980     0.9980


                         Nonlinear OLS Parameter Estimates

                                             Approx                      Approx
           Parameter          Estimate      Std Err     t Value      Pr > |t|

           qf                 2.0413E8       681443      299.55        <.0001
           qb                 4.2263E9      9133179      462.74        <.0001
           k2f                 6451229       867011        7.44        <.0001
           k2r                0.007808      0.00103        7.55        <.0001
           l                  -5.76981       0.4138      -13.94        <.0001
```

Example 20.11. Monte Carlo Simulation

This example illustrates how the form of the error in a ODE model affects the results from a static and dynamic estimation. The differential equation studied is

$$\frac{dy}{dt} = a - ay$$

The analytical solution to this differential equation is

$$y = 1 - \exp(-\text{at})$$

The first data set contains errors that are strictly additive and independent. The data for this estimation are generated by the following DATA step:

```
data drive1;
   a = 0.5;
   do iter=1 to 100;
      do time = 0 to 50;
         y = 1 - exp(-a*time) + 0.1 *rannor(123);
         output;
      end;
   end;
```

The second data set contains errors that are cumulative in form.

```
data drive2;
   a = 0.5;
   yp = 1.0 + 0.01 *rannor(123);
   do iter=1 to 100;
```

```
        do time = 0 to 50;
           y = 1 - exp(-a)*(1 - yp);
           yp = y + 0.01 *rannor(123);
           output;
        end;
     end;
```

The following statements perform the 100 static estimations for each data set:

```
proc model data=drive1 noprint;
   parm a 0.5;
   dert.y = a - a * y;
   fit y / outest=est;
   by iter;
run;
```

Similar code is used to produce 100 dynamic estimations with a fixed and an unknown initial value. The first value in the data set is used to simulate an error in the initial value. The following PROC UNIVARIATE code processes the estimations:

```
proc univariate data=est noprint;
   var a;
   output out=monte mean=mean p5=p5 p95=p95;
run;

proc print data=monte; run;
```

The results of these estimations are summarized in Table 20.5.

Table 20.5. Monte Carlo Summary, A=0.5

Estimation	Additive Error			Cumulative Error		
Type	mean	p95	p5	mean	p95	p5
static	0.77885	1.03524	0.54733	0.57863	1.16112	0.31334
dynamic fixed	0.48785	0.63273	0.37644	3.8546E24	8.88E10	-51.9249
dynamic unknown	0.48518	0.62452	0.36754	641704.51	1940.42	-25.6054

For this example model, it is evident that the static estimation is the least sensitive to misspecification.

Example 20.12. Cauchy Distribution Estimation

In this example a nonlinear model is estimated using the Cauchy distribution. Then a simulation is done for one observation in the data.

The following DATA step creates the data for the model.

```
   /* Generate a Cauchy distributed Y */
data c;
   format date monyy.;
   call streaminit(156789);
```

```
   do t=0 to 20 by 0.1;
      date=intnx('month','01jun90'd,(t*10)-1);
      x=rand('normal');
      e=rand('cauchy') + 10 ;
      y=exp(4*x)+e;
      output;
   end;
run;
```

The model to be estimated is

$$\begin{aligned} y &= e^{-a\,x} + \epsilon \\ \epsilon &\sim \text{Cauchy}(nc) \end{aligned}$$

That is, the residuals of the model are distributed as a Cauchy distribution with non-centrality parameter nc.

The log likelihood for the Cauchy distribution is

$$like = -\log(1 + (x - nc)^2 * \pi)$$

The following SAS statements specify the model and the log-likelihood function.

```
title2 'Cauchy Distribution';

proc model data=c ;
   dependent y;
   parm a -2 nc 4;
   y=exp(-a*x);

      /* Likelihood function for the residuals */
   obj = log(1+(-resid.y-nc)**2 * 3.1415926);

   errormodel y ~ general(obj) cdf=cauchy(nc);

   fit y / outsn=s1 method=marquardt;
   solve y / sdata=s1 data=c(obs=1) random=1000
             seed=256789 out=out1;
run;
```

The FIT statement uses the OUTSN= option to put out the Σ matrix for residuals from the normal distribution. The Σ matrix is 1×1 and has value 1.0 since it is a correlation matrix. The OUTS= matrix is the scalar 2989.0. Because the distribution is univariate (no covariances), the OUTS= would produce the same simulation results. The simulation is performed using the SOLVE statement.

The distribution of y is shown in the following output.

Output 20.12.1. Distribution of Y

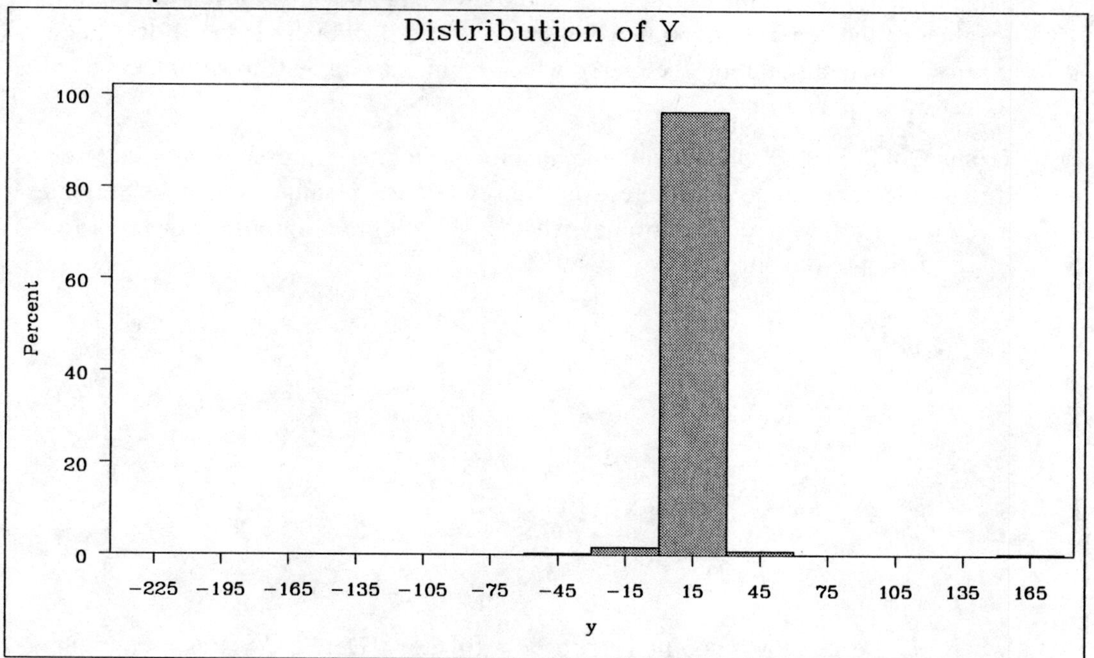

Example 20.13. Switching Regression Example

Take the usual linear regression problem

$$y = X\beta + u$$

where *Y* denotes the *n* column vector of the dependent variable, *X* denotes the ($n \times k$) matrix of independent variables, β denotes the *k* column vector of coefficients to be estimated, *n* denotes the number of observations (*i*=1,2,...,*n*), and *k* denotes the number of independent variables.

You can take this basic equation and split it into two regimes, where the *i* th observation on *y* is generated by one regime or the other.

$$y_i = \sum_{j=1}^{k} \beta_{1j} X_{ji} + u_{1i} = x_i'\beta_1 + u_{1i}$$

$$y_i = \sum_{j=1}^{k} \beta_{2j} X_{ji} + u_{2i} = x_i'\beta_2 + u_{2i}$$

where x_{hi} and x_{hj} are the *i*th and *j*th observations, respec tively, on x_h. The errors, u_{1i} and u_{2i}, are assumed to be distributed normally and independently, with mean zero and constant variance. The variance for the first regime is σ_1^2, and the variance for the second regime is σ_2^2. If $\sigma_1^2 \neq \sigma_2^2$ and $\beta_1 \neq \beta_2$, the regression system given previously is thought to be switching between the two regimes.

The problem is to estimate β_1, β_2, σ_1, and σ_2 without knowing *a priori* which of the n values of the dependent variable, *y*, was generated by which regime. If it is known *a priori* which observations belong to which regime, a simple Chow test can be used to test $\sigma_1^2 = \sigma_2^2$ and $\beta_1 = \beta_2$.

Using Goldfeld and Quandt's D-method for switching regression, you can solve this problem. Assume that there exists observations on some exogenous variables $z_{1i}, z_{2i}, ..., z_{pi}$, where *z* determines whether the *i*th observation is generated from one equation or the other.

$$
\begin{aligned}
y_i &= x_i'\beta_1 + u_{1i} \quad \text{if} \sum_{j=1}^{p} \pi_j z_{ji} \le 0 \\
y_i &= x_i'\beta_2 + u_{2i} \quad \text{if} \sum_{j=1}^{p} \pi_j z_{ji} > 0
\end{aligned}
$$

where π_j are unknown coefficients to be estimated. Define $d(z_i)$ as a continuous approximation to a step function. Replacing the unit step function with a continuous approximation using the cumulative normal integral enables a more practical method that produces consistent estimates.

$$
d(z_i) = \frac{1}{\sqrt{2\pi}\sigma} \int_{-\infty}^{\sum \pi_j z_{ji}} exp\left[-\frac{1}{2}\frac{\xi^2}{\sigma^2} \right] d\xi
$$

D is the *n* dimensional diagonal matrix consisting of $d(z_i)$.

$$
D = \begin{bmatrix} d(z_1) & 0 & 0 & 0 \\ 0 & d(z_2) & 0 & 0 \\ 0 & 0 & \ddots & 0 \\ 0 & 0 & 0 & d(z_n) \end{bmatrix}
$$

The parameters to estimate are now the *k* β_1's, the *k* β_2's, σ_1^2, σ_2^2, *p* π's, and the σ introduced in the $d(z_i)$ equation. The σ can be considered as given *a priori*, or it can be estimated, in which the estimated magnitude provides an estimate of the success in discriminating between the two regimes (Goldfeld and Quandt 1976).

$$
Y = (I - D) X\beta_1 + DX\beta_2 + W
$$

where $W = (I - D)U_1 + DU_2$, and *W* is a vector of unob servable and heteroscedastic error terms. The covariance matrix of *W* is denoted by Ω, where $\Omega = (I - D)^2\sigma_1^2 + D^2\sigma_2^2$. The maximum likelihood parameter estimates maximize the following log-likelihood function.

$$
\begin{aligned}
logL &= -\frac{n}{2}\log 2\pi - \frac{1}{2}\log \mid \Omega \mid - \\
&\frac{1}{2} * \left[[Y-(I-D)X\beta_1 - DX\beta_2]' \, \Omega^{-1} \, [Y-(I-D)X\beta_1 - DX\beta_2] \right]
\end{aligned}
$$

As an example, you now can use this switching regression likelihood to develop a model of housing starts as a function of changes in mortgage interest rates. The data for this example is from the U.S. Census Bureau and covers the period from January 1973 to March 1999. The hypothesis is that there will be different coefficients on your model based on whether the interest rates are going up or down.

So the model for z_i will be the following

$$z_i = p * (rate_i - rate_{i-1})$$

where $rate_i$ is the mortgage interest rate at time i and p is a scale parameter to be estimated.

The regression model will be the following

$$
\begin{aligned}
starts_i &= intercept_1 + ar1 * starts_{i-1} + djf1 * decjanfeb \qquad z_i < 0 \\
starts_i &= intercept_2 + ar2 * starts_{i-1} + djf2 * decjanfeb \qquad z_i >= 0
\end{aligned}
$$

where $starts_i$ is the number of housing starts at month i and $decjanfeb$ is a dummy variable indicating that the current month is one of December, January, or February.

This model is written using the following SAS statements.

```
proc model data=switch;
   parms sig1=10 sig2=10 int1 b11 b13 int2 b21 b23 p;
   bounds 0.0001 < sig1 sig2;

   a = p*dif(rate);          /* Upper bound of integral */
   d = probnorm(a);          /* Normal CDF as an approx of switch */

                             /* Regime 1 */
   y1 = int1 + zlag(starts)*b11 + decjanfeb *b13 ;
                             /* Regime 2 */
   y2 = int2 + zlag(starts)*b21 + decjanfeb *b23 ;
                             /* Composite regression equation */
   starts   = (1 - d)*y1 +  d*y2;

                            /* Resulting log-likelihood function */
   logL = (1/2)*( (313*log(2*3.1415)) +
        log( (sig1**2)*((1-d)**2)+(sig2**2)*(d**2) )
      + (resid.starts*( 1/( (sig1**2)*((1-d)**2)+
        (sig2**2)*(d**2) ) )*resid.starts) ) ;
```

```
      errormodel starts ~ general(logL);

      fit starts / method=marquardt converge=1.0e-5;

        /* Test for significant differences in the parms */
      test int1 = int2 ,/ lm;
      test b11 = b21 ,/ lm;
      test b13 = b23 ,/ lm;
      test sig1 = sig2 ,/ lm;

   run;
```

Four TEST statements were added to test the hypothesis that the parameters were the same in both regimes. The parameter estimates and ANOVA table from this run are shown in the following output.

Output 20.13.1. Parameter Estimates from the Switching Regression

The MODEL Procedure

Nonlinear Liklhood Summary of Residual Errors

Equation	DF Model	DF Error	SSE	MSE	Root MSE	R-Square	Adj R-Sq
starts	9	304	85877.9	282.5	16.8075	0.7806	0.7748

Nonlinear Liklhood Parameter Estimates

Parameter	Estimate	Approx Std Err	t Value	Approx Pr > |t|
sig1	15.47451	0.9475	16.33	<.0001
sig2	19.77797	1.2710	15.56	<.0001
int1	32.82232	5.9070	5.56	<.0001
b11	0.739529	0.0444	16.65	<.0001
b13	-15.456	3.1909	-4.84	<.0001
int2	42.73243	6.8153	6.27	<.0001
b21	0.734112	0.0477	15.37	<.0001
b23	-22.5178	4.2979	-5.24	<.0001
p	25.94332	8.5181	3.05	0.0025

The test results shown in the following output suggest that the variance of the housing starts, SIG1 and SIG2, are significantly different in the two regimes. The tests also show a significant difference in the AR term on the housing starts.

Output 20.13.2. Parameter Estimates from the Switching Regression

The MODEL Procedure

Test Results

Test	Type	Statistic	Pr > ChiSq	Label
Test0	L.M.	0.02	0.8810	int1 = int2
Test1	L.M.	240001	<.0001	b11 = b21
Test2	L.M.	0.02	0.8933	b13 = b23
Test3	L.M.	319354	<.0001	sig1 = sig2

Example 20.14. Simulating from a Mixture of Distributions

This example illustrates how to perform a multivariate simulation using models that have different error distributions. Three models are used. The first model has *t*-distributed errors. The second model is a GARCH(1,1) model with normally distributed errors. The third model has a non-central Cauchy distribution.

The following SAS statements generate the data for this example. The T and the CAUCHY data sets use a common seed so that those two series will be correlated.

```
%let df = 7.5;
%let sig1 = .5;
%let var2 = 2.5;

data t;
   format date monyy.;
   do date='1jun2001'd  to '1nov2002'd;
               /* t-distribution with df,sig1 */
      t = .05 * date + 5000  + &sig1*tinv(ranuni(1234),&df);
      output;
   end;
run;

data normal;
   format date monyy.;
   le = &var2;
   lv = &var2;
   do date='1jun2001'd  to '1nov2002'd;
               /* Normal with GARCH error structure */
      v = 0.0001 + 0.2 * le**2 + .75 * lv;
      e = sqrt( v) * rannor(12345) ;
      normal = 25 + e;
      le = e;
      lv = v;
      output;
   end;
run;

data cauchy;
   format date monyy.;
   PI = 3.1415926;
   do date='1jun2001'd  to '1nov2002'd;
      cauchy = -4 + tan((ranuni(1234) - 0.5) * PI);
      output;
   end;
run;
```

Since the multivariate joint likelihood is unknown, the models must be estimated separately. The residuals for each model are saved using the OUT= option. Also, each model is saved using the OUTMODEL= option. The ID statement is used to provide a variable in the residual data set to merge by. The XLAG function is used to model the GARCH(1,1) process. The XLAG function returns the lag of the first argument if it is nonmissing, otherwise it returns the second argument.

```
proc model data=t outmod=t;
   parms df 10 vt 4;
      t = a * date + c;
   errormodel t ~ t( vt, df );
   fit t / out=tresid;
   id date;
run;

proc model data=normal outmod=normal;
   normal = b0 ;
   h.normal = arch0 + arch1 * xlag(resid.normal **2 , mse.normal)
                + GARCH1 * xlag(h.normal, mse.normal);

   fit normal /fiml out=nresid;
   id date;
run;


proc model data= cauchy outmod=cauchy;
parms nc = 1;
     /* nc is noncentrality parm to Cauchy dist */
   cauchy = nc;
   obj = log(1+resid.cauchy**2 * 3.1415926);
   errormodel cauchy ~ general(obj) cdf=cauchy(nc);

   fit cauchy / out=cresid;
   id date;
run;
```

The simulation requires a covariance matrix created from normal residuals. The following Data Step code uses the inverse CDFs of the *t* and Cauchy distributions to convert the residuals to the normal distribution. The CORR procedure is used to create a correlation matrix using the converted residuals.

```
   /* Merge and normalize the 3 residual data sets */
data c; merge tresid nresid cresid; by date;
   t = probit(cdf("T", t/sqrt(0.2789), 16.58 ));
   cauchy = probit(cdf("CAUCHY", cauchy, -4.0623));
run;

proc corr data=c out=s;
   var t normal cauchy;
run;
```

Now the models can be simulated together using the MODEL procedure SOLVE statement. The data set created by the CORR procedure is used as the correlation matrix. Note that the errormodel statement is not saved with the model and must be restated for this simulation.

```
   /* Create one observation driver data set */
data sim; merge t normal cauchy; by date;
```

```
data sim; set sim(firstobs = 519 );

proc model data=sim model=( t normal cauchy);
   errormodel t ~ t( vt, df );
   errormodel cauchy ~ cauchy(nc);
   solve t cauchy normal / random=2000 seed=1962 out=monte
      sdata=s(where=(_type_="CORR"));
run;
```

An estimation of the joint density of the *t* and Cauchy distribution is created using the KDE procedure. Bounds were placed on the Cauchy dimension because of its fat tail behavior. The joint PDF is shown in the following output.

```
proc kde gridl=5780,-150 gridu=5784,150 data=monte out=density;
   var t cauchy;
run;

title "T and Cauchy Distribution";
proc g3d data=density;
   plot t*cauchy=density;
run;
```

Output 20.14.1. Density of T and CAUCHY Truncated in the CAUCHY dimension

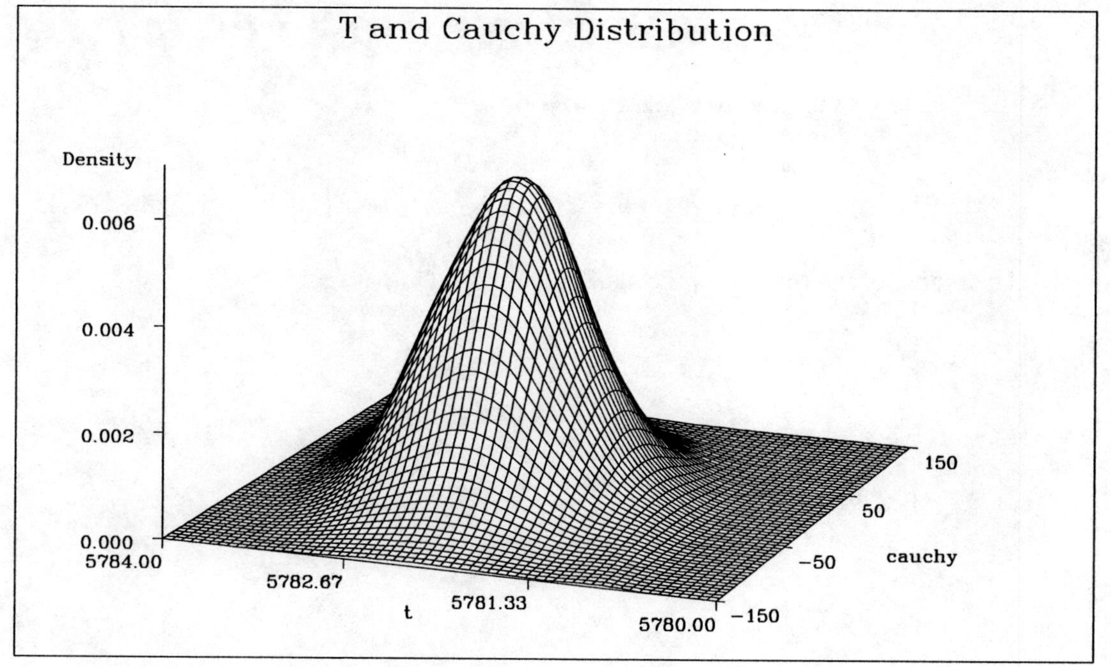

Example 20.15. Simple Linear Regression

This example illustrates how to use SMM to estimate a simple linear regression model for the following process:

$$y = a + bx + \epsilon,\ \epsilon \sim iid\,N(0, s^2).$$

In the following SAS code, $ysim$ is simulated and the first moment and the second moment of $ysim$ is compared with those of the observed endogenous variable y.

```
data _tmpdata;
   do i=1 to 500;
     x = rannor( 1013 );
          Y = 2 + 1.5 * x + 1.5 * rannor( 9871 );
          output;
   end;
run;

proc model data=_tmpdata;
  parms a b s;
       instrument x;

       ysim = (a+b*x) + s * rannor( 8003 );

       y = ysim;
       eq.ysq = y*y - ysim*ysim;

       fit y ysq / gmm ndraw;
       bound s > 0;

run;
```

The output of the MODEL procedure is shown in Output 20.15.1:

Output 20.15.1. PROC MODEL Output

```
                         The MODEL Procedure

                            Model Summary

                      Model Variables               1
                      Parameters                    3
                      Equations                     2
                      Number of Statements          5


                        Model Variables    Y
                             Parameters    a b s
                              Equations    ysq Y


                      The 2 Equations to Estimate

                             Y =   F(a(1), b(x), s)
                           ysq =   F(a, b, s)
                   Instruments     1 x


                         The MODEL Procedure

                  Nonlinear GMM Parameter Estimates

                                            Approx                       Approx
Parameter              Estimate            Std Err      t Value        Pr > |t|

a                      2.065983             0.0657        31.45          <.0001
b                      1.511075             0.0565        26.73          <.0001
s                      1.483358             0.0498        29.78          <.0001
```

Example 20.16. AR(1) Process

This example illustrates how to use SMM to estimate an AR(1) regression model for the following process:

$$
\begin{aligned}
y_t &= a + bx_t + u_t, \\
u_t &= \alpha u_{t-1} + \epsilon_t, \\
\epsilon_t &\sim iid\, N(0, s^2).
\end{aligned}
$$

In the following SAS code, $ysim$ is simulated using this model and the endogenous variable y is set to be equal to $ysim$. The MOMENT statement creates two more moments for the estimation. One is the second moment and the other is the first order autocovariance. The NPREOBS=20 option instructs PROC MODEL to run the simulation 20 times before $ysim$ is compared to the first observation of y. Because the initial $zlag(u)$ is zero, the first $ysim$ is $a + b * x + s * rannor(8003)$. Without the NPREOBS option, this $ysim$ is matched with the first observation of y. With NPREOBS, this $ysim$, along with the next 19 $ysim$, is thrown away, and the moment match starts with the twenty-first $ysim$ with the first observation of y. This way, the initial values do not exert a large inference to the simulated endogenous variables.

```
%let nobs=500;

data _tmpdata;
   lu =0;
   do i=-10 to &nobs;
     x = rannor( 1011 );
           e = rannor( 9887 );
           u = .6 * lu + 1.5 * e;
           Y = 2 + 1.5 * x + u;
           lu = u;
           if i > 0 then output;
   end;
run;


proc model data=_tmpdata ;
  parms a b s 1 alpha .5;
       instrument x;

       u = alpha * zlag(u) + s * rannor( 8003 );

       ysim = a + b * x + u;

       y = ysim;
       eq.ysq = y*y - ysim*ysim;
       eq.ylagy = y * lag(y) - ysim * lag( ysim );

       fit y ysq ylagy / gmm npreobs=10 ndraw=10;
       bound s > 0, 1>alpha>0;

run;
```

The output of the MODEL procedure is shown in Output 20.16.1:

Output 20.16.1. PROC MODEL Output

```
                         The MODEL Procedure

                            Model Summary

                    Model Variables              1
                    Parameters                   4
                    Equations                    3
                    Number of Statements         9
                    Program Lag Length           1


               Model Variables   Y
             Parameters(Value)   a b s(1) alpha(0.5)
                     Equations   ysq ylagy Y


                     The 3 Equations to Estimate

                          Y =  F(a(1), b(x), s, alpha)
                        ysq =  F(a, b, s, alpha)
                      ylagy =  F(a, b, s, alpha)
                Instruments    1 x


                         The MODEL Procedure

                 Nonlinear GMM Parameter Estimates

                                  Approx                        Approx
Parameter          Estimate      Std Err      t Value        Pr > |t|

a                  1.647842       0.1023        16.11          <.0001
b                  1.494174       0.0700        21.36          <.0001
s                  1.418301       0.0919        15.43          <.0001
alpha              0.561595       0.0714         7.87          <.0001
```

Example 20.17. Stochastic Volatility Model

This example illustrates how to use SMM to estimate a stochastic volatility model as in Andersen and Sorensen (1996):

$$
\begin{aligned}
y_t &= \sigma_t z_t, \\
log(\sigma_t^2) &= a + b\,log(\sigma_{t-1}^2) + s u_t, \\
(z_t, u_t) &\sim iid\,N(0, I_2).
\end{aligned}
$$

This model is widely used in modeling the return process of stock prices and foreign exchange rates. This is called the stochastic volatility model because the volatility is stochastic as the random variable u_t appears in the volatility equation. The following SAS code uses three moments: absolute value, the second order moment, and absolute value of the first order autoregressive moment. Note the ADJSMMV option in the FIT statement to request the SMM covariance adjustment for the parameter estimates. Although these moments have closed form solution as shown by Andersen and Sorensen (1996), the simulation approach significantly simplifies the moment conditions.

```
%let nobs=1000;

data _tmpdata;
   a = -0.736; b=0.9; s=0.363;
   ll=sqrt( exp(a/(1-b)));;
   do i=-10 to &nobs;
     u = rannor( 101 );
          z = rannor( 98761 );
          lnssq = a+b*log(ll**2) +s*u;
          st = sqrt(exp(lnssq));
          ll = st;
          y = st * z;
          if i > 0 then output;
   end;
run;


proc model data=_tmpdata ;
  parms a b .5 s 1;
       instrument _exog_ / intonly;

       u = rannor( 8801 );
       z = rannor( 9701 );

       lsigmasq = xlag(sigmasq,exp(a));

       lnsigmasq = a + b * log(lsigmasq) + s * u;
       sigmasq = exp( lnsigmasq );

       ysim = sqrt(sigmasq) * z;

       eq.m1 = abs(y) - abs(ysim);

       eq.m2 = y**2 - ysim**2;

       eq.m5 = abs(y*lag(y))-abs(ysim*lag(ysim));

       fit m1 m2 m5 / gmm npreobs=10 ndraw=10;
       bound s > 0, 1>b>0;

run;
```

The output of the MODEL procedure is shown in Output 20.17.1.

Output 20.17.1. PROC MODEL Output

```
                    The MODEL Procedure

                       Model Summary

                  Parameters                  3
                  Equations                   3
                  Number of Statements       13
                  Program Lag Length          1


               Parameters(Value)    a b(0.5) s(1)
                       Equations    m1 m2 m5


                  The 3 Equations to Estimate

                         m1 =  F(a, b, s)
                         m2 =  F(a, b, s)
                         m5 =  F(a, b, s)
                   Instruments  1



                    The MODEL Procedure

             Nonlinear GMM Parameter Estimates

                                   Approx                   Approx
Parameter          Estimate       Std Err    t Value     Pr > |t|

a                  -2.28945        1.0379      -2.21       0.0276
b                  0.687496        0.1419       4.84       <.0001
s                  0.752418        0.1476       5.10       <.0001
```

Example 20.18. Duration Data Model with Unobserved Heterogeneity

All of the previous three models actually have closed form moment conditions, so the simulation approach is not necessarily required for the estimation. This example illustrates how to use SMM to estimate a model for which there is no closed form solution for the moments and thus the traditional GMM method does not apply. The model is the duration data model with unobserved heterogeneity in Gourieroux and Monfort (1993):

$$
\begin{aligned}
y_i &= -exp(-bx_i - \sigma u_i)log(v_i), \\
u_i &\sim N(0,1) \quad v_i \sim U_{[0,1]}.
\end{aligned}
$$

The SAS code is:

```
%let nobs=1000;

data _tmpdata;
   b=0.9; s=0.5;
```

```
   do i=1 to &nobs;
     u = rannor( 1011 );
          v = ranuni( 9828 );
          x = 2 * ranuni( 7621 );
          y = -exp(-b * x + s * u) * log(v);
          output;
   end;
run;


proc model data=_tmpdata;
  parms b .5 s 1;
       instrument x;

       u = rannor( 9871 );
       v = ranuni( 7003 );

       y = -exp(-b * x + s * u) * log(v);

       moment y = (2 3 4);

       fit y / gmm ndraw=10;

       bound s > 0, b>0;

run;
```

The output of the MODEL procedure is shown in Output 20.18.1.

Output 20.18.1. PROC MODEL Output

```
                    The MODEL Procedure

                       Model Summary

                 Model Variables             1
                 Parameters                  2
                 Equations                   4
                 Number of Statements       10


       Model Variables  y
     Parameters(Value)  b(0.5) s(1)
             Equations  _moment_3 _moment_2 _moment_1 y


                 The 4 Equations to Estimate

                    _moment_3 =  F(b, s)
                    _moment_2 =  F(b, s)
                    _moment_1 =  F(b, s)
                            y =  F(b, s)
                  Instruments    1 x


                    The MODEL Procedure

             Nonlinear GMM Parameter Estimates

                                  Approx                     Approx
Parameter         Estimate       Std Err    t Value     Pr > |t|

b                 0.918135        0.0330      27.80       <.0001
s                 0.310181        0.0426       7.29       <.0001
```

Example 20.19. EMM Estimation of a Stochastic Volatility Model

The Efficient Method of Moments (EMM), introduced by Bansal et al. (1993 and 1995), and Gallant and Tauchen (2001), can be considered a variant of SMM. The idea is to match the efficiency of the Maximum Likelihood (ML) estimation with the flexibility of the SMM procedure. ML itself can be interpreted as a method of moments procedure, where the *score vector*, the vector of derivatives of the log-likelihood function with respect to the parameters, provides the exactly identifying moment conditions. EMM employs an auxiliary (or pseudo) model that closely matches the true model. The score vector of the auxilliary model provides the moment conditions in the SMM step.

This example uses the SMM feature of PROC MODEL to estimate the simple stochastic volatility (SV) model of Example 20.17 with the EMM method.

Suppose that your data are the time series $\{y_1, y_2, \ldots, y_n\}$, and the model that you want to estimate, or the structural model, is characterized by the vector of parameters $\boldsymbol{\theta}$. For the SV model, $\boldsymbol{\theta}$ is given by (a, b, s).

The first step of the EMM method is to fit the data with an auxiliary model (or score generator) that has transition density $f(y_t|Y_{t-1}, \boldsymbol{\eta})$, parametrized by the pseudo parameter $\boldsymbol{\eta}$, where $Y_{t-1} = \{y_{t-1}, \ldots, y_1\}$. The auxiliary model must approximate the true data generating process as closely as possible and be such that ML estimation is feasible.

The only identification requirement is that the dimension of the pseudo parameter $\boldsymbol{\eta}$ be greater than or equal to that of the structural parameter $\boldsymbol{\theta}$.

Andersen, Chung, and Sorensen (1999) showed that the GARCH(1,1) is an appropriate auxiliary model that leads to a good performance of the EMM estimator for the SV model.

The analytical expression for the GARCH(1,1) model with mean zero is

$$
\begin{aligned}
y_t &= \sigma_t z_t \\
\sigma_t^2 &= \omega + \alpha y_{t-1} + \beta \sigma_{t-1}^2
\end{aligned}
$$

The pseudo parameter vector $\boldsymbol{\eta}$ is given by (ω, α, β).

One advantage of such a class of models is that the conditional density of y_t is Gaussian, that is,

$$
f(y_t|Y_{t-1}, \boldsymbol{\eta}) \propto \frac{1}{\sigma_t} \exp\left(-\frac{y_t^2}{2\sigma_t^2}\right)
$$

and therefore the score vector can easily be computed analytically.

The AUTOREG procedure provides the ML estimates, $\hat{\boldsymbol{\eta}}_n$. The output is stored in the garchout data set, while the estimates are stored in the garchest data set.

```
/*
/ estimate GARCH(1,1) model
/ -----------------------------------------------*/
proc autoreg data=_tmpdata(keep=y) outest=garchest noprint covout;
   model y =   / noint garch=(q=1,p=1) ;
   output out=garchout cev=gsigmasq r=resid;
run;
```

If the pseudo model is close enough to the structural model, in a suitable sense, Gallant and Long (1997) showed that a consistent estimator of the asymptotic covariance matrix of the sample pseudo-score vector can be obtained from the formula

$$
\hat{V}_n = \frac{1}{n} \sum_{t=1}^{n} s_f(Y_t, \hat{\boldsymbol{\eta}}_n) s_f(Y_t, \hat{\boldsymbol{\eta}}_n)'
$$

where $s_f(Y_t, \hat{\boldsymbol{\eta}}_n) = (\partial/\partial\boldsymbol{\eta}_n) \log f(y_t|Y_{t-1}, \hat{\boldsymbol{\eta}}_n)$ denotes the score function of the auxiliary model computed at the ML estimates.

The ML estimates of the GARCH(1,1) model are used in the following SAS statements to compute the variance-covariance matrix $\hat{V}_n$.

```
/*
/ compute the V matrix
/ ----------------------------------------------------*/

data vvalues;
   set garchout(keep=y gsigmasq resid);

   /* compute scores of GARCH model */
   score_1 = (-1 + y**2/gsigmasq)/ gsigmasq;
   score_2 = (-1 + y**2/gsigmasq)*lag(gsigmasq) / gsigmasq;
   score_3 = (-1 + y**2/gsigmasq)*lag(y**2) / gsigmasq;

   array score{*} score_1-score_3;
   array v_t{*} v_t_1-v_t_6;
   array v{*} v_1-v_6;

   /* compute external product of score vector */
   do i=1 to 3;
      do j=i to 3;
         v_t{j*(j-1)/2 + i} = score{i}*score{j};
      end;
   end;

   /* average them over t */
   do s=1 to 6;
      v{s}+ v_t{s}/&nobs;
   end;
run;
```

The $\hat{V}$ matrix must be formatted to be used with the VDATA= option of the MODEL procedure. Please see the section "VDATA= Input data set" on page 1160 for more information regarding the VDATA= data set.

```
/*
/ Create a VDATA dataset acceptable to PROC MODEL
/ ------------------------------------------------- */

/* Transpose the last obs in the dataset */
proc transpose data=vvalues(firstobs=&nobs keep=v_1-v_6) out=tempv;
run;

/* Add eq and inst labels */
data vhat;
   set tempv(drop=_name_);
   value = col1;
   drop col1;
   input _type_ $ eq_row $ eq_col $ inst_row $ inst_col $;
   datalines;
      gmm m1 m1 1 1  /* intcpt is the only inst we use */
      gmm m1 m2 1 1
      gmm m2 m2 1 1
      gmm m1 m3 1 1
      gmm m2 m3 1 1
      gmm m3 m3 1 1
   ;
run;
```

The last step of the EMM procedure is to estimate $\boldsymbol{\theta}$ using SMM, where the moment conditions are given by the scores of the auxiliary model.

Given a fixed value of the parameter vector $\boldsymbol{\theta}$, and an arbitrarily large T, one can simulate a series $\{\hat{y}_1(\boldsymbol{\theta}), \hat{y}_2(\boldsymbol{\theta}), \ldots, \hat{y}_T(\boldsymbol{\theta})\}$ from the structural model. The EMM estimator is the value $\hat{\boldsymbol{\theta}}_n$ that minimizes the quantity

$$m_T(\boldsymbol{\theta}, \hat{\boldsymbol{\eta}}_n)' \hat{V}_n^{-1} m_T(\boldsymbol{\theta}, \hat{\boldsymbol{\eta}}_n)$$

where

$$m_T(\boldsymbol{\theta}, \hat{\boldsymbol{\eta}}_n) = \frac{1}{T} \sum_{k=1}^{T} s_f(\hat{Y}_k(\boldsymbol{\theta}), \hat{\boldsymbol{\eta}}_n)$$

is the sample moment condition evaluated at the fixed estimated pseudo parameter $\hat{\boldsymbol{\eta}}_n$. Note that the target function depends on the parameter $\boldsymbol{\theta}$ only through the simulated series $\hat{y}_k$.

The following statements generate a data set that contains $T = 20,000$ replicates of the estimated pseudo parameter $\hat{\boldsymbol{\eta}}_n$ and that is then inputed to the MODEL procedure. The EMM estimates are found using the SMM option of the FIT statement. The $\hat{V}_n$ matrix computed above serves as weighting matrix using the VDATA= option, and the scores of the GARCH(1,1) auxiliary model evaluated at the ML estimates are the moment conditions in the GMM step.

Since the number of structural parameters to estimate (3) is equal to the number of moment equations (3) times the number of instrument (1), the model is exactly identified and the objective function will have value zero at the minimum.

For simplicity, the starting values are set to the true values of the parameters.

```
/*
/ USE SMM TO FIND EMM ESTIMATES
/ ---------------------------------------------------*/

/* Generate dataset of length T */
data emm;
   set garchest(obs=1 keep = _ah_0 _ah_1 _gh_1 _mse_);
   do i=1 to 20000;
      output;
   end;
   drop i;
run;

/* Find the EMM estimates */
proc model data=emm maxiter=1000;
   parms a -0.736 b 0.9 s 0.363;
   instrument _exog_ / intonly;

      /* Describe the structural model */
      u = rannor( 8801 );
      z = rannor( 9701 );
```

```
      lsigmasq = xlag(sigmasq,exp(a));

      lnsigmasq = a + b * log(lsigmasq) + s * u;
      sigmasq = exp( lnsigmasq );

      ysim = sqrt(sigmasq) * z;

      /* Volatility of the GARCH model */
      gsigmasq = _ah_0 + _gh_1*xlag(gsigmasq, _mse_)
                 + _ah_1*xlag(ysim**2, _mse_);

      /* Use scores of the GARCH model as moment conditions */
      eq.m1 = (-1 + ysim**2/gsigmasq)/ gsigmasq;

      eq.m2 = (-1 + ysim**2/gsigmasq)*xlag(gsigmasq, _mse_) / gsigmasq;

      eq.m3 = (-1 + ysim**2/gsigmasq)*xlag(ysim**2, _mse_) / gsigmasq;

   /* Fit scores using SMM and estimated Vhat */
   fit m1 m2 m3 / gmm npreobs=10 ndraw=1 /* smm options */
                  vdata=vhat /* use estimated Vhat */
                  kernel=(bart,0,) /* turn smoothing off */;
                 bounds s > 0, 1>b>0;

run;
```

The output of the MODEL procedure is shown in Output 20.19.1.

Output 20.19.1. PROC MODEL Output

```
                         EMM estimates

                      The MODEL Procedure

                         Model Summary

                 Parameters                   3
                 Equations                    3
                 Number of Statements        14


        Parameters(Value)   a(-0.736) b(0.9) s(0.363)
                Equations   m1 m2 m3


                The 3 Equations to Estimate

                         m1 =  F(a, b, s)
                         m2 =  F(a, b, s)
                         m3 =  F(a, b, s)
                  Instruments  1


                         EMM estimates

                      The MODEL Procedure

               Nonlinear GMM Parameter Estimates

                                        Approx                     Approx
Parameter           Estimate           Std Err      t Value       Pr > |t|

a                    -0.5655            0.0162       -34.93        <.0001
b                   0.921023           0.00219       419.99        <.0001
s                   0.346605           0.00708        48.93        <.0001
```

Example 20.20. Illustration of ODS Graphics (Experimental)

This example illustrates the use of experimental ODS graphics. This is a continuation of the "Nonlinear Regression Analysis" in the section "Getting Started" on page 1003. These graphical displays are requested by specifying the experimental ODS GRAPHICS statement. For general information about ODS graphics, see Chapter 9, "Statistical Graphics Using ODS." For specific information about the graphics available in the MODEL procedure, see the "ODS Graphics" section on page 1166.

The following statements show how to generate ODS graphics plots with the MODEL procedure. The plots are displayed in Output 20.20.1 through Output 20.20.8. Note that the variable date in the ID statement is used to define the horizontal tick mark values when appropriate.

```
ods html;
ods graphics on;

proc model data=sashelp.citimon;
   lhur = 1/(a * ip + b) + c;
```

```
   fit lhur;
   id date;
run;
quit;

ods graphics off;
ods html close;
```

Output 20.20.1. Studentized Residuals Plot (Experimental)

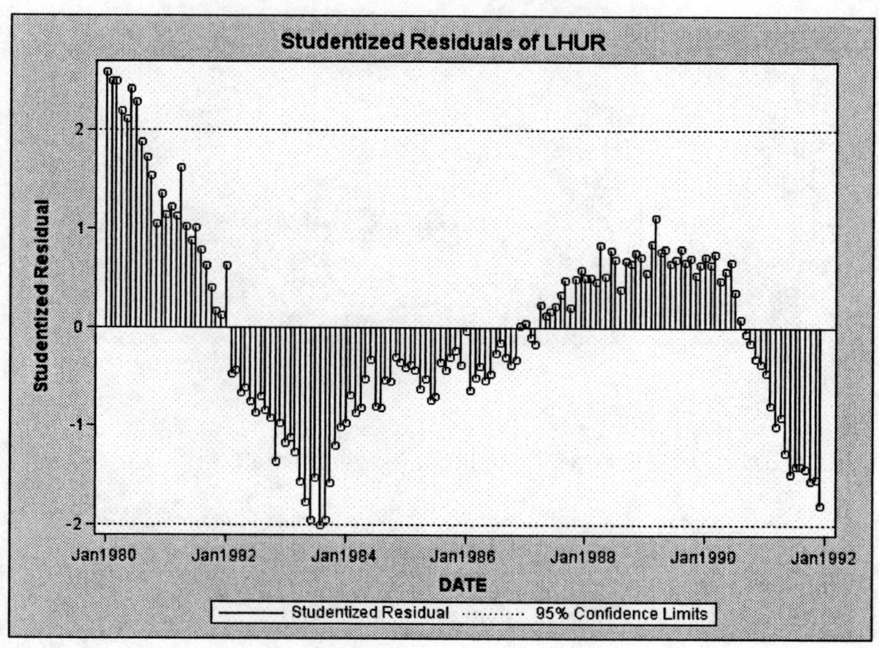

Output 20.20.2. Cook's D Plot (Experimental)

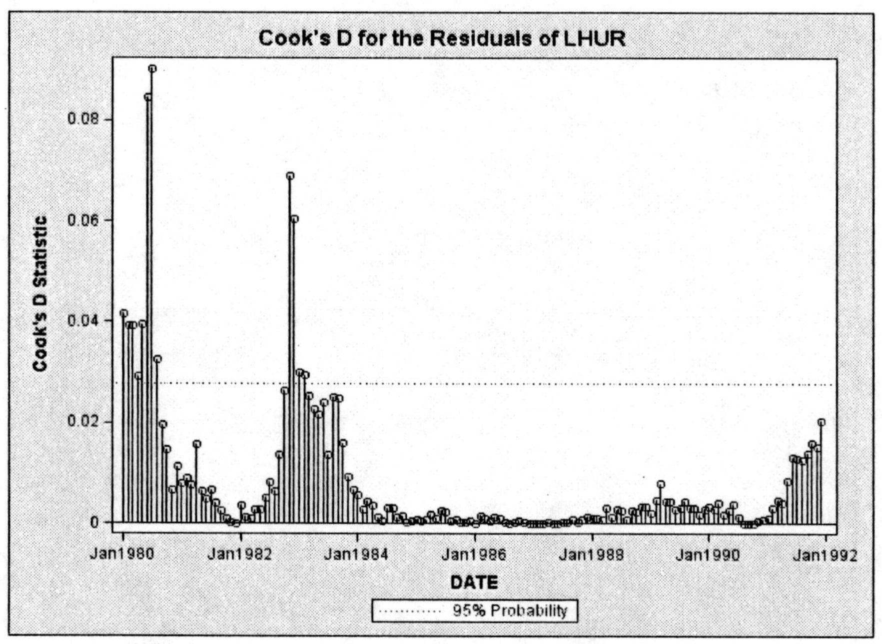

Output 20.20.3. Predicted vs Actual Plot (Experimental)

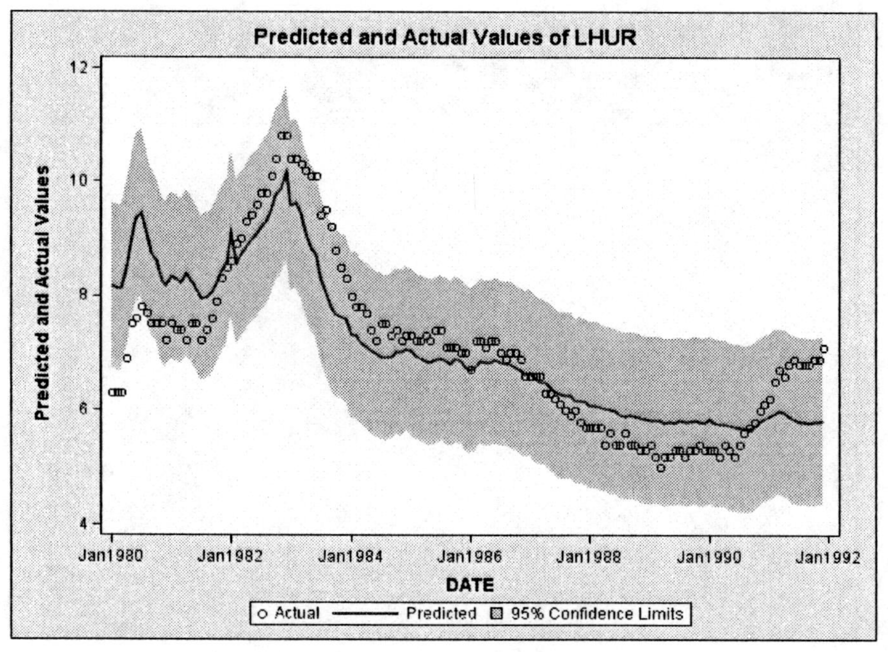

Output 20.20.4. Autocorrelation of Residuals Plot (Experimental)

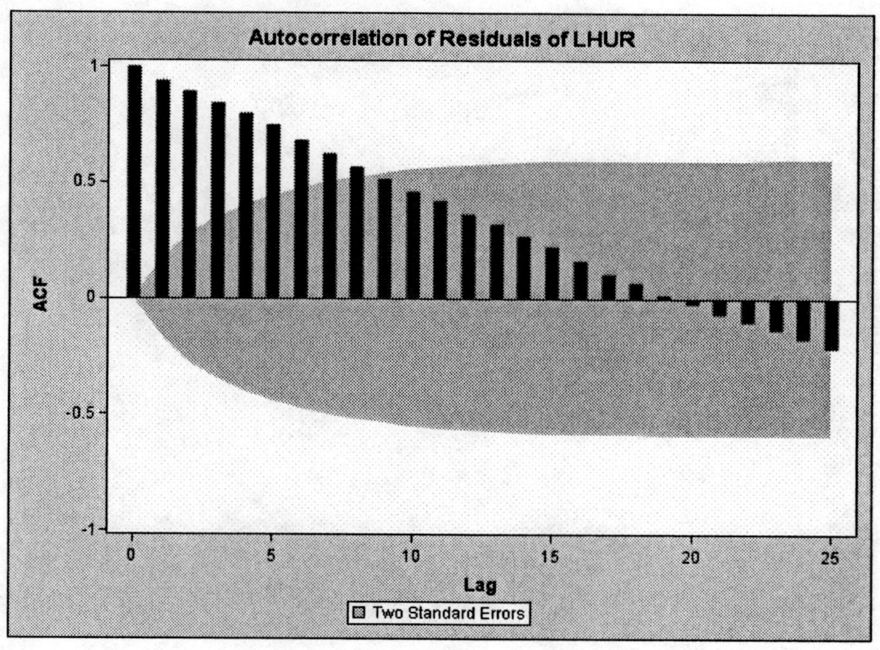

Output 20.20.5. Partial Autocorrelation of Residuals Plot (Experimental)

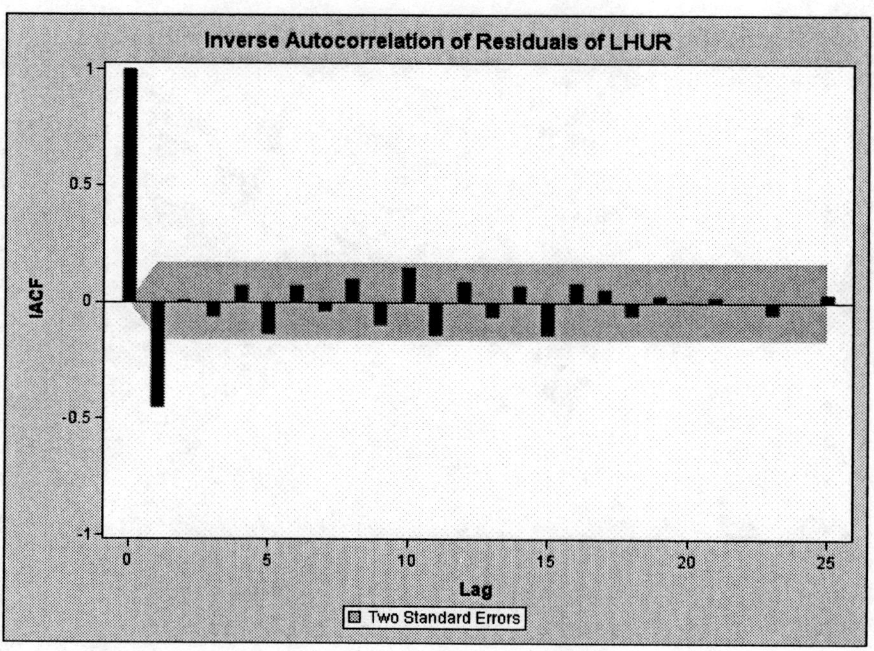

Output 20.20.6. Inverse Autocorrelation of Residuals Plot (Experimental)

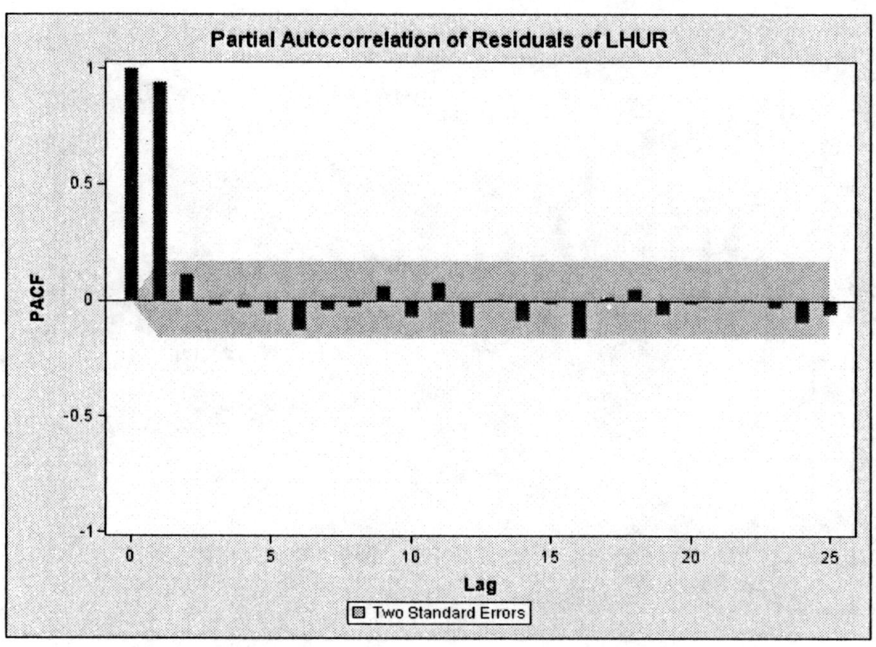

Output 20.20.7. QQ Plot of Residuals (Experimental)

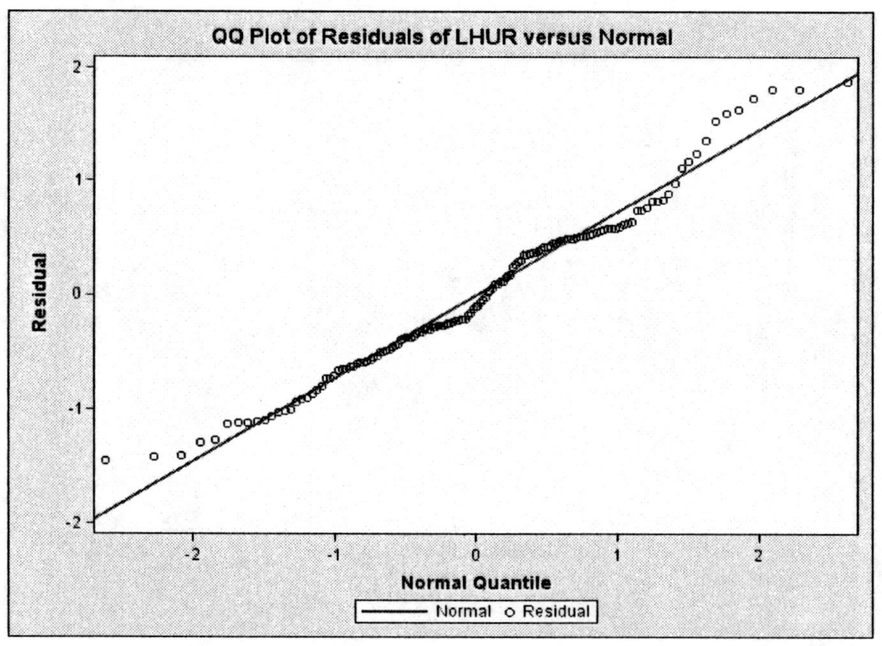

Output 20.20.8. Histogram of Residuals (Experimental)

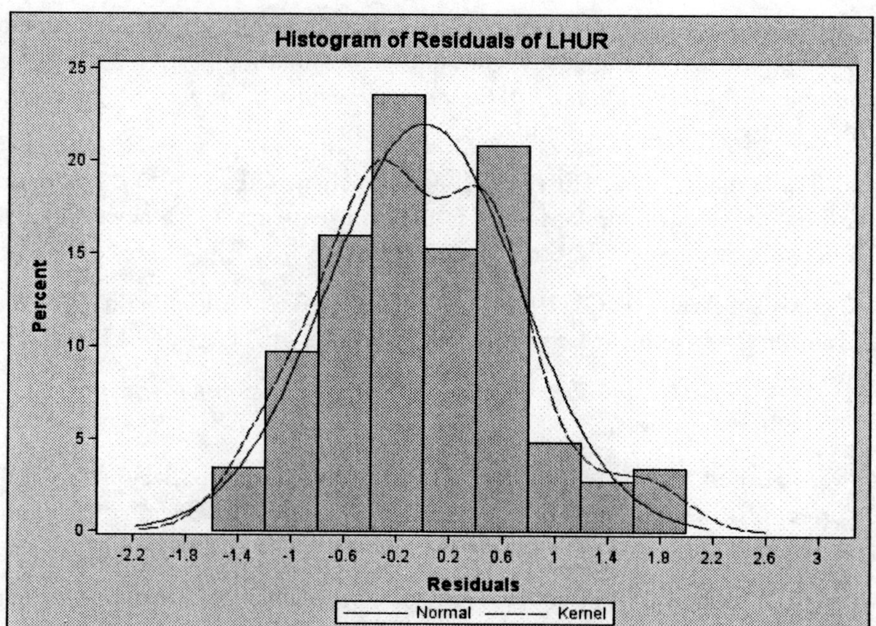

References

Aiken, R.C., ed. (1985), *Stiff Computation,* New York: Oxford University Press.

Amemiya, T. (1974), "The Nonlinear Two-stage Least-squares Estimator," *Journal of Econometrics*, 2, 105–110.

Amemiya, T. (1977), "The Maximum Likelihood Estimator and the Nonlinear Three-Stage Least Squares Estimator in the General Nonlinear Simultaneous Equation Model," *Econometrica*, 45 (4), 955–968.

Amemiya, T. (1985), *Advanced Econometrics*, Cambridge, MA: Harvard University Press.

Andersen, T.G., Chung, H-J., and Sorensen, B.E. (1999), "Efficient Method of Moments Estimation of a Stochastic Volatility Model: A Monte Carlo Study," *Journal of Econometrics*, 91, 61-87.

Andersen, T.G. and Sorensen, B.E. (1996), "GMM Estimation of a Stochastic Volatility Model: A Monte Carlo Study," *Journal of Business and Economic Statistics*, 14, 328–352.

Andrews, D.W.K. (1991), "Heteroscedasticity and Autocorrelation Consistent Covariance Matrix Estimation," *Econometrica*, 59 (3), 817–858.

Andrews, D.W.K. and Monahan, J.C. (1992), "Improved Heteroscedasticity and Autocorrelation Consistent Covariance Matrix Estimator," *Econometrica*, 60 (4), 953–966.

Bard, Yonathan (1974), *Nonlinear Parameter Estimation*, New York: Academic Press, Inc.

Bansal, R., Gallant, A.R., Hussey, R., and Tauchen, G.E. (1993), "Computational Aspects of Nonparametric Simulation Estimation," Belsey, D.A., ed., *Computational Techniques for Econometrics and Economic Analysis*. Boston, MA: Kluwer Academic Publishers, 3-22.

Bansal, R., Gallant, A.R., Hussey, R., and Tauchen, G.E. (1995), "Nonparametric Estimation of Structural Models for High-Frequency Currency Market Data," *Journal of Econometrics*, 66, 251-287.

Bates, D.M. and Watts, D.G. (1981), "A Relative Offset Orthogonality Convergence Criterion for Nonlinear Least Squares," *Technometrics*, 23 (2), 179–183.

Belsley, D.A., Kuh, E., and Welsch, R.E. (1980), *Regression Diagnostics*, New York: John Wiley & Sons, Inc.

Binkley, J.K. and Nelson, G. (1984), "Impact of Alternative Degrees of Freedom Corrections in Two and Three Stage Least Squares," *Journal of Econometrics*, 24 (3) 223–233.

Bowden, R.J. and Turkington, D.A. (1984), *Instrumental Variables*, Cambridge: Cambridge University Press.

Bratley, P., Fox, B.L., and H. Niederreiter (1992), "Implementation and Tests of Low-Discrepancy Sequences," *ACM Transactions on Modeling and Computer Simulation*, 2 (3), 195-213.

Breusch, T.S. and Pagan, A.R., (1979), "A Simple Test for Heteroscedasticity and Random Coefficient Variation," *Econometrica*, 47 (5), 1287–1294.

Breusch, T.S. and Pagan, A.R. (1980), "The Lagrange Multiplier Test and Its Applications to Model Specification in Econometrics," *Review of Econometric Studies*, 47, 239–253.

Byrne, G.D. and Hindmarsh, A.C. (1975), "A Polyalgorithm for the Numerical Solution of ODEs," *ACM TOMS*, 1 (1), 71–96.

Calzolari, G. and Panattoni, L. (1988), "Alternative Estimators of FIML Covariance Matrix: A Monte Carlo Study," *Econometrica*, 56 (3), 701–714.

Chan, K.C., Karolyi, G.A., Longstaff, F.A., and Sanders, A.B. (1992), "An Empirical Comparison of Alternate Models of the Short-Term Interest Rate", *The Journal of Finance*, 47 (3), 1209–1227.

Christensen, L.R., Jorgenson, D.W. and L.J. Lau (1975), "Transcendental Logarithmic Utility Functions," *American Economic Review*, 65, 367–383.

Dagenais, M.G. (1978), "The Computation of FIML Estimates as Iterative Generalized Least Squares Estimates in Linear and Nonlinear Simultaneous Equation Models," *Econometrica*, 46, 6, 1351–1362.

Davidian, M and Giltinan, D.M. (1995), *Nonlinear Models for Repeated Measurement Data*, London: Chapman & Hall.

Davidson, R. and MacKinnon, J.G. (1993), *Estimation and Inference in Econometrics,* New York: Oxford University Press.

Duffie, D. and Singleton, K.J. (1993), "Simulated Moments Estimation of Markov Models of Asset Prices," *Econometrica* 61, 929-952.

Fair, R.C. (1984), *Specification, Estimation, and Analysis of Macroeconometric Models*, Cambridge: Harvard University Press.

Ferson, Wayne E. and Foerster, Stephen R. (1993), "Finite Sample Properties of the Generalized Method of Moments in Tests of Conditional Asset Pricing Models," Working Paper No. 77, University of Washington.

Fox, B.L. (1986), "Algorithm 647: Implementation and Relative Efficiency of Quasirandom Sequence Generators," *ACM Transactions on Mathematical Software,* 12 (4), 362-276.

Gallant, A.R. (1977), "Three-Stage Least Squares Estimation for a System of Simultaneous, Nonlinear, Implicit Equations," *Journal of Econometrics*, 5, 71–88.

Gallant, A.R. (1987), *Nonlinear Statistical Models*, New York: John Wiley and Sons, Inc.

Gallant, A.R. and Holly, A. (1980), "Statistical Inference in an Implicit, Nonlinear, Simultaneous Equation Model in the Context of Maximum Likelihood Estimation," *Econometrica*, 48 (3), 697–720.

Gallant, A.R. and Jorgenson, D.W. (1979), "Statistical Inference for a System of Simultaneous, Nonlinear, Implicit Equations in the Context of Instrumental Variables Estimation," *Journal of Econometrics*, 11, 275–302.

Gallant, A.R. and Long, J. (1997). "Estimating Stochastic Differential Equations Efficiently by Minimum Chi-squared," *Biometrika*, 84, 125-141.

Gallant, A.R. and Tauchen, G.E. (2001), "Efficient Method of Moments," Working Paper, [http://www.econ.duke.edu/~get/wpapers/ee.pdf] accessed 12 September 2001.

Gill, P.E., Murray, W., and Wright, M.H. (1981), *Practical Optimization,* New York: Academic Press Inc.

Godfrey, L.G. (1978a), "Testing Against General Autoregressive and Moving Average Error Models When the Regressors Include Lagged Dependent Variables," *Econometrica*, 46, 1293–1301.

Godfrey, L.G. (1978b), "Testing for Higher Order Serial Correlation in Regression Equations When the Regressors Include Lagged Dependent Variables," *Econometrica*, 46, 1303–1310.

Goldfeld, S.M. and Quandt, R.E. (1972), *Nonlinear Methods in Econometrics*, Amsterdam: North-Holland Publishing Company.

Goldfeld, S.M. and Quandt, R.E. (1973), "A Markov Model for Switching Regressions," *Journal of Econometrics* , 3-16.

Goldfeld, S.M. and Quandt, R.E. (1973), "The Estimation of Structural Shifts by Switching Regressions," *Annals of Economic and Social Measurement*, 2/4.

Goldfeld, S.M. and Quandt, R.E. (1976), *Studies in Nonlinear Estimation*, Cambridge, MA: Ballinger Publishing Company.

Goodnight, J.H. (1979), "A Tutorial on the SWEEP Operator," *The American Statistician*, 33, 149–158.

Gourieroux, C. and Monfort, A. (1993), "Simulation Based Inference: A Survey with Special Reference to Panel Data Models," *Journal of Econometrics*, 59, 5-33.

Greene, William H. (1993), *Econometric Analysis,* New York: Macmillian Publishing Company Inc.

Gregory, A.W. and Veall, M.R. (1985), "On Formulating Wald Tests for Nonlinear Restrictions," *Econometrica*, 53, 1465–1468.

Grunfeld, Y. and Griliches, "Is Aggregation Necessarily Bad ?" *Review of Economics and Statistics*, February 1960, 113–134.

Hansen, L.P. (1982), "Large Sample Properties of Generalized Method of Moments Estimators," *Econometrica*, 50 (4), 1029–1054.

Hansen, L.P. (1985), "A Method for Calculating Bounds on the Asymptotic Covariance Matrices of Generalized Method Of Moments Estimators," *Journal of Econometrics*, 30, 203–238.

Hatanaka, M. (1978), "On the Efficient Estimation Methods for the Macro-Economic Models Nonlinear in Variables," *Journal of Econometrics*, 8, 323–356.

Hausman, J. A. (1978), "Specification Tests in Econometrics," *Econometrica,* 46(6), 1251–1271.

Hausman, J.A. and Taylor, W.E. (1982), "A Generalized Specification Test," *Economics Letters,* 8, 239–245.

Henze, N. and Zirkler, B. (1990), "A Class of Invariant Consistent tests for Multivariate Normality," *Commun. Statist. - Theory Meth.*, 19 (10), 3595–3617.

Johnston, J. (1984), *Econometric Methods*, Third Edition, New York: McGraw-Hill Book Co.

Jorgenson, D.W. and Laffont, J. (1974), "Efficient Estimation of Nonlinear Simultaneous Equations with Additive Disturbances," *Annals of Social and Economic Measurement*, 3, 615–640.

Joy, C., Boyle, P.P., and Tan, K.S. (1996), "Quasi-Monte Carlo Methods in Numerical Finance ", *Management Science*, 42 (6), 926-938.

LaMotte, L.R. (1994), "A Note on the Role of Independence in t Statistics Constructed From Linear Statistics in Regression Models," *The American Statistician*, 48 (3), 238–239.

Lee, B. and Ingram, B. (1991), "Simulation Estimation of Time Series Models," *Journal of Econometrics*, 47, 197-205.

MacKinnon, J.G, and White H. (1985), "Some Heteroskedasticity Consistent Covariance Matrix Estimators with Improved Finite Sample Properties," *Journal of Econometrics*, 29, 305-325.

Maddala, G.S. (1977), *Econometrics*, New York: McGraw-Hill Book Co.

Mardia, K. V. (1980), "Measures of Multivariate Skewness and Kurtosis with Applications," *Biometrika* 57 (3), 519–529.

Mardia, K. V. (1974), "Applications of Some Measures of Multivariate Skewness and Kurtosis in Testing Normality and Robustness Studies," *The Indian Journal of Statistics* 36 (B) pt. 2, 115–128.

Matis, J.H., Miller, T.H., and Allen, D.M. (1991), *Metal Ecotoxicology Concepts and Applications*, ed. M.C Newman and A. W. McIntosh, Chelsea, MI; Lewis Publishers Inc.

Matsumoto, M. and Nishimura, T. (1998), "Mersenne Twister: A 623-Dimensionally Equidistributed Uniform Pseudo-Random Number Generator," *ACM Transactions on Modeling and Computer Simulation*, 8, 3-30.

McFadden, D. (1989), "A Method of Simulated Moments for Estimation of Discrete Response Models without Numerical Integration," *Econometrica* 57, 995-1026.

Messer, K., and White, H. (1994), "A Note on Computing the Heteroskedasticity Consistent Covariance Matrix Using Instrumental Variable Techniques," *Oxford Bulletin of Economics and Statistics*, 46, 181-184.

Mikhail, W.M. (1975), "A Comparative Monte Carlo Study of the Properties of Economic Estimators," *Journal of the American Statistical Association*, 70, 94–104.

Miller, D.M. (1984), "Reducing Transformation Bias in Curve Fitting," *The American Statistician*, 38 (2), 124–126.

Morelock, M.M., Pargellis, C.A., Graham, E.T., Lamarre, D., and Jung, G. (1995), "Time-Resolved Ligand Exchange Reactions: Kinetic Models for competitive Inhibitors with Recombinant Human Renin," *Journal of Medical Chemistry*, 38, 1751–1761.

Nelsen, Roger B. (1999), *Introduction to Copulas*, New York, New York: Springer-Verlag.

Newey, W.K, and West, D. W. (1987), "A Simple, Positive Semi-Definite, Heteroscedasticity and Autocorrelation Consistent Covariance Matrix," *Econometrica*, 55, 703–708.

Noble, B. and Daniel, J.W. (1977), *Applied Linear Algebra,* Englewood Cliffs, NJ: Prentice-Hall.

Ortega, J. M. and Rheinbolt, W.C. (1970), "Iterative Solution of Nonlinear Equations in Several Variables," Burlington, MA: Academic Press.

Pakes, A. and Pollard, D. (1989), "Simulation and the Asymptotics of Optimization Estimators," *Econometrica* 57, 1027-1057.

Parzen, E. (1957), "On Consistent Estimates of the Spectrum of a Stationary Time Series," *Annals of Mathematical Statistics*, 28, 329–348.

Pearlman, J. G. (1980), "An Algorithm for Exact Likelihood of a High-Order Autoregressive-Moving Average Process," *Biometrika*, 67 (1), 232–233.

Petzold, L.R. (1982), "Differential/Algebraic Equations Are Not ODEs," *Siam J. Sci. Stat. Comput.*, 3, 367–384.

Phillips, C.B. and Park, J.Y. (1988), "On Formulating Wald Tests of Nonlinear Restrictions," *Econometrica*, 56, 1065–1083.

Pindyck, R.S. and Rubinfeld, D.L. (1981), *Econometric Models and Economic Forecasts*, Second Edition, New York: McGraw-Hill Book Co.

Savin, N.E. and White, K.J. (1978), "Testing for Autocorrelation with Missing Observations," *Econometrics*, 46, 59–67.

Sobol, I.M., *A Primer for the Monte Carlo Method*, Boca Raton, FL: CRC Press, 1994.

Srivastava, V. and Giles, D.E.A., (1987), "Seemingly Unrelated Regression Equation Models," New York: Marcel Dekker, Inc.

Theil, H. (1971), *Principles of Econometrics*, New York: John Wiley & Sons, Inc.

Thursby, J., (1982), "Misspecification, Heteroscedasticity, and the Chow and Goldfield-Quandt Test," *Review of Economics and Statistics*, 64, 314–321.

Venzon, D.J. and Moolgavkar, S.H. (1988), "A Method for Computing Profile-Likelihood Based Confidence Intervals," *Applied Statistics*, 37, 87–94.

White, Halbert, (1980), "A Heteroskedasticity-Consistent Covariance Matrix Estimator and a Direct Test for Heteroskedasticity," *Econometrica*, 48 (4), 817–838.

Wu, D. M. (July 1973), "Alternative Tests of Independence Between Stochastic Regressors and Disturbances," *Econometrica* , 41 (4), 733–750.

Chapter 21
The PDLREG Procedure

Chapter Contents

Chapter 21

The PDLREG Procedure

Overview

The PDLREG procedure estimates regression models for time series data in which the effects of some of the regressor variables are distributed across time. The distributed lag model assumes that the effect of an input variable X on an output Y is distributed over time. If you change the value of X at time *t*, Y will experience some immediate effect at time *t*, and it will also experience a delayed effect at times $t+1$, $t+2$, and so on up to time $t+p$ for some limit *p*.

The regression model supported by PROC PDLREG can include any number of regressors with distribution lags and any number of covariates. (Simple regressors without lag distributions are called covariates.) For example, the two-regressor model with a distributed lag effect for one regressor is written

$$y_t = \alpha + \sum_{i=0}^{p} \beta_i x_{t-i} + \gamma z_t + u_t$$

Here, x_t is the regressor with a distributed lag effect, z_t is a simple covariate, and u_t is an error term.

The distribution of the lagged effects is modeled by Almon lag polynomials. The coefficients b_i of the lagged values of the regressor are assumed to lie on a polynomial curve. That is,

$$b_i = \alpha_0^* + \sum_{j=1}^{d} \alpha_j^* i^j$$

where $d(\leq p)$ is the degree of the polynomial. For the numerically efficient estimation, the PDLREG procedure uses *orthogonal polynomials*. The preceding equation can be transformed into orthogonal polynomials.

$$b_i = \alpha_0 + \sum_{j=1}^{d} \alpha_j f_j(i)$$

where $f_j(i)$ is a polynomial of degree *j* in the lag length *i*, and α_j is a coefficient estimated from the data.

The PDLREG procedure supports endpoint restrictions for the polynomial. That is, you can constrain the estimated polynomial lag distribution curve so that $b_{-1} = 0$ or

$b_{p+1} = 0$, or both. You can also impose linear restrictions on the parameter estimates for the covariates.

You can specify a minimum degree and a maximum degree for the lag distribution polynomial, and the procedure fits polynomials for all degrees in the specified range. (However, if distributed lags are specified for more that one regressor, you can specify a range of degrees for only one of them.)

The PDLREG procedure can also test for autocorrelated residuals and perform autocorrelated error correction using the autoregressive error model. You can specify any order autoregressive error model and can specify several different estimation methods for the autoregressive model, including exact maximum likelihood.

The PDLREG procedure computes generalized Durbin-Watson statistics to test for autocorrelated residuals. For models with lagged dependent variables, the procedure can produce Durbin h and Durbin t statistics. You can request significance level p-values for the Durbin-Watson, Durbin h, and Durbin t statistics. See Chapter 12, "The AUTOREG Procedure," for details about these statistics.

The PDLREG procedure assumes that the input observations form a time series. Thus, the PDLREG procedure should be used only for ordered and equally spaced time series data.

Getting Started

Use the MODEL statement to specify the regression model. The PDLREG procedure's MODEL statement is written like MODEL statements in other SAS regression procedures, except that a regressor can be followed by a lag distribution specification enclosed in parentheses.

For example, the following MODEL statement regresses Y on X and Z and specifies a distributed lag for X:

```
model y = x(4,2) z;
```

The notation X(4,2) specifies that the model includes X and 4 lags of X, with the coefficients of X and its lags constrained to follow a second-degree (quadratic) polynomial. Thus, the regression model specified by this MODEL statement is

$$y_t = a + b_0 x_t + b_1 x_{t-1} + b_2 x_{t-2} + b_3 x_{t-3} + b_4 x_{t-4} + c z_t + u_t$$

$$b_i = \alpha_0 + \alpha_1 f_1(i) + \alpha_2 f_2(i)$$

where $f_1(i)$ is a polynomial of degree 1 in i and $f_2(i)$ is a polynomial of degree 2 in i.

Lag distribution specifications are enclosed in parentheses and follow the name of the regressor variable. The general form of the lag distribution specification is

regressor-name **(** *length, degree, minimum-degree, end-constraint* **)**

where:

length	is the length of the lag distribution; that is, the number of lags of the regressor to use
degree	is the degree of the distribution polynomial
minimum-degree	is an optional minimum degree for the distribution polynomial
end-constraint	is an optional endpoint restriction specification, which can have the values FIRST, LAST, or BOTH

If the *minimum-degree* option is specified, the PDLREG procedure estimates models for all degrees between *minimum-degree* and *degree*.

Introductory Example

The following statements generate simulated data for variables Y and X. Y depends on the first three lags of X, with coefficients .25, .5, and .25. Thus, the effect of changes of X on Y takes effect 25% after one period, 75% after two periods, and 100% after three periods.

```
data test;
   xl1 = 0; xl2 = 0; xl3 = 0;
   do t = -3 to 100;
      x = ranuni(1234);
      y = 10 + .25 * xl1 + .5 * xl2 + .25 * xl3 + .1 * rannor(1234);
      if t > 0 then output;
      xl3 = xl2; xl2 = xl1; xl1 = x;
      end;
run;
```

The following statements use the PDLREG procedure to regress Y on a distributed lag of X. The length of the lag distribution is 4, and the degree of the distribution polynomial is specified as 3.

```
proc pdlreg data=test;
   model y = x( 4, 3 );
run;
```

The PDLREG procedure first prints a table of statistics for the residuals of the model, as shown in Figure 21.1. See Chapter 12 for an explanation of these statistics.

```
                         The PDLREG Procedure

                       Dependent Variable    y

                   Ordinary Least Squares Estimates

SSE                   0.86604442    DFE                          91
MSE                      0.00952    Root MSE                0.09755
SBC                   -156.72612    AIC                  -169.54786
Regress R-Square          0.7711    Total R-Square           0.7711
Durbin-Watson             1.9920
```

Figure 21.1. Residual Statistics

The PDLREG procedure next prints a table of parameter estimates, standard errors, and *t*-tests, as shown in Figure 21.2.

The PDLREG Procedure

Variable	DF	Estimate	Standard Error	t Value	Approx Pr > |t|
Intercept	1	10.0030	0.0431	231.87	<.0001
x**0	1	0.4406	0.0378	11.66	<.0001
x**1	1	0.0113	0.0336	0.34	0.7377
x**2	1	-0.4108	0.0322	-12.75	<.0001
x**3	1	0.0331	0.0392	0.84	0.4007

Figure 21.2. Parameter Estimates

The preceding table shows the model intercept and the estimated parameters of the lag distribution polynomial. The parameter labeled X**0 is the constant term, α_0, of the distribution polynomial. X**1 is the linear coefficient, α_1, X**2 is the quadratic coefficient, α_2, and X**3 is the cubic coefficient, α_3.

The parameter estimates for the distribution polynomial are not of interest in themselves. Since the PDLREG procedure does not print the orthogonal polynomial basis that it constructs to represent the distribution polynomial, these coefficient values cannot be interpreted.

However, because these estimates are for an orthogonal basis, you can use these results to test the degree of the polynomial. For example, this table shows that the X**3 estimate is not significant; the *p*-value for its *t* ratio is .4007, while the X**2 estimate is highly significant ($p < .0001$). This indicates that a second-degree polynomial may be more appropriate for this data set.

The PDLREG procedure next prints the lag distribution coefficients and a graphical display of these coefficients, as shown in Figure 21.3.

```
                         The PDLREG Procedure

                    Estimate of Lag Distribution

                                    Standard                     Approx
Variable              Estimate         Error     t Value       Pr > |t|

x(0)                 -0.040150        0.0360       -1.12         0.2677
x(1)                  0.324241        0.0307       10.55         <.0001
x(2)                  0.416661        0.0239       17.45         <.0001
x(3)                  0.289482        0.0315        9.20         <.0001
x(4)                 -0.004926        0.0365       -0.13         0.8929

                   Estimate of Lag Distribution

  Variable          -0.04                                    0.4167

  x(0)              |***|                                         |
  x(1)              |   |******************************           |
  x(2)              |   |*****************************************|
  x(3)              |   |***************************              |
  x(4)              |   |                                         |
```

Figure 21.3. Coefficients and Graph of Estimated Lag Distribution

The lag distribution coefficients are the coefficients of the lagged values of X in the regression model. These coefficients lie on the polynomial curve defined by the parameters shown in Figure 21.2. Note that the estimated values for X(1), X(2), and X(3) are highly significant, while X(0) and X(4) are not significantly different from 0. These estimates are reasonably close to the true values used to generate the simulated data.

The graphical display of the lag distribution coefficients plots the estimated lag distribution polynomial reported in Figure 21.2. The roughly quadratic shape of this plot is another indication that a third-degree distribution curve is not needed for this data set.

Syntax

The following statements can be used with the PDLREG procedure:

> **PROC PDLREG** *option* ;
> **BY** *variables* ;
> **MODEL** *dependents = effects / options* ;
> **OUTPUT OUT=** *SAS-data-set keyword = variables* ;
> **RESTRICT** *restrictions* ;

Functional Summary

The statements and options used with the PDLREG procedure are summarized in the following table:

Description	Statement	Option
Data Set Options		
specify the input data set	PDLREG	DATA=
write predicted values to an output data set	OUTPUT	OUT=
BY-Group Processing		
specify BY-group processing	BY	
Printing Control Options		
request all print options	MODEL	ALL
print correlations of the estimates	MODEL	CORRB
print covariances of the estimates	MODEL	COVB
print DW statistics up to order *j*	MODEL	DW=*j*
print the marginal probability of DW statistics	MODEL	DWPROB
print inverse of the crossproducts matrix	MODEL	I
print details at each iteration step	MODEL	ITPRINT
print Durbin *t* statistic	MODEL	LAGDEP
print Durbin *h* statistic	MODEL	LAGDEP=
suppress printed output	MODEL	NOPRINT
print partial autocorrelations	MODEL	PARTIAL
print standardized parameter estimates	MODEL	STB
print crossproducts matrix	MODEL	XPX
Model Estimation Options		
specify order of autoregressive process	MODEL	NLAG=
suppress intercept parameter	MODEL	NOINT
specify convergence criterion	MODEL	CONVERGE=
specify maximum number of iterations	MODEL	MAXITER=
specify estimation method	MODEL	METHOD=
Output Control Options		
specify confidence limit size	OUTPUT	ALPHACLI=
specify confidence limit size for structural predicted values	OUTPUT	ALPHACLM=
output transformed intercept variable	OUTPUT	CONSTANT=
output lower confidence limit for predicted values	OUTPUT	LCL=
output lower confidence limit for structural predicted values	OUTPUT	LCLM=
output predicted values	OUTPUT	P=
output predicted values of the structural part	OUTPUT	PM=
output residuals from the predicted values	OUTPUT	R=
output residuals from the structural predicted values	OUTPUT	RM=

Description	Statement	Option
output transformed variables	OUTPUT	TRANSFORM=
output upper confidence limit for the predicted values	OUTPUT	UCL=
output upper confidence limit for the structural predicted values	OUTPUT	UCLM=

PROC PDLREG Statement

PROC PDLREG *option ;*

The PROC PDLREG statement has the following option:

DATA= *SAS-data-set*
specifies the name of the SAS data set containing the input data. If you do not specify the DATA= option, the most recently created SAS data set is used.

In addition, you can place any of the following MODEL statement options in the PROC PDLREG statement, which is equivalent to specifying the option for every MODEL statement: ALL, CONVERGE=, CORRB, COVB, DW=, DWPROB, ITPRINT, MAXITER=, METHOD=, NOINT, NOPRINT, and PARTIAL.

BY Statement

BY *variables ;*

A BY statement can be used with PROC PDLREG to obtain separate analyses on observations in groups defined by the BY variables.

MODEL Statement

MODEL *dependent = effects / options ;*

The MODEL statement specifies the regression model. The keyword MODEL is followed by the dependent variable name, an equal sign, and a list of independent effects. Only one MODEL statement is allowed.

Every variable in the model must be a numeric variable in the input data set. Specify an independent effect with a variable name optionally followed by a polynomial lag distribution specification.

Specifying Independent Effects

The general form of an effect is

variable (length, degree, minimum-degree, constraint)

The term in parentheses following the variable name specifies a polynomial distributed lag (PDL) for the variable. The PDL specification is as follows:

length specifies the number of lags of the variable to include in the lag distribution.

degree specifies the maximum degree of the distribution polynomial. If not specified, the degree defaults to the lag length.

minimum-degree specifies the minimum degree of the polynomial. By default *minimum-degree* is the same as *degree*.

constraint specifies endpoint restrictions on the polynomial. The value of *constraint* can be FIRST, LAST, or BOTH. If a value is not specified, there are no endpoint restrictions.

If you do not specify the *degree* or *minimum-degree* parameter, but you do specify endpoint restrictions, you must use commas to show which parameter, *degree* or *minimum-degree*, is left out.

MODEL Statement Options

The following options can appear in the MODEL statement after a slash (/):

ALL

prints all the matrices computed during the analysis of the model.

CORRB

prints the matrix of estimated correlations between the parameter estimates.

COVB

prints the matrix of estimated covariances between the parameter estimates.

DW= *j*

prints the generalized Durbin-Watson statistics up to the order of *j*. The default is DW=1. When you specify the LAGDEP or LAGDEP=*name* option, the Durbin-Watson statistic is not printed unless you specify the DW= option.

DWPROB

prints the marginal probability of the Durbin-Watson statistic.

CONVERGE= *value*

sets the convergence criterion. If the maximum absolute value of the change in the autoregressive parameter estimates between iterations is less than this amount, then convergence is assumed. The default is CONVERGE=.001.

I

prints $(\mathbf{X'X})^{-1}$, the inverse of the crossproducts matrix for the model; or, if restrictions are specified, prints $(\mathbf{X'X})^{-1}$ adjusted for the restrictions.

ITPRINT

prints information on each iteration.

LAGDEP
LAGDV

prints the *t* statistic for testing residual autocorrelation when regressors contain lagged dependent variables.

LAGDEP= *name*
LAGDV= *name*

prints the Durbin *h* statistic for testing the presence of first-order autocorrelation when regressors contain the lagged dependent variable whose name is specified as LAGDEP=*name*. When the *h* statistic cannot be computed, the asymptotically equivalent *t* statistic is given.

MAXITER= *number*

sets the maximum number of iterations allowed. The default is MAXITER=50.

METHOD= *value*

specifies the type of estimates for the autoregressive component. The values of the METHOD= option are as follows:

METHOD=ML specifies the maximum likelihood method

METHOD=ULS specifies unconditional least squares

METHOD=YW specifies the Yule-Walker method

METHOD=ITYW specifies iterative Yule-Walker estimates

The default is METHOD=ML if you specified the LAGDEP or LAGDEP= option; otherwise, METHOD=YW is the default.

NLAG= *m*
NLAG= *(number-list)*

specifies the order of the autoregressive process or the subset of autoregressive lags to be fit. If you do not specify the NLAG= option, PROC PDLREG does not fit an autoregressive model.

NOINT

suppresses the intercept parameter from the model.

NOPRINT

suppresses the printed output.

PARTIAL

prints partial autocorrelations if the NLAG= option is specified.

STB

prints standardized parameter estimates. Sometimes known as a standard partial regression coefficient, a *standardized parameter estimate* is a parameter estimate multiplied by the standard deviation of the associated regressor and divided by the standard deviation of the regressed variable.

XPX

prints the crossproducts matrix, **X'X**, used for the model. **X** refers to the transformed matrix of regressors for the regression.

OUTPUT Statement

OUTPUT *OUT= SAS-data-set keyword=option ... ;*

The OUTPUT statement creates an output SAS data set with variables as specified by the following keyword options. The associated computations for these options are described in the section "Predicted Values" in Chapter 12.

ALPHACLI= *number*

sets the confidence limit size for the estimates of future values of the current realization of the response time series to *number*, where *number* is less than one and greater than zero. The resulting confidence interval has 1-*number* confidence. The default value for *number* is .05, corresponding to a 95% confidence interval.

ALPHACLM= *number*

sets the confidence limit size for the estimates of the structural or regression part of the model to *number*, where *number* is less than one and greater than zero. The resulting confidence interval has 1-*number* confidence. The default value for *number* is .05, corresponding to a 95% confidence interval.

OUT= *SAS-data-set*

names the output data.

The following specifications are of the form *KEYWORD=names*, where *KEYWORD=* specifies the statistic to include in the output data set and *names* gives names to the variables that contain the statistics.

CONSTANT= *variable*

writes the transformed intercept to the output data set.

LCL= *name*

requests that the lower confidence limit for the predicted value (specified in the PREDICTED= option) be added to the output data set under the name given.

LCLM= *name*

requests that the lower confidence limit for the structural predicted value (specified in the PREDICTEDM= option) be added to the output data set under the name given.

PREDICTED= *name*
P=*name*

stores the predicted values in the output data set under the name given.

PREDICTEDM= *name*
PM= *name*

stores the structural predicted values in the output data set under the name given. These values are formed from only the structural part of the model.

RESIDUAL= *name*
R= *name*
stores the residuals from the predicted values based on both the structural and time series parts of the model in the output data set under the name given.

RESIDUALM= *name*
RM= *name*
requests that the residuals from the structural prediction be given.

TRANSFORM= *variables*
requests that the specified variables from the input data set be transformed by the autoregressive model and put in the output data set. If you need to reproduce the data suitable for reestimation, you must also transform an intercept variable. To do this, transform a variable that only takes the value 1 or use the CONSTANT= option.

UCL= *name*
stores the upper confidence limit for the predicted value (specified in the PREDICTED= option) in the output data set under the name given.

UCLM= *name*
stores the upper confidence limit for the structural predicted value (specified in the PREDICTEDM= option) in the output data set under the name given.

For example, the SAS statements

```
proc pdlreg data=a;
   model y=x1 x2;
   output out=b p=yhat r=resid;
```

create an output data set named B. In addition to the input data set variables, the data set B contains the variable YHAT, whose values are predicted values of the dependent variable Y, and RESID, whose values are the residual values of Y.

RESTRICT Statement

RESTRICT *equation , ... , equation ;*

The RESTRICT statement places restrictions on the parameter estimates for covariates in the preceding MODEL statement. A parameter produced by a distributed lag cannot be restricted with the RESTRICT statement.

Each restriction is written as a linear equation. If you specify more than one restriction in a RESTRICT statement, the restrictions are separated by commas.

You can refer to parameters by the name of the corresponding regressor variable. Each name used in the equation must be a regressor in the preceding MODEL statement. Use the keyword INTERCEPT to refer to the intercept parameter in the model.

RESTRICT statements can be given labels. You can use labels to distinguish results for different restrictions in the printed output. Labels are specified as follows:

label : **RESTRICT** . . . ;

The following is an example of the use of the RESTRICT statement, in which the coefficients of the regressors X1 and X2 are required to sum to 1.

```
proc pdlreg data=a;
   model y = x1 x2;
   restrict x1 + x2 = 1;
run;
```

Parameter names can be multiplied by constants. When no equal sign appears, the linear combination is set equal to 0. Note that the parameters associated with the variables are restricted, not the variables themselves. Here are some examples of valid RESTRICT statements:

```
restrict x1 + x2 = 1;
restrict x1 + x2 - 1;
restrict 2 * x1 = x2 + x3 , intercept + x4 = 0;
restrict x1 = x2 = x3 = 1;
restrict 2 * x1 - x2;
```

Restricted parameter estimates are computed by introducing a Lagrangian parameter λ for each restriction (Pringle and Raynor 1971). The estimates of these Lagrangian parameters are printed in the parameter estimates table. If a restriction cannot be applied, its parameter value and degrees of freedom are listed as 0.

The Lagrangian parameter, λ, measures the sensitivity of the SSE to the restriction. If the restriction is changed by a small amount ϵ, the SSE is changed by $2\lambda\epsilon$.

The t ratio tests the significance of the restrictions. If λ is zero, the restricted estimates are the same as the unrestricted ones.

You can specify any number of restrictions on a RESTRICT statement, and you can use any number of RESTRICT statements. The estimates are computed subject to all restrictions specified. However, restrictions should be consistent and not redundant.

Details

Missing Values

The PDLREG procedure skips any observations at the beginning of the data set that have missing values. The procedure uses all observations with nonmissing values for all the independent and dependent variables such that the lag distribution has sufficient nonmissing lagged independent variables.

Polynomial Distributed Lag Estimation

The simple finite distributed lag model is expressed in the form

$$y_t = \alpha + \sum_{i=0}^{p} \beta_i x_{t-i} + \epsilon_t$$

When the lag length (*p*) is long, severe multicollinearity can occur. Use the Almon or *polynomial distributed lag* model to avoid this problem, since the relatively low degree *d* (≤*p*) polynomials can capture the true lag distribution. The lag coefficient can be written in the Almon polynomial lag

$$\beta_i = \alpha_0^* + \sum_{j=1}^{d} \alpha_j^* i^j$$

Emerson (1968) proposed an efficient method of constructing orthogonal polynomials from the preceding polynomial equation as

$$\beta_i = \alpha_0 + \sum_{j=1}^{d} \alpha_j f_j(i)$$

where $f_j(i)$ is a polynomial of degree *j* in the lag length *i*. The polynomials $f_j(i)$ are chosen so that they are orthogonal:

$$\sum_{i=1}^{n} w_i f_j(i) f_k(i) = \begin{cases} 1 & \text{if } j = k \\ 0 & \text{if } j \neq k \end{cases}$$

where w_i is the weighting factor, and $n = p + 1$. PROC PDLREG uses the equal weights ($w_i = 1$) for all *i*. To construct the orthogonal polynomials, the following recursive relation is used:

$$f_j(i) = (A_j i + B_j) f_{j-1}(i) - C_j f_{j-2}(i) \qquad j = 1, \ldots, d$$

The constants A_j, B_j, and C_j are determined as follows:

$$\begin{aligned} A_j &= \left\{ \sum_{i=1}^{n} w_i i^2 f_{j-1}^2(i) - \left(\sum_{i=1}^{n} w_i i f_{j-1}^2(i) \right)^2 \right. \\ &\qquad \left. - \left(\sum_{i=1}^{n} w_i i f_{j-1}(i) f_{j-2}(i) \right)^2 \right\}^{-1/2} \\ B_j &= -A_j \sum_{i=1}^{n} w_i i f_{j-1}^2(i) \\ C_j &= A_j \sum_{i=1}^{n} w_i i f_{j-1}(i) f_{j-2}(i) \end{aligned}$$

where $f_{-1}(i) = 0$ and $f_0(i) = 1/\sqrt{\sum_{i=1}^{n} w_i}$.

PROC PDLREG estimates the orthogonal polynomial coefficients, $\alpha_0, \ldots, \alpha_d$, to compute the coefficient estimate of each independent variable (X) with distributed lags. For example, if an independent variable is specified as X(9,3), a third-degree polynomial is used to specify the distributed lag coefficients. The third-degree polynomial is fit as a constant term, a linear term, a quadratic term, and a cubic term. The four terms are constructed to be orthogonal. In the output produced by the PDLREG procedure for this case, parameter estimates with names X**0, X**1, X**2, and X**3 correspond to $\hat{\alpha}_0, \hat{\alpha}_1, \hat{\alpha}_2$, and $\hat{\alpha}_3$, respectively. A test using the *t* statistic and the approximate *p*-value ("Approx Pr > $|t|$") associated with X**3 can determine whether a second-degree polynomial rather than a third-degree polynomial is appropriate. The estimates of the ten lag coefficients associated with the specification X(9,3) are labeled X(0), X(1), X(2), X(3), X(4), X(5), X(6), X(7), X(8), and X(9).

Autoregressive Error Model Estimation

The PDLREG procedure uses the same autoregressive error model estimation methods as the AUTOREG procedure. These two procedures share the same computational resources for computing estimates. See Chapter 12 for details about estimation methods for autoregressive error models.

OUT= Data Set

The OUT= data set produced by the PDLREG procedure's OUTPUT statement is similar in form to the OUT= data set produced by the AUTOREG procedure. See Chapter 12 for details on the OUT= data set.

Printed Output

The PDLREG procedure prints the following items:

1. the name of the dependent variable
2. the ordinary least squares (OLS) estimates
3. the estimates of autocorrelations and of the autocovariance, and if line size permits, a graph of the autocorrelation at each lag. The autocorrelation for lag 0 is 1. These items are printed if you specify the NLAG= option.
4. the partial autocorrelations if the PARTIAL and NLAG= options are specified. The first partial autocorrelation is the autocorrelation for lag 1.
5. the preliminary mean square error, which results from solving the Yule-Walker equations if you specify the NLAG= option
6. the estimates of the autoregressive parameters, their standard errors, and the ratios of estimates to standard errors (*t*) if you specify the NLAG= option
7. the statistics of fit for the final model if you specify the NLAG= option. These include the error sum of squares (SSE), the degrees of freedom for error (DFE), the mean square error (MSE), the root mean square error (Root MSE), the Schwarz information criterion (SBC), the Akaike's information criterion

(AIC), the regression R^2 (Regress R-Square), the total R^2 (Total R-Square), and the Durbin-Watson statistic (Durbin-Watson). See Chapter 12 for details of the regression R^2 and the total R^2.

8. the parameter estimates for the structural model (B), a standard error estimate, the ratio of estimate to standard error (*t*), and an approximation to the significance probability for the parameter being 0 ("Approx Pr > $|t|$")
9. a plot of the lag distribution (estimate of lag distribution)
10. the covariance matrix of the parameter estimates if the COVB option is specified

ODS Table Names

PROC PDLREG assigns a name to each table it creates. You can use these names to reference the table when using the Output Delivery System (ODS) to select tables and create output data sets. These names are listed in the following table. For more information on ODS, see Chapter 8, "Using the Output Delivery System."

Table 21.1. ODS Tables Produced in PROC PDLREG

ODS Table Name	Description	Option
ODS Tables Created by the MODEL Statement		
ARParameterEstimates	Estimates of Autoregressive Parameters	NLAG=
CholeskyFactor	Cholesky Root of Gamma	
Coefficients	Coefficients for First NLAG Observations	NLAG=
ConvergenceStatus	Convergence Status table	default
CorrB	Correlation of Parameter Estimates	CORRB
CorrGraph	Estimates of Autocorrelations	NLAG=
CovB	Covariance of Parameter Estimates	COVB
DependenceEquations	Linear dependence equation	
Dependent	Dependent variable	default
DWTest	Durbin-Watson Statistics	DW=
ExpAutocorr	Expected Autocorrelations	NLAG=
FitSummary	Summary of regression	default
GammaInverse	Gamma Inverse	
IterHistory	Iteration History	ITPRINT
LagDist	Lag Distribution	ALL
ParameterEstimates	Parameter Estimates	default
ParameterEstimatesGivenAR	Parameter estimates assuming AR parameters are given	NLAG=
PartialAutoCorr	Partial autocorrelation	PARTIAL
PreMSE	Preliminary MSE	NLAG=
XPXIMatrix	Inverse X'X Matrix	XPX
XPXMatrix	X'X Matrix	XPX

Table 21.1. (continued)

ODS Table Name	Description	Option
YWIterSSE	Yule-Walker iteration sum of squared error	METHOD=ITYW
ODS Tables Created by the RESTRICT Statement		
Restrict	Restriction table	default

Examples

Example 21.1. Industrial Conference Board Data

In the following example, a second-degree Almon polynomial lag model is fit to a model with a five-period lag, and dummy variables are used for quarter effects. The PDL model is estimated using capital appropriations data series for the period 1952 to 1967. The estimation model is written

$$
\begin{aligned}
CE_t = a_0 + b_1 Q1_t + b_2 Q2_t + b_3 Q3_t \\
+ c_0 CA_t + c_1 CA_{t-1} + \ldots + c_5 CA_{t-5}
\end{aligned}
$$

where CE represents capital expenditures and CA represents capital appropriations.

```
title 'National Industrial Conference Board Data';
title2 'Quarterly Series - 1952Q1 to 1967Q4';

data a;
   input ce ca @@;
   qtr = mod( _n_-1, 4 ) + 1;
   q1  = qtr=1;
   q2  = qtr=2;
   q3  = qtr=3;
cards;
   2072 1660 2077 1926 2078 2181 2043 1897 2062 1695
   2067 1705 1964 1731 1981 2151 1914 2556 1991 3152
   2129 3763 2309 3903 2614 3912 2896 3571 3058 3199
   3309 3262 3446 3476 3466 2993 3435 2262 3183 2011
   2697 1511 2338 1631 2140 1990 2012 1993 2071 2520
   2192 2804 2240 2919 2421 3024 2639 2725 2733 2321
   2721 2131 2640 2552 2513 2234 2448 2282 2429 2533
   2516 2517 2534 2772 2494 2380 2596 2568 2572 2944
   2601 2629 2648 3133 2840 3449 2937 3764 3136 3983
   3299 4381 3514 4786 3815 4094 4093 4870 4262 5344
   4531 5433 4825 5911 5160 6109 5319 6542 5574 5785
   5749 5707 5715 5412 5637 5465 5383 5550 5467 5465
;

proc pdlreg data=a;
```

```
   model ce = q1 q2 q3 ca(5,2) / dwprob;
run;
```

The printed output produced by the PDLREG procedure is shown in Output 21.1.1. The small Durbin-Watson test indicates autoregressive errors.

Output 21.1.1. Printed Output Produced by PROC PDLREG

```
                    National Industrial Conference Board Data
                      Quarterly Series - 1952Q1 to 1967Q4

                             The PDLREG Procedure

                           Dependent Variable    ce


                       Ordinary Least Squares Estimates

   SSE                      1205186.4    DFE                          48
   MSE                          25108    Root MSE              158.45520
   SBC                      733.84921    AIC                  719.797878
   Regress R-Square            0.9834    Total R-Square           0.9834
   Durbin-Watson               0.6157    Pr < DW                  <.0001
   Pr > DW                     1.0000


                                            Standard                   Approx
 Variable        DF      Estimate         Error    t Value     Pr > |t|

 Intercept        1      210.0109       73.2524       2.87       0.0061
 q1               1      -10.5515       61.0634      -0.17       0.8635
 q2               1      -20.9887       59.9386      -0.35       0.7277
 q3               1      -30.4337       59.9004      -0.51       0.6137
 ca**0            1        0.3760      0.007318      51.38       <.0001
 ca**1            1        0.1297        0.0251       5.16       <.0001
 ca**2            1        0.0247        0.0593       0.42       0.6794


                        Estimate of Lag Distribution

                                           Standard                  Approx
  Variable               Estimate            Error    t Value     Pr > |t|

  ca(0)                  0.089467           0.0360       2.49       0.0165
  ca(1)                  0.104317           0.0109       9.56       <.0001
  ca(2)                  0.127237           0.0255       5.00       <.0001
  ca(3)                  0.158230           0.0254       6.24       <.0001
  ca(4)                  0.197294           0.0112      17.69       <.0001
  ca(5)                  0.244429           0.0370       6.60       <.0001

                       Estimate of Lag Distribution


   Variable          0                                             0.2444

   ca(0)             |***************                                    |
   ca(1)             |*****************                                  |
   ca(2)             |*********************                              |
   ca(3)             |**************************                         |
   ca(4)             |********************************                   |
   ca(5)             |****************************************           |
```

The following statements use the REG procedure to fit the same polynomial distributed lag model. A DATA step computes lagged values of the regressor X, and

RESTRICT statements are used to impose the polynomial lag distribution. Refer to Judge, Griffiths, Hill, Lutkepohl, and Lee (1985, pp 357–359) for the restricted least squares estimation of the Almon distributed lag model.

```
data b;
   set a;
   ca_1 = lag( ca );
   ca_2 = lag2( ca );
   ca_3 = lag3( ca );
   ca_4 = lag4( ca );
   ca_5 = lag5( ca );
run;

proc reg data=b;
   model  ce = q1 q2 q3 ca ca_1 ca_2 ca_3 ca_4 ca_5;
   restrict    - ca + 5*ca_1 - 10*ca_2 + 10*ca_3 - 5*ca_4 +    ca_5;
   restrict      ca - 3*ca_1 +  2*ca_2 +  2*ca_3 - 3*ca_4 +    ca_5;
   restrict  -5*ca + 7*ca_1 +  4*ca_2 -  4*ca_3 - 7*ca_4 + 5*ca_5;
run;
```

The REG procedure output is shown in Output 21.1.2.

Output 21.1.2. Printed Output Produced by PROC REG

```
                          The REG Procedure
                            Model: MODEL1
                       Dependent Variable: ce

                         Analysis of Variance

                                    Sum of           Mean
Source                   DF        Squares         Square    F Value    Pr > F

Model                     6       71343377       11890563     473.58    <.0001
Error                    48        1205186          25108
Corrected Total          54       72548564


             Root MSE            158.45520    R-Square     0.9834
             Dependent Mean     3185.69091    Adj R-Sq     0.9813
             Coeff Var             4.97397


                         Parameter Estimates

                         Parameter       Standard
   Variable      DF       Estimate          Error    t Value    Pr > |t|

   Intercept      1      210.01094       73.25236       2.87      0.0061
   q1             1      -10.55151       61.06341      -0.17      0.8635
   q2             1      -20.98869       59.93860      -0.35      0.7277
   q3             1      -30.43374       59.90045      -0.51      0.6137
   ca             1        0.08947        0.03599       2.49      0.0165
   ca_1           1        0.10432        0.01091       9.56      <.0001
   ca_2           1        0.12724        0.02547       5.00      <.0001
   ca_3           1        0.15823        0.02537       6.24      <.0001
   ca_4           1        0.19729        0.01115      17.69      <.0001
   ca_5           1        0.24443        0.03704       6.60      <.0001
   RESTRICT      -1      623.63242          12697       0.05      0.9614*
   RESTRICT      -1          18933          44803       0.42      0.6772*
   RESTRICT      -1          10303          18422       0.56      0.5814*

           * Probability computed using beta distribution.
```

Example 21.2. Money Demand Model

This example estimates the demand for money using the following dynamic specification:

$$m_t = a_0 + b_0 m_{t-1} + \sum_{i=0}^{5} c_i y_{t-i} + \sum_{i=0}^{2} d_i r_{t-i} + \sum_{i=0}^{3} f_i p_{t-i} + u_t$$

where

m_t =log of real money stock (M1)

y_t =log of real GNP

r_t =interest rate (commercial paper rate)

p_t =inflation rate

c_i, d_i, and f_i $(i > 0)$are coefficients for the lagged variables

The following DATA step reads the data and transforms the real money and real GNP variables using the natural logarithm. Refer to Balke and Gordon (1986) for a description of the data.

```
data a;
   input m1 gnp gdf r @@;
   m    = log( 100 * m1 / gdf );
   lagm = lag( m );
   y    = log( gnp );
   p    = log( gdf / lag( gdf ) );
   date = intnx( 'qtr', '1jan1968'd, _n_-1 );
   format date yyqc6.;
   label m      = 'Real Money Stock (M1)'
         lagm = 'Lagged Real Money Stock'
         y      = 'Real GNP'
         r      = 'Commercial Paper Rate'
         p      = 'Inflation Rate';
cards;
   ... data lines are omitted ...
;

proc print data=a(obs=5);
   var date m lagm y r p;
run;
```

Output 21.2.1 shows a partial list of the data set.

Output 21.2.1. Partial List of the Data Set A

Obs	date	m	lagm	y	r	p
1	1968:1	5.44041	.	6.94333	5.58	.
2	1968:2	5.44732	5.44041	6.96226	6.08	0.011513
3	1968:3	5.45815	5.44732	6.97422	5.96	0.008246
4	1968:4	5.46492	5.45815	6.97661	5.96	0.014865
5	1969:1	5.46980	5.46492	6.98855	6.66	0.011005

The regression model is written for the PDLREG procedure with a MODEL statement. The LAGDEP= option is specified to test for the serial correlation in disturbances since regressors contain the lagged dependent variable LAGM.

```
title 'Money Demand Estimation using Distributed Lag Model';
title2 'Quarterly Data - 1968Q2 to 1983Q4';

proc pdlreg data=a;
   model m = lagm y(5,3) r(2, , ,first) p(3,2) / lagdep=lagm;
run;
```

The estimated model is shown in Output 21.2.2 and Output 21.2.3.

Output 21.2.2. Parameter Estimates

Money Demand Estimation using Distributed Lag Model
Quarterly Data - 1968Q2 to 1983Q4

The PDLREG Procedure

Dependent Variable m
Real Money Stock (M1)

Ordinary Least Squares Estimates

SSE	0.00169815	DFE	48
MSE	0.0000354	Root MSE	0.00595
SBC	-404.60169	AIC	-427.4546
Regress R-Square	0.9712	Total R-Square	0.9712
Durbin h	-0.7533	Pr < h	0.2256

Variable	DF	Estimate	Standard Error	t Value	Approx Pr > |t|
Intercept	1	-0.1407	0.2625	-0.54	0.5943
lagm	1	0.9875	0.0425	23.21	<.0001
y**0	1	0.0132	0.004531	2.91	0.0055
y**1	1	-0.0704	0.0528	-1.33	0.1891
y**2	1	0.1261	0.0786	1.60	0.1154
y**3	1	-0.4089	0.1265	-3.23	0.0022
r**0	1	-0.000186	0.000336	-0.55	0.5816
r**1	1	0.002200	0.000774	2.84	0.0065
r**2	1	0.000788	0.000249	3.16	0.0027
p**0	1	-0.6602	0.1132	-5.83	<.0001
p**1	1	0.4036	0.2321	1.74	0.0885
p**2	1	-1.0064	0.2288	-4.40	<.0001

Restriction	DF	L Value	Standard Error	t Value	Approx Pr > |t|
r(-1)	-1	0.0164	0.007275	2.26	0.0223

Output 21.2.3. Estimates for Lagged Variables

```
              Money Demand Estimation using Distributed Lag Model
                         Quarterly Data - 1968Q2 to 1983Q4

                               The PDLREG Procedure

                           Estimate of Lag Distribution

                                          Standard                       Approx
Variable                  Estimate           Error     t Value          Pr > |t|

y(0)                      0.268619          0.0910        2.95            0.0049
y(1)                     -0.196484          0.0612       -3.21            0.0024
y(2)                     -0.163148          0.0537       -3.04            0.0038
y(3)                      0.063850          0.0451        1.42            0.1632
y(4)                      0.179733          0.0588        3.06            0.0036
y(5)                     -0.120276          0.0679       -1.77            0.0827

                          Estimate of Lag Distribution


  Variable        -0.196              0                            0.2686

  y(0)            |                   |*************************|
  y(1)            |*****************|                           |
  y(2)            |    *************|                           |
  y(3)            |                   |******                    |
  y(4)            |                   |*****************         |
  y(5)            |         *********|                          |
```

```
     Money Demand Estimation using Distributed Lag Model
               Quarterly Data - 1968Q2 to 1983Q4

                    The PDLREG Procedure

                Estimate of Lag Distribution

                                  Standard                    Approx
Variable            Estimate         Error    t Value       Pr > |t|

r(0)               -0.001341      0.000388      -3.45         0.0012
r(1)               -0.000751      0.000234      -3.22         0.0023
r(2)                0.001770      0.000754       2.35         0.0230

                Estimate of Lag Distribution

  Variable        -0.001            0                       0.0018

  r(0)            |*****************|                       |
  r(1)            |         *********|                       |
  r(2)            |                 |***********************|


                Estimate of Lag Distribution

                                  Standard                    Approx
Variable            Estimate         Error    t Value       Pr > |t|

p(0)               -1.104051        0.2027      -5.45         <.0001
p(1)                0.082892        0.1257       0.66         0.5128
p(2)                0.263391        0.1381       1.91         0.0624
p(3)               -0.562556        0.2076      -2.71         0.0093

                Estimate of Lag Distribution

  Variable        -1.104                              0   0.2634

  p(0)            |********************************|        |
  p(1)            |                                |***     |
  p(2)            |                                |********|
  p(3)            |                ****************|        |
```

References

Balke, N.S. and Gordon, R.J. (1986), "Historical Data," in *The American Business Cycle*, ed. R.J. Gordon, Chicago: The University of Chicago Press.

Emerson, P.L. (1968), "Numerical Construction of Orthogonal Polynomials from a General Recurrence Formula," *Biometrics*, 24, 695–701.

Gallant, A.R. and Goebel, J.J. (1976), "Nonlinear Regression with Autoregressive Errors," *Journal of the American Statistical Association*, 71, 961–967.

Harvey, A.C. (1981), *The Econometric Analysis of Time Series*, New York: John Wiley & Sons, Inc.

Johnston, J. (1972), *Econometric Methods*, Second Edition, New York: McGraw-Hill Book Co.

Judge, G.G., Griffiths, W.E., Hill, R.C., Lutkepohl, H., and Lee, T.C. (1985), *The Theory and Practice of Econometrics*, Second Edition, New York: John Wiley & Sons, Inc.

Park, R.E. and Mitchell, B.M. (1980), "Estimating the Autocorrelated Error Model with Trended Data," *Journal of Econometrics*, 13, 185–201.

Pringle, R.M. and Raynor, A.A. (1971), *Generalized Inverse Matrices with Applications to Statistics*, New York: Hafner Publishing Company.

Chapter 22
The QLIM Procedure

Chapter Contents

Chapter 22
The QLIM Procedure

Overview

The QLIM (Qualitative and LImited dependent variable Model) procedure analyzes univariate and multivariate limited dependent variable models where dependent variables take discrete values or dependent variables are observed only in a limited range of values. This procedure includes logit, probit, tobit, selection, and multivariate models. The multivariate model can contain discrete choice and limited endogenous variables as well as continuous endogenous variables.

The QLIM procedure supports the following models:

- linear regression model with heteroscedasticity
- probit with heteroscedasticity
- logit with heteroscedasticity
- tobit (censored and truncated) with heteroscedasticity
- Box-Cox regression with heteroscedasticity
- bivariate probit
- bivariate tobit
- sample selection and switching regression models
- multivariate limited dependent variables

Getting Started

The QLIM procedure is similar in use to the other regression or simultaneous equations model procedures in the SAS System. For example, the following statements are used to estimate a binary choice model using the probit probability function:

```
proc qlim data=a;
   model y = x1;
   endogenous y ~ discrete;
run;
```

The response variable, y, is numeric and has discrete values. PROC QLIM enables the user to specify the type of endogenous variables in the ENDOGENOUS statement. The binary probit model can be also specified as follows:

```
model y = x1 / discrete;
```

When multiple endogenous variables are specified in the QLIM procedure, these equations are estimated as a system. Multiple endogenous variables can be specified with one MODEL statement in the QLIM procedure when these models have the same exogenous variables:

```
model y1 y2 = x1 x2 / discrete;
```

The preceding specification is equivalent to

```
proc qlim data=a;
   model y1 = x1 x2;
   model y2 = x1 x2;
   endogenous y1 y2 ~ discrete;
run;
```

The standard tobit model is estimated by specifying the endogenous variable to be truncated or censored. The limits of the dependent variable can be specified with the CENSORED or TRUNCATED option in the ENDOGENOUS or MODEL statement when the data are limited by specific values or variables. For example, the two-limit censored model requires two variables that contain the lower (bottom) and upper (top) bound.

```
proc qlim data=a;
   model y = x1 x2 x3;
   endogenous y ~ censored(lb=bottom ub=top);
run;
```

The bounds can be numbers if they are fixed for all observations in the data set. For example, the standard tobit model can be specified as

```
proc qlim data=a;
   model y = x1 x2 x3;
   endogenous y ~ censored(lb=0);
run;
```

Introductory Example: Binary Probit and Logit Models

The following example illustrates the use of PROC QLIM. The data are originally published by Mroz (1987) and downloaded from Wooldridge (2002). This data set is based on a sample of 753 married white women. The dependent variable is a discrete variable of labor force participation (inlf). Explanatory variables are the number of children ages 5 or younger (kidslt6), the number of children ages 6 to 18 (kidsge6), the woman's age (age), the woman's years of schooling (educ), wife's labor experience (exper), square of experience (expersq), and the family income excluding the wife's wage (nwifeinc). The program (with data values omitted) is illustrated below.

```
title1 "Binary Data";
data mroz;
 input inlf nwifeinc educ exper expersq age kidslt6 kidsge6 lwage;
datalines;
1 10.91006    12 14  196   32  1   0   1.210154

   ...

;
run;


proc qlim data=mroz;
   model inlf = nwifeinc educ exper expersq age kidslt6 kidsge6  / discrete;
run;
```

Results of this analysis are shown in the following four figures. In the first table, shown in Figure 22.1, PROC QLIM provides frequency information on each choice. In this example, 428 women participate in the labor force (inlf=1).

```
                              Binary Data

                          The QLIM Procedure

                  Discrete Response Profile of inlf

        Index           Value             Frequency      Percent

            1               0                   325        43.16
            2               1                   428        56.84
```

Figure 22.1. Choice Frequency Summary

The second table is the estimation summary table shown in Figure 22.2. Included are the number of dependent variables, names of dependent variables, the number of observations, the log-likelihood function value, the maximum absolute gradient, the number of iterations, AIC, and Schwarz criterion.

```
                         Model Fit Summary

          Number of Endogenous Variables                   1
          Endogenous Variable                           inlf
          Number of Observations                         753
          Log Likelihood                          -401.30219
          Maximum Absolute Gradient                0.0004984
          Number of Iterations                            15
          AIC                                      818.60439
          Schwarz Criterion                        855.59691
```

Figure 22.2. Fit Summary Table of Binary Probit

Goodness-of-fit measures are displayed in Figure 22.3. All measures except McKelvey-Zavoina's definition are based on the log-likelihood function value. The likelihood ratio test statistic has chi-square distribution conditional on the null hypothesis that all slope coefficients are zero. In this example, the likelihood ratio statistic is used to test the hypothesis that kidslt6=kidge6=age=educ=exper=expersq=nwifeinc= 0.

```
                          Goodness-of-Fit Measures

Measure                           Value     Formula

Likelihood Ratio (R)             227.14     2 * (LogL - LogL0)
Upper Bound of R (U)             1029.7     - 2 * LogL0
Aldrich-Nelson                   0.2317     R / (R+N)
Cragg-Uhler 1                    0.2604     1 - exp(-R/N)
Cragg-Uhler 2                    0.3494     (1-exp(-R/N)) / (1-exp(-U/N))
Estrella                         0.2888     1 - (1-R/U)^(U/N)
Adjusted Estrella                0.2693     1 - ((LogL-K)/LogL0)^(-2/N*LogL0)
McFadden's LRI                   0.2206     R / U
Veall-Zimmermann                 0.4012     (R * (U+N)) / (U * (R+N))
McKelvey-Zavoina                 0.4025

N = # of observations, K = # of regressors
```

Figure 22.3. Goodness of Fit

Finally, the parameter estimates and standard errors are shown in Figure 22.4.

Parameter Estimates

Parameter	Estimate	Standard Error	t Value	Approx Pr > |t|
Intercept	0.270077	0.508594	0.53	0.5954
nwifeinc	-0.012024	0.004840	-2.48	0.0130
educ	0.130905	0.025254	5.18	<.0001
exper	0.123348	0.018716	6.59	<.0001
expersq	-0.001887	0.000600	-3.15	0.0017
age	-0.052853	0.008477	-6.23	<.0001
kidslt6	-0.868329	0.118522	-7.33	<.0001
kidsge6	0.036005	0.043477	0.83	0.4076

Figure 22.4. Parameter Estimates of Binary Probit

When the error term has a logistic distribution, the binary logit model is estimated. To specify a logistic distribution, add D=LOGIT option as follows,

```
proc qlim data=mroz;
  model inlf = nwifeinc educ exper expersq age kidslt6 kidsge6  / discrete(d=lc
run;
```

The estimated parameters are shown in Figure 22.5.

The QLIM Procedure

Parameter Estimates

Parameter	Estimate	Standard Error	t Value	Approx Pr > |t|
Intercept	0.425452	0.860371	0.49	0.6210
nwifeinc	-0.021345	0.008421	-2.53	0.0113
educ	0.221170	0.043440	5.09	<.0001
exper	0.205870	0.032057	6.42	<.0001
expersq	-0.003154	0.001016	-3.10	0.0019
age	-0.088024	0.014573	-6.04	<.0001
kidslt6	-1.443354	0.203585	-7.09	<.0001
kidsge6	0.060112	0.074790	0.80	0.4215

Figure 22.5. Parameter Estimates of Binary Logit

The heteroscedastic logit model can be estimated using the HETERO statement. If the variance of the logit model is a function of the family income level excluding wife's income (nwifeinc), the variance can be specified as

$$Var(\epsilon_i) = \sigma^2 \exp(\gamma \, \text{nwifeinc}_i)$$

where σ^2 is normalized to 1 because the dependent variable is discrete. The following SAS statements estimate the heteroscedastic logit model:

```
proc qlim data=mroz;
   model inlf = nwifeinc educ exper expersq age kidslt6 kidsge6 / discrete(d=logit);
   hetero inlf ~ nwifeinc / noconst;
run;
```

The parameter estimate (γ) of the heteroscedasticity variable is listed as _H.nwifeinc; see Figure 22.6.

The QLIM Procedure

Parameter Estimates

Parameter	Estimate	Standard Error	t Value	Approx Pr > |t|
Intercept	0.510444	0.983616	0.52	0.6038
nwifeinc	-0.026778	0.012115	-2.21	0.0271
educ	0.255547	0.061765	4.14	<.0001
exper	0.234105	0.046736	5.01	<.0001
expersq	-0.003613	0.001237	-2.92	0.0035
age	-0.100878	0.021524	-4.69	<.0001
kidslt6	-1.645206	0.311737	-5.28	<.0001
kidsge6	0.066941	0.085630	0.78	0.4344
_H.nwifeinc	0.013280	0.013636	0.97	0.3301

Figure 22.6. Parameter Estimates of Binary Logit with Heteroscedasticity

Syntax

The QLIM procedure is controlled by the following statements:

PROC QLIM *options* ;
  BOUNDS *bound1 [, bound2 . . .]* ;
  BY *variables* ;
  CLASS *variables* ;
  ENDOGENOUS *variables ~ options* ;
  HETERO *dependent variables ~ exogenous variables / options* ;
  INIT *initvalue1 [, initvalue2 . . .]* ;
  MODEL *dependent variables = regressors / options* ;
  NLOPTIONS *options* ;
  OUTPUT *options* ;
  RESTRICT *restriction1 [, restriction2 . . .]* ;
  WEIGHT *variable* ;

At least one MODEL statement is required. If more than one MODEL statement is used, the QLIM procedure estimates a system of models. Main effects and higher-order terms can be specified in the MODEL statement, similar to the GLM procedure, and the PROBIT procedure in SAS/STAT. If a CLASS statement is used, it must precede the MODEL statement.

Functional Summary

The statements and options used with the QLIM procedure are summarized in the following table:

Description	Statement	Option
Data Set Options		
specify the input data set	QLIM	DATA=
write parameter estimates to an output data set	QLIM	OUTEST=
write predictions to an output data set	OUTPUT	OUT=
Declaring the Role of Variables		
specify BY-group processing	BY	
specify classification variables	CLASS	
specify a weight variable	WEIGHT	
Printing Control Options		
request all printing options	QLIM	PRINTALL
print correlation matrix of the estimates	QLIM	CORRB
print covariance matrix of the estimates	QLIM	COVB
print a summary iteration listing	QLIM	ITPRINT

Description	Statement	Option
suppress the normal printed output	QLIM	NOPRINT
Options to Control the Optimization Process		
specify the optimization method	QLIM	METHOD=
specify the optimization options	NLOPTIONS	see Chapter 10
set initial values for parameters	INIT	
set linear restrictions on parameters	BOUNDS	
	RESTRICT	
Model Estimation Options		
specify options specific to Box-Cox transformation	MODEL	BOXCOX()
suppress the intercept parameter	MODEL	NOINT
specify a seed for pseudo-random number generation	QLIM	SEED=
specify number of draws for Monte Carlo integration	QLIM	NDRAW=
specify method to calculate parameter covariance	QLIM	COVEST=
Endogenous Variable Options		
specify discrete variable	ENDOGENOUS	DISCRETE()
specify censored variable	ENDOGENOUS	CENSORED()
specify truncated variable	ENDOGENOUS	TRUNCATED()
specify variable selection condition	ENDOGENOUS	SELECT()
Heteroscedasticity Model Options		
specify the function for heteroscedasticity models	HETERO	LINK=
square the function for heteroscedasticity models	HETERO	SQUARE
specify no constant for heteroscedasticity models	HETERO	NOCONST
Output Control Options		
output predicted values	OUTPUT	PREDICTED
output structured part	OUTPUT	XBETA
output residuals	OUTPUT	RESIDUAL
output error standard deviation	OUTPUT	ERRSTD
output marginal effects	OUTPUT	MARGINAL
output probability for the current response	OUTPUT	PROB
output probability for all responses	OUTPUT	PROBALL
output expected value	OUTPUT	EXPECTED
output conditional expected value	OUTPUT	CONDITIONAL
output inverse Mills ratio	OUTPUT	MILLS
include covariances in the OUTEST= data set	QLIM	COVOUT
include correlations in the OUTEST= data set	QLIM	CORROUT

PROC QLIM Statement

PROC QLIM *options* ;

The following options can be used in the PROC QLIM statement:

Data Set Options

DATA= SAS-data-set
specifies the input SAS data set. If the DATA= option is not specified, PROC QLIM uses the most recently created SAS data set.

Output Data Set Options

OUTEST= SAS-data-set
writes the parameter estimates to an output data set.

COVOUT
writes the covariance matrix for the parameter estimates to the OUTEST= data set. This option is valid only if the OUTEST= option is specified.

CORROUT
writes the correlation matrix for the parameter estimates to the OUTEST= data set. This option is valid only if the OUTEST= option is specified.

Printing Options

NOPRINT
suppresses the normal printed output but does not suppress error listings. If NOPRINT option is set, then any other print option is turned off.

PRINTALL
turns on all the printing-control options. The options set by PRINTALL are COVB, CORRB.

CORRB
prints the correlation matrix of the parameter estimates.

COVB
prints the covariance matrix of the parameter estimates.

ITPRINT
prints the initial parameter estimates, convergence criteria, all constraints of the optimization. At each iteration, objective function value, step size, maximum gradient and slope of search direction are printed as well.

Model Estimation Options

COVEST= covariance-option
specify method to calculate the covariance matrix of parameter estimates. The supported covariance types are

OP specifies the covariance from the outer product matrix

HESSIAN	specifies the covariance from the inverse Hessian matrix
QML	specifies the covariance from the outer product and Hessian matrices (the quasi-maximum likelihood estimates)

The default is COVEST=HESSIAN.

NDRAW= value

specify number of draws for Monte Carlo integration.

SEED= value

specify a seed for pseudo-random number generation in Monte Carlo integration.

Options to Control the Optimization Process

PROC QLIM uses the NonLinear Optimization (NLO) subsystem to perform nonlinear optimization tasks. All the NLO options are available from the NLOPTIONS statement. For details, see Chapter 10, "Nonlinear Optimization Methods."

METHOD=*value*

specifies the optimization method. If this option is specified, it overwrites the TECH= option in NLOPTIONS statement. Valid values are

CONGRA	performs a conjugate-gradient optimization
DBLDOG	performs a version of double dogleg optimization
NMSIMP	performs a Nelder-Mead simplex optimization
NEWRAP	performs a Newton-Raphson optimization combining a line-search algorithm with ridging
NRRIDG	performs a Newton-Raphson optimization with ridging
QUANEW	performs a quasi-Newton optimization
TRUREG	performs a trust region optimization

The default method is QUANEW.

BOUNDS Statement

BOUNDS *bound1 [, bound2 ...]* **;**

The BOUNDS statement imposes simple boundary constraints on the parameter estimates. BOUNDS statement constraints refer to the parameters estimated by the QLIM procedure. Any number of BOUNDS statements can be specified.

Each *bound* is composed of variables and constants and inequality operators:

item operator item [operator item [operator item . . .]]

Each *item* is a constant, the name of a parameter, or a list of parameter names. See the "Parameter Names" section for more details on how parameters are named in the QLIM procedure. Each *operator* is '<', '>', '<=', or '>='.

Both the BOUNDS statement and the RESTRICT statement can be used to impose boundary constraints; however, the BOUNDS statement provides a simpler syntax for specifying these kinds of constraints. See the "RESTRICT Statement" section on page 1334 for more information.

The following BOUNDS statement constrains the estimates of the parameters associated with the variable ttime and the variables x1 through x10 to be between zero and one. This example illustrates the use of parameter lists to specify boundary constraints.

```
bounds 0 < ttime x1-x10 < 1;
```

BY Statement

BY *variables* **;**

A BY statement can be used with PROC QLIM to obtain separate analyses on observations in groups defined by the BY variables.

CLASS Statement

CLASS *variables* **;**

The CLASS statement names the classification variables to be used in the analysis. Classification variables can be either character or numeric.

Class levels are determined from the formatted values of the CLASS variables. Thus, you can use formats to group values into levels. See the discussion of the FORMAT procedure in *SAS Language Reference: Dictionary*.

If the CLASS statement is used, it must appear before any of the MODEL statements.

ENDOGENOUS Statement

ENDOGENOUS *variables* ~ *options* **;**

The ENDOGENOUS statement specifies the type of endogenous variables.

Discrete Variable Options

DISCRETE <(*discrete-options*) >

specifies that the endogenous variables in this statement are discrete. Valid *discrete-options* are as follows:

ORDER=DATA | FORMATTED | FREQ | INTERNAL

specifies the sorting order for the levels of the discrete variables specified in the ENDOGENOUS statement. This ordering determines which parameters in the model correspond to each level in the data. The following table shows how PROC QLIM interprets values of the ORDER= option.

Value of ORDER=	Levels Sorted By
DATA	order of appearance in the input data set
FORMATTED	formatted value
FREQ	descending frequency count; levels with the most observations come first in the order
INTERNAL	unformatted value

By default, ORDER=FORMATTED. For the values FORMATTED and INTERNAL, the sort order is machine dependent. For more information on sorting order, see the chapter on the SORT procedure in the *SAS Procedures Guide*.

DISTRIBUTION=*distribution-type*
DIST=*distribution-type*
D=*distribution-type*

specifies the cumulative distribution function used to model the response probabilities. Valid values for *distribution-type* are

NORMAL	the normal distribution for the probit model
LOGISTIC	the logistic distribution for the logit model

By default, DISTRIBUTION=NORMAL.

Censored Variable Options

CENSORED < (*censored-options*) >

specifies that the endogenous variables in this statement are censored. Valid *censored-options* are as follows:

LB=*value or variable*
LOWERBOUND=*value or variable*

specifies the lower bound of the censored variables. If *value* is missing or the value in *variable* is missing, no lower bound is set. By default, no lower bound is set.

UB=*value or variable*
UPPERBOUND=*value or variable*

specifies the upper bound of the censored variables. If *value* is missing or the value in *variable* is missing, no upper bound is set. By default, no upper bound is set.

Truncated Variable Options

TRUNCATED < (*truncated-options*) >

specifies that the endogenous variables in this statement are truncated. Valid *truncated-options* are as follows:

LB=*value or variable*
LOWERBOUND=*value or variable*

specifies the lower bound of the truncated variables. If *value* is missing or the value in *variable* is missing, no lower bound is set. By default, no lower bound is set.

UB=*value or variable*

UPPERBOUND=*value or variable*

specifies the upper bound of the truncated variables. If *value* is missing or the value in *variable* is missing, no upper bound is set. By default, no upper bound is set.

Selection Options

SELECT (*select-option***)**

specifies selection criteria for sample selection model. *Select-option* specifies the condition for the endogenous variable to be selected. It is written as a variable name, followed by an equality operator (=) or an inequality operator (<, >, <=, >=), followed by a number:

variable operator number

The *variable* is the endogenous variable that the selection is based on. The *operator* can be =, <, >, <= , or >=. Multiple *select-options* can be combined with the logic operators: AND, OR. This example illustrates the use of SELECT option.

```
endogenous y1 ~ select(z=0);
endogenous y2 ~ select(z=1 and z=2);
```

HETERO Statement

HETERO *dependent variables* ~ *exogenous variables / options***;**

The HETERO statement specifies variables that are related to the heteroscedasticity of the residuals and the way these variables are used to model the error variance. The heteroscedastic regression model supported by PROC QLIM is

$$y_i = \mathbf{x}_i'\boldsymbol{\beta} + \epsilon_i$$

$$\epsilon_i \sim \mathrm{N}(0, \sigma_\mathrm{i}^2)$$

See the section "Heteroscedasticity" on page 1340 for more details on the specification of functional forms.

LINK=*value*

The functional form can be specified using the LINK= option. The following option values are allowed:

EXP specifies exponential link function

$$\sigma_i^2 = \sigma^2(1 + \exp(\mathbf{z}_i'\gamma))$$

LINEAR specifies linear link function

$$\sigma_i^2 = \sigma^2(1 + \mathbf{z}_i'\gamma)$$

When the LINK= option is not specified, the exponential link function is specified by default.

NOCONST
specifies that there is no constant in linear or exponential heteroscedasticity model.

$$\sigma_i^2 = \sigma^2(\mathbf{z}_i'\gamma)$$
$$\sigma_i^2 = \sigma^2\exp(\mathbf{z}_i'\gamma)$$

SQUARE
estimates the model using the square of linear heteroscedasticity function. For example, you can specify the following heteroscedasticity function:

$$\sigma_i^2 = \sigma^2(1 + (\mathbf{z}_i'\gamma)^2)$$

```
model y = x1 x2 / discrete;
hetero y ~ z1 / link=linear square;
```

The option SQUARE does not apply to exponential heteroscedasticity function because the square of an exponential function of $\mathbf{z}_i'\gamma$ is the same the exponetial of $2\mathbf{z}_i'\gamma$. Hence the only difference is that all γ estimates are divided by two.

INIT Statement

INIT *initvalue1 [, initvalue2 . . .]* **;**

The INIT statement is used to set initial values for parameters in the optimization. Any number of INIT statements can be specified.

Each *initvalue* is written as a parameter or parameter list, followed by an optional equality operator (=), followed by a number:

parameter <=> number

MODEL Statement

MODEL *dependent = regressors / options ;*

The MODEL statement specifies the dependent variable and independent regressor variables for the regression model.

The following options can be used in the MODEL statement after a slash (/).

LIMIT1=*value*
specifies the restriction of the threshold value of the first category when the ordinal probit or logit model is estimated. LIMIT1=ZERO is the default option. When LIMIT1=VARYING is specified, the threshold value is estimated.

NOINT
suppresses the intercept parameter.

Endogenous Variable Options

The endogenous variable options are the same as the options specified in the ENDOGENOUS statement. If an endogenous variable has endogenous option specified in both MODEL statement and ENDOGENOUS statement, the option in ENDOGENOUS statement is used.

BOXCOX Estimation Options

BOXCOX (*option-list*)
specifies options that are used for Box-Cox regression or regressor transformation. For example, the Box-Cox regression is specified as

```
model y = x1 x2 / boxcox(y=lambda,x1 x2)
```

PROC QLIM estimates the following Box-Cox regression model:

$$y_i^{(\lambda)} = \beta_0 + \beta_1 x_{1i}^{(\lambda_2)} + \beta_2 x_{2i}^{(\lambda_2)} + \epsilon_i$$

The *option-list* takes the form of *variable-list* < = varname > separated by ','. The *variable-list* specifies the list of variables to have the same Box-Cox transformation. *varname* specifies the name of this Box-Cox coefficient. If *varname* is not specified, the coefficient is called _Lambda*i* where *i* increments sequentially.

NLOPTIONS Statement

NLOPTIONS *< options >* ;

PROC QLIM uses the NonLinear Optimization (NLO) subsystem to perform nonlinear optimization tasks. For a list of all the options of the NLOPTIONS statement, see Chapter 10, "Nonlinear Optimization Methods."

OUTPUT Statement

OUTPUT *<OUT=SAS-data-set>* *<output-options>*;

The OUTPUT statement creates a new SAS data set containing all variables in the input data set and, optionally, the estimates of $\mathbf{x}'\beta$, predicted value, residual, marginal effects, probability, standard deviation of the error, expected value, conditional expected value, inverse Mills ratio. When the response values are missing for the observation, all output estimates except residual are still computed as long as none of the explanatory variables is missing. This enables you to compute these statistics for prediction. You can only specify one OUTPUT statement.

Details on the specifications in the OUTPUT statement are as follows:

CONDITIONAL
output estimates of conditional expected values of continuous endogenous variables.

ERRSTD
output estimates of σ_j, the standard deviation of the error term.

EXPECTED
output estimates of expected values of continuous endogenous variables.

MARGINAL
output marginal effects.

MILLS
output estimates of inverse Mills ratios of continuous endogenous variables.

OUT=*SAS-data-set*
names the output data set.

PREDICTED
output estimates of predicted endogenous variables.

PROB
output estimates of probability of discrete endogenous variables taking the current observed responses.

PROBALL
output estimates of probability of discrete endogenous variables for all possible responses.

RESIDUAL
output estimates of residuals of continuous endogenous variables.

XBETA
output estimates of $\mathbf{x}'\beta$.

RESTRICT Statement

RESTRICT *restriction1 [, restriction2 ...]* ;

The RESTRICT statement is used to impose linear restrictions on the parameter estimates. Any number of RESTRICT statements can be specified.

Each *restriction* is written as an expression, followed by an equality operator (=) or an inequality operator (<, >, <=, >=), followed by a second expression:

expression operator expression

The *operator* can be =, <, >, <= , or >=. The operator and second expression are optional.

Restriction expressions can be composed of parameter names, times ($*$), plus ($+$) and minus ($-$) operators, and constants. Parameters named in restriction expressions must be among the parameters estimated by the model. The restriction expressions must be a linear function of the parameters.

The following is an example of the use of the RESTRICT statement:

```
proc qlim data=one;
model y = x1-x10 / discrete;
restrict x1*2 <= x2 + x3;
run;
```

WEIGHT Statement

WEIGHT *variable* ;

The WEIGHT statement specifies a variable to supply weighting values to use for each observation in estimating parameters.

If the weight of an observation is nonpositive, that observation is not used in the estimation.

Details

Ordinal Discrete Choice Modeling

Binary Probit and Logit Model

The binary choice model is

$$y_i^* = \mathbf{x}_i'\beta + \epsilon_i$$

where the sign of the dependent variable is only observed as follows:

$$\begin{aligned} y_i &= 1 \quad \text{if } \mathrm{y_i^*} > 0 \\ &= 0 \quad \text{otherwise} \end{aligned}$$

The disturbance, ϵ_i, of the probit model has standard normal distribution with the distribution function (CDF)

$$\Phi(x) = \int_{-\infty}^{x} \frac{1}{\sqrt{2\pi}} \exp(-t^2/2)dt$$

The disturbance of the logit model has standard logistic distribution with the CDF

$$\Lambda(x) = \frac{\exp(x)}{1+\exp(x)} = \frac{1}{1+\exp(-x)}$$

The binary discrete choice model has the following probability that the event $\{y_i = 1\}$ occurs:

$$P(y_i = 1) = F(\mathbf{x}_i'\boldsymbol{\beta}) = \begin{cases} \Phi(\mathbf{x}_i'\boldsymbol{\beta}) & \text{(probit)} \\ \Lambda(\mathbf{x}_i'\boldsymbol{\beta}) & \text{(logit)} \end{cases}$$

The log-likelihood function is

$$\ell = \sum_{i=1}^{N} \{y_i \log[F(\mathbf{x}_i'\boldsymbol{\beta})] + (1-y_i)\log[1-F(\mathbf{x}_i'\boldsymbol{\beta})]\}$$

where the CDF $F(x)$ is defined as $\Phi(x)$ for the probit model while $F(x) = \Lambda(x)$ for logit. The first order derivative of the logit model are

$$\frac{\partial \ell}{\partial \boldsymbol{\beta}} = \sum_{i=1}^{N} (y_i - \Lambda(\mathbf{x}_i'\boldsymbol{\beta}))\mathbf{x}_i$$

The probit model has more complicated derivatives

$$\frac{\partial \ell}{\partial \boldsymbol{\beta}} = \sum_{i=1}^{N} \left[\frac{(2y_i - 1)\phi((2y_i - 1)\mathbf{x}_i'\boldsymbol{\beta})}{\Phi((2y_i - 1)\mathbf{x}_i'\boldsymbol{\beta})} \right] \mathbf{x}_i = \sum_{i=1}^{N} r_i \mathbf{x}_i$$

where

$$r_i = \frac{(2y_i - 1)\phi((2y_i - 1)\mathbf{x}_i'\boldsymbol{\beta})}{\Phi((2y_i - 1)\mathbf{x}_i'\boldsymbol{\beta})}$$

Note that logit maximum likelihood estimates are greater than probit maximum likelihood estimates by approximately $\frac{\pi}{\sqrt{3}}$, since the probit parameter estimates ($\boldsymbol{\beta}$) are standardized and the error term with logistic distribution has a variance of $\frac{\pi^2}{3}$.

Ordinal Probit/Logit

When the dependent variable is observed in sequence with M categories, binary discrete choice modeling is not appropriate for data analysis. McKelvey and Zavoina (1975) proposed the ordinal (or ordered) probit model.

Consider the following regression equation:

$$y_i^* = \mathbf{x}_i'\boldsymbol{\beta} + \epsilon_i$$

where error disturbances, ϵ_i, have the distribution function F. The unobserved continuous random variable, y_i^*, is identified as M categories. Suppose there are $M+1$ real numbers, $\mu_0, \cdots, \mu_M$, where $\mu_0 = -\infty$, $\mu_1 = 0$, $\mu_M = \infty$, and $\mu_0 \leq \mu_1 \leq \cdots \leq \mu_M$. Define that

$$R_{i,j} = \mu_j - \mathbf{x}_i'\boldsymbol{\beta}$$

The probability that the unobserved dependent variable is contained in the jth category can be written as

$$P[\mu_{j-1} < y_i^* \leq \mu_j] = F(R_{i,j}) - F(R_{i,j-1})$$

The log-likelihood function is

$$\ell = \sum_{i=1}^{N}\sum_{j=1}^{M} d_{ij} \log\left[F(R_{i,j}) - F(R_{i,j-1})\right]$$

where

$$d_{ij} = \begin{cases} 1 & \text{if } \mu_{j-1} < y_i \leq \mu_j \\ 0 & \text{otherwise} \end{cases}$$

The first derivatives are written as

$$\frac{\partial \ell}{\partial \boldsymbol{\beta}} = \sum_{i=1}^{N}\sum_{j=1}^{M} d_{ij}\left[\frac{f(R_{i,j-1}) - f(R_{i,j})}{F(R_{i,j}) - F(R_{i,j-1})}\mathbf{x}_i\right]$$

$$\frac{\partial \ell}{\partial \mu_k} = \sum_{i=1}^{N}\sum_{j=1}^{M} d_{ij}\left[\frac{\delta_{j,k} f(R_{i,j}) - \delta_{j-1,k} f(R_{i,j-1})}{F(R_{i,j}) - F(R_{i,j-1})}\right]$$

where $f(x) = \frac{dF(x)}{dx}$ and $\delta_{j,k} = 1$ if $j = k$. When the ordinal probit is estimated, it is assumed that $F(R_{i,j}) = \Phi(R_{i,j})$. The ordinal logit model is estimated if $F(R_{i,j}) = \Lambda(R_{i,j})$. The first threshold parameter, μ_1, is estimated when the LIMIT1=VARYING option is specified. By default (LIMIT1=ZERO), so that $M-2$ threshold parameters $(\mu_2, \ldots, \mu_{M-1})$ are estimated.

The ordered probit models are analyzed by Aitchison and Silvey (1957), and Cox (1970) discussed ordered response data using the logit model. They defined the probability that y_i^* belongs to jth category as

$$P[\mu_{j-1} < y_i \le \mu_j] = F(\mu_j + \mathbf{x}_i'\boldsymbol{\theta}) - F(\mu_{j-1} + \mathbf{x}_i'\boldsymbol{\theta})$$

where $\mu_0 = -\infty$ and $\mu_M = \infty$. Therefore, the ordered response model analyzed by Aitchison and Silvey can be estimated if the LIMIT1=VARYING option is specified. Note that $\boldsymbol{\theta} = -\boldsymbol{\beta}$.

Goodness-of-Fit Measures

McFadden (1974) suggested a likelihood ratio index that is analogous to the R^2 in the linear regression model.

$$R_M^2 = 1 - \frac{\ln L}{\ln L_0}$$

where L is the value of the maximum likelihood function and L_0 is a likelihood function when regression coefficients except an intercept term are zero. It can be shown that L_0 can be written as

$$L_0 = \sum_{j=1}^{M} N_j \ln(\frac{N_j}{N}),$$

where N_j is the number of responses in category j.

Estrella (1998) proposes the following requirements for a goodness-of-fit measure to be desirable in discrete choice modeling:

- The measure must take values in $[0, 1]$, where 0 represents no fit and 1 corresponds to perfect fit.
- The measure should be directly related to the valid test statistic for significance of all slope coefficients.
- The derivative of the measure with respect to the test statistic should comply with corresponding derivatives in a linear regression.

Estrella's measure is written

$$R_{E1}^2 = 1 - \left(\frac{\ln L}{\ln L_0}\right)^{-\frac{2}{N}\ln L_0}$$

An alternative measure suggested by Estrella is

$$R_{E2}^2 = 1 - [(\ln L - K)/\ln L_0]^{-\frac{2}{N}\ln L_0}$$

where $\ln L_0$ is computed with null slope parameter values, N is the number observations used, and K represents the number of estimated parameters.

Other goodness-of-fit measures are summarized as follows:

$$R^2_{CU1} = 1 - \left(\frac{L_0}{L}\right)^{\frac{2}{N}} \quad \text{(Cragg-Uhler 1)}$$

$$R^2_{CU2} = \frac{1 - (L_0/L)^{\frac{2}{N}}}{1 - L_0^{\frac{2}{N}}} \quad \text{(Cragg-Uhler 2)}$$

$$R^2_A = \frac{2(\ln L - \ln L_0)}{2(\ln L - \ln L_0) + N} \quad \text{(Aldrich-Nelson)}$$

$$R^2_{VZ} = R^2_A \frac{2\ln L_0 - N}{2\ln L_0} \quad \text{(Veall-Zimmermann)}$$

$$R^2_{MZ} = \frac{\sum_{i=1}^{N}(\hat{y}_i - \bar{\hat{y}}_i)^2}{N + \sum_{i=1}^{N}(\hat{y}_i - \bar{\hat{y}}_i)^2} \quad \text{(McKelvey-Zavoina)}$$

where $\hat{y}_i = \mathbf{x}_i'\hat{\boldsymbol{\beta}}$ and $\bar{\hat{y}}_i = \sum_{i=1}^{N} \hat{y}_i/N$.

Limited Dependent Variable Models

Censored Regression Models

When the dependent variable is censored, values in a certain range are all transformed to a single value. For example, the standard tobit model can be defined as

$$y_i^* = \mathbf{x}_i'\boldsymbol{\beta} + \epsilon_i$$

$$y_i = \begin{cases} y_i^* & \text{if } y_i^* > 0 \\ 0 & \text{if } y_i^* \le 0 \end{cases}$$

where $\epsilon_i \sim iidN(0, \sigma^2)$. The log-likelihood function of the standard censored regression model is

$$\ell = \sum_{i \in \{y_i = 0\}} \ln[1 - \Phi(\mathbf{x}_i'\boldsymbol{\beta}/\sigma)] + \sum_{i \in \{y_i > 0\}} \ln\left[\frac{\phi((y_i - \mathbf{x}_i'\boldsymbol{\beta})/\sigma)}{\sigma}\right]$$

where $\Phi(\cdot)$ is the cumulative density function of the standard normal distribution and $\phi(\cdot)$ is the probability density function of the standard normal distribution.

The tobit model can be generalized to handle observation-by-observation censoring. The censored model on both of the lower and upper limits can be defined as follows

$$y_i = \begin{cases} R_i & \text{if } y_i^* \geq R_i \\ y_i^* & \text{if } L_i < y_i^* < R_i \\ L_i & \text{if } y_i^* \leq L_i \end{cases}$$

The log-likelihood function can be written as

$$\begin{aligned} \ell \; = \; & \sum_{i \in \{L_i < y_i < R_i\}} \ln \phi(\frac{y_i - \mathbf{x}_i'\boldsymbol{\beta}}{\sigma})/\sigma + \sum_{i \in \{y_i = R_i\}} \ln \Phi(-\frac{R_i - \mathbf{x}_i'\boldsymbol{\beta}}{\sigma}) + \\ & \sum_{i \in \{y_i = L_i\}} \ln \Phi(\frac{L_i - \mathbf{x}_i'\boldsymbol{\beta}}{\sigma}) \end{aligned}$$

Log-likelihood functions of the lower- or upper-limit censored model are easily derived from the two-limit censored model. The log-likelihood function of the lower-limit censored model is

$$\ell = \sum_{i \in \{y_i > L_i\}} \ln \phi(\frac{y_i - \mathbf{x}_i'\boldsymbol{\beta}}{\sigma})/\sigma + \sum_{i \in \{y_i = L_i\}} \ln \Phi(\frac{L_i - \mathbf{x}_i'\boldsymbol{\beta}}{\sigma})$$

The log-likelihood function of the upper-limit censored model is

$$\ell = \sum_{i \in \{y_i < R_i\}} \ln \phi(\frac{y_i - \mathbf{x}_i'\boldsymbol{\beta}}{\sigma})/\sigma + \sum_{i \in \{y_i = R_i\}} \ln \left[1 - \Phi(\frac{R_i - \mathbf{x}_i'\boldsymbol{\beta}}{\sigma})\right]$$

Truncated Regression Models

In truncated model, the observed sample is a subset of the population where the dependent variable falls in a certain range. For example, when neither a dependent variable nor exogenous variables are observed for $y_i^* \leq 0$, the truncated regression model can be specified. The log-likelihood function of the truncated regression model is

$$\ell = \sum_{i \in \{y_i > 0\}} \left\{ -\ln \Phi(\mathbf{x}_i'\boldsymbol{\beta}/\sigma) + \ln \left[\frac{\phi((y_i - \mathbf{x}_i'\boldsymbol{\beta})/\sigma)}{\sigma}\right] \right\}$$

The two-limit truncation model is defined as

$$y_i = y_i^* \quad \text{if } L_i < y_i^* < R_i$$

The log-likelihood function of the two-limit truncated regression model is

$$\ell = \sum_{i=1}^{N} \left\{ \ln \phi(\frac{y_i - \mathbf{x}_i'\boldsymbol{\beta}}{\sigma})/\sigma - \ln \left[\Phi(\frac{R_i - \mathbf{x}_i'\boldsymbol{\beta}}{\sigma}) - \Phi(\frac{L_i - \mathbf{x}_i'\boldsymbol{\beta}}{\sigma})\right] \right\}$$

The log-likelihood functions of the lower- and upper-limit truncation model are

$$\ell = \sum_{i=1}^{N} \left\{ \ln \left[\phi\left(\frac{y_i - \mathbf{x}_i'\boldsymbol{\beta}}{\sigma}\right)/\sigma \right] - \ln \left[1 - \Phi\left(\frac{L_i - \mathbf{x}_i'\boldsymbol{\beta}}{\sigma}\right) \right] \right\} \quad \text{(lower)}$$

$$\ell = \sum_{i=1}^{N} \left\{ \ln \left[\phi\left(\frac{y_i - \mathbf{x}_i'\boldsymbol{\beta}}{\sigma}\right)/\sigma \right] - \ln \left[\Phi\left(\frac{R_i - \mathbf{x}_i'\boldsymbol{\beta}}{\sigma}\right) \right] \right\} \quad \text{(upper)}$$

Heteroscedasticity and Box-Cox Transformation

Heteroscedasticity

If the variance of regression disturbance (ϵ_i) is heteroscedastic, the variance can be specified as a function of variables

$$E(\epsilon_i^2) = \sigma_i^2 = f(\mathbf{z}_i'\gamma)$$

The following table shows various functional forms of heteroscedasticity and the corresponding options to request each model.

No.	Model	Options
1	$f(\mathbf{z}_i'\gamma) = \sigma^2(1+\exp(\mathbf{z}_i'\gamma))$	link=EXP (default)
2	$f(\mathbf{z}_i'\gamma) = \sigma^2\exp(\mathbf{z}_i'\gamma)$	link=EXP noconst
3	$f(\mathbf{z}_i'\gamma) = \sigma^2(1+\sum_{l=1}^{L}\gamma_l z_{li})$	link=LINEAR
4	$f(\mathbf{z}_i'\gamma) = \sigma^2(1+(\sum_{l=1}^{L}\gamma_l z_{li})^2)$	link=LINEAR square
5	$f(\mathbf{z}_i'\gamma) = \sigma^2(\sum_{l=1}^{L}\gamma_l z_{li})$	link=LINEAR noconst
6	$f(\mathbf{z}_i'\gamma) = \sigma^2((\sum_{l=1}^{L}\gamma_l z_{li})^2)$	link=LINEAR square noconst

For discrete choice models, σ^2 is normalized ($\sigma^2 = 1$) since this parameter is not identified. Note that in models 3 and 5, it may be possible that variances of some observations are negative. Although the QLIM procedure assigns a large penalty to move the optimization away from such regions, sometimes the optimization may stuck in such regions. Signs of such outcome include extremely small likelihood values or missing standard errors in the estimates. In models 2 and 6, variances are guaranteed to be greater or equal to zero but it may be possible that variances of some observations are very close to zero. In these scenarios, standard errors may be missing. Models 1 and 4 do not have such problems. Variances in these models are always positive and never close to zero.

The heteroscedastic regression model is estimated using the following log-likelihood function:

$$\ell = -\frac{N}{2}\ln(2\pi) - \sum_{i=1}^{N}\frac{1}{2}\ln(\sigma_i^2) - \frac{1}{2}\sum_{i=1}^{N}\left(\frac{e_i}{\sigma_i}\right)^2$$

where $e_i = y_i - \mathbf{x}_i'\boldsymbol{\beta}$.

Box-Cox Modeling

The Box-Cox transformation on x is defined as

$$x^{(\lambda)} = \begin{cases} \frac{x^{\lambda}-1}{\lambda} & \text{if } \lambda \neq 0 \\ \ln(x) & \text{if } \lambda = 0 \end{cases}$$

The Box-Cox regression model with heteroscedasticity is written

$$\begin{aligned} y_i^{(\lambda_0)} &= \beta_0 + \sum_{k=1}^{K} \beta_k x_{ki}^{(\lambda_k)} + \epsilon_i \\ &= \mu_i + \epsilon_i \end{aligned}$$

where $\epsilon_i \sim N(0, \sigma_i^2)$ and transformed variables must be positive. In practice, too many transformation parameters cause numerical problems in model fitting. It is common to have the same Box-Cox transformation performed on all the variables, that is, $\lambda_0 = \lambda_1 = \cdots = \lambda_K$. It is required for the magnitude of transformed variables to be in the tolerable range if the corresponding transformation parameters are $|\lambda| > 1$.

The log-likelihood function of the Box-Cox regression model is written

$$\ell = -\frac{N}{2}\ln(2\pi) - \sum_{i=1}^{N}\ln(\sigma_i) - \frac{1}{2\sigma_i^2}\sum_{i=1}^{N} e_i^2 + (\lambda_0 - 1)\sum_{i=1}^{N}\ln(y_i)$$

where $e_i = y_i^{(\lambda_0)} - \mu_i$.

When the dependent variable is discrete, censored, or truncated, the Box-Cox transformation can only be applied to explanatory variables.

Bivariate Limited Dependent Variable Modeling

The generic form of a bivariate limited dependent variable model is

$$\begin{aligned} y_{1i}^* &= \mathbf{x}_{1i}'\boldsymbol{\beta}_1 + \epsilon_{1i} \\ y_{2i}^* &= \mathbf{x}_{2i}'\boldsymbol{\beta}_2 + \epsilon_{2i} \end{aligned}$$

where the disturbances, ϵ_{1i} and ϵ_{2i}, have normal distribution with zero mean, standard deviations σ_1 and σ_2, and correlation of ρ. y_1^* and y_2^* are latent variables. The dependent variables y_1 and y_2 are observed if the latent variables y_1^* and y_2^* fall in certain ranges.

$$\begin{aligned} y_1 = y_{1i} & \quad \text{if} \quad y_{1i}^* \in D_1(y_{1i}) \\ y_2 = y_{2i} & \quad \text{if} \quad y_{2i}^* \in D_2(y_{2i}) \end{aligned}$$

D is a transformation from (y_{1i}^*, y_{2i}^*) to (y_{1i}, y_{2i}). For example, if $y1$ and $y2$ are censored variables with lower bound 0, then

$$y_1 = y_{1i} \quad \text{if} \quad y_{1i}^* > 0, \qquad y_1 = 0 \quad \text{if} \quad y_{1i}^* \le 0$$
$$y_2 = y_{2i} \quad \text{if} \quad y_{2i}^* > 0, \qquad y_2 = 0 \quad \text{if} \quad y_{2i}^* \le 0$$

There are three cases for the log likelihood of (y_{1i}, y_{2i}). The first case is that $y_{1i} = y_{1i}^*$ and $y_{2i} = y_{2i}^*$. That is, this observation is mapped to one point in the space of latent variables. The log likelihood is computed from a bivariate normal density,

$$\ell_i = \ln \phi_2(\frac{y_1 - \mathbf{x_1}'\boldsymbol{\beta}_1}{\sigma_1}, \frac{y_2 - \mathbf{x_2}'\boldsymbol{\beta}_2}{\sigma_2}, \rho) - \ln \sigma_1 - \ln \sigma_2$$

where $\phi_2(u, v, \rho)$ is the density function for standardized bivariate normal distribution with correlation ρ,

$$\phi_2(u, v, \rho) = \frac{e^{-(1/2)(u^2+v^2-2\rho uv)/(1-\rho^2)}}{2\pi(1-\rho^2)^{1/2}}$$

The second case is that one observed dependent variable is mapped to a point of its latent variable and the other dependent variable is mapped to a segment in the space of its latent variable. For example, in the bivariate censored model specified, if observed $y1 > 0$ and $y2 = 0$, then $y1^* = y1$ and $y2^* \in (-\infty, 0]$. In general, the log likelihood for one observation can be written as follows (the subscript i is dropped for simplicity): If one set is a single point and the other set is a range, without loss of generality, let $D_1(y_1) = \{y_1\}$ and $D_2(y_2) = [L_2, R_2]$,

$$\begin{aligned} \ell_i &= \ln \phi(\frac{y_1 - \mathbf{x_1}'\boldsymbol{\beta}_1}{\sigma_1}) - \ln \sigma_1 \\ &+ \ln[\Phi(\frac{R_2 - \mathbf{x_2}'\boldsymbol{\beta}_2 - \rho\frac{y_1 - \mathbf{x_1}'\boldsymbol{\beta}_1}{\sigma_1}}{\sigma_2}) - \Phi(\frac{L_2 - \mathbf{x_2}'\boldsymbol{\beta}_2 - \rho\frac{y_1 - \mathbf{x_1}'\boldsymbol{\beta}_1}{\sigma_1}}{\sigma_2})] \end{aligned}$$

where ϕ and Φ are the density function and the cumulative probability function for standardized univariate normal distribution.

The third case is that both dependent variables are mapped to segments in the space of latent variables. For example, in the bivariate censored model specified, if observed $y1 = 0$ and $y2 = 0$, then $y1^* \in (-\infty, 0]$ and $y2^* \in (-\infty, 0]$. In general, if $D_1(y_1) = [L_1, R_1]$ and $D_2(y_2) = [L_2, R_2]$, the log likelihood is

$$\ell_i = \ln \int_{\frac{L_1 - \mathbf{x_1}'\boldsymbol{\beta}_1}{\sigma_1}}^{\frac{R_1 - \mathbf{x_1}'\boldsymbol{\beta}_1}{\sigma_1}} \int_{\frac{L_2 - \mathbf{x_2}'\boldsymbol{\beta}_2}{\sigma_2}}^{\frac{R_2 - \mathbf{x_2}'\boldsymbol{\beta}_2}{\sigma_2}} \phi_2(u, v, \rho)\, du\, dv$$

Selection Models

In sample selection models, one or several dependent variables are observed when another variable takes certain values. For example, the standard Heckman selection model can be defined as

$$z_i^* = \mathbf{w}_i'\gamma + u_i$$

$$z_i = \begin{cases} 1 & \text{if } z_i^* > 0 \\ 0 & \text{if } z_i^* \leq 0 \end{cases}$$

$$y_i = \mathbf{x}_i'\boldsymbol{\beta} + \epsilon_i \text{ if } z_i = 1$$

where u_i and ϵ_i are jointly normal with zero mean, standard deviations of 1 and σ, and correlation of ρ. z is the variable that the selection is based on and y is observed when z has a value of 1. Least squares regression using the observed data of y produces inconsistent estimates of $\boldsymbol{\beta}$. Maximum likelihood method is used to estimate selection models. The log-likelihood function of the Heckman selection model is written as

$$\begin{aligned} \ell &= \sum_{i \in \{z_i=0\}} \ln[1 - \Phi(\mathbf{w}_i'\gamma)] \\ &+ \sum_{i \in \{z_i=1\}} \{\ln \phi(\frac{y_i - \mathbf{x_i}'\boldsymbol{\beta}}{\sigma}) - \ln \sigma + \ln \Phi(\mathbf{w}_i'\gamma + \rho\frac{y_i - \mathbf{x_i}'\boldsymbol{\beta}}{\sigma})\} \end{aligned}$$

Only one variable is allowed for the selection to be based on, but the selection may lead to several variables. For example, in the following switch regression model,

$$z_i^* = \mathbf{w}_i'\gamma + u_i$$

$$z_i = \begin{cases} 1 & \text{if } z_i^* > 0 \\ 0 & \text{if } z_i^* \leq 0 \end{cases}$$

$$\begin{aligned} y_{1i} &= \mathbf{x}_{1i}'\boldsymbol{\beta}_1 + \epsilon_{1i} \text{ if } z_i = 0 \\ y_{2i} &= \mathbf{x}_{2i}'\boldsymbol{\beta}_2 + \epsilon_{2i} \text{ if } z_i = 1 \end{aligned}$$

z is the variable that the selection is based on. If $z = 0$, then y_1 is observed. If $z = 1$, then y_2 is observed. Because it is never the case that $y1$ and $y2$ are observed at the same time, the correlation between y_1 and y_2 cannot be estimated. Only the correlation between z and y_1 and the correlation between z and y_2 can be estimated. This estimation uses the maximum likelihood method.

Multivariate Limited Dependent Models

The multivariate model is similar to bivariate models. The generic form of the multivariate limited dependent variable model is

$$\begin{aligned} y_{1i}^{*} &= \mathbf{x}_{1i}'\boldsymbol{\beta}_1 + \epsilon_{1i} \\ y_{2i}^{*} &= \mathbf{x}_{2i}'\boldsymbol{\beta}_2 + \epsilon_{2i} \\ &\cdots \\ y_{mi}^{*} &= \mathbf{x}_{mi}'\boldsymbol{\beta}_m + \epsilon_{mi} \end{aligned}$$

where m is the number of models to be estimated. The vector ϵ has multivariate normal distribution with mean 0 and variance-covariance matrix Σ. Similar to bivariate models, the likelihood may involve computing multivariate normal integrations. This is done using Monte Carlo integration. (See Genz 1992; Hajivassiliou and McFadden D. 1998).

When the number of equations N increases in a system, the number of parameters increases at the rate of N^2 because of the correlation matrix. When the number of parameters is large, sometimes the optimization converges but some of the standard deviations are missing. This usually means that the model is overparameterized. The default method for computing the covariance is to use the inverse Hessian matrix. Hessian is computed by finite differences, and in overparameterized cases, the inverse cannot be computed. It is recommended to reduce the number of parameters in such cases. Sometimes using the outer product covariance matrix (COVEST=OP option) may also help.

Output

XBeta, Predicted, Residual

Xbeta is the structural part on the right-hand side of the model. Predicted value is the predicted dependent variable value. For censored variables, if the predicted value is outside the boundaries, it is reported as the closest boundary. For discrete variables, it is the level whose boundaries Xbeta falls in between. Residual is only defined for continuous variables and is defined as

$$Residual = Observed - Predicted$$

Error Standard Deviation

Error standard deviation is σ_i in the model. It only varies when the HETERO statement is used.

Marginal Effects

Marginal effect is the contribution of one control variable to the response variable. For the binary choice model and ordinal response model with M categories, specify

$M+1$ real numbers, $\mu_0, \cdots, \mu_M$, where $\mu_0 = -\infty$, $\mu_1 = 0$ (or estimated when LIMIT1=VARYING), $\mu_M = \infty$, and $\mu_0 \leq \mu_1 \leq \cdots \leq \mu_M$. Define that

$$R_{i,j} = \mu_j - \mathbf{x}_i'\boldsymbol{\beta}$$

The probability that the unobserved dependent variable is contained in the jth category can be written

$$P[\mu_{j-1} < y_i^* \leq \mu_j] = F(R_{i,j}) - F(R_{i,j-1})$$

The marginal effect of changes in the regressors on the probability of $y_i = j$ is then

$$\frac{\partial Prob[y_i = j]}{\partial \mathbf{x}} = [f(\mu_{j-1} - \mathbf{x}_i'\boldsymbol{\beta}) - f(\mu_j - \mathbf{x}_i'\boldsymbol{\beta})]\boldsymbol{\beta}$$

where $f(x) = \frac{dF(x)}{dx}$. In particular,

$$f(x) = \frac{dF(x)}{dx} = \begin{cases} \frac{1}{\sqrt{2\pi}} e^{-x^2/2} & \text{(probit)} \\ \frac{e^{-x}}{[1+e^{(-x)}]^2} & \text{(logit)} \end{cases}$$

The marginal effects in the Box-Cox regression model are

$$\frac{\partial E[y_i]}{\partial \mathbf{x}} = \boldsymbol{\beta} \frac{x^{\lambda_k - 1}}{y^{\lambda_0 - 1}}$$

The marginal effects in the truncated regression model are

$$\frac{\partial E[y_i | L_i < y_i^* < R_i]}{\partial \mathbf{x}} = \boldsymbol{\beta} \left[1 - \frac{(\phi(a_i) - \phi(b_i))^2}{(\Phi(b_i) - \Phi(a_i))^2} + \frac{a_i \phi(a_i) - b_i \phi(b_i)}{\Phi(b_i) - \Phi(a_i)} \right]$$

where $a_i = \frac{L_i - \mathbf{x}_i'\boldsymbol{\beta}}{\sigma_i}$ and $b_i = \frac{R_i - \mathbf{x}_i'\boldsymbol{\beta}}{\sigma_i}$.

The marginal effects in the censored regression model are

$$\frac{\partial E[y|\mathbf{x}_i]}{\partial \mathbf{x}} = \boldsymbol{\beta} \times Prob[L_i < y_i^* < R_i]$$

Inverse Mills Ratio, Expected and Conditionally Expected Values

These values only apply to continuous variables. Let L_i and R_i be the lower boundary and upper boundary for the y_i. Define $a_i = \frac{L_i - \mathbf{x}_i'\boldsymbol{\beta}}{\sigma_i}$ and $b_i = \frac{R_i - \mathbf{x}_i'\boldsymbol{\beta}}{\sigma_i}$. Then the Inverse Mills Ratio is defined as

$$\lambda = \frac{(\phi(a_i) - \phi(b_i))}{(\Phi(b_i) - \Phi(a_i))}$$

The expected value is the unconditional expectation of the dependent variable. For a censored variable, it is

$$E[y_i] = \Phi(a_i)L_i + (\mathbf{x}_i'\boldsymbol{\beta} + \lambda\sigma_i)(\Phi(a_i) - \Phi(b_i) + (1 - \Phi(b_i))R_i$$

For a noncensored variable, this is

$$E[y_i] = \mathbf{x}_i'\boldsymbol{\beta}$$

The conditional expected value is the expectation given that the variable is inside the boundaries.

$$E[y_i|L_i < y_i < R_i] = \mathbf{x}_i'\boldsymbol{\beta} + \lambda\sigma_i$$

Probability

Probability is only for discrete responses. It is the marginal probability that the discrete response is taking the value of the observation. If the PROBALL option is specified, then the probability for all of the possible responses of the discrete variables are computed.

Naming

Naming of Parameters

When there is only one equation in the estimation, parameters are named in the same way as other SAS procedures such as REG, PROBIT, etc. The constant in the regression equation is called Intercept. The coefficients on independent variables are named by the independent variables. The standard deviation of the errors is called _Sigma. If there are Box-Cox transformations, the coefficients are named _Lambda$i$, where i increments from 1, or as specified by the user. The limits for the discrete dependent variable are named _Limit$i$. If the LIMIT=varying option is specified, then _Limit$i$ starts from 1. If the LIMIT=varying option is not specified, then _Limit1 is set to 0 and the limit parameters start from $i = 2$. If the HETERO statement is included, the coefficients of the independent variables in the hetero equation are called _H.x where x is the name of the independent variable.

When there are multiple equations in the estimation, the parameters in the main equation are named in the format of $y.x$ where y is the name of the dependent variable and x is the name of the independent variable. The standard deviation of the errors is call _Sigma.y. Box-Cox parameters are called _Lambda$i.y$ and limit variables are called _Limit$i.y$. Parameters in the HETERO statement are named as _H.$y.x$. In the OUTEST= data set, all variables are changed from '.' to '_'.

Naming of Output Variables

The following table shows the option in the Output statement, with the corresponding variable names and their explanation.

Option	Name	Explanation
PREDICTED	P_y	Predicted value of y
RESIDUAL	RESID_y	Residual of y, (y-PredictedY)
XBETA	XBETA_y	Structure part ($\mathbf{x}'\beta$) of y equation
ERRSTD	ERRSTD_y	Standard deviation of error term
PROB	PROB_y	Probability that y is taking the observed value in this observation. (Discrete y only)
PROBALL	PROBi_y	Probability that y is taking the ith value. (Discrete y only)
MILLS	MILLS_y	Inverse Mills ratio for y
EXPECTED	EXPCT_y	Unconditional expected value of y
CONDITIONAL	CEXPCT_y	Conditional expected value of y, condition on the truncation.
MARGINAL	MEFF_x	Marginal effect of x on y ($\frac{\partial y}{\partial x}$) with single equation
	MEFF_y_x	Marginal effect of x on y ($\frac{\partial y}{\partial x}$) with multiple equations
	MEFF_Pi_x	Marginal effect of x on y ($\frac{\partial Prob(y=i)}{\partial x}$) with single equation and discrete y
	MEFF_Pi_y_x	Marginal effect of x on y ($\frac{\partial Prob(y=i)}{\partial x}$) with multiple equations and discrete y

If you prefer to name the output variables differently, you can use the RENAME option in the data set. For example, the following statement renames the residual of y to *Resid*.

```
proc qlim data=one;
model y = x1-x10 / censored;
output out=outds(rename=(resid_y=resid)) residual;
run;
```

ODS Table Names

PROC QLIM assigns a name to each table it creates. You can use these names to denote the table when using the Output Delivery System (ODS) to select tables and create output data sets. These names are listed in the following table. For more information on ODS, see Chapter 8, "Using the Output Delivery System."

Table 22.1. ODS Tables Produced in PROC QLIM

ODS Table Name	Description	Option
	ODS Tables Created by the Model Statement	
FitSummary	Summary of Nonlinear Estimation	default
ResponseProfile	Response Profile	default
GoodnessOfFit	Pseudo-R^2 Measures	default

Table 22.1. (continued)

ODS Table Name	Description	Option
ParameterEstimates	Parameter Estimates	default
CovB	Covariance of Parameter Estimates	COVB
CorrB	Correlation of Parameter Estimates	CORRB

Examples

Example 22.1. Ordered Data Modeling

Cameron and Trivedi (1986) studied an Australian Health Survey data. Variable definitions are given in Cameron and Trivedi (1998, p. 68). The dependent variable, dvisits, has nine ordered values. The following SAS statements estimate the ordinal probit model:

```
data docvisit;
   input sex age agesq income levyplus freepoor freerepa
         illness actdays hscore chcond1 chcond2 dvisits;
   y = (dvisits > 0);
   if ( dvisits > 8 ) then dvisits = 8;

  ...

 0 0.72 0.5184 0.25  0  0  1  0  0  0  0  0  0
;


title1 "Ordered Discrete Responses";
proc qlim data=docvisit;
  model dvisits = sex age agesq income levyplus
   freepoor freerepa illness actdays hscore
   chcond1 chcond2 / discrete;
run;
```

The output of the QLIM procedure for Ordered Data Modeling is shown in Output 22.1.1.

Output 22.1.1. Ordered Data Modeling

Ordered Discrete Responses

The QLIM Procedure

Discrete Response Profile of dvisits

Index	Value	Frequency	Percent
1	0	4141	79.79
2	1	782	15.07
3	2	174	3.35
4	3	30	0.58
5	4	24	0.46
6	5	9	0.17
7	6	12	0.23
8	7	12	0.23
9	8	6	0.12

Output 22.1.1. (continued)

Ordered Discrete Responses

Model Fit Summary

Number of Endogenous Variables	1
Endogenous Variable	dvisits
Number of Observations	5190
Log Likelihood	-3138
Maximum Absolute Gradient	0.0006844
Number of Iterations	88
AIC	6316
Schwarz Criterion	6447

Goodness-of-Fit Measures

Measure	Value	Formula
Likelihood Ratio (R)	789.73	2 * (LogL - LogL0)
Upper Bound of R (U)	7065.9	- 2 * LogL0
Aldrich-Nelson	0.1321	R / (R+N)
Cragg-Uhler 1	0.1412	1 - exp(-R/N)
Cragg-Uhler 2	0.1898	(1-exp(-R/N)) / (1-exp(-U/N))
Estrella	0.149	1 - (1-R/U)^(U/N)
Adjusted Estrella	0.1416	1 - ((LogL-K)/LogL0)^(-2/N*LogL0)
McFadden's LRI	0.1118	R / U
Veall-Zimmermann	0.2291	(R * (U+N)) / (U * (R+N))
McKelvey-Zavoina	0.2036	

N = # of observations, K = # of regressors

Parameter Estimates

Parameter	Estimate	Standard Error	t Value	Approx Pr > |t|
Intercept	-1.378704	0.147412	-9.35	<.0001
sex	0.131885	0.043785	3.01	0.0026
age	-0.534198	0.815897	-0.65	0.5126
agesq	0.857317	0.898353	0.95	0.3399
income	-0.062211	0.068017	-0.91	0.3604
levyplus	0.137031	0.053262	2.57	0.0101
freepoor	-0.346045	0.129638	-2.67	0.0076
freerepa	0.178382	0.074348	2.40	0.0164
illness	0.150485	0.015747	9.56	<.0001
actdays	0.100575	0.005850	17.19	<.0001
hscore	0.031862	0.009201	3.46	0.0005
chcond1	0.061602	0.049024	1.26	0.2089
chcond2	0.135322	0.067711	2.00	0.0457
_Limit2	0.938884	0.031219	30.07	<.0001
_Limit3	1.514288	0.049329	30.70	<.0001
_Limit4	1.711660	0.058148	29.44	<.0001
_Limit5	1.952860	0.072010	27.12	<.0001
_Limit6	2.087422	0.081643	25.57	<.0001
_Limit7	2.333787	0.101746	22.94	<.0001
_Limit8	2.789795	0.156177	17.86	<.0001

By default, ordinal probit/logit models are estimated assuming that the first threshold or limit parameter (μ_1) is 0. However, this parameter can also be estimated when the

LIMIT1=VARYING option is specified. The probability that y_i^* belongs to the jth category is defined as

$$P[\mu_{j-1} < y_i^* < \mu_j] = F(\mu_j - \mathbf{x}_i'\boldsymbol{\beta}) - F(\mu_{j-1} - \mathbf{x}_i'\boldsymbol{\beta})$$

where $F(\cdot)$ is the logistic or standard normal CDF, $\mu_0 = -\infty$ and $\mu_9 = \infty$. Output 22.1.2 lists ordinal or cumulative logit estimates. Note that the intercept term is suppressed for model identification when μ_1 is estimated.

Output 22.1.2. Ordinal Probit Parameter Estimates with LIMIT1=VARYING

Ordered Discrete Responses

The QLIM Procedure

Parameter Estimates

Parameter	Estimate	Standard Error	t Value	Approx Pr > |t|
sex	0.131885	0.043785	3.01	0.0026
age	-0.534187	0.815944	-0.65	0.5127
agesq	0.857306	0.898403	0.95	0.3400
income	-0.062211	0.068018	-0.91	0.3604
levyplus	0.137031	0.053262	2.57	0.0101
freepoor	-0.346045	0.129638	-2.67	0.0076
freerepa	0.178382	0.074348	2.40	0.0164
illness	0.150485	0.015747	9.56	<.0001
actdays	0.100575	0.005850	17.19	<.0001
hscore	0.031862	0.009201	3.46	0.0005
chcond1	0.061602	0.049024	1.26	0.2089
chcond2	0.135321	0.067711	2.00	0.0457
_Limit1	1.378705	0.147419	9.35	<.0001
_Limit2	2.317589	0.150209	15.43	<.0001
_Limit3	2.892994	0.155200	18.64	<.0001
_Limit4	3.090366	0.158249	19.53	<.0001
_Limit5	3.331566	0.164040	20.31	<.0001
_Limit6	3.466128	0.168746	20.54	<.0001
_Limit7	3.712493	0.179694	20.66	<.0001
_Limit8	4.168501	0.215683	19.33	<.0001

Example 22.2. Tobit Analysis

The following table shows a subset of the Mroz (1987) data set. In this data, Hours is the number of hours the wife worked outside the household in a given year, Yrs_Ed is the years of education, and Yrs_Exp is the years of work experience. A Tobit model will be fit to the hours worked with years of education and experience as covariates.

```
title1 "Estimating a tobit model";

data subset;
      input Hours Yrs_Ed Yrs_Exp @@;
      if Hours eq 0
         then Lower=.;
         else Lower=Hours;
```

```
datalines;
0 8 9 0 8 12 0 9 10 0 10 15 0 11 4 0 11 6
1000 12 1 1960 12 29 0 13 3 2100 13 36
3686 14 11 1920 14 38 0 15 14 1728 16 3
1568 16 19 1316 17 7 0 17 15
;
run;


proc qlim data=subset;
  model hours = yrs_ed yrs_exp;
  endogenous hours ~ censored(lb=0);
run;
```

The output of the QLIM procedure is shown in Output 22.2.1.

Output 22.2.1. Tobit Analysis

```
                    Estimating a tobit model

                      The QLIM Procedure

                      Model Fit Summary

          Number of Endogenous Variables               1
          Endogenous Variable                      hours
          Number of Observations                      17
          Log Likelihood                       -74.93700
          Maximum Absolute Gradient           1.18953E-6
          Number of Iterations                        23
          AIC                                  157.87400
          Schwarz Criterion                    161.20685


                     Parameter Estimates

                                  Standard                  Approx
Parameter        Estimate            Error    t Value    Pr > |t|

Intercept    -5598.295129        27.692304    -202.16      <.0001
Yrs_Ed         373.123254        53.989108       6.91      <.0001
Yrs_Exp         63.336247        36.551332       1.73      0.0831
_Sigma        1582.859635       390.074877       4.06      <.0001
```

Example 22.3. Bivariate Probit Analysis

This example shows how to estimate a bivariate probit model. Note the INIT statement in the code that set the initial values for some parameters in the optimization.

```
data a;
  keep y1 y2 x1 x2;
  do i = 1 to 500;
    x1 = rannor( 19283 );
    x2 = rannor( 98721 );
```

```
          u1 = rannor( 76527 );
          u2 = rannor( 65721 );
          y11 = 1 + 2 * x1 + 3 * x2 + u1;
          y21 = 3 + 4 * x1 - 2 * x2 + u1*.2 + u2;
          if ( y11 > 0 ) then y1 = 1;
          else  y1 = 0;
          if ( y21 > 0 ) then y2 = 1;
          else  y2 = 0;
          output;
       end;
    run;

proc qlim data=a method=qn;
   init y1.x1 2.8, y1.x2 2.1,
        _rho .1;
   model y1 = x1 x2;
   model y2 = x1 x2;
   endogenous y1 y2 ~ discrete;
run;
```

The output of the QLIM procedure is shown in Output 22.3.1.

Output 22.3.1. Bivariate Probit Analysis

The QLIM Procedure

Model Fit Summary

Number of Endogenous Variables	2
Endogenous Variable	y1 y2
Number of Observations	500
Log Likelihood	-134.90796
Maximum Absolute Gradient	3.23486E-7
Number of Iterations	17
AIC	283.81592
Schwarz Criterion	313.31817

Parameter Estimates

Parameter	Estimate	Standard Error	t Value	Approx Pr > |t|
y1.Intercept	1.003639	0.153677	6.53	<.0001
y1.x1	2.244374	0.256058	8.77	<.0001
y1.x2	3.273441	0.341576	9.58	<.0001
y2.Intercept	3.621164	0.457164	7.92	<.0001
y2.x1	4.551525	0.576533	7.89	<.0001
y2.x2	-2.442769	0.332290	-7.35	<.0001
_Rho	0.144097	0.336458	0.43	0.6685

Example 22.4. Sample Selection Model

The following example illustrates the use of PROC QLIM for sample selection models. The data set is the same one from Mroz (1987). The goal is to estimate a wage offer function for married women, accounting for potential selection bias. Of the 753 women, the wage is observed for 428 working women. The labor force participation equation estimated in the introductory example is used for selection. The wage equation use log wage (lwage) as dependent variable. The explanatory variables in the wage equation are the woman's years of schooling (educ), wife's labor experience (exper), square of experience (expersq). The program is illustrated below.

```
proc qlim data=mroz;
  model inlf = nwifeinc educ exper expersq age kidslt6 kidsge6 /discrete;
  model lwage = educ exper expersq / select(inlf=1);
run;
```

The output of the QLIM procedure is shown in Output 22.4.1.

Output 22.4.1. Sample Selection

The QLIM Procedure

Model Fit Summary

Number of Endogenous Variables	2
Endogenous Variable	inlf lwage
Number of Observations	753
Log Likelihood	-832.88509
Maximum Absolute Gradient	0.00524
Number of Iterations	81
AIC	1694
Schwarz Criterion	1759

Parameter Estimates

Parameter	Estimate	Standard Error	t Value	Approx Pr > |t|
lwage.Intercept	-0.552698	0.260378	-2.12	0.0338
lwage.educ	0.108350	0.014861	7.29	<.0001
lwage.exper	0.042837	0.014879	2.88	0.0040
lwage.expersq	-0.000837	0.000417	-2.01	0.0449
_Sigma.lwage	0.663397	0.022707	29.21	<.0001
inlf.Intercept	0.266450	0.508958	0.52	0.6006
inlf.nwifeinc	-0.012132	0.004877	-2.49	0.0129
inlf.educ	0.131341	0.025382	5.17	<.0001
inlf.exper	0.123282	0.018724	6.58	<.0001
inlf.expersq	-0.001886	0.000600	-3.14	0.0017
inlf.age	-0.052829	0.008479	-6.23	<.0001
inlf.kidslt6	-0.867397	0.118651	-7.31	<.0001
inlf.kidsge6	0.035873	0.043475	0.83	0.4093
_Rho	0.026605	0.147078	0.18	0.8565

Note the correlation estimate is insignificant. This indicates that selection bias is not a big problem in the estimation of wage equation.

References

Abramowitz, M. and Stegun, A. (1970), *Handbook of Mathematical Functions*, New York: Dover Press.

Aitchison, J. and Silvey, S. (1957), "The Generalization of Probit Analysis to the Case of Multiple Responses," *Biometrika*, 44, 131–140.

Amemiya, T. (1978), "The Estimation of a Simultaneous Equation Generalized Probit Model," *Econometrica*, 46, 1193–1205.

Amemiya, T. (1978), "On a Two-Step Estimate of a Multivariate Logit Model," *Journal of Econometrics*, 8, 13–21.

Amemiya, T. (1981), "Qualitative Response Models: A Survey," *Journal of Economic Literature*, 19, 483–536.

Amemiya, T. (1984), "Tobit Models: A Survey," *Journal of Econometrics*, 24, 3–61.

Amemiya, T. (1985), *Advanced Econometrics*, Cambridge: Harvard University Press.

Ben-Akiva, M. and Lerman, S.R. (1987), *Discrete Choice Analysis*, Cambridge: MIT Press.

Bera, A.K., Jarque, C.M., and Lee, L.-F. (1984), "Testing the Normality Assumption in Limited Dependent Variable Models," *International Economic Review*, 25, 563–578.

Bloom, D.E. and Killingsworth, M.R. (1985), "Correcting for Truncation Bias Caused by a Latent Truncation Variable," *Journal of Econometrics*, 27, 131–135.

Box, G.E.P. and Cox, D.R. (1964), "An Analysis of Transformations," *Journal of the Royal Statistical Society, Series B.*, 26, 211–252.

Cameron, A.C. and Trivedi, P.K. (1986), "Econometric Models Based on Count Data: Comparisons and Applications of Some Estimators," *Journal of Applied Econometrics*, 1, 29–53.

Cameron, A.C. and Trivedi, P.K. (1998), *Regression Analysis of Count Data*, Cambridge: Cambridge University Press.

Copley, P.A., Doucet, M.S., and Gaver, K.M. (1994), "A Simultaneous Equations Analysis of Quality Control Review Outcomes and Engagement Fees for Audits of Recipients of Federal Financial Assistance," *The Accounting Review*, 69, 244–256.

Cox, D.R. (1970), *Analysis of Binary Data*, London: Metheun.

Cox, D.R. (1972), "Regression Models and Life Tables," *Journal of the Royal Statistical Society, Series B*, 20, 187–220.

Cox, D.R. (1975), "Partial Likelihood," *Biometrika*, 62, 269–276.

Deis, D.R. and Hill, R.C. (1998), "An Application of the Bootstrap Method to the Simultaneous Equations Model of the Demand and Supply of Audit Services," *Contemporary Accounting Research*, 15, 83–99.

Estrella, A. (1998), "A New Measure of Fit for Equations with Dichotomous Dependent Variables," *Journal of Business and Economic Statistics*, 16, 198–205.

Genz, A. (1992), "Numerical Computation of Multivariate Normal Probabilities," *Journal of Computational and Graphical Statistics*, 1, 141–150.

Godfrey, L.G. (1988), *Misspecification Tests in Econometrics*, Cambridge: Cambridge University Press.

Gourieroux, C., Monfort, A., Renault, E., and Trognon, A. (1987), "Generalized Residuals," *Journal of Econometrics*, 34, 5–32.

Green, W.H. (1997), *Econometric Analysis*, Upper Saddle River, N.J.: Prentice Hall.

Hajivassiliou, V.A. (1993), "Simulation Estimation Methods for Limited Dependent Variable Models," in *Handbook of Statistics*, Vol. 11, ed. G.S. Maddala, C.R. Rao, and H.D. Vinod, New York: Elsevier Science Publishing.

Hajivassiliou, V.A., and McFadden, D. (1998), "The Method of Simulated Scores for the Estimation of LDV Models," *Econometrica*, 66, 863–896.

Heckman, J.J. (1978), "Dummy Endogenous Variables in a Simultaneous Equation System," *Econometrica*, 46, 931–959.

Hinkley, D.V. (1975), "On Power Transformations to Symmetry," *Biometrika*, 62, 101–111.

Kim, M. and Hill, R.C. (1993), "The Box-Cox Transformation-of-Variables in Regression," *Empirical Economics*, 18, 307–319.

King, G. (1989b), *Unifying Political Methodology: The Likelihood Theory and Statistical Inference*, Cambridge: Cambridge University Press.

Lee, L.-F. (1981), "Simultaneous Equations Models with Discrete and Censored Dependent Variables," in *Structural Analysis of Discrete Data with Econometric Applications*, ed. C.F. Manski and D. McFadden, Cambridge: MIT Press

Long, J.S. (1997), *Regression Models for Categorical and Limited Dependent Variables*, Thousand Oaks, CA: Sage Publications, Inc.

McFadden, D. (1974), "Conditional Logit Analysis of Qualitative Choice Behavior," in *Frontiers in Econometrics*, ed. P. Zarembka, New York: Academic Press.

McFadden, D. (1981), "Econometric Models of Probabilistic Choice," in *Structural Analysis of Discrete Data with Econometric Applications*, ed. C.F. Manski and D. McFadden, Cambridge: MIT Press.

McKelvey, R.D. and Zavoina, W. (1975), "A Statistical Model for the Analysis of Ordinal Level Dependent Variables," *Journal of Mathematical Sociology*, 4, 103–120.

Mroz, T.A. (1987), "The Sensitivity of an Empirical Model of Married Women's Hours of Work to Economic and Statistical Assumptions," *Econometrica*, 55, 765–799.

Mroz, T.A. (1999), "Discrete Factor Approximations in Simultaneous Equation Models: Estimating the Impact of a Dummy Endogenous Variable on a Continuous Outcome," *Journal of Econometrics*, 92, 233–274.

Nawata, K. (1994), "Estimation of Sample Selection Bias Models by the Maximum Likelihood Estimator and Heckman's Two-Step Estimator," *Economics Letters*, 45, 33–40.

Parks, R.W. (1967), "Efficient Estimation of a System of Regression Equations When Disturbances Are Both Serially and Contemporaneously Correlated," *Journal of the American Statistical Association*, 62, 500–509.

Powers, D.A. and Xie, Y. (2000), *Statistical Methods for Categorical Data Analysis*, San Diego: Academic Press.

Wooldridge, J.M. (2002), *Econometric Analysis of Cross Section of Panel Data*, Cambridge, MA: MIT Press.

Chapter 23
The SIMLIN Procedure

Chapter Contents

Chapter 23
The SIMLIN Procedure

Overview

The SIMLIN procedure reads the coefficients for a set of linear structural equations, which are usually produced by the SYSLIN procedure. PROC SIMLIN then computes the reduced form and, if input data are given, uses the reduced form equations to generate predicted values. PROC SIMLIN is especially useful when dealing with sets of structural difference equations. The SIMLIN procedure can perform simulation or forecasting of the endogenous variables.

The SIMLIN procedure can be applied only to models that are:

- linear with respect to the parameters
- linear with respect to the variables
- square (as many equations as endogenous variables)
- nonsingular (the coefficients of the endogenous variables form an invertible matrix)

Getting Started

The SIMLIN procedure processes the coefficients in a data set created by the SYSLIN procedure using the OUTEST= option or by another regression procedure such as PROC REG. To use PROC SIMLIN you must first produce the coefficient data set and then specify this data set on the EST= option of the PROC SIMLIN statement. You must also tell PROC SIMLIN which variables are endogenous and which variables are exogenous. List the endogenous variables in an ENDOGENOUS statement, and list the exogenous variables in an EXOGENOUS statement.

The following example illustrates the creation of an OUTEST= data set with PROC SYSLIN and the computation and printing of the reduced form coefficients for the model with PROC SIMLIN.

```
proc syslin data=in outest=e;
   model y1 = y2 x1;
   model y2 = y1 x2;
run;

proc simlin est=e;
   endogenous y1 y2;
   exogenous x1 x2;
run;
```

If the model contains lagged endogenous variables you must also use a LAGGED statement to tell PROC SIMLIN which variables contain lagged values, which endogenous variables they are lags of, and the number of periods of lagging. For dynamic models, the TOTAL and INTERIM= options can be used on the PROC SIMLIN statement to compute and print total and impact multipliers. (See "Dynamic Multipliers" later in this section for an explanation of multipliers.)

In the following example the variables Y1LAG1, Y2LAG1, and Y2LAG2 contain lagged values of the endogenous variables Y1 and Y2. Y1LAG1 and Y2LAG1 contain values of Y1 and Y2 for the previous observation, while Y2LAG2 contains 2 period lags of Y2. The LAGGED statement specifies the lagged relationships, and the TOTAL and INTERIM= options request multiplier analysis. The INTERIM=2 option prints matrices showing the impact that changes to the exogenous variables have on the endogenous variables after 1 and 2 periods.

```
data in; set in;
  y1lag1 = lag(y1);
  y2lag1 = lag(y2);
  y2lag2 = lag2(y2);
run;

proc syslin data=in outest=e;
   model y1 = y2 y1lag1 y2lag2 x1;
   model y2 = y1 y2lag1 x2;
run;

proc simlin est=e total interim=2;
   endogenous y1 y2;
   exogenous x1 x2;
   lagged y1lag1 y1 1 y2lag1 y2 1 y2lag2 y2 2;
run;
```

After the reduced form of the model is computed, the model can be simulated by specifying an input data set on the PROC SIMLIN statement and using an OUTPUT statement to write the simulation results to an output data set. The following example modifies the PROC SIMLIN step from the preceding example to simulate the model and stores the results in an output data set.

```
proc simlin est=e total interim=2 data=in;
   endogenous y1 y2;
   exogenous x1 x2;
   lagged y1lag1 y1 1 y2lag1 y2 1 y2lag2 y2 2;
   output out=sim predicted=y1hat y2hat
                  residual=y1resid y2resid;
run;
```

Prediction and Simulation

If an input data set is specified with the DATA= option in the PROC SIMLIN statement, the procedure reads the data and uses the reduced form equations to compute predicted and residual values for each of the endogenous variables. (If no data set is specified with the DATA= option, no simulation of the system is performed, and only the reduced form and multipliers are computed.)

The character of the prediction is based on the START= value. Until PROC SIMLIN encounters the START= observation, actual endogenous values are found and fed into the lagged endogenous terms. Once the START= observation is reached, dynamic simulation begins, where predicted values are fed into lagged endogenous terms until the end of the data set is reached.

The predicted and residual values generated here are different from those produced by the SYSLIN procedure since PROC SYSLIN uses the structural form with actual endogenous values. The predicted values computed by the SIMLIN procedure solve the simultaneous equation system. These reduced-form predicted values are functions only of the exogenous and lagged endogenous variables and do not depend on actual values of current period endogenous variables.

Syntax

The following statements can be used with PROC SIMLIN:

PROC SIMLIN *options*;
BY *variables*;
ENDOGENOUS *variables*;
EXOGENOUS *variables*;
ID *variables*;
LAGGED *lag-var endogenous-var number ellipsis* ;
OUTPUT *OUT=SAS-data-set options*;

Functional Summary

The statements and options controlling the SIMLIN procedure are summarized in the following table.

Description	Statement	Option
Data Set Options		
specify input data set containing structural coefficients	PROC SIMLIN	EST=
specify type of estimates read from EST= data set	PROC SIMLIN	TYPE=
write reduced form coefficients and multipliers to an output data set	PROC SIMLIN	OUTEST=
specify the input data set for simulation	PROC SIMLIN	DATA=
write predicted and residual values to an output data set	OUTPUT	
Printing Control Options		
print the structural coefficients	PROC SIMLIN	ESTPRINT
suppress printing of reduced form coefficients	PROC SIMLIN	NORED
suppress all printed output	PROC SIMLIN	NOPRINT
Dynamic Multipliers		
compute interim multipliers	PROC SIMLIN	INTERIM=
compute total multipliers	PROC SIMLIN	TOTAL
Declaring the Role of Variables		
specify BY-group processing	BY	
specify the endogenous variables	ENDOGENOUS	
specify the exogenous variables	EXOGENOUS	
specify identifying variables	ID	
specify lagged endogenous variables	LAGGED	

Description	Statement	Option
Controlling the Simulation		
specify the starting observation for dynamic simulation	PROC SIMLIN	START=

PROC SIMLIN Statement

PROC SIMLIN *options;*

The following options can be used in the PROC SIMLIN statement:

DATA= *SAS-data-set*
specifies the SAS data set containing input data for the simulation. If the DATA= option is used, the data set specified must supply values for all exogenous variables throughout the simulation. If the DATA= option is not specified, no simulation of the system is performed, and only the reduced form and multipliers are computed.

EST= *SAS-data-set*
specifies the input data set containing the structural coefficients of the system. If EST= is omitted the most recently created SAS data set is used. The EST= data set is normally a "TYPE=EST" data set produced by the OUTEST= option of PROC SYSLIN. However, you can also build the EST= data set with a SAS DATA step. See "The EST= Data Set" later in this chapter for details.

ESTPRINT
prints the structural coefficients read from the EST= data set.

INTERIM= *n*
rssbjixinterim multipliersSIMLIN procedure requests that interim multipliers be computed for interims 1 through *n*. If not specified, no interim multipliers are computed. This feature is available only if there are no lags greater than 1.

NOPRINT
suppresses all printed output.

NORED
suppresses the printing of the reduced form coefficients.

OUTEST= *SAS-data-set*
specifies an output SAS data set to contain the reduced form coefficients and multipliers, in addition to the structural coefficients read from the EST= data set. The OUTEST= data set has the same form as the EST= data set. If the OUTEST= option is not specified, the reduced form coefficients and multipliers are not written to a data set.

START= *n*

specifies the observation number in the DATA= data set where the dynamic simulation is to be started. By default, the dynamic simulation starts with the first observation in the DATA= data set for which all variables (including lags) are not missing.

TOTAL

requests that the total multipliers be computed. This feature is available only if there are no lags greater than 1.

TYPE= *value*

specifies the type of estimates to be read from the EST= data set. The TYPE= value must match the value of the _TYPE_ variable for the observations that you want to select from the EST= data set (TYPE=2SLS, for example).

BY Statement

BY *variables;*

A BY statement can be used with PROC SIMLIN to obtain separate analyses for groups of observations defined by the BY variables.

The BY statement can be applied to one or both of the EST= and the DATA= input data set. When a BY statement is used and both an EST= and a DATA= input data set are specified, PROC SIMLIN checks to see if one or both of the data sets contain the BY variables.

Thus, there are three ways of using the BY statement with PROC SIMLIN:

1. If the BY variables are found in the EST= data set only, PROC SIMLIN simulates over the entire DATA= data set once for each set of coefficients read from the BY groups in the EST= data set.
2. If the BY variables are found in the DATA= data set only, PROC SIMLIN performs separate simulations over each BY group in the DATA= data set, using the single set of coefficients in the EST= data set.
3. If the BY variables are found in both the EST= and the DATA= data sets, PROC SIMLIN performs separate simulations over each BY group in the DATA= data set using the coefficients from the corresponding BY group in the EST= data set.

ENDOGENOUS Statement

ENDOGENOUS *variables;*

List the names of the endogenous (jointly dependent) variables in the ENDOGENOUS statement. The ENDOGENOUS statement can be abbreviated as ENDOG or ENDO.

EXOGENOUS Statement

EXOGENOUS *variables;*

List the names of the exogenous (independent) variables in the EXOGENOUS statement. The EXOGENOUS statement can be abbreviated as EXOG or EXO.

ID Statement

ID *variables;*

The ID statement can be used to restrict the variables copied from the DATA= data set to the OUT= data set. Use the ID statement to list the variables you want copied to the OUT= data set besides the exogenous, endogenous, lagged endogenous, and BY variables. If the ID statement is omitted, all the variables in the DATA= data set are copied to the OUT= data set.

LAGGED Statement

LAGGED *lag-var endogenous-var number ellipsis ;*

For each lagged endogenous variable, specify the name of the lagged variable, the name of the endogenous variable that was lagged, and the degree of the lag. Only one LAGGED statement is allowed.

The following is an example of the use of the LAGGED statement:

```
proc simlin est=e;
   endog y1 y2;
   lagged y1lag1 y1 1  y2lag1 y2 1  y2lag3 y2 3;
```

This statement specifies that the variable Y1LAG1 contains the values of the endogenous variable Y1 lagged one period; the variable Y2LAG1 refers to the values of Y2 lagged one period; and the variable Y2LAG3 refers to the values of Y2 lagged three periods.

OUTPUT Statement

OUTPUT *OUT= SAS-data-set options;*

The OUTPUT statement specifies that predicted and residual values be put in an output data set. A DATA= input data set must be supplied if the OUTPUT statement is used, and only one OUTPUT statement is allowed. The following options can be used in the OUTPUT statement:

OUT= *SAS-data-set*
names the output SAS data set to contain the predicted values and residuals. If OUT= is not specified, the output data set is named using the DATA*n* convention.

PREDICTED= *names*
P= *names*
names the variables in the output data set that contain the predicted values of the simulation. These variables correspond to the endogenous variables in the order in which they are specified in the ENDOGENOUS statement. Specify up to as many names as there are endogenous variables. If you specify names on the PREDICTED= option for only some of the endogenous variables, predicted values for the remaining variables are not output. The names must not match any variable name in the input data set.

RESIDUAL= *names*
R= *names*
names the variables in the output data set that contain the residual values from the simulation. The residuals are the differences between the actual values of the endogenous variables from the DATA= data set and the predicted values from the simulation. These variables correspond to the endogenous variables in the order in which they are specified in the ENDOGENOUS statement. Specify up to as many names as there are endogenous variables. The names must not match any variable name in the input data set.

The following is an example of the use of the OUTPUT statement. This example outputs predicted values for Y1 and Y2 and outputs residuals for Y1.

```
proc simlin est=e;
   endog y1 y2;
   output out=b predicted=y1hat y2hat residual=y1resid;
```

Details

The following sections explain the structural and reduced forms, dynamic multipliers, input data sets, and the model simulation process in more detail.

Defining the Structural Form

An EST= input data set supplies the coefficients of the equation system. The data set containing the coefficients is normally a "TYPE=EST" data set created by the OUTEST= option of PROC SYSLIN or another regression procedure. The data set contains the special variables _TYPE_, _DEPVAR_, and INTERCEPT. You can also supply the structural coefficients of the system to PROC SIMLIN in a data set produced by a SAS DATA step as long as the data set is of the form TYPE=EST. Refer to SAS/STAT software documentation for a discussion of the special TYPE=EST type of SAS data set.

Suppose that there is a $g \times 1$ vector of endogenous variables $\mathbf{y}_t$, an $l \times 1$ vector of lagged endogenous variables $\mathbf{y}_t^L$, and a $k \times 1$ vector of exogenous variables $\mathbf{x}_t$, including the intercept. Then, there are g structural equations in the simultaneous system that can be written

$$\mathbf{G}\mathbf{y}_t = \mathbf{C}\mathbf{y}_t^L + \mathbf{B}\mathbf{x}_t$$

where $\mathbf{G}$ is the matrix of coefficients of current period endogenous variables, $\mathbf{C}$ is the matrix of coefficients of lagged endogenous variables, and $\mathbf{B}$ is the matrix of coefficients of exogenous variables. $\mathbf{G}$ is assumed to be nonsingular.

Computing the Reduced Form

First, the SIMLIN procedure computes reduced form coefficients by premultiplying by $\mathbf{G}^{-1}$:

$$\mathbf{y}_t = \mathbf{G}^{-1}\mathbf{C}\mathbf{y}_t^L + \mathbf{G}^{-1}\mathbf{B}\mathbf{x}_t$$

This can be written as

$$\mathbf{y}_t = \Pi_1\mathbf{y}_t^L + \Pi_2\mathbf{x}_t$$

where $\Pi_1 = \mathbf{G}^{-1}\mathbf{C}$ and $\Pi_2 = \mathbf{G}^{-1}\mathbf{B}$ are the reduced form coefficient matrices.

The reduced form matrices $\Pi_1 = \mathbf{G}^{-1}\mathbf{C}$ and $\Pi_2 = \mathbf{G}^{-1}\mathbf{B}$ are printed unless the NORED option is specified in the PROC SIMLIN statement. The structural coefficient matrices $\mathbf{G}$, $\mathbf{C}$, and $\mathbf{B}$ are printed when the ESTPRINT option is specified.

Dynamic Multipliers

For models that have only first-order lags, the equation of the reduced form of the system can be rewritten

$$\mathbf{y}_t = \mathbf{D}\mathbf{y}_{t-1} + \Pi_2 \mathbf{x}_t$$

D is a matrix formed from the columns of Π_1 plus some columns of zeros, arranged in the order in which the variables meet the lags. The elements of Π_2 are called *impact multipliers* because they show the immediate effect of changes in each exogenous variable on the values of the endogenous variables. This equation can be rewritten as

$$\mathbf{y}_t = \mathbf{D}^2\mathbf{y}_{t-2} + \mathbf{D}\Pi_2\mathbf{x}_{t-1} + \Pi_2 \mathbf{x}_t$$

The matrix formed by the product $\mathbf{D}\Pi_2$ shows the effect of the exogenous variables one lag back; the elements in this matrix are called *interim multipliers* and are computed and printed when the INTERIM= option is specified in the PROC SIMLIN statement. The *i*th period interim multipliers are formed by $\mathbf{D}^i\Pi_2$.

The series can be expanded as

$$\mathbf{y}_t = \mathbf{D}^{\infty}\mathbf{y}_{t-\infty} + \sum_{i=0}^{\infty} \mathbf{D}^i \Pi_2 \mathbf{x}_{t-i}$$

A permanent and constant setting of a value for x has the following cumulative effect:

$$\left(\sum_{i=0}^{\infty} \mathbf{D}^i\right) \Pi_2 \mathbf{x} = (\mathbf{I} - \mathbf{D})^{-1}\Pi_2 \mathbf{x}$$

The elements of $(\mathbf{I}\text{-}\mathbf{D})^{-1}\Pi_2$ are called the *total multipliers*. Assuming that the sum converges and that **(I-D)** is invertible, PROC SIMLIN computes the total multipliers when the TOTAL option is specified in the PROC SIMLIN statement.

Multipliers for Higher Order Lags

The dynamic multiplier options require the system to have no lags of order greater than one. This limitation can be circumvented, since any system with lags greater than one can be rewritten as a system where no lag is greater than one by forming new endogenous variables that are single-period lags.

For example, suppose you have the third-order single equation

$$y_t = a y_{t-3} + b\mathbf{x}_t$$

This can be converted to a first-order three-equation system by introducing two additional endogenous variables, $y_{1,t}$ and $y_{2,t}$, and computing corresponding first-order lagged variables for each endogenous variable: y_{t-1}, $y_{1,t-1}$, and $y_{2,t-1}$. The higher order lag relations are then produced by adding identities to link the endogenous and identical lagged endogenous variables:

$$y_{1,t} = y_{t-1}$$

$$y_{2,t} = y_{1,t-1}$$

$$y_t = a y_{2,t-1} + b\mathbf{X}_t$$

This conversion using the SYSLIN and SIMLIN procedures requires three steps:

1. Add the extra endogenous and lagged endogenous variables to the input data set using a DATA step. Note that two copies of each lagged endogenous variable are needed for each lag reduced, one to serve as an endogenous variable and one to serve as a lagged endogenous variable in the reduced system.
2. Add IDENTITY statements to the PROC SYSLIN step to equate each added endogenous variable to its lagged endogenous variable copy.
3. In the PROC SIMLIN step, declare the added endogenous variables in the ENDOGENOUS statement and define the lag relations in the LAGGED statement.

See Example 23.2 for an illustration of how to convert an equation system with higher-order lags into a larger system with only first-order lags.

EST= Data Set

Normally, PROC SIMLIN uses an EST= data set produced by PROC SYSLIN with the OUTEST= option. This data set is in the form expected by PROC SIMLIN. If there is more than one set of estimates produced by PROC SYSLIN, you must use the TYPE= option in the PROC SIMLIN statement to select the set to be simulated. Then PROC SIMLIN reads from the EST= data set only those observations with a _TYPE_ value corresponding to the TYPE= option (for example, TYPE=2SLS) or with a _TYPE_ value of IDENTITY.

The SIMLIN procedure can only solve square, nonsingular systems. If you have fewer equations than endogenous variables, you must specify IDENTITY statements in the PROC SYSLIN step to bring the system up to full rank. If there are *g* endogenous variables and *m*<*g* stochastic equations with unknown parameters, then you use *m* MODEL statements to specify the equations with parameters to be estimated and you must use *g*-*m* IDENTITY statements to complete the system.

You can build your own EST= data set with a DATA step rather than use PROC SYSLIN. The EST= data set must contain the endogenous variables, the lagged endogenous variables (if any), and the exogenous variables in the system (if any). If any of the equations have intercept terms, the variable INTERCEPT must supply these coefficients. The EST= data set should also contain the special character variable comp _DEPVAR_ to label the equations.

The EST= data set must contain one observation for each equation in the system. The values of the lagged endogenous variables must contain the **C** coefficients. The values of the exogenous variables and the INTERCEPT variable must contain the **B** coefficients. The values of the endogenous variables, however, must contain the negatives of the **G** coefficients. This is because the SYSLIN procedure writes the coefficients to the OUTEST= data set in the form

$$0 = \mathbf{H}\mathbf{y}_t + \mathbf{C}\mathbf{y}_t^L + \mathbf{B}\mathbf{x}_t$$

where **H=-G**.

See "Multipliers for Higher Order Lags" and Example 23.2 later in this chapter for more information on building the EST= data set.

DATA= Data Set

The DATA= data set must contain all of the exogenous variables. Values for all of the exogenous variables are required for each observation for which predicted endogenous values are desired. To forecast past the end of the historical data, the DATA= data set should contain nonmissing values for all of the exogenous variables and missing values for the endogenous variables for the forecast periods, in addition to the historical data. (See Example 23.1 for an illustration.)

In order for PROC SIMLIN to output residuals and compute statistics of fit, the DATA= data set must also contain the endogenous variables with nonmissing actual values for each observation for which residuals and statistics are to be computed.

If the system contains lags, initial values must be supplied for the lagged variables. This can be done by including either the lagged variables or the endogenous variables, or both, in the DATA= data set. If the lagged variables are not in the DATA= data set or if they have missing values in the early observations, PROC SIMLIN prints a warning and uses the endogenous variable values from the early observations to initialize the lags.

OUTEST= Data Set

The OUTEST= data set contains all the variables read from the EST= data set. The variables in the OUTEST= data set are as follows.

- the BY statement variables, if any
- _TYPE_, a character variable that identifies the type of observation
- _DEPVAR_, a character variable containing the name of the dependent variable for the observation
- the endogenous variables

- the lagged endogenous variables
- the exogenous variables
- INTERCEPT, a numeric variable containing the intercept values
- _MODEL_, a character variable containing the name of the equation
- _SIGMA_, a numeric variable containing the estimated error variance of the equation (output only if present in the EST= data set)

The observations read from the EST= data set that supply the structural coefficients are copied to the OUTEST= data set, except that the signs of endogenous coefficients are reversed. For these observations, the _TYPE_ variable values are the same as in the EST= data set.

In addition, the OUTEST= data set contains observations with the following _TYPE_ values:

REDUCED — the reduced form coefficients. The endogenous variables for this group of observations contain the inverse of the endogenous coefficient matrix **G**. The lagged endogenous variables contain the matrix $\Pi_1=\mathbf{G}^{-1}\mathbf{C}$. The exogenous variables contain the matrix $\Pi_2=\mathbf{G}^{-1}\mathbf{B}$.

IMULT*i* — the interim multipliers, if the INTERIM= option is specified. There are *gn* observations for the interim multipliers, where *g* is the number of endogenous variables and *n* is the value of the INTERIM=*n* option. For these observations the _TYPE_ variable has the value IMULT*i*, where the interim number *i* ranges from 1 to *n*.

The exogenous variables in groups of *g* observations that have a _TYPE_ value of IMULT*i* contain the matrix $\mathbf{D}^i\Pi_2$ of multipliers at interim *i*. The endogenous and lagged endogenous variables for this group of observations are set to missing.

TOTAL — the total multipliers, if the TOTAL option is specified. The exogenous variables in this group of observations contain the matrix $(\mathbf{I}\text{-}\mathbf{D})^{-1}\Pi_2$. The endogenous and lagged endogenous variables for this group of observations are set to missing.

OUT= Data Set

The OUT= data set normally contains all of the variables in the input DATA= data set, plus the variables named in the PREDICTED= and RESIDUAL= options in the OUTPUT statement.

You can use an ID statement to restrict the variables that are copied from the input data set. If an ID statement is used, the OUT= data set contains only the BY variables (if any), the ID variables, the endogenous and lagged endogenous variables (if any), the exogenous variables, plus the PREDICTED= and RESIDUAL= variables.

The OUT= data set contains an observation for each observation in the DATA= data set. When the actual value of an endogenous variable is missing in the DATA= data set, or when the DATA= data set does not contain the endogenous variable, the corresponding residual is missing.

Printed Output

Structural Form

The following items are printed as they are read from the EST= input data set. Structural zeros are printed as dots in the listing of these matrices.

1. Structural Coefficients for Endogenous Variables. This is the **G** matrix, with g rows and g columns.
2. Structural Coefficients for Lagged Endogenous Variables. These coefficients make up the **C** matrix, with g rows and l columns.
3. Structural Coefficients for Exogenous Variables. These coefficients make up the **B** matrix, with g rows and k columns.

Reduced Form

1. The reduced form coefficients are obtained by inverting **G** so that the endogenous variables can be directly expressed as functions of only lagged endogenous and exogenous variables.
2. Inverse Coefficient Matrix for Endogenous Variables. This is the inverse of the **G** matrix.
3. Reduced Form for Lagged Endogenous Variables. This is $\Pi_1 = \mathbf{G}^{-1}\mathbf{C}$, with g rows and l columns. Each value is a dynamic multiplier that shows how past values of lagged endogenous variables affect values of each of the endogenous variables.
4. Reduced Form for Exogenous Variables. This is $\Pi_2 = \mathbf{G}^{-1}\mathbf{B}$, with g rows and k columns. Its values are called *impact multipliers* because they show the immediate effect of each exogenous variable on the value of the endogenous variables.

Multipliers

Interim and total multipliers show the effect of a change in an exogenous variable over time.

1. Interim Multipliers. These are the interim multiplier matrices. They are formed by multiplying Π_2 by powers of **D**. The dth interim multiplier is $\mathbf{D}^d\Pi_2$. The interim multiplier of order d shows the effects of a change in the exogenous variables after d periods. Interim multipliers are only available if the maximum lag of the endogenous variables is 1.
2. Total Multipliers. This is the matrix of total multipliers, $\mathrm{T}=(\mathbf{I}\text{-}\mathbf{D})^{-1}\Pi_2$. This matrix shows the cumulative effect of changes in the exogenous variables. Total multipliers are only available if the maximum lag is one.

Statistics of Fit

If the DATA= option is used and the DATA= data set contains endogenous variables, PROC SIMLIN prints a statistics-of-fit report for the simulation. The statistics printed include the following. (Summations are over the observations for which both y_t and $\hat{y}_t$ are nonmissing.)

1. the number of nonmissing errors. (Number of observations for which both y_t and $\hat{y}_t$ are nonmissing.)
2. the mean error: $\frac{1}{n}\sum(y_t - \hat{y}_t)$
3. the mean percent error: $\frac{100}{n}\sum\frac{(y_t-\hat{y}_t)}{y_t}$
4. the mean absolute error: $\frac{1}{n}\sum|y_t - \hat{y}_t|$
5. the mean absolute percent error $\frac{100}{n}\sum\frac{|y_t-\hat{y}_t|}{y_t}$
6. the root mean square error: $\sqrt{\frac{1}{n}\sum(y_t - \hat{y}_t)^2}$
7. the root mean square percent error: $\sqrt{\frac{100}{n}\sum(\frac{(y_t-\hat{y}_t)}{y_t})^2}$

ODS Table Names

PROC SIMLIN assigns a name to each table it creates. You can use these names to reference the table when using the Output Delivery System (ODS) to select tables and create output data sets. These names are listed in the following table. For more information on ODS, see Chapter 8, "Using the Output Delivery System."

Table 23.1. ODS Tables Produced in PROC SIMLIN

ODS Table Name	Description	Option
Endogenous	Structural Coefficients for Endogenous Variables	default
LaggedEndogenous	Structural Coefficients for Lagged Endogenous Variables	default
Exogenous Structural	Coefficients for Exogenous Variables	default
InverseCoeff	Inverse Coefficient Matrix for Endogenous Variables	default
RedFormLagEndo	Reduced Form for Lagged Endogenous Variables	default
RedFormExog	Reduced Form for Exogenous Variables	default
InterimMult	Interim Multipliers	INTERIM= option
TotalMult	Total Multipliers	TOTAL= option
FitStatistics	Fit statistics	default

Examples

Example 23.1. Simulating Klein's Model I

In this example, the SIMLIN procedure simulates a model of the U.S. economy called Klein's Model I. The SAS data set KLEIN, shown in Output 23.1.1, is used as input to the SYSLIN and SIMLIN procedures.

```
data klein;
   input year c p w i x wp g t k wsum;
   date=mdy(1,1,year);
   format date year.;
   y    =c+i+g-t;
   yr   =year-1931;
   klag=lag(k);
   plag=lag(p);
   xlag=lag(x);
   if year>=1921;
   label c    ='consumption'
         p    ='profits'
         w    ='private wage bill'
         i    ='investment'
         k    ='capital stock'
         y    ='national income'
         x    ='private production'
         wsum='total wage bill'
         wp   ='govt wage bill'
         g    ='govt demand'
         t    ='taxes'
         klag='capital stock lagged'
         plag='profits lagged'
         xlag='private product lagged'
         yr   ='year-1931';
   datalines;
  ... data lines omitted ...
proc print data=klein;
run;
```

Output 23.1.1. PROC PRINT Listing of Input Data Set KLEIN

Obs	year	c	p	w	i	x	wp	g	t	k	wsum	date	y	yr	klag	plag	xlag
1	1921	41.9	12.4	25.5	-0.2	45.6	2.7	3.9	7.7	182.6	28.2	1921	37.9	-10	182.8	12.7	44.9
2	1922	45.0	16.9	29.3	1.9	50.1	2.9	3.2	3.9	184.5	32.2	1922	46.2	-9	182.6	12.4	45.6
3	1923	49.2	18.4	34.1	5.2	57.2	2.9	2.8	4.7	189.7	37.0	1923	52.5	-8	184.5	16.9	50.1
4	1924	50.6	19.4	33.9	3.0	57.1	3.1	3.5	3.8	192.7	37.0	1924	53.3	-7	189.7	18.4	57.2
5	1925	52.6	20.1	35.4	5.1	61.0	3.2	3.3	5.5	197.8	38.6	1925	55.5	-6	192.7	19.4	57.1
6	1926	55.1	19.6	37.4	5.6	64.0	3.3	3.3	7.0	203.4	40.7	1926	57.0	-5	197.8	20.1	61.0
7	1927	56.2	19.8	37.9	4.2	64.4	3.6	4.0	6.7	207.6	41.5	1927	57.7	-4	203.4	19.6	64.0
8	1928	57.3	21.1	39.2	3.0	64.5	3.7	4.2	4.2	210.6	42.9	1928	60.3	-3	207.6	19.8	64.4
9	1929	57.8	21.7	41.3	5.1	67.0	4.0	4.1	4.0	215.7	45.3	1929	63.0	-2	210.6	21.1	64.5
10	1930	55.0	15.6	37.9	1.0	61.2	4.2	5.2	7.7	216.7	42.1	1930	53.5	-1	215.7	21.7	67.0
11	1931	50.9	11.4	34.5	-3.4	53.4	4.8	5.9	7.5	213.3	39.3	1931	45.9	0	216.7	15.6	61.2
12	1932	45.6	7.0	29.0	-6.2	44.3	5.3	4.9	8.3	207.1	34.3	1932	36.0	1	213.3	11.4	53.4
13	1933	46.5	11.2	28.5	-5.1	45.1	5.6	3.7	5.4	202.0	34.1	1933	39.7	2	207.1	7.0	44.3
14	1934	48.7	12.3	30.6	-3.0	49.7	6.0	4.0	6.8	199.0	36.6	1934	42.9	3	202.0	11.2	45.1
15	1935	51.3	14.0	33.2	-1.3	54.4	6.1	4.4	7.2	197.7	39.3	1935	47.2	4	199.0	12.3	49.7
16	1936	57.7	17.6	36.8	2.1	62.7	7.4	2.9	8.3	199.8	44.2	1936	54.4	5	197.7	14.0	54.4
17	1937	58.7	17.3	41.0	2.0	65.0	6.7	4.3	6.7	201.8	47.7	1937	58.3	6	199.8	17.6	62.7
18	1938	57.5	15.3	38.2	-1.9	60.9	7.7	5.3	7.4	199.9	45.9	1938	53.5	7	201.8	17.3	65.0
19	1939	61.6	19.0	41.6	1.3	69.5	7.8	6.6	8.9	201.2	49.4	1939	60.6	8	199.9	15.3	60.9
20	1940	65.0	21.1	45.0	3.3	75.7	8.0	7.4	9.6	204.5	53.0	1940	66.1	9	201.2	19.0	69.5
21	1941	69.7	23.5	53.3	4.9	88.4	8.5	13.8	11.6	209.4	61.8	1941	76.8	10	204.5	21.1	75.7
22	1942	.	.	.	.	.	8.5	13.8	11.6	.	.	1942	.	11	209.4	23.5	88.4
23	1943	.	.	.	.	.	8.5	13.8	12.6	.	.	1943	.	12	.	.	.
24	1944	.	.	.	.	.	8.5	13.8	11.6	.	.	1944	.	13	.	.	.
25	1945	.	.	.	.	.	8.5	13.8	11.6	.	.	1945	.	14	.	.	.
26	1946	.	.	.	.	.	8.5	13.8	11.6	.	.	1946	.	15	.	.	.
27	1947	.	.	.	.	.	8.5	13.8	11.6	.	.	1947	.	16	.	.	.

First, the model is specified and estimated using the SYSLIN procedure, and the parameter estimates are written to an OUTEST= data set. The printed output produced by the SYSLIN procedure is not shown here; see Example 26.1 in Chapter 26 for the printed output of the PROC SYSLIN step.

```
title1 'Simulation of Klein''s Model I using SIMLIN';
proc syslin 3sls data=klein outest=a;

   instruments klag plag xlag wp g t yr;
   endogenous c p w i x wsum k y;

   consume: model     c = p plag wsum;
   invest:  model     i = p plag klag;
   labor:   model     w = x xlag yr;

   product: identity x = c + i + g;
   income:  identity y = c + i + g - t;
   profit:  identity p = x - w - t;
   stock:   identity k = klag + i;
   wage:    identity wsum = w + wp;
run;

proc print data=a;
run;
```

The OUTEST= data set A created by the SYSLIN procedure contains parameter estimates to be used by the SIMLIN procedure. The OUTEST= data set is shown in Output 23.1.2.

Output 23.1.2. The OUTEST= Data Set Created by PROC SYSLIN

Simulation of Klein's Model I using SIMLIN

Obs	_TYPE_	_STATUS_	_MODEL_	_DEPVAR_	_SIGMA_	Intercept	klag	plag	xlag
1	INST	0 Converged	FIRST	c	2.11403	58.3018	-0.14654	0.74803	0.23007
2	INST	0 Converged	FIRST	p	2.18298	50.3844	-0.21610	0.80250	0.02200
3	INST	0 Converged	FIRST	w	1.75427	43.4356	-0.12295	0.87192	0.09533
4	INST	0 Converged	FIRST	i	1.72376	35.5182	-0.19251	0.92639	-0.11274
5	INST	0 Converged	FIRST	x	3.77347	93.8200	-0.33906	1.67442	0.11733
6	INST	0 Converged	FIRST	wsum	1.75427	43.4356	-0.12295	0.87192	0.09533
7	INST	0 Converged	FIRST	k	1.72376	35.5182	0.80749	0.92639	-0.11274
8	INST	0 Converged	FIRST	y	3.77347	93.8200	-0.33906	1.67442	0.11733
9	3SLS	0 Converged	CONSUME	c	1.04956	16.4408	.	0.16314	.
10	3SLS	0 Converged	INVEST	i	1.60796	28.1778	-0.19485	0.75572	.
11	3SLS	0 Converged	LABOR	w	0.80149	1.7972	.	.	0.18129
12	IDENTITY	0 Converged	PRODUCT	x	.	0.0000	.	.	.
13	IDENTITY	0 Converged	INCOME	y	.	0.0000	.	.	.
14	IDENTITY	0 Converged	PROFIT	p	.	0.0000	.	.	.
15	IDENTITY	0 Converged	STOCK	k	.	0.0000	1.00000	.	.
16	IDENTITY	0 Converged	WAGE	wsum	.	0.0000	.	.	.

Obs	wp	g	t	yr	c	p	w	i	x	wsum	k	y
1	0.19327	0.20501	-0.36573	0.70109	-1	.	.	.	.	.	.	.
2	-0.07961	0.43902	-0.92310	0.31941	.	-1.00000	.	.	.	.	.	.
3	-0.44373	0.86622	-0.60415	0.71358	.	.	-1	.	.	.	.	.
4	-0.71661	0.10023	-0.16152	0.33190	.	.	.	-1	.	.	.	.
5	-0.52334	1.30524	-0.52725	1.03299	.	.	.	.	-1.00000	.	.	.
6	0.55627	0.86622	-0.60415	0.71358	.	.	.	.	.	-1.00000	.	.
7	-0.71661	0.10023	-0.16152	0.33190	.	.	.	.	.	.	-1	.
8	-0.52334	1.30524	-1.52725	1.03299	.	.	.	.	.	.	.	-1
9	.	.	.	.	-1	0.12489	.	.	.	0.79008	.	.
10	.	.	.	.	.	-0.01308	.	-1	.	.	.	.
11	.	.	.	0.14967	.	.	-1	.	0.40049	.	.	.
12	.	1.00000	.	.	1	.	.	1	-1.00000	.	.	.
13	.	1.00000	-1.00000	.	1	.	.	1	.	.	.	-1
14	.	.	-1.00000	.	.	-1.00000	-1	.	1.00000	.	.	.
15	.	.	.	.	.	.	.	1	.	.	-1	.
16	1.00000	.	.	.	.	.	1	.	.	-1.00000	.	.

Using the OUTEST= data set A produced by the SYSLIN procedure, the SIMLIN procedure can now compute the reduced form and simulate the model. The following statements perform the simulation.

```
proc simlin est=a data=klein type=3sls
            estprint total interim=2 outest=b;
   endogenous c p w i x wsum k y;
   exogenous  wp g t yr;
   lagged  klag k 1   plag p 1   xlag x 1;
   id year;
   output out=c p=chat phat what ihat xhat wsumhat khat yhat
                r=cres pres wres ires xres wsumres kres yres;
run;
```

The reduced form coefficients and multipliers are added to the information read from EST= data set A and written to the OUTEST= data set B. The predicted and residual values from the simulation are written to the OUT= data set C specified in the OUTPUT statement.

The SIMLIN procedure first prints the structural coefficient matrices read from the EST= data set, as shown in Output 23.1.3.

Output 23.1.3. SIMLIN Procedure Output – Structural Coefficients

Simulation of Klein's Model I using SIMLIN

The SIMLIN Procedure

Structural Coefficients for Endogenous Variables

Variable	c	p	w	i
c	1.0000	-0.1249	.	.
i	.	0.0131	.	1.0000
w	.	.	1.0000	.
x	-1.0000	.	.	-1.0000
y	-1.0000	.	.	-1.0000
p	.	1.0000	1.0000	.
k	.	.	.	-1.0000
wsum	.	.	-1.0000	.

Structural Coefficients for Endogenous Variables

Variable	x	wsum	k	y
c	.	-0.7901	.	.
i	.	.	.	.
w	-0.4005	.	.	.
x	1.0000	.	.	.
y	.	.	.	1.0000
p	-1.0000	.	.	.
k	.	.	1.0000	.
wsum	.	1.0000	.	.

Simulation of Klein's Model I using SIMLIN

The SIMLIN Procedure

Structural Coefficients for Lagged Endogenous Variables

Variable	klag	plag	xlag
c	.	0.1631	.
i	-0.1948	0.7557	.
w	.	.	0.1813
x	.	.	.
y	.	.	.
p	.	.	.
k	1.0000	.	.
wsum	.	.	.

Structural Coefficients for Exogenous Variables

Variable	wp	g	t	yr	Intercept
c	.	.	.	.	16.4408
i	.	.	.	.	28.1778
w	.	.	.	0.1497	1.7972
x	.	1.0000	.	.	0
y	.	1.0000	-1.0000	.	0
p	.	.	-1.0000	.	0
k	.	.	.	.	0
wsum	1.0000	.	.	.	0

The SIMLIN procedure then prints the inverse of the endogenous variables coefficient matrix, as shown in Output 23.1.4.

Output 23.1.4. SIMLIN Procedure Output – Inverse Coefficient Matrix

Simulation of Klein's Model I using SIMLIN

The SIMLIN Procedure

Inverse Coefficient Matrix for Endogenous Variables

Variable	c	i	w	x
c	1.6347	0.6347	1.0957	0.6347
p	0.9724	0.9724	-0.3405	0.9724
w	0.6496	0.6496	1.4406	0.6496
i	-0.0127	0.9873	0.004453	-0.0127
x	1.6219	1.6219	1.1001	1.6219
wsum	0.6496	0.6496	1.4406	0.6496
k	-0.0127	0.9873	0.004453	-0.0127
y	1.6219	1.6219	1.1001	0.6219

Inverse Coefficient Matrix for Endogenous Variables

Variable	y	p	k	wsum
c	0	0.1959	0	1.2915
p	0	1.1087	0	0.7682
w	0	0.0726	0	0.5132
i	0	-0.0145	0	-0.0100
x	0	0.1814	0	1.2815
wsum	0	0.0726	0	1.5132
k	0	-0.0145	1.0000	-0.0100
y	1.0000	0.1814	0	1.2815

The SIMLIN procedure next prints the reduced form coefficient matrices, as shown in Output 23.1.5.

Output 23.1.5. SIMLIN Procedure Output – Reduced Form Coefficients

Simulation of Klein's Model I using SIMLIN

The SIMLIN Procedure

Reduced Form for Lagged Endogenous Variables

Variable	klag	plag	xlag
c	-0.1237	0.7463	0.1986
p	-0.1895	0.8935	-0.0617
w	-0.1266	0.5969	0.2612
i	-0.1924	0.7440	0.000807
x	-0.3160	1.4903	0.1994
wsum	-0.1266	0.5969	0.2612
k	0.8076	0.7440	0.000807
y	-0.3160	1.4903	0.1994

Reduced Form for Exogenous Variables

Variable	wp	g	t	yr	Intercept
c	1.2915	0.6347	-0.1959	0.1640	46.7273
p	0.7682	0.9724	-1.1087	-0.0510	42.7736
w	0.5132	0.6496	-0.0726	0.2156	31.5721
i	-0.0100	-0.0127	0.0145	0.000667	27.6184
x	1.2815	1.6219	-0.1814	0.1647	74.3457
wsum	1.5132	0.6496	-0.0726	0.2156	31.5721
k	-0.0100	-0.0127	0.0145	0.000667	27.6184
y	1.2815	1.6219	-1.1814	0.1647	74.3457

The multiplier matrices (requested by the INTERIM=2 and TOTAL options) are printed next, as shown in Output 23.1.6.

Output 23.1.6. SIMLIN Procedure Output – Multipliers

Simulation of Klein's Model I using SIMLIN

The SIMLIN Procedure

Interim Multipliers for Interim 1

Variable	wp	g	t	yr	Intercept
c	0.829130	1.049424	-0.865262	-.0054080	43.27442
p	0.609213	0.771077	-0.982167	-.0558215	28.39545
w	0.794488	1.005578	-0.710961	0.0125018	41.45124
i	0.574572	0.727231	-0.827867	-.0379117	26.57227
x	1.403702	1.776655	-1.693129	-.0433197	69.84670
wsum	0.794488	1.005578	-0.710961	0.0125018	41.45124
k	0.564524	0.714514	-0.813366	-.0372452	54.19068
y	1.403702	1.776655	-1.693129	-.0433197	69.84670

Interim Multipliers for Interim 2

Variable	wp	g	t	yr	Intercept
c	0.663671	0.840004	-0.968727	-.0456589	28.36428
p	0.350716	0.443899	-0.618929	-.0401446	10.79216
w	0.658769	0.833799	-0.925467	-.0399178	28.33114
i	0.345813	0.437694	-0.575669	-.0344035	10.75901
x	1.009485	1.277698	-1.544396	-.0800624	39.12330
wsum	0.658769	0.833799	-0.925467	-.0399178	28.33114
k	0.910337	1.152208	-1.389035	-.0716486	64.94969
y	1.009485	1.277698	-1.544396	-.0800624	39.12330

Simulation of Klein's Model I using SIMLIN

The SIMLIN Procedure

Total Multipliers

Variable	wp	g	t	yr	Intercept
c	1.881667	1.381613	-0.685987	0.1789624	41.3045
p	0.786945	0.996031	-1.286891	-.0748290	15.4770
w	1.094722	1.385582	-0.399095	0.2537914	25.8275
i	0.000000	0.000000	-0.000000	0.0000000	0.0000
x	1.881667	2.381613	-0.685987	0.1789624	41.3045
wsum	2.094722	1.385582	-0.399095	0.2537914	25.8275
k	2.999365	3.796275	-4.904859	-.2852032	203.6035
y	1.881667	2.381613	-1.685987	0.1789624	41.3045

The last part of the SIMLIN procedure output is a table of statistics of fit for the simulation, as shown in Output 23.1.7.

Output 23.1.7. SIMLIN Procedure Output – Simulation Statistics

Simulation of Klein's Model I using SIMLIN

The SIMLIN Procedure

Fit Statistics

Variable	N	Mean Error	Mean Pct Error	Mean Abs Error	Mean Abs Pct Error	RMS Error	RMS Pct Error
c	21	0.1367	-0.3827	3.5011	6.69769	4.3155	8.1701
p	21	0.1422	-4.0671	2.9355	19.61400	3.4257	26.0265
w	21	0.1282	-0.8939	3.1247	8.92110	4.0930	11.4709
i	21	0.1337	105.8529	2.4983	127.13736	2.9980	252.3497
x	21	0.2704	-0.9553	5.9622	10.40057	7.1881	12.5653
wsum	21	0.1282	-0.6669	3.1247	7.88988	4.0930	10.1724
k	21	-0.1424	-0.1506	3.8879	1.90614	5.0036	2.4209
y	21	0.2704	-1.3476	5.9622	11.74177	7.1881	14.2214

The OUTEST= output data set contains all the observations read from the EST= data set, and in addition contains observations for the reduced form and multiplier matrices. The following statements produce a partial listing of the OUTEST= data set, as shown in Output 23.1.8.

```
proc print data=b;
   where _type_ = 'REDUCED' | _type_ = 'IMULT1';
run;
```

Output 23.1.8. Partial Listing of OUTEST= Data Set

Simulation of Klein's Model I using SIMLIN

Obs	_TYPE_	_DEPVAR_	_MODEL_	_SIGMA_	c	p	w	i	x	wsum	k	y
9	REDUCED	c		.	1.63465	0.63465	1.09566	0.63465	0	0.19585	0	1.29151
10	REDUCED	p		.	0.97236	0.97236	-0.34048	0.97236	0	1.10872	0	0.76825
11	REDUCED	w		.	0.64957	0.64957	1.44059	0.64957	0	0.07263	0	0.51321
12	REDUCED	i		.	-0.01272	0.98728	0.00445	-0.01272	0	-0.01450	0	-0.01005
13	REDUCED	x		.	1.62194	1.62194	1.10011	1.62194	0	0.18135	0	1.28146
14	REDUCED	wsum		.	0.64957	0.64957	1.44059	0.64957	0	0.07263	0	1.51321
15	REDUCED	k		.	-0.01272	0.98728	0.00445	-0.01272	0	-0.01450	1	-0.01005
16	REDUCED	y		.	1.62194	1.62194	1.10011	0.62194	1	0.18135	0	1.28146
17	IMULT1	c		.	.	.	.	.	.	.	.	.
18	IMULT1	p		.	.	.	.	.	.	.	.	.
19	IMULT1	w		.	.	.	.	.	.	.	.	.
20	IMULT1	i		.	.	.	.	.	.	.	.	.
21	IMULT1	x		.	.	.	.	.	.	.	.	.
22	IMULT1	wsum		.	.	.	.	.	.	.	.	.
23	IMULT1	k		.	.	.	.	.	.	.	.	.
24	IMULT1	y		.	.	.	.	.	.	.	.	.

Obs	klag	plag	xlag	wp	g	t	yr	Intercept
9	-0.12366	0.74631	0.19863	1.29151	0.63465	-0.19585	0.16399	46.7273
10	-0.18946	0.89347	-0.06173	0.76825	0.97236	-1.10872	-0.05096	42.7736
11	-0.12657	0.59687	0.26117	0.51321	0.64957	-0.07263	0.21562	31.5721
12	-0.19237	0.74404	0.00081	-0.01005	-0.01272	0.01450	0.00067	27.6184
13	-0.31603	1.49034	0.19944	1.28146	1.62194	-0.18135	0.16466	74.3457
14	-0.12657	0.59687	0.26117	1.51321	0.64957	-0.07263	0.21562	31.5721
15	0.80763	0.74404	0.00081	-0.01005	-0.01272	0.01450	0.00067	27.6184
16	-0.31603	1.49034	0.19944	1.28146	1.62194	-1.18135	0.16466	74.3457
17	.	.	.	0.82913	1.04942	-0.86526	-0.00541	43.2744
18	.	.	.	0.60921	0.77108	-0.98217	-0.05582	28.3955
19	.	.	.	0.79449	1.00558	-0.71096	0.01250	41.4512
20	.	.	.	0.57457	0.72723	-0.82787	-0.03791	26.5723
21	.	.	.	1.40370	1.77666	-1.69313	-0.04332	69.8467
22	.	.	.	0.79449	1.00558	-0.71096	0.01250	41.4512
23	.	.	.	0.56452	0.71451	-0.81337	-0.03725	54.1907
24	.	.	.	1.40370	1.77666	-1.69313	-0.04332	69.8467

The actual and predicted values for the variable C are plotted in Output 23.1.9.

```
title2 h=1 'Plots of Simulation Results';
symbol1 i=none v=star;
symbol2 i=join v=circle;
proc gplot data=c;
   plot c*year=1 chat*year=2 / overlay href=1941.5;
run;
```

Output 23.1.9. Plot of Actual and Predicted Consumption

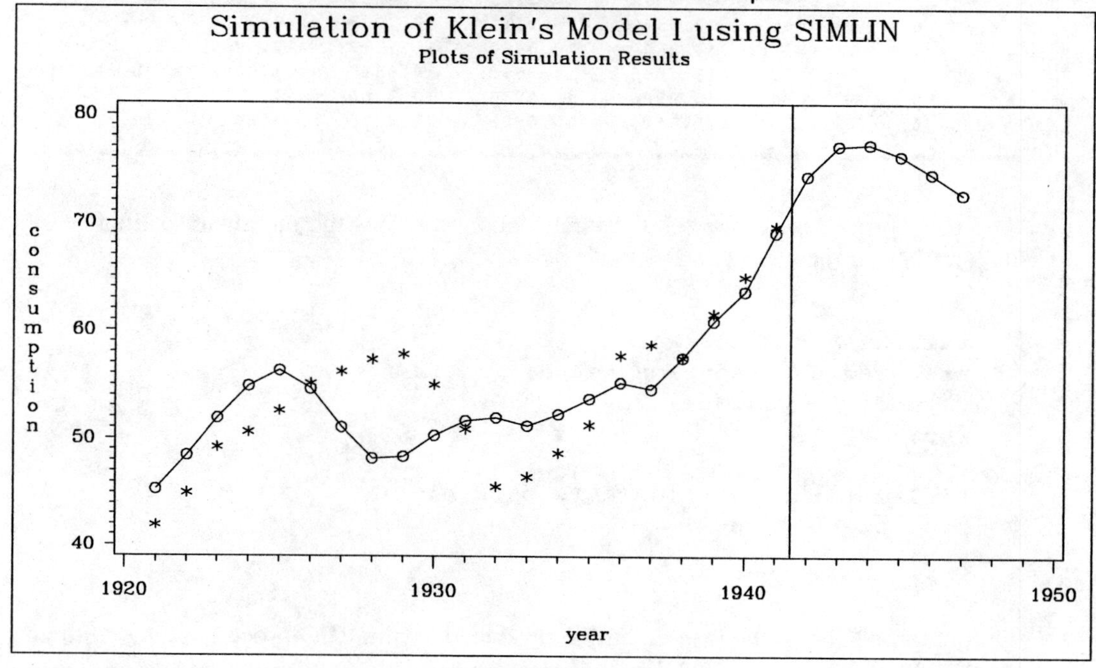

Example 23.2. Multipliers for a Third-Order System

This example shows how to fit and simulate a single equation dynamic model with third-order lags. It then shows how to convert the third-order equation into a three equation system with only first-order lags, so that the SIMLIN procedure can compute multipliers. (See the section "Multipliers for Higher Order Lags" earlier in this chapter for more information.)

The input data set TEST is created from simulated data. A partial listing of the data set TEST produced by PROC PRINT is shown in Output 23.2.1.

```
title1 'Simulate Equation with Third-Order Lags';
title2 'Listing of Simulated Input Data';
proc print data=test(obs=10);
run;
```

Output 23.2.1. Partial Listing of Input Data Set

Simulate Equation with Third-Order Lags
Listing of Simulated Input Data

Obs	y	ylag1	ylag2	ylag3	x	n
1	8.2369	8.5191	6.9491	7.8800	-1.2593	1
2	8.6285	8.2369	8.5191	6.9491	-1.6805	2
3	10.2223	8.6285	8.2369	8.5191	-1.9844	3
4	10.1372	10.2223	8.6285	8.2369	-1.7855	4
5	10.0360	10.1372	10.2223	8.6285	-1.8092	5
6	10.3560	10.0360	10.1372	10.2223	-1.3921	6
7	11.4835	10.3560	10.0360	10.1372	-2.0987	7
8	10.8508	11.4835	10.3560	10.0360	-1.8788	8
9	11.2684	10.8508	11.4835	10.3560	-1.7154	9
10	12.6310	11.2684	10.8508	11.4835	-1.8418	10

The REG procedure processes the input data and writes the parameter estimates to the OUTEST= data set A.

```
title2 'Estimated Parameters';
proc reg data=test outest=a;
   model y=ylag3 x;
run;

title2 'Listing of OUTEST= Data Set';
proc print data=a;
run;
```

Output 23.2.2 shows the printed output produced by the REG procedure, and Output 23.2.3 displays the OUTEST= data set A produced.

Output 23.2.2. Estimates and Fit Information from PROC REG

```
                 Simulate Equation with Third-Order Lags
                          Estimated Parameters

                           The REG Procedure
                             Model: MODEL1
                         Dependent Variable: y

                          Analysis of Variance

                                  Sum of           Mean
Source                   DF      Squares         Square    F Value    Pr > F

Model                     2    173.98377       86.99189    1691.98    <.0001
Error                    27      1.38818        0.05141
Corrected Total          29    175.37196


             Root MSE              0.22675    R-Square     0.9921
             Dependent Mean       13.05234    Adj R-Sq     0.9915
             Coeff Var             1.73721


                          Parameter Estimates

                       Parameter       Standard
     Variable     DF    Estimate          Error    t Value    Pr > |t|

     Intercept     1     0.14239        0.23657       0.60      0.5523
     ylag3         1     0.77121        0.01723      44.77      <.0001
     x             1    -1.77668        0.10843     -16.39      <.0001
```

Output 23.2.3. The OUTEST= Data Set Created by PROC REG

```
                 Simulate Equation with Third-Order Lags
                      Listing of OUTEST= Data Set

Obs  _MODEL_  _TYPE_  _DEPVAR_   _RMSE_   Intercept   ylag3        x      y

 1   MODEL1   PARMS      y      0.22675    0.14239   0.77121  -1.77668   -1
```

The SIMLIN procedure processes the TEST data set using the estimates from PROC REG. The following statements perform the simulation and write the results to the OUT= data set OUT2.

```
title2 'Simulation of Equation';
proc simlin est=a data=test nored;
   endogenous y;
   exogenous  x;
   lagged ylag3 y 3;
   id n;
   output out=out1 predicted=yhat residual=yresid;
run;
```

The printed output from the SIMLIN procedure is shown in Output 23.2.4.

Output 23.2.4. Output Produced by PROC SIMLIN

```
                    Simulate Equation with Third-Order Lags
                            Simulation of Equation

                             The SIMLIN Procedure

                                Fit Statistics

                          Mean   Mean Pct  Mean Abs    Mean Abs         RMS    RMS Pct
Variable         N       Error      Error     Error   Pct Error       Error      Error

y               30     -0.0233    -0.2268    0.2662     2.05684      0.3408     2.6159
```

The following statements plot the actual and predicted values, as shown in Output 23.2.5.

```
title2 'Plots of Simulation Results';
symbol1 i=none v=star;
symbol2 i=join v=circle;
proc gplot data=out1;
   plot yhat*n=1 y*n=2 / overlay;
run;
```

Output 23.2.5. Plot of Predicted and Actual Values

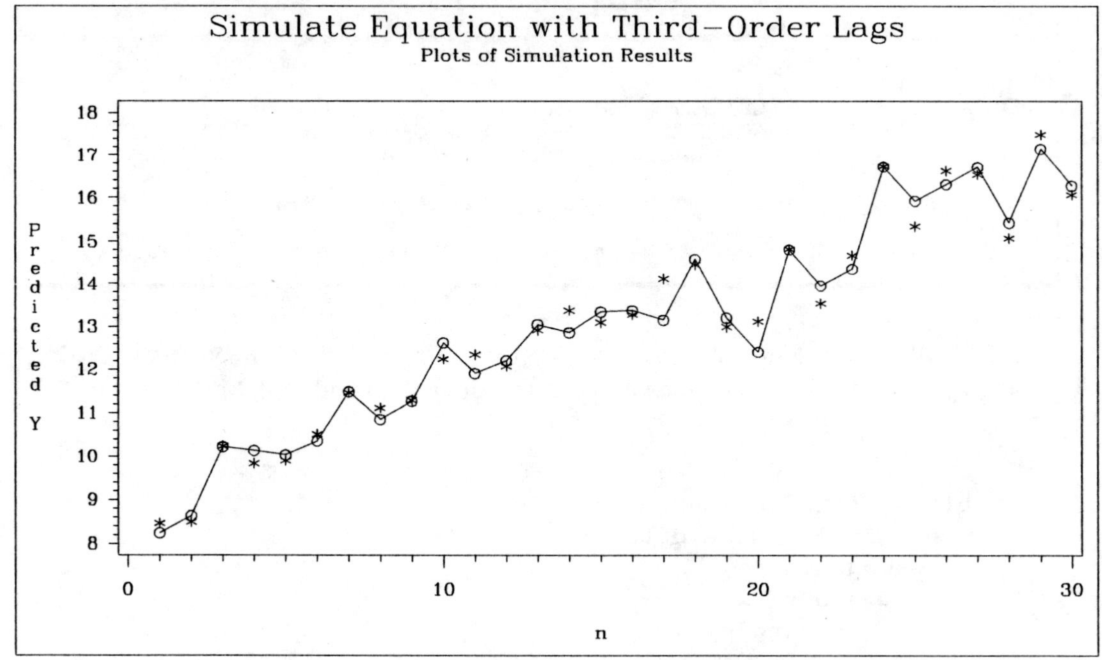

Next, the input data set TEST is modified by creating two new variables, YLAG1X and YLAG2X, that are equal to YLAG1 and YLAG2. These variables are used in the SYSLIN procedure. (The estimates produced by PROC SYSLIN are the same as before and are not shown.) A listing of the OUTEST= data set B created by PROC SYSLIN is shown in Output 23.2.6.

```
data test2;
   set test;
   ylag1x=ylag1;
   ylag2x=ylag2;
run;

title2 'Estimation of parameters and definition of identities';
proc syslin data=test2 outest=b;
   endogenous y ylag1x ylag2x;
   model y=ylag3 x;
   identity ylag1x=ylag1;
   identity ylag2x=ylag2;
run;

title2 'Listing of OUTEST= data set from PROC SYSLIN';
proc print data=b;
run;
```

Output 23.2.6. Listing of OUTEST= Data Set Created from PROC SYSLIN

Simulate Equation with Third-Order Lags
Listing of OUTEST= data set from PROC SYSLIN

Obs	_TYPE_	_STATUS_	_MODEL_	_DEPVAR_	_SIGMA_	Intercept	ylag3	x	ylag1	ylag2	y	ylag1x	ylag2x
1	OLS	0 Converged	y	y	0.22675	0.14239	0.77121	-1.77668	.	.	-1	.	.
2	IDENTITY	0 Converged		ylag1x	.	0.00000	.	.	1	.	.	-1	.
3	IDENTITY	0 Converged		ylag2x	.	0.00000	.	.	.	1	.	.	-1

The SIMLIN procedure is used to compute the reduced form and multipliers. The OUTEST= data set B from PROC SYSLIN is used as the EST= data set for the SIMLIN procedure. The following statements perform the multiplier analysis.

```
title2 'Simulation of transformed first-order equation system';

proc simlin est=b data=test2 total interim=2;
   endogenous y ylag1x ylag2x;
   exogenous  x;
   lagged  ylag1 y 1  ylag2 ylag1x 1  ylag3 ylag2x 1;
   id n;
   output out=out2 predicted=yhat residual=yresid;
run;
```

Output 23.2.7 shows the interim 2 and total multipliers printed by the SIMLIN procedure.

Output 23.2.7. Interim 2 and Total Multipliers

```
                 Simulate Equation with Third-Order Lags
         Simulation of transformed first-order equation system

                         The SIMLIN Procedure

                  Interim Multipliers for Interim 2

             Variable                x      Intercept

             y                0.000000      0.0000000
             ylag1x           0.000000      0.0000000
             ylag2x          -1.776682      0.1423865


                          Total Multipliers

             Variable                x      Intercept

             y               -7.765556      0.6223455
             ylag1x          -7.765556      0.6223455
             ylag2x          -7.765556      0.6223455
```

References

Maddala, G.S (1977), *Econometrics*, New York: McGraw-Hill Book Co.

Pindyck, R.S. and Rubinfeld, D.L. (1991), *Econometric Models and Economic Forecasts*, Third Edition, New York: McGraw-Hill Book Co.

Theil, H. (1971), *Principles of Econometrics*, New York: John Wiley & Sons, Inc.

Chapter 24
The SPECTRA Procedure

Chapter Contents

Chapter 24
The SPECTRA Procedure

Overview

The SPECTRA procedure performs spectral and cross-spectral analysis of time series. You can use spectral analysis techniques to look for periodicities or cyclical patterns in data.

The SPECTRA procedure produces estimates of the spectral and cross-spectral densities of a multivariate time series. Estimates of the spectral and cross-spectral densities of a multivariate time series are produced using a finite Fourier transform to obtain periodograms and cross-periodograms. The periodogram ordinates are smoothed by a moving average to produce estimated spectral and cross-spectral densities. PROC SPECTRA can also test whether or not the data are white noise.

PROC SPECTRA uses the finite Fourier transform to decompose data series into a sum of sine and cosine waves of different amplitudes and wavelengths. The Fourier transform decomposition of the series x_t is

$$x_t = \frac{a_0}{2} + \sum_{k=1}^{m} [a_k cos(\omega_k t) + b_k sin(\omega_k t)]$$

where

t	is the time subscript, $t = 1, 2, \ldots, n$
x_t	are the data
n	is the number of observations in the time series
m	is the number of of frequencies in the Fourier decomposition: $m = \frac{n}{2}$ if n is even; $m = \frac{n-1}{2}$ if n is odd
a_0	is the mean term: $a_0 = 2\overline{x}$
a_k	are the cosine coefficients
b_k	are the sine coefficients
ω_k	are the Fourier frequencies: $\omega_k = \frac{2\pi k}{n}$

Functions of the Fourier coefficients a_k and b_k can be plotted against frequency or against wave length to form *periodograms*. The amplitude periodogram J_k is defined as follows:

$$J_k = \frac{n}{2}(a_k^2 + b_k^2)$$

Several definitions of the term periodogram are used in the spectral analysis literature. The following discussion refers to the J_k sequence as the periodogram.

The periodogram can be interpreted as the contribution of the *k*th harmonic ω_k to the total sum of squares, in an analysis of variance sense, for the decomposition of the process into two-degree-of-freedom components for each of the m frequencies. When n is even, $sin(\omega_{\frac{n}{2}})$ is zero, and thus the last periodogram value is a one-degree-of-freedom component.

The periodogram is a volatile and inconsistent estimator of the spectrum. The spectral density estimate is produced by smoothing the periodogram. Smoothing reduces the variance of the estimator but introduces a bias. The weight function used for the smoothing process, W(), often called the kernel or spectral window, is specified with the WEIGHTS statement. It is related to another weight function, $w()$, the lag window, that is used in other methods to taper the correlogram rather than to smooth the periodogram. Many specific weighting functions have been suggested in the literature (Fuller 1976, Jenkins and Watts 1968, Priestly 1981). Table 24.1 later in this chapter gives the formulas relevant when the WEIGHTS statement is used.

Letting *i* represent the imaginary unit $\sqrt{-1}$, the cross-periodogram is defined as follows:

$$J_k^{xy} = \frac{n}{2}(a_k^x a_k^y + b_k^x b_k^y) + i\frac{n}{2}(a_k^x b_k^y - b_k^x a_k^y)$$

The cross-spectral density estimate is produced by smoothing the cross-periodogram in the same way as the periodograms are smoothed using the spectral window specified by the WEIGHTS statement.

The SPECTRA procedure creates an output SAS data set whose variables contain values of the periodograms, cross-periodograms, estimates of spectral densities, and estimates of cross-spectral densities. The form of the output data set is described in the section "OUT= Data Set" later in this chapter.

Getting Started

To use the SPECTRA procedure, specify the input and output data sets and options for the analysis you want on the PROC SPECTRA statement, and list the variables to analyze in the VAR statement.

For example, to take the Fourier transform of a variable X in a data set A, use the following statements:

```
proc spectra data=a out=b coef;
   var x;
run;
```

This PROC SPECTRA step writes the Fourier coefficients a_k and b_k to the variables COS_01 and SIN_01 in the output data set B.

When a WEIGHTS statement is specified, the periodogram is smoothed by a weighted moving average to produce an estimate for the spectral density of the series. The following statements write a spectral density estimate for X to the variable S_01 in the output data set B.

```
proc spectra data=a out=b s;
   var x;
   weights 1 2 3 4 3 2 1;
run;
```

When the VAR statement specifies more than one variable, you can perform cross-spectral analysis by specifying the CROSS option. The CROSS option by itself produces the cross-periodograms. For example, the following statements write the real and imaginary parts of the cross-periodogram of X and Y to the variable RP_01_02 and IP_01_02 in the output data set B.

```
proc spectra data=a out=b cross;
   var x y;
run;
```

To produce cross-spectral density estimates, combine the CROSS option and the S option. The cross-periodogram is smoothed using the weights specified by the WEIGHTS statement in the same way as the spectral density. The squared coherency and phase estimates of the cross-spectrum are computed when the K and PH options are used.

The following example computes cross-spectral density estimates for the variables X and Y.

```
proc spectra data=a out=b cross s;
   var x y;
   weights 1 2 3 4 3 2 1;
run;
```

The real part and imaginary part of the cross-spectral density estimates are written to the variable CS_01_02 and QS_01_02, respectively.

Syntax

The following statements are used with the SPECTRA procedure.

PROC SPECTRA *options*;
  BY *variables*;
  VAR *variables*;
  WEIGHTS *constants*;

Functional Summary

The statements and options controlling the SPECTRA procedure are summarized in the following table.

Description	Statement	Option
Statements		
specify BY-group processing	BY	
specify the variables to be analyzed	VAR	
specify weights for spectral density estimates	WEIGHTS	
Data Set Options		
specify the input data set	PROC SPECTRA	DATA=
specify the output data set	PROC SPECTRA	OUT=
Output Control Options		
output the amplitudes of the cross-spectrum	PROC SPECTRA	A
output the Fourier coefficients	PROC SPECTRA	COEF
output the periodogram	PROC SPECTRA	P
output the spectral density estimates	PROC SPECTRA	S
output cross-spectral analysis results	PROC SPECTRA	CROSS
output squared coherency of the cross-spectrum	PROC SPECTRA	K
output the phase of the cross-spectrum	PROC SPECTRA	PH
Smoothing Options		
specify the Bartlett kernel	WEIGHTS	BART
specify the Parzen kernel	WEIGHTS	PARZEN
specify the Quadratic Spectral kernel	WEIGHTS	QS
specify the Tukey-Hanning kernel	WEIGHTS	TUKEY
specify the Truncated kernel	WEIGHTS	TRUNCAT

Description	Statement	Option
Other Options		
subtract the series mean	PROC SPECTRA	ADJMEAN
specify an alternate quadrature spectrum estimate	PROC SPECTRA	ALTW
request tests for white noise	PROC SPECTRA	WHITETEST

PROC SPECTRA Statement

PROC SPECTRA *options;*

The following options can be used in the PROC SPECTRA statement.

A

outputs the amplitude variables (A_*nn*_*mm*) of the cross-spectrum.

ADJMEAN
CENTER

subtracts the series mean before performing the Fourier decomposition. This sets the first periodogram ordinate to 0 rather than 2*n* times the squared mean. This option is commonly used when the periodograms are to be plotted to prevent a large first periodogram ordinate from distorting the scale of the plot.

ALTW

specifies that the quadrature spectrum estimate is computed at the boundaries in the same way as the spectral density estimate and the cospectrum estimate are computed.

COEF

outputs the Fourier cosine and sine coefficients of each series, in addition to the periodogram.

CROSS

is used with the P and S options to output cross-periodograms and cross-spectral densities.

DATA= *SAS-data-set*

names the SAS data set containing the input data. If the DATA= option is omitted, the most recently created SAS data set is used.

K

outputs the squared coherency variables (K_*nn*_*mm*) of the cross-spectrum. The K_*nn*_*mm* variables are identically 1 unless weights are given in the WEIGHTS statement and the S option is specified.

OUT= *SAS-data-set*

names the output data set created by PROC SPECTRA to store the results. If the OUT= option is omitted, the output data set is named using the DATA*n* convention.

P

outputs the periodogram variables. The variables are named P_*nn*, where *nn* is an index of the original variable with which the periodogram variable is associated. When both the P and CROSS options are specified, the cross-periodogram variables RP_*nn*_*mm* and IP_*nn*_*mm* are also output.

PH

outputs the phase variables (PH_*nn*_*mm*) of the cross-spectrum.

S

outputs the spectral density estimates. The variables are named S_*nn*, where *nn* is an index of the original variable with which the estimate variable is associated. When both the S and CROSS options are specified, the cross-spectral variables CS_*nn*_*mm* and QS_*nn*_*mm* are also output.

WHITETEST

prints a test of the hypothesis that the series are white noise. See "White Noise Test" later in this chapter for details.

Note that the CROSS, A, K, and PH options are only meaningful if more than one variable is listed in the VAR statement.

BY Statement

BY *variables;*

A BY statement can be used with PROC SPECTRA to obtain separate analyses for groups of observations defined by the BY variables.

VAR Statement

VAR *variables;*

The VAR statement specifies one or more numeric variables containing the time series to analyze. The order of the variables in the VAR statement list determines the index, *nn*, used to name the output variables. The VAR statement is required.

WEIGHTS Statement

WEIGHTS *constant-specification | kernel-specification;*

The WEIGHTS statement specifies the relative weights used in the moving average applied to the periodogram ordinates to form the spectral density estimates. A WEIGHTS statement must be used to produce smoothed spectral density estimates. If the WEIGHTS statement is not used, only the periodogram is produced.

Using Constant Specifications

Any number of weighting constants can be specified. The constants should be positive and symmetric about the middle weight. The middle constant, (or the constant to the right of the middle if an even number of weight constants are specified), is the relative weight of the current periodogram ordinate. The constant immediately following the middle one is the relative weight of the next periodogram ordinate, and so on. The actual weights used in the smoothing process are the weights specified in the WEIGHTS statement scaled so that they sum to $\frac{1}{4\pi}$.

The moving average reflects at each end of the periodogram. The first periodogram ordinate is not used; the second periodogram ordinate is used in its place.

For example, a simple triangular weighting can be specified using the following WEIGHTS statement:

```
weights 1 2 3 2 1;
```

Using Kernel Specifications

You can specify five different kernels in the WEIGHTS statement. The syntax for the statement is

WEIGHTS [PARZEN][BART][TUKEY][TRUNCAT][QS] [c e];

where $c >= 0$ and $e >= 0$ are used to compute the bandwidth parameter as

$$\mathrm{l(q) = cq^e}$$

and q is the number of periodogram ordinates +1:

$$q = \mathrm{floor(n/2)} + 1$$

To specify the bandwidth explicitly, set $c =$ to the desired bandwidth and $e = 0$.

For example, a Parzen kernel can be specified using the following WEIGHTS statement:

```
weights parzen 0.5 0;
```

For details, see the "Kernels" section on page 1400, later in this chapter.

Details

Input Data

Observations in the data set analyzed by the SPECTRA procedure should form ordered, equally spaced time series. No more than 99 variables can be included in the analysis.

Data are often de-trended before analysis by the SPECTRA procedure. This can be done by using the residuals output by a SAS regression procedure. Optionally, the data can be centered using the ADJMEAN option in the PROC SPECTRA statement, since the zero periodogram ordinate corresponding to the mean is of little interest from the point of view of spectral analysis.

Missing Values

Missing values are essentially excluded from the analysis by the SPECTRA procedure. If the SPECTRA procedure encounters missing values for any variable listed in the VAR statement, the procedure determines the longest contiguous span of data that has no missing values for the variables listed in the VAR statement and uses it for the analysis.

Computational Method

If the number of observations n factors into prime integers that are less than or equal to 23, and the product of the square-free factors of n is less than 210, then PROC SPECTRA uses the Fast Fourier Transform developed by Cooley and Tukey and implemented by Singleton (1969). If n cannot be factored in this way, then PROC SPECTRA uses a Chirp-Z algorithm similar to that proposed by Monro and Branch (1976). To reduce memory requirements, when n is small the Fourier coefficients are computed directly using the defining formulas.

Kernels

Kernels are used to smooth the periodogram by using a weighted moving average of nearby points. A smoothed periodogram is defined by the following equation.

$$\hat{J}_i(\mathrm{l(q)}) = \sum_{\tau=-\mathrm{l(q)}}^{\mathrm{l(q)}} \mathrm{w}\left(\frac{\tau}{\mathrm{l(q)}}\right) \tilde{\mathrm{J}}_{\mathrm{i}+\tau}$$

where $\mathrm{w(x)}$ is the kernel or weight function. At the endpoints, the moving average is computed cyclically; that is,

$$\tilde{J}_{i+\tau} = \begin{cases} J_{i+\tau} & 0 <= \mathrm{i}+\tau <= \mathrm{q} \\ J_{-(i+\tau)} & \mathrm{i}+\tau < 0 \\ J_{q-(i+\tau)} & \mathrm{i}+\tau > \mathrm{q} \end{cases}$$

The SPECTRA procedure supports the following kernels. They are listed with their default bandwidth functions.

Bartlett: KERNEL BART

$$\begin{aligned} \mathrm{w(x)} &= \begin{cases} 1-|x| & |x|\leq 1 \\ 0 & \text{otherwise} \end{cases} \\ \mathrm{l(q)} &= \frac{1}{2}q^{1/3} \end{aligned}$$

Parzen: KERNEL PARZEN

$$\begin{aligned} \mathrm{w(x)} &= \begin{cases} 1-6|x|^2+6|x|^3 & 0\leq|x|\leq\frac{1}{2} \\ 2(1-|x|)^3 & \frac{1}{2}\leq|x|\leq 1 \\ 0 & \text{otherwise} \end{cases} \\ \mathrm{l(q)} &= q^{1/5} \end{aligned}$$

Quadratic Spectral: KERNEL QS

$$\begin{aligned} \mathrm{w(x)} &= \frac{25}{12\pi^2x^2}\left(\frac{sin(6\pi x/5)}{6\pi x/5} - cos(6\pi x/5)\right) \\ \mathrm{l(q)} &= \frac{1}{2}q^{1/5} \end{aligned}$$

Tukey-Hanning: KERNEL TUKEY

$$\begin{aligned} \mathrm{w(x)} &= \begin{cases} (1+cos(\pi x))/2 & |x|\leq 1 \\ 0 & \text{otherwise} \end{cases} \\ \mathrm{l(q)} &= \frac{2}{3}q^{1/5} \end{aligned}$$

Truncated: KERNEL TRUNCAT

$$\begin{aligned} \mathrm{w(x)} &= \begin{cases} 1 & |x|\leq 1 \\ 0 & \text{otherwise} \end{cases} \\ \mathrm{l(q)} &= \frac{1}{4}q^{1/5} \end{aligned}$$

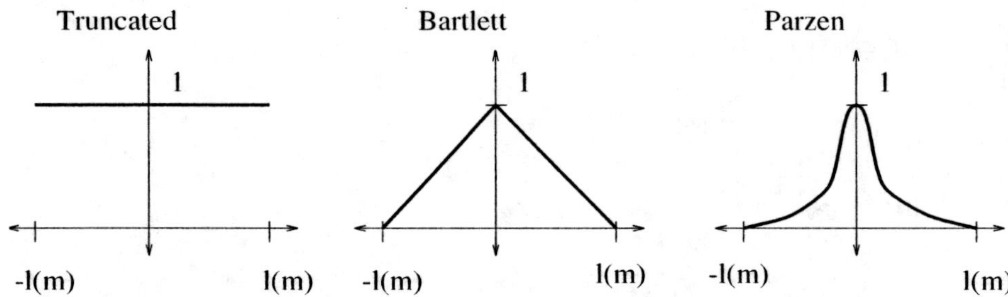

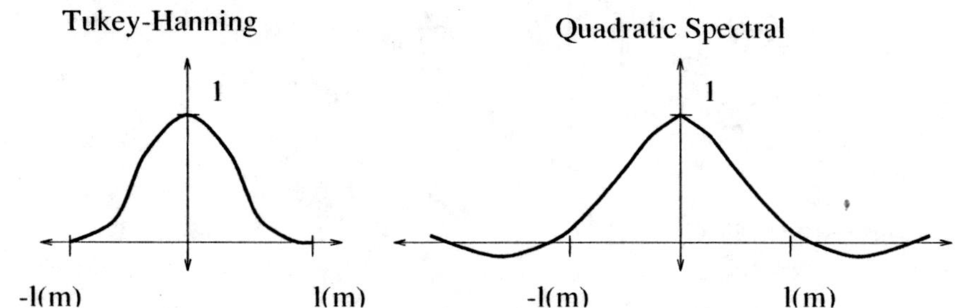

Figure 24.1. Kernels for Smoothing

Refer to Andrews (1991) for details on the properties of these kernels.

White Noise Test

PROC SPECTRA prints two test statistics for white noise when the WHITETEST option is specified: Fisher's Kappa (Davis 1941, Fuller 1976) and Bartlett's Kolmogorov-Smirnov statistic (Bartlett 1966, Fuller 1976, Durbin 1967).

If the time series is a sequence of independent random variables with mean 0 and variance σ^2, then the periodogram, J_k, will have the same expected value for all k. For a time series with nonzero autocorrelation, each ordinate of the periodogram, J_k, will have different expected values. The Fisher's Kappa statistic tests whether the largest J_k can be considered different from the mean of the J_k. Critical values for the Fisher's Kappa test can be found in Fuller 1976 and *SAS/ETS Software: Applications Guide 1*.

The Kolmogorov-Smirnov statistic reported by PROC SPECTRA has the same asymptotic distribution as Bartlett's test (Durbin 1967). The Kolmogorov-Smirnov statistic compares the normalized cumulative periodogram with the cumulative distribution function of a uniform(0,1) random variable. The normalized cumulative periodogram, F_j, of the series is

$$F_j = \frac{\sum_{k=1}^{j} J_k}{\sum_{k=1}^{m} J_k}, j = 1, 2 \ldots, m-1$$

where $m = \frac{n}{2}$ if n is even or $m = \frac{n-1}{2}$ if n is odd. The test statistic is the maximum absolute difference of the normalized cumulative periodogram and the uniform cumulative distribution function. For $m-1$ greater than 100, if Bartlett's Kolmogorov-Smirnov statistic exceeds the critical value

$$\frac{a}{\sqrt{m-1}}$$

where $a = 1.36$ or $a = 1.63$ corresponding to 5% or 1% significance levels respectively, then reject the null hypothesis that the series represents white noise. Critical values for $m - 1 < 100$ can be found in a table of significance points of the Kolmogorov-Smirnov statistics with sample size $m-1$ (Miller 1956, Owen 1962).

Transforming Frequencies

The variable FREQ in the data set created by the SPECTRA procedure ranges from 0 to π. Sometimes it is preferable to express frequencies in cycles per observation period, which is equal to $\frac{2}{\pi}$FREQ.

To express frequencies in cycles per unit time (for example, in cycles per year), multiply FREQ by $\frac{d}{2\pi}$, where *d* is the number of observations per unit of time. For example, for monthly data, if the desired time unit is years then *d* is 12. The period of the cycle is $\frac{2\pi}{d \times \mathrm{FREQ}}$, which ranges from $\frac{2}{d}$ to infinity.

OUT= Data Set

The OUT= data set contains $\frac{n}{2}+1$ observations, if *n* is even, or $\frac{n+1}{2}$ observations, if *n* is odd, where *n* is the number of observations in the time series.

The variables in the new data set are named according to the following conventions. Each variable to be analyzed is associated with an index. The first variable listed in the VAR statement is indexed as 01, the second variable as 02, and so on. Output variables are named by combining indexes with prefixes. The prefix always identifies the nature of the new variable, and the indices identify the original variables from which the statistics were obtained.

Variables containing spectral analysis results have names consisting of a prefix, an underscore, and the index of the variable analyzed. For example, the variable S_01 contains spectral density estimates for the first variable in the VAR statement. Variables containing cross-spectral analysis results have names consisting of a prefix, an underscore, the index of the first variable, another underscore, and the index of the second variable. For example, the variable A_01_02 contains the amplitude of the cross-spectral density estimate for the first and second variables in the VAR statement.

Table 24.1 shows the formulas and naming conventions used for the variables in the OUT= data set. Let X be variable number *nn* in the VAR statement list and let Y be variable number *mm* in the VAR statement list. Table 24.1 shows the output variables containing the results of the spectral and cross-spectral analysis of X and Y.

In Table 24.1 the following notation is used. Let W_j be the vector of $2p+1$ smoothing weights given by the WEIGHTS statement, normalized to sum to $\frac{1}{4\pi}$. The subscript of W_j runs from W_{-p} to W_p, so that W_0 is the middle weight in the WEIGHTS statement list. Let $\omega_k = \frac{2\pi k}{n}$, where $k = 0, 1, \ldots, \mathrm{floor}(\frac{n}{2})$.

Table 24.1. Variables Created by PROC SPECTRA

Variable	Description
FREQ	frequency in radians from 0 to π (Note: Cycles per observation is $\frac{\text{FREQ}}{2\pi}$.)
PERIOD	period or wavelength: $\frac{2\pi}{\text{FREQ}}$ (Note: PERIOD is missing for FREQ=0.)
COS_X COS_WAVE	cosine transform of X: $a_k^x = \frac{2}{n}\sum_{t=1}^{n} X_t\cos(\omega_k(t-1))$
SIN_X SIN_WAVE	sine transform of X: $b_k^x = \frac{2}{n}\sum_{t=1}^{n} X_t\sin(\omega_k(t-1))$
P_*nn*	periodogram of X: $J_k^x = \frac{n}{2}[(a_k^x)^2 + (b_k^x)^2]$
S_*nn*	spectral density estimate of X: $F_k^x = \sum_{j=-p}^{p} W_j J_{k+j}^x$ (except across endpoints)
RP_*nn*_*mm*	real part of cross-periodogram X and Y: $\mathrm{real}(\mathrm{J}_\mathrm{k}^{\mathrm{xy}}) = \frac{\mathrm{n}}{2}(\mathrm{a}_\mathrm{k}^\mathrm{x}\mathrm{a}_\mathrm{k}^\mathrm{y} + \mathrm{b}_\mathrm{k}^\mathrm{x}\mathrm{b}_\mathrm{k}^\mathrm{y})$
IP_*nn*_*mm*	imaginary part of cross-periodogram of X and Y: $\mathrm{imag}(\mathrm{J}_\mathrm{k}^{\mathrm{xy}}) = \frac{\mathrm{n}}{2}(\mathrm{a}_\mathrm{k}^\mathrm{x}\mathrm{b}_\mathrm{k}^\mathrm{y} - \mathrm{b}_\mathrm{k}^\mathrm{x}\mathrm{a}_\mathrm{k}^\mathrm{y})$
CS_*nn*_*mm*	cospectrum estimate (real part of cross-spectrum) of X and Y: $C_k^{xy} = \sum_{j=-p}^{p} W_j \mathrm{real}(\mathrm{J}_{\mathrm{k+j}}^{\mathrm{xy}})$ (except across endpoints)
QS_*nn*_*mm*	quadrature spectrum estimate (imaginary part of cross-spectrum) of X and Y: $Q_k^{xy} = \sum_{j=-p}^{p} W_j \mathrm{imag}(\mathrm{J}_{\mathrm{k+j}}^{\mathrm{xy}})$ (except across endpoints)
A_*nn*_*mm*	amplitude (modulus) of cross-spectrum of X and Y: $A_k^{xy} = \sqrt{(C_k^{xy})^2 + (Q_k^{xy})^2}$
K_*nn*_*mm*	coherency squared of X and Y: $K_k^{xy} = (A_k^{xy})^2/(F_k^x F_k^y)$
PH_*nn*_*mm*	phase spectrum in radians of X and Y: $\Phi_k^{xy} = \arctan(Q_k^{xy}/C_k^{xy})$

Printed Output

By default PROC SPECTRA produced no printed output.

When the WHITETEST option is specified, the SPECTRA procedure prints the following statistics for each variable in the VAR statement:

1. the name of the variable
2. M-1, the number of two-degree-of-freedom periodogram ordinates used in the tests
3. MAX(P(*)), the maximum periodogram ordinate
4. SUM(P(*)), the sum of the periodogram ordinates
5. Fisher's Kappa statistic
6. Bartlett's Kolmogorov-Smirnov test statistic

See "White Noise Test" earlier in this chapter for details.

ODS Table Names

PROC SPECTRA assigns a name to each table it creates. You can use these names to reference the table when using the Output Delivery System (ODS) to select tables and create output data sets. These names are listed in the following table. For more information on ODS, see Chapter 8, "Using the Output Delivery System."

Table 24.2. ODS Tables Produced in PROC SPECTRA

ODS Table Name	Description	Option
WhiteNoiseTest	White Noise Test	WHITETEST
Kappa	Fishers Kappa	WHITETEST
Bartlett	Bartletts Kolmogorov-Smirnov Statistic	WHITETEST

Examples

Example 24.1. Spectral Analysis of Sunspot Activity

This example analyzes Wolfer's sunspot data (Anderson 1971). The following statements read and plot the data.

```
title "Wolfer's Sunspot Data";
data sunspot;
   input year wolfer @@;
   datalines;
1749  809 1750  834 1751  477 1752  478 1753  307 1754  122 1755   96
1756  102 1757  324 1758  476 1759  540 1760  629 1761  859 1762  612
1763  451 1764  364 1765  209 1766  114 1767  378 1768  698 1769 1061
1770 1008 1771  816 1772  665 1773  348 1774  306 1775   70 1776  198
1777  925 1778 1544 1779 1259 1780  848 1781  681 1782  385 1783  228
1784  102 1785  241 1786  829 1787 1320 1788 1309 1789 1181 1790  899
1791  666 1792  600 1793  469 1794  410 1795  213 1796  160 1797   64
1798   41 1799   68 1800  145 1801  340 1802  450 1803  431 1804  475
1805  422 1806  281 1807  101 1808   81 1809   25 1810    0 1811   14
1812   50 1813  122 1814  139 1815  354 1816  458 1817  411 1818  304
1819  239 1820  157 1821   66 1822   40 1823   18 1824   85 1825  166
1826  363 1827  497 1828  625 1829  670 1830  710 1831  478 1832  275
1833   85 1834  132 1835  569 1836 1215 1837 1383 1838 1032 1839  858
1840  632 1841  368 1842  242 1843  107 1844  150 1845  401 1846  615
1847  985 1848 1243 1849  959 1850  665 1851  645 1852  542 1853  390
1854  206 1855   67 1856   43 1857  228 1858  548 1859  938 1860  957
1861  772 1862  591 1863  440 1864  470 1865  305 1866  163 1867   73
1868  373 1869  739 1870 1391 1871 1112 1872 1017 1873  663 1874  447
1875  171 1876  113 1877  123 1878   34 1879   60 1880  323 1881  543
1882  597 1883  637 1884  635 1885  522 1886  254 1887  131 1888   68
1889   63 1890   71 1891  356 1892  730 1893  849 1894  780 1895  640
1896  418 1897  262 1898  267 1899  121 1900   95 1901   27 1902   50
1903  244 1904  420 1905  635 1906  538 1907  620 1908  485 1909  439
1910  186 1911   57 1912   36 1913   14 1914   96 1915  474 1916  571
1917 1039 1918  806 1919  636 1920  376 1921  261 1922  142 1923   58
1924  167
;

symbol1 i=splines v=dot;
proc gplot data=sunspot;
   plot wolfer*year;
run;
```

The plot of the sunspot series is shown in Output 24.1.1.

Output 24.1.1. Plot of Original Data

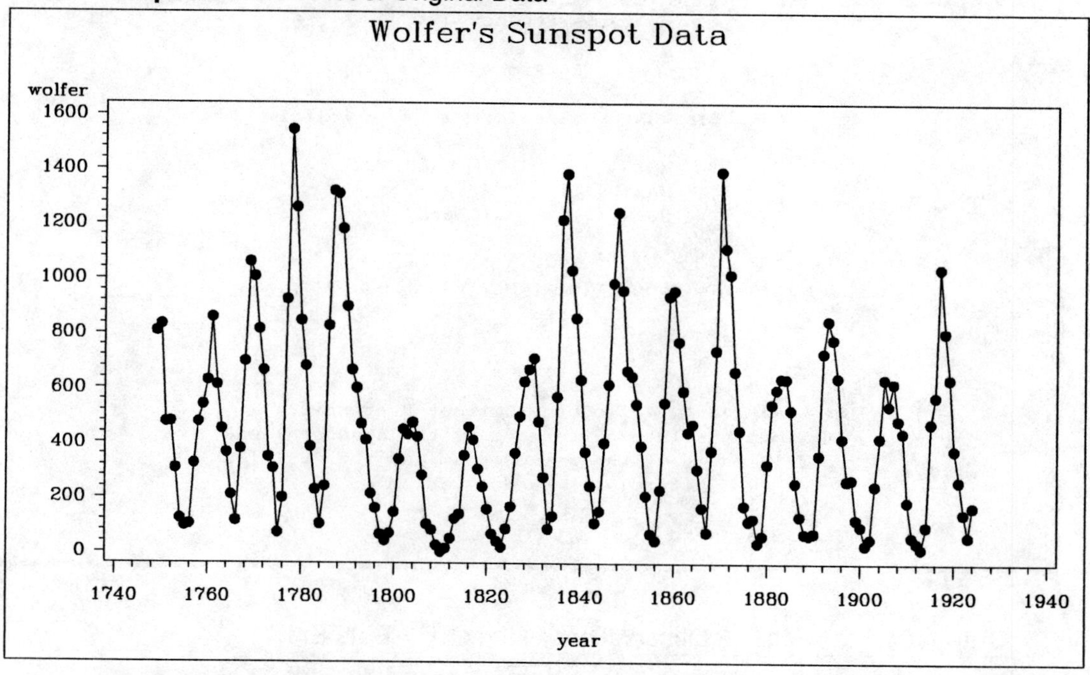

The spectral analysis of the sunspot series is performed by the following statements:

```
proc spectra data=sunspot out=b p s adjmean whitetest;
   var wolfer;
   weights 1 2 3 4 3 2 1;
run;

proc print data=b(obs=12);
run;
```

The PROC SPECTRA statement specifies the P and S options to write the periodogram and spectral density estimates to the OUT= data set B. The WEIGHTS statement specifies a triangular spectral window for smoothing the periodogram to produce the spectral density estimate. The ADJMEAN option zeros the frequency 0 value and avoids the need to exclude that observation from the plots. The WHITETEST option prints tests for white noise.

The Fisher's Kappa test statistic of 16.070 is larger than the 5% critical value of 7.2, so the null hypothesis that the sunspot series is white noise is rejected.

The Bartlett's Kolmogorov-Smirnov statistic of 0.6501 is greater than

$$a\sqrt{1/(m-1)} = 1.36\sqrt{1/87} = 0.1458$$

so reject the null hypothesis that the spectrum represents white noise.

The printed output produced by PROC SPECTRA is shown in Output 24.1.2. The output data set B created by PROC SPECTRA is shown in part in Output 24.1.3.

Output 24.1.2. White Noise Test Results

```
                    Wolfer's Sunspot Data

                      SPECTRA Procedure

             Test for White Noise for Variable wolfer

                    M-1                 87
                    Max(P(*))      4062267
                    Sum(P(*))     21156512


            Fisher's Kappa: (M-1)*Max(P(*))/Sum(P(*))

                      Kappa     16.70489


            Bartlett's Kolmogorov-Smirnov Statistic:
         Maximum absolute difference of the standardized
         partial sums of the periodogram and the CDF of a
                  uniform(0,1) random variable.

         Test Statistic                              0.650055
```

Output 24.1.3. First 12 Observations of the OUT= Data Set

Wolfer's Sunspot Data

Obs	FREQ	PERIOD	P_01	S_01
1	0.00000	.	0.00	59327.52
2	0.03570	176.000	3178.15	61757.98
3	0.07140	88.000	2435433.22	69528.68
4	0.10710	58.667	1077495.76	66087.57
5	0.14280	44.000	491850.36	53352.02
6	0.17850	35.200	2581.12	36678.14
7	0.21420	29.333	181163.15	20604.52
8	0.24990	25.143	283057.60	15132.81
9	0.28560	22.000	188672.97	13265.89
10	0.32130	19.556	122673.94	14953.32
11	0.35700	17.600	58532.93	16402.84
12	0.39270	16.000	213405.16	18562.13

The following statements plot the periodogram and spectral density estimate:

```
proc gplot data=b;
   plot p_01 * freq;
   plot p_01 * period;
   plot s_01 * freq;
   plot s_01 * period;
run;
```

The periodogram is plotted against frequency in Output 24.1.4 and plotted against period in Output 24.1.5. The spectral density estimate is plotted against frequency in Output 24.1.6 and plotted against period in Output 24.1.7.

Output 24.1.4. Plot of Periodogram by Frequency

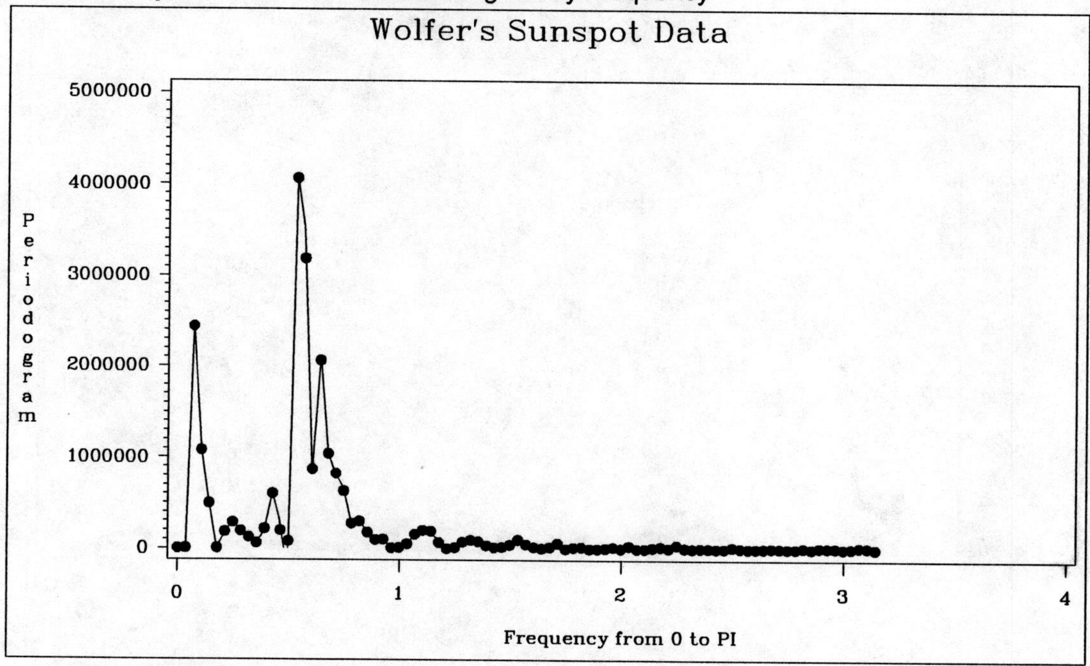

Output 24.1.5. Plot of Periodogram by Period

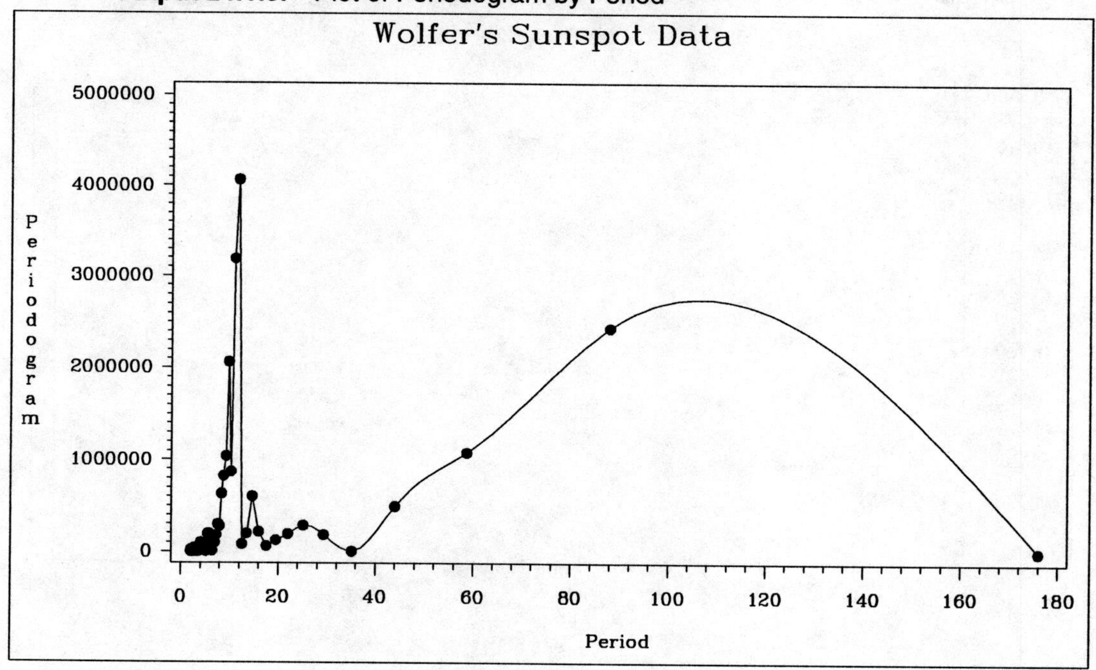

Output 24.1.6. Plot of Spectral Density Estimate by Frequency

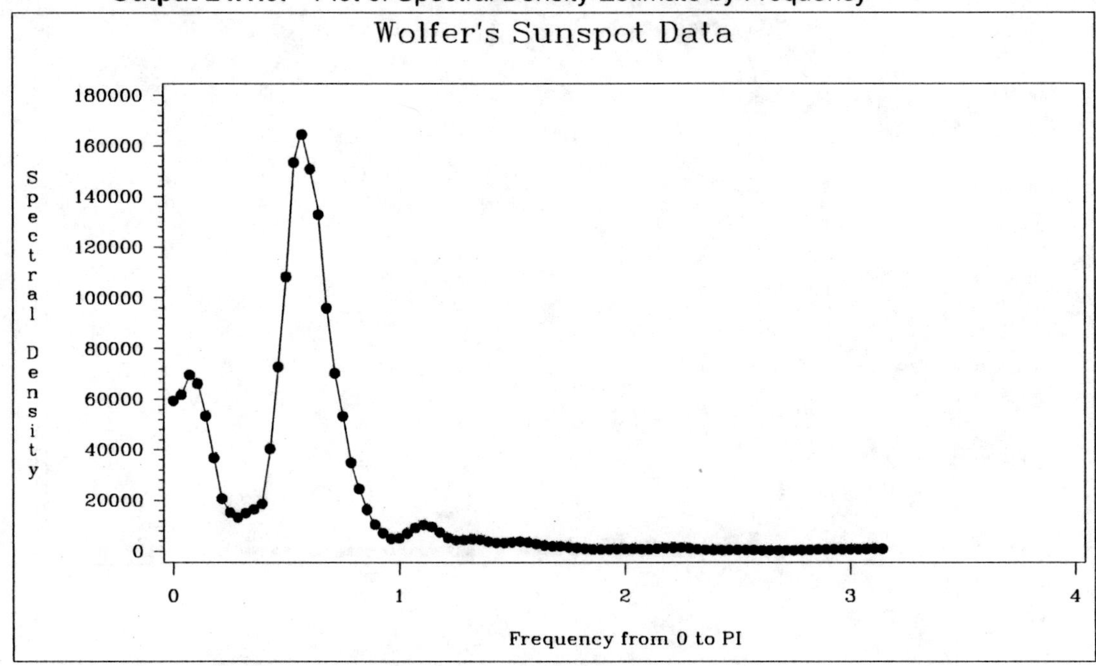

Output 24.1.7. Plot of Spectral Density Estimate by Period

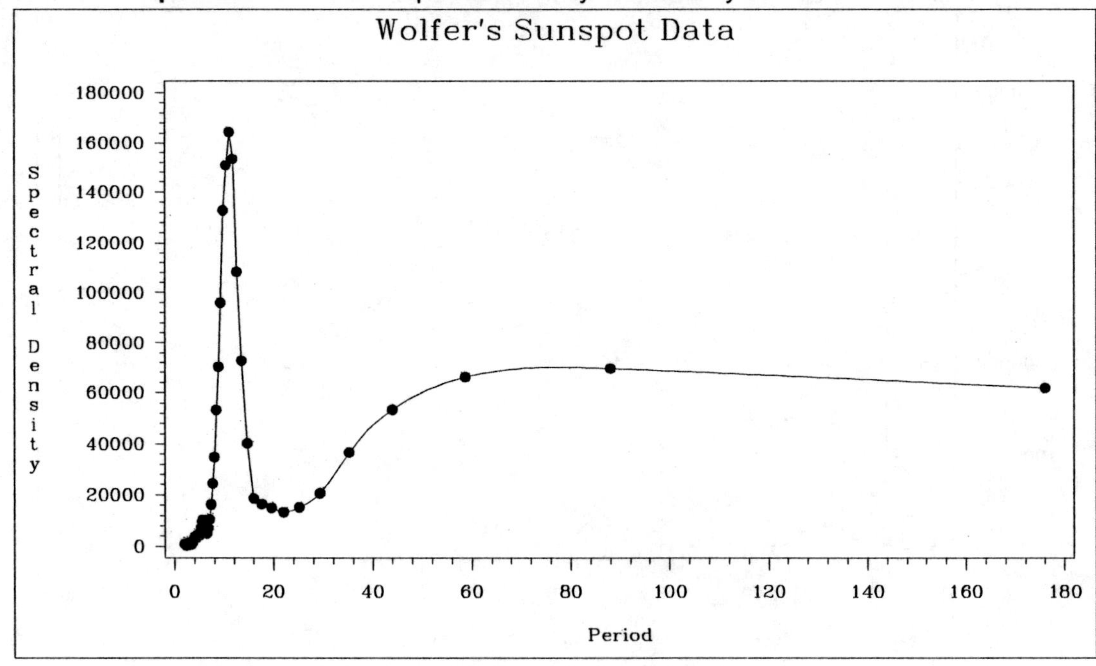

Since PERIOD is the reciprocal of frequency, the plot axis for PERIOD is stretched for low frequencies and compressed at high frequencies. One way to correct for this is to use a WHERE statement to restrict the plots and exclude the low frequency components. The following statements plot the spectral density for periods less than 50.

```
proc gplot data=b;
   where period < 50;
```

```
    plot s_01 * period / href=11;
run;
```

The spectral analysis of the sunspot series confirms a strong 11-year cycle of sunspot activity. The plot makes this clear by drawing a reference line at the 11 year period, which highlights the position of the main peak in the spectral density.

Output 24.1.8 shows the plot. Contrast Output 24.1.8 with Output 24.1.7.

Output 24.1.8. Plot of Spectral Density Estimate by Period to 50 Years

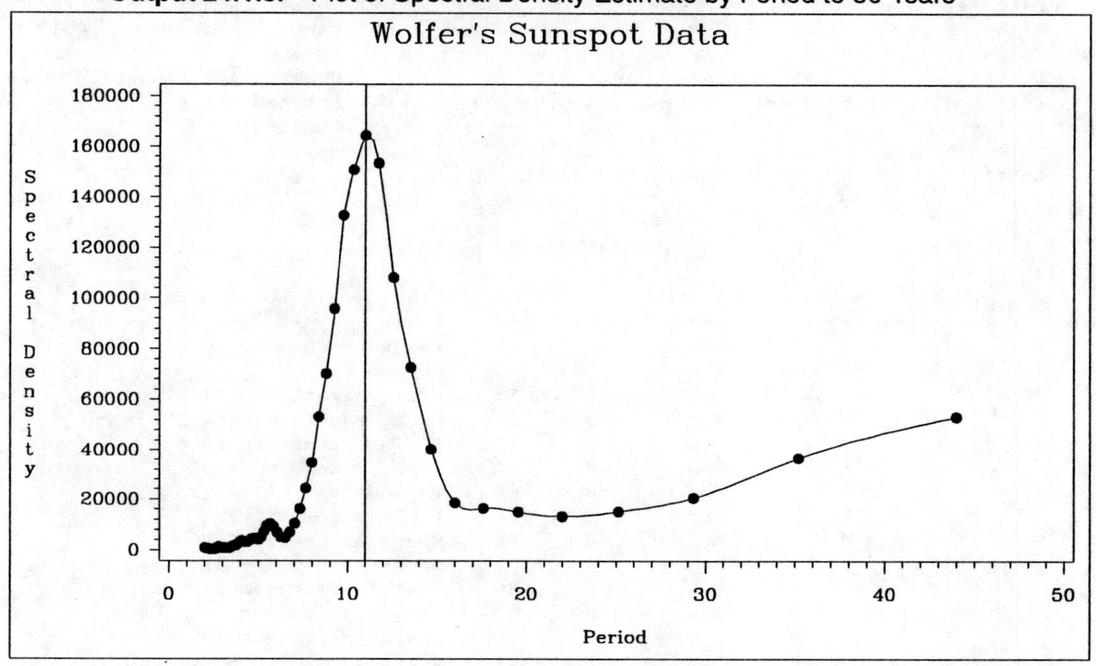

Example 24.2. Cross-Spectral Analysis

This example shows cross-spectral analysis for two variables X and Y using simulated data. X is generated by an AR(1) process; Y is generated as white noise plus an input from X lagged 2 periods. All output options are specified on the PROC SPECTRA statement. PROC CONTENTS shows the contents of the OUT= data set.

```
data a;
   xl = 0; xll = 0;
   do i = - 10 to 100;
      x = .4 * xl  + rannor(123);
      y = .5 * xll + rannor(123);
      if i > 0 then output;
      xll = xl; xl = x;
      end;
run;

proc spectra data=a out=b cross coef a k p ph s;
   var x y;
   weights 1 1.5 2 4 8 9 8 4 2 1.5 1;
```

```
run;

proc contents data=b position;
run;
```

The PROC CONTENTS report for the output data set B is shown in Output 24.2.1.

Output 24.2.1. Contents of PROC SPECTRA OUT= Data Set

```
                              The CONTENTS Procedure

Data Set Name: WORK.B                                       Observations:          51
Member Type:   DATA                                         Variables:             17
Engine:        V8                                           Indexes:               0
Created:       12:39 Wednesday, April 28, 1999              Observation Length:    136
Last Modified: 12:39 Wednesday, April 28, 1999              Deleted Observations:  0
Protection:                                                 Compressed:            NO
Data Set Type: DATA                                         Sorted:                NO
Label:         Spectral Density Estimates


                    -----Variables Ordered by Position-----

      #    Variable     Type    Len    Pos    Label
     ------------------------------------------------------------------------
      1    FREQ         Num       8      0    Frequency from 0 to PI
      2    PERIOD       Num       8      8    Period
      3    COS_01       Num       8     16    Cosine Transform of x
      4    SIN_01       Num       8     24    Sine Transform of x
      5    COS_02       Num       8     32    Cosine Transform of y
      6    SIN_02       Num       8     40    Sine Transform of y
      7    P_01         Num       8     48    Periodogram of x
      8    P_02         Num       8     56    Periodogram of y
      9    S_01         Num       8     64    Spectral Density of x
     10    S_02         Num       8     72    Spectral Density of y
     11    RP_01_02     Num       8     80    Real Periodogram of x by y
     12    IP_01_02     Num       8     88    Imag Periodogram of x by y
     13    CS_01_02     Num       8     96    Cospectra of x by y
     14    QS_01_02     Num       8    104    Quadrature of x by y
     15    K_01_02      Num       8    112    Coherency**2 of x by y
     16    A_01_02      Num       8    120    Amplitude of x by y
     17    PH_01_02     Num       8    128    Phase of x by y
```

The following statements plot the amplitude of the cross-spectrum estimate against frequency and against period for periods less than 25.

```
symbol1 i=splines v=dot;
proc gplot data=b;
   plot a_01_02 * freq;
run;

proc gplot data=b;
   plot a_01_02 * period;
   where period < 25;
run;
```

The plot of the amplitude of the cross-spectrum estimate against frequency is shown in Output 24.2.2. The plot of the cross-spectrum amplitude against period for periods less than 25 observations is shown in Output 24.2.3.

Output 24.2.2. Plot of Cross-Spectrum Amplitude by Frequency

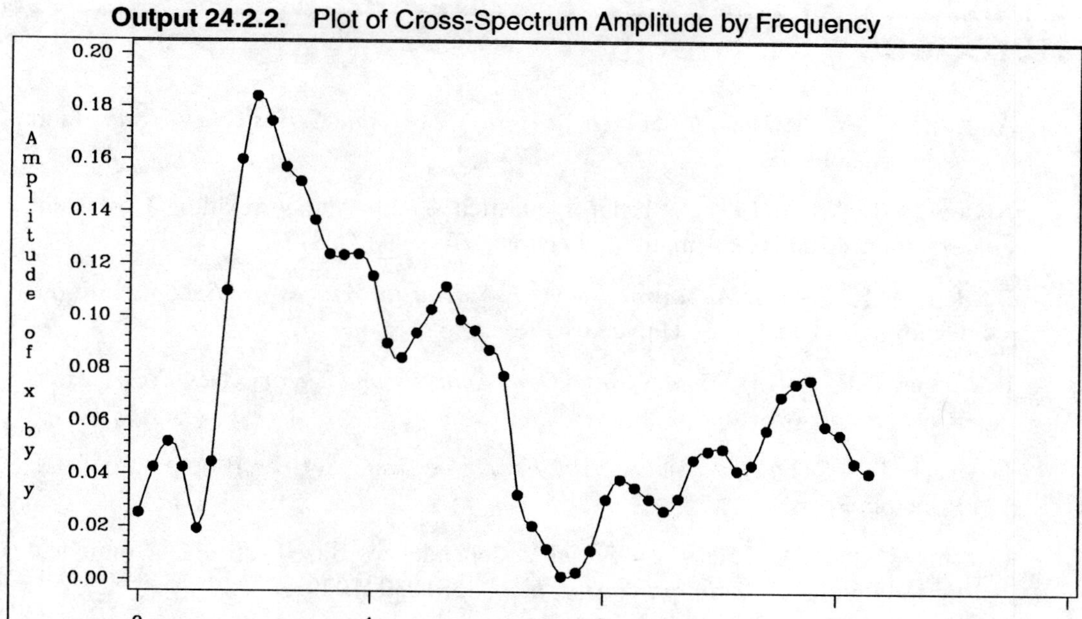

Output 24.2.3. Plot of Cross-Spectrum Amplitude by Period

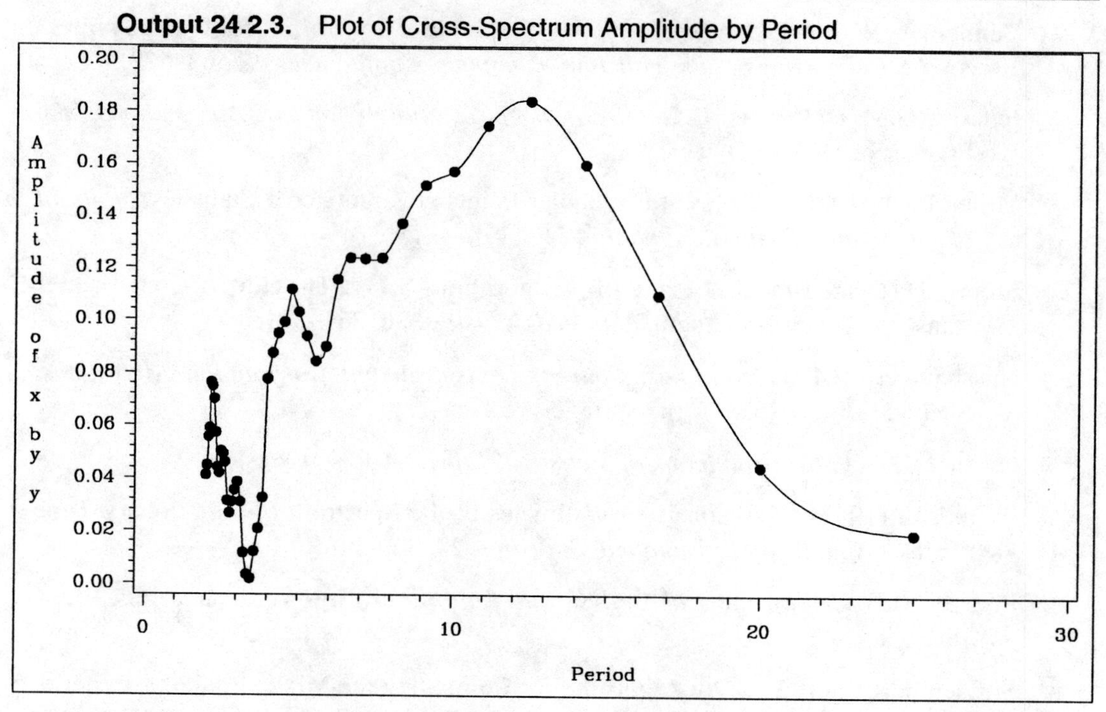

References

Anderson, T.W. (1971), *The Statistical Analysis of Time Series*, New York: John Wiley & Sons, Inc.

Andrews, D.W.K. (1991), "Heteroscedasticity and Autocorrelation Consistent Covariance Matrix Estimation," *Econometrica*, 59 (3), 817-858.

Bartlett, M.S. (1966), *An Introduction to Stochastic Processes*, Second Edition, Cambridge: Cambridge University Press.

Brillinger, D.R. (1975), *Time Series: Data Analysis and Theory*, New York: Holt, Rinehart and Winston, Inc.

Davis, H.T. (1941), *The Analysis of Economic Time Series*, Bloomington, IN: Principia Press.

Durbin, J. (1967), "Tests of Serial Independence Based on the Cumulated Periodogram," *Bulletin of Int. Stat. Inst.*, 42, 1039–1049.

Fuller, W.A. (1976), *Introduction to Statistical Time Series*, New York: John Wiley & Sons, Inc.

Gentleman, W.M. and Sande, G. (1966), "Fast Fourier transforms–for fun and profit," *AFIPS Proceedings of the Fall Joint Computer Conference*, 19, 563–578.

Jenkins, G.M. and Watts, D.G. (1968), *Spectral Analysis and Its Applications*, San Francisco: Holden-Day.

Miller, L. H. (1956), "Tables of Percentage Points of Kolmogorov Statistics," *Journal of American Statistic Association*, 51, 111.

Monro, D.M. and Branch, J.L. (1976), "Algorithm AS 117. The chirp discrete Fourier transform of general length," *Applied Statistics*, 26, 351–361.

Nussbaumer, H.J. (1982), *Fast Fourier Transform and Convolution Algorithms*, Second Edition, New York: Springer-Verlag.

Owen, D. B. (1962), *Handbook of Statistical Tables*, Addison Wesley.

Parzen, E. (1957), "On Consistent Estimates of the Spectrum of a Stationary Time Series," *Annals of Mathematical Statistics*, 28, 329-348.

Priestly, M.B. (1981), *Spectral Analysis and Time Series*, New York: Academic Press, Inc.

Singleton, R.C. (1969), "An Algorithm for Computing the Mixed Radix Fast Fourier Transform," *I.E.E.E. Transactions of Audio and Electroacoustics*, AU-17, 93–103.

Chapter 25
The STATESPACE Procedure

Chapter Contents

Chapter 25
The STATESPACE Procedure

Overview

The STATESPACE procedure analyzes and forecasts multivariate time series using the state space model. The STATESPACE procedure is appropriate for jointly forecasting several related time series that have dynamic interactions. By taking into account the autocorrelations among the whole set of variables, the STATESPACE procedure may give better forecasts than methods that model each series separately.

By default, the STATESPACE procedure automatically selects a state space model appropriate for the time series, making the procedure a good tool for automatic forecasting of multivariate time series. Alternatively, you can specify the state space model by giving the form of the state vector and the state transition and innovation matrices.

The methods used by the STATESPACE procedure assume that the time series are jointly stationary. Nonstationary series must be made stationary by some preliminary transformation, usually by differencing. The STATESPACE procedure allows you to specify differencing of the input data. When differencing is specified, the STATESPACE procedure automatically integrates forecasts of the differenced series to produce forecasts of the original series.

The State Space Model

The *state space model* represents a multivariate time series through auxiliary variables, some of which may not be directly observable. These auxiliary variables are called the *state vector*. The state vector summarizes all the information from the present and past values of the time series relevant to the prediction of future values of the series. The observed time series are expressed as linear combinations of the state variables. The state space model is also called a Markovian representation, or a canonical representation, of a multivariate time series process. The state space approach to modeling a multivariate stationary time series is summarized in Akaike (1976).

The state space form encompasses a very rich class of models. Any Gaussian multivariate stationary time series can be written in a state space form, provided that the dimension of the predictor space is finite. In particular, any autoregressive moving average (ARMA) process has a state space representation and, conversely, any state space process can be expressed in an ARMA form (Akaike 1974). More details on the relation of the state space and ARMA forms are given in "Relation of ARMA and State Space Forms" later in this chapter.

Let $\mathbf{x}_t$ be the $r \times 1$ vector of observed variables, after differencing (if differencing is specified) and subtracting the sample mean. Let $\mathbf{z}_t$ be the state vector of dimension s, $s \geq r$, where the first r components of $\mathbf{z}_t$ consist of $\mathbf{x}_t$. Let the notation $\mathbf{x}_{t+k|t}$

represent the conditional expectation (or prediction) of $\mathbf{x}_{t+k}$ based on the information available at time t. Then the last $s-r$ elements of $\mathbf{z}_t$ consist of elements of $\mathbf{x}_{t+k|t}$, where k>0 is specified or determined automatically by the procedure.

There are various forms of the state space model in use. The form of the state space model used by the STATESPACE procedure is based on Akaike (1976). The model is defined by the following *state transition equation*:

$$\mathbf{z}_{t+1} = \mathbf{F}\mathbf{z}_t + \mathbf{G}\mathbf{e}_{t+1}$$

In the state transition equation, the $s \times s$ coefficient matrix $\mathbf{F}$ is called the *transition matrix*; it determines the dynamic properties of the model.

The $s \times r$ coefficient matrix $\mathbf{G}$ is called the *input matrix*; it determines the variance structure of the transition equation. For model identification, the first r rows and columns of $\mathbf{G}$ are set to an $r \times r$ identity matrix.

The input vector $\mathbf{e}_t$ is a sequence of independent normally distributed random vectors of dimension r with mean $\mathbf{0}$ and covariance matrix $\Sigma_{\mathbf{ee}}$. The random error $\mathbf{e}_t$ is sometimes called the innovation vector or shock vector.

In addition to the state transition equation, state space models usually include a *measurement equation* or *observation equation* that gives the observed values $\mathbf{x}_t$ as a function of the state vector $\mathbf{z}_t$. However, since PROC STATESPACE always includes the observed values $\mathbf{x}_t$ in the state vector $\mathbf{z}_t$, the measurement equation in this case merely represents the extraction of the first r components of the state vector.

The measurement equation used by the STATESPACE procedure is

$$\mathbf{x}_t = [\mathbf{I}_r \mathbf{0}]\mathbf{z}_t$$

where $\mathbf{I}_r$ is an $r \times r$ identity matrix. In practice, PROC STATESPACE performs the extraction of $\mathbf{x}_t$ from $\mathbf{z}_t$ without reference to an explicit measurement equation.

In summary:

$\mathbf{x}_t$ is an observation vector of dimension r.

$\mathbf{z}_t$ is a state vector of dimension s, whose first r elements are $\mathbf{x}_t$ and whose last $s-r$ elements are conditional prediction of future $\mathbf{x}_t$.

$\mathbf{F}$ is an $s \times s$ transition matrix.

$\mathbf{G}$ is an $s \times r$ input matrix, with the identity matrix $\mathbf{I}_r$ forming the first r rows and columns.

$\mathbf{e}_t$ is a sequence of independent normally distributed random vectors of dimension r with mean $\mathbf{0}$ and covariance matrix $\Sigma_{\mathbf{ee}}$.

How PROC STATESPACE Works

The design of the STATESPACE procedure closely follows the modeling strategy proposed by Akaike (1976). This strategy employs canonical correlation analysis for the automatic identification of the state space model.

Following Akaike (1976), the procedure first fits a sequence of unrestricted vector autoregressive (VAR) models and computes Akaike's information criterion (AIC) for each model. The vector autoregressive models are estimated using the sample autocovariance matrices and the Yule-Walker equations. The order of the VAR model producing the smallest Akaike information criterion is chosen as the order (number of lags into the past) to use in the canonical correlation analysis.

The elements of the state vector are then determined via a sequence of canonical correlation analyses of the sample autocovariance matrices through the selected order. This analysis computes the sample canonical correlations of the past with an increasing number of steps into the future. Variables that yield significant correlations are added to the state vector; those that yield insignificant correlations are excluded from further consideration. The importance of the correlation is judged on the basis of another information criterion proposed by Akaike. See the section "Canonical Correlation Analysis" for details. If you specify the state vector explicitly, these model identification steps are omitted.

Once the state vector is determined, the state space model is fit to the data. The free parameters in the $\mathbf{F}$, $\mathbf{G}$, and $\mathbf{\Sigma_{ee}}$ matrices are estimated by approximate maximum likelihood. By default, the $\mathbf{F}$ and $\mathbf{G}$ matrices are unrestricted, except for identifiability requirements. Optionally, conditional least-squares estimates can be computed. You can impose restrictions on elements of the $\mathbf{F}$ and $\mathbf{G}$ matrices.

After the parameters are estimated, forecasts are produced from the fitted state space model using the Kalman filtering technique. If differencing was specified, the forecasts are integrated to produce forecasts of the original input variables.

Getting Started

The following introductory example uses simulated data for two variables X and Y. The following statements generate the X and Y series.

```
data in;
   x=10;  y=40;
   x1=0; y1=0;
   a1=0; b1=0;
   iseed=123;
   do t=-100 to 200;
      a=rannor(iseed);
      b=rannor(iseed);
      dx = 0.5*x1 + 0.3*y1 + a - 0.2*a1 - 0.1*b1;
      dy = 0.3*x1 + 0.5*y1 + b;
      x = x + dx + .25;
      y = y + dy + .25;
      if t >= 0 then output;
      x1 = dx; y1 = dy;
      a1 = a; b1 = b;
   end;
   keep t x y;
run;
```

The simulated series X and Y are shown in Figure 25.1.

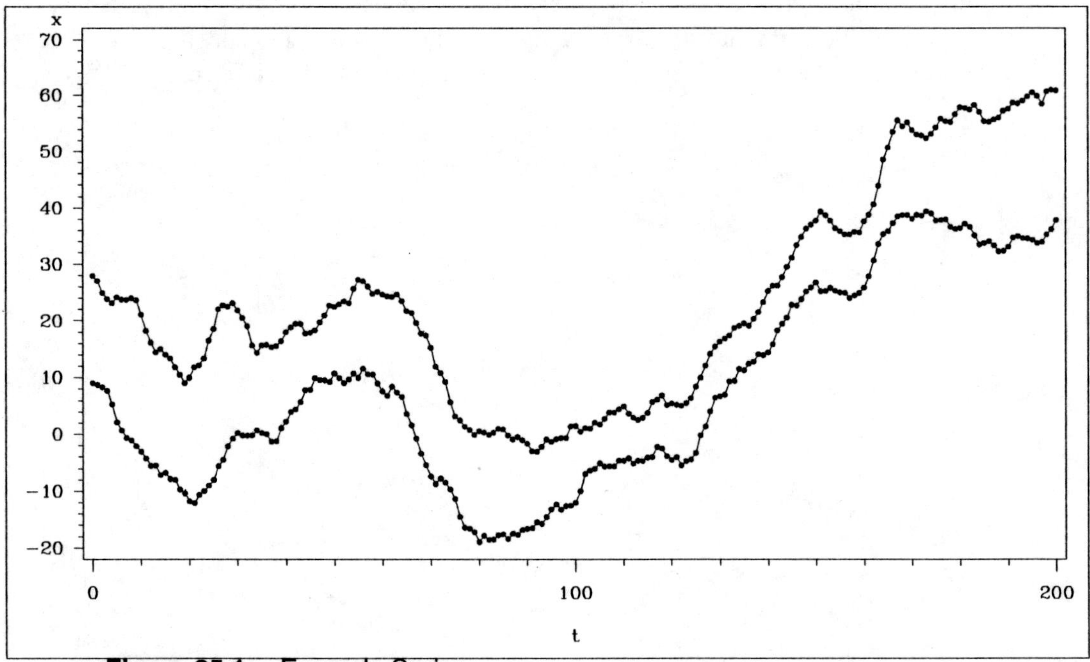

Figure 25.1. Example Series

Automatic State Space Model Selection

The STATESPACE procedure is designed to automatically select the best state space model for forecasting the series. You can specify your own model if you wish, and you can use the output from PROC STATESPACE to help you identify a state space model. However, the easiest way to use PROC STATESPACE is to let it choose the model.

Stationarity and Differencing

Although PROC STATESPACE selects the state space model automatically, it does assume that the input series are stationary. If the series are nonstationary, then the process may fail. Therefore the first step is to examine your data and test to see if differencing is required. (See the section "Stationarity and Differencing" later in this chapter for further discussion of this issue.)

The series shown in Figure 25.1 are nonstationary. In order to forecast X and Y with a state space model, you must difference them (or use some other de-trending method). If you fail to difference when needed and try to use PROC STATESPACE with nonstationary data, an inappropriate state space model may be selected, and the model estimation may fail to converge.

The following statements identify and fit a state space model for the first differences of X and Y, and forecast X and Y 10 periods ahead:

```
proc statespace data=in out=out lead=10;
   var x(1) y(1);
   id t;
run;
```

The DATA= option specifies the input data set and the OUT= option specifies the output data set for the forecasts. The LEAD= option specifies forecasting 10 observations past the end of the input data. The VAR statement specifies the variables to forecast and specifies differencing. The notation X(1) Y(1) specifies that the state space model analyzes the first differences of X and Y.

Descriptive Statistics and Preliminary Autoregressions

The first page of the printed output produced by the preceding statements is shown in Figure 25.2.

```
                              The STATESPACE Procedure

                           Number of Observations    200

                                         Standard
         Variable            Mean           Error

         x               0.144316        1.233457     Has been differenced.
                                                      With period(s) = 1.
         y               0.164871        1.304358     Has been differenced.
                                                      With period(s) = 1.


                              The STATESPACE Procedure

                  Information Criterion for Autoregressive Models

   Lag=0     Lag=1     Lag=2     Lag=3     Lag=4     Lag=5     Lag=6     Lag=7     Lag=8

149.697 8.387786 5.517099 12.05986 15.36952 21.79538 24.00638 29.88874 33.55708

                                    Information
                                   Criterion for
                                  Autoregressive
                                      Models

                                 Lag=9        Lag=10

                              41.17606     47.70222


                   Schematic Representation of Correlations

   Name/Lag        0     1     2     3     4     5     6     7     8     9    10

   x              ++    ++    ++    ++    ++    ++    +.    ..    +.    +.    ..
   y              ++    ++    ++    ++    ++    +.    +.    +.    +.    ..    ..

             + is > 2*std error,  - is < -2*std error,  . is between
```

Figure 25.2. Descriptive Statistics and VAR Order Selection

Descriptive statistics are printed first, giving the number of nonmissing observations after differencing, and the sample means and standard deviations of the differenced series. The sample means are subtracted before the series are modeled (unless the NOCENTER option is specified), and the sample means are added back when the forecasts are produced.

Let X_t and Y_t be the observed values of X and Y, and let x_t and y_t be the values of X and Y after differencing and subtracting the mean difference. The series $\mathbf{x}_t$ modeled by the STATEPSPACE procedure is

$$\mathbf{x}_t = \begin{bmatrix} x_t \\ y_t \end{bmatrix} = \begin{bmatrix} (1-B)X_t - 0.144316 \\ (1-B)Y_t - 0.164871 \end{bmatrix}$$

where B represents the backshift operator.

After the descriptive statistics, PROC STATESPACE prints the Akaike information criterion (AIC) values for the autoregressive models fit to the series. The smallest AIC value, in this case 5.517 at lag 2, determines the number of autocovariance matrices analyzed in the canonical correlation phase.

A schematic representation of the autocorrelations is printed next. This indicates which elements of the autocorrelation matrices at different lags are significantly greater or less than 0.

The second page of the STATESPACE printed output is shown in Figure 25.3.

```
                        The STATESPACE Procedure

           Schematic Representation of Partial Autocorrelations

Name/Lag       1      2      3      4      5      6      7      8      9      10

x              ++     +.     ..     ..     ..     ..     ..     ..     ..     ..
y              ++     ..     ..     ..     ..     ..     ..     ..     ..     ..

          + is > 2*std error,   - is < -2*std error,   . is between


                   Yule-Walker Estimates for Minimum AIC

                  --------Lag=1-------        --------Lag=2-------
                         x           y               x           y

         x        0.257438    0.202237        0.170812    0.133554
         y        0.292177    0.469297        -0.00537    -0.00048
```

Figure 25.3. Partial Autocorrelations and VAR Model

Figure 25.3 shows a schematic representation of the partial autocorrelations, similar to the autocorrelations shown in Figure 25.2. The selection of a second order autoregressive model by the AIC statistic looks reasonable in this case because the partial autocorrelations for lags greater than 2 are not significant.

Next, the Yule-Walker estimates for the selected autoregressive model are printed. This output shows the coefficient matrices of the vector autoregressive model at each lag.

Selected State Space Model Form and Preliminary Estimates

After the autoregressive order selection process has determined the number of lags to consider, the canonical correlation analysis phase selects the state vector. By default, output for this process is not printed. You can use the CANCORR option to print details of the canonical correlation analysis. See the section "Canonical Correlation Analysis" later in this chapter for an explanation of this process.

Once the state vector is selected the state space model is estimated by approximate maximum likelihood. Information from the canonical correlation analysis and from the preliminary autoregression is used to form preliminary estimates of the state space model parameters. These preliminary estimates are used as starting values for the iterative estimation process.

The form of the state vector and the preliminary estimates are printed next, as shown in Figure 25.4.

```
                  The STATESPACE Procedure
    Selected Statespace Form and Preliminary Estimates

                       State Vector

      x(T;T)           y(T;T)           x(T+1;T)


               Estimate of Transition Matrix

            0                0                1
     0.291536         0.468762         -0.00411
      0.24869          0.24484         0.204257


               Input Matrix for Innovation

                    1                0
                    0                1
             0.257438         0.202237


              Variance Matrix for Innovation

             0.945196         0.100786
             0.100786         1.014703
```

Figure 25.4. Preliminary Estimates of State Space Model

Figure 25.4 first prints the state vector as X[T;T] Y[T;T] X[T+1;T]. This notation indicates that the state vector is

$$\mathbf{z}_t = \begin{bmatrix} x_{t|t} \\ y_{t|t} \\ x_{t+1|t} \end{bmatrix}$$

The notation $x_{t+1|t}$ indicates the conditional expectation or prediction of x_{t+1} based on the information available at time *t*, and $x_{t|t}$ and $y_{t|t}$ are x_t and y_t respectively.

The remainder of Figure 25.4 shows the preliminary estimates of the transition matrix **F**, the input matrix **G**, and the covariance matrix $\Sigma_{\mathbf{ee}}$.

Estimated State Space Model

The next page of the STATESPACE output prints the final estimates of the fitted model, as shown in Figure 25.5. This output has the same form as in Figure 25.4, but shows the maximum likelihood estimates instead of the preliminary estimates.

```
                        The STATESPACE Procedure
                Selected Statespace Form and Fitted Model

                              State Vector

          x(T;T)                y(T;T)               x(T+1;T)


                     Estimate of Transition Matrix

                        0                  0                  1
                 0.297273            0.47376           -0.01998
                   0.2301           0.228425           0.256031


                     Input Matrix for Innovation

                                1                  0
                                0                  1
                         0.257284           0.202273


                    Variance Matrix for Innovation

                         0.945188           0.100752
                         0.100752           1.014712
```

Figure 25.5. Fitted State Space Model

The estimated state space model shown in Figure 25.5 is

$$
\begin{bmatrix} x_{t+1|t+1} \\ y_{t+1|t+1} \\ x_{t+2|t+1} \end{bmatrix} = \begin{bmatrix} 0 & 0 & 1 \\ 0.297 & 0.474 & -0.020 \\ 0.230 & 0.228 & 0.256 \end{bmatrix} \begin{bmatrix} x_t \\ y_t \\ x_{t+1|t} \end{bmatrix} + \begin{bmatrix} 1 & 0 \\ 0 & 1 \\ 0.257 & 0.202 \end{bmatrix} \begin{bmatrix} e_{t+1} \\ n_{t+1} \end{bmatrix}
$$

$$
var \begin{bmatrix} e_{t+1} \\ n_{t+1} \end{bmatrix} = \begin{bmatrix} 0.945 & 0.101 \\ 0.101 & 1.015 \end{bmatrix}
$$

The next page of the STATESPACE output lists the estimates of the free parameters in the **F** and **G** matrices with standard errors and *t* statistics, as shown in Figure 25.6.

```
                        The STATESPACE Procedure

                          Parameter Estimates

                                          Standard
        Parameter      Estimate              Error      t Value

        F(2,1)         0.297273           0.129995         2.29
        F(2,2)         0.473760           0.115688         4.10
        F(2,3)         -0.01998           0.313025        -0.06
        F(3,1)         0.230100           0.126226         1.82
        F(3,2)         0.228425           0.112978         2.02
        F(3,3)         0.256031           0.305256         0.84
        G(3,1)         0.257284           0.071060         3.62
        G(3,2)         0.202273           0.068593         2.95
```

Figure 25.6. Final Parameter Estimates

Convergence Failures

The maximum likelihood estimates are computed by an iterative nonlinear maximization algorithm, which may not converge. If the estimates fail to converge, warning messages are printed in the output.

If you encounter convergence problems, you should recheck the stationarity of the data and ensure that the specified differencing orders are correct. Attempting to fit state space models to nonstationary data is a common cause of convergence failure. You can also use the MAXIT= option to increase the number of iterations allowed, or experiment with the convergence tolerance options DETTOL= and PARMTOL=.

Forecast Data Set

The following statements print the output data set. The WHERE statement excludes the first 190 observations from the output, so that only the forecasts and the last 10 actual observations are printed.

```
proc print data=out;
   id t;
   where t > 190;
run;
```

The PROC PRINT output is shown in Figure 25.7.

t	x	FOR1	RES1	STD1	y	FOR2	RES2	STD2
191	34.8159	33.6299	1.18600	0.97221	58.7189	57.9916	0.72728	1.00733
192	35.0656	35.6598	-0.59419	0.97221	58.5440	59.7718	-1.22780	1.00733
193	34.7034	35.5530	-0.84962	0.97221	59.0476	58.5723	0.47522	1.00733
194	34.6626	34.7597	-0.09707	0.97221	59.7774	59.2241	0.55330	1.00733
195	34.4055	34.8322	-0.42664	0.97221	60.5118	60.1544	0.35738	1.00733
196	33.8210	34.6053	-0.78434	0.97221	59.8750	60.8260	-0.95102	1.00733
197	34.0164	33.6230	0.39333	0.97221	58.4698	59.4502	-0.98046	1.00733
198	35.3819	33.6251	1.75684	0.97221	60.6782	57.9167	2.76150	1.00733
199	36.2954	36.0528	0.24256	0.97221	60.9692	62.1637	-1.19450	1.00733
200	37.8945	37.1431	0.75142	0.97221	60.8586	61.4085	-0.54984	1.00733
201	.	38.5068	.	0.97221	.	61.3161	.	1.00733
202	.	39.0428	.	1.59125	.	61.7509	.	1.83678
203	.	39.4619	.	2.28028	.	62.1546	.	2.62366
204	.	39.8284	.	2.97824	.	62.5099	.	3.38839
205	.	40.1474	.	3.67689	.	62.8275	.	4.12805
206	.	40.4310	.	4.36299	.	63.1139	.	4.84149
207	.	40.6861	.	5.03040	.	63.3755	.	5.52744
208	.	40.9185	.	5.67548	.	63.6174	.	6.18564
209	.	41.1330	.	6.29673	.	63.8435	.	6.81655
210	.	41.3332	.	6.89383	.	64.0572	.	7.42114

Figure 25.7. OUT= Data Set Produced by PROC STATESPACE

The OUT= data set produced by PROC STATESPACE contains the VAR and ID statement variables. In addition, for each VAR statement variable, the OUT= data set contains the variables FOR*i*, RES*i*, and STD*i*. These variables contain the predicted values, residuals, and forecast standard errors for the *i*th variable in the VAR statement list. In this case, X is listed first in the VAR statement, so FOR1 contains the forecasts of X, while FOR2 contains the forecasts of Y.

The following statements plot the forecasts and actuals for the series.

```
proc gplot data=out;
   plot for1*t=1 for2*t=1 x*t=2 y*t=2 /
        overlay href=200.5;
   symbol1 v=circle i=join;
   symbol2 v=star i=none;
   where t > 150;
run;
```

The forecast plot is shown in Figure 25.8. The last 50 observations are also plotted to provide context, and a reference line is drawn between the historical and forecast periods. The actual values are plotted with asterisks.

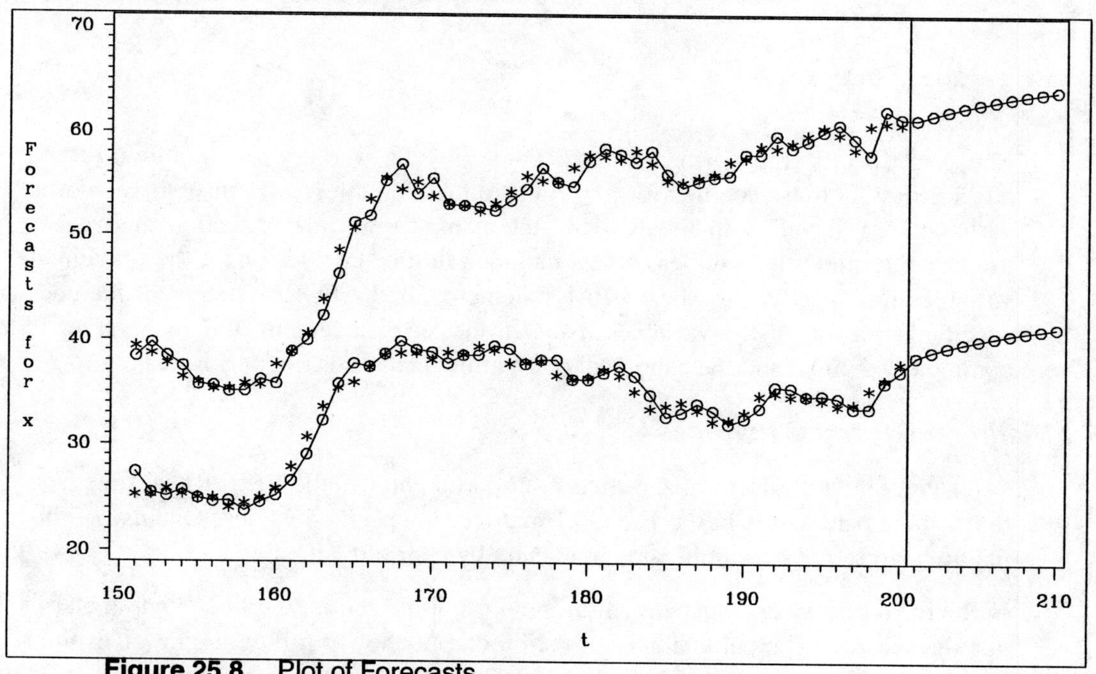

Figure 25.8. Plot of Forecasts

Controlling Printed Output

By default, the STATESPACE procedure produces a large amount of printed output. The NOPRINT option suppresses all printed output. You can suppress the printed output for the autoregressive model selection process with the PRINTOUT=NONE option. The descriptive statistics and state space model estimation output are still printed when PRINTOUT=NONE is specified. You can produce more detailed output with the PRINTOUT=LONG option and by specifying the printing control options CANCORR, COVB, and PRINT.

Specifying the State Space Model

Instead of allowing the STATESPACE procedure to select the model automatically, you can use FORM and RESTRICT statements to specify a state space model.

Specifying the State Vector

Use the FORM statement to control the form of the state vector. You can use this feature to force PROC STATESPACE to estimate and forecast a model different from the model it would select automatically. You can also use this feature to reestimate the automatically selected model (possibly with restrictions) without repeating the canonical correlation analysis.

The FORM statement specifies the number of lags of each variable to include in the state vector. For example, the statement FORM X 3; forces the state vector to include $x_{t|t}$, $x_{t+1|t}$, and $x_{t+2|t}$. The following statement specifies the state vector $(x_{t|t}, y_{t|t}, x_{t+1|t})$, which is the same state vector selected in the preceding example:

```
form x 2 y 1;
```

You can specify the form for only some of the variables and allow PROC STATESPACE to select the form for the other variables. If only some of the variables are specified in the FORM statement, canonical correlation analysis is used to determine the number of lags included in the state vector for the remaining variables not specified by the FORM statement. If the FORM statement includes specifications for all the variables listed in the VAR statement, the state vector is completely defined and the canonical correlation analysis is not performed.

Restricting the F and G matrices

After you know the form of the state vector, you can use the RESTRICT statement to fix some parameters in the **F** and **G** matrices to specified values. One use of this feature is to remove insignificant parameters by restricting them to 0.

In the introductory example shown in the preceding section, the F[2,3] parameter is not significant. (The parameters estimation output shown in Figure 25.6 gives the *t* statistic for F[2,3] as -0.06. F[3,3] and F[3,1] also have low significance with $t < 2$.)

The following statements reestimate this model with F[2,3] restricted to 0. The FORM statement is used to specify the state vector and thus bypass the canonical correlation analysis.

```
proc statespace data=in out=out lead=10;
   var x(1) y(1);
   id t;
   form x 2 y 1;
   restrict f(2,3)=0;
run;
```

The final estimates produced by these statements are shown in Figure 25.9.

```
                    The STATESPACE Procedure
           Selected Statespace Form and Fitted Model

                         State Vector

x(T;T)               y(T;T)               x(T+1;T)


                 Estimate of Transition Matrix

            0               0                    1
     0.290051        0.467468                    0
     0.227051        0.226139              0.26436


                 Input Matrix for Innovation

                    1               0
                    0               1
             0.256826        0.202022


               Variance Matrix for Innovation

             0.945175        0.100696
             0.100696        1.014733
```

```
                    The STATESPACE Procedure

                      Parameter Estimates

                                  Standard
Parameter       Estimate             Error      t Value

F(2,1)          0.290051          0.063904         4.54
F(2,2)          0.467468          0.060430         7.74
F(3,1)          0.227051          0.125221         1.81
F(3,2)          0.226139          0.111711         2.02
F(3,3)          0.264360          0.299537         0.88
G(3,1)          0.256826          0.070994         3.62
G(3,2)          0.202022          0.068507         2.95
```

Figure 25.9. Results using RESTRICT Statement

Syntax

The STATESPACE procedure uses the following statements:

PROC STATESPACE *options*;
BY *variable . . .* ;
FORM *variable value . . .* ;
ID *variable*;
INITIAL **F***(row,column)=value . . .* **G***(row,column)=value ...* ;
RESTRICT **F***(row,column)=value . . .* **G***(row,column)=value ...* ;
VAR *variable (difference, difference, . . .) ...* ;

Functional Summary

The statements and options used by PROC STATESPACE are summarized in the following table.

Description	Statement	Option
Input Data Set Options		
specify the input data set	PROC STATESPACE	DATA=
prevent subtraction of sample mean	PROC STATESPACE	NOCENTER
specify the ID variable	ID	
specify the observed series and differencing	VAR	
Options for Autoregressive Estimates		
specify the maximum order	PROC STATESPACE	ARMAX=
specify maximum lag for autocovariances	PROC STATESPACE	LAGMAX=
output only minimum AIC model	PROC STATESPACE	MINIC
specify the amount of detail printed	PROC STATESPACE	PRINTOUT=
write preliminary AR models to a data set	PROC STATESPACE	OUTAR=
Options for Canonical Correlation Analysis		
print the sequence of canonical correlations	PROC STATESPACE	CANCORR
specify upper limit of dimension of state vector	PROC STATESPACE	DIMMAX=
specify the minimum number of lags	PROC STATESPACE	PASTMIN=
specify the multiplier of the degrees of freedom	PROC STATESPACE	SIGCORR=
Options for State Space Model Estimation		
specify starting values	INITIAL	
print covariance matrix of parameter estimates	PROC STATESPACE	COVB
specify the convergence criterion	PROC STATESPACE	DETTOL=
specify the convergence criterion	PROC STATESPACE	PARMTOL=

Description	Statement	Option
print the details of the iterations	PROC STATESPACE	ITPRINT
specify an upper limit of the number of lags	PROC STATESPACE	KLAG=
specify maximum number of iterations allowed	PROC STATESPACE	MAXIT=
suppress the final estimation	PROC STATESPACE	NOEST
write the state space model parameter estimates to an output data set	PROC STATESPACE	OUTMODEL=
use conditional least squares for final estimates	PROC STATESPACE	RESIDEST
specify criterion for testing for singularity	PROC STATESPACE	SINGULAR=
Options for Forecasting		
start forecasting before end of the input data	PROC STATESPACE	BACK=
specify the time interval between observations	PROC STATESPACE	INTERVAL=
specify multiple periods in the time series	PROC STATESPACE	INTPER=
specify how many periods to forecast	PROC STATESPACE	LEAD=
specify the output data set for forecasts	PROC STATESPACE	OUT=
print forecasts	PROC STATESPACE	PRINT
Options to Specify the State Space Model		
specify the state vector	FORM	
specify the parameter values	RESTRICT	
BY Groups		
specify BY-group processing	BY	
Printing		
suppresses all printed output	NOPRINT	

PROC STATESPACE Statement

PROC STATESPACE *options*;

The following options can be specified in the PROC STATESPACE statement.

Printing Options

NOPRINT

suppresses all printed output.

Input Data Options

DATA= *SAS-data-set*

specifies the name of the SAS data set to be used by the procedure. If the DATA= option is omitted, the most recently created SAS data set is used.

LAGMAX= *k*

specifies the number of lags for which the sample autocovariance matrix is computed. The LAGMAX= option controls the number of lags printed in the schematic representation of the autocorrelations.

The sample autocovariance matrix of lag *i*, denoted as $\mathbf{C}_i$, is computed as

$$\mathbf{C}_i = \frac{1}{N-1} \sum_{t=1+i}^{N} \mathbf{x}_t \mathbf{x}'_{t-i}$$

where $\mathbf{x}_t$ is the differenced and centered data and N is the number of observations. (If the NOCENTER option is specified, 1 is not subtracted from N.) LAGMAX= *k* specifies that $\mathbf{C}_0$ through $\mathbf{C}_k$ are computed. The default is LAGMAX=10.

NOCENTER

prevents subtraction of the sample mean from the input series (after any specified differencing) before the analysis.

Options for Preliminary Autoregressive Models

ARMAX= *n*

specifies the maximum order of the preliminary autoregressive models. The ARMAX= option controls the autoregressive orders for which information criteria are printed, and controls the number of lags printed in the schematic representation of partial autocorrelations. The default is ARMAX=10. See "Preliminary Autoregressive Models" later in this chapter for details.

MINIC

writes to the OUTAR= data set only the preliminary Yule-Walker estimates for the VAR model producing the minimum AIC. See "OUTAR= Data Set" later in this chapter for details.

OUTAR= *SAS-data-set*

writes the Yule-Walker estimates of the preliminary autoregressive models to a SAS data set. See "OUTAR= Data Set" later in this chapter for details.

PRINTOUT= SHORT | LONG | NONE

determines the amount of detail printed. PRINTOUT=LONG prints the lagged covariance matrices, the partial autoregressive matrices, and estimates of the residual covariance matrices from the sequence of autoregressive models. PRINTOUT=NONE suppresses the output for the preliminary autoregressive models. The descriptive statistics and state space model estimation output are still printed when PRINTOUT=NONE is specified. PRINTOUT=SHORT is the default.

Canonical Correlation Analysis Options

CANCORR

prints the canonical correlations and information criterion for each candidate state vector considered. See "Canonical Correlation Analysis" later in this chapter for details.

DIMMAX= *n*

specifies the upper limit to the dimension of the state vector. The DIMMAX= option can be used to limit the size of the model selected. The default is DIMMAX=10.

PASTMIN= *n*

specifies the minimum number of lags to include in the canonical correlation analysis. The default is PASTMIN=0. See "Canonical Correlation Analysis" later in this chapter for details.

SIGCORR= *value*

specifies the multiplier of the degrees of freedom for the penalty term in the information criterion used to select the state space form. The default is SIGCORR=2. The larger the value of the SIGCORR= option, the smaller the state vector tends to be. Hence, a large value causes a simpler model to be fit. See "Canonical Correlations Analysis" later in this chapter for details.

State Space Model Estimation Options

COVB

prints the inverse of the observed information matrix for the parameter estimates. This matrix is an estimate of the covariance matrix for the parameter estimates.

DETTOL= *value*

specifies the convergence criterion. The DETTOL= and PARMTOL= option values are used together to test for convergence of the estimation process. If, during an iteration, the relative change of the parameter estimates is less than the PARMTOL= value and the relative change of the determinant of the innovation variance matrix is less than the DETTOL= value, then iteration ceases and the current estimates are accepted. The default is DETTOL=1E-5.

ITPRINT

prints the iterations during the estimation process.

KLAG= *n*

sets an upper limit for the number of lags of the sample autocovariance matrix used in computing the approximate likelihood function. If the data have a strong moving average character, a larger KLAG= value may be necessary to obtain good estimates. The default is KLAG=15. See "Parameter Estimation" later in this chapter for details.

MAXIT= *n*

sets an upper limit to the number of iterations in the maximum likelihood or conditional least-squares estimation. The default is MAXIT=50.

NOEST

suppresses the final maximum likelihood estimation of the selected model.

OUTMODEL= *SAS-data-set*

writes the parameter estimates and their standard errors to a SAS data set. See "OUTMODEL= Data Set" later in this chapter for details.

PARMTOL= *value*

specifies the convergence criterion. The DETTOL= and PARMTOL= option values are used together to test for convergence of the estimation process. If, during an iteration, the relative change of the parameter estimates is less than the PARMTOL= value and the relative change of the determinant of the innovation variance matrix is less than the DETTOL= value, then iteration ceases and the current estimates are accepted. The default is PARMTOL=.001.

RESIDEST

computes the final estimates using conditional least squares on the raw data. This type of estimation may be more stable than the default maximum likelihood method but is usually more computationally expensive. See "Parameter Estimation" later in this chapter for details of the conditional least squares method.

SINGULAR= *value*

specifies the criterion for testing for singularity of a matrix. A matrix is declared singular if a scaled pivot is less than the SINGULAR= value when sweeping the matrix. The default is SINGULAR=1E-7.

Forecasting Options

BACK= *n*

starts forecasting *n* periods before the end of the input data. The BACK= option value must not be greater than the number of observations. The default is BACK=0.

INTERVAL= *interval*

specifies the time interval between observations. The INTERVAL= value is used in conjunction with the ID variable to check that the input data are in order and have no missing periods. The INTERVAL= option is also used to extrapolate the ID values past the end of the input data. See Chapter 3, "Date Intervals, Formats, and Functions," for details on the INTERVAL= values allowed.

INTPER= *n*

specifies that each input observation corresponds to *n* time periods. For example, the options INTERVAL=MONTH and INTPER=2 specify bimonthly data and are equivalent to specifying INTERVAL=MONTH2. If the INTERVAL= option is not specified, the INTPER= option controls the increment used to generate ID values for the forecast observations. The default is INTPER=1.

LEAD= *n*

specifies how many forecast observations are produced. The forecasts start at the point set by the BACK= option. The default is LEAD=0, which produces no forecasts.

OUT= *SAS-data-set*

writes the residuals, actual values, forecasts, and forecast standard errors to a SAS data set. See "OUT= Data Set" later in this chapter for details.

PRINT

prints the forecasts.

BY Statement

BY *variable ...* **;**

A BY statement can be used with the STATESPACE procedure to obtain separate analyses on observations in groups defined by the BY variables.

FORM Statement

FORM *variable value ...* **;**

The FORM statement specifies the number of times a variable is included in the state vector. Values can be specified for any variable listed in the VAR statement. If a value is specified for each variable in the VAR statement, the state vector for the state space model is entirely specified, and automatic selection of the state space model is not performed.

The FORM statement forces the state vector, $\mathbf{z}_t$, to contain a specific variable a given number of times. For example, if Y is one of the variables in $\mathbf{x}_t$, then the statement

```
form y 3;
```

forces the state vector to contain $Y_t, Y_{t+1|t}$, and $Y_{t+2|t}$, possibly along with other variables.

The following statements illustrate the use of the FORM statement:

```
proc statespace data=in;
   var x y;
   form x 3 y 2;
run;
```

These statements fit a state space model with the following state vector:

$$\mathbf{z_t} = \begin{bmatrix} x_{t|t} \\ y_{t|t} \\ x_{t+1|t} \\ y_{t+1|t} \\ x_{t+2|t} \end{bmatrix}$$

ID Statement

ID *variable*;

The ID statement specifies a variable that identifies observations in the input data set. The variable specified in the ID statement is included in the OUT= data set. The values of the ID variable are extrapolated for the forecast observations based on the values of the INTERVAL= and INTPER= options.

INITIAL Statement

INITIAL F *(row,column)= value ...* **G***(row, column)= value ...* ;

The INITIAL statement gives initial values to the specified elements of the **F** and **G** matrices. These initial values are used as starting values for the iterative estimation.

Parts of the **F** and **G** matrices represent fixed structural identities. If an element specified is a fixed structural element instead of a free parameter, the corresponding initialization is ignored.

The following is an example of an INITIAL statement:

```
initial f(3,2)=0 g(4,1)=0 g(5,1)=0;
```

RESTRICT Statement

RESTRICT F*(row,column)= value ...* **G***(row,column)= value ...* ;

The RESTRICT statement restricts the specified elements of the **F** and **G** matrices to the specified values.

To use the restrict statement you need to know the form of the model. Either specify the form of the model with the FORM statement, or do a preliminary run, perhaps with the NOEST option, to find the form of the model that PROC STATESPACE selects for the data.

The following is an example of a RESTRICT statement:

```
restrict f(3,2)=0 g(4,1)=0 g(5,1)=0 ;
```

Parts of the **F** and **G** matrices represent fixed structural identities. If a restriction is specified for an element that is a fixed structural element instead of a free parameter, the restriction is ignored.

VAR Statement

VAR *variable (difference, difference, ...) ... ;*

The VAR statement specifies the variables in the input data set to model and forecast. The VAR statement also specifies differencing of the input variables. The VAR statement is required.

Differencing is specified by following the variable name with a list of difference periods separated by commas. See the section "Stationarity and Differencing" for more information on differencing of input variables.

The order in which variables are listed in the VAR statement controls the order in which variables are included in the state vector. Usually, potential inputs should be listed before potential outputs.

For example, assuming the input data are monthly, the following VAR statement specifies modeling and forecasting of the one period and seasonal second difference of X and Y:

```
var x(1,12) y(1,12);
```

In this example, the vector time series analyzed is

$$\mathbf{x}_t = \begin{bmatrix} (1-B)(1-B^{12})X_t - \overline{x} \\ (1-B)(1-B^{12})Y_t - \overline{y} \end{bmatrix}$$

where B represents the back shift operator, and $\overline{x}$ and $\overline{y}$ represent the means of the differenced series. If the NOCENTER option is specified the mean differences are not subtracted.

Details

Missing Values

The STATESPACE procedure does not support missing values. The procedure uses the first contiguous group of observations with no missing values for any of the VAR statement variables. Observations at the beginning of the data set with missing values for any VAR statement variable are not used or included in the output data set.

Stationarity and Differencing

The state space model used by the STATESPACE procedure assumes that the time series are stationary. Hence, the data should be checked for stationarity. One way to check for stationarity is to plot the series. A graph of series over time can show a time trend or variability changes.

You can also check stationarity by using the sample autocorrelation functions displayed by the ARIMA procedure. The autocorrelation functions of nonstationary series tend to decay slowly. See Chapter 11, "The ARIMA Procedure," for more information.

Another alternative is to use the STATIONARITY= option on the IDENTIFY statement in PROC ARIMA to apply Dickey-Fuller tests for unit roots in the time series. See Chapter 11, "The ARIMA Procedure," for more information on Dickey-Fuller unit root tests.

The most popular way to transform a nonstationary series to stationarity is by differencing. Differencing of the time series is specified in the VAR statement. For example, to take a simple first difference of the series X, use this statement:

```
var x(1);
```

In this example, the change in X from one period to the next is analyzed. When the series has a seasonal pattern, differencing at a period equal to the length of the seasonal cycle may be desirable. For example, suppose the variable X is measured quarterly and shows a seasonal cycle over the year. You can use the following statement to analyze the series of changes from the same quarter in the previous year:

```
var x(4);
```

To difference twice, add another differencing period to the list. For example, the following statement analyzes the series of second differences $(X_t - X_{t-1}) - (X_{t-1} - X_{t-2}) = X_t - 2X_{t-1} + X_{t-2}$:

```
var x(1,1);
```

The following statement analyzes the seasonal second difference series.

```
var x(1,4);
```

The series modeled is the 1-period difference of the 4-period difference: $(X_t - X_{t-4}) - (X_{t-1} - X_{t-5}) = X_t - X_{t-1} - X_{t-4} + X_{t-5}$.

Another way to obtain stationary series is to use a regression on time to de-trend the data. If the time series has a deterministic linear trend, regressing the series on time produces residuals that should be stationary. The following statements write residuals of X and Y to the variable RX and RY in the output data set DETREND.

```
data a;
   set a;
   t=_n_;
run;

proc reg data=a;
   model x y = t;
   output out=detrend r=rx ry;
run;
```

You then use PROC STATESPACE to forecast the de-trended series RX and RY. A disadvantage of this method is that you need to add the trend back to the forecast series in an additional step. A more serious disadvantage of the de-trending method is that it assumes a deterministic trend. In practice, most time series appear to have a stochastic rather than a deterministic trend. Differencing is a more flexible and often more appropriate method.

There are several other methods to handle nonstationary time series. For more information and examples, refer to Brockwell and Davis (1991).

Preliminary Autoregressive Models

After computing the sample autocovariance matrices, PROC STATESPACE fits a sequence of vector autoregressive models. These preliminary autoregressive models are used to estimate the autoregressive order of the process and limit the order of the autocovariances considered in the state vector selection process.

Yule-Walker Equations for Forward and Backward Models

Unlike a univariate autoregressive model, a multivariate autoregressive model has different forms, depending on whether the present observation is being predicted from the past observations or from the future observations.

Let $\mathbf{x}_t$ be the r-component stationary time series given by the VAR statement after differencing and subtracting the vector of sample means. (If the NOCENTER option is specified, the mean is not subtracted.) Let n be the number of observations of $\mathbf{x}_t$ from the input data set.

Let $\mathbf{e}_t$ be a vector white noise sequence with mean vector $\mathbf{0}$ and variance matrix $\mathbf{\Sigma}_p$, and let $\mathbf{n}_t$ be a vector white noise sequence with mean vector $\mathbf{0}$ and variance matrix $\mathbf{\Omega}_p$. Let p be the order of the vector autoregressive model for $\mathbf{x}_t$.

The forward autoregressive form based on the past observations is written as follows:

$$\mathbf{x}_t = \sum_{i=1}^{p} \mathbf{\Phi}_i^p \mathbf{x}_{t-i} + \mathbf{e}_t$$

The backward autoregressive form based on the future observations is written as follows:

$$\mathbf{x}_t = \sum_{i=1}^{p} \mathbf{\Psi}_i^p \mathbf{x}_{t+i} + \mathbf{n}_t$$

Letting E denote the expected value operator, the autocovariance sequence for the $\mathbf{x}_t$ series, $\mathbf{\Gamma}_i$, is

$$\mathbf{\Gamma}_i = E\mathbf{x}_t\mathbf{x}'_{t-i}$$

The Yule-Walker equations for the autoregressive model that matches the first p elements of the autocovariance sequence are

$$\begin{bmatrix} \mathbf{\Gamma}_0 & \mathbf{\Gamma}_1 & \cdots & \mathbf{\Gamma}_{p-1} \\ \mathbf{\Gamma}'_1 & \mathbf{\Gamma}_0 & \cdots & \mathbf{\Gamma}_{p-2} \\ \vdots & \vdots & & \vdots \\ \mathbf{\Gamma}'_{p-1} & \mathbf{\Gamma}'_{p-2} & \cdots & \mathbf{\Gamma}_0 \end{bmatrix} \begin{bmatrix} \mathbf{\Phi}_1^p \\ \mathbf{\Phi}_2^p \\ \vdots \\ \mathbf{\Phi}_p^p \end{bmatrix} = \begin{bmatrix} \mathbf{\Gamma}_1 \\ \mathbf{\Gamma}_2 \\ \vdots \\ \mathbf{\Gamma}_p \end{bmatrix}$$

and

$$\begin{bmatrix} \mathbf{\Gamma}_0 & \mathbf{\Gamma}'_1 & \cdots & \mathbf{\Gamma}'_{p-1} \\ \mathbf{\Gamma}_1 & \mathbf{\Gamma}_0 & \cdots & \mathbf{\Gamma}'_{p-2} \\ \vdots & \vdots & & \vdots \\ \mathbf{\Gamma}_{p-1} & \mathbf{\Gamma}_{p-2} & \cdots & \mathbf{\Gamma}_0 \end{bmatrix} \begin{bmatrix} \mathbf{\Psi}_1^p \\ \mathbf{\Psi}_2^p \\ \vdots \\ \mathbf{\Psi}_p^p \end{bmatrix} = \begin{bmatrix} \mathbf{\Gamma}'_1 \\ \mathbf{\Gamma}'_2 \\ \vdots \\ \mathbf{\Gamma}'_p \end{bmatrix}$$

Here $\mathbf{\Phi}_i^p$ are the coefficient matrices for the past observation form of the vector autoregressive model, and $\mathbf{\Psi}_i^p$ are the coefficient matrices for the future observation form. More information on the Yule-Walker equations in the multivariate setting can be found in Whittle (1963) and Ansley and Newbold (1979).

The innovation variance matrices for the two forms can be written as follows:

$$\mathbf{\Sigma}_p = \mathbf{\Gamma}_0 - \sum_{i=1}^{p} \mathbf{\Phi}_i^p \mathbf{\Gamma}'_i$$

$$\boldsymbol{\Omega}_p = \boldsymbol{\Gamma}_0 - \sum_{i=1}^{p} \boldsymbol{\Psi}_i^p \boldsymbol{\Gamma}_i$$

The autoregressive models are fit to the data using the preceding Yule-Walker equations with $\boldsymbol{\Gamma}_i$ replaced by the sample covariance sequence $\mathbf{C}_i$. The covariance matrices are calculated as

$$\mathbf{C}_i = \frac{1}{N-1} \sum_{t=i+1}^{N} \mathbf{x}_t \mathbf{x}_{t-i}'$$

Let $\widehat{\boldsymbol{\Phi}}_p$, $\widehat{\boldsymbol{\Psi}}_p$, $\widehat{\boldsymbol{\Sigma}}_p$, and $\widehat{\boldsymbol{\Omega}}_p$ represent the Yule-Walker estimates of $\boldsymbol{\Phi}_p$, $\boldsymbol{\Psi}_p$, $\boldsymbol{\Sigma}_p$, and $\boldsymbol{\Omega}_p$ respectively. These matrices are written to an output data set when the OUTAR= option is specified.

When the PRINTOUT=LONG option is specified, the sequence of matrices $\widehat{\boldsymbol{\Sigma}}_p$ and the corresponding correlation matrices are printed. The sequence of matrices $\widehat{\boldsymbol{\Sigma}}_p$ is used to compute Akaike information criteria for selection of the autoregressive order of the process.

Akaike Information Criterion

The Akaike information criterion, or AIC, is defined as -2(*maximum of log likelihood*)+2(*number of parameters*). Since the vector autoregressive models are estimates from the Yule-Walker equations, not by maximum likelihood, the exact likelihood values are not available for computing the AIC. However, for the vector autoregressive model the maximum of the log likelihood can be approximated as

$$\ln(L) \approx -\frac{n}{2} \ln(|\widehat{\boldsymbol{\Sigma}}_p|)$$

Thus, the AIC for the order p model is computed as

$$AIC_p = n\ln(|\widehat{\boldsymbol{\Sigma}}_p|) + 2pr^2$$

You can use the printed AIC array to compute a likelihood ratio test of the autoregressive order. The log-likelihood ratio test statistic for testing the order p model against the order $p-1$ model is

$$-n\ln(|\widehat{\boldsymbol{\Sigma}}_p|) + n\ln(|\widehat{\boldsymbol{\Sigma}}_{p-1}|)$$

This quantity is asymptotically distributed as a χ^2 with r^2 degrees of freedom if the series is autoregressive of order $p-1$. It can be computed from the AIC array as

$$AIC_{p-1} - AIC_p + 2r^2$$

You can evaluate the significance of these test statistics with the PROBCHI function in a SAS DATA step, or with a χ^2 table.

Determining the Autoregressive Order

Although the autoregressive models can be used for prediction, their primary value is to aid in the selection of a suitable portion of the sample covariance matrix for use in computing canonical correlations. If the multivariate time series $\mathbf{x}_t$ is of autoregressive order p, then the vector of past values to lag p is considered to contain essentially all the information relevant for prediction of future values of the time series.

By default, PROC STATESPACE selects the order, p, producing the autoregressive model with the smallest AIC_p. If the value p for the minimum AIC_p is less than the value of the PASTMIN= option, then p is set to the PASTMIN= value. Alternatively, you can use the ARMAX= and PASTMIN= options to force PROC STATESPACE to use an order you select.

Significance Limits for Partial Autocorrelations

The STATESPACE procedure prints a schematic representation of the partial autocorrelation matrices indicating which partial autocorrelations are significantly greater or significantly less than 0. Figure 25.10 shows an example of this table.

```
                         The STATESPACE Procedure

           Schematic Representation of Partial Autocorrelations

Name/Lag        1     2     3     4     5     6     7     8     9    10

x               ++    +.    ..    ..    ..    ..    ..    ..    ..    ..
y               ++    ..    ..    ..    ..    ..    ..    ..    ..    ..

         + is > 2*std error,   - is < -2*std error,   . is between
```

Figure 25.10. Significant Partial Autocorrelations

The partial autocorrelations are from the sample partial autoregressive matrices $\hat{\mathbf{\Phi}}^p_p$. The standard errors used for the significance limits of the partial autocorrelations are computed from the sequence of matrices $\mathbf{\Sigma}_p$ and $\mathbf{\Omega}_p$.

Under the assumption that the observed series arises from an autoregressive process of order $p-1$, the pth sample partial autoregressive matrix $\hat{\mathbf{\Phi}}^p_p$ has an asymptotic variance matrix $\frac{1}{n}\mathbf{\Omega}_p^{-1} \otimes \mathbf{\Sigma}_p$.

The significance limits for $\hat{\mathbf{\Phi}}^p_p$ used in the schematic plot of the sample partial autoregressive sequence are derived by replacing $\mathbf{\Omega}_p$ and $\mathbf{\Sigma}_p$ with their sample estimators to produce the variance estimate, as follows:

$$\widehat{Var}\left(\hat{\mathbf{\Phi}}^p_p\right) = \left(\frac{1}{n-rp}\right)\hat{\mathbf{\Omega}}_p^{-1} \otimes \hat{\mathbf{\Sigma}}_p$$

Canonical Correlation Analysis

Given the order p, let $\mathbf{p}_t$ be the vector of current and past values relevant to prediction of $\mathbf{x}_{t+1}$:

$$\mathbf{p}_t = (\mathbf{x}'_t, \mathbf{x}'_{t-1}, \cdots, \mathbf{x}'_{t-p})'$$

Let $\mathbf{f}_t$ be the vector of current and future values:

$$\mathbf{f}_t = (\mathbf{x}'_t, \mathbf{x}'_{t+1}, \cdots, \mathbf{x}'_{t+p})'$$

In the canonical correlation analysis, consider submatrices of the sample covariance matrix of $\mathbf{p}_t$ and $\mathbf{f}_t$. This covariance matrix, $\mathbf{V}$, has a block Hankel form:

$$\mathbf{V} = \begin{bmatrix} \mathbf{C}_0 & \mathbf{C}'_1 & \mathbf{C}'_2 & \cdots & \mathbf{C}'_p \\ \mathbf{C}'_1 & \mathbf{C}'_2 & \mathbf{C}'_3 & \cdots & \mathbf{C}'_{p+1} \\ \vdots & \vdots & \vdots & & \vdots \\ \mathbf{C}'_p & \mathbf{C}'_{p+1} & \mathbf{C}'_{p+2} & \cdots & \mathbf{C}'_{2p} \end{bmatrix}$$

State Vector Selection Process

The canonical correlation analysis forms a sequence of potential state vectors, $\mathbf{z}^j_t$. Examine a sequence, $\mathbf{f}^j_t$, of subvectors of $\mathbf{f}_t$, and form the submatrix, $\mathbf{V}^j$, consisting of the rows and columns of $\mathbf{V}$ corresponding to the components of $\mathbf{f}^j_t$, and compute its canonical correlations.

The smallest canonical correlation of $\mathbf{V}^j$ is then used in the selection of the components of the state vector. The selection process is described in the following. For more details about this process, refer to Akaike (1976).

In the following discussion, the notation $\mathbf{x}_{t+k|t}$ denotes the wide sense conditional expectation (best linear predictor) of $\mathbf{x}_{t+k}$, given all $\mathbf{x}_s$ with s less than or equal to t. In the notation $x_{i,t+1}$, the first subscript denotes the ith component of $\mathbf{x}_{t+1}$.

The initial state vector $\mathbf{z}^1_t$ is set to $\mathbf{x}_t$. The sequence $\mathbf{f}^j_t$ is initialized by setting

$$\mathbf{f}^1_t = (\mathbf{z}^{1'}_t, x_{1,t+1|t})' = (\mathbf{x}'_t, x_{1,t+1|t})'$$

That is, start by considering whether to add $x_{1,t+1|t}$ to the initial state vector $\mathbf{z}^1_t$.

The procedure forms the submatrix $\mathbf{V}^1$ corresponding to $\mathbf{f}^1_t$ and computes its canonical correlations. Denote the smallest canonical correlation of $\mathbf{V}^1$ as ρ_{min}. If ρ_{min} is significantly greater than 0, $x_{1,t+1|t}$ is added to the state vector.

If the smallest canonical correlation of $\mathbf{V}^1$ is not significantly greater than 0, then a linear combination of $\mathbf{f}_t^1$ is uncorrelated with the past, $\mathbf{p}_t$. Assuming that the determinant of $\mathbf{C}_0$ is not 0, (that is, no input series is a constant), you can take the coefficient of $x_{1,t+1|t}$ in this linear combination to be 1. Denote the coefficients of $\mathbf{z}_t^1$ in this linear combination as ℓ. This gives the relationship:

$$x_{1,t+1|t} = \ell' \mathbf{x}_t$$

Therefore, the current state vector already contains all the past information useful for predicting $x_{1,t+1}$ and any greater leads of $x_{1,t}$. The variable $x_{1,t+1|t}$ is not added to the state vector, nor are any terms $x_{1,t+k|t}$ considered as possible components of the state vector. The variable x_1 is no longer active for state vector selection.

The process described for $x_{1,t+1|t}$ is repeated for the remaining elements of $\mathbf{f}_t$. The next candidate for inclusion in the state vector is the next component of $\mathbf{f}_t$ corresponding to an active variable. Components of $\mathbf{f}_t$ corresponding to inactive variables that produced a zero ρ_{min} in a previous step are skipped.

Denote the next candidate as $x_{l,t+k|t}$. The vector $\mathbf{f}_t^j$ is formed from the current state vector and $x_{l,t+k|t}$ as follows:

$$\mathbf{f}_t^j = (\mathbf{z}_t^{j'}, x_{l,t+k|t})'$$

The matrix $\mathbf{V}^j$ is formed from $\mathbf{f}_t^j$ and its canonical correlations are computed. The smallest canonical correlation of $\mathbf{V}^j$ is judged to be either greater than or equal to 0. If it is judged to be greater than 0, $x_{l,t+k|t}$ is added to the state vector. If it is judged to be 0, then a linear combination of $\mathbf{f}_t^j$ is uncorrelated with the $\mathbf{p}_t$, and the variable x_l is now inactive.

The state vector selection process continues until no active variables remain.

Testing Significance of Canonical Correlations

For each step in the canonical correlation sequence, the significance of the smallest canonical correlation, ρ_{min}, is judged by an information criterion from Akaike (1976). This information criterion is

$$-n\ln(1 - \rho_{min}^2) - \lambda(r(p+1) - q + 1)$$

where q is the dimension of $\mathbf{f}_t^j$ at the current step, r is the order of the state vector, p is the order of the vector autoregressive process, and λ is the value of the SIGCORR= option. The default is SIGCORR=2. If this information criterion is less than or equal to 0, ρ_{min} is taken to be 0; otherwise, it is taken to be significantly greater than 0. (Do not confuse this information criterion with the AIC.)

Variables in $\mathbf{x}_{t+p|t}$ are not added in the model, even with positive information criterion, because of the singularity of $\mathbf{V}$. You can force the consideration of more candidate state variables by increasing the size of the $\mathbf{V}$ matrix by specifying a PASTMIN= option value larger than p.

Printing the Canonical Correlations

To print the details of the canonical correlation analysis process, specify the CANCORR option in the PROC STATESPACE statement. The CANCORR option prints the candidate state vectors, the canonical correlations, and the information criteria for testing the significance of the smallest canonical correlation.

Bartlett's χ^2 and its degrees of freedom are also printed when the CANCORR option is specified. The formula used for Bartlett's χ^2 is

$$\chi^2 = -(n - .5(r(p+1) - q + 1))\ln(1 - \rho^2_{min})$$

with $r(p+1) - q + 1$ degrees of freedom.

Figure 25.11 shows the output of the CANCORR option for the introductory example shown in the "Getting Started" section of this chapter.

The STATESPACE Procedure
Canonical Correlations Analysis

x(T;T)	y(T;T)	x(T+1;T)	Information Criterion	Chi Square	DF
1	1	0.237045	3.566167	11.4505	4

x(T;T)	y(T;T)	x(T+1;T)	y(T+1;T)	Information Criterion	Chi Square	DF
1	1	0.238244	0.056565	-5.35906	0.636134	3

x(T;T)	y(T;T)	x(T+1;T)	x(T+2;T)	Information Criterion	Chi Square	DF
1	1	0.237602	0.087493	-4.46312	1.525353	3

Figure 25.11. Canonical Correlations Analysis

New variables are added to the state vector if the information criteria are positive. In this example, $\mathbf{y}_{t+1|t}$ and $\mathbf{x}_{t+2|t}$ are not added to the state space vector because the information criteria for these models are negative.

If the information criterion is nearly 0, then you may want to investigate models that arise if the opposite decision is made regarding ρ_{min}. This investigation can be accomplished by using a FORM statement to specify part or all of the state vector.

Preliminary Estimates of F

When a candidate variable $x_{l,t+k|t}$ yields a zero ρ_{min} and is not added to the state vector, a linear combination of $\mathbf{f}_t^j$ is uncorrelated with the $\mathbf{p}_t$. Because of the method used to construct the $\mathbf{f}_t^j$ sequence, the coefficient of $x_{l,t+k|t}$ in $\mathbf{l}$ can be taken as 1. Denote the coefficients of $\mathbf{z}_t^j$ in this linear combination as $\mathbf{l}$.

This gives the relationship:

$$x_{l,t+k|t} = \mathbf{l}'\mathbf{z}_t^j$$

The vector $\mathbf{l}$ is used as a preliminary estimate of the first r columns of the row of the transition matrix $\mathbf{F}$ corresponding to $x_{l,t+k-1|t}$.

Parameter Estimation

The model is $\mathbf{z}_{t+1} = \mathbf{F}\mathbf{z}_t + \mathbf{G}\mathbf{e}_{t+1}$, where $\mathbf{e}_t$ is a sequence of independent multivariate normal innovations with mean vector $\mathbf{0}$ and variance $\Sigma_{\mathbf{ee}}$. The observed sequence, $\mathbf{x}_t$, composes the first r components of $\mathbf{z}_t$ and, thus, $\mathbf{x}_t = \mathbf{H}\mathbf{z}_t$, where $\mathbf{H}$ is the $r \times s$ matrix $[\mathbf{I}_r\ \mathbf{0}]$.

Let $\mathbf{E}$ be the $r \times n$ matrix of innovations:

$$\mathbf{E} = \begin{bmatrix} \mathbf{e}_1 & \cdots & \mathbf{e}_n \end{bmatrix}$$

If the number of observations, n, is reasonably large, the log likelihood, L, can be approximated up to an additive constant as follows:

$$L = -\frac{n}{2}\ln(|\boldsymbol{\Sigma}_{\mathbf{ee}}|) - \frac{1}{2}trace(\boldsymbol{\Sigma}_{\mathbf{ee}}^{-1}\mathbf{E}\mathbf{E}')$$

The elements of $\boldsymbol{\Sigma}_{\mathbf{ee}}$ are taken as free parameters and are estimated as follows:

$$\mathbf{S}_0 = \frac{1}{n}\mathbf{E}\mathbf{E}'$$

Replacing $\boldsymbol{\Sigma}_{\mathbf{ee}}$ by $\mathbf{S}_0$ in the likelihood equation, the log likelihood, up to an additive constant, is

$$\mathbf{L} = -\frac{n}{2}\ln(|\mathbf{S}_0|)$$

Letting B be the backshift operator, the formal relation between $\mathbf{x}_t$ and $\mathbf{e}_t$ is

$$\mathbf{x}_t = \mathbf{H}(\mathbf{I} - B\mathbf{F})^{-1}\mathbf{G}\mathbf{e}_t$$

$$\mathbf{e}_t = (\mathbf{H}(\mathbf{I} - B\mathbf{F})^{-1}\mathbf{G})^{-1}\mathbf{x}_t = \sum_{i=0}^{\infty} \boldsymbol{\Xi}_i \mathbf{x}_{t-i}$$

Letting $\mathbf{C}_i$ be the ith lagged sample covariance of $\mathbf{x}_t$, and neglecting end effects, the matrix $\mathbf{S}_0$ is

$$\mathbf{S}_0 = \sum_{i,j=0}^{\infty} \mathbf{\Xi}_i \mathbf{C}_{-i+j} \mathbf{\Xi}_j'$$

For the computation of $\mathbf{S}_0$, the infinite sum is truncated at the value of the KLAG= option. The value of the KLAG= option should be large enough that the sequence $\mathbf{\Xi}_i$ is approximately 0 beyond that point.

Let θ be the vector of free parameters in the $\mathbf{F}$ and $\mathbf{G}$ matrices. The derivative of the log likelihood with respect to the parameter θ is

$$\frac{\partial L}{\partial \theta} = -\frac{n}{2}\,\mathrm{trace}\left(\mathbf{S}_0^{-1}\frac{\partial \mathbf{S}_0}{\partial \theta}\right)$$

The second derivative is

$$\frac{\partial^2 \mathbf{L}}{\partial \theta \partial \theta'} = \frac{n}{2}\left(\mathrm{trace}\left(\mathbf{S}_0^{-1}\frac{\partial \mathbf{S}_0}{\partial \theta'}\mathbf{S}_0^{-1}\frac{\partial \mathbf{S}_0}{\partial \theta}\right) - \mathrm{trace}\left(\mathbf{S}_0^{-1}\frac{\partial^2 \mathbf{S}_0}{\partial \theta \partial \theta'}\right)\right)$$

Near the maximum, the first term is unimportant and the second term can be approximated to give the following second derivative approximation:

$$\frac{\partial^2 L}{\partial \theta \partial \theta'} \cong -n\,\mathrm{trace}\left(\mathbf{S}_0^{-1}\frac{\partial \mathbf{E}}{\partial \theta}\frac{\partial \mathbf{E}'}{\partial \theta'}\right)$$

The first derivative matrix and this second derivative matrix approximation are computed from the sample covariance matrix $\mathbf{C}_0$ and the truncated sequence $\mathbf{\Xi}_i$. The approximate likelihood function is maximized by a modified Newton-Raphson algorithm employing these derivative matrices.

The matrix $\mathbf{S}_0$ is used as the estimate of the innovation covariance matrix, $\mathbf{\Sigma}_{\mathbf{ee}}$. The negative of the inverse of the second derivative matrix at the maximum is used as an approximate covariance matrix for the parameter estimates. The standard errors of the parameter estimates printed in the parameter estimates tables are taken from the diagonal of this covariance matrix. The parameter covariance matrix is printed when the COVB option is specified.

If the data are nearly nonstationary, a better estimate of $\mathbf{\Sigma}_{\mathbf{ee}}$ and the other parameters can sometimes be obtained by specifying the RESIDEST option. The RESIDEST option estimates the parameters using conditional least squares instead of maximum likelihood.

The residuals are computed using the state space equation and the sample mean values of the variables in the model as start-up values. The estimate of $\mathbf{S}_0$ is then computed using the residuals from the *i*th observation on, where *i* is the maximum number of times any variable occurs in the state vector. A multivariate Gauss-Marquardt algorithm is used to minimize $|\mathbf{S}_0|$. Refer to Harvey (1981a) for a further description of this method.

Forecasting

Given estimates of $\mathbf{F}$, $\mathbf{G}$, and $\mathbf{\Sigma_{ee}}$, forecasts of $\mathbf{x}_t$ are computed from the conditional expectation of $\mathbf{z}_t$.

In forecasting, the parameters $\mathbf{F}$, $\mathbf{G}$, and $\mathbf{\Sigma_{ee}}$ are replaced with the estimates or by values specified in the RESTRICT statement. One-step-ahead forecasting is performed for the observation $\mathbf{x}_t$, where $t \leq n - b$. Here n is the number of observations and b is the value of the BACK= option. For the observation $\mathbf{x}_t$, where $t > n - b$, m-step-ahead forecasting is performed for $m = t - n + b$. The forecasts are generated recursively with the initial condition $\mathbf{z}_0 = 0$.

The m-step-ahead forecast of $\mathbf{z}_{t+m}$ is $\mathbf{z}_{t+m|t}$, where $\mathbf{z}_{t+m|t}$ denotes the conditional expectation of $\mathbf{z}_{t+m}$ given the information available at time t. The m-step-ahead forecast of $\mathbf{x}_{t+m}$ is $\mathbf{x}_{t+m|t} = \mathbf{H}\mathbf{z}_{t+m|t}$, where the matrix $\mathbf{H} = [\mathbf{I}_r \mathbf{0}]$.

Let $\mathbf{\Psi}_i = \mathbf{F}^i\mathbf{G}$. Note that the last $s - r$ elements of $\mathbf{z}_t$ consist of the elements of $\mathbf{x}_{u|t}$ for $u > t$.

The state vector $\mathbf{z}_{t+m}$ can be represented as

$$\mathbf{z}_{t+m} = \mathbf{F}^m\mathbf{z}_t + \sum_{i=0}^{m-1} \mathbf{\Psi}_i \mathbf{e}_{t+m-i}$$

Since $\mathbf{e}_{t+i|t} = \mathbf{0}$ for $i > 0$, the m-step-ahead forecast $\mathbf{z}_{t+m|t}$ is

$$\mathbf{z}_{t+m|t} = \mathbf{F}^m\mathbf{z}_t = \mathbf{F}\mathbf{z}_{t+m-1|t}$$

Therefore, the m-step-ahead forecast of $\mathbf{x}_{t+m}$ is

$$\mathbf{x}_{t+m|t} = \mathbf{H}\mathbf{z}_{t+m|t}$$

The m-step-ahead forecast error is

$$\mathbf{z}_{t+m} - \mathbf{z}_{t+m|t} = \sum_{i=0}^{m-1} \mathbf{\Psi}_i \mathbf{e}_{t+m-i}$$

The variance of the m-step-ahead forecast error is

$$\mathbf{V}_{z,m} = \sum_{i=0}^{m-1} \mathbf{\Psi}_i \mathbf{\Sigma}_{\mathbf{ee}} \mathbf{\Psi}_i'$$

Letting $\mathbf{V}_{z,0} = \mathbf{0}$, the variance of the m-step-ahead forecast error of $\mathbf{z}_{t+m}$, $\mathbf{V}_{z,m}$, can be computed recursively as follows:

$$\mathbf{V}_{z,m} = \mathbf{V}_{z,m-1} + \mathbf{\Psi}_{m-1} \mathbf{\Sigma}_{\mathbf{ee}} \mathbf{\Psi}_{m-1}'$$

The variance of the m-step-ahead forecast error of $\mathbf{x}_{t+m}$ is the $r \times r$ left upper submatrix of $\mathbf{V}_{z,m}$; that is,

$$\mathbf{V}_{x,m} = \mathbf{H}\mathbf{V}_{z,m}\mathbf{H}'$$

Unless the NOCENTER option is specified, the sample mean vector is added to the forecast. When differencing is specified, the forecasts $\mathbf{x}_{t+m|t}$ plus the sample mean vector are integrated back to produce forecasts for the original series.

Let $\mathbf{y}_t$ be the original series specified by the VAR statement, with some 0 values appended corresponding to the unobserved past observations. Let B be the backshift operator, and let $\mathbf{\Delta}(B)$ be the $s \times s$ matrix polynomial in the backshift operator corresponding to the differencing specified by the VAR statement. The off-diagonal elements of $\mathbf{\Delta}_i$ are 0. Note that $\mathbf{\Delta}_0 = \mathbf{I}_s$, where $\mathbf{I}_s$ is the $s \times s$ identity matrix. Then $\mathbf{z}_t = \mathbf{\Delta}(B)\mathbf{y}_t$.

This gives the relationship

$$\mathbf{y}_t = \mathbf{\Delta}^{-1}(B)\mathbf{z}_t = \sum_{i=0}^{\infty} \mathbf{\Lambda}_i \mathbf{z}_{t-i}$$

where $\mathbf{\Delta}^{-1}(B) = \sum_{i=0}^{\infty} \mathbf{\Lambda}_i B^i$ and $\mathbf{\Lambda}_0 = \mathbf{I}_s$.

The m-step-ahead forecast of $\mathbf{y}_{t+m}$ is

$$\mathbf{y}_{t+m|t} = \sum_{i=0}^{m-1} \mathbf{\Lambda}_i \mathbf{z}_{t+m-i|t} + \sum_{i=m}^{\infty} \mathbf{\Lambda}_i \mathbf{z}_{t+m-i}$$

The m-step-ahead forecast error of $\mathbf{y}_{t+m}$ is

$$\sum_{i=0}^{m-1} \mathbf{\Lambda}_i \left(\mathbf{z}_{t+m-i} - \mathbf{z}_{t+m-i|t}\right) = \sum_{i=0}^{m-1} \left(\sum_{u=0}^{i} \mathbf{\Lambda}_u \mathbf{\Psi}_{i-u} \right) \mathbf{e}_{t+m-i}$$

Letting $\mathbf{V}_{y,0} = \mathbf{0}$, the variance of the m-step-ahead forecast error of $\mathbf{y}_{t+m}$, $\mathbf{V}_{y,m}$, is

$$\begin{aligned}\mathbf{V}_{y,m} &= \sum_{i=0}^{m-1}\left(\sum_{u=0}^{i}\mathbf{\Lambda}_u\mathbf{\Psi}_{i-u}\right)\mathbf{\Sigma}_{\mathbf{ee}}\left(\sum_{u=0}^{i}\mathbf{\Lambda}_u\mathbf{\Psi}_{i-u}\right)' \\ &= \mathbf{V}_{y,m-1} + \left(\sum_{u=0}^{m-1}\mathbf{\Lambda}_u\mathbf{\Psi}_{m-1-u}\right)\mathbf{\Sigma}_{\mathbf{ee}}\left(\sum_{u=0}^{m-1}\mathbf{\Lambda}_u\mathbf{\Psi}_{m-1-u}\right)'\end{aligned}$$

Relation of ARMA and State Space Forms

Every state space model has an ARMA representation, and conversely every ARMA model has a state space representation. This section discusses this equivalence. The following material is adapted from Akaike (1974), where there is a more complete discussion. Pham-Dinh-Tuan (1978) also contains a discussion of this material.

Suppose you are given the following ARMA model:

$$\mathbf{\Phi}(B)\mathbf{x}_t = \mathbf{\Theta}(B)\mathbf{e}_t$$

or, in more detail

$$\mathbf{x}_t - \mathbf{\Phi}_1\mathbf{x}_{t-1} - \cdots - \mathbf{\Phi}_p\mathbf{x}_{t-p} = \mathbf{e}_t + \mathbf{\Theta}_1\mathbf{e}_{t-1} + \cdots + \mathbf{\Theta}_q\mathbf{e}_{t-q} \qquad (1)$$

where $\mathbf{e}_t$ is a sequence of independent multivariate normal random vectors with mean $\mathbf{0}$ and variance matrix $\mathbf{\Sigma}_{\mathbf{ee}}$; B is the backshift operator ($B\mathbf{x}_t = \mathbf{x}_{t-1}$); $\mathbf{\Phi}(B)$ and $\mathbf{\Theta}(B)$ are matrix polynomials in B; and $\mathbf{x}_t$ is the observed process.

If the roots of the determinantial equation $|\mathbf{\Phi}(B)| = 0$ are outside the unit circle in the complex plane, the model can also be written as

$$\mathbf{x}_t = \mathbf{\Phi}^{-1}(B)\mathbf{\Theta}(B)\mathbf{e}_t = \sum_{i=0}^{\infty}\mathbf{\Psi}_i\mathbf{e}_{t-i}$$

The $\mathbf{\Psi}_i$ matrices are known as the impulse response matrices and can be computed as $\mathbf{\Phi}^{-1}(B)\mathbf{\Theta}(B)$.

You can assume $p > q$ since, if this is not initially true, you can add more terms $\mathbf{\Phi}_i$ that are identically 0 without changing the model.

To write this set of equations in a state space form, proceed as follows. Let $\mathbf{x}_{t+i|t}$ be the conditional expectation of $\mathbf{x}_{t+i}$ given $\mathbf{x}_w$ for $w \leq t$. The following relations hold:

$$\mathbf{x}_{t+i|t} = \sum_{j=i}^{\infty}\mathbf{\Psi}_j\mathbf{e}_{t+i-j}$$

$$\mathbf{x}_{t+i|t+1} = \mathbf{x}_{t+i|t} + \mathbf{\Psi}_{i-1}\mathbf{e}_{t+1}$$

However, from equation (1) you can derive the following relationship:

$$\mathbf{x}_{t+p|t} = \mathbf{\Phi}_1\mathbf{x}_{t+p-1|t} + \cdots + \mathbf{\Phi}_p\mathbf{x}_t \tag{2}$$

Hence, when $i = p$, you can substitute for $\mathbf{x}_{t+p|t}$ in the right-hand side of equation (2) and close the system of equations.

This substitution results in the following model in the state space form $\mathbf{z}_{t+1} = \mathbf{F}\mathbf{z}_t + \mathbf{G}\mathbf{e}_{t+1}$:

$$\begin{bmatrix} \mathbf{x}_{t+1} \\ \mathbf{x}_{t+2|t+1} \\ \vdots \\ \mathbf{x}_{t+p|t+1} \end{bmatrix} = \begin{bmatrix} 0 & \mathbf{I} & 0 & \cdots & 0 \\ 0 & 0 & \mathbf{I} & \cdots & 0 \\ \vdots & \vdots & \vdots & & \vdots \\ \mathbf{\Phi}_p & \mathbf{\Phi}_{p-1} & & \cdots & \mathbf{\Phi}_1 \end{bmatrix} \begin{bmatrix} \mathbf{x}_t \\ \mathbf{x}_{t+1|t} \\ \vdots \\ \mathbf{x}_{t+p-1|t} \end{bmatrix} + \begin{bmatrix} \mathbf{I} \\ \mathbf{\Psi}_1 \\ \vdots \\ \mathbf{\Psi}_{p-1} \end{bmatrix} \mathbf{e}_{t+1}$$

Note that the state vector $\mathbf{z}_t$ is composed of conditional expectations of $\mathbf{x}_t$ and the first *r* components of $\mathbf{z}_t$ are equal to $\mathbf{x}_t$.

The state space form can be cast into an ARMA form by solving the system of difference equations for the first *r* components.

When converting from an ARMA form to a state space form, you can generate a state vector larger than needed; that is, the state space model may not be a minimal representation. When going from a state space form to an ARMA form, you can have nontrivial common factors in the autoregressive and moving average operators that yield an ARMA model larger than necessary.

If the state space form used is not a minimal representation, some but not all components of $\mathbf{x}_{t+i|t}$ may be linearly dependent. This situation corresponds to $[\mathbf{\Phi}_p\mathbf{\Theta}_{p-1}]$ being of less than full rank when $\mathbf{\Phi}(B)$ and $\mathbf{\Theta}(B)$ have no common nontrivial left factors. In this case, $\mathbf{z}_t$ consists of a subset of the possible components of $[\mathbf{x}_{t+i|t}]$ $i = 1, 2, \cdots, p-1$. However, once a component of $\mathbf{x}_{t+i|t}$ (for example, the *j*th one) is linearly dependent on the previous conditional expectations, then all subsequent *j*th components of $\mathbf{x}_{t+k|t}$ for $k > i$ must also be linearly dependent. Note that in this case, equivalent but seemingly different structures can arise if the order of the components within $\mathbf{x}_t$ is changed.

OUT= Data Set

The forecasts are contained in the output data set specified by the OUT= option on the PROC STATESPACE statement. The OUT= data set contains the following variables:

- the BY variables
- the ID variable

- the VAR statement variables. These variables contain the actual values from the input data set.
- FOR*i*, numeric variables containing the forecasts. The variable FOR*i* contains the forecasts for the *i*th variable in the VAR statement list. Forecasts are one-step-ahead predictions until the end of the data or until the observation specified by the BACK= option.
- RES*i*, numeric variables containing the residual for the forecast of the *i*th variable in the VAR statement list. For forecast observations, the actual values are missing and the RES*i* variables contain missing values.
- STD*i*, numeric variables containing the standard deviation for the forecast of the *i*th variable in the VAR statement list. The values of the STD*i* variables can be used to construct univariate confidence limits for the corresponding forecasts. However, such confidence limits do not take into account the covariance of the forecasts.

OUTAR= Data Set

The OUTAR= data set contains the estimates of the preliminary autoregressive models. The OUTAR= data set contains the following variables:

- ORDER, a numeric variable containing the order p of the autoregressive model that the observation represents
- AIC, a numeric variable containing the value of the information criterion AIC_p
- SIGF*l*, numeric variables containing the estimate of the innovation covariance matrices for the forward autoregressive models. The variable SIGF*l* contains the *l*th column of $\hat{\mathbf{\Sigma}}_p$ in the observations with ORDER=p.
- SIGB*l*, numeric variables containing the estimate of the innovation covariance matrices for the backward autoregressive models. The variable SIGB*l* contains the *l*th column of $\hat{\mathbf{\Omega}}_p$ in the observations with ORDER=p.
- FOR*k*_*l*, numeric variables containing the estimates of the autoregressive parameter matrices for the forward models. The variable FOR*k*_*l* contains the *l*th column of the lag k autoregressive parameter matrix $\hat{\mathbf{\Phi}}_k^p$ in the observations with ORDER=p.
- BAC*k*_*l*, numeric variables containing the estimates of the autoregressive parameter matrices for the backward models. The variable BAC*k*_*l* contains the *l*th column of the lag k autoregressive parameter matrix $\hat{\mathbf{\Psi}}_k^p$ in the observations with ORDER=p.

The estimates for the order p autoregressive model can be selected as those observations with ORDER=p. Within these observations, the *k*,*l*th element of $\mathbf{\Phi}_i^p$ is given by the value of the FOR*i*_*l* variable in the *k*th observation. The *k*,*l*th element of $\mathbf{\Psi}_i^p$ is given by the value of BAC*i*_*l* variable in the *k*th observation. The *k*,*l*th element of $\mathbf{\Sigma}_p$ is given by SIGF*l* in the *k*th observation. The *k*,*l*th element of $\mathbf{\Omega}_p$ is given by SIGB*l* in the *k*th observation.

Table 25.1 shows an example of the OUTAR= data set, with ARMAX=3 and $\mathbf{x}_t$ of dimension 2. In Table 25.1, (i, j) indicate the *i,j*th element of the matrix.

Table 25.1. Values in the OUTAR= Data Set

Obs	ORDER	AIC	SIGF1	SIGF2	SIGB1	SIGB2	FOR1_1	FOR1_2	FOR2_1	FOR2_2	FOR3_1
1	0	AIC_0	$\boldsymbol{\Sigma}_{0(1,1)}$	$\boldsymbol{\Sigma}_{0(1,2)}$	$\boldsymbol{\Omega}_{0(1,1)}$	$\boldsymbol{\Omega}_{0(1,2)}$	.	.	.	.	.
2	0	AIC_0	$\boldsymbol{\Sigma}_{0(2,1)}$	$\boldsymbol{\Sigma}_{0(2,2)}$	$\boldsymbol{\Omega}_{0(2,1)}$	$\boldsymbol{\Omega}_{0(2,2)}$	.	.	.	.	.
3	1	AIC_1	$\boldsymbol{\Sigma}_{1(1,1)}$	$\boldsymbol{\Sigma}_{1(1,2)}$	$\boldsymbol{\Omega}_{1(1,1)}$	$\boldsymbol{\Omega}_{1(1,2)}$	$\boldsymbol{\Phi}^1_{1(1,1)}$	$\boldsymbol{\Phi}^1_{1(1,2)}$	.	.	.
4	1	AIC_1	$\boldsymbol{\Sigma}_{1(2,1)}$	$\boldsymbol{\Sigma}_{1(1,2)}$	$\boldsymbol{\Omega}_{1(2,1)}$	$\boldsymbol{\Omega}_{1(1,2)}$	$\boldsymbol{\Phi}^1_{1(2,1)}$	$\boldsymbol{\Phi}^1_{1(2,2)}$	.	.	.
5	2	AIC_2	$\boldsymbol{\Sigma}_{2(1,1)}$	$\boldsymbol{\Sigma}_{2(1,2)}$	$\boldsymbol{\Omega}_{2(1,1)}$	$\boldsymbol{\Omega}_{2(1,2)}$	$\boldsymbol{\Phi}^2_{1(1,1)}$	$\boldsymbol{\Phi}^2_{1(1,2)}$	$\boldsymbol{\Phi}^2_{2(1,1)}$	$\boldsymbol{\Phi}^2_{2(1,2)}$	.
6	2	AIC_2	$\boldsymbol{\Sigma}_{2(2,1)}$	$\boldsymbol{\Sigma}_{2(1,2)}$	$\boldsymbol{\Omega}_{2(2,1)}$	$\boldsymbol{\Omega}_{2(1,2)}$	$\boldsymbol{\Phi}^2_{1(2,1)}$	$\boldsymbol{\Phi}^2_{1(2,2)}$	$\boldsymbol{\Phi}^2_{2(2,1)}$	$\boldsymbol{\Phi}^2_{2(2,2)}$	.
7	3	AIC_3	$\boldsymbol{\Sigma}_{3(1,1)}$	$\boldsymbol{\Sigma}_{3(1,2)}$	$\boldsymbol{\Omega}_{3(1,1)}$	$\boldsymbol{\Omega}_{3(1,2)}$	$\boldsymbol{\Phi}^3_{1(1,1)}$	$\boldsymbol{\Phi}^3_{1(1,2)}$	$\boldsymbol{\Phi}^3_{2(1,1)}$	$\boldsymbol{\Phi}^3_{2(1,2)}$	$\boldsymbol{\Phi}^3_{3(1,1)}$
8	3	AIC_3	$\boldsymbol{\Sigma}_{3(2,1)}$	$\boldsymbol{\Sigma}_{3(1,2)}$	$\boldsymbol{\Omega}_{3(2,1)}$	$\boldsymbol{\Omega}_{3(1,2)}$	$\boldsymbol{\Phi}^3_{1(2,1)}$	$\boldsymbol{\Phi}^3_{1(2,2)}$	$\boldsymbol{\Phi}^3_{2(2,1)}$	$\boldsymbol{\Phi}^3_{2(2,2)}$	$\boldsymbol{\Phi}^3_{3(2,1)}$

Obs	FOR3_2	BACK1_1	BACK1_2	BACK2_1	BACK2_2	BACK3_1	BACK3_2
1	.	.	.	.	.	.	.
2	.	.	.	.	.	.	.
3	.	$\boldsymbol{\Psi}^1_{1(1,1)}$	$\boldsymbol{\Psi}^1_{1(1,2)}$	.	.	.	.
4	.	$\boldsymbol{\Psi}^1_{1(2,1)}$	$\boldsymbol{\Psi}^1_{1(2,2)}$	.	.	.	.
5	.	$\boldsymbol{\Psi}^2_{1(1,1)}$	$\boldsymbol{\Psi}^2_{1(1,2)}$	$\boldsymbol{\Psi}^2_{2(1,1)}$	$\boldsymbol{\Psi}^2_{2(1,2)}$	.	.
6	.	$\boldsymbol{\Psi}^2_{1(2,1)}$	$\boldsymbol{\Psi}^2_{1(2,2)}$	$\boldsymbol{\Psi}^2_{2(2,1)}$	$\boldsymbol{\Psi}^2_{2(2,2)}$	.	.
7	$\boldsymbol{\Phi}^3_{3(1,2)}$	$\boldsymbol{\Psi}^3_{1(1,1)}$	$\boldsymbol{\Psi}^3_{1(1,2)}$	$\boldsymbol{\Psi}^3_{2(1,1)}$	$\boldsymbol{\Psi}^3_{2(1,2)}$	$\boldsymbol{\Psi}^3_{3(1,1)}$	$\boldsymbol{\Psi}^3_{3(1,2)}$
8	$\boldsymbol{\Phi}^3_{3(2,2)}$	$\boldsymbol{\Psi}^3_{1(2,1)}$	$\boldsymbol{\Psi}^3_{1(2,2)}$	$\boldsymbol{\Psi}^3_{2(2,1)}$	$\boldsymbol{\Psi}^3_{2(2,2)}$	$\boldsymbol{\Psi}^3_{3(2,1)}$	$\boldsymbol{\Psi}^3_{3(2,2)}$

The estimated autoregressive parameters can be used in the IML procedure to obtain autoregressive estimates of the spectral density function or forecasts based on the autoregressive models.

OUTMODEL= Data Set

The OUTMODEL= data set contains the estimates of the $\mathbf{F}$ and $\mathbf{G}$ matrices and their standard errors, the names of the components of the state vector, and the estimates of the innovation covariance matrix. The variables contained in the OUTMODEL= data set are as follows:

- the BY variables
- STATEVEC, a character variable containing the name of the component of the state vector corresponding to the observation. The STATEVEC variable has the value STD for standard deviations observations, which contain the standard errors for the estimates given in the preceding observation.
- F_*j*, numeric variables containing the columns of the $\mathbf{F}$ matrix. The variable F_*j* contains the *j*th column of $\mathbf{F}$. The number of F_*j* variables is equal to the value of the DIMMAX= option. If the model is of smaller dimension, the extraneous variables are set to missing.
- G_*j*, numeric variables containing the columns of the $\mathbf{G}$ matrix. The variable G_*j* contains the *j*th column of $\mathbf{G}$. The number of G_*j* variables is equal to *r*, the dimension of $\mathbf{x}_t$ given by the number of variables in the VAR statement.
- SIG_*j*, numeric variables containing the columns of the innovation covariance matrix. The variable SIG_*j* contains the *j*th column of $\boldsymbol{\Sigma}_{ee}$. There are *r* variables SIG_*j*.

Table 25.2 shows an example of the OUTMODEL= data set, with $\mathbf{x}_t = (x_t, y_t)'$, $\mathbf{z}_t = (x_t, y_t, x_{t+1|t})'$, and DIMMAX=4. In Table 25.2, $\mathbf{F}_{i,j}$ and $\mathbf{G}_{i,j}$ are the *i,j*th elements of $\mathbf{F}$ and $\mathbf{G}$ respectively. Note that all elements for F_4 are missing because $\mathbf{F}$ is a 3×3 matrix.

Table 25.2. Value in the OUTMODEL= Data Set

Obs	STATEVEC	F_1	F_2	F_3	F_4	G_1	G_2	SIG_1	SIG_2
1	X(T;T)	0	0	1	.	1	0	$\Sigma_{1,1}$	$\Sigma_{1,2}$
2	STD	.	.	.	.	.	.	.	.
3	Y(T;T)	$F_{2,1}$	$F_{2,2}$	$F_{2,3}$	.	0	1	$\Sigma_{2,1}$	$\Sigma_{2,2}$
4	STD	std $F_{2,1}$	std $F_{2,2}$	std $F_{2,3}$	.	.	.	.	.
5	X(T+1;T)	$F_{3,1}$	$F_{3,2}$	$F_{3,3}$	.	$G_{3,1}$	$G_{3,2}$	.	.
6	STD	std $F_{3,1}$	std $F_{3,2}$	std $F_{3,3}$	.	std $G_{3,1}$	std $G_{3,2}$	.	.

Printed Output

The printed output produced by the STATESPACE procedure is described in the following:

1. descriptive statistics, which include the number of observations used, the names of the variables, their means and standard deviations (Std), and the differencing operations used.
2. the Akaike information criteria for the sequence of preliminary autoregressive models
3. if the PRINTOUT=LONG option is specified, the sample autocovariance matrices of the input series at various lags.
4. if the PRINTOUT=LONG option is specified, the sample autocorrelation matrices of the input series.
5. a schematic representation of the autocorrelation matrices, showing the significant autocorrelations.
6. if the PRINTOUT=LONG option is specified, the partial autoregressive matrices. (These are Φ_p^p as described in "Preliminary Autoregressive Models" earlier in this chapter.)
7. a schematic representation of the partial autocorrelation matrices, showing the significant partial autocorrelations.
8. the Yule-Walker estimates of the autoregressive parameters for the autoregressive model with the minimum AIC.
9. if the PRINTOUT=LONG option is specified, the autocovariance matrices of the residuals of the minimum AIC model. This is the sequence of estimated innovation variance matrices for the solutions of the Yule-Walker equations.
10. if the PRINTOUT=LONG option is specified, the autocorrelation matrices of the residuals of the minimum AIC model.
11. If the CANCORR option is specified, the canonical correlations analysis for each potential state vector considered in the state vector selection process. This includes the potential state vector, the canonical correlations, the information criterion for the smallest canonical correlation, Bartlett's χ^2 statistic ("Chi Square") for the smallest canonical correlation, and the degrees of freedom of Bartlett's χ^2.
12. the components of the chosen state vector.
13. the preliminary estimate of the transition matrix, **F**, the input matrix, **G**, and the variance matrix for the innovations, Σ_{ee}.

14. if the ITPRINT option is specified, the iteration history of the likelihood maximization. For each iteration, this shows the iteration number, the number of step halvings, the determinant of the innovation variance matrix, the damping factor Lambda, and the values of the parameters.
15. the state vector, printed again to aid interpretation of the following listing of **F** and **G**.
16. the final estimate of the transition matrix, **F**.
17. the final estimate of the input matrix, **G**.
18. the final estimate of the variance matrix for the innovations, $\boldsymbol{\Sigma}_{\mathbf{ee}}$.
19. a table listing the estimates of the free parameters in **F** and **G** and their standard errors and *t* statistics.
20. if the COVB option is specified, the covariance matrix of the parameter estimates.
21. if the COVB option is specified, the correlation matrix of the parameter estimates.
22. if the PRINT option is specified, the forecasts and their standard errors.

ODS Table Names

PROC STATESPACE assigns a name to each table it creates. You can use these names to reference the table when using the Output Delivery System (ODS) to select tables and create output data sets. These names are listed in the following table. For more information on ODS, see Chapter 8, "Using the Output Delivery System."

Table 25.3. ODS Tables Produced in PROC STATESPACE

ODS Table Name	Description	Option
NObs	Number of observations	default
Summary	Simple summary statistics table	default
InfoCriterion	Information criterion table	default
CovLags	Covariance Matrices of Input Series	PRINTOUT=LONG
CorrLags	Correlation Matrices of Input Series	PRINTOUT=LONG
PartialAR	Partial Autoregressive Matrices	PRINTOUT=LONG
YWEstimates	Yule-Walker Estimates for Minimum AIC	default
CovResiduals	Covariance of Residuals	PRINTOUT=LONG
CorrResiduals	Residual Correlations from AR Models	PRINTOUT=LONG
StateVector	State vector table	default
CorrGraph	Schematic Representation of Correlations	default
TransitionMatrix	Transition Matrix	default
InputMatrix	Input Matrix	default
VarInnov	Variance Matrix for the Innovation	default
CovB	Covariance of Parameter Estimates	COVB
CorrB	Correlation of Parameter Estimates	COVB
CanCorr	Canonical Correlation Analysis	CANCORR
IterHistory	Iterative Fitting table	ITPRINT
ParameterEstimates	Parameter Estimates Table	default

Table 25.3. (continued)

ODS Table Name	Description	Option
Forecasts	Forecasts Table	PRINT
ConvergenceStatus	Convergence Status Table	default

Examples

Example 25.1. Series J from Box and Jenkins

This example analyzes the gas furnace data (series J) from Box and Jenkins. (The data are not shown. Refer to Box and Jenkins (1976) for the data.)

First, a model is selected and fit automatically using the following statements.

```
title1 'Gas Furnace Data';
title2 'Box & Jenkins Series J';
title3 'Automatically Selected Model';

proc statespace data=seriesj cancorr;
   var x y;
run;
```

The results for the automatically selected model are shown in Output 25.1.1.

Output 25.1.1. Results for Automatically Selected Model

```
                    Gas Furnace Data
                 Box & Jenkins Series J
               Automatically Selected Model

                The STATESPACE Procedure

             Number of Observations     296

                                         Standard
             Variable         Mean          Error

             x            -0.05683       1.072766
             y            53.50912       3.202121


                    Gas Furnace Data
                 Box & Jenkins Series J
               Automatically Selected Model

                The STATESPACE Procedure

       Information Criterion for Autoregressive Models

  Lag=0     Lag=1     Lag=2     Lag=3     Lag=4     Lag=5     Lag=6     Lag=7     Lag=8

651.3862 -1033.57 -1632.96 -1645.12 -1651.52 -1648.91 -1649.34 -1643.15 -1638.56

                      Information
                     Criterion for
                    Autoregressive
                        Models

                    Lag=9       Lag=10

                   -1634.8    -1633.59


         Schematic Representation of Correlations

 Name/Lag      0     1     2     3     4     5     6     7     8     9    10

 x            +-    +-    +-    +-    +-    +-    +-    +-    +-    +-    +-
 y            -+    -+    -+    -+    -+    -+    -+    -+    -+    -+    -+

        + is > 2*std error,  - is < -2*std error,  . is between
```

```
                              Gas Furnace Data
                           Box & Jenkins Series J
                        Automatically Selected Model

                          The STATESPACE Procedure

            Schematic Representation of Partial Autocorrelations

     Name/Lag      1     2     3     4     5     6     7     8     9    10

     x            +.    -.    +.    ..    ..    -.    ..    ..    ..    ..
     y            -+    --    -.    .+    ..    ..    ..    ..    ..    .+

          + is > 2*std error,  - is < -2*std error,  . is between


                  Yule-Walker Estimates for Minimum AIC

       ------Lag=1------ ------Lag=2------ ------Lag=3------ ------Lag=4------
              x        y        x        y        x        y        x        y

x      1.925887 -0.00124 -1.20166 0.004224 0.116918 -0.00867 0.104236 0.003268
y      0.050496 1.299793 -0.02046  -0.3277 -0.71182 -0.25701 0.195411 0.133417
```

```
                              Gas Furnace Data
                           Box & Jenkins Series J
                        Automatically Selected Model

                          The STATESPACE Procedure
                      Canonical Correlations Analysis

                                              Information          Chi
       x(T;T)        y(T;T)     x(T+1;T)        Criterion       Square        DF

            1             1     0.804883         292.9228     304.7481         8


                                                          Information          Chi
  x(T;T)        y(T;T)     x(T+1;T)      y(T+1;T)           Criterion       Square        DF

       1             1     0.906681      0.607529            122.3358     134.7237         7


                                                    Information        Chi
  x(T;T)     y(T;T)   x(T+1;T)   y(T+1;T)   x(T+2;T)    Criterion     Square     DF

       1          1   0.909434   0.610278   0.186274     -1.54701   10.34705      6


                                                    Information        Chi
  x(T;T)     y(T;T)   x(T+1;T)   y(T+1;T)   y(T+2;T)    Criterion     Square     DF

       1          1    0.91014   0.618937   0.206823     0.940392   12.80924      6


                                                          Information      Chi
x(T;T)    y(T;T) x(T+1;T) y(T+1;T) y(T+2;T) y(T+3;T)    Criterion   Square    DF

     1         1 0.912963 0.628785 0.226598 0.083258     -7.94103 2.041584     5
```

Gas Furnace Data
Box & Jenkins Series J
Automatically Selected Model

The STATESPACE Procedure
Selected Statespace Form and Preliminary Estimates

State Vector

x(T;T)	y(T;T)	x(T+1;T)	y(T+1;T)	y(T+2;T)

Estimate of Transition Matrix

0	0	1	0	0
0	0	0	1	0
-0.84718	0.026794	1.711715	-0.05019	0
0	0	0	0	1
-0.19785	0.334274	-0.18174	-1.23557	1.787475

Input Matrix for Innovation

1	0
0	1
1.925887	-0.00124
0.050496	1.299793
0.142421	1.361696

Gas Furnace Data
Box & Jenkins Series J
Automatically Selected Model

The STATESPACE Procedure
Selected Statespace Form and Preliminary Estimates

Variance Matrix for Innovation

0.035274	-0.00734
-0.00734	0.097569

```
                         Gas Furnace Data
                       Box & Jenkins Series J
                    Automatically Selected Model

                      The STATESPACE Procedure
               Selected Statespace Form and Fitted Model

                            State Vector

 x(T;T)         y(T;T)         x(T+1;T)        y(T+1;T)        y(T+2;T)


                    Estimate of Transition Matrix

        0              0              1              0              0
        0              0              0              1              0
 -0.86192       0.030609       1.724235       -0.05483              0
        0              0              0              0              1
 -0.34839       0.292124       -0.09435       -1.09823       1.671418


                     Input Matrix for Innovation

                                 1              0
                                 0              1
                           1.92442       -0.00416
                          0.015621       1.258495
                           0.08058       1.353204
```

```
                         Gas Furnace Data
                       Box & Jenkins Series J
                    Automatically Selected Model

                      The STATESPACE Procedure
               Selected Statespace Form and Fitted Model

                  Variance Matrix for Innovation

                      0.035579       -0.00728
                      -0.00728       0.095577


                        Parameter Estimates

                                      Standard
              Parameter    Estimate      Error    t Value

              F(3,1)       -0.86192   0.072961     -11.81
              F(3,2)       0.030609   0.026167       1.17
              F(3,3)       1.724235   0.061599      27.99
              F(3,4)       -0.05483   0.030169      -1.82
              F(5,1)       -0.34839   0.135253      -2.58
              F(5,2)       0.292124   0.046299       6.31
              F(5,3)       -0.09435   0.096527      -0.98
              F(5,4)       -1.09823   0.109525     -10.03
              F(5,5)       1.671418   0.083737      19.96
              G(3,1)       1.924420   0.058162      33.09
              G(3,2)       -0.00416   0.035255      -0.12
              G(4,1)       0.015621   0.095771       0.16
              G(4,2)       1.258495   0.055742      22.58
              G(5,1)       0.080580   0.151622       0.53
              G(5,2)       1.353204   0.091388      14.81
```

The two series are believed to have a transfer function relation with the gas rate (variable X) as the input and the CO_2 concentration (variable Y) as the output. Since the parameter estimates shown in Output 25.1.1 support this kind of model, the model is reestimated with the feedback parameters restricted to 0. The following statements fit the transfer function (no feedback) model.

```
title3 'Transfer Function Model';
proc statespace data=seriesj printout=none;
   var x y;
   restrict f(3,2)=0 f(3,4)=0
            g(3,2)=0 g(4,1)=0 g(5,1)=0;
run;
```

The last two pages of the output are shown in Output 25.1.2.

Output 25.1.2. STATESPACE Output for Transfer Function Model

```
                              Gas Furnace Data
                           Box & Jenkins Series J
                           Transfer Function Model

                          The STATESPACE Procedure
                   Selected Statespace Form and Fitted Model

                                State Vector

x(T;T)            y(T;T)            x(T+1;T)          y(T+1;T)          y(T+2;T)


                      Estimate of Transition Matrix

          0                 0                 1                 0                 0
          0                 0                 0                 1                 0
   -0.68882                 0          1.598717                 0                 0
          0                 0                 0                 0                 1
   -0.35944          0.284179           -0.0963          -1.07313          1.650047


                         Input Matrix for Innovation

                                   1                 0
                                   0                 1
                            1.923446                 0
                                   0          1.260856
                                   0          1.346332
```

```
                         Gas Furnace Data
                       Box & Jenkins Series J
                      Transfer Function Model

                      The STATESPACE Procedure
              Selected Statespace Form and Fitted Model

                   Variance Matrix for Innovation

                       0.036995         -0.0072
                        -0.0072        0.095712


                        Parameter Estimates

                                         Standard
             Parameter      Estimate        Error       t Value

             F(3,1)         -0.68882     0.050549        -13.63
             F(3,3)         1.598717     0.050924         31.39
             F(5,1)         -0.35944     0.229044         -1.57
             F(5,2)         0.284179     0.096944          2.93
             F(5,3)         -0.09630     0.140876         -0.68
             F(5,4)         -1.07313     0.250385         -4.29
             F(5,5)         1.650047     0.188533          8.75
             G(3,1)         1.923446     0.056328         34.15
             G(4,2)         1.260856     0.056464         22.33
             G(5,2)         1.346332     0.091086         14.78
```

References

Akaike, H. (1974), "Markovian Representation of Stochastic Processes and Its Application to the Analysis of Autoregressive Moving Average Processes," *Annals of the Institute of Statistical Mathematics*, 26, 363-387.

Akaike, H. (1976), "Canonical Correlations Analysis of Time Series and the Use of an Information Criterion," in *Advances and Case Studies in System Identification*, eds. R. Mehra and D.G. Lainiotis, New York: Academic Press.

Anderson, T.W. (1971), *The Statistical Analysis of Time Series*, New York: John Wiley & Sons.

Ansley, C.F. and Newbold, P. (1979), "Multivariate Partial Autocorrelations," *Proceedings of the Business and Economic Statistics Section*, American Statistical Association, 349-353.

Box, G.E.P. and Jenkins, G. (1976), *Time Series Analysis: Forecasting and Control*, San Francisco: Holden-Day.

Brockwell, P.J. and Davis, R.A. (1991), *Time Series: Theory and Methods,* 2nd Edition, Springer-Verlag.

Hannan, E.J. (1970), *Multiple Time Series*, New York: John Wiley & Sons.

Hannan, E.J. (1976), "The Identification and Parameterization of ARMAX and State Space Forms," *Econometrica*, 44, 713-722.

Harvey, A.C. (1981a), *The Econometric Analysis of Time Series*, New York: John Wiley & Sons.

Harvey, A.C. (1981b), *Time Series Models*, New York: John Wiley & Sons.

Jones, R.H. (1974), "Identification and Autoregressive Spectrum Estimation," *IEEE Transactions on Automatic Control*, AC-19, 894-897.

Pham-Dinh-Tuan (1978), "On the Fitting of Multivariate Processes of the Autoregressive-Moving Average Type," *Biometrika*, 65, 99-107.

Priestley, M.B. (1980), "System Identification, Kalman Filtering, and Stochastic Control," in *Directions in Time Series,* eds. D.R. Brillinger and G.C. Tiao, Institute of Mathematical Statistics.

Whittle, P. (1963), "On the Fitting of Multivariate Autoregressions and the Approximate Canonical Factorization of a Spectral Density Matrix," *Biometrika*, 50, 129-134.

Chapter 26

The SYSLIN Procedure

Chapter Contents

Chapter 26
The SYSLIN Procedure

Overview

The SYSLIN procedure estimates parameters in an interdependent system of linear regression equations.

Ordinary least squares (OLS) estimates are biased and inconsistent when current period endogenous variables appear as regressors in other equations in the system. The errors of a set of related regression equations are often correlated, and the efficiency of the estimates can be improved by taking these correlations into account. The SYSLIN procedure provides several techniques which produce consistent and asymptotically efficient estimates for systems of regression equations.

The SYSLIN procedure provides the following estimation methods:

- ordinary least squares (OLS)
- two-stage least squares (2SLS)
- limited information maximum likelihood (LIML)
- K-class
- seemingly unrelated regressions (SUR)
- iterated seemingly unrelated regressions (ITSUR)
- three-stage least squares (3SLS)
- iterated three-stage least squares (IT3SLS)
- full information maximum likelihood (FIML)
- minimum expected loss (MELO)

Other features of the SYSLIN procedure enable you to:

- impose linear restrictions on the parameter estimates.
- test linear hypotheses about the parameters.
- write predicted and residual values to an output SAS data set.
- write parameter estimates to an output SAS data set.
- write the crossproducts matrix (SSCP) to an output SAS data set.
- use raw data, correlations, covariances, or cross products as input.

Experimental graphics are now available with the SYSLIN procedure. For more information, see the "ODS Graphics" section on page 1514.

Getting Started

This section introduces the use of the SYSLIN procedure. The problem of dependent regressors is introduced using a supply-demand example. This section explains the terminology used for variables in a system of regression equations and introduces the SYSLIN procedure statements for declaring the roles the variables play. The syntax used for the different estimation methods and the output produced is shown.

An Example Model

In simultaneous systems of equations, endogenous variables are determined jointly rather than sequentially. Consider the following demand and supply functions for some product:

$$Q_D = a_1 + b_1 P + c_1 Y + d_1 S + \epsilon_1 \qquad \text{(demand)}$$

$$Q_S = a_2 + b_2 P + c_2 U + \epsilon_2 \qquad \text{(supply)}$$

$$Q = Q_D = Q_S \qquad \text{(market equilibrium)}$$

The variables in this system are as follows:

Q_D	quantity demanded
Q_S	quantity supplied
Q	the observed quantity sold, which equates quantity supplied and quantity demanded in equilibrium
P	price per unit
Y	income
S	price of substitutes
U	unit cost
ϵ_1	the random error term for the demand equation
ϵ_2	the random error term for the supply equation

In this system, quantity demanded depends on price, income, and the price of substitutes. Consumers normally purchase more of a product when prices are lower and when income and the price of substitute goods are higher. Quantity supplied depends on price and the unit cost of production. Producers will supply more when price is high and when unit cost is low. The actual price and quantity sold are determined jointly by the values that equate demand and supply.

Since price and quantity are jointly endogenous variables, both structural equations are necessary to adequately describe the observed values. A critical assumption of OLS is that the regressors are uncorrelated with the residual. When current endogenous variables appear as regressors in other equations (endogenous variables depend on each other), this assumption is violated and the OLS parameter estimates are biased and inconsistent. The bias caused by the violated assumptions is called *Simultaneous equation bias*. Neither the demand nor supply equation can be estimated consistently by OLS.

Variables in a System of Equations

Before explaining how to use the SYSLIN procedure, it is useful to define some terms. The variables in a system of equations can be classified as follows:

- *Endogenous variables*, which are also called *jointly dependent* or *response variables*, are the variables determined by the system. Endogenous variables can also appear on the right-hand side of equations.
- *Exogenous variables* are independent variables that do not depend on any of the endogenous variables in the system.
- *Predetermined variables* include both the exogenous variables and *lagged endogenous variables*, which are past values of endogenous variables determined at previous time periods. PROC SYSLIN does not compute lagged values; any lagged endogenous variables must be computed in a preceding DATA step.
- *Instrumental variables* are predetermined variables used in obtaining predicted values for the current period endogenous variables by a first-stage regression. The use of instrumental variables characterizes estimation methods such as two-stage least squares and three-stage least squares. Instrumental variables estimation methods substitute these first-stage predicted values for endogenous variables when they appear as regressors in model equations.

Using PROC SYSLIN

First specify the input data set and estimation method on the PROC SYSLIN statement. If any model uses dependent regressors, and you are using an instrumental variables regression method, declare the dependent regressors with an ENDOGENOUS statement and declare the instruments with an INSTRUMENTS statement. Next, use MODEL statements to specify the structural equations of the system.

The use of different estimation methods is shown by the following examples. These examples use the simulated dataset WORK.IN given below.

```
data in;
  label q = \quotes{Quantity}
        p = \quotes{Price}
        s = \quotes{Price of Substitutes}
        y = \quotes{Income}
        u = \quotes{Unit Cost};
  drop i e1 e2;
  p = 0; q = 0;
  do i = 1 to 60;
     y = 1 + .05*i   + .15*rannor(123);
     u = 2           + .05*rannor(123) + .05*rannor(123);
```

```
         s = 4 - .001*(i-10)*(i-110) + .5*rannor(123);
         e1 = .15 * rannor(123);
         e2 = .15 * rannor(123);
         demandx = 1 + .3 * y + .35 * s + e1;
         supplyx = -1 - 1 * u + e2 - .4*e1;
         q = 1.4/2.15 * demandx + .75/2.15 * supplyx;
         p = ( - q + supplyx ) / -1.4;
         output;
      end;
   run;
```

OLS Estimation

PROC SYSLIN performs OLS regression if you do not specify a method of estimation in the PROC SYSLIN statement. OLS does not use instruments, so the ENDOGENOUS and INSTRUMENTS statements can be omitted.

The following statements estimate the supply and demand model shown previously:

```
proc syslin data=in;
   demand: model q = p y s;
   supply: model q = p u;
run;
```

The PROC SYSLIN output for the demand equation is shown in Figure 26.1, and the output for the supply equation is shown in Figure 26.2.

The SYSLIN Procedure
Ordinary Least Squares Estimation

Model	DEMAND
Dependent Variable	q
Label	Quantity

Analysis of Variance

Source	DF	Sum of Squares	Mean Square	F Value	Pr > F
Model	3	9.587891	3.195964	398.31	<.0001
Error	56	0.449336	0.008024		
Corrected Total	59	10.03723			

Root MSE	0.08958	R-Square	0.95523
Dependent Mean	1.30095	Adj R-Sq	0.95283
Coeff Var	6.88541		

Parameter Estimates

Variable	DF	Parameter Estimate	Standard Error	t Value	Pr > |t|	Variable Label
Intercept	1	-0.47677	0.210239	-2.27	0.0272	Intercept
p	1	0.123324	0.105177	1.17	0.2459	Price
y	1	0.201282	0.032403	6.21	<.0001	Income
s	1	0.167258	0.024091	6.94	<.0001	Price of Substitutes

Figure 26.1. OLS Results for Demand Equation

```
                          The SYSLIN Procedure
                     Ordinary Least Squares Estimation

                       Model                      SUPPLY
                       Dependent Variable              q
                       Label                    Quantity


                          Analysis of Variance

                                     Sum of          Mean
   Source                  DF       Squares        Square    F Value    Pr > F

   Model                    2      9.033890      4.516945     256.61    <.0001
   Error                   57      1.003337      0.017602
   Corrected Total         59      10.03723


           Root MSE                0.13267     R-Square        0.90004
           Dependent Mean          1.30095     Adj R-Sq        0.89653
           Coeff Var              10.19821


                          Parameter Estimates

                 Parameter Standard                    Variable
Variable      DF  Estimate     Error t Value Pr > |t| Label

Intercept      1  -0.30390 0.471397    -0.64   0.5217 Intercept
p              1  1.218743 0.053914    22.61   <.0001 Price
u              1  -1.07757 0.234150    -4.60   <.0001 Unit Cost
```

Figure 26.2. OLS Results for Supply Equation

For each MODEL statement, the output first shows the model label and dependent variable name and label. This is followed by an Analysis of Variance table for the model, which shows the model, error, and total mean squares, and an F test for the no-regression hypothesis. Next, the procedure prints the root mean square error, dependent variable mean and coefficient of variation, and the R^2 and adjusted R^2 statistics.

Finally, the table of parameter estimates shows the estimated regression coefficients, standard errors, and t-tests. You would expect the price coefficient in a demand equation to be negative. However, note that the OLS estimate of the price coefficient P in the demand equation (.1233) has a positive sign. This could be caused by simultaneous equation bias.

Two-Stage Least Squares Estimation

In the supply and demand model, P is an endogenous variable, and consequently the OLS estimates are biased. The following example estimates this model using two-stage least squares.

```
proc syslin data=in 2sls;
   endogenous  p;
   instruments y u s;
   demand: model q = p y s;
   supply: model q = p u;
run;
```

The 2SLS option on the PROC SYSLIN statement specifies the two-stage least-squares method. The ENDOGENOUS statement specifies that P is an endogenous regressor for which first-stage predicted values are substituted. You only need to declare an endogenous variable in the ENDOGENOUS statement if it is used as a regressor; thus although Q is endogenous in this model, it is not necessary to list it in the ENDOGENOUS statement.

Usually, all predetermined variables that appear in the system are used as instruments. The INSTRUMENTS statement specifies that the exogenous variables Y, U, and S are used as instruments for the first-stage regression to predict P.

The 2SLS results are shown in Figure 26.3 and Figure 26.4. The first-stage regressions are not shown. To see the first-stage regression results, use the FIRST option on the MODEL statement.

```
                        The SYSLIN Procedure
                 Two-Stage Least Squares Estimation

                  Model                        DEMAND
                  Dependent Variable                q
                  Label                      Quantity


                        Analysis of Variance

                                  Sum of          Mean
Source                  DF       Squares        Square    F Value    Pr > F

Model                    3      9.670882      3.223627     115.58    <.0001
Error                   56      1.561944      0.027892
Corrected Total         59      10.03723


         Root MSE              0.16701    R-Square        0.86095
         Dependent Mean        1.30095    Adj R-Sq        0.85350
         Coeff Var            12.83740


                        Parameter Estimates

                  Parameter Standard                        Variable
Variable      DF  Estimate      Error t Value Pr > |t|  Label

Intercept      1  1.901040 1.171224      1.62   0.1102 Intercept
p              1  -1.11518 0.607391     -1.84   0.0717 Price
y              1  0.419544 0.117954      3.56   0.0008 Income
s              1  0.331475 0.088472      3.75   0.0004 Price of Substitutes
```

Figure 26.3. 2SLS Results for Demand Equation

```
                          The SYSLIN Procedure
                   Two-Stage Least Squares Estimation

                     Model                     SUPPLY
                     Dependent Variable             q
                     Label                   Quantity


                          Analysis of Variance

                                    Sum of          Mean
Source                    DF       Squares        Square    F Value    Pr > F

Model                      2      9.646098      4.823049     253.96    <.0001
Error                     57      1.082503      0.018991
Corrected Total           59      10.03723


         Root MSE                0.13781     R-Square        0.89910
         Dependent Mean          1.30095     Adj R-Sq        0.89556
         Coeff Var              10.59291


                          Parameter Estimates

                 Parameter Standard                        Variable
Variable      DF  Estimate     Error t Value Pr > |t|  Label

Intercept      1  -0.51878 0.490999    -1.06   0.2952 Intercept
p              1  1.333080 0.059271    22.49   <.0001 Price
u              1  -1.14623 0.243491    -4.71   <.0001 Unit Cost
```

Figure 26.4. 2SLS Results for Supply Equation

The 2SLS output is similar in form to the OLS output. However, the 2SLS results are based on predicted values for the endogenous regressors from the first stage instrumental regressions. This makes the analysis of variance table and the R^2 statistics difficult to interpret. See the sections "ANOVA Table for Instrumental Variables Methods" and "The R^2 Statistics" later in this chapter for details.

Note that, unlike the OLS results, the 2SLS estimate for the P coefficient in the demand equation (-1.115) is negative.

LIML, K-Class, and MELO Estimation

To obtain limited information maximum likelihood, general K-class, or minimum expected loss estimates, use the ENDOGENOUS, INSTRUMENTS, and MODEL statements as in the 2SLS case but specify the LIML, K=, or MELO option instead of 2SLS in the PROC SYSLIN statement. The following statements show this for K-class estimation.

```
proc syslin data=in k=.5;
   endogenous  p;
   instruments y u s;
   demand: model q = p y s;
   supply: model q = p u;
run;
```

For more information on these estimation methods see the "Estimation Methods" in the "Details" section and consult econometrics textbooks.

SUR, 3SLS, and FIML Estimation

In a multivariate regression model, the errors in different equations may be correlated. In this case the efficiency of the estimation may be improved by taking these cross-equation correlations into account.

Seemingly Unrelated Regression

Seemingly unrelated regression (SUR), also called joint generalized least squares (JGLS) or Zellner estimation, is a generalization of OLS for multi-equation systems. Like OLS, the SUR method assumes that all the regressors are independent variables, but SUR uses the correlations among the errors in different equations to improve the regression estimates. The SUR method requires an initial OLS regression to compute residuals. The OLS residuals are used to estimate the cross-equation covariance matrix.

The SUR option on the PROC SYSLIN statement specifies seemingly unrelated regression, as shown in the following statements:

```
proc syslin data=in sur;
   demand: model q = p y s;
   supply: model q = p u;
run;
```

INSTRUMENTS and ENDOGENOUS statements are not needed for SUR, since the SUR method assumes there are no endogenous regressors. For SUR to be effective, the models must use different regressors. SUR produces the same results as OLS unless the model contains at least one regressor not used in the other equations.

Three-Stage Least Squares

The three-stage least-squares method generalizes the two-stage least-squares method to take account of the correlations between equations in the same way that SUR generalizes OLS. Three-stage least squares requires three steps: first-stage regressions to get predicted values for the endogenous regressors; a two-stage least-squares step to get residuals to estimate the cross-equation correlation matrix; and the final 3SLS estimation step.

The 3SLS option on the PROC SYSLIN statement specifies the three-stage least-squares method, as shown in the following statements.

```
proc syslin data=in 3sls;
   endogenous  p;
   instruments y u s;
   demand: model q = p y s;
   supply: model q = p u;
run;
```

The 3SLS output begins with a two-stage least-squares regression to estimate the cross-model correlation matrix. This output is the same as the 2SLS results shown in Figure 26.3 and Figure 26.4, and is not repeated here. The next part of the 3SLS output prints the cross-model correlation matrix computed from the 2SLS residuals. This output is shown in Figure 26.5 and includes the cross-model covariances, correlations, the inverse of the correlation matrix, and the inverse covariance matrix.

```
                  The SYSLIN Procedure
         Three-Stage Least Squares Estimation

                 Cross Model Covariance

                      DEMAND          SUPPLY

   DEMAND           0.027892         -.011283
   SUPPLY           -.011283         0.018991


                 Cross Model Correlation

                      DEMAND          SUPPLY

   DEMAND            1.00000         -0.49022
   SUPPLY           -0.49022          1.00000


             Cross Model Inverse Correlation

                      DEMAND          SUPPLY

   DEMAND            1.31634          0.64530
   SUPPLY            0.64530          1.31634


             Cross Model Inverse Covariance

                      DEMAND          SUPPLY

   DEMAND            47.1945          28.0380
   SUPPLY            28.0380          69.3130
```

Figure 26.5. Estimated Cross-Model Covariances used for 3SLS Estimates

The final 3SLS estimates are shown in Figure 26.6.

```
                    The SYSLIN Procedure
            Three-Stage Least Squares Estimation

           System Weighted MSE                0.5711
           Degrees of freedom                    113
           System Weighted R-Square           0.9627

               Model                       DEMAND
               Dependent Variable               q
               Label                     Quantity


                    Parameter Estimates

             Parameter Standard                   Variable
Variable     DF  Estimate     Error t Value Pr > |t| Label

Intercept     1  1.980261 1.169169     1.69   0.0959 Intercept
p             1  -1.17654 0.605012    -1.94   0.0568 Price
y             1  0.404115 0.117179     3.45   0.0011 Income
s             1  0.359204 0.085077     4.22   <.0001 Price of Substitutes


               Model                       SUPPLY
               Dependent Variable               q
               Label                     Quantity


                    Parameter Estimates

             Parameter Standard                   Variable
Variable     DF  Estimate     Error t Value Pr > |t| Label

Intercept     1  -0.51878 0.490999    -1.06   0.2952 Intercept
p             1  1.333080 0.059271    22.49   <.0001 Price
u             1  -1.14623 0.243491    -4.71   <.0001 Unit Cost
```

Figure 26.6. Three-Stage Least Squares Results

This output first prints the system weighted mean square error and system weighted R^2 statistics. The system weighted MSE and system weighted R^2 measure the fit of the joint model obtained by stacking all the models together and performing a single regression with the stacked observations weighted by the inverse of the model error variances. See the section "The R^2 Statistics" for details.

Next, the table of 3SLS parameter estimates for each model is printed. This output has the same form as for the other estimation methods.

Note that the 3SLS and 2SLS results may be the same in some cases. This results from the same principle that causes OLS and SUR results to be identical unless an equation includes a regressor not used in the other equations of the system. However, the application of this principle is more complex when instrumental variables are used. When all the exogenous variables are used as instruments, linear combinations of all the exogenous variables appear in the third-stage regressions through substitution of first-stage predicted values.

In this example, 3SLS produces different (and, it is hoped, more efficient) estimates for the demand equation. However, the 3SLS and 2SLS results for the supply equation are the same. This is because the supply equation has one endogenous regressor and one exogenous regressor not used in other equations. In contrast, the demand equation has fewer endogenous regressors than exogenous regressors not used in other equations in the system.

Full Information Maximum Likelihood

The FIML option on the PROC SYSLIN statement specifies the full information maximum likelihood method, as shown in the following statements.

```
proc syslin data=in fiml;
   endogenous  p q;
   instruments y u s;
   demand: model q = p y s;
   supply: model q = p u;
run;
```

The FIML results are shown in Figure 26.7.

```
                         The SYSLIN Procedure
             Full-Information Maximum Likelihood Estimation

     NOTE: Convergence criterion met at iteration 3.


                      Model                         DEMAND
                      Dependent Variable                 q
                      Label                       Quantity


                          Parameter Estimates

                   Parameter Standard                      Variable
Variable        DF  Estimate     Error t Value Pr > |t| Label

Intercept        1  1.988529 1.233625     1.61   0.1126 Intercept
p                1  -1.18147 0.652274    -1.81   0.0755 Price
y                1  0.402310 0.107269     3.75   0.0004 Income
s                1  0.361345 0.103816     3.48   0.0010 Price of Substitutes


                      Model                         SUPPLY
                      Dependent Variable                 q
                      Label                       Quantity


                          Parameter Estimates

                   Parameter Standard                      Variable
Variable        DF  Estimate     Error t Value Pr > |t| Label

Intercept        1  -0.52443 0.479522    -1.09   0.2787 Intercept
p                1  1.336083 0.057939    23.06   <.0001 Price
u                1  -1.14804 0.237793    -4.83   <.0001 Unit Cost
```

Figure 26.7. FIML Results

Computing Reduced-Form Estimates

A system of structural equations with endogenous regressors can be represented as functions only of the predetermined variables. For this to be possible, there must be as many equations as endogenous variables. If there are more endogenous variables than regression models, you can use IDENTITY statements to complete the system. See "Reduced-Form Estimates" in the "Computational Details" section later in this chapter for details.

The REDUCED option on the PROC SYSLIN statement prints reduced form estimates. The following statements show this using the 3SLS estimates of the structural parameters.

```
proc syslin data=in 3sls reduced;
    endogenous  p;
    instruments y u s;
    demand: model q = p y s;
    supply: model q = p u;
run;
```

The first four pages of this output were as shown previously and are not repeated here. (See Figure 26.3, Figure 26.4, Figure 26.5, and Figure 26.6.) The final page of the output from this example contains the reduced-form coefficients from the 3SLS structural estimates, as shown in Figure 26.8.

```
                    The SYSLIN Procedure
           Three-Stage Least Squares Estimation

                    Endogenous Variables

                            p               q

           DEMAND        1.176539           1
           SUPPLY        -1.33308           1


                    Exogenous Variables

          Intercept             y               s               u

DEMAND     1.980261      0.404115        0.359204               0
SUPPLY     -0.51878             0               0        -1.14623


              Inverse Endogenous Variables

                       DEMAND          SUPPLY

             p       0.398467        -0.39847
             q       0.531188        0.468812


                       Reduced Form

        Intercept             y               s               u

  p      0.995786      0.161027        0.143131        0.456736
  q       0.80868      0.214661        0.190805        -0.53737
```

Figure 26.8. Reduced-Form 3SLS Results

Restricting Parameter Estimates

You can impose restrictions on the parameter estimates with RESTRICT and SRESTRICT statements. The RESTRICT statement imposes linear restrictions on parameters in the equation specified by the preceding MODEL statement. The SRESTRICT statement imposes linear restrictions that relate parameters in different models.

To impose restrictions involving parameters in different equations, use the SRESTRICT statement. Specify the parameters in the linear hypothesis as *model-label.regressor-name*. (If the MODEL statement does not have a label, you can use the dependent variable name as the label for the model, provided the dependent variable uniquely labels the model.)

Tests for the significance of the restrictions are printed when RESTRICT or SRESTRICT statements are used. You can label RESTRICT and SRESTRICT statements to identify the restrictions in the output.

The RESTRICT statement in the following example restricts the price coefficient in the demand equation to equal .015. The SRESTRICT statement restricts the estimate of the income coefficient in the demand equation to be .01 times the estimate of the unit cost coefficient in the supply equation.

```
proc syslin data=in 3sls;
   endogenous  p;
   instruments y u s;
   demand: model q = p y s;
   peq015: restrict p = .015;
   supply: model q = p u;
   yeq01u: srestrict demand.y = .01 * supply.u;
run;
```

The restricted estimation results are shown in Figure 26.9.

The SYSLIN Procedure
Three-Stage Least Squares Estimation

Model	DEMAND
Dependent Variable	q
Label	Quantity

Parameter Estimates

Variable	DF	Parameter Estimate	Standard Error	t Value	Pr > |t|	Variable Label
Intercept	1	-0.46584	0.053307	-8.74	<.0001	Intercept
p	1	0.015000	0	.	.	Price
y	1	-0.00679	0.002357	-2.88	0.0056	Income
s	1	0.325589	0.009872	32.98	<.0001	Price of Substitutes
RESTRICT	-1	50.59341	7.464990	6.78	<.0001	PEQ015

Model	SUPPLY
Dependent Variable	q
Label	Quantity

Parameter Estimates

Variable	DF	Parameter Estimate	Standard Error	t Value	Pr > |t|	Variable Label
Intercept	1	-1.31894	0.477633	-2.76	0.0077	Intercept
p	1	1.291718	0.059101	21.86	<.0001	Price
u	1	-0.67887	0.235679	-2.88	0.0056	Unit Cost

Parameter Estimates

Variable	DF	Parameter Estimate	Standard Error	t Value	Pr > |t|	Variable Label
RESTRICT	-1	342.3611	38.12103	8.98	<.0001	YEQ01U

Figure 26.9. Restricted Estimates

The standard error for P in the demand equation is 0, since the value of the P coefficient was specified by the RESTRICT statement and not estimated from the data. The Parameter Estimates table for the demand equation contains an additional row for the restriction specified by the RESTRICT statement. The "parameter estimate" for the restriction is the value of the Lagrange multiplier used to impose the restriction.

The restriction is highly "significant" ($t = 6.777$), which means that the data are not consistent with the restriction, and the model does not fit as well with the restriction imposed. See the section "RESTRICT Statement" for more information.

After the Parameter Estimates table for the supply equation, the results for the cross model restrictions are printed. This shows that the restriction specified by the SRESTRICT statement is not consistent with the data ($t = 8.98$). See the section "SRESTRICT Statement" for more information.

Testing Parameters

You can test linear hypotheses about the model parameters with TEST and STEST statements. The TEST statement tests hypotheses about parameters in the equation specified by the preceding MODEL statement. The STEST statement tests hypotheses that relate parameters in different models.

For example, the following statements test the hypothesis that the price coefficient in the demand equation is equal to .015.

```
proc syslin data=in 3sls;
   endogenous  p;
   instruments y u s;
   demand: model q = p y s;
   test_1: test p = .015;
   supply: model q = p u;
run;
```

The TEST statement results are shown in Figure 26.10. This reports an *F*-test for the hypothesis specified by the TEST statement. In this case the *F* statistic is 6.79 (3.879/.571) with 1 and 113 degrees of freedom. The *p*-value for this *F* statistic is .0104, which indicates that the hypothesis tested is almost but not quite rejected at the .01 level. See the section "TEST Statement" for more information.

```
                    The SYSLIN Procedure
              Three-Stage Least Squares Estimation

             System Weighted MSE               0.5711
             Degrees of freedom                   113
             System Weighted R-Square          0.9627

                 Model                        DEMAND
                 Dependent Variable                q
                 Label                      Quantity

                       Parameter Estimates

                 Parameter Standard                    Variable
Variable      DF  Estimate     Error t Value Pr > |t| Label

Intercept      1  1.980261 1.169169     1.69   0.0959 Intercept
p              1  -1.17654 0.605012    -1.94   0.0568 Price
y              1  0.404115 0.117179     3.45   0.0011 Income
s              1  0.359204 0.085077     4.22   <.0001 Price of Substitutes

                 Test Results for Variable TEST_1

              Num DF       Den DF     F Value     Pr > F

                   1          113        6.79     0.0104
```

Figure 26.10. TEST Statement Results

To test hypotheses involving parameters in different equations, use the STEST statement. Specify the parameters in the linear hypothesis as *model-label.regressor-name*. (If the MODEL statement does not have a label, you can use the dependent variable name as the label for the model, provided the dependent variable uniquely labels the model.)

For example, the following statements test the hypothesis that the income coefficient in the demand equation is .01 times the unit cost coefficient in the supply equation:

```
proc syslin data=in 3sls;
   endogenous  p;
   instruments y u s;
   demand: model q = p y s;
   supply: model q = p u;
   stest1: stest demand.y = .01 * supply.u;
run;
```

The STEST statement results are shown in Figure 26.11. The form and interpretation of the STEST statement results is like the TEST statement results. In this case, the F-test produces a p-value less than .0001, and strongly rejects the hypothesis tested. See the section “STEST Statement” for more information.

```
                     The SYSLIN Procedure
               Three-Stage Least Squares Estimation

              System Weighted MSE                0.5711
              Degrees of freedom                    113
              System Weighted R-Square           0.9627


                   Model                    DEMAND
                   Dependent Variable            q
                   Label                  Quantity


                        Parameter Estimates

                 Parameter Standard                      Variable
Variable      DF  Estimate     Error t Value Pr > |t|  Label

Intercept      1  1.980261 1.169169     1.69   0.0959  Intercept
p              1  -1.17654 0.605012    -1.94   0.0568  Price
y              1  0.404115 0.117179     3.45   0.0011  Income
s              1  0.359204 0.085077     4.22   <.0001  Price of Substitutes


                   Model                    SUPPLY
                   Dependent Variable            q
                   Label                  Quantity


                        Parameter Estimates

                 Parameter Standard                      Variable
Variable      DF  Estimate     Error t Value Pr > |t|  Label

Intercept      1  -0.51878 0.490999    -1.06   0.2952  Intercept
p              1  1.333080 0.059271    22.49   <.0001  Price
u              1  -1.14623 0.243491    -4.71   <.0001  Unit Cost


                 Test Results for Variable STEST1

              Num DF       Den DF     F Value      Pr > F

                   1          113       22.46      0.0001
```

Figure 26.11. STEST Statement Results

You can combine TEST and STEST statements with RESTRICT and SRESTRICT statements to perform hypothesis tests for restricted models. Of course, the validity of the TEST and STEST statement results will depend on the correctness of any restrictions you impose on the estimates.

Saving Residuals and Predicted Values

You can store predicted values and residuals from the estimated models in a SAS data set. Specify the OUT= option on the PROC SYSLIN statement and use the OUTPUT statement to specify names for new variables to contain the predicted and residual values.

For example, the following statements store the predicted quantity from the supply and demand equations in a data set PRED:

```
proc syslin data=in out=pred 3sls;
   endogenous  p;
   instruments y u s;
   demand: model q = p y s;
   output predicted=q_demand;
   supply: model q = p u;
   output predicted=q_supply;
run;
```

Plotting Residuals

You can plot the residuals against the regressors by specifying the PLOT option on the MODEL statement. For example, the following statements plot the 2SLS residuals for the demand model against price, income, price of substitutes, and the intercept.

```
proc syslin data=in 2sls;
   endogenous  p;
   instruments y u s;
   demand: model q = p y s / plot;
run;
```

The plot for price is shown in Figure 26.12. The other plots are not shown.

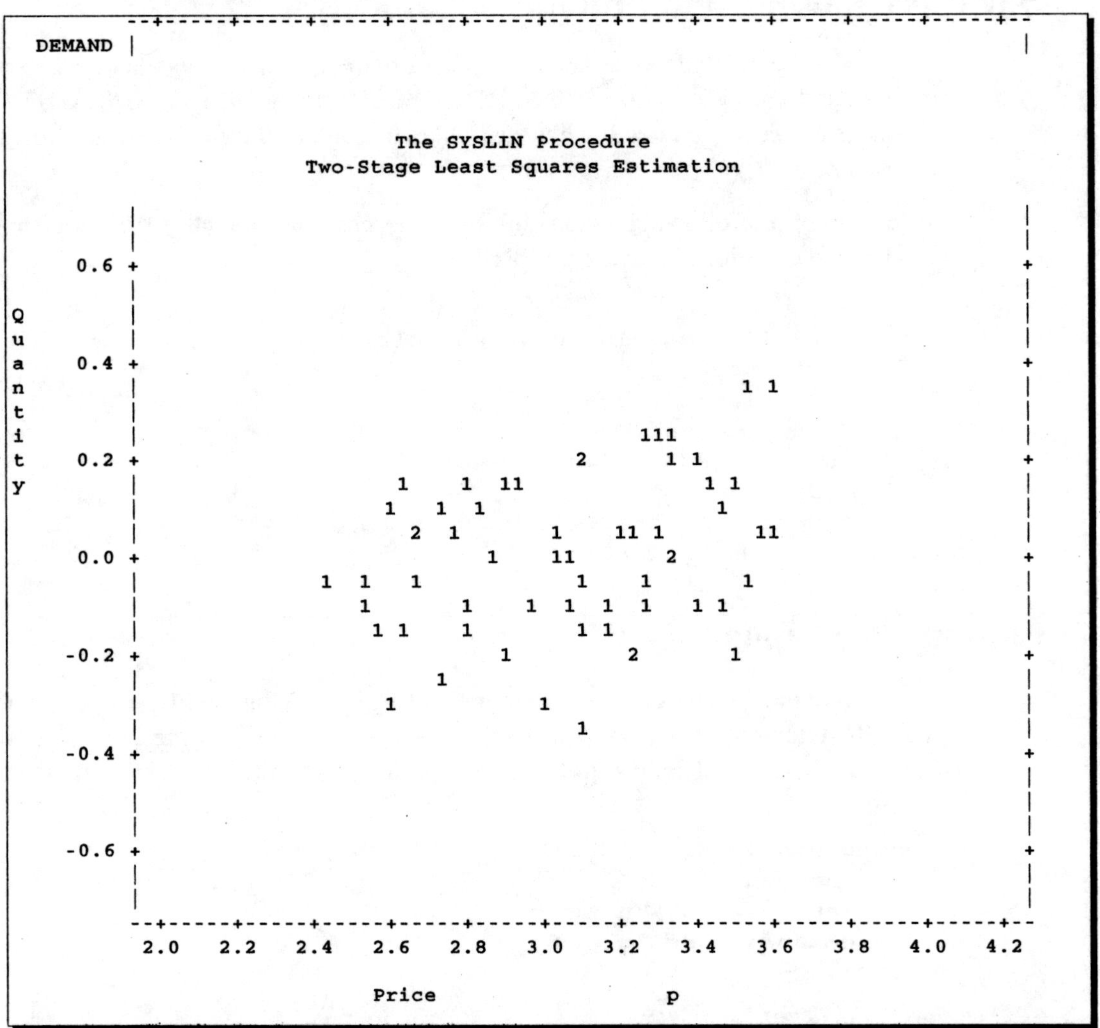

Figure 26.12. PLOT Option Output for P

Syntax

The SYSLIN procedure uses the following statements:

PROC SYSLIN *options* ;
  BY *variables* ;
  ENDOGENOUS *variables* ;
  IDENTITY *identities* ;
  INSTRUMENTS *variables* ;
  MODEL *response = regressors / options* ;
  OUTPUT PREDICTED= *variable* **RESIDUAL=** *variable* ;
  RESTRICT *restrictions* ;
  SRESTRICT *restrictions* ;
  STEST *equations* ;
  TEST *equations* ;
  VAR *variables* ;
  WEIGHT *variable* ;

Functional Summary

The SYSLIN procedure statements and options are summarized in the following table.

Description	Statement	Option
Data Set Options		
specify the input data set	PROC SYSLIN	DATA=
specify the output data set	PROC SYSLIN	OUT=
write parameter estimates to an output data set	PROC SYSLIN	OUTEST=
write covariances to the OUTEST= data set	PROC SYSLIN	OUTCOV OUTCOV3
write the SSCP matrix to an output data set	PROC SYSLIN	OUTSSCP=
Estimation Method Options		
specify full information maximum likelihood estimation	PROC SYSLIN	FIML
specify iterative SUR estimation	PROC SYSLIN	ITSUR
specify iterative 3SLS estimation	PROC SYSLIN	IT3SLS
specify K-class estimation	PROC SYSLIN	K=
specify limited information maximum likelihood estimation	PROC SYSLIN	LIML
specify minimum expected loss estimation	PROC SYSLIN	MELO
specify ordinary least squares estimation	PROC SYSLIN	OLS
specify seemingly unrelated estimation	PROC SYSLIN	SUR

Description	Statement	Option
specify two-stage least-squares estimation	PROC SYSLIN	2SLS
specify three-stage least-squares estimation	PROC SYSLIN	3SLS
specify Fuller's modification to LIML	PROC SYSLIN	ALPHA=
specify convergence criterion	PROC SYSLIN	CONVERGE=
specify maximum number of iterations	PROC SYSLIN	MAXIT=
use diagonal of **S** instead of **S**	PROC SYSLIN	SDIAG
exclude RESTRICT statements in final stage	PROC SYSLIN	NOINCLUDE
specify criterion for testing for singularity	PROC SYSLIN	SINGULAR=
specify denominator for variance estimates	PROC SYSLIN	VARDEF=
Printing Control Options		
print first-stage regression statistics	PROC SYSLIN	FIRST
print estimates and SSE at each iteration	PROC SYSLIN	ITPRINT
print the restricted reduced-form estimates	PROC SYSLIN	REDUCED
print descriptive statistics	PROC SYSLIN	SIMPLE
print uncorrected SSCP matrix	PROC SYSLIN	USSCP
print correlations of the parameter estimates	MODEL	CORRB
print covariances of the parameter estimates	MODEL	COVB
print Durbin-Watson statistics	MODEL	DW
print Basmann's test	MODEL	OVERID
plot residual values against regressors	MODEL	PLOT
print standardized parameter estimates	MODEL	STB
print unrestricted parameter estimates	MODEL	UNREST
print the model crossproducts matrix	MODEL	XPX
print the inverse of the crossproducts matrix	MODEL	I
suppress printed output	MODEL	NOPRINT
suppress all printed output	PROC SYSLIN	NOPRINT
Model Specification		
specify structural equations	MODEL	
suppress the intercept parameter	MODEL	NOINT
specify linear relationship among variables	IDENTITY	
perform weighted regression	WEIGHT	
Tests and Restrictions on Parameters		
place restrictions on parameter estimates	RESTRICT	
place restrictions on parameter estimates	SRESTRICT	
test linear hypothesis	STEST	
test linear hypothesis	TEST	
Other Statements		

Description	Statement	Option
specify BY-group processing	BY	
specify the endogenous variables	ENDOGENOUS	
specify instrumental variables	INSTRUMENTS	
write predicted and residual values to a data set	OUTPUT	
name variable for predicted values	OUTPUT	PREDICTED=
name variable for residual values	OUTPUT	RESIDUAL=
include additional variables in $X'X$ matrix	VAR	

PROC SYSLIN Statement

PROC SYSLIN *options;*

The following options can be used with the PROC SYSLIN statement.

Data Set Options

DATA= *SAS-data-set*

specifies the input data set. If the DATA= option is omitted, the most recently created SAS data set is used. In addition to ordinary SAS data sets, PROC SYSLIN can analyze data sets of TYPE=CORR, TYPE=COV, TYPE=UCORR, TYPE=UCOV, and TYPE=SSCP. See "Special TYPE= Input Data Set" in the "Input Data Set" section later in this chapter for more information.

OUT= *SAS-data-set*

specifies an output SAS data set for residuals and predicted values. The OUT= option is used in conjunction with the OUTPUT statement. See the section "OUT= Data Set" later in this chapter for more details.

OUTEST= *SAS-data-set*

writes the parameter estimates to an output data set. See the section "OUTEST= Data Set" later in this chapter for details.

OUTCOV
COVOUT

writes the covariance matrix of the parameter estimates to the OUTEST= data set in addition to the parameter estimates.

OUTCOV3
COV3OUT

writes covariance matrices for each model in a system to the OUTEST= data set when the 3SLS, SUR, or FIML option is used.

OUTSSCP= *SAS-data-set*
writes the sum-of-squares-and-crossproducts matrix to an output data set. See the section "OUTSSCP= Data Set" later in this chapter for details.

Estimation Method Options

2SLS
specifies the two-stage least-squares estimation method.

3SLS
specifies the three-stage least-squares estimation method.

FIML
specifies the full information maximum likelihood estimation method.

ITSUR
specifies the iterative seemingly unrelated estimation method.

IT3SLS
specifies the iterative three-stage least-squares estimation method.

K= *value*
specifies the K-class estimation method.

LIML
specifies the limited information maximum likelihood estimation method.

MELO
specifies the minimum expected loss estimation method.

OLS
specifies the ordinary least squares estimation method. This is the default.

SUR
specifies the seemingly unrelated estimation method.

Printing and Control Options

ALL
specifies the CORRB, COVB, DW, I, OVERID, PLOT, STB, and XPX options for every MODEL statement.

ALPHA= *value*
specifies Fuller's modification to the LIML estimation method. See "Fuller's Modification to LIML *K* Value" later in this chapter for details.

CONVERGE= *value*
specifies the convergence criterion for the iterative estimation methods IT3SLS, ITSUR, and FIML. The default is CONVERGE=.0001.

FIRST
prints first-stage regression statistics for the endogenous variables regressed on the instruments. This output includes sums of squares, estimates, variances, and standard deviations.

ITPRINT

prints parameter estimates, system-weighted residual sum of squares, and R^2 at each iteration for the IT3SLS and ITSUR estimation methods. For the FIML method, the ITPRINT option prints parameter estimates, negative of log likelihood function, and norm of gradient vector at each iteration.

MAXITER= *n*

specifies the maximum number of iterations allowed for the IT3SLS, ITSUR, and FIML estimation methods. The MAXITER= option can be abbreviated as MAXIT=. The default is MAXITER=30.

NOINCLUDE

excludes the RESTRICT statements from the final stage for the 3SLS, IT3SLS, SUR, ITSUR estimation methods.

NOPRINT

suppresses all printed output. Specifying NOPRINT in the PROC SYSLIN statement is equivalent to specifying NOPRINT in every MODEL statement.

REDUCED

prints the reduced-form estimates. If the REDUCED option is specified, you should specify any IDENTITY statements needed to make the system square. See "Reduced-Form Estimates" in the section "Computational Details" later in this chapter for more information.

SDIAG

uses the diagonal of **S** instead of **S** to do the estimation, where **S** is the covariance matrix of equation errors. See "Uncorrelated Errors Across Equations" in the section "Computational Details" later in this chapter for more information.

SIMPLE

prints descriptive statistics for the dependent variables. The statistics printed include the sum, mean, uncorrected sum of squares, variance, and standard deviation.

SINGULAR= *value*

specifies a criterion for testing singularity of the crossproducts matrix. This is a tuning parameter used to make PROC SYSLIN more or less sensitive to singularities. The value must be between 0 and 1. The default is SINGULAR=1E-8.

USSCP

prints the uncorrected sum-of-squares-and-crossproducts matrix.

USSCP2

prints the uncorrected sum-of-squares-and-crossproducts matrix for all variables used in the analysis, including predicted values of variables generated by the procedure.

VARDEF= DF | N | WEIGHT | WGT

specifies the denominator to use in calculating cross-equation error covariances and parameter standard errors and covariances. The default is VARDEF=DF, which corrects for model degrees of freedom. VARDEF=N specifies no degrees-of-freedom correction. VARDEF=WEIGHT specifies the sum of the observation weights. VARDEF=WGT specifies the sum of the observation weights minus the model degrees of freedom. See "Computation of Standard Errors" in the section "Computational Details" later in this chapter for more information.

BY Statement

BY *variables ;*

A BY statement can be used with PROC SYSLIN to obtain separate analyses on observations in groups defined by the BY variables.

ENDOGENOUS Statement

ENDOGENOUS *variables ;*

The ENDOGENOUS statement declares the jointly dependent variables that are projected in the first-stage regression through the instrument variables. The ENDOGENOUS statement is not needed for the SUR, ITSUR, or OLS estimation methods. The default ENDOGENOUS list consists of all the dependent variables in the MODEL and IDENTITY statements that do not appear in the INSTRUMENTS statement.

IDENTITY Statement

IDENTITY *equation ;*

The IDENTITY statement specifies linear relationships among variables to write to the OUTEST= data set. It provides extra information in the OUTEST= data set but does not create or compute variables. The OUTEST= data set can be processed by the SIMLIN procedure in a later step.

The IDENTITY statement is also used to compute reduced-form coefficients when the REDUCED option in the PROC SYSLIN statement is specified. See "Reduced-Form Estimates" in the section "Computational Details" later in this chapter for more information.

The *equation* given by the IDENTITY statement has the same form as equations in the MODEL statement. A label can be specified for an IDENTITY statement as follows:

label: **IDENTITY** . . . ;

INSTRUMENTS Statement

INSTRUMENTS *variables ;*

The INSTRUMENTS statement declares the variables used in obtaining first-stage predicted values. All the instruments specified are used in each first-stage regression. The INSTRUMENTS statement is required for the 2SLS, 3SLS, IT3SLS, LIML, MELO, and K-class estimation methods. The INSTRUMENTS statement is not needed for the SUR, ITSUR, OLS, or FIML estimation methods.

MODEL Statement

MODEL *response = regressors / options ;*

The MODEL statement regresses the response variable on the left side of the equal sign against the regressors listed on the right side.

Models can be given labels. Model labels are used in the printed output to identify the results for different models. Model labels are also used in SRESTRICT and STEST statements to refer to parameters in different models. If no label is specified, the response variable name is used as the label for the model. The model label is specified as follows:

label: **MODEL** . . . ;

The following options can be used in the MODEL statement after a slash (/).

ALL
specifies the CORRB, COVB, DW, I, OVERID, PLOT, STB, and XPX options.

ALPHA= *value*
specifies the α parameter for Fuller's modification to the LIML estimation method. See "Fuller's Modification to LIML" in the section "Computational Details" later in this chapter for more information.

CORRB
prints the matrix of estimated correlations between the parameter estimates.

COVB
prints the matrix of estimated covariances between the parameter estimates.

DW
prints Durbin-Watson statistics and autocorrelation coefficients for the residuals. If there are missing values, d' is calculated according to Savin and White (1978). Use the DW option only if the data set to be analyzed is an ordinary SAS data set with time series observations sorted in time order. The Durbin-Watson test is not valid for models with lagged dependent regressors.

I
prints the inverse of the crossproducts matrix for the model, $(\mathbf{X}'\mathbf{X})^{-1}$. If restrictions are specified, the crossproducts matrix printed is adjusted for the restrictions. See the section "Computational Details" for more information.

K= *value*
specifies K-class estimation.

NOINT
suppresses the intercept parameter from the model.

NOPRINT
suppresses the normal printed output.

OVERID
prints Basmann's (1960) test for over identifying restrictions. See "Over Identification Restrictions" in the section "Computational Details" later in this chapter for more information.

PLOT
plots residual values against regressors. A plot of the residuals for each regressor is printed.

STB
prints standardized parameter estimates. Sometimes known as a standard partial regression coefficient, a standardized parameter estimate is a parameter estimate multiplied by the standard deviation of the associated regressor and divided by the standard deviation of the response variable.

UNREST
prints parameter estimates computed before restrictions are applied. The UNREST option is valid only if a RESTRICT statement is specified.

XPX
prints the model crossproducts matrix, $X'X$. See the section "Computational Details" for more information.

OUTPUT Statement

OUTPUT PREDICTED=*variable* **RESIDUAL=***variable* **;**

The OUTPUT statement writes predicted values and residuals from the preceding model to the data set specified by the OUT= option on the PROC SYSLIN statement. An OUTPUT statement must come after the MODEL statement to which it applies. The OUT= option must be specified in the PROC SYSLIN statement.

The following options can be specified in the OUTPUT statement:

PREDICTED= *variable*
names a new variable to contain the predicted values for the response variable. The PREDICTED= option can be abbreviated as PREDICT=, PRED=, or P=.

RESIDUAL= *variable*
names a new variable to contain the residual values for the response variable. The RESIDUAL= option can be abbreviated as RESID= or R=.

For example, the following statements create an output data set named B. In addition to the variables in the input data set, the data set B contains the variable YHAT, with values that are predicted values of the response variable Y, and YRESID, with values that are the residual values of Y.

```
proc syslin data=a out=b;
   model y = x1 x2;
   output p=yhat r=yresid;
run;
```

For example, the following statements create an output data set named PRED. In addition to the variables in the input data set, the data set PRED contains the variables Q_DEMAND and Q_SUPPLY, with values that are predicted values of the response variable Q for the demand and supply equations respectively, and R_DEMAND and R_SUPPLY, with values that are the residual values of the demand and supply equations.

```
proc syslin data=in out=pred;
   demand: model q = p y s;
   output p=q_demand r=r_demand;
   supply: model q = p u;
   output p=q_supply r=r_supply;
run;
```

See the section "OUT= Data Set" later in this chapter for more details.

RESTRICT Statement

RESTRICT *equation , ... , equation ;*

The RESTRICT statement places restrictions on the parameter estimates for the preceding MODEL statement. Any number of restrict statements can follow a MODEL statement. Each restriction is written as a linear equation. If more than one restriction is specified in a single RESTRICT statement, the restrictions are separated by commas.

Parameters are referred to by the name of the corresponding regressor variable. Each name used in the equation must be a regressor in the preceding MODEL statement. The keyword INTERCEPT is used to refer to the intercept parameter in the model.

RESTRICT statements can be given labels. The labels are used in the printed output to distinguish results for different restrictions. Labels are specified as follows:

label : **RESTRICT** . . . ;

The following is an example of the use of the RESTRICT statement, in which the coefficients of the regressors X1 and X2 are required to sum to 1.

```
proc syslin data=a;
   model y = x1 x2;
   restrict x1 + x2 = 1;
run;
```

Variable names can be multiplied by constants. When no equal sign appears, the linear combination is set equal to 0. Note that the parameters associated with the variables are restricted, not the variables themselves. Here are some examples of valid RESTRICT statements:

```
restrict x1 + x2 = 1;
restrict x1 + x2 - 1;
restrict 2 * x1 = x2 + x3 , intercept + x4 = 0;
restrict x1 = x2 = x3 = 1;
restrict 2 * x1 - x2;
```

Restricted parameter estimates are computed by introducing a Lagrangian parameter λ for each restriction (Pringle and Raynor 1971). The estimates of these Lagrangian parameters are printed in the parameter estimates table. If a restriction cannot be applied, its parameter value and degrees of freedom are listed as 0.

The Lagrangian parameter, λ, measures the sensitivity of the SSE to the restriction. If the restriction is changed by a small amount ϵ, the SSE is changed by $2\lambda\epsilon$.

The *t*-ratio tests the significance of the restrictions. If λ is zero, the restricted estimates are the same as the unrestricted.

Any number of restrictions can be specified on a RESTRICT statement, and any number of RESTRICT statements can be used. The estimates are computed subject to all restrictions specified. However, restrictions should be consistent and not redundant.

Note: The RESTRICT statement is not supported for the FIML estimation method.

SRESTRICT Statement

SRESTRICT *equation , ... , equation ;*

The SRESTRICT statement imposes linear restrictions involving parameters in two or more MODEL statements. The SRESTRICT statement is like the RESTRICT statement but is used to impose restrictions across equations, whereas the RESTRICT statement only applies to parameters in the immediately preceding MODEL statement.

Each restriction is written as a linear equation. Parameters are referred to as *label.variable*, where *label* is the model label and *variable* is the name of the regressor to which the parameter is attached. (If the MODEL statement does not have a label, you can use the dependent variable name as the label for the model, provided the dependent variable uniquely labels the model.) Each variable name used must be a regressor in the indicated MODEL statement. The keyword INTERCEPT is used to refer to intercept parameters.

SRESTRICT statements can be given labels. The labels are used in the printed output to distinguish results for different restrictions. Labels are specified as follows:

label : **SRESTRICT** . . . ;

The following is an example of the use of the SRESTRICT statement, in which the coefficient for the regressor X2 is constrained to be the same in both models.

```
proc syslin data=a 3sls;
   endogenous y1 y2;
   instruments x1 x2;
   model y1 = y2 x1 x2;
   model y2 = y1 x2;
   srestrict y1.x2 = y2.x2;
run;
```

When no equal sign is used, the linear combination is set equal to 0. Thus the restriction in the preceding example can also be specified as

```
   srestrict y1.x2 - y2.x2;
```

Any number of restrictions can be specified on an SRESTRICT statement, and any number of SRESTRICT statements can be used. The estimates are computed subject to all restrictions specified. However, restrictions should be consistent and not redundant.

When a system restriction is requested for a single equation estimation method (such as OLS or 2SLS), PROC SYSLIN produces the restricted estimates by actually using a corresponding system method. For example, when SRESTRICT is specified along with OLS, PROC SYSLIN produces the restricted OLS estimates via a two-step process equivalent to using SUR estimation with the SDIAG option. First of all, the unrestricted OLS results are produced. Then the GLS (SUR) estimation with the system restriction is performed using the diagonal of the covariance matrix of the residuals. When SRESTRICT is specified along with 2SLS, PROC SYSLIN produces the restricted 2SLS estimates via a multistep process equivalent to using 3SLS estimation with the SDIAG option. First of all, the unrestricted 2SLS results are produced. Then the GLS (3SLS) estimation with the system restriction is performed using the diagonal of the covariance matrix of the residuals.

The results of the SRESTRICT statements are printed after the parameter estimates for all the models in the system. The format of the SRESTRICT statement output is the same as the parameter estimates table. In this output the "Parameter Estimate" is the Lagrangian parameter, λ, used to impose the restriction.

The Lagrangian parameter, λ, measures the sensitivity of the system sum of square errors to the restriction. The system SSE is the system MSE shown in the printed output multiplied by the degrees of freedom. If the restriction is changed by a small amount ϵ, the system SSE is changed by $2\lambda\epsilon$.

The *t*-ratio tests the significance of the restriction. If λ is zero, the restricted estimates are the same as the unrestricted estimates.

The model degrees of freedom are not adjusted for the cross-model restrictions imposed by SRESTRICT statements.

Note: The SRESTRICT statement is not supported for the LIML and the FIML estimation methods.

STEST Statement

STEST *equation , ... , equation / options ;*

The STEST statement performs an F-test for the joint hypotheses specified in the statement.

The hypothesis is represented in matrix notation as

$$\mathbf{L}\beta = \mathbf{c}$$

and the F-test is computed as

$$\frac{(\mathbf{L}b - \mathbf{c})'(\mathbf{L}(\mathbf{X}'\mathbf{X})^{-1}\mathbf{L}')^{-1}(\mathbf{L}b - \mathbf{c})}{m\hat{\sigma}^2}$$

where b is the estimate of β, m is the number of restrictions, and $\hat{\sigma}^2$ is the system weighted mean square error. See the section "Computational Details" for information on the matrix $\mathbf{X}'\mathbf{X}$.

Each hypothesis to be tested is written as a linear equation. Parameters are referred to as *label.variable*, where *label* is the model label and *variable* is the name of the regressor to which the parameter is attached. (If the MODEL statement does not have a label, you can use the dependent variable name as the label for the model, provided the dependent variable uniquely labels the model.) Each variable name used must be a regressor in the indicated MODEL statement. The keyword INTERCEPT is used to refer to intercept parameters.

STEST statements can be given labels. The label is used in the printed output to distinguish different tests. Any number of STEST statements can be specified. Labels are specified as follows:

label: **STEST** . . . ;

The following is an example of the STEST statement:

```
proc syslin data=a 3sls;
   endogenous y1 y2;
   instruments x1 x2;
   model y1 = y2 x1 x2;
   model y2 = y1 x2;
   stest y1.x2 = y2.x2;
run;
```

The test performed is exact only for ordinary least squares, given the OLS assumptions of the linear model. For other estimation methods, the F-test is based on large sample theory and is only approximate in finite samples.

If RESTRICT or SRESTRICT statements are used, the tests computed by the STEST statement are conditional on the restrictions specified. The validity of the tests may be compromised if incorrect restrictions are imposed on the estimates.

The following are examples of STEST statements:

```
stest a.x1 + b.x2 = 1;
stest 2 * b.x2 = c.x3 + c.x4 ,
      a.intercept + b.x2 = 0;
stest a.x1 = c.x2 = b.x3 = 1;
stest 2 * a.x1 - b.x2 = 0;
```

The PRINT option can be specified in the STEST statement after a slash (/):

PRINT

prints intermediate calculations for the hypothesis tests.

Note: The STEST statement is not supported for the FIML estimation method.

TEST Statement

TEST *equation , ... , equation / options ;*

The TEST statement performs *F*-tests of linear hypotheses about the parameters in the preceding MODEL statement. Each equation specifies a linear hypothesis to be tested. If more than one equation is specified, the equations are separated by commas.

Variable names must correspond to regressors in the preceding MODEL statement, and each name represents the coefficient of the corresponding regressor. The keyword INTERCEPT is used to refer to the model intercept.

TEST statements can be given labels. The label is used in the printed output to distinguish different tests. Any number of TEST statements can be specified. Labels are specified as follows:

label: **TEST** . . . ;

The following is an example of the use of TEST statement, which tests the hypothesis that the coefficients of X1 and X2 are the same:

```
proc syslin data=a;
   model y = x1 x2;
   test x1 = x2;
run;
```

The following statements perform *F*-tests for the hypothesis that the coefficients of X1 and X2 are equal, and that the sum of the X1 and X2 coefficients is twice the intercept, and for the joint hypothesis.

```
proc syslin data=a;
   model y = x1 x2;
   x1eqx2:   test x1 = x2;
   sumeq2i: test x1 + x2 = 2 * intercept;
   joint:    test x1 = x2, x1 + x2 = 2 * intercept;
run;
```

The following are additional examples of TEST statements:

```
test x1 + x2 = 1;
test x1 = x2 = x3 = 1;
test 2 * x1 = x2 + x3, intercept + x4 = 0;
test 2 * x1 - x2;
```

The TEST statement performs an F-test for the joint hypotheses specified. The hypothesis is represented in matrix notation as follows:

$$\mathbf{L}\beta = \mathbf{c}$$

The F test is computed as

$$\frac{(\mathbf{L}b - \mathbf{c})'(\mathbf{L}(\mathbf{X}'\mathbf{X})^{-}\mathbf{L}')^{-1}(\mathbf{L}b - \mathbf{c})}{m\hat{\sigma}^2}$$

where b is the estimate of β, m is the number of restrictions, and $\hat{\sigma}^2$ is the model mean square error. See the section "Computational Details" for information on the matrix $\mathbf{X}'\mathbf{X}$.

The test performed is exact only for ordinary least squares, given the OLS assumptions of the linear model. For other estimation methods, the F-test is based on large sample theory and is only approximate in finite samples.

If RESTRICT or SRESTRICT statements are used, the tests computed by the TEST statement are conditional on the restrictions specified. The validity of the tests may be compromised if incorrect restrictions are imposed on the estimates.

The PRINT option can be specified in the TEST statement after a slash (/):

PRINT

prints intermediate calculations for the hypothesis tests.

Note: The TEST statement is not supported for the FIML estimation method.

VAR Statement

VAR *variables ;*

The VAR statement is used to include variables in the crossproducts matrix that are not specified in any MODEL statement. This statement is rarely used with PROC SYSLIN and is used only with the OUTSSCP= option in the PROC SYSLIN statement.

WEIGHT Statement

WEIGHT *variable ;*

The WEIGHT statement is used to perform weighted regression. The WEIGHT statement names a variable in the input data set whose values are relative weights for a weighted least-squares fit. If the weight value is proportional to the reciprocal of the variance for each observation, the weighted estimates are the best linear unbiased estimates (BLUE).

Details

Input Data Set

PROC SYSLIN does not compute new values for regressors. For example, if you need a lagged variable, you must create it with a DATA step. No values are computed by IDENTITY statements; all values must be in the input data set.

Special TYPE= Input Data Set

The input data set for most applications of the SYSLIN procedure contains standard rectangular data. However, PROC SYSLIN can also process input data in the form of a crossproducts, covariance, or correlation matrix. Data sets containing such matrices are identified by values of the TYPE= data set option.

These special kinds of input data sets can be used to save computer time. It takes nk^2 operations, where n is the number of observations and k is the number of variables, to calculate cross products; the regressions are of the order k^3. When n is in the thousands and k is much smaller, you can save most of the computer time in later runs of PROC SYSLIN by reusing the SSCP matrix rather than recomputing it.

The SYSLIN procedure can process TYPE= CORR, COV, UCORR, UCOV, or SSCP data sets. TYPE=CORR and TYPE=COV data sets, usually created by the CORR procedure, contain means and standard deviations, and correlations or covariances. TYPE=SSCP data sets, usually created in previous runs of PROC SYSLIN, contain sums of squares and cross products. Refer to *SAS/STAT User's Guide* for more information on special SAS data sets.

When special SAS data sets are read, you must specify the TYPE= data set option. PROC CORR and PROC SYSLIN automatically set the type for output data sets; however, if you create the data set by some other means, you must specify its type with the TYPE= data set option.

When the special data sets are used, the DW (Durbin-Watson test) and PLOT options in the MODEL statement cannot be performed, and the OUTPUT statements are not valid.

Estimation Methods

A brief description of the methods used by the SYSLIN procedure follows. For more information on these methods, see the references at the end of this chapter.

There are two fundamental methods of estimation for simultaneous equations: least squares and maximum likelihood. There are two approaches within each of these categories: single equation methods, also referred to as limited information methods, and system methods, or full information methods. System methods take into account cross-equation correlations of the disturbances in estimating parameters, while single equation methods do not.

OLS, 2SLS, MELO, K-class, SUR, ITSUR, 3SLS, and IT3SLS use the least-squares method; LIML and FIML use the maximum likelihood method.

OLS, 2SLS, MELO, K-class and LIML are single equation methods. The system methods are SUR, ITSUR, 3SLS, IT3SLS, and FIML.

Single Equation Estimation Methods

Single equation methods do not take into account correlations of errors across equations. As a result, these estimators are not asymptotically efficient compared to full information methods, however, there are instances in which they may be preferred. (See "Choosing a Method for Simultaneous Equations" later in this chapter for more information.)

Let $\mathbf{y}_i$ be the dependent endogenous variable in equation i, and X_i and Y_i be the matrices of exogenous and endogenous variables appearing as regressors in the same equation.

The 2SLS method owes its name to the fact that, in a first stage, the instrumental variables are used as regressors to obtain a projected value $\hat{Y}_i$ that is uncorrelated with the residual in equation i. In a second stage, $\hat{Y}_i$ replaces Y_i on the right hand side to obtain consistent least squares estimators.

Normally, the predetermined variables of the system are used as the instruments. It is possible to use variables other than predetermined variables from your system as instruments, however, the estimation may not be as efficient. For consistent estimates, the instruments must be uncorrelated with the residual and correlated with the endogenous variables.

The LIML method results in consistent estimates that are equal to the 2SLS estimates when an equation is exactly identified. LIML can be viewed as a least-variance ratio estimation or as a maximum likelihood estimation. LIML involves minimizing the ratio $\lambda = (rvar\_eq)/(rvar\_sys)$, where $rvar\_eq$ is the residual variance associated with regressing the weighted endogenous variables on all predetermined variables appearing in that equation, and $rvar\_sys$ is the residual variance associated with regressing weighted endogenous variables on all predetermined variables in the system.

The MELO method computes the minimum expected loss estimator. MELO estimators "minimize the posterior expectation of generalized quadratic loss functions for structural coefficients of linear structural models" (Judge et al. 1985, p. 635).

K-class estimators are a class of estimators that depends on a user-specified parameter k. A K-value less than 1 is recommended but not required. k may be deterministic or stochastic, but its probability limit must equal 1 for consistent parameter estimates. When all the predetermined variables are listed as instruments, they include all the other single equation estimators supported by PROC SYSLIN. The instance when some of the predetermined variables are not listed among the instruments is not supported by PROC SYSLIN for the general K-class estimation. It is, however, supported for the other methods.

For $k = 1$, the K-class estimator is the 2SLS estimator, while for $k = 0$, the K-class estimator is the OLS estimator. The K-class interpretation of LIML is that $k = \lambda$. Note that k is stochastic in the LIML method, unlike for OLS and 2SLS.

MELO is a Bayesian K-class estimator. It yields estimates that can be expressed as a matrix-weighted average of the OLS and 2SLS estimates. MELO estimators have finite second moments and hence finite risk. Other frequently used K-class estimators may not have finite moments under some commonly encountered circumstances and hence there can be infinite risk relative to quadratic and other loss functions.

One way of comparing K-class estimators is to note that when k=1, the correlation between regressor and the residual is completely corrected for. In all other cases, it is only partially corrected for.

See "Computational Details" later in this section for more details on K-class estimators.

SUR and 3SLS Estimation Methods

SUR may improve the efficiency of parameter estimates when there is contemporaneous correlation of errors across equations. In practice, the contemporaneous correlation matrix is estimated using OLS residuals. Under two sets of circumstances, SUR parameter estimates are the same as those produced by OLS: when there is no contemporaneous correlation of errors across equations (the estimate of contemporaneous correlation matrix is diagonal,) and when the independent variables are the same across equations.

Theoretically, SUR parameter estimates will always be at least as efficient as OLS in large samples, provided that your equations are correctly specified. However, in small samples the need to estimate the covariance matrix from the OLS residuals increases the sampling variability of the SUR estimates, and this effect can cause SUR to be less efficient than OLS. If the sample size is small and the across-equation correlations are small, then OLS should be preferred to SUR. The consequences of specification error are also more serious with SUR than with OLS.

The 3SLS method combines the ideas of the 2SLS and SUR methods. Like 2SLS, the 3SLS method uses $\hat{Y}$ instead of Y for endogenous regressors, which results in consistent estimates. Like SUR, the 3SLS method takes the cross-equation error correlations into account to improve large sample efficiency. For 3SLS, the 2SLS residuals are used to estimate the cross-equation error covariance matrix.

The SUR and 3SLS methods can be iterated by recomputing the estimate of the cross-equation covariance matrix from the SUR or 3SLS residuals and then computing new SUR or 3SLS estimates based on this updated covariance matrix estimate. Continuing this iteration until convergence produces ITSUR or IT3SLS estimates.

FIML Estimation Method

The FIML estimator is a system generalization of the LIML estimator. The FIML method involves minimizing the determinant of the covariance matrix associated with residuals of the reduced form of the equation system. From a maximum likelihood standpoint, the LIML method involves assuming that the errors are normally distributed and then maximizing the likelihood function subject to restrictions on a particular equation. FIML is similar, except that the likelihood function is maximized subject to restrictions on all of the parameters in the model, not just those in the equation being estimated.

Note: the RESTRICT, SRESTRICT, TEST, and STEST statements are not supported when the FIML method is used.

Choosing a Method for Simultaneous Equations

A number of factors should be taken into account in choosing an estimation method. Although system methods are asymptotically most efficient in the absence of specification error, system methods are more sensitive to specification error than single equation methods.

In practice, models are never perfectly specified. It is a matter of judgment whether the misspecification is serious enough to warrant avoidance of system methods.

Another factor to consider is sample size. With small samples, 2SLS may be preferred to 3SLS. In general, it is difficult to say much about the small sample properties of K-class estimators because this depends on the regressors used.

LIML and FIML are invariant to the normalization rule imposed but are computationally more expensive than 2SLS or 3SLS.

If the reason for contemporaneous correlation among errors across equations is a common omitted variable, it is not necessarily best to apply SUR. SUR parameter estimates are more sensitive to specification error than OLS. OLS may produce better parameter estimates under these circumstances. SUR estimates are also affected by the sampling variation of the error covariance matrix. There is some evidence from Monte Carlo studies that SUR is less efficient than OLS in small samples.

ANOVA Table for Instrumental Variables Methods

In the instrumental variables methods (2SLS, LIML, K-class, MELO), first-stage predicted values are substituted for the endogenous regressors. As a result, the regression sum of squares (RSS) and the error sum of squares (ESS) do not sum to the total corrected sum of squares for the dependent variable (TSS). The "Analysis of Variance" table printed for the second-stage results serves to display these sums of squares and the mean squares used for the F-test, but this table is not a variance decomposition in the usual analysis of variance sense.

The F-test shown in the instrumental variables case is a valid test of the no-regression hypothesis that the true coefficients of all regressors are 0. However, because of the first-stage projection of the regression mean square, this is a Wald-type test statistic, which is asymptotically F but not exactly F-distributed in finite samples. Thus, for small samples the F-test is only approximate when instrumental variables are used.

The R^2 Statistics

As explained in the section "ANOVA Table for Instrumental Variables Methods" on page 1505 when instrumental variables are used, the regression sum of squares (RSS) and the error sum of squares (ESS) do not sum to the total corrected sum of squares. In this case, there are several ways that the R^2 statistic can be defined.

The definition of R^2 used by the SYSLIN procedure is

$$\mathrm{R}^2 = \frac{\mathrm{RSS}}{\mathrm{RSS} + \mathrm{ESS}}$$

This definition is consistent with the F-test of the null hypothesis that the true coefficients of all regressors are zero. However, this R^2 may not be a good measure of the goodness of fit of the model.

System Weighted R^2 and System Weighted Mean Square Error

The system weighted R^2, printed for the 3SLS, IT3SLS, SUR, ITSUR, and FIML methods, is computed as follows.

$$\mathrm{R}^2 = \mathbf{Y'WR(X'X)^{-1}R'WY/Y'WY}$$

In this equation the matrix **X'X** is $\mathbf{R'WR}$, and **W** is the projection matrix of the instruments:

$$\mathbf{W} = \mathbf{S}^{-1} \otimes \mathbf{Z(Z'Z)^{-1}Z'}$$

The matrix **Z** is the instrument set, **R** is the the regressor set, and **S** is the estimated cross-model covariance matrix.

The system weighted MSE, printed for the 3SLS, IT3SLS, SUR, ITSUR, and FIML methods, is computed as follows:

$$MSE = \frac{1}{tdf}(\mathbf{Y'WY} - \mathbf{Y'WR}(\mathbf{X'X})^{-1}\mathbf{R'WY})$$

In this equation *tdf* is the sum of the error degrees of freedom for the equations in the system.

Computational Details

This section discusses various computational details.

Computation of Least Squares-Based Estimators

Let the system be composed of G equations, and the ith equation be expressed in this form:

$$\mathbf{y}_i = Y_i\boldsymbol{\beta}_i + X_i\boldsymbol{\gamma}_i + \mathbf{u}$$

where

- $\mathbf{y}_i$ is the vector of observations on the dependent variable
- Y_i is the matrix of observations on the endogenous variables included in the equation
- $\boldsymbol{\beta}_i$ is the vector of parameters associated with Y_i
- X_i is the matrix of observations on the predetermined variables included in the equation
- $\boldsymbol{\gamma}_i$ is the vector of parameters associated with X_i
- $\mathbf{u}$ is a vector of errors

Let $\hat{V}_i = Y_i - \hat{Y}_i$, where $\hat{Y}_i$ is the projection of Y_i onto the space spanned by the instruments matrix Z.

Let

$$\boldsymbol{\delta}_i = \begin{bmatrix} \boldsymbol{\beta}_i \\ \boldsymbol{\gamma}_i \end{bmatrix}$$

be the vector of parameters associated with both the endogenous and exogenous variables.

The K class of estimators (Theil 1971) is defined by

$$\hat{\boldsymbol{\delta}}_{i,k} = \begin{bmatrix} Y_i'Y_i - k\hat{V}_i'\hat{V}_i & Y_i'X_i \\ X_i'Y_i & X_i'X_i \end{bmatrix}^{-1} \begin{bmatrix} (Y_i - kV_i)'y_i \\ X_i'y_i \end{bmatrix}$$

where k is a user-defined value.

Let

$$R = [Y_i \;\; X_i]$$

and

$$\hat{R} = [\hat{Y}_i \;\; X_i]$$

The 2SLS estimator is defined as

$$\hat{\delta}_{i,2SLS} = [\hat{R}_i' \hat{R}_i]^{-1} \hat{R}_i' y_i$$

Let $\mathbf{y}$ and $\boldsymbol{\delta}$ be the vectors obtained by stacking the vectors of dependent variables and parameters for all G equations, and let R and $\hat{R}$ be the block diagonal matrices formed by R_i and $\hat{R}_i$, respectively.

The SUR and ITSUR estimators are defined as

$$\hat{\delta}_{(IT)SUR} = \left[R' \left(\hat{\Sigma}^{-1} \otimes I\right) R\right]^{-1} R' \left(\hat{\Sigma}^{-1} \otimes I\right) \mathbf{y}$$

while the 3SLS and IT3SLS estimators are defined as

$$\hat{\delta}_{(IT)3SLS} = \left[\hat{R}' \left(\hat{\Sigma}^{-1} \otimes I\right) \hat{R}\right]^{-1} \hat{R}' \left(\hat{\Sigma}^{-1} \otimes I\right) \mathbf{y}$$

where I is the identity matrix, and $\hat{\Sigma}$ is an estimator of the cross-equation correlation matrix. For 3SLS, $\hat{\Sigma}$ is obtained from the 2SLS estimation, while for SUR it is derived from the OLS estimation. For IT3SLS and ITSUR, it is obtained iteratively from the previous estimation step, until convergence.

Computation of Standard Errors

The VARDEF= option in the PROC SYSLIN statement controls the denominator used in calculating the cross-equation covariance estimates and the parameter standard errors and covariances. The values of the VARDEF= option and the resulting denominator are as follows:

N	uses the number of nonmissing observations.
DF	uses the number of nonmissing observations less the degrees of freedom in the model.
WEIGHT	uses the sum of the observation weights given by the WEIGHTS statement.
WDF	uses the sum of the observation weights given by the WEIGHTS statement less the degrees of freedom in the model.

The VARDEF= option does not affect the model mean square error, root mean square error, or R^2 statistics. These statistics are always based on the error degrees of freedom, regardless of the VARDEF= option. The VARDEF= option also does not affect the dependent variable coefficient of variation (C.V.).

Reduced-Form Estimates

The REDUCED option on the PROC SYSLIN statement computes estimates of the reduced-form coefficients. The REDUCED option requires that the equation system be square. If there are fewer models than endogenous variables, IDENTITY statements can be used to complete the equation system.

The reduced-form coefficients are computed as follows. Represent the equation system, with all endogenous variables moved to the left-hand side of the equations and identities, as

$$\mathbf{BY} = \mathbf{\Gamma X}$$

Here **B** is the estimated coefficient matrix for the endogenous variables **Y**, and $\mathbf{\Gamma}$ is the estimated coefficient matrix for the exogenous (or predetermined) variables **X**.

The system can be solved for **Y** as follows, provided **B** is square and nonsingular:

$$\mathbf{Y} = \mathbf{B}^{-1}\mathbf{\Gamma X}$$

The reduced-form coefficients are the matrix $\mathbf{B}^{-1}\mathbf{\Gamma}$.

Uncorrelated Errors Across Equations

The SDIAG option in the PROC SYSLIN statement computes estimates assuming uncorrelated errors across equations. As a result, when the SDIAG option is used, the 3SLS estimates are identical to 2SLS estimates, and the SUR estimates are the same as the OLS estimates.

Over Identification Restrictions

The OVERID option in the MODEL statement can be used to test for over identifying restrictions on parameters of each equation. The null hypothesis is that the predetermined variables not appearing in any equation have zero coefficients. The alternative hypothesis is that at least one of the assumed zero coefficients is nonzero. The test is approximate and rejects the null hypothesis too frequently for small sample sizes.

The formula for the test is given as follows. Let $y_i = \beta_i \mathbf{Y}_i + \gamma_i \mathbf{Z}_i + e_i$ be the *i*th equation. $\mathbf{Y}_i$ are the endogenous variables that appear as regressors in the *i*th equation, and $\mathbf{Z}_i$ are the instrumental variables that appear as regressors in the *i*th equation. Let N_i be the number of variables in $\mathbf{Y}_i$ and $\mathbf{Z}_i$.

Let $v_i = y_i - \mathbf{Y}_i \hat{\beta}_i$. Let **Z** represent all instrumental variables, *T* be the total number of observations, and *K* be the total number of instrumental variables. Define $\hat{l}$ as follows:

$$\hat{l} = \frac{v'_i(\mathbf{I} - \mathbf{Z}_i(\mathbf{Z}'_i\mathbf{Z}_i)^{-1}\mathbf{Z}'_i)v_i}{v'_i(\mathbf{I} - \mathbf{Z}(\mathbf{Z}'\mathbf{Z})^{-1}\mathbf{Z}')v_i}$$

Then the test statistic

$$\frac{T-K}{K-N_i}(\hat{l}-1)$$

is distributed approximately as an F with $K - N_i$ and $T - K$ degrees of freedom. Refer to Basmann (1960) for more information.

Fuller's Modification to LIML

The ALPHA= option in the PROC SYSLIN and MODEL statements parameterizes Fuller's modification to LIML. This modification is $k = \gamma - (\alpha/(n-g))$, where α is the value of the ALPHA= option, γ is the LIML k value, n is the number of observations, and g is the number of predetermined variables. Fuller's modification is not used unless the ALPHA= option is specified. Refer to Fuller (1977) for more information.

Missing Values

Observations having a missing value for any variable in the analysis are excluded from the computations.

OUT= Data Set

The output SAS data set produced by the OUT= option in the PROC SYSLIN statement contains all the variables in the input data set and the variables containing predicted values and residuals specified by OUTPUT statements.

The residuals are computed as actual values minus predicted values. Predicted values never use lags of other predicted values, as would be desirable for dynamic simulation. For these applications, PROC SIMLIN is available to predict or simulate values from the estimated equations.

OUTEST= Data Set

The OUTEST= option produces a TYPE=EST output SAS data set containing estimates from the regressions. The variables in the OUTEST= data set are as follows:

BY variables — the BY statement variables are included in the OUTEST= data set

TYPE — identifies the estimation type for the observations. The _TYPE_ value INST indicates first-stage regression estimates. Other values indicate the estimation method used: 2SLS indicates two-stage least squares results, 3SLS indicates three-stage least squares results, LIML indicates limited information maximum likelihood results, and so forth. Observations added by IDENTITY statements have the _TYPE_ value IDENTITY.

MODEL — the model label. The model label is the label specified on the MODEL statement or the dependent variable name if no label is specified. For first-stage regression estimates, _MODEL_ has the value FIRST.

DEPVAR	the name of the dependent variable for the model
NAME	the names of the regressors for the rows of the covariance matrix, if the COVOUT option is specified. _NAME_ has a blank value for the parameter estimates observations. The _NAME_ variable is not included in the OUTEST= data set unless the COVOUT option is used to output the covariance of parameter estimates matrix.
SIGMA	contains the root mean square error for the model, which is an estimate of the standard deviation of the error term. The _SIGMA_ variable contains the same values reported as Root MSE in the printed output.
INTERCEPT	the intercept parameter estimates
regressors	the regressor variables from all the MODEL statements are included in the OUTEST= data set. Variables used in IDENTIFY statements are also included in the OUTEST= data set.

The parameter estimates are stored under the names of the regressor variables. The intercept parameters are stored in the variable INTERCEP. The dependent variable of the model is given a coefficient of -1. Variables not in a model have missing values for the OUTEST= observations for that model.

Some estimation methods require computation of preliminary estimates. All estimates computed are output to the OUTEST= data set. For each BY group and each estimation, the OUTEST= data set contains one observation for each MODEL or IDENTITY statement. Results for different estimations are identified by the _TYPE_ variable.

For example, consider the following statements:

```
proc syslin data=a outest=est 3sls;
   by b;
   endogenous y1 y2;
   instruments x1-x4;
   model y1 = y2 x1 x2;
   model y2 = y1 x3 x4;
   identity x1 = x3 + x4;
run;
```

The 3SLS method requires both a preliminary 2SLS stage and preliminary first stage regressions for the endogenous variable. The OUTEST= data set thus contains 3 different kinds of estimates. The observations for the first-stage regression estimates have the _TYPE_ value INST. The observations for the 2SLS estimates have the _TYPE_ value 2SLS. The observations for the final 3SLS estimates have the _TYPE_ value 3SLS.

Since there are 2 endogenous variables in this example, there are 2 first-stage regressions and 2 _TYPE_=INST observations in the OUTEST= data set. Since there are 2 model statements, there are 2 OUTEST= observations with _TYPE_=2SLS and 2 observations with _TYPE_=3SLS. In addition, the OUTEST= data set contains an observation with the _TYPE_ value IDENTITY containing the coefficients specified by the IDENTITY statement. All these observations are repeated for each BY-group in the input data set defined by the values of the BY variable B.

When the COVOUT option is specified, the estimated covariance matrix for the parameter estimates is included in the OUTEST= data set. Each observation for parameter estimates is followed by observations containing the rows of the parameter covariance matrix for that model. The row of the covariance matrix is identified by the variable _NAME_. For observations that contain parameter estimates, _NAME_ is blank. For covariance observations, _NAME_ contains the regressor name for the row of the covariance matrix, and the regressor variables contain the covariances.

See Example 26.1 for an example of the OUTEST= data set.

OUTSSCP= Data Set

The OUTSSCP= option produces a TYPE=SSCP output SAS data set containing sums of squares and cross products. The data set contains all variables used in the MODEL, IDENTITY, and VAR statements. Observations are identified by the variable _NAME_.

The OUTSSCP= data set can be useful when a large number of observations are to be explored in many different SYSLIN runs. The sum-of-squares-and-crossproducts matrix can be saved with the OUTSSCP= option and used as the DATA= data set on subsequent SYSLIN runs. This is much less expensive computationally because PROC SYSLIN never reads the original data again. In the step that creates the OUTSSCP= data set, include in the VAR statement all the variables you expect to use.

Printed Output

The printed output produced by the SYSLIN procedure is as follows:

1. If the SIMPLE option is used, a table of descriptive statistics is printed showing the sum, mean, sum of squares, variance, and standard deviation for all the variables used in the models.
2. First-stage regression results are printed if the FIRST option is specified and an instrumental variables method is used. This shows the regression of each endogenous variable on the variables in the INSTRUMENTS list.
3. The results of the second-stage regression are printed for each model. (See "Printed Output for Each Model," which follows.)
4. If a systems method like 3SLS, SUR, or FIML is used, the cross-equation error covariance matrix is printed. This matrix is shown four ways: the covariance matrix itself, the correlation matrix form, the inverse of the correlation matrix, and the inverse of the covariance matrix.
5. If a systems method like 3SLS, SUR, or FIML is used, the system weighted mean square error and system weighted R^2 statistics are printed. The system weighted MSE and R^2 measure the fit of the joint model obtained by stacking

all the models together and performing a single regression with the stacked observations weighted by the inverse of the model error variances.

6. If a systems method like 3SLS, SUR, or FIML is used, the final results are printed for each model.
7. If the REDUCED option is used, the reduced-form coefficients are printed. This consists of the structural coefficient matrix for the endogenous variables, the structural coefficient matrix for the exogenous variables, the inverse of the endogenous coefficient matrix, and the reduced-form coefficient matrix. The reduced-form coefficient matrix is the product of the inverse of the endogenous coefficient matrix and the exogenous structural coefficient matrix.

Printed Output for Each Model

The results printed for each model include the "Analysis of Variance" table, the "Parameter Estimates" table, and optional items requested by TEST statements or by options on the MODEL statement.

The printed output produced for each model is described in the following.

The Analysis of Variance table includes the following:

- the model degrees of freedom, sum of squares, and mean square
- the error degrees of freedom, sum of squares, and mean square. The error mean square is computed by dividing the error sum of squares by the error degrees of freedom and is not effected by the VARDEF= option.
- the corrected total degrees of freedom and total sum of squares. Note that for instrumental variables methods the model and error sums of squares do not add to the total sum of squares.
- the F-ratio, labeled "F Value," and its significance, labeled "PROB>F," for the test of the hypothesis that all the nonintercept parameters are 0
- the root mean square error. This is the square root of the error mean square.
- the dependent variable mean
- the coefficient of variation (C.V.) of the dependent variable
- the R^2 statistic. This R^2 is computed consistently with the calculation of the F statistic. It is valid for hypothesis tests but may not be a good measure of fit for models estimated by instrumental variables methods.
- the R^2 statistic adjusted for model degrees of freedom, labeled "Adj R-SQ"

The Parameter Estimates table includes the following.

- estimates of parameters for regressors in the model and the Lagrangian parameter for each restriction specified
- a degrees of freedom column labeled DF. Estimated model parameters have 1 degree of freedom. Restrictions have a DF of -1. Regressors or restrictions dropped from the model due to collinearity have a DF of 0.

- the standard errors of the parameter estimates
- the t statistics, which are the parameter estimates divided by the standard errors
- the significance of the *t*-tests for the hypothesis that the true parameter is 0, labeled "Pr > |t|." As previously noted, the significance tests are strictly valid in finite samples only for OLS estimates but are asymptotically valid for the other methods.
- the standardized regression coefficients, if the STB option is specified. This is the parameter estimate multiplied by the ratio of the standard deviation of the regressor to the standard deviation of the dependent variable.
- the labels of the regressor variables or restriction labels

In addition to the Analysis of Variance table and the Parameter Estimates table, the results printed for each model may include the following:

1. If TEST statements are specified, the test results are printed.
2. If the DW option is specified, the Durbin-Watson statistic and first-order autocorrelation coefficient are printed.
3. If the OVERID option is specified, the results of Basmann's test for overidentifying restrictions are printed.
4. If the PLOT option is used, plots of residual against each regressor are printed.
5. If the COVB or CORRB options are specified, the results for each model also include the covariance or correlation matrix of the parameter estimates. For systems methods like 3SLS and FIML, the COVB and CORB output is printed for the whole system after the output for the last model, instead of separately for each model.

The third stage output for 3SLS, SUR, IT3SLS, ITSUR, and FIML does not include the Analysis of Variance table. When a systems method is used, the second stage output does not include the optional output, except for the COVB and CORB matrices.

ODS Table Names

PROC SYSLIN assigns a name to each table it creates. You can use these names to reference the table when using the Output Delivery System (ODS) to select tables and create output data sets. These names are listed in the following table. For more information on ODS, see Chapter 8, "Using the Output Delivery System."

Table 26.1. ODS Tables Produced in PROC SYSLIN

ODS Table Name	Description	Option
ANOVA	Summary of the SSE, MSE for the equations	default
AugXPXMat	Model Crossproducts	XPX
AutoCorrStat	Autocorrelation Statistics	default
ConvCrit	Convergence criteria for estimation	default
ConvergenceStatus	Convergence status	default
CorrB	Correlations of parameters	CORRB
CorrResiduals	Correlations of residuals	CORRS
CovB	Covariance of parameters	COVB
CovResiduals	Covariance of residuals	
EndoMat	Endogenous Variables	
Equations	Listing of equations to estimate	default
ExogMat	Exogenous Variables	
FitStatistics	Statistics of Fit	default
InvCorrResiduals	Inverse Correlations of residuals	CORRS
InvCovResiduals	InvCovariance of residuals	COVS
InvEndoMat	Inverse Endogenous Variables	
InvXPX	$X'X$ inverse for System	I
IterHistory	Iteration printing	ITALL/ITPRINT
MissingValues	Missing values generated by the program	default
ModelVars	Name and label for the Model	default
ParameterEstimates	Parameter Estimates	default
RedMat	Reduced Form	REDUCED
SimpleStatistics	Descriptive statistics	SIMPLE
SSCP	Model Crossproducts	
TestResults	Test for Overidentifying Restrictions	
Weight	Weighted Model Statistics	
YPY	Y'Y matrices	USSCP2

ODS Graphics (Experimental)

This section describes the use of ODS for creating graphics with the SYSLIN procedure. These graphics are experimental in this release, meaning that both the graphical results and the syntax for specifying them are subject to change in a future release.

ODS Graph Names

PROC SYSLIN assigns a name to each graph it creates using ODS. You can use these names to reference the graphs when using ODS. The names are listed in Table 26.2.

To request these graphs, you must specify the ODS GRAPHICS statement. For more information on the ODS GRAPHICS statement, see Chapter 9, "Statistical Graphics Using ODS."

Table 26.2. ODS Graphics Produced by PROC SYSLIN

ODS Graph Name	Plot Description
ActualByPredicted	Predicted vs actual plot
QQPlot	QQ plot of residuals
ResidualHistogram	Histogram of the residuals
ResidualPlot	Residual plot

Examples

Example 26.1. Klein's Model I Estimated with LIML and 3SLS

This example uses PROC SYSLIN to estimate the classic Klein Model I. For a discussion of this model, see Theil (1971). The following statements read the data.

```
*---------------------------Klein's Model I----------------------------*
| By L.R. Klein, Economic Fluctuations in the United States, 1921-1941 |
| (1950), NY: John Wiley.   A macro-economic model of the U.S. with    |
| three behavioral equations, and several identities. See Theil, p.456.|
*----------------------------------------------------------------------*;
data klein;
input year c p w i x wp g t k wsum;
   date=mdy(1,1,year);
   format date monyy.;
   y   =c+i+g-t;
   yr  =year-1931;
   klag=lag(k);
   plag=lag(p);
   xlag=lag(x);
   label year='Year'
         date='Date'
         c   ='Consumption'
         p   ='Profits'
         w   ='Private Wage Bill'
         i   ='Investment'
         k   ='Capital Stock'
         y   ='National Income'
         x   ='Private Production'
         wsum='Total Wage Bill'
         wp  ='Govt Wage Bill'
         g   ='Govt Demand'
         i   ='Taxes'
         klag='Capital Stock Lagged'
         plag='Profits Lagged'
         xlag='Private Product Lagged'
         yr  ='YEAR-1931';
  datalines;
1920    .   12.7    .     .   44.9    .     .     .   182.8    .
1921  41.9  12.4  25.5 -0.2  45.6   2.7   3.9   7.7   182.6  28.2
1922  45.0  16.9  29.3  1.9  50.1   2.9   3.2   3.9   184.5  32.2
1923  49.2  18.4  34.1  5.2  57.2   2.9   2.8   4.7   189.7  37.0
1924  50.6  19.4  33.9  3.0  57.1   3.1   3.5   3.8   192.7  37.0
1925  52.6  20.1  35.4  5.1  61.0   3.2   3.3   5.5   197.8  38.6
1926  55.1  19.6  37.4  5.6  64.0   3.3   3.3   7.0   203.4  40.7
1927  56.2  19.8  37.9  4.2  64.4   3.6   4.0   6.7   207.6  41.5
1928  57.3  21.1  39.2  3.0  64.5   3.7   4.2   4.2   210.6  42.9
```

```
1929  57.8  21.7  41.3  5.1  67.0  4.0   4.1   4.0  215.7  45.3
1930  55.0  15.6  37.9  1.0  61.2  4.2   5.2   7.7  216.7  42.1
1931  50.9  11.4  34.5 -3.4  53.4  4.8   5.9   7.5  213.3  39.3
1932  45.6   7.0  29.0 -6.2  44.3  5.3   4.9   8.3  207.1  34.3
1933  46.5  11.2  28.5 -5.1  45.1  5.6   3.7   5.4  202.0  34.1
1934  48.7  12.3  30.6 -3.0  49.7  6.0   4.0   6.8  199.0  36.6
1935  51.3  14.0  33.2 -1.3  54.4  6.1   4.4   7.2  197.7  39.3
1936  57.7  17.6  36.8  2.1  62.7  7.4   2.9   8.3  199.8  44.2
1937  58.7  17.3  41.0  2.0  65.0  6.7   4.3   6.7  201.8  47.7
1938  57.5  15.3  38.2 -1.9  60.9  7.7   5.3   7.4  199.9  45.9
1939  61.6  19.0  41.6  1.3  69.5  7.8   6.6   8.9  201.2  49.4
1940  65.0  21.1  45.0  3.3  75.7  8.0   7.4   9.6  204.5  53.0
1941  69.7  23.5  53.3  4.9  88.4  8.5  13.8  11.6  209.4  61.8
;
run;
```

The following statements estimate the Klein model using the limited information maximum likelihood method. In addition, the parameter estimates are written to a SAS data set with the OUTEST= option.

```
proc syslin data=klein outest=b liml;
   endogenous c p w i x wsum k y;
   instruments klag plag xlag wp g t yr;
   consume: model c = p plag  wsum;
   invest:  model i = p plag  klag;
   labor:   model w = x xlag  yr;
run;


proc print data=b; run;
```

The PROC SYSLIN estimates are shown in Output 26.1.1 through Output 26.1.3.

Output 26.1.1. LIML Estimates for Consumption

The SYSLIN Procedure
Limited-Information Maximum Likelihood Estimation

Model	CONSUME
Dependent Variable	c
Label	Consumption

Analysis of Variance

Source	DF	Sum of Squares	Mean Square	F Value	Pr > F
Model	3	854.3541	284.7847	118.42	<.0001
Error	17	40.88419	2.404952		
Corrected Total	20	941.4295			

Root MSE	1.55079	R-Square	0.95433
Dependent Mean	53.99524	Adj R-Sq	0.94627
Coeff Var	2.87209		

Parameter Estimates

Variable	DF	Parameter Estimate	Standard Error	t Value	Pr > |t|	Variable Label
Intercept	1	17.14765	2.045374	8.38	<.0001	Intercept
p	1	-0.22251	0.224230	-0.99	0.3349	Profits
plag	1	0.396027	0.192943	2.05	0.0558	Profits Lagged
wsum	1	0.822559	0.061549	13.36	<.0001	Total Wage Bill

Output 26.1.2. LIML Estimates for Investments

```
                 Limited-Information Maximum Likelihood Estimation

                          Model                        INVEST
                          Dependent Variable                i
                          Label                         Taxes


                               Analysis of Variance

                                      Sum of           Mean
      Source                  DF     Squares         Square     F Value    Pr > F

      Model                    3    210.3790       70.12634       34.06    <.0001
      Error                   17    34.99649       2.058617
      Corrected Total         20    252.3267


              Root MSE              1.43479    R-Square        0.85738
              Dependent Mean        1.26667    Adj R-Sq        0.83221
              Coeff Var           113.27274


                               Parameter Estimates

                    Parameter  Standard                        Variable
 Variable       DF   Estimate     Error  t Value  Pr > |t|  Label

 Intercept       1   22.59083  9.498146     2.38    0.0294  Intercept
 p               1   0.075185  0.224712     0.33    0.7420  Profits
 plag            1   0.680386  0.209145     3.25    0.0047  Profits Lagged
 klag            1   -0.16826  0.045345    -3.71    0.0017  Capital Stock Lagged
```

Output 26.1.3. LIML Estimates for Labor

Limited-Information Maximum Likelihood Estimation

Model	LABOR
Dependent Variable	w
Label	Private Wage Bill

Analysis of Variance

Source	DF	Sum of Squares	Mean Square	F Value	Pr > F
Model	3	696.1485	232.0495	393.62	<.0001
Error	17	10.02192	0.589525		
Corrected Total	20	794.9095			

Root MSE	0.76781	R-Square	0.98581
Dependent Mean	36.36190	Adj R-Sq	0.98330
Coeff Var	2.11156		

Parameter Estimates

Variable	DF	Parameter Estimate	Standard Error	t Value	Pr > |t|	Variable Label
Intercept	1	1.526187	1.320838	1.16	0.2639	Intercept
x	1	0.433941	0.075507	5.75	<.0001	Private Production
xlag	1	0.151321	0.074527	2.03	0.0583	Private Product Lagged
yr	1	0.131593	0.035995	3.66	0.0020	YEAR-1931

The OUTEST= data set is shown in part in Output 26.1.4. Note that the data set contains the parameter estimates and root mean square errors, _SIGMA_, for the first stage instrumental regressions as well as the parameter estimates and σ for the LIML estimates for the three structural equations.

Output 26.1.4. The OUTEST= Data Set

Obs	_TYPE_	_STATUS_	_MODEL_	_DEPVAR_	_SIGMA_	Intercept	klag	plag
1	LIML	0 Converged	CONSUME	c	1.55079	17.1477	.	0.39603
2	LIML	0 Converged	INVEST	i	1.43479	22.5908	-0.16826	0.68039
3	LIML	0 Converged	LABOR	w	0.76781	1.5262	.	.

Obs	xlag	wp	g	t	yr	c	p	w	i	x	wsum	k	y
1	.	.	.	.	.	-1	-0.22251	.	.	.	0.82256	.	.
2	.	.	.	.	.	.	0.07518	.	-1	.	.	.	.
3	0.15132	.	.	.	0.13159	.	.	-1	.	0.43394	.	.	.

The following statements estimate the model using the 3SLS method. The reduced-form estimates are produced by the REDUCED option; IDENTITY statements are used to make the model complete.

```
proc syslin data=klein 3sls reduced;
   endogenous c p w i x wsum k y;
   instruments klag plag xlag wp g t yr;
   consume: model    c = p plag wsum;
   invest:  model    i = p plag klag;
   labor:   model    w = x xlag yr;
   product: identity x = c + i + g;
   income:  identity y = c + i + g - t;
   profit:  identity p = y - w;
   stock:   identity k = klag + i;
   wage:    identity wsum = w + wp;
run;
```

The preliminary 2SLS results and estimated cross-model covariance matrix are not shown. The 3SLS estimates are shown in Output 26.1.5 through Output 26.1.7. The reduced-form estimates are shown in Output 26.1.8 through Output 26.1.11.

Output 26.1.5. 3SLS Estimates for Consumption

```
                              The SYSLIN Procedure
                       Three-Stage Least Squares Estimation

                      System Weighted MSE              5.9342
                      Degrees of freedom                   51
                      System Weighted R-Square         0.9550


                        Model                       CONSUME
                        Dependent Variable                c
                        Label                   Consumption


                              Parameter Estimates

                         Parameter  Standard                          Variable
Variable          DF     Estimate      Error  t Value  Pr > |t|  Label

Intercept          1     16.44079   1.449925    11.34    <.0001  Intercept
p                  1     0.124890   0.120179     1.04    0.3133  Profits
plag               1     0.163144   0.111631     1.46    0.1621  Profits Lagged
wsum               1     0.790081   0.042166    18.74    <.0001  Total Wage Bill
```

Output 26.1.6. 3SLS Estimates for Investments

Three-Stage Least Squares Estimation

Model	INVEST
Dependent Variable	i
Label	Taxes

Parameter Estimates

Variable	DF	Parameter Estimate	Standard Error	t Value	Pr > |t|	Variable Label
Intercept	1	28.17785	7.550853	3.73	0.0017	Intercept
p	1	-0.01308	0.179938	-0.07	0.9429	Profits
plag	1	0.755724	0.169976	4.45	0.0004	Profits Lagged
klag	1	-0.19485	0.036156	-5.39	<.0001	Capital Stock Lagged

Output 26.1.7. 3SLS Estimates for Labor

Three-Stage Least Squares Estimation

Model	LABOR
Dependent Variable	w
Label	Private Wage Bill

Output 26.1.8. Reduced-Form Estimates

Three-Stage Least Squares Estimation

Endogenous Variables

	c	p	w	i
CONSUME	1	-0.12489	0	0
INVEST	0	0.013079	0	1
LABOR	0	0	1	0
PRODUCT	-1	0	0	-1
INCOME	-1	0	0	-1
PROFIT	0	1	1	0
STOCK	0	0	0	-1
WAGE	0	0	-1	0

Endogenous Variables

	x	wsum	k	y
CONSUME	0	-0.79008	0	0
INVEST	0	0	0	0
LABOR	-0.40049	0	0	0
PRODUCT	1	0	0	0
INCOME	0	0	0	1
PROFIT	0	0	0	-1
STOCK	0	0	1	0
WAGE	0	1	0	0

Output 26.1.9. Reduced-Form Estimates

Three-Stage Least Squares Estimation

Exogenous Variables

	Intercept	plag	klag	xlag
CONSUME	16.44079	0.163144	0	0
INVEST	28.17785	0.755724	-0.19485	0
LABOR	1.797218	0	0	0.181291
PRODUCT	0	0	0	0
INCOME	0	0	0	0
PROFIT	0	0	0	0
STOCK	0	0	1	0
WAGE	0	0	0	0

Exogenous Variables

	yr	g	t	wp
CONSUME	0	0	0	0
INVEST	0	0	0	0
LABOR	0.149674	0	0	0
PRODUCT	0	1	0	0
INCOME	0	1	-1	0
PROFIT	0	0	0	0
STOCK	0	0	0	0
WAGE	0	0	0	1

Output 26.1.10. Reduced-Form Estimates

Three-Stage Least Squares Estimation

Inverse Endogenous Variables

	CONSUME	INVEST	LABOR	PRODUCT
c	1.634654	0.634654	1.095657	0.438802
p	0.972364	0.972364	-0.34048	-0.13636
w	0.649572	0.649572	1.440585	0.576943
i	-0.01272	0.987282	0.004453	0.001783
x	1.621936	1.621936	1.10011	1.440585
wsum	0.649572	0.649572	1.440585	0.576943
k	-0.01272	0.987282	0.004453	0.001783
y	1.621936	1.621936	1.10011	0.440585

Inverse Endogenous Variables

	INCOME	PROFIT	STOCK	WAGE
c	0.195852	0.195852	9.2E-17	1.291509
p	1.108721	1.108721	5.51E-17	0.768246
w	0.072629	0.072629	3.68E-17	0.513215
i	-0.0145	-0.0145	1.85E-20	-0.01005
x	0.181351	0.181351	9.2E-17	1.281461
wsum	0.072629	0.072629	1.08E-16	1.513215
k	-0.0145	-0.0145	1	-0.01005
y	1.181351	0.181351	9.2E-17	1.281461

Output 26.1.11. Reduced-Form Estimates

Three-Stage Least Squares Estimation

Reduced Form

	Intercept	plag	klag	xlag
c	46.7273	0.746307	-0.12366	0.198633
p	42.77363	0.893474	-0.18946	-0.06173
w	31.57207	0.596871	-0.12657	0.261165
i	27.6184	0.744038	-0.19237	0.000807
x	74.3457	1.490345	-0.31603	0.19944
wsum	31.57207	0.596871	-0.12657	0.261165
k	27.6184	0.744038	0.80763	0.000807
y	74.3457	1.490345	-0.31603	0.19944

Reduced Form

	yr	g	t	wp
c	0.163991	0.634654	-0.19585	1.291509
p	-0.05096	0.972364	-1.10872	0.768246
w	0.215618	0.649572	-0.07263	0.513215
i	0.000667	-0.01272	0.014501	-0.01005
x	0.164658	1.621936	-0.18135	1.281461
wsum	0.215618	0.649572	-0.07263	1.513215
k	0.000667	-0.01272	0.014501	-0.01005
y	0.164658	1.621936	-1.18135	1.281461

Example 26.2. Grunfeld's Model Estimated with SUR

The following example was used by Zellner in his classic 1962 paper on seemingly unrelated regressions. Different stock prices often move in the same direction at a given point in time. The SUR technique may provide more efficient estimates than OLS in this situation.

The following statements read the data. (The prefix GE stands for General Electric and WH stands for Westinghouse.)

```
*---------Zellner's Seemingly Unrelated Technique------------*
| A. Zellner, "An Efficient Method of Estimating Seemingly    |
| Unrelated Regressions and Tests for Aggregation Bias,"      |
| JASA 57(1962) pp.348-364                                    |
|                                                             |
| J.C.G. Boot, "Investment Demand: an Empirical Contribution  |
| to the Aggregation Problem," IER 1(1960) pp.3-30.           |
|                                                             |
| Y. Grunfeld, "The Determinants of Corporate Investment,"    |
| Unpublished thesis, Chicago, 1958                           |
*-------------------------------------------------------------*;

data grunfeld;
   input year ge_i ge_f ge_c wh_i wh_f wh_c;
   label ge_i = 'Gross Investment, GE'
         ge_c = 'Capital Stock Lagged, GE'
         ge_f = 'Value of Outstanding Shares Lagged, GE'
         wh_i = 'Gross Investment, WH'
         wh_c = 'Capital Stock Lagged, WH'
         wh_f = 'Value of Outstanding Shares Lagged, WH';
   datalines;
1935     33.1      1170.6    97.8      12.93     191.5     1.8
1936     45.0      2015.8    104.4     25.90     516.0     .8
1937     77.2      2803.3    118.0     35.05     729.0     7.4
1938     44.6      2039.7    156.2     22.89     560.4     18.1
1939     48.1      2256.2    172.6     18.84     519.9     23.5
1940     74.4      2132.2    186.6     28.57     628.5     26.5
1941     113.0     1834.1    220.9     48.51     537.1     36.2
1942     91.9      1588.0    287.8     43.34     561.2     60.8
1943     61.3      1749.4    319.9     37.02     617.2     84.4
1944     56.8      1687.2    321.3     37.81     626.7     91.2
1945     93.6      2007.7    319.6     39.27     737.2     92.4
1946     159.9     2208.3    346.0     53.46     760.5     86.0
1947     147.2     1656.7    456.4     55.56     581.4     111.1
1948     146.3     1604.4    543.4     49.56     662.3     130.6
1949     98.3      1431.8    618.3     32.04     583.8     141.8
1950     93.5      1610.5    647.4     32.24     635.2     136.7
1951     135.2     1819.4    671.3     54.38     723.8     129.7
1952     157.3     2079.7    726.1     71.78     864.1     145.5
1953     179.5     2371.6    800.3     90.08     1193.5    174.8
1954     189.6     2759.9    888.9     68.60     1188.9    213.5
;
```

The following statements compute the SUR estimates for the Grunfeld model.

```
proc syslin data=grunfeld sur;
   ge:      model ge_i = ge_f ge_c;
```

```
    westing: model wh_i = wh_f wh_c;
run;
```

The PROC SYSLIN output is shown in Output 26.2.1.

Output 26.2.1. PROC SYSLIN Output for SUR

```
                         The SYSLIN Procedure
                    Ordinary Least Squares Estimation

               Model                                      GE
               Dependent Variable                       ge_i
               Label                   Gross Investment, GE


                         Analysis of Variance

                                  Sum of        Mean
   Source                 DF     Squares      Square    F Value    Pr > F

   Model                   2    31632.03    15816.02      20.34    <.0001
   Error                  17    13216.59    777.4463
   Corrected Total        19    44848.62

            Root MSE            27.88272    R-Square       0.70531
            Dependent Mean     102.29000    Adj R-Sq       0.67064
            Coeff Var           27.25850


                         Parameter Estimates

                     Parameter Standard                    Variable
Variable        DF   Estimate      Error t Value Pr > |t|  Label

Intercept        1   -9.95631 31.37425   -0.32   0.7548  Intercept
ge_f             1   0.026551 0.015566    1.71   0.1063  Value of Outstanding Shares
                                                         Lagged, GE
ge_c             1   0.151694 0.025704    5.90   <.0001  Capital Stock Lagged, GE
```

The SYSLIN Procedure
Ordinary Least Squares Estimation

Model	WESTING
Dependent Variable	wh_i
Label	Gross Investment, WH

Analysis of Variance

Source	DF	Sum of Squares	Mean Square	F Value	Pr > F
Model	2	5165.553	2582.776	24.76	<.0001
Error	17	1773.234	104.3079		
Corrected Total	19	6938.787			

Root MSE	10.21312	R-Square	0.74445
Dependent Mean	42.89150	Adj R-Sq	0.71438
Coeff Var	23.81153		

Parameter Estimates

Variable	DF	Parameter Estimate	Standard Error	t Value	Pr > |t|	Variable Label
Intercept	1	-0.50939	8.015289	-0.06	0.9501	Intercept
wh_f	1	0.052894	0.015707	3.37	0.0037	Value of Outstanding Shares Lagged, WH
wh_c	1	0.092406	0.056099	1.65	0.1179	Capital Stock Lagged, WH

The SYSLIN Procedure
Seemingly Unrelated Regression Estimation

Cross Model Covariance

	GE	WESTING
GE	777.446	207.587
WESTING	207.587	104.308

Cross Model Correlation

	GE	WESTING
GE	1.00000	0.72896
WESTING	0.72896	1.00000

Cross Model Inverse Correlation

	GE	WESTING
GE	2.13397	-1.55559
WESTING	-1.55559	2.13397

Cross Model Inverse Covariance

	GE	WESTING
GE	0.002745	-.005463
WESTING	-.005463	0.020458

The SYSLIN Procedure
Seemingly Unrelated Regression Estimation

System Weighted MSE	0.9719
Degrees of freedom	34
System Weighted R-Square	0.6284

Model	GE
Dependent Variable	ge_i
Label	Gross Investment, GE

Parameter Estimates

Variable	DF	Parameter Estimate	Standard Error	t Value	Pr > |t|	Variable Label
Intercept	1	-27.7193	29.32122	-0.95	0.3577	Intercept
ge_f	1	0.038310	0.014415	2.66	0.0166	Value of Outstanding Shares Lagged, GE
ge_c	1	0.139036	0.024986	5.56	<.0001	Capital Stock Lagged, GE

```
                    The SYSLIN Procedure
            Seemingly Unrelated Regression Estimation

            Model                                  WESTING
            Dependent Variable                        wh_i
            Label                     Gross Investment, WH


                        Parameter Estimates

                 Parameter Standard                      Variable
Variable      DF  Estimate     Error t Value Pr > |t| Label

Intercept      1  -1.25199 7.545217    -0.17   0.8702 Intercept
wh_f           1  0.057630 0.014546     3.96   0.0010 Value of Outstanding Shares
                                                      Lagged, WH
wh_c           1  0.063978 0.053041     1.21   0.2443 Capital Stock Lagged, WH
```

Example 26.3. Illustration of ODS Graphics (Experimental)

This example illustrates the use of experimental ODS graphics. This is a continuation of Example 26.1 on page 1515. These graphical displays are requested by specifying the experimental ODS GRAPHICS statement. For general information about ODS graphics, see Chapter 9, "Statistical Graphics Using ODS." For specific information about the graphics available in the SYSLIN procedure, see the "ODS Graphics" section on page 1514.

The following statements show how to generate ODS graphics plots with the SYSLIN procedure. The plots of residuals for each one of the equations in the model are displayed in Output 26.3.1 through Output 26.3.3.

```
ods html;
ods graphics on;

proc syslin data=klein outest=b liml;
   endogenous c p w i x wsum k y;
   instruments klag plag xlag wp g t yr;
   consume: model c = p plag  wsum;
   invest:  model i = p plag  klag;
   labor:   model w = x xlag  yr;
run;

ods graphics off;
ods html close;
```

Output 26.3.1. Residuals Plot for Consumption (Experimental)

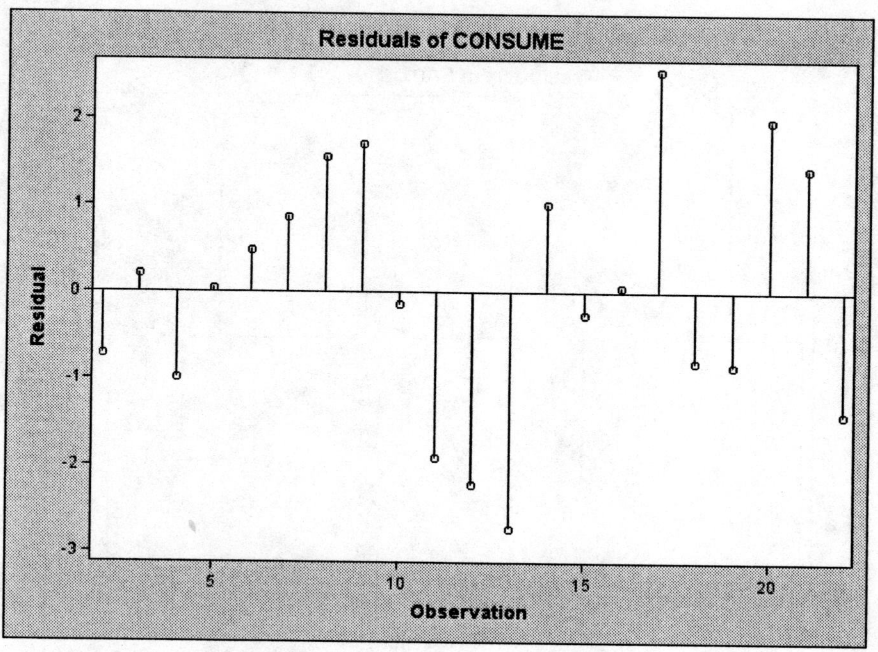

Output 26.3.2. Residuals Plot for Investments (Experimental)

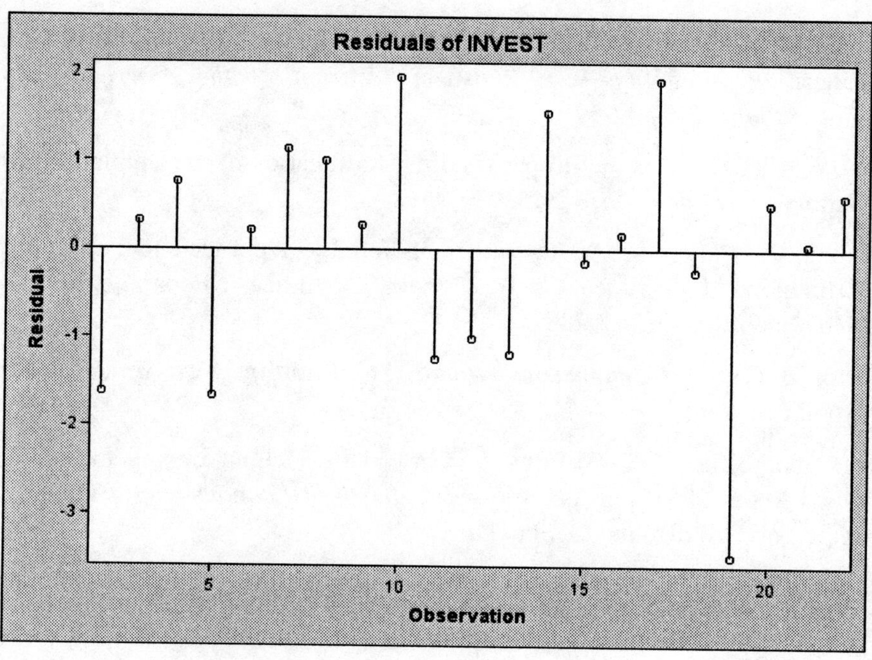

Output 26.3.3. Residuals Plot for Labor (Experimental)

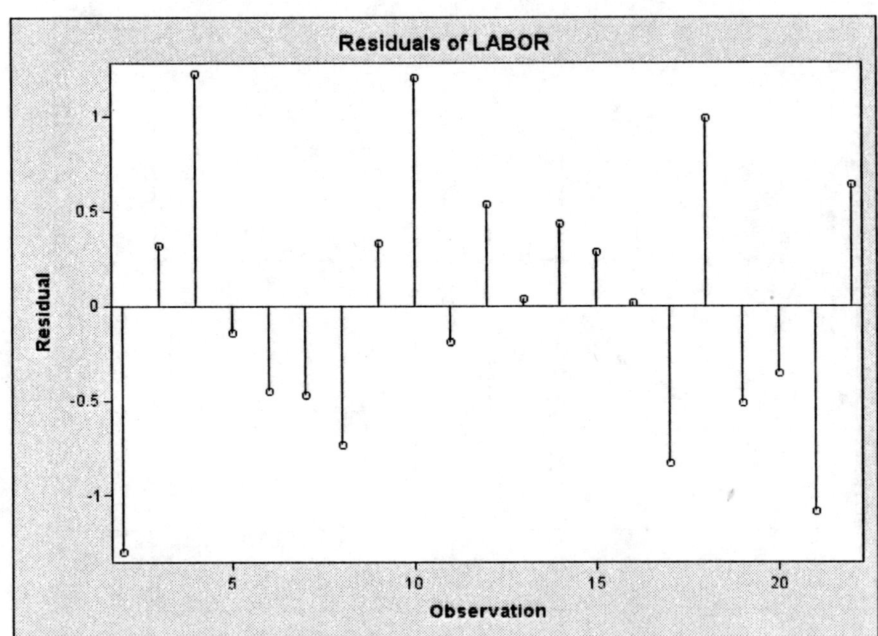

References

Basmann, R.L. (1960), "On Finite Sample Distributions of Generalized Classical Linear Identifiability Test Statistics," *Journal of the American Statistical Association*, 55, 650-659.

Fuller, W.A. (1977), "Some Properties of a Modification of the Limited Information Estimator," *Econometrica*, 45, 939-952.

Hausman, J.A. (1975), "An Instrumental Variable Approach to Full Information Estimators for Linear and Certain Nonlinear Econometric Models," *Econometrica*, 43, 727-738.

Johnston, J. (1984), *Econometric Methods*, Third Edition, New York: McGraw-Hill Book Company.

Judge, George G., W. E. Griffiths, R. Carter Hill, Helmut Lutkepohl, and Tsoung-Chao Lee (1985), *The Theory and Practice of Econometrics*, Second Edition, New York: John Wiley & Sons, Inc.

Maddala, G.S. (1977), *Econometrics*, New York: McGraw-Hill Book Company.

Park, S.B. (1982), "Some Sampling Properties of Minimum Expected Loss (MELO) Estimators of Structural Coefficients," *Journal of the Econometrics*, 18, 295-311.

Pindyck, R.S. and Rubinfeld, D.L. (1981), *Econometric Models and Economic Forecasts*, Second Edition, New York: McGraw-Hill Book Company.

Pringle, R.M. and Raynor, A.A. (1971), *Generalized Inverse Matrices with Applications to Statistics*, New York: Hafner Publishing Company.

Rao, P. (1974), "Specification Bias in Seemingly Unrelated Regressions," in *Essays in Honor of Tinbergen*, Volume 2, New York: International Arts and Sciences Press.

Savin, N.E. and White, K.J. (1978), "Testing for Autocorrelation with Missing Observations," *Econometrics*, 46, 59-66.

Theil, H. (1971), *Principles of Econometrics*, New York: John Wiley & Sons, Inc.

Zellner, A. (1962), "An Efficient Method of Estimating Seemingly Unrelated Regressions and Tests for Aggregation Bias," *Journal of the American Statistical Association*, 57, 348-368.

Zellner, A. (1978), "Estimation of Functions of Population Means and Regression Coefficients: A Minimum Expected Loss (MELO) Approach," *Journal of the Econometrics*, 8, 127-158.

Zellner, A. and Park, S. (1979), "Minimum Expected Loss (MELO) Estimators for Functions of Parameters and Structural Coefficients of Econometric Models," *Journal of the American Statistical Association*, 74, 185-193.

Chapter 27
The TSCSREG Procedure

Chapter Contents

Chapter 27
The TSCSREG Procedure

Overview

The TSCSREG (**T**ime **S**eries **C**ross **S**ection **Reg**ression) procedure analyzes a class of linear econometric models that commonly arise when time series and cross-sectional data are combined. The TSCSREG procedure deals with panel data sets that consist of time series observations on each of several cross-sectional units.

Such models can be viewed as two-way designs with covariates

$$y_{it} = \sum_{k=1}^{K} X_{itk}\beta_k + u_{it} \quad i = 1, \ldots, N; \quad t = 1, \ldots, T$$

where *N* is the number of cross sections, *T* is the length of the time series for each cross section, and *K* is the number of exogenous or independent variables.

The performance of any estimation procedure for the model regression parameters depends on the statistical characteristics of the error components in the model. The TSCSREG procedure estimates the regression parameters in the preceding model under several common error structures. The error structures and the corresponding methods the TSCSREG procedure uses to analyze them are as follows:

- one and two-way fixed and random effects models. If the specification is dependent only on the cross section to which the observation belongs, such a model is referred to as a model with one-way effects. A specification that depends on both the cross section and the time series to which the observation belongs is called a model with two-way effects.
- Therefore, the specifications for the one-way model are

  $$u_{it} = \nu_i + \epsilon_{it}$$

  and the specifications for the two-way model are

  $$u_{it} = \nu_i + e_t + \epsilon_{it}$$

  where ϵ_{it} is a classical error term with zero mean and a homoscedastic covariance matrix.
- Apart from the possible one-way or two-way nature of the effect, the other dimension of difference between the possible specifications is that of the nature of the cross-sectional or time-series effect. The models are referred to as fixed effects models if the effects are nonrandom and as random effects models otherwise.

- first-order autoregressive model with contemporaneous correlation

$$u_{it} = \rho_i u_{i,t-1} + \epsilon_{it}$$

- The Parks method is used to estimate this model. This model assumes a first-order autoregressive error structure with contemporaneous correlation between cross sections. The covariance matrix is estimated by a two-stage procedure leading to the estimation of model regression parameters by GLS.
- mixed variance-component moving average error process

$$u_{it} = a_i + b_t + e_{it}$$

$$e_{it} = \alpha_0 \epsilon_t + \alpha_1 \epsilon_{t-1} + \ldots + \alpha_m \epsilon_{t-m}$$

- The Da Silva method is used to estimate this model. The Da Silva method estimates the regression parameters using a two-step GLS-type estimator.

The TSCSREG procedure analyzes panel data sets that consist of multiple time series observations on each of several individuals or cross-sectional units. The input data set must be in time series cross-sectional form. See Chapter 2, "Working with Time Series Data," for a discussion of how time series related by a cross-sectional dimension are stored in SAS data sets. The TSCSREG procedure requires that the time series for each cross section have the same number of observations and cover the same time range.

Getting Started

Specifying the Input Data

The input data set used by the TSCSREG procedure must be sorted by cross section and by time within each cross section. Therefore, the first step in using PROC TSCSREG is to make sure that the input data set is sorted. Normally, the input data set contains a variable that identifies the cross section for each observation and a variable that identifies the time period for each observation.

To illustrate, suppose that you have a data set A containing data over time for each of several states. You want to regress the variable Y on regressors X1 and X2. Cross sections are identified by the variable STATE, and time periods are identified by the variable DATE. The following statements sort the data set A appropriately:

```
proc sort data=a;
   by state date;
run;
```

The next step is to invoke the TSCSREG procedure and specify the cross section and time series variables in an ID statement. List the variables in the ID statement exactly as they are listed in the BY statement.

```
proc tscsreg data=a;
   id state date;
```

Alternatively, you can omit the ID statement and use the CS= and TS= options on the PROC TSCSREG statement to specify the number of cross sections in the data set and the number of time series observations in each cross section.

Unbalanced Data

In the case of fixed effects and random effects models, the TSCSREG procedure is capable of processing data with different numbers of time series observations across different cross sections. You must specify the ID statement to estimate models using unbalanced data. The missing time series observations are recognized by the absence of time series id variable values in some of the cross sections in the input data set. Moreover, if an observation with a particular time series id value and cross-sectional id value is present in the input data set, but one or more of the model variables are missing, that time series point is treated as missing for that cross section.

Also, when PROC TSCSREG is processing balanced data, you now need to specify only the CS= parameter if you do not specify an ID statement. The TS= parameter is not required, since it can be inferred from the number of observations if the data is balanced.

Specifying the Regression Model

Next, specify the linear regression model with a MODEL statement. The MODEL statement in PROC TSCSREG is specified like the MODEL statement in other SAS regression procedures: the dependent variable is listed first, followed by an equal sign, followed by the list of regressor variables.

```
proc tscsreg data=a;
   id state date;
   model y = x1 x2;
run;
```

The reason for using PROC TSCSREG instead of other SAS regression procedures is that you can incorporate a model for the structure of the random errors. It is important to consider what kind of error structure model is appropriate for your data and to specify the corresponding option in the MODEL statement.

The error structure options supported by the TSCSREG procedure are FIXONE, FIXTWO, RANONE, RANTWO, FULLER, PARKS, and DASILVA. See the "Details" section later in this chapter for more information about these methods and the error structures they assume.

By default, the Fuller-Battese method is used. Thus, the preceding example is the same as specifying the FULLER option, as shown in the following statements:

```
proc tscsreg data=a;
   id state date;
```

```
      model y = x1 x2 / fuller;
   run;
```

You can specify more than one error structure option in the MODEL statement; the analysis is repeated using each method specified. You can use any number of MODEL statements to estimate different regression models or estimate the same model using different options. See Example 27.1 in the section "Examples."

In order to aid in model specification within this class of models, the procedure provides two specification test statistics. The first is an F statistic that tests the null hypothesis that the fixed effects parameters are all zero. The second is a Hausman m-statistic that provides information about the appropriateness of the random effects specification. It is based on the idea that, under the null hypothesis of no correlation between the effects variables and the regressors, OLS and GLS are consistent, but OLS is inefficient. Hence, a test can be based on the result that the covariance of an efficient estimator with its difference from an inefficient estimator is zero. Rejection of the null hypothesis might suggest that the fixed effects model is more appropriate.

The procedure also provides the Buse R-squared measure, which is the most appropriate goodness-of-fit measure for models estimated using GLS. This number is interpreted as a measure of the proportion of the transformed sum of squares of the dependent variable that is attributable to the influence of the independent variables. In the case of OLS estimation, the Buse R-squared measure is equivalent to the usual R-squared measure.

Estimation Techniques

If the effects are fixed, the models are essentially regression models with dummy variables corresponding to the specified effects. For fixed effects models, ordinary least squares (OLS) estimation is best linear unbiased.

The other alternative is to assume that the effects are random. In the one-way case, $E(\nu_i) = 0$, $E(\nu_i^2) = \sigma_\nu^2$, and

$E(\nu_i \nu_j) = 0$ for $i \neq j$, and ν_i is uncorrelated with ϵ_{it} for all i and t. In the two-way case, in addition to all of the preceding, $E(e_t) = 0$, $E(e_t^2) = \sigma_e^2$, and

$E(e_t e_s) = 0$ for $t \neq s$, and the e_t are uncorrelated with the ν_i and the ϵ_{it} for all $i$and t. Thus, the model is a variance components model, with the variance components σ_ν^2 and σ_e^2, as well as σ_ϵ^2, to be estimated. A crucial implication of such a specification is that the effects are independent of the regressors. For random effects models, the estimation method is an estimated generalized least squares (EGLS) procedure that involves estimating the variance components in the first stage and using the estimated variance covariance matrix thus obtained to apply generalized least squares (GLS) to the data.

Introductory Example

The following example uses the cost function data from Greene (1990) to estimate the variance components model. The variable OUTPUT is the log of output in millions of kilowatt-hours, and COST is the log of cost in millions of dollars. Refer to Greene (1990) for details.

```
data greene;
   input firm year output cost @@;
cards;
     1 1955    5.36598   1.14867  1 1960    6.03787   1.45185
     1 1965    6.37673   1.52257  1 1970    6.93245   1.76627
     2 1955    6.54535   1.35041  2 1960    6.69827   1.71109
     2 1965    7.40245   2.09519  2 1970    7.82644   2.39480
     3 1955    8.07153   2.94628  3 1960    8.47679   3.25967
     3 1965    8.66923   3.47952  3 1970    9.13508   3.71795
     4 1955    8.64259   3.56187  4 1960    8.93748   3.93400
     4 1965    9.23073   4.11161  4 1970    9.52530   4.35523
     5 1955    8.69951   3.50116  5 1960    9.01457   3.68998
     5 1965    9.04594   3.76410  5 1970    9.21074   4.05573
     6 1955    9.37552   4.29114  6 1960    9.65188   4.59356
     6 1965   10.21163   4.93361  6 1970   10.34039   5.25520
;

proc sort data=greene;
   by firm year;
run;
```

Usually you cannot explicitly specify all the explanatory variables that affect the dependent variable. The omitted or unobservable variables are summarized in the error disturbances. The TSCSREG procedure used with the Fuller-Battese method adds the individual and time-specific random effects to the error disturbances, and the parameters are efficiently estimated using the GLS method. The variance components model used by the Fuller-Battese method is

$$y_{it} = \sum_{k=1}^{K} X_{itk}\beta_k + v_i + e_t + \epsilon_{it} \quad i = 1, \ldots, N; \quad t = 1, \ldots, T$$

The following statements fit this model. Since the Fuller-Battese is the default method, no options are required.

```
proc tscsreg data=greene;
   model cost = output;
   id firm year;
run;
```

The TSCSREG procedure output is shown in Figure 27.1. A model description is printed first, which reports the estimation method used and the number of cross sections and time periods. The variance components estimates are printed next. Finally, the table of regression parameter estimates shows the estimates, standard errors, and *t*-tests.

```
                         The TSCSREG Procedure

Dependent Variable: cost

                           Model Description

              Estimation Method                          RanTwo
              Number of Cross Sections                        6
              Time Series Length                              4

                            Fit Statistics

        SSE                0.3481     DFE                      22
        MSE                0.0158     Root MSE             0.1258
        R-Square           0.8136

                      Variance Component Estimates

        Variance Component for Cross Sections      0.046907
        Variance Component for Time Series          0.00906
        Variance Component for Error               0.008749

                            Hausman Test for
                             Random Effects

                          DF     m Value     Pr > m

                           1       26.46     <.0001

                          Parameter Estimates

                                                Standard
    Variable          DF      Estimate           Error      t Value      Pr > |t|

    Intercept          1      -2.99992          0.6478        -4.63        0.0001
    output             1      0.746596          0.0762         9.80        <.0001
```

Figure 27.1. The Variance Components Estimates

Syntax

The following statements are used with the TSCSREG procedure.

PROC TSCSREG *options*;
  BY *variables*;
  ID *cross-section-id-variable time-series-id-variable*;
  MODEL *dependent = regressor-variables / options*;
  label: **TEST** *equation [,equation...]*;

Functional Summary

The statements and options used with the TSCSREG procedure are summarized in the following table.

Description	Statement	Option
Data Set Options		
specify the input data set	TSCSREG	DATA=
write parameter estimates to an output data set	TSCSREG	OUTEST=
include correlations in the OUTEST= data set	TSCSREG	CORROUT
include covariances in the OUTEST= data set	TSCSREG	COVOUT
specify number of time series observations	TSCSREG	TS=
specify number of cross sections	TSCSREG	CS=
Declaring the Role of Variables		
specify BY-group processing	BY	
specify the cross section and time ID variables	ID	
Printing Control Options		
print correlations of the estimates	MODEL	CORRB
print covariances of the estimates	MODEL	COVB
suppress printed output	MODEL	NOPRINT
perform tests of linear hypotheses	TEST	
Model Estimation Options		
specify the one-way fixed effects model	MODEL	FIXONE
specify the two-way fixed effects model	MODEL	FIXTWO
specify the one-way random effects model	MODEL	RANONE
specify the one-way random effects model	MODEL	RANTWO
specify Fuller-Battese method	MODEL	FULLER
specify PARKS	MODEL	PARKS
specify Da Silva method	MODEL	DASILVA
specify order of the moving average error process for Da Silva method	MODEL	M=
print Φ matrix for Parks method	MODEL	PHI
print autocorrelation coefficients for Parks method	MODEL	RHO
suppress the intercept term	MODEL	NOINT
control check for singularity	MODEL	SINGULAR=

PROC TSCSREG Statement

PROC TSCSREG *options;*

The following options can be specified on the PROC TSCSREG statement.

DATA= *SAS-data-set*
names the input data set. The input data set must be sorted by cross section and by time period within cross section. If you omit DATA=, the most recently created SAS data set is used.

TS= *number*
specifies the number of observations in the time series for each cross section. The TS= option value must be greater than 1. The TS= option is required unless an ID statement is used. Note that the number of observations for each time series must be the same for each cross section and must cover the same time period.

CS= *number*
specifies the number of cross sections. The CS= option value must be greater than 1. The CS= option is required unless an ID statement is used.

OUTEST= *SAS-data-set*
names an output data set to contain the parameter estimates. When the OUTEST= option is not specified, the OUTEST= data set is not created. See the section "OUTEST= Data Set" later in this chapter for details on the structure of the OUTEST= data set.

OUTCOV
COVOUT
writes the covariance matrix of the parameter estimates to the OUTEST= data set. See the section "OUTEST= Data Set" later in this chapter for details.

OUTCORR
CORROUT
writes the correlation matrix of the parameter estimates to the OUTEST= data set. See the section "OUTEST= Data Set" later in this chapter for details.

In addition, any of the following MODEL statement options can be specified in the PROC TSCSREG statement: CORRB, COVB, FIXONE, FIXTWO, RANONE, RANTWO, FULLER, PARKS, DASILVA, NOINT, NOPRINT, M=, PHI, RHO, and SINGULAR=. When specified in the PROC TSCSREG statement, these options are equivalent to specifying the options for every MODEL statement. See the section "MODEL Statement" for a complete description of each of these options.

BY Statement

BY *variables ;*

A BY statement can be used with PROC TSCSREG to obtain separate analyses on observations in groups defined by the BY variables. When a BY statement appears, the input data set must be sorted by the BY variables as well as by cross section and time period within the BY groups.

When both an ID statement and a BY statement are specified, the input data set must be sorted first with respect to BY variables and then with respect to the cross section and time series ID variables. For example,

```
proc sort data=a;
   by byvar1 byvar2 csid tsid;
run;

proc tscsreg data=a;
   by byvar1 byvar2;
   id csid tsid;
   ...
run;
```

When both a BY statement and an ID statement are used, the data set may have a different number of cross sections or a different number of time periods in each BY group. If no ID statement is used, the CS=*N* and TS=*T* options must be specified and each BY group must contain $N \times T$ observations.

ID Statement

ID *cross-section-id-variable time-series-id-variable;*

The ID statement is used to specify variables in the input data set that identify the cross section and time period for each observation.

When an ID statement is used, the TSCSREG procedure verifies that the input data set is sorted by the cross section ID variable and by the time series ID variable within each cross section. The TSCSREG procedure also verifies that the time series ID values are the same for all cross sections.

To make sure the input data set is correctly sorted, use PROC SORT with a BY statement with the variables listed exactly as they are listed in the ID statement to sort the input data set.

```
proc sort data=a;
   by csid tsid;
run;

proc tscsreg data=a;
   id csid tsid;
   ... etc. ...
run;
```

If the ID statement is not used, the TS= and CS= options must be specified on the PROC TSCSREG statement. Note that the input data must be sorted by time within cross section, regardless of whether the cross section structure is given by an ID statement or by the options TS= and CS=.

If an ID statement is specified, the time series length *T* is set to the minimum number of observations for any cross section, and only the first *T* observations in each cross section are used. If both the ID statement and the TS= and CS= options are specified, the TS= and CS= options are ignored.

MODEL Statement

MODEL *response = regressors / options;*

The MODEL statement specifies the regression model and the error structure assumed for the regression residuals. The response variable on the left side of the equal sign is regressed on the independent variables listed after the equal sign. Any number of MODEL statements can be used. For each model statement only one response variable can be specified on the left side of the equal sign.

The error structure is specified by the FULLER, PARKS, and DASILVA options. More than one of these three options can be used, in which case the analysis is repeated for each error structure model specified.

Models can be given labels. Model labels are used in the printed output to identify the results for different models. If no label is specified, the response variable name is used as the label for the model. The model label is specified as follows:

label **: MODEL . . . ;**

The following options can be specified on the MODEL statement after a slash (/).

CORRB
CORR
prints the matrix of estimated correlations between the parameter estimates.

COVB
VAR
prints the matrix of estimated covariances between the parameter estimates.

FIXONE
specifies that a one-way fixed effects model be estimated.

FIXTWO
specifies that a two-way fixed effects model be estimated.

RANONE
specifies that a one-way random effects model be estimated.

RANTWO
specifies that a two-way random effects model be estimated.

FULLER
specifies that the model be estimated using the Fuller-Battese method, which assumes a variance components model for the error structure. See "Fuller-Battese Method" later in this chapter for details. FULLER is the default.

PARKS
specifies that the model be estimated using the Parks method, which assumes a first-order autoregressive model for the error structure. See "Parks Method" later in this chapter for details.

DASILVA

specifies that the model be estimated using the Da Silva method, which assumes a mixed variance-component moving average model for the error structure. See "Da Silva Method" later in this chapter for details.

M= *number*

specifies the order of the moving average process in the Da Silva method. The M= value must be less than $T-1$. The default is M=1.

PHI

prints the Φ matrix of estimated covariances of the observations for the Parks method. The PHI option is relevant only when the PARKS option is used. See "Parks Method" later in this chapter for details.

RHO

prints the estimated autocorrelation coefficients for the Parks method.

NOINT
NOMEAN

suppresses the intercept parameter from the model.

NOPRINT

suppresses the normal printed output.

SINGULAR= *number*

specifies a singularity criterion for the inversion of the matrix. The default depends on the precision of the computer system.

TEST Statement

label: **TEST** *equation [,equation...]*;

The TEST statement performs F-tests of linear hypotheses about the regression parameters in the preceding MODEL statement. Each equation specifies a linear hypothesis to be tested. All hypotheses in one TEST statement are tested jointly. Variable names in the equations must correspond to regressors in the preceding MODEL statement, and each name represents the coefficient of the corresponding regressor. The keyword INTERCEPT refers to the coefficient of the intercept.

The following illustrates the use of the TEST statement:

```
proc tscsreg;
   model y = x1 x2 x3;
   test x1 = 0, x2/2 + 2*x3= 0;
   test_int: test intercept=0, x3 = 0;
```

Details

Notation

The discussion here is in the context of the usual panel structure,

$$y_{it} = \sum_{k=1}^{K} x_{itk}\beta_k + u_{it} \quad i = 1, \ldots N; \quad t = 1, \ldots T_i$$

with the specification of u_{it} dependent on the particular model. The total number of observations $M = \sum_{i=1}^{N} T_i$. For the balanced data case, $T_i = T$ for all i. The $M \times M$ covariance matrix of u_{it} is denoted by $\mathbf{V}$. Let $\mathbf{X}$ and $\mathbf{y}$ be the independent and dependent variables arranged by cross section and by time within each cross section. Let $\mathbf{X}_s$ be the X matrix without the intercept. Generally, all other notation is specific to each section.

The One-Way Fixed Effects Model

The specification for the one-way fixed effects model is

$$u_{it} = \nu_i + \epsilon_{it}$$

where the ν_is are nonrandom. Since including both the intercept and all the ν_is induces a redundancy (unless the intercept is suppressed with the NOINT option), the ν_i estimates are reported under the restriction that $\nu_N = 0$.

Let $\mathbf{Q}_0 = diag(\mathbf{E}_{T_i})$, with $\bar{\mathbf{J}}_{T_i} = \mathbf{J}_{T_i}/T_i$ and $\mathbf{E}_{T_i} = \mathbf{I}_{T_i} - \bar{\mathbf{J}}_{T_i}$.

The estimators for the intercept and the fixed effects are given by the usual OLS expressions.

If $\tilde{\mathbf{X}}_s = \mathbf{Q}_0\mathbf{X}_s$ and $\tilde{\mathbf{y}} = \mathbf{Q}_0\mathbf{y}$, the estimator of the slope coefficients is given by

$$\tilde{\beta}_s = (\tilde{\mathbf{X}}_s'\tilde{\mathbf{X}}_s)^{-1}\tilde{\mathbf{X}}_s'\tilde{\mathbf{y}}$$

The estimator of the error variance is

$$\hat{\sigma}_\epsilon = \tilde{\mathbf{u}}'\mathbf{Q}_0\tilde{\mathbf{u}}/(M - N - (K - 1))$$

where the residuals $\tilde{\mathbf{u}}$ are given by $\tilde{\mathbf{u}} = (\mathbf{I}_M - \mathbf{J}_M\mathbf{j}'_M/M)(\mathbf{y} - \mathbf{X}_s\tilde{\beta}_s)$ if there is an intercept and by $\tilde{\mathbf{u}} = (\mathbf{y} - \mathbf{X}_s\tilde{\beta}_s)$if there is not.

The Two-Way Fixed Effects Model

The specification for the two-way fixed effects model is

$$u_{it} = \nu_i + e_t + \epsilon_{it}$$

where the ν_is and e_ts are nonrandom. If you do not specify the NOINT option, which suppresses the intercept, the estimates for the fixed effects are reported under the restriction that $\nu_N = 0$ and $e_T = 0$. If you specify the NOINT option to suppress the intercept, only the restriction $e_T = 0$ is imposed.

Let $\mathbf{X}_*$ and $\mathbf{y}_*$ be the independent and dependent variables arranged by time and by cross section within each time period. (Note that the input data set used by the TSCSREG procedure must be sorted by cross section and then by time within each cross section.) Let M_t be the number of cross sections observed in year t and let $\sum_t M_t = M$. Let $\mathbf{D}_t$ be the $M_t \times N$ matrix obtained from the $N \times N$ identity matrix from which rows corresponding to cross sections not observed at time t have been omitted. Consider

$$\mathbf{Z} = (\mathbf{Z}_1, \mathbf{Z}_2)$$

where $\mathbf{Z}_1 = (\mathbf{D}_1', \mathbf{D}_2', \ldots .\mathbf{D}_T')'$ and $\mathbf{Z}_2 = diag(\mathbf{D}_1\mathbf{j}_N, \mathbf{D}_2\mathbf{j}_N, \ldots\ldots \mathbf{D}_T\mathbf{j}_N)$. The matrix $\mathbf{Z}$ gives the dummy variable structure for the two-way model.

Let

$$\Delta_N = \mathbf{Z}_1'\mathbf{Z}_1, \quad \Delta_T = \mathbf{Z}_2'\mathbf{Z}_2, \quad \mathbf{A} = \mathbf{Z}_2'\mathbf{Z}_1$$

$$\bar{\mathbf{Z}} = \mathbf{Z}_2 - \mathbf{Z}_1\Delta_N^{-1}\mathbf{A}'$$

$$\mathbf{Q} = \Delta_T - \mathbf{A}\Delta_N^{-1}\mathbf{A}'$$

$$\mathbf{P} = (\mathbf{I}_M - \mathbf{Z}_1\Delta_N^{-1}\mathbf{Z}_1') - \bar{\mathbf{Z}}\mathbf{Q}^{-}\bar{\mathbf{Z}}'$$

The estimators for the intercept and the fixed effects are given by the usual OLS expressions.

The estimate of the regression slope coefficients is given by

$$\tilde{\beta}_s = (\mathbf{X}_{*s}'\mathbf{P}\mathbf{X}_{*s})^{-1}\mathbf{X}_{*s}'\mathbf{P}\mathbf{y}_*$$

where $\mathbf{X}_{*s}$ is the $\mathbf{X}_*$ matrix without the vector of 1s.

The estimator of the error variance is

$$\hat{\sigma}_\epsilon^2 = \tilde{\mathbf{u}}'\mathbf{P}\tilde{\mathbf{u}}/(M - T - N + 1 - (K - 1))$$

where the residuals are given by $\tilde{\mathbf{u}} = (\mathbf{I}_M - \mathbf{j}_M\mathbf{j}_M'/M)(\mathbf{y}_* - \mathbf{X}_{*s}\tilde{\beta}_s)$if there is an intercept in the model and by $\tilde{\mathbf{u}} = \mathbf{y}_* - \mathbf{X}_{*s}\tilde{\beta}_s$if there is no intercept.

The One-Way Random Effects Model

The specification for the one-way random effects model is

$$u_{it} = \nu_i + \epsilon_{it}$$

Let $\mathbf{Z}_0 = diag(\mathbf{j}_{T_i})$, $\mathbf{P}_0 = diag(\bar{\mathbf{J}}_{T_i})$, and $\mathbf{Q}_0 = diag(\mathbf{E}_{T_i})$, with $\bar{\mathbf{J}}_{T_i} = \mathbf{J}_{T_i}/T_i$ and $\mathbf{E}_{T_i} = \mathbf{I}_{T_i} - \bar{\mathbf{J}}_{T_i}$. Define $\tilde{\mathbf{X}}_s = \mathbf{Q}_0\mathbf{X}_s$ and $\tilde{\mathbf{y}} = \mathbf{Q}_0\mathbf{y}$.

The fixed effects estimator of σ^2_ϵ is still unbiased under the random effects assumptions, so you need to calculate only the estimate of σ_ν.

In the balanced data case, the estimation method for the variance components is the fitting constants method as applied to the one way model; refer to Baltagi and Chang (1994). Fuller and Battese (1974) apply this method to the two-way model.

Let

$$R(\nu) = \mathbf{y}'\mathbf{Z}_0(\mathbf{Z}_0'\mathbf{Z}_0)^{-1}\mathbf{Z}_0'\mathbf{y}$$

$$R(\beta|\nu) = ((\tilde{\mathbf{X}}_s'\tilde{\mathbf{X}}_s)^{-1}\tilde{\mathbf{X}}_s'\tilde{\mathbf{y}})'(\tilde{\mathbf{X}}_s'\tilde{\mathbf{y}})$$

$$R(\beta) = (\mathbf{X}'\mathbf{y})'(\mathbf{X}'\mathbf{X})^{-1}\mathbf{X}'\mathbf{y}$$

$$R(\nu|\beta) = R(\beta|\nu) + R(\nu) - R(\beta)$$

The estimator of the error variance is given by

$$\hat{\sigma}^2_\epsilon = (\mathbf{y}'\mathbf{y} - R(\beta|\nu) - R(\nu))/(M - N - (K-1))$$

and the estimator of the cross-sectional variance component is given by

$$\hat{\sigma}^2_\nu = (R(\nu|\beta) - (N-1)\hat{\sigma}^2_\epsilon)/(M - \mathrm{tr}(\mathbf{Z}_0'\mathbf{X}(\mathbf{X}'\mathbf{X})^{-1}\mathbf{X}'\mathbf{Z}_0))$$

The estimation of the one-way unbalanced data model is performed using a specialization (Baltagi and Chang 1994) of the approach used by Wansbeek and Kapteyn (1989) for unbalanced two-way models.

The estimation of the variance components is performed by using a quadratic unbiased estimation (QUE) method. This involves focusing on quadratic forms of the centered residuals, equating their expected values to the realized quadratic forms, and solving for the variance components.

Let

$$q_1 = \tilde{\mathbf{u}}'\mathbf{Q}_0\tilde{\mathbf{u}}$$

$$q_2 = \tilde{\mathbf{u}}'\mathbf{P}_0\tilde{\mathbf{u}}$$

where the residuals $\tilde{\mathbf{u}}$ are given by $\tilde{\mathbf{u}} = (\mathbf{I}_M - \mathbf{j}_M\mathbf{j}'_M/M)(\mathbf{y} - \mathbf{X}_s\tilde{\mathbf{X}}'_s\tilde{\mathbf{X}}_s)^{-1}\tilde{\mathbf{X}}_s'\tilde{\mathbf{y}})$ if there is an intercept and by $tilde\mathbf{u} = (\mathbf{y} - \mathbf{X}_s(\tilde{\mathbf{X}}'_s\tilde{\mathbf{X}}_s)^{-1}\tilde{\mathbf{X}}'_s\tilde{\mathbf{y}})$ if there is not.

Consider the expected values

$$E(q_1) = (M - N - (K-1))\sigma_\epsilon^2$$

$$E(q_2) = (N - 1 + \mathrm{tr}[(\mathbf{X}_s'\mathbf{Q}_0\mathbf{X}_s)^{-1}\mathbf{X}_s'\mathbf{P}_0\mathbf{X}_s] - \mathrm{tr}[(\mathbf{X}_s'\mathbf{Q}_0\mathbf{X}_s)^{-1}\mathbf{X}_s'\bar{\mathbf{J}}_M\mathbf{X}_s])\sigma_\epsilon^2$$

$$+[M - (\sum_i T_i^2/M)]\sigma_\nu^2$$

$\hat{\sigma}_\epsilon^2$ and $\hat{\sigma}_\nu^2$ are obtained by equating the quadratic forms to their expected values.

The estimated generalized least squares procedure substitutes the QUE estimates into the covariance matrix of u_{it}, which is given by

$$\mathbf{V} = \sigma_\nu^2 I_M + \sigma_\epsilon^2 \mathbf{Z}_0\mathbf{Z}_0'$$

The Two-Way Random Effects Model

The specification for the two way model is

$$u_{it} = \nu_i + e_t + \epsilon_{it}$$

For balanced data, the two-way random effects model is estimated using the method of Fuller and Battese (1974), so in this case, the RANTWO option is equivalent to the FULLER option already existing in PROC TSCSREG.

The following method (Wansbeek and Kapteyn 1989) is used to handle unbalanced data.

Let $\mathbf{X}_*$ and $\mathbf{y}_*$ be the independent and dependent variables arranged by time and by cross section within each time period. (Note that the input data set used by the TSCSREG procedure must be sorted by cross section and then by time within each cross section.) Let M_t be the number of cross sections observed in time t and $\sum_t M_t = M$. Let $\mathbf{D}_t$ be the $M_t \times N$ matrix obtained from the $N \times N$ identity matrix from which rows corresponding to cross sections not observed at time t have been omitted. Consider

$$\mathbf{Z} = (\mathbf{Z}_1, \mathbf{Z}_2)$$

where $\mathbf{Z}_1 = (\mathbf{D}_1', \mathbf{D}_2', \ldots..\mathbf{D}_T')'$ and $\mathbf{Z}_2 = diag(\mathbf{D}_1\mathbf{j}_N, \mathbf{D}_2\mathbf{j}_N, \ldots\ldots \mathbf{D}_T\mathbf{j}_N)$.

The matrix $\mathbf{Z}$ gives the dummy variable structure for the two-way model.

Let

$$\Delta_N = \mathbf{Z}_1'\mathbf{Z}_1, \quad \Delta_T = \mathbf{Z}_2'\mathbf{Z}_2, \quad \mathbf{A} = \mathbf{Z}_2'\mathbf{Z}_1$$

$$\bar{\mathbf{Z}} = \mathbf{Z}_2 - \mathbf{Z}_1 \Delta_N^{-1} \mathbf{A}'$$

$$\mathbf{Q} = \Delta_T - \mathbf{A} \Delta_N^{-1} \mathbf{A}'$$

$$\mathbf{P} = (\mathbf{I}_M - \mathbf{Z}_1 \Delta_N^{-1} \mathbf{Z}_1') - \bar{\mathbf{Z}} \mathbf{Q} - \bar{\mathbf{Z}}'$$

The estimator of the error variance is

$$\hat{\sigma}_\epsilon^2 = \tilde{\mathbf{u}}' \mathbf{P} \tilde{\mathbf{u}} / M - T - N + 1 - (K - 1))$$

where the $\tilde{\mathbf{u}}$ are given by $\tilde{\mathbf{u}} = (\mathbf{I}_M - \mathbf{j}_M \mathbf{j}'_M / M)(\mathbf{y}_* - \mathbf{X}_{*s}(\mathbf{X}'_{*s} \mathbf{P} \mathbf{X}_{*s})^{-1} \mathbf{X}_{*s}' \mathbf{P} \mathbf{y}_*)$ if there is an intercept and by $\tilde{\mathbf{u}} = (\mathbf{y}_* - \mathbf{X}_{*s}(\mathbf{X}'_{*s} \mathbf{P} \mathbf{X}_{*s})^{-1} \mathbf{X}'_{*s} \mathbf{P} \mathbf{y}_*$if there is not.

The estimation of the variance components is performed by using a quadratic unbiased estimation (QUE) method that involves focusing on quadratic forms of the residuals $\tilde{\mathbf{u}}$, equating their expected values to the realized quadratic forms, and solving for the variance components.

Let

$$q_N = \tilde{\mathbf{u}}' \mathbf{Z}_2 \Delta_T^{-1} \mathbf{Z}_2' \tilde{\mathbf{u}}$$

$$q_T = \tilde{\mathbf{u}}' \mathbf{Z}_1 \Delta_N^{-1} \mathbf{Z}_1' \tilde{\mathbf{u}}$$

Consider the expected values

$$E(q_N) = (T + k_N - (1 + k_0))\sigma^2 + (T - \frac{\lambda_1}{M})\sigma_\nu^2 + (M - \frac{\lambda_2}{M})\sigma_e^2$$

$$E(q_T) = (N + k_T - (1 + k_0))\sigma^2 + (M - \frac{\lambda_1}{M})\sigma_\nu^2 + (N - \frac{\lambda_2}{M})\sigma_e^2$$

where

$$k_0 = \mathbf{j}_M' \mathbf{X}_{*s} (\mathbf{X}_{*s}' \mathbf{P} \mathbf{X}_{*s})^{-1} \mathbf{X}_{*s}' \mathbf{j}_M / M$$

$$k_N = tr((\mathbf{X}_{*s}' \mathbf{P} \mathbf{X}_{*s})^{-1} \mathbf{X}_{*s}' \mathbf{Z}_2 \Delta_T^{-1} \mathbf{Z}_2' \mathbf{X}_{*s})$$

$$k_T = tr((\mathbf{X}_{*s}' \mathbf{P} \mathbf{X}_{*s})^{-1} \mathbf{X}_{*s}' \mathbf{Z}_1 \Delta_N^{-1} \mathbf{Z}_1' \mathbf{X}_{*s})$$

$$\lambda_1 = \mathbf{j}_M' \mathbf{Z}_1 \mathbf{Z}_1' \mathbf{j}_M$$

$$\lambda_2 = \mathbf{j}_M' \mathbf{Z}_2 \mathbf{Z}_2' \mathbf{j}_M$$

The quadratic unbiased estimators for σ_ν^2 and σ_e^2 are obtained by equating the expected values to the quadratic forms and solving for the two unknowns.

The estimated generalized least squares procedure substitute the QUE estimates into the covariance matrix of the composite error term u_{it}, which is given by

$$\mathbf{V} = \sigma_\epsilon^2 \mathbf{I}_M + \sigma_\nu^2 \mathbf{Z}_1\mathbf{Z}_1' + \sigma_e^2 \mathbf{Z}_2\mathbf{Z}_2'$$

Parks Method (Autoregressive Model)

Parks (1967) considered the first-order autoregressive model in which the random errors u_{it}, $i = 1, 2, \ldots, N$, $t = 1, 2, \ldots, T$, have the structure

$$\begin{aligned} E(u_{it}^2) &= \sigma_{ii} && \text{(heteroscedasticity)} \\ E(u_{it}u_{jt}) &= \sigma_{ij} && \text{(contemporaneously correlated)} \\ u_{it} &= \rho_i u_{i,t-1} + \epsilon_{it} && \text{(autoregression)} \end{aligned}$$

where

$$\begin{aligned} E(\epsilon_{it}) &= 0 \\ E(u_{i,t-1}\epsilon_{jt}) &= 0 \\ E(\epsilon_{it}\epsilon_{jt}) &= \phi_{ij} \\ E(\epsilon_{it}\epsilon_{js}) &= 0 \qquad (s \neq t) \\ E(u_{i0}) &= 0 \\ E(u_{i0}u_{j0}) &= \sigma_{ij} = \phi_{ij}/(1 - \rho_i\rho_j) \end{aligned}$$

The model assumed is first-order autoregressive with contemporaneous correlation between cross sections. In this model, the covariance matrix for the vector of random errors **u** can be expressed as

$$E(\mathbf{u}\mathbf{u}') = \mathbf{V} = \begin{bmatrix} \sigma_{11}P_{11} & \sigma_{12}P_{12} & \ldots & \sigma_{1N}P_{1N} \\ \sigma_{21}P_{21} & \sigma_{22}P_{22} & \ldots & \sigma_{2N}P_{2N} \\ \vdots & \vdots & \vdots & \vdots \\ \sigma_{N1}P_{N1} & \sigma_{N2}P_{N2} & \ldots & \sigma_{NN}P_{NN} \end{bmatrix}$$

where

$$P_{ij} = \begin{bmatrix} 1 & \rho_j & \rho_j^2 & \ldots & \rho_j^{T-1} \\ \rho_i & 1 & \rho_j & \ldots & \rho_j^{T-2} \\ \rho_i^2 & \rho_i & 1 & \ldots & \rho_j^{T-3} \\ \vdots & \vdots & \vdots & \vdots & \vdots \\ \rho_i^{T-1} & \rho_i^{T-2} & \rho_i^{T-3} & \ldots & 1 \end{bmatrix}$$

The matrix $\mathbf{V}$ is estimated by a two-stage procedure, and β is then estimated by generalized least squares. The first step in estimating $\mathbf{V}$ involves the use of ordinary least squares to estimate β and obtain the fitted residuals, as follows:

$$\hat{\mathbf{u}} = \mathbf{y} - \mathbf{X}\hat{\beta}_{OLS}$$

A consistent estimator of the first-order autoregressive parameter is then obtained in the usual manner, as follows:

$$\hat{\rho}_i = \left(\sum_{t=2}^{T} \hat{u}_{it}\hat{u}_{i,t-1} \right) \Big/ \left(\sum_{t=2}^{T} \hat{u}_{i,t-1}^2 \right) \quad i = 1, 2, \ldots, N$$

Finally, the autoregressive characteristic of the data can be removed (asymptotically) by the usual transformation of taking weighted differences. That is, for $i = 1, 2, \ldots, N$,

$$y_{i1}\sqrt{1-\hat{\rho}_i^2} = \sum_{k=1}^{p} X_{i1k}\beta_k\sqrt{1-\hat{\rho}_i^2} + u_{i1}\sqrt{1-\hat{\rho}_i^2}$$

$$y_{it} - \hat{\rho}_i y_{i,t-1} = \sum_{k=1}^{p} (X_{itk} - \hat{\rho}_i \mathbf{X}_{i,t-1,k})\beta_k + u_{it} - \hat{\rho}_i u_{i,t-1} \quad t = 2, \ldots, T$$

which is written

$$y_{it}^* = \sum_{k=1}^{p} X_{itk}^*\beta_k + u_{it}^* \quad i = 1, 2, \ldots, N; \quad t = 1, 2, \ldots, T$$

Notice that the transformed model has not lost any observations (Seely and Zyskind 1971).

The second step in estimating the covariance matrix **V** is to apply ordinary least squares to the preceding transformed model, obtaining

$$\hat{\mathbf{u}}^* = \mathbf{y}^* - \mathbf{X}^* \beta^*_{OLS}$$

from which the consistent estimator of σ_{ij} is calculated:

$$s_{ij} = \frac{\hat{\phi}_{ij}}{(1 - \hat{\rho}_i \hat{\rho}_j)}$$

where

$$\hat{\phi}_{ij} = \frac{1}{(T-p)} \sum_{t=1}^{T} \hat{u}^*_{it} \hat{u}^*_{jt}$$

EGLS then proceeds in the usual manner,

$$\hat{\beta}_P = (\mathbf{X}'\hat{\mathbf{V}}^{-1}\mathbf{X})^{-1}\mathbf{X}'\hat{\mathbf{V}}^{-1}\mathbf{y}$$

where $\hat{\mathbf{V}}$ is the derived consistent estimator of **V**. For computational purposes, it should be pointed out that $\hat{\beta}_P$ is obtained directly from the transformed model,

$$\hat{\beta}_P = (\mathbf{X}^{*'}(\hat{\Phi}^{-1} \otimes I_T)\mathbf{X}^*)^{-1}\mathbf{X}^{*'}(\hat{\Phi}^{-1} \otimes I_T)\mathbf{y}^*$$

where $\hat{\Phi} = [\hat{\phi}_{ij}]_{i,j=1,\ldots,N}$.

The preceding procedure is equivalent to Zellner's two-stage methodology applied to the transformed model (Zellner 1962).

Parks demonstrates that his estimator is consistent and asymptotically, normally distributed with

$$\mathrm{Var}(\hat{\beta}_{\mathrm{P}}) = (\mathbf{X}'\mathbf{V}^{-1}\mathbf{X})^{-1}$$

Standard Corrections

For the PARKS option, the first-order autocorrelation coefficient must be estimated for each cross section. Let ρ be the $N * 1$ vector of true parameters and $R = (r_1, \ldots, r_N)'$ be the corresponding vector of estimates. Then, to ensure that only range-preserving estimates are used in PROC TSCSREG, the following modification for R is made:

$$r_i = \begin{cases} r_i & \text{if } |r_i| < 1 \\ max(.95, rmax) & \text{if } r_i \geq 1 \\ min(-.95, rmin) & \text{if } r_i \leq -1 \end{cases}$$

where

$$rmax = \begin{cases} 0 & \text{if } r_i < 0 \text{ or } r_i \geq 1 \text{ for all i} \\ \underset{j}{max}[r_j : 0 \leq r_j < 1] & \text{otherwise} \end{cases}$$

and

$$rmin = \begin{cases} 0 & \text{if } r_i > 0 \text{ or } r_i \leq -1 \text{ for all i} \\ \underset{j}{max}[r_j : -1 < r_j \leq 0] & \text{otherwise} \end{cases}$$

Whenever this correction is made, a warning message is printed.

Da Silva Method (Variance-Component Moving Average Model)

Suppose you have a sample of observations at *T* time points on each of *N* cross-sectional units. The Da Silva method assumes that the observed value of the dependent variable at the *t*th time point on the *i*th cross-sectional unit can be expressed as

$$y_{it} = \mathbf{x}_{it}^{'}\beta + a_i + b_t + e_{it} \quad i = 1, \ldots, N; \quad t = 1, \ldots, T$$

where

$\mathbf{x}_{it}^{'} = (x_{it1}, \ldots, x_{itp})$is a vector of explanatory variables for the *t*th time point and *i*th cross-sectional unit

$\beta = (\beta_1, \ldots, \beta_p)'$ is the vector of parameters

a_i is a time-invariant, cross-sectional unit effect

b_t is a cross-sectionally invariant time effect

e_{it} is a residual effect unaccounted for by the explanatory variables and the specific time and cross-sectional unit effects

Since the observations are arranged first by cross sections, then by time periods within cross sections, these equations can be written in matrix notation as

$$\mathbf{y} = \mathbf{X}\beta + \mathbf{u}$$

where

$$\mathbf{u} = (\mathbf{a} \otimes \mathbf{1}_T) + (\mathbf{1}_N \otimes \mathbf{b}) + \mathbf{e}$$

$$\mathbf{y} = (y_{11}, \ldots, y_{1T}, y_{21}, \ldots, y_{NT})'$$

$$\mathbf{X} = (\mathbf{x}_{11}, \ldots, \mathbf{x}_{1T}, \mathbf{x}_{21}, \ldots, \mathbf{x}_{NT})'$$

$$\mathbf{a} = (a_1 \ldots a_N)'$$

$$\mathbf{b} = (b_1 \ldots b_T)'$$

$$\mathbf{e} = (e_{11}, \ldots, e_{1T}, e_{21}, \ldots, e_{NT})'$$

Here $\mathbf{1}_N$ is an $N \times 1$ vector with all elements equal to 1, and $\otimes$ denotes the Kronecker product.

It is assumed that

1. $\mathbf{x}_{it}$ is a sequence of nonstochastic, known $p{\times}1$ vectors in $\Re^p$ whose elements are uniformly bounded in $\Re^p$. The matrix $\mathbf{X}$ has a full column rank p.
2. β is a $p \times 1$ constant vector of unknown parameters.
3. $\mathbf{a}$ is a vector of uncorrelated random variables such that $E(a_i) = 0$ and $var(a_i) = \sigma_a^2, \sigma_a^2 > 0, i = 1, \ldots, N$.
4. $\mathbf{b}$ is a vector of uncorrelated random variables such that $E(b_t) = 0$ and $var(b_t) = \sigma_b^2, \sigma_b^2 > 0, t = 1, \ldots, T$.
5. $\mathbf{e}_i = (e_{i1}, \ldots, e_{iT})'$ is a sample of a realization of a finite moving average time series of order $m < T - 1$ for each i; hence,

$$e_{it} = \alpha_0 \epsilon_t + \alpha_1 \epsilon_{t-1} + \ldots + \alpha_m \epsilon_{t-m}, \quad t = 1, \ldots, T; \quad i = 1, \ldots, N$$

   where $\alpha_0, \alpha_1, \ldots, \alpha_m$ are unknown constants such that $\alpha_0 \neq 0$ and $\alpha_m \neq 0$, and $\{\epsilon_j\}_{j=-\infty}^{j=\infty}$ is a white noise process, that is, a sequence of uncorrelated random variables with $E(\epsilon_t) = 0, E(\epsilon_t^2) = \sigma_\epsilon^2$, and $\sigma_\epsilon^2 > 0$.
6. The sets of random variables $\{a_i\}_{i=1}^N$, $\{b_t\}_{t=1}^T$, and $\{e_{it}\}_{t=1}^T$ for $i = 1, \ldots, N$ are mutually uncorrelated.
7. The random terms have normal distributions: $a_i \sim N(0, \sigma_a^2)$, $b_t \sim N(0, \sigma_b^2)$,and $\epsilon_{t-k} \sim N(0, \sigma_\epsilon^2)$, for $i = 1, \ldots, N; t = 1, \ldots T; k = 1, \ldots, m$.

If assumptions 1-6 are satisfied, then

$$E(\mathbf{y}) = \mathbf{X}\beta$$

and

$$var(\mathbf{y}) = \sigma_a^2 (I_N \otimes J_T) + \sigma_b^2 (J_N \otimes I_T) + (I_N \otimes \Gamma_T)$$

where Γ_T is a $T \times T$ matrix with elements γ_{ts} as follows:

$$cov(e_{it}e_{is}) = \begin{cases} \gamma(|t-s|) & \text{if } |t-s| \leq \text{m} \\ 0 & \text{if } |t-s| > \text{m} \end{cases}$$

where $\gamma(k) = \sigma_\epsilon^2 \sum_{j=0}^{m-k} \alpha_j \alpha_{j+k}$ for $k = |t-s|$. For the definition of I_N, I_T, J_N, and J_T, see the "Fuller-Battese Method" section earlier in this chapter.

The covariance matrix, denoted by **V**, can be written in the form

$$\mathbf{V} = \sigma_a^2(I_N \otimes J_T) + \sigma_b^2(J_N \otimes I_T) + \sum_{k=0}^{m} \gamma(k)(I_N \otimes \Gamma_T^{(k)})$$

where $\Gamma_T^{(0)} = I_T$, and, for *k*=1,. . ., *m*, $\Gamma_T^{(k)}$ is a band matrix whose *k*th off-diagonal elements are 1's and all other elements are 0's.

Thus, the covariance matrix of the vector of observations **y** has the form

$$var(\mathbf{y}) = \sum_{k=1}^{m+3} \nu_k V_k$$

where

$$\begin{aligned} \nu_1 &= \sigma_a^2 \\ \nu_2 &= \sigma_b^2 \\ \nu_k &= \gamma(k-3) \qquad k = 3, \ldots, m+3 \\ V_1 &= I_N \otimes J_T \\ V_2 &= J_N \otimes I_T \\ V_k &= I_N \otimes \Gamma_T^{(k-3)} \qquad k = 3, \ldots, m+3 \end{aligned}$$

The estimator of β is a two-step GLS-type estimator, that is, GLS with the unknown covariance matrix replaced by a suitable estimator of **V**. It is obtained by substituting Seely estimates for the scalar multiples ν_k, $k = 1, 2, \ldots, m+3$.

Seely (1969) presents a general theory of unbiased estimation when the choice of estimators is restricted to finite dimensional vector spaces, with a special emphasis on quadratic estimation of functions of the form $\sum_{i=1}^{n} \delta_i \nu_i$.

The parameters ν_i (*i*=1,. . ., n) are associated with a linear model E(**y**)=**X**β with covariance matrix $\sum_{i=1}^{n} \nu_i V_i$ where V_i (*i*=1, . . ., n) are real symmetric matrices. The method is also discussed by Seely (1970a,1970b) and Seely and Zyskind (1971). Seely and Soong (1971) consider the MINQUE principle, using an approach along the lines of Seely (1969).

Linear Hypothesis Testing

For a linear hypothesis of the form $\mathbf{R}\ \beta$=$\mathbf{r}$ where $\mathbf{R}$ is $J \times L$ and $\mathbf{r}$ is $J \times 1$, the *F*-statistic with $J, M - L$ degrees of freedom is computed as

$$(\mathbf{R}\beta - \mathbf{r})'[\mathbf{R}(\mathbf{X}'\hat{\mathbf{V}}^{-1}\mathbf{X})^{-1}\mathbf{R}']^{-1}\mathbf{R}(\mathbf{R}\beta - \mathbf{r})$$

R-squared

The conventional R-squared measure is inappropriate for all models that the TSCSREG procedure estimates using GLS since a number outside the 0-to-1 range may be produced. Hence, a generalization of the R-squared measure is reported. The following goodness-of-fit measure (Buse 1973) is reported:

$$R^2 = 1 - \frac{\hat{\mathbf{u}}'\hat{\mathbf{V}}^{-1}\hat{\mathbf{u}}}{\mathbf{y}'\mathbf{D}'\hat{\mathbf{V}}^{-1}\mathbf{D}\mathbf{y}}$$

where $\hat{\mathbf{u}}$ are the residuals of the transformed model, $\hat{\mathbf{u}} = \mathbf{y} - \mathbf{X}(\mathbf{X}'\hat{\mathbf{V}}^{-1}\mathbf{X})^{-1}\mathbf{X}'\hat{\mathbf{V}}^{-1}\mathbf{y}$, and $\mathbf{D} = \mathbf{I}_M - \mathbf{j}_M\mathbf{j}_M'(\frac{\hat{\mathbf{V}}^{-1}}{\mathbf{j}_M'\hat{\mathbf{V}}^{-1}\mathbf{j}_M})$.

This is a measure of the proportion of the transformed sum of squares of the dependent variable that is attributable to the influence of the independent variables.

If there is no intercept in the model, the corresponding measure (Theil 1961) is

$$R^2 = 1 - \frac{\hat{\mathbf{u}}'\hat{\mathbf{V}}^{-1}\hat{\mathbf{u}}}{\mathbf{y}'\hat{\mathbf{V}}^{-1}\mathbf{y}}$$

Clearly, in the case of OLS estimation, both the R-squared formulas given here reduce to the usual R-squared formula.

Specification Tests

The TSCSREG procedure outputs the results of one specification test for fixed effects and one specification test for random effects.

For fixed effects, let β_f be the n dimensional vector of fixed effects parameters. The specification test reported is the conventional *F*-statistic for the hypothesis $\beta_f = \mathbf{0}$. The *F*-statistic with $n, M - K$ degrees of freedom is computed as

$$\hat{\beta}_f\hat{\mathbf{S}}_f^{-1}\hat{\beta}_f/n$$

where $\hat{\mathbf{S}}_f$ is the estimated covariance matrix of the fixed effects parameters.

Hausman's (1978) specification test or *m*-statistic can be used to test hypotheses in terms of bias or inconsistency of an estimator. This test was also proposed by Wu

(1973) and further extended in Hausman and Taylor (1982). Hausman's m-statistic is as follows.

Consider two estimators, $\hat{\beta}_a$ and $\hat{\beta}_b$, which under the null hypothesis are both consistent, but only $\hat{\beta}_a$ is asymptotically efficient. Under the alternative hypothesis, only $\hat{\beta}_b$ is consistent. The m-statistic is

$$m = (\hat{\beta}_b - \hat{\beta}_a)'(\hat{\mathbf{S}}_b - \hat{\mathbf{S}}_a)^{-}(\hat{\beta}_b - \hat{\beta}_a)$$

where $\hat{\mathbf{S}}_b$ and $\hat{\mathbf{S}}_a$ are consistent estimates of the asymptotic covariance matrices of $\hat{\beta}_b$ and $\hat{\beta}_a$. Then m is distributed χ^2 with k degrees of freedom, where k is the dimension of $\hat{\beta}_a$ and $\hat{\beta}_b$.

In the random effects specification, the null hypothesis of no correlation between effects and regressors implies that the OLS estimates of the slope parameters are consistent and inefficient but the GLS estimates of the slope parameters are consistent and efficient. This facilitates a Hausman specification test. The reported χ^2 statistic has degrees of freedom equal to the number of slope parameters.

OUTEST= Data Set

PROC TSCSREG writes the parameter estimates to an output data set when the OUTEST= option is specified. The OUTEST= data set contains the following variables:

MODEL — a character variable containing the label for the MODEL statement if a label is specified

METHOD — a character variable identifying the estimation method. Current methods are FULLER, PARKS, and DASILVA.

TYPE — a character variable that identifies the type of observation. Values of the _TYPE_ variable are CORRB, COVB, CSPARMS, and PARMS; the CORRB observation contains correlations of the parameter estimates; the COVB observation contains covariances of the parameter estimates; the CSPARMS observation contains cross-sectional parameter estimates; and the PARMS observation contains parameter estimates.

NAME — a character variable containing the name of a regressor variable for COVB and CORRB observations and left blank for other observations. The _NAME_ variable is used in conjunction with the _TYPE_ values COVB and CORRB to identify rows of the correlation or covariance matrix.

DEPVAR — a character variable containing the name of the response variable

MSE — the mean square error of the transformed model

CSID — the value of the cross section ID for CSPARMS observations. _CSID_ is used with the _TYPE_ value CSPARMS to identify the cross section for the first order autoregressive parameter estimate contained in the observation. _CSID_ is missing for observations with other _TYPE_ values. (Currently only the _A_1 variable contains values for CSPARMS observations.)

VARCS — the variance component estimate due to cross sections. _VARCS_ is included in the OUTEST= data set when either the FULLER or DASILVA option is specified.

VARTS — the variance component estimate due to time series. _VARTS_ is included in the OUTEST= data set when either the FULLER or DASILVA option is specified.

VARERR — the variance component estimate due to error. _VARERR_ is included in the OUTEST= data set when the FULLER option is specified.

_A_1 — the first order autoregressive parameter estimate. _A_1 is included in the OUTEST= data set when the PARKS option is specified. The values of _A_1 are cross-sectional parameters, meaning that they are estimated for each cross section separately. _A_1 has a value only for _TYPE_=CSPARMS observations. The cross section to which the estimate belongs is indicated by the _CSID_ variable.

INTERCEP — the intercept parameter estimate. (INTERCEP will be missing for models for which the NOINT option is specified.)

regressors — the regressor variables specified in the MODEL statement. The regressor variables in the OUTEST= data set contain the corresponding parameter estimates for the model identified by _MODEL_ for _TYPE_=PARMS observations, and the corresponding covariance or correlation matrix elements for _TYPE_=COVB and _TYPE_=CORRB observations. The response variable contains the value -1 for the _TYPE_=PARMS observation for its model.

Printed Output

For each MODEL statement, the printed output from PROC TSCSREG includes the following:

1. a model description, which gives the estimation method used, the model statement label if specified, the number of cross sections and the number of observations in each cross section, and the order of moving average error process for the DASILVA option
2. the estimates of the underlying error structure parameters
3. the regression parameter estimates and analysis. For each regressor, this includes the name of the regressor, the degrees of freedom, the parameter estimate, the standard error of the estimate, a *t* statistic for testing whether the estimate is significantly different from 0, and the significance probability of the *t* statistic. Whenever possible, the notation of the original reference is followed.

Optionally, PROC TSCSREG prints the following:

4. the covariance and correlation of the resulting regression parameter estimates for each model and assumed error structure
5. the $\hat{\Phi}$ matrix that is the estimated contemporaneous covariance matrix for the PARKS option

ODS Table Names

PROC TSCSREG assigns a name to each table it creates. You can use these names to reference the table when using the Output Delivery System (ODS) to select tables and create output data sets. These names are listed in the following table. For more information on ODS, see Chapter 8, "Using the Output Delivery System."

Table 27.1. ODS Tables Produced in PROC TSCSREG

ODS Table Name	Description	Option
ODS Tables Created by the MODEL Statement		
ModelDescription	Model Description	
FitStatistics	Fit Statistics	
FixedEffectsTest	F Test for No Fixed Effects	
ParameterEstimates	Parameter Estimates	
CovB	Covariance of Parameter Estimates	
CorrB	Correlations of Parameter Estimates	
VarianceComponents	Variance Component Estimates	
RandomEffectsTest	Hausman Test for Random Effects	
AR1Estimates	First Order Autoregressive Parameter Estimates	
EstimatedPhiMatrix	Estimated Phi Matrix	PARKS
EstimatedAutocovariances	Estimates of Autocovariances	PARKS
ODS Tables Created by the TEST Statement		
TestResults	Test Results	

Example

Example 27.1. Analyzing Demand for Liquid Assets

In this example, the demand equations for liquid assets are estimated. The demand function for the demand deposits is estimated under three error structures while demand equations for time deposits and savings and loan (S & L) association shares are calculated using the Parks method. The data for seven states (CA, DC, FL, IL, NY, TX, and WA) are selected out of 49 states. Refer to Feige (1964) for data description. All variables were transformed via natural logarithm. The first five observations of the data set A are shown in Output 27.1.1.

```
data a;
   input state $ year d t s y rd rt rs;
   label d = 'Per Capita Demand Deposits'
         t = 'Per Capita Time Deposits'
         s = 'Per Capita S & L Association Shares'
         y = 'Permanent Per Capita Personal Income'
         rd = 'Service Charge on Demand Deposits'
         rt = 'Interest on Time Deposits'
         rs = 'Interest on S & L Association Shares';
datalines;
   ... data lines are omitted ...
;

proc print data=a(obs=5);
run;
```

Output 27.1.1. A Sample of Liquid Assets Data

Obs	state	year	d	t	s	y	rd	rt	rs
1	CA	1949	6.2785	6.1924	4.4998	7.2056	-1.0700	0.1080	1.0664
2	CA	1950	6.4019	6.2106	4.6821	7.2889	-1.0106	0.1501	1.0767
3	CA	1951	6.5058	6.2729	4.8598	7.3827	-1.0024	0.4008	1.1291
4	CA	1952	6.4785	6.2729	5.0039	7.4000	-0.9970	0.4492	1.1227
5	CA	1953	6.4118	6.2538	5.1761	7.4200	-0.8916	0.4662	1.2110

The SORT procedure is used to sort the data into the required time series cross-sectional format. Then PROC TSCSREG analyzes the data.

```
proc sort data=a;
   by state year;
run;

title 'Demand for Liquid Assets';
proc tscsreg data=a;
   model d = y rd rt rs / fuller parks dasilva m=7;
   model t = y rd rt rs / parks;
   model s = y rd rt rs / parks;
   id state year;
run;
```

The income elasticities for liquid assets are greater than 1 except for the demand deposit income elasticity (0.692757) estimated by the Da Silva method. In Output 27.1.2, Output 27.1.3 and Output 27.1.4, the coefficient estimates (-0.29094, -0.43591, and -0.27736) of demand deposits (RD) imply that demand deposits increase significantly as the service charge is reduced. The price elasticities (0.227152 and 0.408066) for time deposits (RT) and S & L association shares (RS) have the expected sign and thus an increase in the interest rate on time deposits or S & L shares will increase the demand for the corresponding liquid asset. Demand deposits and S & L shares appear to be substitutes (Output 27.1.2, Output 27.1.3, Output 27.1.4, and Output 27.1.6). Time deposits are also substitutes for S & L shares in the time deposit demand equation (Output 27.1.5), while these liquid assets are independent of each other in Output 27.1.6 (insignificant coefficient estimate of RT, -0.02705). Demand deposits and time deposits appear to be weak complements in Output 27.1.3 and Output 27.1.4, while the cross elasticities between demand deposits and time deposits are not significant in Output 27.1.2 and Output 27.1.5.

Output 27.1.2. Demand for Demand Deposits – Fuller-Battese Method

```
                          Demand for Liquid Assets

                           The TSCSREG Procedure
                    Fuller and Battese Method Estimation

Dependent Variable: d Per Capita Demand Deposits

                            Model Description

                    Estimation Method                Fuller
                    Number of Cross Sections              7
                    Time Series Length                   11


                              Fit Statistics

             SSE                 0.0795    DFE                     72
             MSE                 0.0011    Root MSE            0.0332
             R-Square            0.6786


                       Variance Component Estimates

             Variance Component for Cross Sections      0.03427
             Variance Component for Time Series         0.00026
             Variance Component for Error               0.00111


                             Hausman Test for
                              Random Effects

                           DF    m Value    Pr > m

                            4       5.51    0.2385


                           Parameter Estimates

                                     Standard
 Variable        DF   Estimate        Error   t Value   Pr > |t|   Label

 Intercept        1   -1.23606       0.7252     -1.70     0.0926   Intercept
 y                1   1.064058       0.1040     10.23     <.0001   Permanent Per Capita
                                                                   Personal Income
 rd               1   -0.29094       0.0526     -5.53     <.0001   Service Charge on
                                                                   Demand Deposits
 rt               1   0.039388       0.0278      1.42     0.1603   Interest on Time
                                                                   Deposits
 rs               1   -0.32662       0.1140     -2.86     0.0055   Interest on S & L
                                                                   Association Shares
```

Output 27.1.3. Demand for Demand Deposits – Parks Method

Demand for Liquid Assets

The TSCSREG Procedure
Parks Method Estimation

Dependent Variable: d Per Capita Demand Deposits

Model Description

Estimation Method	Parks
Number of Cross Sections	7
Time Series Length	11

Fit Statistics

SSE	73.3696	DFE	72
MSE	1.0190	Root MSE	1.0095
R-Square	0.9263		

Parameter Estimates

Variable	DF	Estimate	Standard Error	t Value	Pr > |t|	Label
Intercept	1	-2.66565	0.3139	-8.49	<.0001	Intercept
y	1	1.222569	0.0423	28.87	<.0001	Permanent Per Capita Personal Income
rd	1	-0.43591	0.0201	-21.71	<.0001	Service Charge on Demand Deposits
rt	1	0.041237	0.0210	1.97	0.0530	Interest on Time Deposits
rs	1	-0.26683	0.0654	-4.08	0.0001	Interest on S & L Association Shares

Output 27.1.4. Demand for Demand Deposits – Da Silva Method

```
                      Demand for Liquid Assets

                       The TSCSREG Procedure
                     Da Silva Method Estimation

Dependent Variable: d Per Capita Demand Deposits

                          Model Description

              Estimation Method                 DaSilva
              Number of Cross Sections                7
              Time Series Length                     11
              Order of MA Error Process               7


                            Fit Statistics

        SSE           21609.8923    DFE                      72
        MSE             300.1374    Root MSE            17.3245
        R-Square          0.4995


                    Variance Component Estimates

        Variance Component for Cross Sections      0.03063
        Variance Component for Time Series        0.000148


                             Estimates of
                            Autocovariances
                         Lag             Gamma

                         0         0.0008558553
                         1         0.0009081747
                         2         0.0008494797
                         3         0.0007889687
                         4         0.0013281983
                         5         0.0011091685
                         6         0.0009874973
                         7         0.0008462601
```

```
                      Demand for Liquid Assets

                       The TSCSREG Procedure
                     Da Silva Method Estimation

Dependent Variable: d Per Capita Demand Deposits

                         Parameter Estimates

                              Standard
 Variable       DF  Estimate     Error  t Value  Pr > |t|  Label

 Intercept       1  1.281084    0.0824    15.55    <.0001  Intercept
 y               1  0.692757   0.00677   102.40    <.0001  Permanent Per Capita
                                                           Personal Income
 rd              1  -0.27736   0.00274  -101.18    <.0001  Service Charge on
                                                           Demand Deposits
 rt              1  0.009378   0.00171     5.49    <.0001  Interest on Time
                                                           Deposits
 rs              1  -0.09942   0.00601   -16.53    <.0001  Interest on S & L
                                                           Association Shares
```

Output 27.1.5. Demand for Time Deposits – Parks Method

Demand for Liquid Assets

The TSCSREG Procedure
Parks Method Estimation

Dependent Variable: t Per Capita Time Deposits

Model Description

Estimation Method	Parks
Number of Cross Sections	7
Time Series Length	11

Fit Statistics

SSE	63.3807	DFE	72
MSE	0.8803	Root MSE	0.9382
R-Square	0.9517		

Parameter Estimates

Variable	DF	Estimate	Standard Error	t Value	Pr > |t|	Label
Intercept	1	-5.33334	0.5007	-10.65	<.0001	Intercept
y	1	1.516344	0.0810	18.72	<.0001	Permanent Per Capita Personal Income
rd	1	-0.04791	0.0294	-1.63	0.1082	Service Charge on Demand Deposits
rt	1	0.227152	0.0332	6.85	<.0001	Interest on Time Deposits
rs	1	-0.42569	0.1262	-3.37	0.0012	Interest on S & L Association Shares

Output 27.1.6. Demand for Savings and Loan Shares – Parks Method

```
                              Demand for Liquid Assets

                               The TSCSREG Procedure
                              Parks Method Estimation

Dependent Variable: s Per Capita S & L Association Shares

                                 Model Description

                        Estimation Method                    Parks
                        Number of Cross Sections                 7
                        Time Series Length                      11


                                  Fit Statistics

                SSE              71.9675    DFE                  72
                MSE               0.9995    Root MSE         0.9998
                R-Square          0.9017


                                Parameter Estimates

                                    Standard
 Variable       DF    Estimate        Error    t Value    Pr > |t|    Label

 Intercept       1    -8.09632       0.7850     -10.31      <.0001    Intercept
 y               1    1.832988       0.1157      15.84      <.0001    Permanent Per Capita
                                                                      Personal Income
 rd              1    0.576723       0.0435      13.26      <.0001    Service Charge on
                                                                      Demand Deposits
 rt              1    -0.02705       0.0312      -0.87      0.3891    Interest on Time
                                                                      Deposits
 rs              1    0.408066       0.1092       3.74      0.0004    Interest on S & L
                                                                      Association Shares
```

Acknowledgments

The TSCSREG procedure was developed by Douglas J. Drummond and A. Ronald Gallant, and contributed to the Version 5 SUGI Supplemental Library in 1979.

Dr. Drummond, now deceased, was with the Center for Survey Statistics, Research Triangle Park, NC. Dr. Drummond programmed the Parks and Fuller-Battese methods. Professor Gallant, who is currently with the University of North Carolina at Chapell Hill, programmed the Da Silva method and generously contributed his time to the support of PROC TSCSREG after Dr. Drummond's death.

The version of PROC TSCSREG documented here was produced by converting the older SUGI Supplemental Library version of the procedure to Version 6 of SAS software. This conversion work was performed by SAS Institute, which now supports the procedure. Although several features were added during the conversion (such as the OUTEST= option, ID statement, and BY statement), credit for the statistical aspects and general design of the TSCSREG procedure belongs to Dr. Drummond and Professor Gallant.

References

Baltagi, B. H. and Chang, Y. (1994), "Incomplete Panels: A Comparative Study of Alternative Estimators for the Unbalanced One-way Error Component Regression Model," *Journal of Econometrics,* 62(2), 67-89.

Buse, A. (1973), "Goodness of Fit in Generalized Least Squares Estimation," *American Statistician,* 27, 106-108.

Da Silva, J.G.C. (1975), "The Analysis of Cross-Sectional Time Series Data," Ph.D. dissertation, Department of Statistics, North Carolina State University.

SAS Institute Inc. (1979), *SAS Technical Report S-106, TSCSREG: A SAS Procedure for the Analysis of Time-Series Cross-Section Data*, Cary, NC: SAS Institute Inc.

Feige, E.L. (1964), *The Demand for Liquid Assets: A Temporal Cross-Section Analysis*, Englewood Cliffs: Prentice-Hall.

Feige, E.L. and Swamy, P.A.V. (1974), "A Random Coefficient Model of the Demand for Liquid Assets," *Journal of Money, Credit, and Banking*, 6, 241-252.

Fuller, W.A. and Battese, G.E. (1974), "Estimation of Linear Models with Crossed-Error Structure," *Journal of Econometrics*, 2, 67-78.

Greene, W.H. (1990), *Econometric Analysis*, New York: Macmillan Publishing Company.

Hausman, J.A. (1978), "Specification Tests in Econometrics," *Econometrica*, 46, 1251-1271.

Hausman, J.A. and Taylor, W.E. (1982), "A Generalized Specification Test," *Economics Letters,* 8, 239-245.

Hsiao, C. (1986), *Analysis of Panel Data*, Cambridge: Cambridge University Press.

Judge, G.G., Griffiths, W.E., Hill, R.C., Lutkepohl, H., and Lee, T.C. (1985), *The Theory and Practice of Econometrics*, Second Edition, New York: John Wiley & Sons.

Kmenta, J. (1971), *Elements of Econometrics*, New York: MacMillan Publishing Company, Inc.

Maddala, G.S. (1977), *Econometrics*, New York: McGraw-Hill Co.

Parks, R.W. (1967), "Efficient Estimation of a System of Regression Equations when Disturbances Are Both Serially and Contemporaneously Correlated," *Journal of the American Statistical Association*, 62, 500-509.

Searle S.R. (1971), "Topics in Variance Component Estimation," *Biometrics*, 26, 1-76.

Seely, J. (1969), "Estimation in Finite-Dimensional Vector Spaces with Application to the Mixed Linear Model," Ph.D. dissertation, Department of Statistics, Iowa State University.

Seely, J. (1970a), "Linear Spaces and Unbiased Estimation," *Annals of Mathematical Statistics*, 41, 1725-1734.

Seely, J. (1970b), "Linear Spaces and Unbiased Estimation - Application to the Mixed Linear Model," *Annals of Mathematical Statistics*, 41, 1735-1748.

Seely, J. and Soong, S. (1971), "A Note on MINQUE's and Quadratic Estimability," Corvallis, Oregon: Oregon State University.

Seely, J. and Zyskind, G. (1971), "Linear Spaces and Minimum Variance Unbiased Estimation," *Annals of Mathematical Statistics*, 42, 691-703.

Theil, H. (1961), *Economic Forecasts and Policy*, Second Edition, Amsterdam: North-Holland, 435-437.

Wansbeek, T., and Kapteyn, Arie (1989), "Estimation of the Error-Components Model with Incomplete Panels," *Journal of Econometrics,* 41, 341-361.

Wu, D. M. (1973), "Alternative Tests of Independence between Stochastic Regressors and Disturbances," *Econometrica,* 41(4), 733-750.

Zellner, A. (1962), "An Efficient Method of Estimating Seemingly Unrelated Regressions and Tests for Aggregation Bias," *Journal of the American Statistical Association*, 57, 348-368.

Chapter 28

The TIMESERIES Procedure

Chapter Contents

Chapter 28
The TIMESERIES Procedure

Overview

The TIMESERIES procedure analyzes time-stamped transactional data with respect to time and accumulates the data into a time series format. The procedure can perform trend and seasonal analysis on the transactions. Once the transactional data are accumulated, time domain and frequency domain analysis can be performed on the accumulated time series.

For seasonal analysis of the transaction data, various statistics can be computed for each season. For trend analysis of the transaction data, various statistics can be computed for each time period. The analysis is similar to applying the MEANS procedure of Base SAS software to each season or time period of concern.

Once the transactional data are accumulated to form a time series and any missing values are interpreted, the accumulated time series can be functionally transformed using log, square root, logistic, or Box-Cox transformations. The time series can be further transformed using simple and/or seasonal differencing. After functional and difference transformations have been applied, the accumulated and transformed time series can be stored in an output data set. This working time series can then be analyzed further using various time series analysis techniques provided by this procedure or other SAS/ETS procedures.

Time series analyses performed by the TIMESERIES procedure include:

- Descriptive (Global) Statistics
- Seasonal Decomposition/Adjustment Analysis
- Correlation Analysis
- Cross-correlation Analysis

All results of the transactional or time series analysis can be stored in output data sets or printed using the Output Delivery System (ODS).

Experimental graphics are now available with the TIMESERIES procedure. For more information, see the "ODS Graphics" section on page 1603.

The TIMESERIES procedure can process large amounts of time-stamped transactional data. Therefore, the analysis results are useful for large-scale time series analysis or (temporal) data mining. All of the results can be stored in output data sets in either a time series format (default) or in coordinate format (transposed). The time series format is useful for preparing the data for subsequent analysis using other SAS/ETS procedures. For example, the working time series can be further analyzed, modeled, and forecast using other SAS/ETS procedures. The coordinate format is useful when using this procedure with SAS/STAT procedures or Enterprise Miner. For example, clustering time-stamped transactional data can be achieved by using the results of this procedure with the clustering procedures of SAS/STAT and the nodes of Enterprise Miner.

The EXPAND procedure can be used for the frequency conversion and transformations of time series output from this procedure.

Getting Started

This section outlines the use of the TIMESERIES procedure and gives a cursory description of some of the analysis techniques that can be performed on time-stamped transactional data.

Given an input data set that contains numerous transaction variables recorded over time at no specific frequency, the TIMESERIES procedure can form time series as follows:

```
PROC TIMESERIES DATA=<input-data-set> OUT=<output-data-set>;
   ID <time-ID-variable> INTERVAL=<frequency>
                         ACCUMULATE=<statistic>;
   VAR <time-series-variables>;
RUN;
```

The TIMESERIES procedure forms time series from the input time-stamped transactional data. It can provide results in output data sets or in other output formats using the Output Delivery System (ODS). The following examples are more fully illustrated in the "Examples" section on page 1606.

Time-stamped transactional data are often recorded at no fixed interval. Analysts often want to use time series analysis techniques that require fixed-time intervals. Therefore, the transactional data must be accumulated to form a fixed-interval time series.

Suppose that a bank wishes to analyze the transactions associated with each of its customers over time. Further, suppose that the data set WORK.TRANSACTIONS contains four variables related to these transactions: CUSTOMER, DATE, WITHDRAWAL, and DEPOSITS. The following examples illustrate possible ways to analyze these transactions using the TIMESERIES procedure.

The following statements illustrate how to use the TIMESERIES procedure to accumulate time-stamped transactional data to form a daily time series based on the accumulated daily totals of each type of transaction (WITHDRAWALS and DEPOSITS).

```
proc timeseries data=transactions out=timeseries;
   by customer;
   id date interval=day accumulate=total;
   var withdrawals deposits;
run;
```

The OUT=TIMESERIES option specifies that the resulting time series data for each customer is to be stored in the data set WORK.TIMESERIES. The INTERVAL=DAY option specifies that the transactions are to accumulated on a daily basis. The ACCUMULATE=TOTAL option specifies that the sum of the transactions are to be accumulated. Once the transactional data are accumulated into a time series format, many of the procedures provided with SAS/ETS software can be used to analyze the time series data.

For example, the ARIMA procedure can be used to model and forecast each customer's transactions using an ARIMA(0,1,1)(0,1,1)$_s$ model (where the number of seasons is s=7 days in a week) using the following statements:

```
proc arima data=timeseries;
   identify var=withdrawals(1,7) noprint;
   estimate q=(1,7) outest=estimates noprint;
   forecast id=date interval=day out=forecasts;
quit;
```

The OUTEST=ESTIMATES data set will contain the parameter estimates of the model specified. The OUT=FORECASTS data set will contain forecasts based on the model specified. See the ARIMA procedure for more detail.

A single set of transactions can be very large and must be summarized in order to analyze them effectively. Analysts often want to examine transactional data for trends and seasonal variation. To analyze transactional data for trends and seasonality, statistics must be computed for each time period and season of concern. For each observation, the time period and season must be determined and the data must be analyzed based on this determination.

The following statements illustrate how to use the TIMESERIES procedure to perform trend and seasonal analysis of time-stamped transactional data.

```
proc timeseries data=transactions out=out
      outseason=season outtrend=trend;
   by customer;
   id date interval=day accumulate=total;
   var withdrawals deposits;
run;
```

Since the INTERVAL=DAY option is specified, the length of the seasonal cycle is seven (7) where the first season is Sunday and the last season is Saturday. The output data set specified by the OUTSEASON=SEASON option contains the seasonal statistics for each day of the week by each customer. The output data set specified by the OUTTREND=TREND option contains the trend statistics for each day of the calendar by each customer.

Often it is desired to seasonally decompose into seasonal, trend, cycle, and irregular components or seasonally adjust a time series. These techniques describe how the changing seasons influence the time series.

The following statements illustrate how to use the TIMESERIES procedure to perform seasonal adjustment/decomposition analysis of time-stamped transactional data.

```
proc timeseries data=transactions out=out outdecomp=decompose;
   by customer;
   id date interval=day accumulate=total;
   var withdrawals deposits;
run;
```

The output data set specified by the OUTDECOMP=DECOMPOSE data set contains the decomposed/adjusted time series for each customer.

A single time series can be very large. Often, a time series must be summarized with respect to time lags in order to be efficiently analyzed. Analysts often want to analyze time series data using time domain techniques. These techniques help describe how a current observation is related to the past observations with respect to the time (season) lag.

The following statements illustrate how to use the TIMESERIES procedure to perform time domain analysis of time-stamped transactional data.

```
proc timeseries data=transactions out=out outcorr=timedomain;
   by customer;
   id date interval=day accumulate=total;
   var withdrawals deposits;
run;
```

The output data set specified by the OUTCORR=TIMEDOMAIN data set contains the time domain statistics by each customer.

Syntax

The following statements are used with the TIMESERIES procedure.

PROC TIMESERIES *options*;
  BY *variables*;
  CORR *statistics-list / options*;
  CROSSCORR *statistics-list / options*;
  DECOMP *component-list / options*;
  SEASON *statistics-list / options*;
  TREND *statistics-list / options*;
  VAR *variable-list / options*;
  CROSSVAR *variable-list / options*;
  ID *variable* **INTERVAL=** *interval options*;

Functional Summary

The statements and options controlling the TIMESERIES procedure are summarized in the following table.

Description	Statement	Option
Statements		
specify BY-group processing	BY	
specify variables to analyze	VAR	
specify cross-variables to analyze	CROSSVAR	
specify the time ID variable	ID	
specify correlation options	CORR	
specify cross-correlation optons	CROSSCORR	
specify decomposition optons	DECOMP	
specify seasonal statistics optons	SEASON	
specify trend statistics optons	TREND	
Data Set Options		
specify the input data set	PROC TIMESERIES	DATA=
specify the output data set	PROC TIMESERIES	OUT=
specify correlations output data set	PROC TIMESERIES	OUTCORR=
specify cross-correlations output data set	PROC TIMESERIES	OUTCROSSCORR=
specify decomposition output data set	PROC TIMESERIES	OUTDECOMP=
specify seasonal statistics output data set	PROC TIMESERIES	OUTSEASON=
specify summary statistics output data set	PROC TIMESERIES	OUTSUM=
specify trend statistics output data set	PROC TIMESERIES	OUTTREND=
Accumulation and Seasonality Options		
specify accumulation frequency	ID	INTERVAL=
specify length of seasonal cycle	PROC TIMESERIES	SEASONALITY=
specify interval alignment	ID	ALIGN=
specify time ID variable values are not sorted	ID	NOTSORTED
specify starting time ID value	ID	START=
specify ending time ID value	ID	END=
specify accumulation statistic	ID, VAR, CROSSVAR	ACCUMULATE=

Description	Statement	Option
specify missing value interpretation	ID, VAR, CROSSVAR	SETMISS=
Time-Stamped Data Seasonal Statistics Options		
specify the form of the output data set	SEASON	TRANSPOSE=
Time-Stamped Data Trend Statistics Options		
specify the form of the output data set	TREND	TRANSPOSE=
specify the number of time periods to be stored	TREND	NPERIODS=
Time Series Transformation Options		
specify simple differencing	VAR, CROSSVAR	DIF=
specify seasonal differencing	VAR, CROSSVAR	SDIF=
specify transformation	VAR, CROSSVAR	TRANSFORM=
Time Series Correlation Options		
specify the list of lags	CORR	LAGS=
specify the number of lags	CORR	NLAG=
specify the number of parameters	CORR	NPARMS=
specify the form of the output data set	CORR	TRANSPOSE=
Time Series Cross-correlation Options		
specify the list of lags	CROSSCORR	LAGS=
specify the number of lags	CROSSCORR	NLAG=
specify the form of the output data set	CROSSCORR	TRANSPOSE=
Time Series Decomposition Options		
specify mode of decomposition	DECOMP	MODE=
specify the Hodrick-Prescott filter parameter	DECOMP	LAMBDA=
specify the number of time periods to be stored	DECOMP	NPERIODS=
specify the form of the output data set	DECOMP	TRANSPOSE=
Printing Control Options		
specify time ID format	ID	FORMAT=
specify printed output	PROC TIMESERIES	PRINT=
specify detailed printed output	PROC TIMESERIES	PRINTDETAILS
Miscellaneous Options		
specify that analysis variables are processed in sorted order	PROC TIMESERIES	SORTNAMES

Description	Statement	Option
limits error and warning messages	PROC TIMESERIES	MAXERROR=

PROC TIMESERIES Statement

PROC TIMESERIES *options*;

The following options can be used in the PROC TIMESERIES statement.

DATA= *SAS-data-set*
names the SAS data set containing the input data for the procedure to create time series. If the DATA= option is not specified, the most recently created SAS data set is used.

MAXERROR= *number*
limits the number of warning and error messages produced during the execution of the procedure to the specified value. The default is MAXERRORS=50. This option is particularly useful in BY-group processing where it can be used to suppress the recurring messages.

OUT= *SAS-data-set*
names the output data set to contain the the time series variables specified in the subsequent VAR statements. If an ID variable is specified, it will also be included in the OUT= data set. The values are accumulated based on the ID statement INTERVAL= and/ or ACCUMULATE= option. The OUT= data set is particularly useful when you wish to further analyze, model, or forecast the resulting time series with other SAS/ETS procedures.

OUTCORR= *SAS-data-set*
names the output data set to contain the univariate time domain statistics.

OUTCROSSCORR= *SAS-data-set*
names the output data set to contain the cross-correlation statistics.

OUTDECOMP= *SAS-data-set*
names the output data set to contain the decomposed and/or seasonally adjusted time series.

OUTSEASON= *SAS-data-set*
names the output data set to contain the seasonal statistics. The statistics are computed for each season as specified by the INTERVAL= option or the SEASONALITY= option. The OUTSEASON= data set is particularly useful when analyzing transactional data for seasonal variations.

OUTSUM= *SAS-data-set*
names the output data set to contain the descriptive statistics. The descriptive statistics are based on the accumulated time series when the ACCUMULATE= or

SETMISSING= options are specified. The OUTSUM= data set is particularly useful when analyzing large numbers of series and a summary of the results are needed.

OUTTREND= *SAS-data-set*

names the output data set to contain the trend statistics. The statistics are computed for each time period as specified by the INTERVAL= option. The OUTTREND= data set is particularly useful when analyzing transactional data for trends.

PRINT= *option* **|** (*options*)

specifies the printed output desired. By default, the TIMESERIES procedure produces no printed output. The following printing options are available:

DECOMP	prints the seasonal decomposition/adjustment table. (OUTDECOMP= data set)
SEASONS	prints the seasonal statistics table. (OUTSEASON= data set)
DESCSTATS	prints the descriptive statistics for the accumulated time series. (OUTSUM= data set)
SUMMARY	prints the descriptive statistics table for all time series. (OUTSUM= data set)
TRENDS	prints the trend statistics table. (OUTTREND= data set)

For example, PRINT=SEASONS prints the seasonal statistics. The PRINT= option produces printed output for these results utilizing the Output Delivery System (ODS). The PRINT= option produces results similar to the data sets listed next to the above options in parenthesis.

PRINTDETAILS

specifies that output requested with the PRINT= option be printed in greater detail.

SEASONALITY= *number*

specifies the length of the seasonal cycle. For example, SEASONALITY=3 means that every group of three time periods forms a seasonal cycle. By default, the length of the seasonal cycle is one (no seasonality) or the length implied by the INTERVAL= option specified in the ID statement. For example, INTERVAL=MONTH implies that the length of the seasonal cycle is twelve.

SORTNAMES

specifies that the variables specified in the VAR statements are processed in sorted order by the variable names.

BY Statement

BY *variables;*

A BY statement can be used with PROC TIMESERIES to obtain separate analyses for groups of observations defined by the BY variables.

CORR Statement

CORR *statistics / options*;

A CORR statement can be used with the TIMESERIES procedure to specify options related to time domain analysis of the accumulated time series. Only one CORR statement is allowed.

The following time domain statistics are available:

LAG	Time lag
N	Number of Variance Products
ACOV	Autocovariances
ACF	Autocorrelations
ACFSTD	Autocorrelation Standard Errors
ACF2STD	Indicates ACF Beyond Two Standard Errors
ACFNORM	Normalized Autocorrelations
ACFPROB	Autocorrelation Probabilities
ACFLPROB	Autocorrelation Log Probabilities
PACF	Partial Autocorrelations
PACFSTD	Partial Autocorrelation Standard Errors
PACF2STD	Indicates PACF Beyond Two Standard Errors
PACFNORM	Partial Normalized Autocorrelations
PACFPROB	Partial Autocorrelation Probabilities
PACFLPROB	Partial Autocorrelation Log Probabilities
IACF	Inverse Autocorrelations
IACFSTD	Inverse Autocorrelation Standard Errors
IACF2STD	Indicates IACF Beyond Two Standard Errors
IACFNORM	Normalized Inverse Autocorrelations
IACFPROB	Inverse Autocorrelation Probabilities
IACFLPROB	Inverse Autocorrelation Log Probabilities
WN	White Noise Test Statistics
WNPROB	White Noise Test Probabilities
WNLPROB	White Noise Test Log Probabilities

If none of the correlation statistics are specified, the default is as follows:

```
corr lag n acov acf acfstd pacf pacfstd iacf iacfstd wn wnprob;
```

The following options can be specified in the CORR statement following the slash (/):

NLAG= *number*
LAGS= *(numlist)*
specifies the number of lags or list of lags to be stored in OUTCORR= data set or printed. The default is 24 or three times the length of the seasonal cycle whichever is smaller.

NPARMS= *number*
specifies the number of parameters used in the model that created the residual time series. The number of parameters determines the degrees of freedom associated with the Ljung-Box statistics. The default is NPARMS=0.

TRANSPOSE=NO | YES
TRANSPOSE=YES specifies that the OUTCORR= data set is recorded with the lags as the column names instead of the correlation statistics as the column names. The TRANSPOSE=NO option is particularly useful for graphing the correlation results using SAS/GRAPH procedures. The TRANSPOSE=YES option is particularly useful for analyzing the correlation results using other SAS/STAT procedures or Enterprise Miner. The default is TRANSPOSE=NO.

CROSSCORR Statement

CROSSCORR *statistics / options*;

A CROSSCORR statement can be used with the TIMESERIES procedure to specify options related to cross-correlation analysis of the accumulated time series. Only one CROSSCORR statement is allowed.

The following time domain statistics are available:

LAG	Time lag
N	Number of Variance Products
CCOV	Cross-Covariances
CCF	Cross-correlations
CCFSTD	Cross-correlation Standard Errors
CCF2STD	Indicates CCF Beyond Two Standard Errors
CCFNORM	Normalized Cross-correlations
CCFPROB	Cross-correlations Probabilities
CCFLPROB	Cross-correlations Log Probabilities

If none of the correlation statistics are specified, the default is as follows:

```
crosscorr lag n ccov ccf ccfstd;
```

The following options can be specified in the CROSSCORR statement following the slash (/):

NLAG= *number*
LAGS= *(numlist)*

specifies the number of lags or list of lags to be stored in OUTCROSSCORR= data set or printed. The default is 24 or three times the length of the seasonal cycle whichever is smaller.

TRANSPOSE=NO | YES

TRANSPOSE=YES specifies that the OUTCROSSCORR= data set is recorded with the lags as the column names instead of the cross-correlation statistics as the column names. The TRANSPOSE=NO option is particularly useful for graphing the cross-correlation results using SAS/GRAPH procedures. The TRANSPOSE=YES option is particularly useful for analyzing the cross-correlation results using other SAS/STAT procedures or Enterprise Miner. The default is TRANSPOSE=NO.

DECOMP Statement

DECOMP *components / options*;

A DECOMP statement can be used with the TIMESERIES procedure to specify options related to classical seasonal decomposition of the time series data. Only one DECOMP statement is allowed. The options specified affects all variables specified in the VAR statements. Decomposition can be performed only when the length of the seasonal cycle implied by the INTERVAL= option or specified by the SEASONALITY= option is greater than one.

The following seasonal decomposition components are available:

ORIG|ORIGINAL	Original Series
TCC|TRENDCYCLE	Trend-Cycle Component
SIC|SEASONIRREGULAR	Seasonal-Irregular Component
SC|SEASONAL	Seasonal Component
SCSTD	Seasonal Component Standard Errors
TCS|TRENDCYCLESEASON	Trend-Cycle-Seasonal Component
IC|IRREGULAR	Irregular Component
SA|ADJUSTED	Seasonal Adjusted
PCSA	Percent Change Seasonal Adjusted
TC	Trend Component
CC|CYCLE	Cycle Component

If none of the components are specified, the default is as follows:

```
decomp orig tcc sc ic sa;
```

The following options can be specified in the DECOMP statement following the slash (/):

MODE=ADD|ADDITIVE
MODE=MULT|MULTIPLICATIVE
MODE=LOGADD|LOGADDITIVE
MODE=PSEUDOADD|PSEUDOADDITIVE
MODE=MULTORADD

specifies the type of decomposition is to be used to decompose the time series. Multiplicative and log additive decomposition requires a positive-valued time series. If the accumulated time series contains nonpositive values and the MODE=MULT or MODE=LOGADD option is specified, an error results. Pseudo-additive decomposition requires a nonnegative-valued time series. If the accumulated time series contains negative values and the MODE=PSEUDOADD option is specified, an error results. The MODE=MULTORADD option specifies that multiplicative decomposition is used when the accumulated time series contains only positive values, that pseudo-additive decomposition is used when the accumulated time series contains only nonnegative values, and that additive decomposition is used otherwise. The default is MODE=MULTORADD.

LAMBDA= *number*

specifies the Hodrick-Prescott filter parameter for trend-cycle decomposition. The default is LAMBDA=1600. If filtering is not specified this option is ignored.

NPERIODS= *number*

specifies the number of time periods to be stored in the OUTDECOMP= data set when the TRANSPOSE=YES option is specified. If the TRANSPOSE=NO option is specified, the NPERIODS= option is ignored. If the NPERIODS= option is positive the first or beginning time periods are recorded. If the NPERIODS= option is negative the last or ending time periods are recorded. The NPERIODS= option specifies the number of OUTDECOMP= data set variables to contain the seasonal decomposition and is therefore limited to the maximum allowable number of SAS variables. If the number of time periods exceeds this limit a warning is printed in the log and the number periods stored is reduced to the limit.

If NPERIODS= option is not specified, all of the periods specified between the ID statement START= and END= options are stored. If either of the START= or END= options are not specified, the default magnitude is the seasonality specified by the TIMESERIES statement SEASONALITY= option or implied by the INTERVAL= option. If only the START= option is specified, the default sign is positive. If only the END= option is specified, the default sign is negative.

```
/* NPERIODS=10 because there are ten months between
   the specified start and end dates */
   id date interval=month accumulate=total
      start='01JAN2000'D end='01OCT2000'D;
   decomp / transpose=yes;

/* NPERIODS=10 because there are ten months between
   the specified start and end dates */
```

```
   id date interval=month accumulate=total
      start='01JAN2000'D end='01OCT2000'D;
   decomp / transpose=yes nperiods=100;

/* NPERIODS=12 because there are twelve months in a year
   and only the start date is specified */
   id date interval=month accumulate=total
      start='01JAN2000'D;
   decomp / transpose=yes;

/* NPERIODS=-12 because there are twelve months in a year
   and only the end date is specified */
   id date interval=month accumulate=total
      end='01OCT2000'D;
   decomp / transpose=yes;
```

TRANSPOSE=NO | YES

TRANSPOSE=YES specifies that the OUTDECOMP= data set is recorded with the time periods as the column names instead of the statistics as the column names. The first and last time period stored in the OUTDECOMP= data set corresponds to the period of the ID statement START= option and END= option, respectively. If only the ID statement END= option is specified, the last time ID value of each accumulated time series corresponds to the last time period column. If only the ID statement START= option is specified, the first time ID value of each accumulated time series corresponds to the first time period column. If neither the START= option or END= option is specified with the ID statement, the first time ID value of each accumulated time series corresponds to the first time period column. The TRANSPOSE=NO option is particularly useful for analyzing the decomposition results using other SAS/ETS procedures or graphing the decomposition results using SAS/GRAPH procedures such as the GPLOT procedure. The TRANSPOSE=YES option is particularly useful for analyzing the decomposition results using other SAS/STAT procedures or Enterprise Miner. The default is TRANSPOSE=NO.

ID Statement

ID *variable* **INTERVAL=** *interval options*;

The ID statement names a numeric variable that identifies observations in the input and output data sets. The ID variable's values are assumed to be SAS date, time, or datetime values. In addition, the ID statement specifies the (desired) frequency associated with the time series. The ID statement options also specify how the observations are accumulated and how the time ID values are aligned to form the time series. The information specified affects all variables specified in subsequent VAR statements. If the ID statement is specified, the INTERVAL= option must also be specified. If an ID statement is not specified, the observation number, with respect to the BY group, is used as the time ID.

The following options can be used with the ID statement.

ACCUMULATE= *option*

specifies how the data set observations are accumulated within each time period. The frequency (width of each time interval) is specified by the INTERVAL= option. The ID variable contains the time ID values. Each time ID variable value corresponds to a specific time period. The accumulated values form the time series, which is used in subsequent analysis.

The ACCUMULATE= option is particularly useful when there are zero or more than one input observations coinciding with a particular time period (e.g., time-stamped transactional data). The EXPAND procedure offers additional frequency conversions and transformations that can also be useful in creating a time series.

The following options determine how the observations are accumulated within each time period based on the ID variable and the frequency specified by the INTERVAL= option:

NONE	No accumulation occurs; the ID variable values must be equally spaced with respect to the frequency. This is the default option.
TOTAL	Observations are accumulated based on the total sum of their values.
AVERAGE | AVG	Observations are accumulated based on the average of their values.
MINIMUM | MIN	Observations are accumulated based on the minimum of their values.
MEDIAN | MED	Observations are accumulated based on the median of their values.
MAXIMUM | MAX	Observations are accumulated based on the maximum of their values.
N	Observations are accumulated based on the number of non-missing observations.
NMISS	Observations are accumulated based on the number of missing observations.
NOBS	Observations are accumulated based on the number of observations.
FIRST	Observations are accumulated based on the first of their values.
LAST	Observations are accumulated based on the last of their values.
STDDEV |STD	Observations are accumulated based on the standard deviation of their values.
CSS	Observations are accumulated based on the corrected sum of squares of their values.
USS	Observations are accumulated based on the uncorrected sum of squares of their values.

If the ACCUMULATE= option is specified, the SETMISSING= option is useful for specifying how accumulated missing values are treated. If missing values should be interpreted as zero, then SETMISSING=0 should be used. The DETAILS section describes accumulation in greater detail.

ALIGN= *option*

controls the alignment of SAS dates used to identify output observations. The ALIGN= option accepts the following values: BEGINNING|BEG|B, MIDDLE|MID|M, and ENDING|END|E. BEGINNING is the default.

END= *option*

specifies a SAS date, datetime, or time value that represents the end of the data. If the last time ID variable value is less than the END= value, the series is extended with missing values. If the last time ID variable value is greater than the END= value, the series is truncated. For example, END="&sysdate"D uses the automatic macro variable SYSDATE to extend or truncate the series to the current date. This START= and END= option can be used to ensure that data associated within each BY group contains the same number of observations.

FORMAT= *format*

specifies the SAS format for the time ID values. If the FORMAT= option is not specified, the default format is implied from the INTERVAL= option.

INTERVAL= *interval*

specifies the frequency of the accumulated time series. For example, if the input data set consists of quarterly observations, then INTERVAL=QTR should be used. If the SEASONALITY= option is not specified, the length of the seasonal cycle is implied from the INTERVAL= option. For example, INTERVAL=QTR implies a seasonal cycle of length 4. If the ACCUMULATE= option is also specified, the INTERVAL= option determines the time periods for the accumulation of observations.

NOTSORTED

specifies that the time ID values are not in sorted order. The TIMESERIES procedure will sort the data with respect to the time ID prior to analysis.

SETMISSING= *option* **|** *number*

specifies how missing values (either actual or accumulated) are interpreted in the accumulated time series. If a number is specified, missing values are set to number. If a missing value indicates an unknown value, this option should not be used. If a missing value indicates no value, a SETMISSING=0 should be used. You would typically use SETMISSING=0 for transactional data because no recorded data usually implies no activity. The following options can also be used to determine how missing values are assigned:

MISSING	Missing values are set to missing. This is the default option.
AVERAGE | AVG	Missing values are set to the accumulated average value.
MINIMUM | MIN	Missing values are set to the accumulated minimum value.
MEDIAN | MED	Missing values are set to the accumulated median value.

MAXIMUM | MAX	Missing values are set to the accumulated maximum value.
FIRST	Missing values are set to the accumulated first non-missing value.
LAST	Missing values are set to the accumulated last non-missing value.
PREVIOUS | PREV	Missing values are set to the previous period's accumulated non-missing value. Missing values at the beginning of the accumulated series remain missing.
NEXT	Missing values are set to the next period's accumulated non-missing value. Missing values at the end of the accumulated series remain missing.

START= *option*

specifies a SAS date, datetime, or time value that represents the beginning of the data. If the first time ID variable value is greater than the START= value, the series is prepended with missing values. If the first time ID variable value is less than the START= value, the series is truncated. This START= and END= option can be used to ensure that data associated with each by group contains the same number of observations.

SEASON Statement

SEASON *statistics / options*;

A SEASON statement can be used with the TIMESERIES procedure to specify options related to seasonal analysis of the time-stamped transactional data. Only one SEASON statement is allowed. The options specified affects all variables specified in the VAR statements. Seasonal analysis can be performed only when the length of the seasonal cycle implied by the INTERVAL= option or specified by the SEASONALITY= option is greater than one.

The following seasonal statistics are available:

NOBS	Number of Observations
N	Number of Non-Missing Observations
NMISS	Number of Missing Observations
MINIMUM	Minimum Value
MAXIMUM	Maximum Value
RANGE	Range Value
SUM	Summation Value
MEAN	Mean Value
STDDEV	Standard Deviation
CSS	Corrected Sum of Squares
USS	Uncorrected Sum of Squares

MEDIAN	Median Value

If none of the season statistics is specified, the default is as follows:

```
season n min max mean std;
```

The following options can be specified in the SEASON statement following the slash (/):

TRANSPOSE=NO | YES
TRANSPOSE=YES specifies that the OUTSEASON= data set is recorded with the seasonal indices as the column names instead of the statistics as the column names. The TRANSPOSE=NO option is particularly useful for graphing the seasonal analysis results using SAS/GRAPH procedures. The TRANSPOSE=YES option is particularly useful for analyzing the seasonal analysis results using other SAS/STAT procedures or Enterprise Miner. The default is TRANSPOSE=NO.

TREND Statement

TREND *statistics / options;*

A TREND statement can be used with the TIMESERIES procedure to specify options related to trend analysis of the time-stamped transactional data. Only one TREND statement is allowed. The options specified affects all variables specified in the VAR statements.

The following trend statistics are available:

NOBS	Number of Observations
N	Number of Non-Missing Observations
NMISS	Number of Missing Observations
MINIMUM	Minimum Value
MAXIMUM	Maximum Value
RANGE	Range Value
SUM	Summation Value
MEAN	Mean Value
STDDEV	Standard Deviation
CSS	Corrected Sum of Squares
USS	Uncorrected Sum of Squares
MEDIAN	Median Value

If none of the trend statistics is specified, the default is as follows:

```
trend n min max mean std;
```

The following options can be specified in the TREND statement following the slash (/):

NPERIODS= *number*
Specifies the number of time periods to be stored in the OUTTREND= data set when the TRANSPOSE option is specified. If the TRANSPOSE option is not specified, the NPERIODS= option is ignored. The NPERIODS= option specifies the number of OUTTREND= data set variables to contain the trend statistics and is therefore limited to the maximum allowable number of SAS variables.

If NPERIODS= option is not specified, all of the periods specified between the ID statement START= and END= options are stored. If either of the START= or END= options are not specified, the default is the seasonality specified by the ID statement SEASONALITY= option or implied by the INTERVAL= option. If the seasonality is zero, the default is NPERIODS=5.

TRANSPOSE=NO | YES
TRANSPOSE=YES specifies that the OUTTREND= data set is recorded with the time periods as the column names instead of the statistics as the column names. The first and last time period stored in the OUTTREND= data set corresponds to the period of the ID statement START= option and END= option, respectively. If only the ID statement END= option is specified, the last time ID value of each accumulated time series corresponds to the last time period column. If only the ID statement START= option is specified, the first time ID value of each accumulated time series corresponds to the first time period column. If neither the START= option or END= option is specified with the ID statement, the first time ID value of each accumulated time series corresponds to the first time period column. The TRANSPOSE=NO option is particularly useful for analyzing the trend analysis results using other SAS/ETS procedures or graphing the trend analysis results using SAS/GRAPH procedures such as the GPLOT procedure. The TRANSPOSE=YES option is particularly useful for analyzing the trend analysis results using other SAS/STAT procedures or Enterprise Miner. The default is TRANSPOSE=YES.

VAR and CROSSVAR Statements

VAR *variable-list / options*;

CROSSVAR *variable-list / options*;

The VAR and CROSSVAR statement lists the numeric variables in the DATA= data set whose values are to be accumulated to form the time series.

An input data set variable can be specified in only one VAR or CROSSVAR statement. Any number of VAR and CROSSVAR statements can be used. The following options can be used with the VAR and CROSSVAR statement.

ACCUMULATE= *option*
specifies how the data set observations are accumulated within each time period for the variables listed in the VAR statement. If the ACCUMULATE= option is not specified in the VAR statement, accumulation is determined by the ACCUMULATE=

option of the ID statement. See the ID statement ACCUMULATE= option for more details.

DIF= *numlist*

specifies the differencing to be applied to the accumulated time series.

SDIF= *numlist*

specifies the seasonal differencing to be applied to the accumulated time series.

SETMISS= *option* | *number*
SETMISSING= *option* | *number*

option specifies how missing values (either actual or accumulated) are interpreted in the accumulated time series for variables listed in the VAR statement. If the SETMISSING= option is not specified in the VAR statement, missing values are set based on the SETMISSING= option of the ID statement. See the ID statement SETMISSING= option for more details.

TRANSFORM= *option*

specifies the time series transformation to be applied to the accumulated time series. The following transformations are provided:

NONE	No transformation is applied. This option is the default.
LOG	Logarithmic transformation
SQRT	Square-root transformation
LOGISTIC	Logistic transformation
BOXCOX(*n*)	Box-Cox transformation with parameter number where number is between -5 and 5

When the TRANSFORM= option is specified the time series must be strictly positive.

Details

The TIMESERIES procedure can be used to perform trend and seasonal analysis on transactional data. For trend analysis, various sample statistics are computed for each time period defined by the time ID variable and INTERVAL= option. For seasonal analysis, various sample statistics are computed for each season defined by the INTERVAL= or the SEASONALITY= option. For example, if the transactional data ranges from June 1990 to January 2000 and the data are to be accumulated on a monthly basis, then the trend statistics are computed for every month: June 1990, July 1990, ..., January 2000. The seasonal statistics are computed for each season: January, February, ..., December.

The TIMESERIES procedure can be used to form time series data from transactional data. The accumulated time series can then be analyzed using time series techniques.

1. Accumulation	ACCUMULATE= option
2. Missing Value Interpretation	SETMISSING= option
3. Time Series Transformation	TRANSFORM= option
4. Time Series Differencing	DIF= and SDIF= option
5. Descriptive Statistics	OUTSUM= option, PRINT=DESCSTATS
6. Seasonal Decomposition	DECOMP statement, OUTDECOMP= option
7. Correlation Analysis	CORR statement, OUTCORR= option
8. Cross-correlation Analysis	CROSSCORR statement, OUTCROSSCORR= option

Accumulation

If the ACCUMULATE= option is specified, data set observations are accumulated within each time period. The frequency (width of each time interval) is specified by the INTERVAL= option. The ID variable contains the time ID values. Each time ID value corresponds to a specific time period. Accumulation is particularly useful when the input data set contains transactional data, whose observations are not spaced with respect to any particular time interval. The accumulated values form the time series, which is used in subsequent analyses.

For example, suppose a data set contains the following observations:

```
19MAR1999    10
19MAR1999    30
11MAY1999    50
12MAY1999    20
23MAY1999    20
```

If the INTERVAL=MONTH is specified, all of the above observations fall within three time periods of March 1999, April 1999, and May 1999. The observations are accumulated within each time period as follows:

If the ACCUMULATE=NONE option is specified, an error is generated because the ID variable values are not equally spaced with respect to the specified frequency (MONTH).

If the ACCUMULATE=TOTAL option is specified:

```
O1MAR1999    40
O1APR1999     .
O1MAY1999    90
```

If the ACCUMULATE=AVERAGE option is specified:

```
O1MAR1999    20
O1APR1999     .
O1MAY1999    30
```

If the ACCUMULATE=MINIMUM option is specified:

```
O1MAR1999    10
O1APR1999     .
O1MAY1999    20
```

If the ACCUMULATE=MEDIAN option is specified:

```
O1MAR1999    20
O1APR1999     .
O1MAY1999    20
```

If the ACCUMULATE=MAXIMUM option is specified:

```
O1MAR1999    30
O1APR1999     .
O1MAY1999    50
```

If the ACCUMULATE=FIRST option is specified:

```
O1MAR1999    10
O1APR1999     .
O1MAY1999    50
```

If the ACCUMULATE=LAST option is specified:

```
O1MAR1999    30
O1APR1999     .
O1MAY1999    20
```

If the ACCUMULATE=STDDEV option is specified:

```
01MAR1999    14.14
01APR1999     .
01MAY1999    17.32
```

As can be seen from the above examples, even though the data set observations contained no missing values, the accumulated time series may have missing values.

Missing Value Interpretation

Sometimes missing values should be interpreted as unknown values. But sometimes missing values are known, such as when missing values are created from accumulation and no observations should be interpreted as no value, i.e. zero. In the former case, the SETMISSING= option can be used to interpret how missing values are treated. The SETMISSING=0 option should be used when missing observations are to be treated as no (zero) values. In other cases, missing values should be interpreted as global values, such as minimum or maximum values of the accumulated series. The accumulated and interpreted time series is used in subsequent analyses.

Time Series Transformation

There are four transformations available, for strictly positive series only. Let $y_t > 0$ be the original time series, and let w_t be the transformed series. The transformations are defined as follows:

Log — is the logarithmic transformation.

$$w_t = \ln(\mathrm{y_t})$$

Logistic — is the logistic transformation.

$$w_t = \ln(\mathrm{c}\mathrm{y_t}/(1 - \mathrm{c}\mathrm{y_t}))$$

where the scaling factor c is

$$c = (1 - 10^{-6})10^{-\mathrm{ceil}(\log_{10}(\max(\mathrm{y_t})))}$$

and $\mathrm{ceil}(\mathrm{x})$ is the smallest integer greater than or equal to x.

Square Root — is the square root transformation.

$$w_t = \sqrt{y_t}$$

Box Cox — is the Box-Cox transformation.

$$w_t = \begin{cases} \frac{y_t^{\lambda}-1}{\lambda}, & \lambda \neq 0 \\ \ln(\mathrm{y_t}), & \lambda = 0 \end{cases}$$

More complex time series transformations can be performed using the EXPAND procedure of SAS/ETS.

Time Series Differencing

After optionally transforming the series, the accumulated series can be simply or seasonally differenced using the VAR statement DIF= and SDIF= option. For example, suppose y_t is a monthly time series, the following examples of the DIF= and SDIF= options demonstrate how to simply and seasonally difference the time series.

```
dif=(1) sdif=(1)
dif=(1,12)
```

Additionally assuming y_t is strictly positive, the VAR statement TRANSFORM= option, DIF= and SDIF= options can be combined.

Descriptive Statistics

Descriptive statistics can be computed from the working series by specifying the OUTSUM= option or the PRINT=DESCSTATS.

Seasonal Decomposition

Seasonal decomposition/analysis can be performed on the working series by specifying the OUTDECOMP= option, the PRINT=DECOMP option, or one of the PLOT= option associated with decomposition. The DECOMP statement enables you to specify options related to decomposition. The TIMESERIES procedure uses classical decomposition. More complex seasonal decomposition/adjustment analysis can be performed using the X11 or the X12 procedure of SAS/ETS.

The DECOMP statement MODE= option determines the mode of the seasonal adjustment decomposition to be performed. There are four modes: multiplicative (MODE=MULT), additive (MODE=ADD), pseudo-additive (MODE=PSEUDOADD), and log-additive (MODE=LOGADD) decomposition. The default is MODE=MULTORADD which specifies MODE=MULT for series that are strictly positive, MODE=PSEUDOADD for series that are nonnegative, and MODE=ADD for series that are not.

When MODE=LOGADD is specified, the components are exponentiated to the original metric.

The DECOMP statement LAMBDA= option specifies the Hodrick-Prescott filter parameter. The default is LAMBDA=1600. The Hodrick-Prescott filter is used to decompose the trend-cycle component into the trend component and cycle component in an additive fashion. A smaller parameter assigns less significance to the cycle, that is, LAMBDA=0 implies no cycle component.

The notation and keywords associated with seasonal decomposition/adjustment analysis are defined as follows:

Table 28.1. Seasonal Adjustment Formulas

Component	Keyword	MULT	ADD	LOGADD	PSEUDOADD
Original	ORIGINAL	$O_t = TC_t S_t I_t$	$O_t = TC_t + S_t + I_t$	$log(O_t) = TC_t + S_t + I_t$	$O_t = TC_t(S_t + I_t - 1)$
Trend-Cycle Component	TCC	Centered Moving Average of O_t	Centered Moving Average of O_t	Centered Moving Average of $log(O_t)$	Centered Moving Average of O_t
Seasonal-Irregular Component	SIC	$SI_t = S_t I_t = O_t/TC_t$	$SI_t = S_t + I_t = O_t - TC_t$	$SI_t = S_t + I_t = log(O_t) - TC_t$	$SI_t = S_t + I_t - 1 = O_t/TC_t$
Seasonal Component	SC	Seasonal Averages of SI_t	Seasonal Averages of SI_t	Seasonal Averages of SI_t	Seasonal Averages of SI_t
Irregular Component	IC	$I_t = SI_t/S_t$	$I_t = SI_t - S_t$	$I_t = SI_t - S_t$	$I_t = SI_t - S_t + 1$
Trend-Cycle-Seasonal Component	TCS	$TCS_t = TC_t S_t = O_t/I_t$	$TCS_t = TC_t + S_t = O_t - I_t$	$TCS_t = TC_t + S_t = O_t - I_t$	$TCS_t = TC_t S_t$
Trend Component	TC	$T_t = TC_t - C_t$	$T_t = TC_t - C_t$	$T_t = TC_t - C_t$	$T_t = TC_t - C_t$
Cycle Component	CC	$C_t = TC_t - T_t$	$C_t = TC_t - T_t$	$C_t = TC_t - T_t$	$C_t = TC_t - T_t$
Seasonal Adjusted	SA	$SA_t = O_t/S_t = TC_t I_t$	$SA_t = O_t - S_t = TC_t + I_t$	$SA_t = O_t/exp(S_t) = exp(TC_t + I_t)$	$SA_t = TC_t I_t$

Correlation Analysis

Correlation analysis can be performed on the working series by specifying the OUTCORR= option or one of the PLOT= options associated with correlation. The CORR statement enables you to specify options related to correlation analysis.

Autocovariance Statistics

LAGS	$h \in \{0, \ldots, H\}$
N	N_h is the number of observed products at lag h ignoring missing values
ACOV	$\hat{\gamma}(h) = \frac{1}{T}\sum_{t=h+1}^{T}(y_t - \overline{y})(y_{t-h} - \overline{y})$
ACOV	$\hat{\gamma}(h) = \frac{1}{N_h}\sum_{t=h+1}^{T}(y_t - \overline{y})(y_{t-h} - \overline{y})$ embedded missing values

Autocorrelation Statistics

ACF	$\hat{\rho}(h) = \hat{\gamma}(h)/\hat{\gamma}(0)$
ACFSTD	$Std(\hat{\rho}(h)) = \sqrt{\frac{1}{T}\left(1 + 2\sum_{j=1}^{h-1}\hat{\rho}(j)^2\right)}$
ACFNORM	$Norm(\hat{\rho}(h)) = \hat{\rho}(h)/Std(\hat{\rho}(h))$
ACFPROB	$Prob(\hat{\rho}(h)) = 2\left(1 - \Phi\left(\lvert Norm(\hat{\rho}(h))\rvert\right)\right)$
ACFLPROB	$LogProb(\hat{\rho}(h)) = -\log_{10}(Prob(\hat{\rho}(h))$
ACF2STD	$Flag(\hat{\rho}(h)) = \begin{cases} 1 & \hat{\rho}(h) > 2Std(\hat{\rho}(h)) \\ 0 & -2Std(\hat{\rho}(h)) < \hat{\rho}(h) < 2Std(\hat{\rho}(h)) \\ -1 & \hat{\rho}(h) < -2Std(\hat{\rho}(h)) \end{cases}$

Partial Autocorrelation Statistics

PACF	$\hat{\varphi}(h) = \Gamma_{(0,h-1)}\{\gamma_j\}_{j=1}^{h}$
PACFSTD	$Std(\hat{\varphi}(h)) = 1/\sqrt{N_0}$
PCFNORM	$Norm(\hat{\varphi}(h)) = \hat{\varphi}(h)/Std(\hat{\varphi}(h))$
PACFPROB	$Prob(\hat{\varphi}(h)) = 2\left(1 - \Phi\left(\lvert Norm(\hat{\varphi}(h))\rvert\right)\right)$
PACFLPROB	$LogProb(\hat{\varphi}(h)) = -\log_{10}(Prob(\hat{\varphi}(h))$
PACF2STD	$Flag(\hat{\varphi}(h)) = \begin{cases} 1 & \hat{\varphi}(h) > 2Std(\hat{\varphi}(h)) \\ 0 & -2Std(\hat{\varphi}(h)) < \hat{\varphi}(h) < 2Std(\hat{\varphi}(h)) \\ -1 & \hat{\varphi}(h) < -2Std(\hat{\varphi}(h)) \end{cases}$

Inverse Autocorrelation Statistics

IACF	$\hat{\theta}(h)$
IACFSTD	$Std(\hat{\theta}(h)) = 1/\sqrt{N_0}$
IACFNORM	$Norm(\hat{\theta}(h)) = \hat{\theta}(h)/Std(\hat{\theta}(h))$
IACFPROB	$Prob(\hat{\theta}(h)) = 2\left(1 - \Phi\left(\lvert Norm(\hat{\theta}(h))\rvert\right)\right)$

IACFLPROB $LogProb(\hat{\theta}(h)) = -\log_{10}(Prob(\hat{\theta}(h))$

IACF2STD $Flag(\hat{\theta}(h)) = \begin{cases} 1 & \hat{\theta}(h) > 2Std(\hat{\theta}(h)) \\ 0 & -2Std(\hat{\theta}(h)) < \hat{\theta}(h) < 2Std(\hat{\theta}(h)) \\ -1 & \hat{\theta}(h) < -2Std(\hat{\theta}(h)) \end{cases}$

White Noise Statistics

WN $Q(h) = T(T+2)\sum_{j=1}^{h} \rho(j)^2/(T-j)$

WN $Q(h) = \sum_{j=1}^{h} N_j \rho(j)^2$ embedded missing values

WNPROB $Prob(Q(h)) = \chi_{\max(1,h-p)}(Q(h))$

WNLPROB $LogProb(Q(h)) = -\log_{10}(Prob(Q(h))$

Cross-correlation Analysis

Cross-correlation analysis can be performed on the working series by specifying the OUTCROSSCORR= option or one of the CROSSPLOT= options associated with cross-correlation. The CROSSCORR statement enables you to specify options related to cross-correlation analysis.

Cross-correlation Statistics

LAGS $h \in \{0, \ldots, H\}$

N N_h is the number of observed products at lag h ignoring missing values

CCOV $\hat{\gamma}_{x,y}(h) = \frac{1}{T}\sum_{t=h+1}^{T}(x_t - \overline{x})(y_{t-h} - \overline{y})$

CCOV $\hat{\gamma}_{x,y}(h) = \frac{1}{N_h}\sum_{t=h+1}^{T}(x_t - \overline{x})(y_{t-h} - \overline{y})$ embedded missing values

CCF $\hat{\rho}_{x,y}(h) = \hat{\gamma}_{x,y}(h)/\sqrt{\hat{\gamma}_x(0)\hat{\gamma}_y(0)}$

CCFSTD $Std(\hat{\rho}_{x,y}(h)) = 1/\sqrt{N_0}$

CCFNORM $Norm(\hat{\rho}_{x,y}(h)) = \hat{\rho}_{x,y}(h)/Std(\hat{\rho}_{x,y}(h))$

CCFPROB $Prob(\hat{\rho}_{x,y}(h)) = 2\left(1 - \Phi\left(|Norm(\hat{\rho}_{x,y}(h))|\right)\right)$

CCFLPROB $LogProb(\hat{\rho}_{x,y}(h)) = -\log_{10}(Prob(\hat{\rho}_{x,y}(h))$

CCF2STD $Flag(\hat{\rho}_{x,y}(h)) = \begin{cases} 1 & \hat{\rho}_{x,y}(h) > 2Std(\hat{\rho}_{x,y}(h)) \\ 0 & -2Std(\hat{\rho}_{x,y}(h)) < \hat{\rho}_{x,y}(h) < 2Std(\hat{\rho}_{x,y}(h)) \\ -1 & \hat{\rho}_{x,y}(h) < -2Std(\hat{\rho}_{x,y}(h)) \end{cases}$

Data Set Output

The TIMESERIES procedure can create the OUT=, and OUTSUM= data sets. In general, these data sets will contain the variables listed in the BY statement. In general, if an analysis step related to an output data step fails, the values of this step are not recorded or are set to missing in the related output data set, and appropriate error and/or warning messages are recorded in the log.

OUT= Data Set

The OUT= data set contains the variables specified in the BY, ID, and VAR statements. If the ID statement is specified, the ID variable values are aligned and extended based on the ALIGN= and INTERVAL= options. The values of the variables specified in the VAR statements are accumulated based on the ACCUMULATE= option and missing values are interpreted based on the SETMISSING= option.

OUTCORR= Data Set

The OUTCORR= data set contains the variables specified in the BY statement as well as the variables listed below. The OUTCORR= data set records the correlations for each variable specified in a VAR statement.

When the CORR statement TRANSPOSE=NO option is specified, the variable *names* are related to correlation statistics specified in the CORR statement options; the variable *values* are related to the NLAG= or LAGS= options.

NAME	Variable name
LAG	Time lag
N	Number of Variance Products
ACOV	Autocovariances
ACF	Autocorrelations
ACFSTD	Autocorrelation Standard Errors
ACF2STD	Indicates ACF Beyond Two Standard Errors
ACFNORM	Normalized Autocorrelations
ACFPROB	Autocorrelation Probabilities
ACFLPROB	Autocorrelation Log Probabilities
PACF	Partial Autocorrelations
PACFSTD	Partial Autocorrelation Standard Errors
PACF2STD	Indicates PACF Beyond Two Standard Errors
PACFNORM	Partial Normalized Autocorrelations
PACFPROB	Partial Autocorrelation Probabilities
PACFLPROB	Partial Autocorrelation Log Probabilities
IACF	Inverse Autocorrelations
IACFSTD	Inverse Autocorrelation Standard Errors
IACF2STD	Indicates IACF Beyond Two Standard Errors
IACFNORM	Normalized Inverse Autocorrelations
IACFPROB	Inverse Autocorrelation Probabilities
IACFLPROB	Inverse Autocorrelation Log Probabilities
WN	White Noise Test Statistics

WNPROB	White Noise Test Probabilities
WNLPROB	White Noise Test Log Probabilities

The above correlation statistics are computed for each specified time lag.

When the CORR statement TRANSPOSE=YES option is specified, the variable *values* are related to correlation statistics specified in the CORR statement; the variable *names* are related to the NLAG= or LAGS= options.

NAME	Variable name
STAT	Correlation statistic name
LABEL	Correlation statistic label
LAG*h*	Correlation statistics for lag *h*

OUTCROSSCORR= Data Set

The OUTCROSSCORR= data set contains the variables specified in the BY statement as well as the variables listed below. The OUTCROSSCORR= data set records the cross-correlations for each variable specified in a VAR statement.

When the CROSSCORR statement TRANSPOSE=NO option is specified, the variable *names* are related to cross-correlation statistics specified in the CROSSCORR statement options; the variable *values* are related to the NLAG= or LAGS= options.

NAME	Variable name
CROSS	Cross Variable name
LAG	Time lag
N	Number of Variance Products
CCOV	Cross-Covariances
CCF	Cross-correlations
CCFSTD	Cross-correlation Standard Errors
CCF2STD	Indicates CCF Beyond Two Standard Errors
CCFNORM	Normalized Cross-correlations
CCFPROB	Cross-correlation Probabilities
CCFLPROB	Cross-correlation Log Probabilities

The above cross-correlation statistics are computed for each specified time lag.

When the CROSSCORR statement TRANSPOSE=YES option is specified, the variable *values* are related to cross-correlation statistics specified in the CROSSCORR statement; the variable *names* are related to the NLAG= or LAGS= options.

NAME	Variable name
CROSS	Cross Variable name
STAT	Cross-correlation statistic name
LABEL	Cross-correlation statistic label
LAG*h*	Cross-correlation statistics for lag *h*

OUTDECOMP= Data Set

The OUTDECOMP= data set contains the variables specified in the BY statement as well as the variables listed below. The OUTDECOMP= data set records the seasonal decomposition/adjustments for each variable specified in a VAR statement.

When the DECOMP statement TRANSPOSE=NO option is specified, the variable *names* are related to decomposition/adjustments specified in the DECOMP statement; the variable *values* are related to the INTERVAL= and SEASONALITY= options.

NAME	Variable name
MODE	Mode of decomposition
TIMEID	Time ID values
SEASON	Seasonal index
ORIGINAL	Original series values
TCC	Trend-Cycle Component
SIC	Seasonal-Irregular Component
SC	Seasonal Component
SCSTD	Seasonal Component Standard Errors
TCS	Trend-Cycle-Seasonal Component
IC	Irregular Component
SA	Seasonal Adjusted Component
PCSA	Percent Change Seasonal Adjusted Component
TC	Trend Component
CC	CYCLE Component

The above decomposition components are computed for each time period.

When the DECOMP statement TRANSPOSE=YES option is specified, the variable *values* are related to decomposition/adjustments specified in the DECOMP statement; the variable *names* are related to the INTERVAL=, SEASONALITY=, and NPERIODS= options.

NAME	Variable name
MODE	Mode of decomposition name

COMP	Decomposition component name
LABEL	Decomposition component label
PERIOD*t*	Decomposition component value for time period *t*

OUTSEASON= Data Set

The OUTSEASON= data set contains the variables specified in the BY statement as well as the variables listed below. The OUTSEASON= data set records the seasonal statistics for each variable specified in a VAR statement.

When the SEASON statement TRANSPOSE=NO option is specified, the variable *names* are related to seasonal statistics specified in the SEASON statement; the variable *values* are related to the INTERVAL= or SEASONALITY= options.

NAME	Variable name
TIMEID	Time ID values
SEASON	Seasonal index
NOBS	Number of Observations
N	Number of Non-Missing Observations
NMISS	Number of Missing Observations
MINIMUM	Minimum Value
MAXIMUM	Maximum Value
RANGE	Maximum Value
SUM	Summation Value
MEAN	Mean Value
STDDEV	Standard Deviation
CSS	Corrected Sum of Squares
USS	Uncorrected Sum of Squares
MEDIAN	Median Value

The above statistics are computed for each season.

When the SEASON statement TRANSPOSE=YES option is specified, the variable *values* are related to seasonal statistics specified in the SEASON statement; the variable *names* are related to the INTERVAL= or SEASONALITY= options.

NAME	Variable name
STAT	Season statistic name
LABEL	Season statistic name
SEASON*s*	Season statistic value for season *s*

OUTSUM= Data Set

The OUTSUM= data set contains the variables specified in the BY statement as well as the variables listed below. The OUTSUM= data set records the descriptive statistics for each variable specified in a VAR statement.

Variables related to descripive statistics are based on the ACCUMULATE= and SETMISSING= options:

NAME	Variable name
STATUS	Status flag that indicates whether the requested analyses were successful
NOBS	Number of Observations
N	Number of Non-Missing Observations
NMISS	Number of Missing Observations
MINIMUM	Minimum Value
MAXIMUM	Maximum Value
AVG	Average Value
STDDEV	Standard Deviation

The OUTSUM= data set contains the descriptive statistics of the (accumulated) time series.

OUTTREND= Data Set

The OUTTREND= data set contains the variables specified in the BY statement as well as the variables listed below. The OUTTREND= data set records the trend statistics for each variable specified in a VAR statement.

When the TREND statement TRANSPOSE=NO option is specified, the variable *names* are related to trend statistics specified in the TREND statement; the variable *values* are related to the INTERVAL= or SEASONALITY= options.

NAME	Variable name
TIMEID	Time ID values
SEASON	Seasonal index
NOBS	Number of Observations
N	Number of Non-Missing Observations
NMISS	Number of Missing Observations
MINIMUM	Minimum Value
MAXIMUM	Maximum Value
RANGE	Maximum Value
SUM	Summation Value

MEAN	Mean Value
STDDEV	Standard Deviation
CSS	Corrected Sum of Squares
USS	Uncorrected Sum of Squares
MEDIAN	Median Value

The above statistics are computed for each time period.

When the TREND statement TRANSPOSE=YES option is specified, the variable *values* related to trend statistics specified in the TREND statement; the variable *name* are related to the INTERVAL=, SEASONALITY=, and NPERIODS= options.

NAME	Variable name
STAT	Trend statistic name
LABEL	Trend statistic name
PERIOD*t*	Trend statistic value for time period *t*

Printed Output

The TIMESERIES procedure optionally produces printed output for these results utilizing the Output Delivery System (ODS). By default, the procedure produces no printed output. All output is controlled by the PRINT= and PRINTDETAILS options associated with the PROC TIMESERIES statement. In general, if an analysis step related to printed output fails, the values of this step are not printed and appropriate error and/or warning messages are recorded in the log. The printed output is similar to the output data set and these similarities are described below.

PRINT=DECOMP

prints the seasonal decomposition similar to the OUTDECOMP= data set.

PRINT=DESCSTATS

prints a table of descriptive statistics for each variable.

PRINT=SEASONS

prints the seasonal statistics similar to the OUTSEASON= data set.

PRINT=SUMMARY

prints the summary statistics similar to the OUTSUM= data set.

PRINT=TRENDS

prints the trend statistics similar to the OUTTREND= data set.

PRINTDETAILS

The PRINTDETAILS option prints each table with greater detail.

Specifically, if PRINT=SEASONS and the PRINTDETAILS options are specified, all seasonal statistics are printed.

ODS Table Names

The table below relates the PRINT= options to ODS tables:

Table 28.2. ODS Tables Produced in PROC TIMESERIES

ODS Table Name	Description	Option
ODS Tables Created by the PRINT=DECOMP option		
SeasonalDecomposition	Seasonal Decomposition	
ODS Tables Created by the PRINT=DESCSTATS option		
DescStats	Descriptive Statistics	
ODS Tables Created by the PRINT=SEASONS option		
GlobalStatistics	Global Statistics	
SeasonStatistics	Season Statistics	
ODS Tables Created by the PRINT=SUMMARY option		
StatisticsSummary	Statistics Summary	
ODS Tables Created by the PRINT=TRENDS option		
GlobalStatistics	Global Statistics	
TrendStatistics	Trend Statistics	

The tables are related to a single series within a BY group.

ODS Graphics (Experimental)

This section describes the use of ODS for creating graphics with the TIMESERIES procedure. These graphics are experimental in this release, meaning that both the graphical results and the syntax for specifying them are subject to change in a future release.

To request these graphs, you must specify the ODS GRAPHICS statement. In addition, you can specify the PLOT= or CROSSPLOT= option in the TIMESERIES statement according to the following syntax. For more information on the ODS GRAPHICS statement, see Chapter 9, “Statistical Graphics Using ODS.”

PLOT= *option* **|** **(***options***)**

specifies the univariate graphical output desired. By default, the TIMESERIES procedure produces no graphical output. The following plotting options are available:

SERIES	plots time series graphics. (OUT= data set)
RESIDUAL	plots residual time series graphics. (OUT= data set)
CORR	plots correlation panel graphics. (OUTCORR= data set)

ACF	plots autocorrelation function graphics. (OUTCORR= data set)
PACF	plots partial autocorrelation function graphics. (OUTCORR= data set)
IACF	plots inverse autocorrelation function graphics. (OUTCORR= data set)
WN	plots white noise graphics. (OUTCORR= data set)
DECOMP	plots seasonal adjustment panel graphics. (OUTDECOMP= data set)
TCS	plots the trend-cycle-seasonal component graphics. (OUTDECOMP= data set)
TCC	plots the trend-cycle component graphics. (OUTDECOMP= data set)
SIC	plots the seasonal-irregular component graphics. (OUTDECOMP= data set)
SC	plots the seasonal component graphics. (OUTDECOMP= data set)
SA	plots the seasonal adjusted graphics. (OUTDECOMP= data set)
PCSA	plots the percent change seasonal adjusted graphics. (OUTDECOMP= data set)
IC	plots the irregular component graphics. (OUTDECOMP= data set)
TC	plots the trend component graphics. (OUTDECOMP= data set)
CC	plots the cycle component graphics. (OUTDECOMP= data set)
ALL	Same as PLOT=(SERIES ACF PACF IACF WN).

For example, PLOT=SERIES plots the time series. The PLOT= option produces graphical output for these results utilizing the Output Delivery System (ODS). The PLOT= option produces results similar to the data sets listed next to the above options in parenthesis.

CROSSPLOT= *option* **|** (*options*)

specifies the cross-variable graphical output desired. By default, the TIMESERIES procedure produces no graphical output. The following plotting options are available:

SERIES	plots time series graphics. (OUT= data set)
CCF	plots autocorrelation function graphics. (OUTCORR= data set)
ALL	Same as PLOT=(SERIES CCF).

For example, CROSSPLOT=SERIES plots the two time series. The CROSSPLOT= option produces graphical output for these results utilizing the Output Delivery System (ODS). The CROSSPLOT= option produces results similar to the data sets listed next to the above options in parenthesis.

ODS Graph Names

PROC TIMESERIES assigns a name to each graph it creates using ODS. You can use these names to reference the graphs when using ODS. The names are listed in Table 28.3.

To request these graphs, you must specify the ODS GRAPHICS statement. In addition, you can specify the PLOT= or CROSSPLOT= option in the TIMESERIES statement. For more information on the ODS GRAPHICS statement, see Chapter 9, "Statistical Graphics Using ODS."

Table 28.3. ODS Graphics Produced by PROC TIMESERIES

ODS Graph Name	Plot Description	Statement	PLOT= Option
ACFPlot	Autocorrelation Function	TIMESERIES	PLOT=ACF
ACFNORMPlot	Standardized Autocorrelation Function	TIMESERIES	PLOT=ACF
CCFNORMPlot	Standardized Cross-correlation Function	TIMESERIES	CROSSPLOT=CCF
CCFPlot	Cross-correlation Function	TIMESERIES	CROSSPLOT=CCF
CorrelationPlots	Correlation Graphics Panel	TIMESERIES	PLOT=CORR
CrossSeriesPlot	Cross Series Plot	TIMESERIES	CROSSPLOT=SERIES
CycleComponentPlot	Cycle Component	TIMESERIES	PLOT=CC
DecompositionPlots	Decomposition Graphiics Panel	TIMESERIES	PLOT=DECOMP
IACFPlot	Inverse Autocorrelation Function	TIMESERIES	PLOT=IACF
IACFNORMPlot	Standardized Inverse Autocorrelation Function	TIMESERIES	PLOT=IACF
IrregularComponentPlot	Irregular Component	TIMESERIES	PLOT=IC
PACFPlot	Partial Autocorrelation Function	TIMESERIES	PLOT=PACF
PACFNORMPlot	Standardized Partial Autocorrelation Function	TIMESERIES	PLOT=PACF
PercentChangeAdjustedplot	Percent-Change Seasonally Adjusted	TIMESERIES	PLOT=SA
ResidualPlot	Residual Time Series Plot	TIMESERIES	PLOT=RESIDUAL
SeasonalAdjusted	Seasonally Adjusted	TIMESERIES	PLOT=SA
SeasonalComponentPlot	Seasonal Component	TIMESERIES	PLOT=SC
SeasonalIrregularComponentPlot	Seasonal-Irregular Component	TIMESERIES	PLOT=SIC
SeriesPlot	Time Series Plot	TIMESERIES	PLOT=SERIES

Table 28.3. (continued)

ODS Graph Name	Plot Description	Statement	Option
TrendComponentPlot	Trend Component	TIMESERIES	PLOT=TC
TrendCycleComponentPlot	Trend-Cycle Component	TIMESERIES	PLOT=TCC
TrendCycleSeasonalPlot	Trend-Cycle-Seasonal Component	TIMESERIES	PLOT=TCS
WhiteNoiseLogProb	White Noise Log Probability	TIMESERIES	PLOT=WN
WhiteNoiseProbability	White Noise Probability	TIMESERIES	PLOT=WN

Examples

Example 28.1. Accumulating Transactional Data into Time Series Data

This example illustrates the accumulation of time-stamped transactional data that has been recorded at no particular frequency into time series data at a specific frequency using the TIMESERIES procedure. Once the time series is created, the various SAS/ETS procedures related to time series analysis, seasonal adjustment/decomposition, modeling, and forecasting can be used to further analyze the time series data.

Suppose that the input data set WORK.RETAIL contains variables STORE and TIMESTAMP and numerous other numeric transaction variables. The BY variable STORE contains values that break up the transactions into groups (BY groups). The time ID variable TIMESTAMP contains SAS date values recorded at no particular frequency. The other data set variables contain the numeric transaction values to be analyzed. It is further assumed that the input data set is sorted by the variables STORE and TIMESTAMP.

The following statements form monthly time series from the transactional data based on the median value (ACCUMULATE=MEDIAN) of the transactions recorded with each time period. Also, the accumulated time series values for time periods with no transactions are set to zero instead of missing (SETMISS=0) and only transactions recorded between the first day of 1998 (START='01JAN1998'D) and last day of 2000 (END='31JAN2000'D).are considered and if needed extended to include this range.

```
proc timeseries data=work.retail out=mseries;
   by store;
   id timestamp interval=month accumulate=median setmiss=0
      start='01jan1998'd
      end  ='31dec2000'd;
   var _ALL_;
run;
```

The monthly time series data are stored in the data WORK.MSERIES. Each BY group associated with the BY variable STORE will contain an observation for each of the 36 months associated with the years 1998, 1999, and 2000. Each observation will contain the variable STORE, TIMESTAMP, and each of the analysis variables in the input data set.

Once each set of transactions has been accumulated to form corresponding time series, accumulated time series can be analyzed using various time series analysis techniques. For example, exponentially weighted moving averages can be used to smooth each series. The following statements use the EXPAND procedure to smooth the analysis variable named STOREITEM.

```
proc expand data=mseries out=smoothed from=month;
   by store;
   id date;
   convert storeitem=smooth / transform=(ewma 0,1);
run;
```

The decomposed series are stored in the data set WORK.SMOOTHED. The variable SMOOTH contains the smoothed series.

If the time ID variable TIMESTAMP contained SAS datetime values instead of SAS date values, the INTERVAL= , START=, and END= option must be changed accordingly and the following statements could be used.

```
proc timeseries data=work.retail out=tseries;
   by store;
   id timestamp interval=dtmonth accumulate=median setmiss=0
      start='01jan1998:00:00:00'dt
      end  ='31dec2000:00:00:00'dt;
   var _ALL_;
run;
```

The monthly time series data are stored in the data WORK.TSERIES and the time ID values use a SAS datetime representation.

Example 28.2. Trend and Seasonal Analysis

This example illustrates trend and seasonal analysis of time-stamped transactional data using the TIMESERIES procedure.

Suppose that the data set SASHELP.AIR contains two variable DATE and AIR. The variable DATE contains sorted SAS date values recorded at no particular frequency. The variable AIR contains the transaction values to be analyzed.

The following statements accumulate the transactional data on an average basis to form a quarterly time series and perform trend and seasonal analysis on the transactions.

```
proc timeseries data=sashelp.air out=series
                outtrend=trend outseason=season print=seasons;
   id date interval=qtr accumulate=avg;
   var air;
run;
```

The time series is stored in the data set WORK.SERIES, the trend statistics are stored in the data set WORK.TREND, and the seasonal statistics are stored in the data set WORK.SEASON. Additionally, the seasonal statistics are printed (PRINT=SEASONS) and the results of the seasonal analysis are shown in Output 28.2.1.

Output 28.2.1. Seasonal Statistics Table

The TIMESERIES Procedure

Season Statistics for Variable AIR

Season Index	N	Minimum	Maximum	Sum	Mean	Standard Deviation
1	36	112.0000	419.0000	8963.00	248.9722	95.65189
2	36	121.0000	535.0000	10207.00	283.5278	117.61839
3	36	136.0000	622.0000	12058.00	334.9444	143.97935
4	36	104.0000	461.0000	9135.00	253.7500	101.34732

Using the trend statistics stored in the WORK.TREND data set, the following statements plot various trend statistics associated with each time period over time.

```
title1 "Trend Statistics";
legend1 value=("Maximum" "Mean" "Median" "Minimum");
symbol interpol=spline;
axis2 label=none;
proc gplot data=trend;
   plot max    *date
        mean   *date
        median *date
        min    *date
        / overlay vaxis=axis2 legend=legend1;
 run;
```

The results of this trend analysis are shown in Output 28.2.2.

Output 28.2.2. Trend Statistics Plot

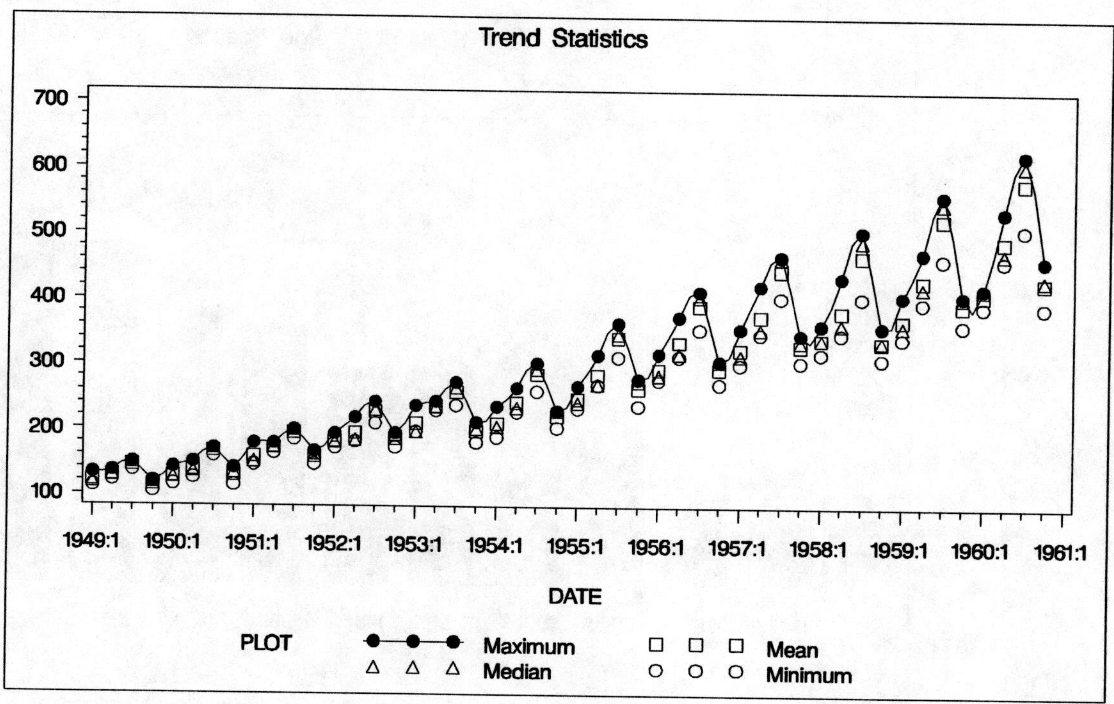

Using the trend statistics stored in the WORK.TREND data set, the following statements chart the sum of the transactions associated with each time period for the second season over time.

```
title1 "Trend Statistics for 2nd Season";
proc gchart data=trend;
   where _season_ = 2;
   vbar date / sumvar=sum discrete;
run;
quit;
```

The results of this trend analysis are shown in Output 28.2.3.

Output 28.2.3. Trend Statistics Plot

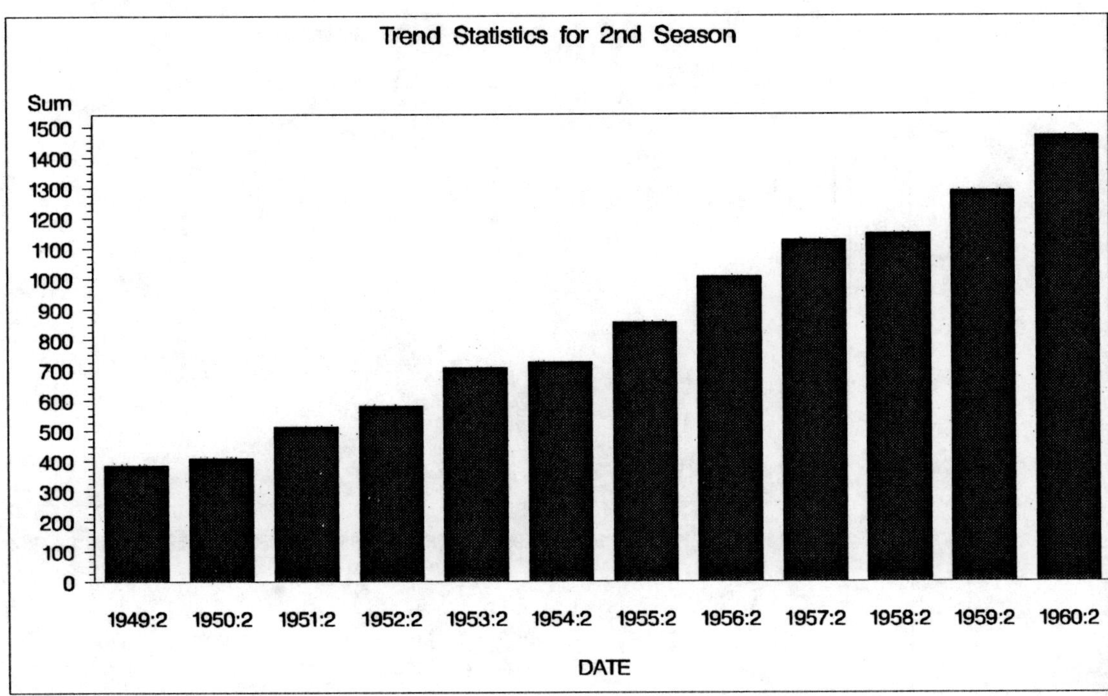

Using the trend statistics stored in the WORK.TREND data set, the following statements plot the mean of the transactions associated with each time period by each year over time.

```
data trend;
   set trend;
   year = year(date);
run;

title1 "Trend Statistics by Year";
symbol interpol=spline;
axis1 value=('Qtr 1' 'Qtr 2' 'Qtr 3' 'Qtr 4' );
proc gplot data=trend;
  plot mean*_season_=year / haxis=axis1;
run;
```

The results of this trend analysis are shown in Output 28.2.4.

Output 28.2.4. Trend Statistics

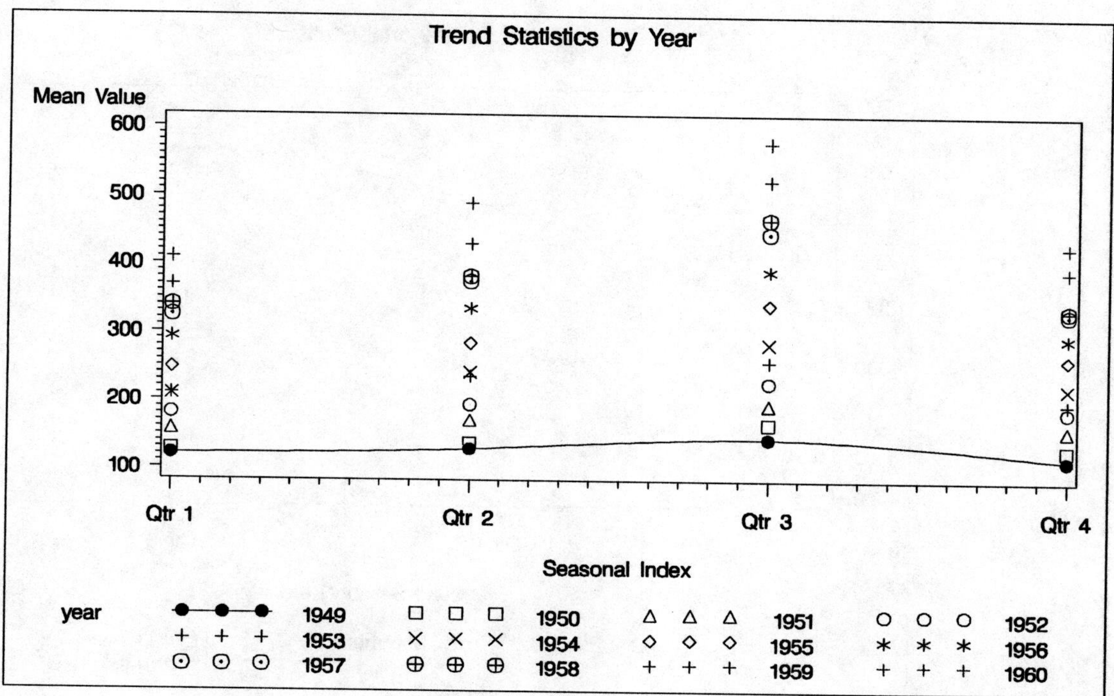

Using the season statistics stored in the WORK.SEASON data set, the following statements plot various season statistics for each season.

```
title1 "Seasonal Statistics";
legend1 value=("Maximum" "Mean" "Median" "Minimum");
symbol interpol=spline;
axis1 value=('Qtr 1' 'Qtr 2' 'Qtr 3' 'Qtr 4' );
axis2 label=none;
proc gplot data=season;
   plot max    *_season_
        mean   *_season_
        median *_season_
        min    *_season_
        / overlay haxis=axis1 vaxis=axis2 legend=legend1;
run;
```

The results of this seasonal analysis are shown in Output 28.2.5.

Output 28.2.5. Seasonal Statistics Plot

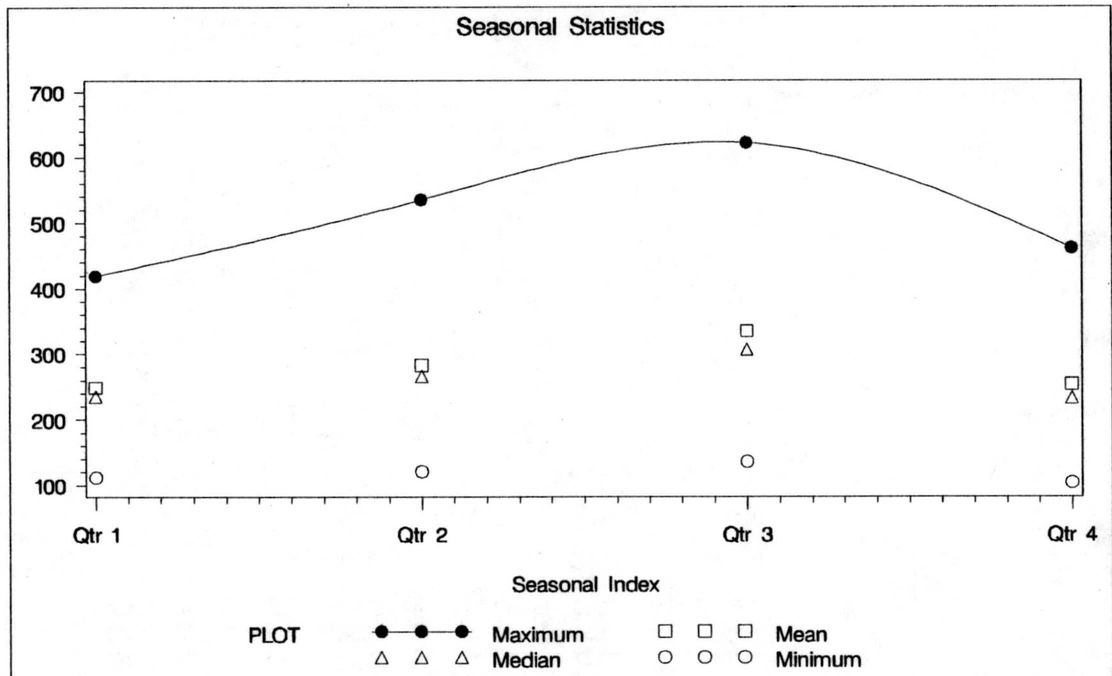

Example 28.3. Illustration of ODS Graphics (Experimental)

This example illustrates the use of experimental ODS graphics.

The following statements utilize the SASHELP.WORKERS data set to study the time series of electrical workers, and its interaction with the series of masonry workers. The series plot, the correlation panel, the seasonal adjustment panel, and all cross-series plots are requested. Output 28.3.1 through Output 28.3.4 show a selection of the plots created.

The graphical displays are requested by specifying the experimental ODS GRAPHICS statement and the experimental PLOT= or CROSSPLOT= options in the PROC TIMESERIES statement. For general information about ODS graphics, see Chapter 9, "Statistical Graphics Using ODS." For specific information about the graphics available in the TIMESERIES procedure, see the "ODS Graphics" section on page 1603.

```
ods html;
ods graphics on;

title "Illustration of ODS Graphics";
proc timeseries data=sashelp.workers out=_null_
   plot=(series corr decomp)
   crossplot=all;
   id date interval=month;
```

```
    var electric;
    crossvar masonry;
run;

ods graphics off;
ods html close;
```

Output 28.3.1. Series Plot (Experimental)

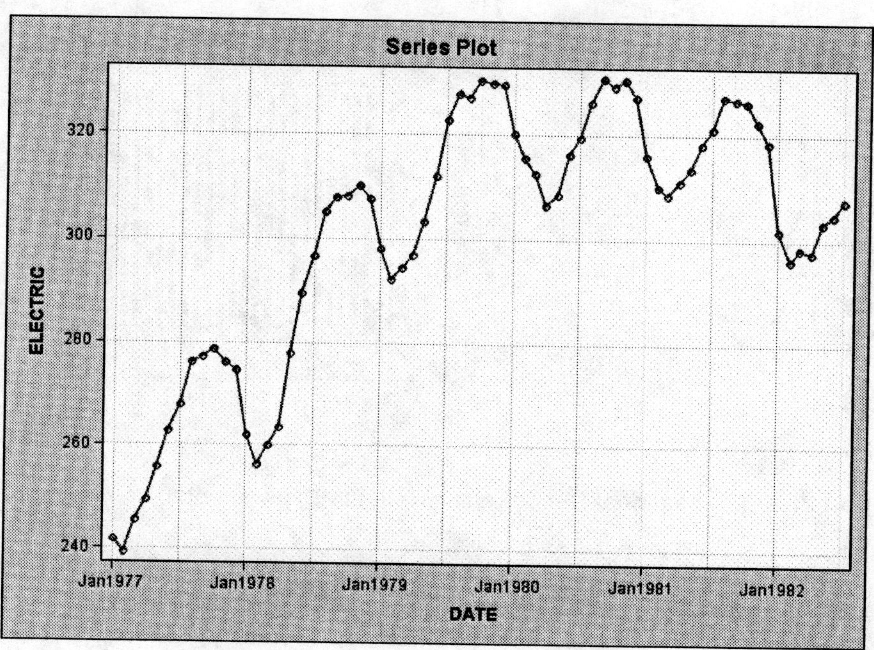

Output 28.3.2. Correlation Panel (Experimental)

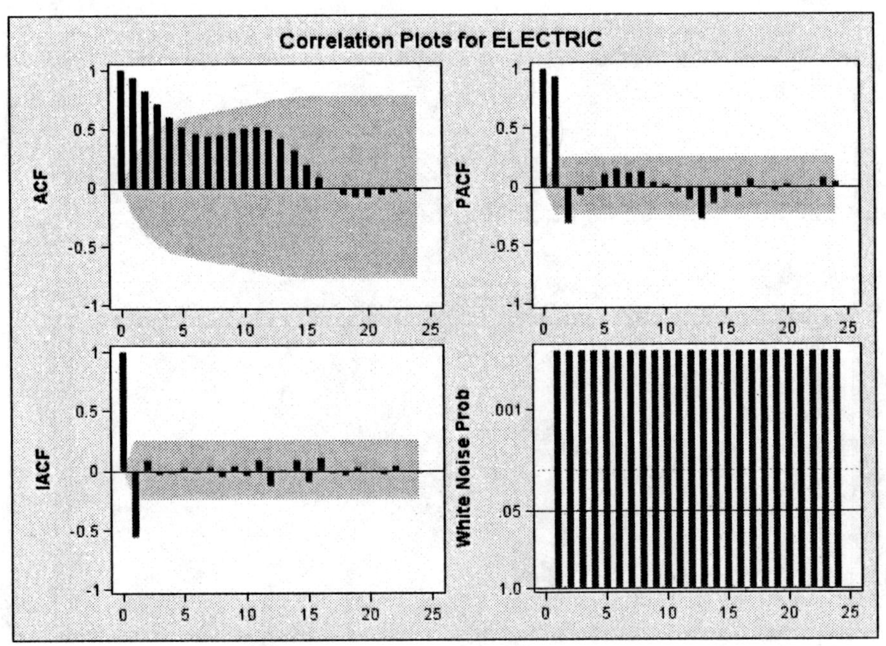

Output 28.3.3. Seasonal Decomposition Panel (Experimental)

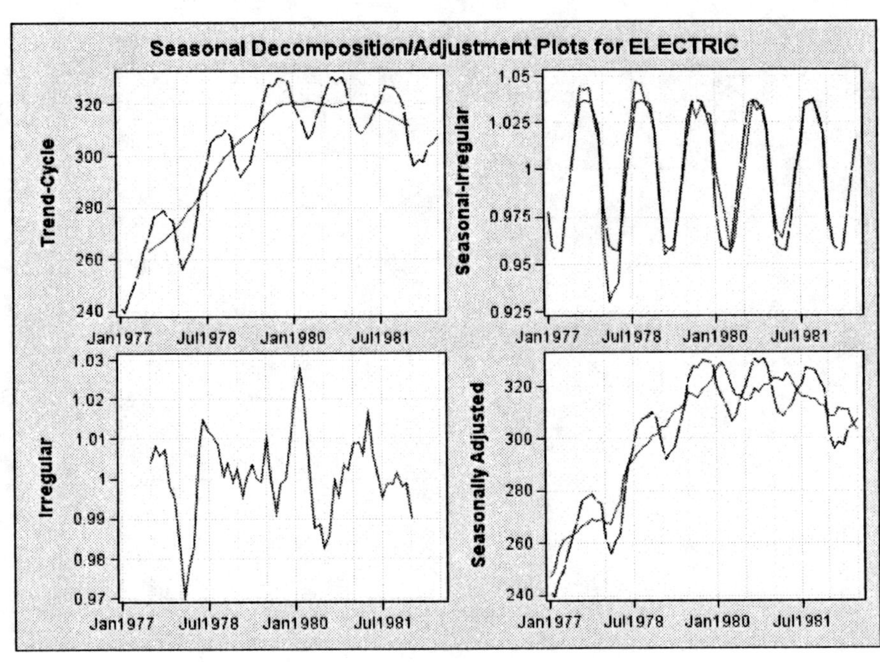

Output 28.3.4. Cross Correlation Plot (Experimental)

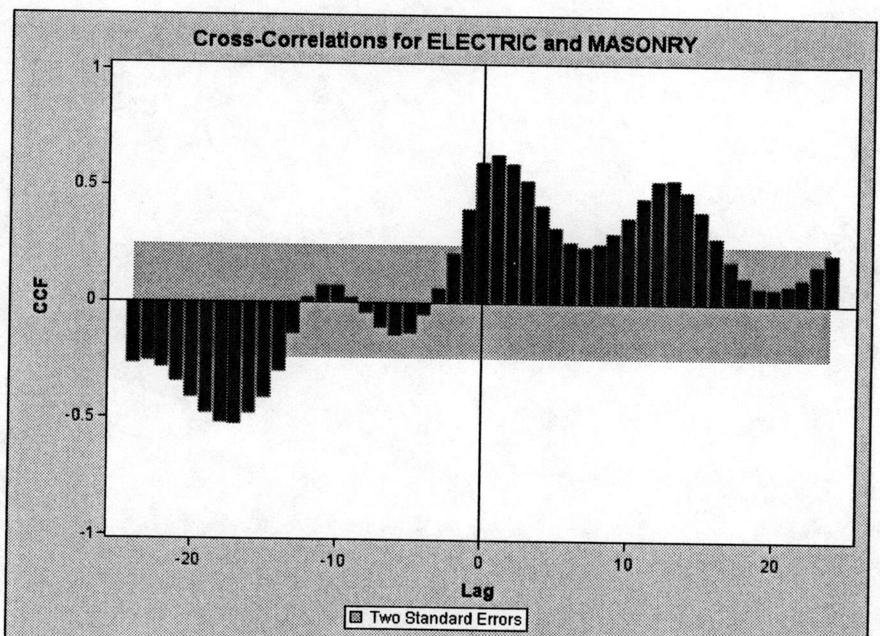

References

Greene, W.H. (1999), *Econometric Analysis*, Fourth Edition, New York: Macmillan.

Hodrick, R. and Prescott, E. (1980), "Post-War U.S. Business Cycles: An Empirical Investigation," Discussion Paper 451, Carnegie Mellon University.

Makridakis, S. and Wheelwright, S.C. (1978), *Interactive Forecasting: Univariate and Multivariate Methods*, Second Edition, San Francisco: Holden-Day, 198-201.

Pyle, D. (1999), *Data Preparation for Data Mining*, San Francisco: Morgan Kaufman Publishers, Inc.

Stoffer, D.S., Toloi, C.M.C. (1992), "A Note on the Ljung-Box-Pierce Portmanteau Statistic with Missing Data," *Statistics and Probability Letters* 13, 391-396.

Wheelwright, S.C. and Makridakis, S. (1973), *Forecasting Methods for Management*, Third Edition, New York: Wiley-Interscience, 123-133.

Chapter 29
The UCM Procedure

Chapter Contents

Chapter 29
The UCM Procedure

Overview

The UCM procedure analyzes and forecasts equally spaced univariate time series data using the Unobserved Components Models (UCM). The UCMs are also called *Structural Models* in the time series literature. A UCM decomposes the response series into components such as trend, seasonals, cycles, and the regression effects due to predictor series. The components in the model are supposed to capture the salient features of the series that are useful in *explaining* and *predicting* its behavior. Harvey (1989) is a good reference for time series modeling using the UCMs. Harvey calls the components in a UCM the "stylized facts" about the series under consideration. Traditionally, the ARIMA models and, to some limited extent, the Exponential Smoothing models, have been the main tools in the analysis of this type of time series data. It is fair to say that the UCMs capture the versatility of the ARIMA models while possessing the interpretability of the smoothing models. A thorough discussion of the correspondence between the ARIMA models and the UCMs, and the relative merits of the UCM and ARIMA modeling is given in Harvey (1989). The UCMs are also very similar to another set of models, called the *Dynamic Models*, that are popular in the Bayesian time series literature (West and Harrison 1999). In SAS/ETS you can use PROC ARIMA for the ARIMA modeling and the Time Series Forecasting System for a point-and-click interface to the ARIMA and exponential smoothing modeling.

You can use the UCM procedure to fit a wide range of UCMs that can incorporate complex trend, seasonal, and cyclical patterns and can include multiple predictors. It provides a variety of diagnostic tools to assess the fitted model and to suggest the possible extensions or modifications. The components in the UCM provide a succinct description of the underlying mechanism governing the series. You can print, save, or plot the estimates of these component series. Along with the standard forecast and residual plots, the study of these component plots is an essential part of the time series analysis using the UCMs. Once a suitable UCM is found for the series under consideration, it can be used for a variety purposes. For example, it can be used for

- forecasting the values of the response series and the component series in the model
- obtaining a model-based seasonal decomposition of the series
- obtaining a "denoised" version and interpolating the missing values of the response series in the historical period
- obtaining the full sample or "smoothed" estimates of the component series in the model

Experimental graphics are now available with the UCM procedure. For more information, see the "ODS Graphics" section on page 1664.

Getting Started

The analysis of time series using the UCMs involves recognizing the salient features present in the series and modeling them suitably. The UCM procedure provides a variety of models for modeling the commonly observed features in time series. These models are discussed in detail later in this section. First the procedure is illustrated using a few examples.

A Seasonal Series with a Linear Trend

The airline passenger series, given as Series G in Box and Jenkins (1976), is often used in time series literature as an example of a nonstationary seasonal time series. This series is a monthly series consisting of the number of airline passengers who traveled during the years 1949 to 1960. Its main features are a continual rise in the number of passengers from year to year and the seasonal variation in the numbers during any given year. It also exhibits an increase in variability around the trend. A log transformation is used to stabilize this variability. These trend and seasonal features of the series are apparent in the following plot (Figure 29.1):

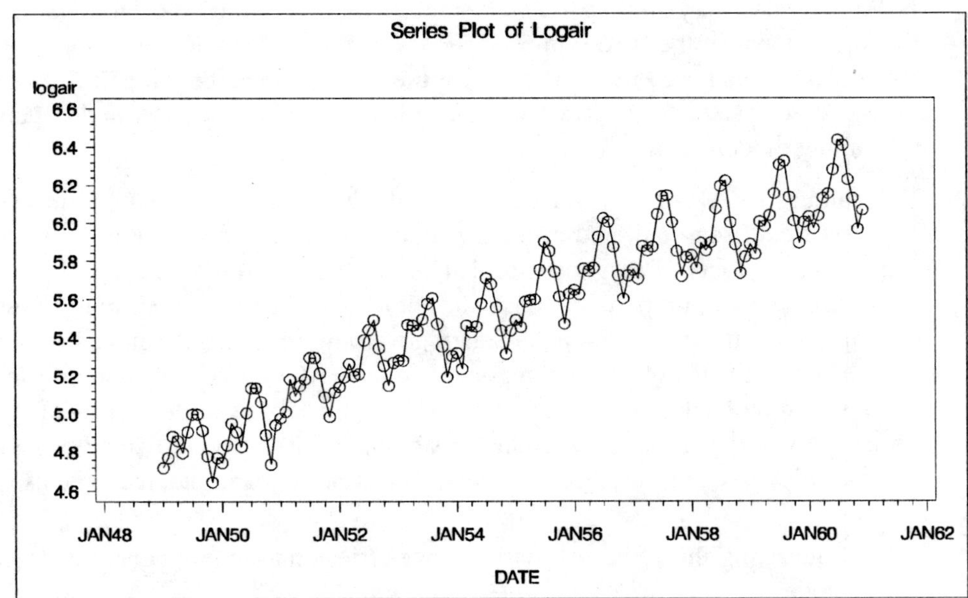

Figure 29.1. Series Plot of Log Transformed Airline Passenger Series

In this example this series will be modeled using an unobserved component model called the Basic Structural Model (BSM). The BSM models a time series as a sum of three stochastic components; a trend component μ_t, a seasonal component γ_t, and random error ϵ_t. Formally, a BSM for a response series y_t can be described as

$$y_t = \mu_t + \gamma_t + \epsilon_t$$

Each of the stochastic components in the model is modeled separately. The random error ϵ_t, also called the *irregular component*, is modeled simply as a sequence of independent, identically distributed (i.i.d.) zero mean Gaussian random variables. The trend and the seasonal components can be modeled in a few different ways. The model for trend used here is called a *locally linear time trend*. This trend model can be written as follows:

$$\begin{aligned} \mu_t &= \mu_{t-1} + \beta_{t-1} + \eta_t, \quad && \eta_t \sim i.i.d.\ N(0, \sigma_\eta^2) \\ \beta_t &= \beta_{t-1} + \xi_t, && \xi_t \sim i.i.d.\ N(0, \sigma_\xi^2) \end{aligned}$$

These equations specify a trend where the level μ_t as well as the slope β_t is allowed to vary over time. This variation in slope and level is governed by the variances of the disturbance terms η_t and ξ_t in their respective equations. Some interesting special cases of this model arise by manipulating these disturbance variances. For example, if the variance of ξ_t is zero, the slope will be constant (equal to β_0) and, if in addition, the variance of η_t is also zero, μ_t will be a deterministic trend given by the line $\mu_0 + \beta_0 t$. The seasonal model used in this example is called a trigonometric seasonal. The stochastic equations governing a trigonometric seasonal are explained later. However, it is interesting to note here that this seasonal model reduces to the familiar regression with deterministic seasonal dummies if the variance of the disturbance terms in its equations is equal to zero. The following SAS statements specify a BSM with these three components:

```
proc ucm data=series_g;
      id date interval=month;
      model logair;
      irregular;
      level;
      slope;
      season length=12 type=trig print=smooth;
      estimate;
      forecast lead=24 print=decomp;
run;
```

The PROC statement signifies the start of the UCM procedure and the input data set containing the dependent series is specified there. The optional ID statement is used to specify a date, datetime, or time identification variable, *date* in this example, to label the observations. The INTERVAL=MONTH option in the ID statement indicates that the measurements were collected on a monthly basis. The model specification begins with the MODEL statement, where the dependent series is specified (*logair* in this case). After this the components in the model are specified using separate statements that enable controlling their individual properties. The IRREGULAR statement is used to specify the irregular component ϵ_t, and the trend component μ_t is specified using the LEVEL and SLOPE statements. The seasonal component γ_t is specified using the SEASON statement. The specifics of the seasonal characteristics such as its season length, its stochastic evolution properties, etc, are specified using the options in the SEASON statement. The seasonal used in this example has season length 12, corresponding to the monthly seasonality, and is of the *trigonometric* type (different types of seasonals are explained later in this section). The parameters of this model are the variances of the disturbance terms in the evolution equations of μ_t, β_t and γ_t and the variance of the *irregular* component ϵ_t. These parameters are estimated by maximizing the likelihood of the data. The ESTIMATE statement options can be used to specify the span of data used in parameter estimation and to display and save the results of the estimation step and the model diagnostics. You can use the estimated model to obtain the forecasts of the series as well as the components. The options in the individual component statements can be used to display the component forecasts, for example, PRINT=SMOOTH option in the SEASON statement requests the displaying of smoothed forecasts of the seasonal component γ_t. The series forecasts and forecasts of the sum of components can be requested using the FORECAST statement. The option PRINT=DECOMP in the FORECAST statement requests the printing of the smoothed trend μ_t and the trend plus seasonal $(\mu_t + \gamma_t)$.

The parameter estimates for this model are displayed in Figure 29.2.

The UCM Procedure

Final Estimates of the Free Parameters

Component	Parameter	Estimate	Approx Std Error	t Value	Approx Pr > |t|
Irregular	Error Variance	0.00023436	0.0001079	2.17	0.0298
Level	Error Variance	0.00029828	0.0001057	2.82	0.0048
Slope	Error Variance	9.8572E-13	6.7141E-10	0.00	0.9988
Season	Error Variance	0.00000356	1.32347E-6	2.69	0.0072

Figure 29.2. BSM for the Logair Series

The estimates suggest that except for the slope component the disturbance variances of all the components are significant, that is, all these components are stochastic. The slope component, however, appears to be deterministic because its error variance is quite insignificant. It may then be useful to check if the slope component can be dropped from the model, that is if $\beta_0 = 0$. This can be checked by examining the significance analysis table of the components given in Figure 29.3.

Significance Analysis of Components (Based on the Final State)			
Component	DF	Chi-Square	Pr > ChiSq
Irregular	1	0.08	0.7747
Level	1	117867	<.0001
Slope	1	43.78	<.0001
Season	11	507.75	<.0001

Figure 29.3. Component Significance Analysis for the Logair Series

This table provides the significance of the components in the model at the end of the estimation span. If a component is deterministic, this analysis is equivalent to checking whether the corresponding regression effect is significant. However, if a component is stochastic then this analysis only pertains to the portion of the series near the end of the estimation span. In this example the slope appears quite significant and should be retained in the model, possibly as a deterministic component. Note that, on the basis of this table, the irregular component's contribution appears insignificant towards the end of the estimation span, however, since it is a *stochastic* component it cannot be dropped from the model on the basis of this analysis alone. The slope component can be made deterministic by holding the value of its error variance fixed at zero. This is done by modifying the SLOPE statement as follows:

```
slope variance=0 noest;
```

After a tentative model is fit its adequacy can be checked by examining different Goodness of Fit measures and other diagnostic tests and plots that are based on the model residuals. The table given in Figure 29.4 shows the goodness fit statistics that are computed using the one step ahead prediction errors (see "Statistics of Fit"). These measures indicate a good agreement between the model and the data. Additional diagnostics measures are also printed by default but are not shown here.

The UCM Procedure

Fit Statistics Based on Residuals	
Mean Squared Error	0.00147
Root Mean Squared Error	0.03830
Mean Absolute Percentage Error	0.54132
Maximum Percent Error	2.19097
R-Square	0.99061
Adjusted R-Square	0.99046
Random Walk R-Square	0.99220
Amemiya's Adjusted R-Square	0.99017

Number of non-missing residuals used for computing the fit statistics = 131

Figure 29.4. Fit Statistics for the Logair Series

Once the model appears satisfactory, it can be used for forecasting. An interesting feature of the UCM procedure is that, apart from the series forecasts, you can request the forecasts of the individual components in the model. The plots of component forecasts can be useful in understanding their contributions to the series. In what follows, a few such plots are shown. The first plot (Figure 29.5) shows the smoothed trend of the series.

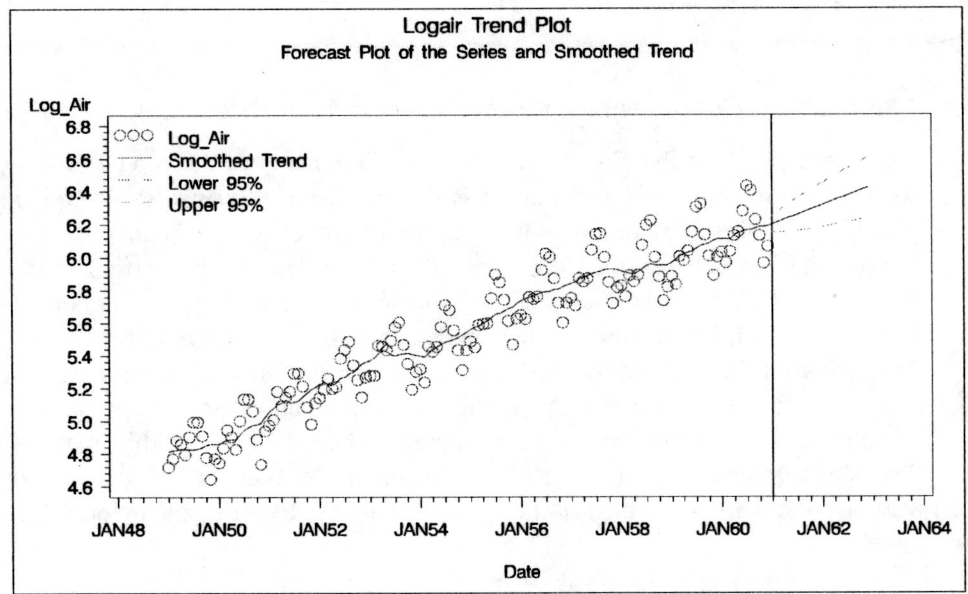

Figure 29.5. Smoothed Trend in the Logair Series

The second plot (Figure 29.6) shows the seasonal component by itself.

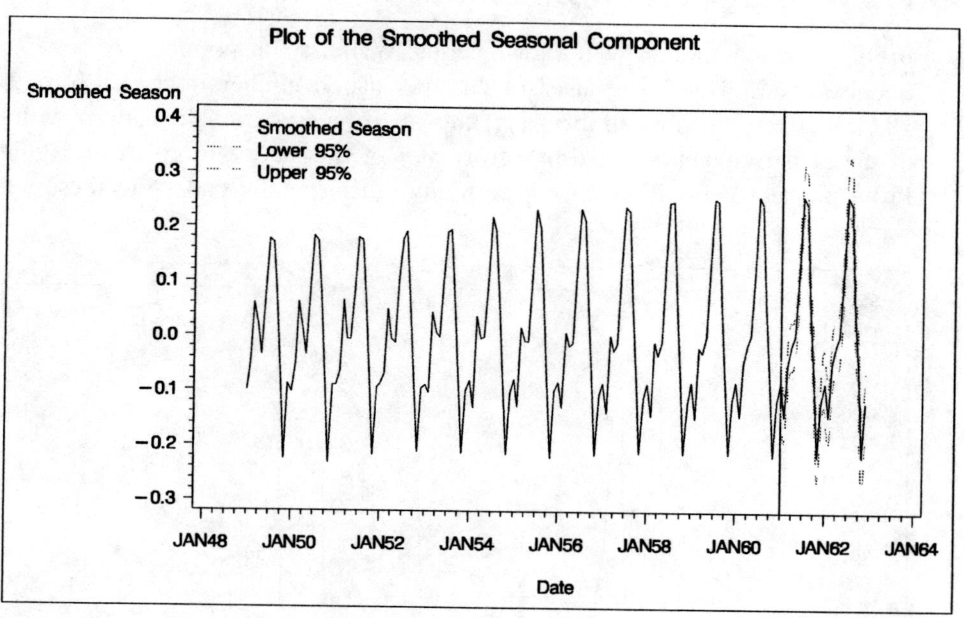

Figure 29.6. Smoothed Seasonal in the Logair Series

The plot of the sum of trend and seasonal is shown in Figure 29.7. You can see that, at least visually, the model seems to fit the data well. In all these decomposition plots the component estimates are extrapolated for two years in the future.

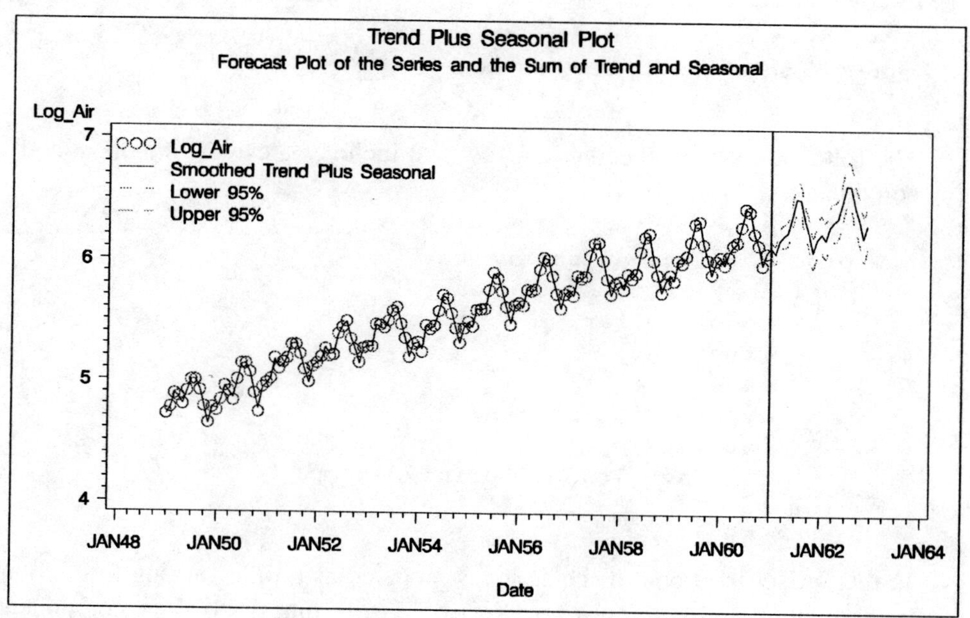

Figure 29.7. Smoothed Trend plus Seasonal in the Logair Series

A Series with Cyclical Component

In this example another well known series, Wolfer's sunspot data (Anderson 1971), is considered. The data consist of yearly sunspot numbers recorded from 1749 to 1924. These sunspot numbers are known to have a cyclical pattern with period of about eleven years. A time series plot of this series is given in Figure 29.8. From the plot it is difficult to discern any other specific pattern to these numbers.

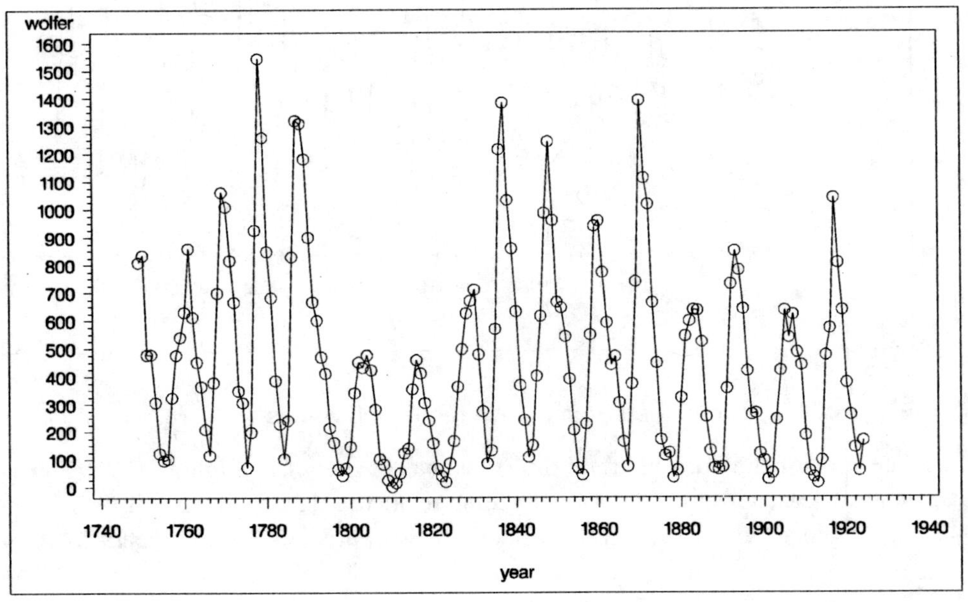

Figure 29.8. Wolfer Sunspot Numbers

The following syntax specifies a UCM that includes a cycle component and a level component.

```
proc ucm data=sunspot;
     id year interval=year;
     model wolfer;
     irregular;
     level;
     cycle print=smooth;
     estimate;
     forecast lead=12 print=decomp;
run;
```

In this model the trend of the series is modeled as a time-varying level component without any persistent upward or downward drift, that is, no slope component is included. The cyclical behavior of the series is modeled using a cycle component that is a damped sinusoidal with fixed period and time varying amplitude. The parameters of the cycle are its period, the damping factor, and the variance of the disturbance terms in its stochastic equations. They are estimated from the data. In this case the estimate of the cycle period turns out to be approximately 10.58 years, consistent with the known results. As in the earlier example, it is informative to see the decomposition plots of the series. The first plot (Figure 29.9) shows the smoothed trend of the series.

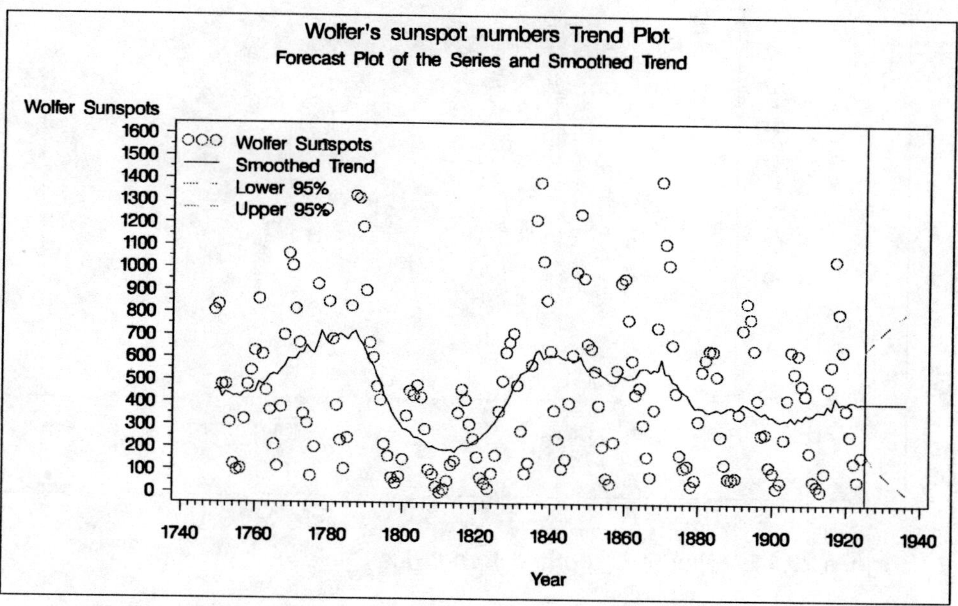

Figure 29.9. Smoothed Trend

The second plot shows the cycle component (Figure 29.10).

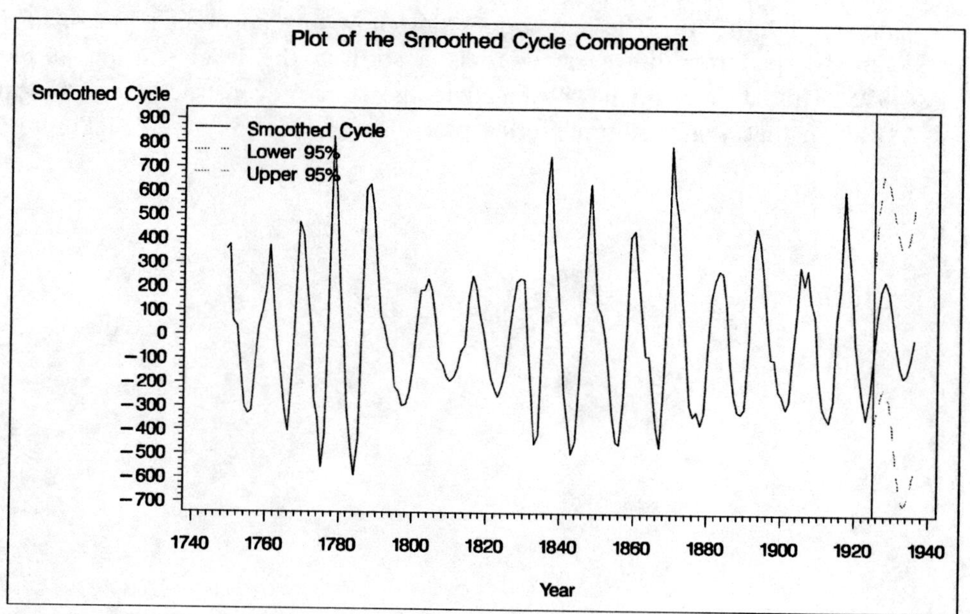

Figure 29.10. Smoothed Cycle

The plot of sum of trend and cycle is shown in Figure 29.11.

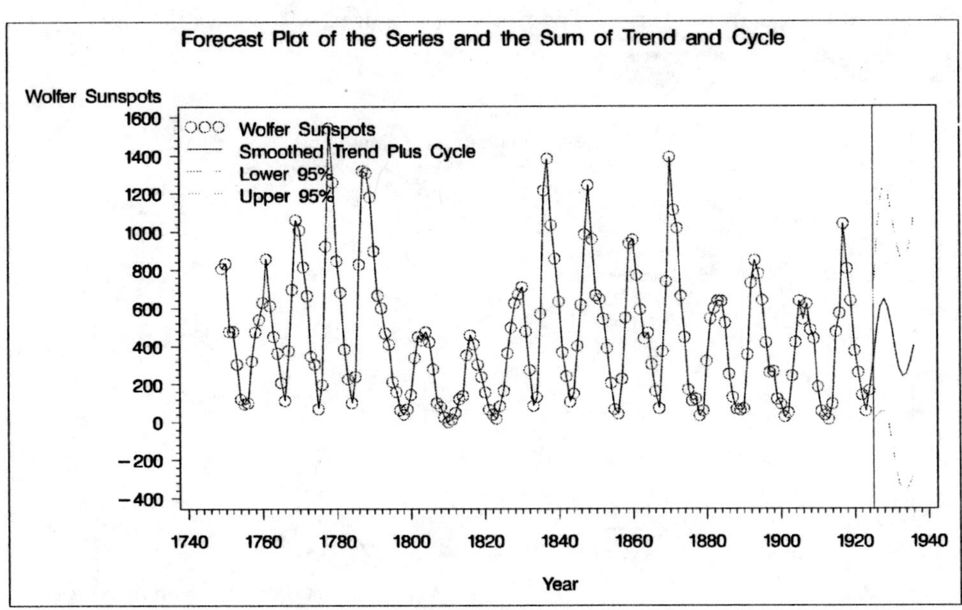

Figure 29.11. Plot of Smoothed Trend Plus Cycle

A Series with Level Shift

In this example the series consists of the yearly level readings of the river Nile recorded at Aswan (see Cobb 1978). The data consists of readings from the years 1871 to 1970. The series does not show any apparent trend or any other distinctive patterns; however, there is a shift in the level starting at the year 1899. This shift could be attributed to the start of construction of a dam near Aswan in that year. A time series plot of this series is given in Figure 29.12.

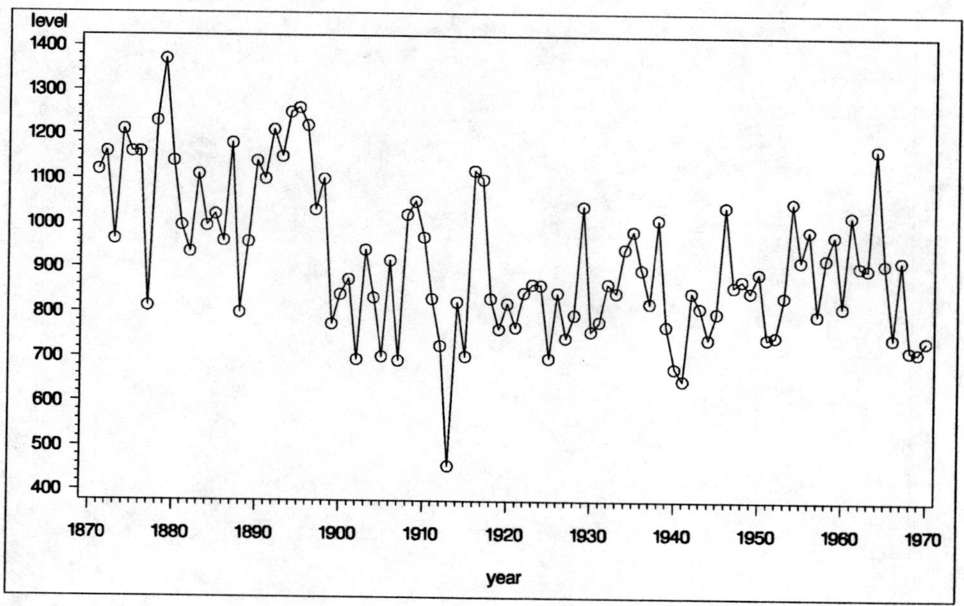

Figure 29.12. Nile River Level

The following syntax specifies a UCM that models the level of the river as a locally constant series with a shift in the year 1899, represented by a dummy regressor (Shift1899).

```
proc ucm data=nile;
   id year interval=year;
   model nile_level = shift1899;
   irregular;
   level;
   estimate;
   forecast print=decomp;
run;
```

The decomposition plots of this model can be easily obtained. However, it is instructive to see the plot of the smoothed trend obtained without using this regressor in the model. This plot is given in Figure 29.13. The plot shows a noticeable drop in the smoothed river level around 1899.

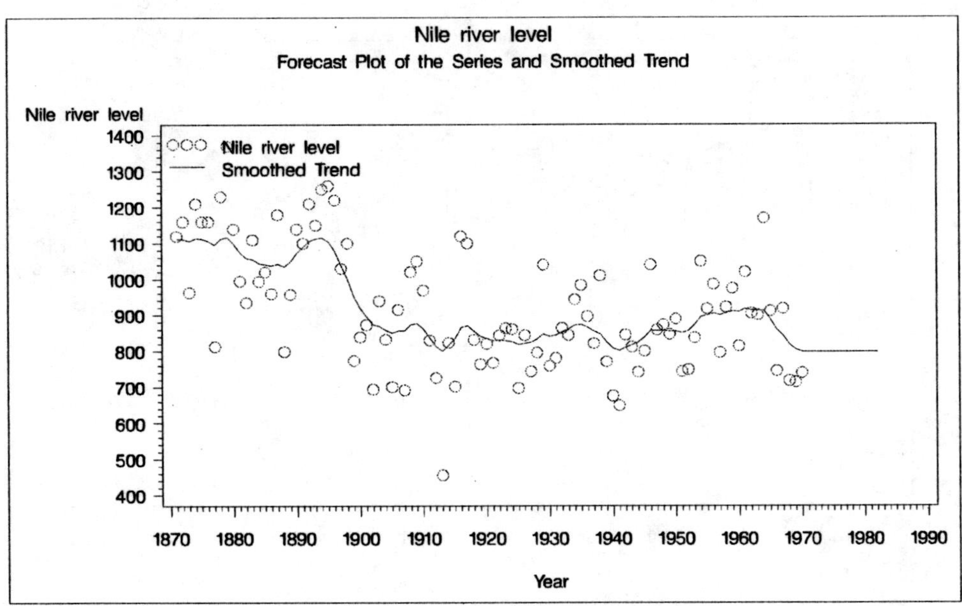

Figure 29.13. Smoothed Trend without the Shift of 1899

The second plot shows the smoothed trend including the correction due to the shift in the year 1899 (Figure 29.14). Notice the simplicity in the shape of the smoothed curve after the incorporation of the shift information.

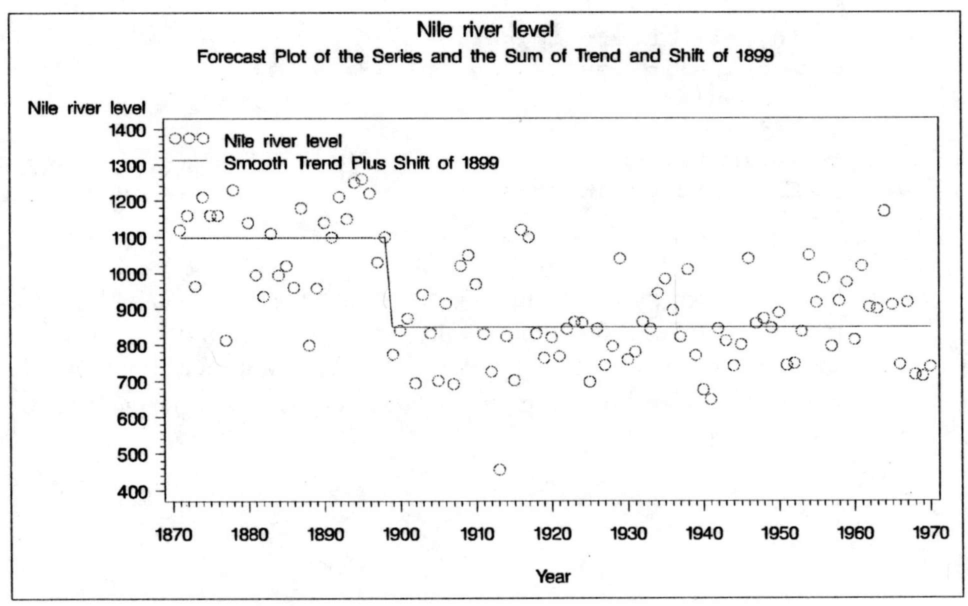

Figure 29.14. Smoothed Trend Plus Shift of 1899

An Introduction to Unobserved Component Models

A general UCM considered in this procedure can be described as

$$
\begin{aligned}
y_t &= \mu_t + \gamma_t + \psi_t + r_t + \sum_{i=1}^{p} \phi_i y_{t-i} + \sum_{j=1}^{m} \beta_j x_{jt} + \epsilon_t \\
\epsilon_t &\sim i.i.d.\ N(0, \sigma_\epsilon^2)
\end{aligned}
$$

The terms μ_t, γ_t, ψ_t, and r_t represent the trend, seasonal, cyclical and the autoregressive components, respectively. In fact the model can contain multiple seasonals and cycles, and the seasonals can be of different types. For simplicity of discussion the above model contains only one of each of these components. The regression term, $\sum_{j=1}^{m} \beta_j x_{jt}$, includes variables with values supplied in the input dataset. The $\sum_{i=1}^{p} \phi_i y_{t-i}$ is a regression term involving the lags of the dependent variable. It is written separately because its mathematical treatment is slightly different (see "Details"). The disturbance term ϵ_t, also called the *irregular* component, is assumed to be a Gaussian white noise with variance σ_ϵ^2. By controlling the presence or absence of various terms and by choosing the proper flavor of the included terms, the UCMs can generate a rich variety of time series patterns. A UCM can be applied to variables after transforming them by transforms such as *log* and *difference*.

The components μ_t, γ_t, ψ_t, and r_t model structurally different aspects of the time series. For example, the trend μ_t models the natural tendency of the series in the absence of any other perturbing effects such as seasonality, cyclical components, and the effects of exogenous variables while the seasonal component γ_t models the correction to the level due to the seasonal effects. These components are assumed to be statistically independent of each other and independent of the irregular component. All of the component models can be thought of as stochastic generalizations of the relevant deterministic patterns in time. This way the deterministic cases emerge as special cases of the stochastic models. The different models available for these unobserved components are discussed next.

Modeling the Trend

As mentioned earlier, the trend in a series can be loosely defined as the natural tendency of the series in the absence of any other perturbing effects. The UCM procedure offers two ways to model the trend component μ_t. The first model, called the Random Walk (RW) model, implies that the trend remains roughly constant throughout the life of the series without any persistent upward or downward drift. In the second model the trend is modeled as a locally linear time trend (LLT). The RW model can be described as

$$
\mu_t = \mu_{t-1} + \eta_t, \quad \eta_t \sim i.i.d.\ N(0, \sigma_\eta^2)
$$

Note that if $\sigma_\eta^2 = 0$ then the model becomes $\mu_t = constant$. In the LLT model the trend is locally linear, consisting of both the *level* and *slope*. The model for μ_t is

$$
\begin{aligned}
\mu_t &= \mu_{t-1} + \beta_{t-1} + \eta_t, & \eta_t &\sim i.i.d.\ N(0, \sigma_\eta^2) \\
\beta_t &= \beta_{t-1} + \xi_t, & \xi_t &\sim i.i.d.\ N(0, \sigma_\xi^2)
\end{aligned}
$$

The disturbances η_t and ξ_t are assumed to be independent. There are some interesting special cases of this model obtained by setting one or both of the disturbance variances σ^2_η and σ^2_ξ equal to zero. If σ^2_ξ is set equal to zero then you get a linear trend model with fixed slope. If σ^2_η is set to zero then the resulting model usually has a smoother trend. If both the variances are set to zero then the resulting model is the deterministic linear time trend: $\mu_t = \mu_0 + \beta_0 t$.

These trend patterns can be incorporated in your model using the LEVEL and SLOPE statements in PROC UCM.

Modeling a Cycle

A deterministic cycle ψ_t with frequency λ, $0 < \lambda < \pi$, can be written as

$$\psi_t = \alpha \cos(\lambda t) + \beta \sin(\lambda t)$$

If the argument t is measured on a continuous scale, ψ_t is a periodic function with period $2\pi/\lambda$, amplitude $(\alpha^2 + \beta^2)^{1/2}$, and phase $\tan^{-1}(\beta/\alpha)$. However, if ψ_t is measured only at the integer values it is not exactly periodic, unless $\lambda = (2\pi j)/k$ for some integers j and k. The cycles in their pure form are not used very often in practice. However, they are very useful as building blocks for more complex periodic patterns. It is well known that the periodic pattern of any complexity can be written as a sum of pure cycles of different frequencies and amplitudes. In time series situations it is useful to generalize this simple cyclical pattern to a stochastic cycle that has a fixed period but time varying amplitude and phase. The stochastic cycle considered here is motivated by the following recursive formula for computing ψ_t:

$$\begin{bmatrix} \psi_t \\ \psi_t^* \end{bmatrix} = \begin{bmatrix} \cos\lambda & \sin\lambda \\ -\sin\lambda & \cos\lambda \end{bmatrix} \begin{bmatrix} \psi_{t-1} \\ \psi_{t-1}^* \end{bmatrix}$$

starting with $\psi_0 = \alpha$ and $\psi_0^* = \beta$. Note that ψ_t and ψ_t^* satisfy the relation

$$\psi_t^2 + \psi_t^{*2} = \alpha^2 + \beta^2 \quad \text{for all } t$$

A stochastic generalization of the cycle ψ_t can be obtained by adding random noise to this recursion and by introducing a damping factor, ρ, for additional modeling flexibility. This model can be described as follows:

$$\begin{bmatrix} \psi_t \\ \psi_t^* \end{bmatrix} = \rho \begin{bmatrix} \cos\lambda & \sin\lambda \\ -\sin\lambda & \cos\lambda \end{bmatrix} \begin{bmatrix} \psi_{t-1} \\ \psi_{t-1}^* \end{bmatrix} + \begin{bmatrix} \nu_t \\ \nu_t^* \end{bmatrix}$$

where $0 \le \rho \le 1$, and the disturbances ν_t and ν_t^* are independent $N(0, \sigma^2_\nu)$ variables. The resulting stochastic cycle has a fixed period but time varying amplitude and phase. The stationarity properties of the random sequence ψ_t depend on the damping factor ρ. If $\rho < 1$, ψ_t has a stationary distribution with mean zero and variance $\sigma^2_\nu/(1 - \rho^2)$. If $\rho = 1$, ψ_t is non-stationary.

A cycle is incorporated in a UCM by using a CYCLE statement in PROC UCM. Multiple cycles can be included in the model using separate CYCLE statements for each included cycle.

As mentioned before, the cycles are very useful as building blocks for constructing more complex periodic patterns. Periodic patterns of almost any complexity can be created by superimposing cycles of different periods and amplitudes. In particular, the seasonal patterns, general periodic patterns with integer periods, can be constructed as sums of cycles. This important topic of modeling the seasonals is considered next.

Modeling a Seasonal

The seasonal fluctuations are a common source of variation in the time series data. These fluctuations arise because of the regular changes in seasons or some other periodic events. The seasonal effects are regarded as corrections to the general trend of the series due to the seasonal variations, and these effects sum to zero when summed over the full season cycle. Therefore the seasonal component γ_t is modeled as a stochastic periodic pattern of an integer period s such that the sum $\sum_{i=0}^{s-1} \gamma_{t-i}$ is always zero in the mean. The period s is called the season length. Two different models for the seasonal component are considered here. The first model is called the *dummy* variable form of the seasonal component. It is described by the equation

$$\sum_{i=0}^{s-1} \gamma_{t-i} = \omega_t, \qquad \omega_t \sim i.i.d.\ N(0, \sigma_\omega^2)$$

The other type of model is called the *trigonometric* form of the seasonal component. In this case γ_t is modeled as a sum of cycles of different frequencies. This model is given as follows:

$$\gamma_t = \sum_{j=1}^{[s/2]} \gamma_{j,t}$$

where $[s/2]$ equals $s/2$ if s is even and equals $(s-1)/2$ if it is odd. The cycles $\gamma_{j,t}$ have frequencies $\lambda_j = 2\pi j/s$ and are specified by the matrix equation

$$\begin{bmatrix} \gamma_{j,t} \\ \gamma_{j,t}^* \end{bmatrix} = \begin{bmatrix} \cos\lambda_j & \sin\lambda_j \\ -\sin\lambda_j & \cos\lambda_j \end{bmatrix} \begin{bmatrix} \gamma_{j,t-1} \\ \gamma_{j,t-1}^* \end{bmatrix} + \begin{bmatrix} \omega_{j,t} \\ \omega_{j,t}^* \end{bmatrix}$$

where the disturbances $\omega_{j,t}$ and $\omega_{j,t}^*$ are assumed to be independent and, for fixed j, $\omega_{j,t}$ and $\omega_{j,t}^* \sim N(0, \sigma_\omega^2)$. If s is even then the equation for $\gamma_{s/2,t}^*$ is not needed and $\gamma_{s/2,t}$ is given by

$$\gamma_{s/2,t} = -\gamma_{s/2,t-1} + \omega_{s/2,t}$$

The cycles $\gamma_{j,t}$ are called *harmonics*. If the seasonal is deterministic, the decomposition of the seasonal effects into these harmonics is identical to its Fourier decomposition. In this case the sum of squares of the seasonal factors equals the sum of squares of the amplitudes of these harmonics. In many practical situations, the contribution of the high frequency harmonics is negligible and can be ignored, giving rise to a simpler description of the seasonal. In the case of stochastic seasonals the situation may not be so transparent; however, similar considerations still apply. Note that, if the disturbance variance $\sigma_\omega^2 = 0$ then both the dummy and the trigonometric forms of seasonal components reduce to constant seasonal effects. That is, the seasonal component reduces to a deterministic function that is completely determined by its first $s - 1$ values.

The dummy and the trigonometric type seasonals defined above can be considered as *saturated* seasonals that put no restrictions on the $s - 1$ seasonal values. In some cases a more parsimonious representation of the seasonal may be more appropriate. This is particularly useful for seasonals with large season lengths. Parsimonious representations of the seasonals can be obtained in several different ways. Some of these ways involve the reuse of the already introduced cycle and seasonal components. One possibility is to consider special cases of the trigonometric seasonals obtained by deleting a few of the $[s/2]$ harmonics used in the sum. For example, a slightly smoother seasonal of length 12, corresponding to the monthly seasonality, can be obtained by deleting the highest frequency harmonic of period 2. That is, such a seasonal will be a sum of five stochastic cycles that have periods 12, 6, 4, 3, and 2.4. Another possibility is to consider a seasonal of a large season length as a sum of two or more seasonals that are each of much smaller season lengths. One more possibility is to restrict the seasonal values within certain blocks to be the same. An example of such a situation is as follows: Consider an hourly series that may show periodic variation that is attributable to the day of the week, and to the hour of the day. The hour of the day effect can be modeled as a simple saturated seasonal of season length 24. The day of the week effect could be modeled as a seasonal of season length 168 that restricts the seasonal values within a given day to be equal. Such a seasonal could be called a block-seasonal of season length 7 and block length 24.

These different types of seasonal patterns can be included in a UCM using a combination of SEASON, BLOCKSEASON, and CYCLE statements in PROC UCM.

Modeling the Autoregression

An autoregression of order one can be thought of as a special case of a cycle when the frequency λ is either 0 or π. Modeling this special case separately helps interpretation and parameter estimation. The auto-regression component r_t is modeled as follows:

$$r_t = \rho r_{t-1} + \nu_t, \qquad \nu_t \sim i.i.d.\ N(0, \sigma_\nu^2)$$

where $-1 \le \rho < 1$.

The Regression Terms

The regression terms $\sum_{j=1}^m \beta_j x_{jt}$ and $\sum_{i=1}^p \phi_i y_{t-i}$ supply additional flexibility to the model. Lags, differences, and other transformations can be applied to the variables.

The Model Parameters

The parameter vector in a UCM consists of the variances of the disturbance terms of the unobserved components, the damping coefficients and frequencies in the cycles, the damping coefficient in the autoregression, and the regression coefficients in the regression terms. These parameters are estimated by maximizing the likelihood. It is possible to restrict the values of the model parameters to user specified values.

Model Specification

A UCM is specified by describing the components in the model. For example, consider the model

$$y_t = \mu_t + \gamma_t + \epsilon_t$$

consisting of the irregular, level, slope, and the seasonal components. This model is called the Basic Structural Model (BSM) by Harvey. The syntax for a BSM with monthly seasonality of trigonometric type is

```
model y;
   irregular;
   level;
   slope;
   season length=12 type=trig;
```

Similarly the syntax

```
model y = x;
   irregular;
   level;
   slope variance=0 noest;
   season length=12 type=dummy;
```

specifies a BSM with dependent variable y, a regressor x and dummy type monthly seasonality. Moreover, the disturbance variance of the slope component is restricted to zero, giving rise to a local linear trend with fixed slope.

A model can contain multiple cycle and seasonal components. In such cases the model syntax contains a separate statement for each of these multiple cycle or seasonal components; for example, the syntax for model containing irregular and level components along with two cycle components could be as follows:

```
model y = x;
   irregular;
   level;
   cycle;
   cycle;
```

Syntax

Syntax

The UCM procedure uses the following statements.

PROC UCM *options*;
  BY *variables*;
  ID *variable options*;
  MODEL *dependent variable < = regressors >* ;
  IRREGULAR *options*;
  LEVEL *options*;
  SLOPE *options*;
  SEASON *options*;
  BLOCKSEASON *options*;
  CYCLE *options*;
  AUTOREG *options*;
  DEPLAG *options*;
  ESTIMATE *options*;
  FORECAST *options*;
  NLOPTIONS *options*;

Functional Summary

The statements and options controlling the UCM procedure are summarized in the following table.

Description	Statement	Option
Data Set Options		
specify the input data set	PROC UCM	DATA=
write parameter estimates to an output data set	ESTIMATE	OUTEST=
write forecasts and smoothed values of the response series and components to an output data set	FORECAST	OUTFOR=
BY Groups		
specify BY-group processing	BY	
ID Variable		
specify a date or time identification variable	ID	
specify the time interval between observations	ID	INTERVAL=
control the alignment of SAS Date values	ID	ALIGN=
Options for Specifying the Model		

Description	Statement	Option
specify the response series and, optionally, the predictor series	MODEL	
specify the initial value for the disturbance variance of the irregular component	IRREGULAR	VARIANCE=
fix the value of the disturbance variance of the irregular component to the specified initial value	IRREGULAR	NOEST
specify the initial value for the disturbance variance of the level component	LEVEL	VARIANCE=
fix the value of the disturbance variance of the level component to the specified initial value	LEVEL	NOEST
specify the initial value for the disturbance variance of the slope component	SLOPE	VARIANCE=
fix the value of the disturbance variance of the slope component to the specified initial value	SLOPE	NOEST
specify the season length of a seasonal component	SEASON	LENGTH=
specify the type of a seasonal component	SEASON	TYPE=
specify the initial value for the disturbance variance of a seasonal component	SEASON	VARIANCE=
fix the value of the disturbance variance of the seasonal component to the specified initial value	SEASON	NOEST
specify the block size of a block seasonal component	BLOCKSEASON	BLOCKSIZE=
specify the number of blocks of a block seasonal component	BLOCKSEASON	NBLOCKS=
specify the relative position of the first observation within the block of a block seasonal component	BLOCKSEASON	OFFSET=
specify the initial value for the disturbance variance of a block seasonal component	BLOCKSEASON	VARIANCE=
fix the value of the disturbance variance of the block seasonal component to the specified initial value	BLOCKSEASON	NOEST
specify the initial value for the period of a cycle component	CYCLE	PERIOD=
specify the initial value for the damping factor of a cycle component	CYCLE	RHO=
specify the initial value for the disturbance variance of the cycle component	CYCLE	VARIANCE=
fix the values of the parameters of the cycle component to the specified initial values	CYCLE	NOEST=
specify the initial value for the damping factor of the autoreg component	AUTOREG	RHO=
specify the initial value for the disturbance variance of the autoreg component	AUTOREG	VARIANCE=
fix the values of the parameters of the autoreg component to the specified initial values	AUTOREG	NOEST=

Description	Statement	Option
specify the lags of the response series to be included in the model	DEPLAG	LAGS=
specify the initial values for the lag coefficients for the response lags	DEPLAG	PHI=
fix the values of lag coefficients to the specified initial values	DEPLAG	NOEST
Options to Control the Nonlinear Optimization in Estimation Process		
specify an optimization algorithm	NLOPTIONS	TECH=
limit number of iterations during the optimization	NLOPTIONS	MAXITER=
limit number of function evaluations	NLOPTIONS	MAXFUNC=
specify function convergence criteria	NLOPTIONS	ABSFTOL=
specify gradient convergence criteria	NLOPTIONS	ABSGTOL=
specify parameter convergence criteria	NLOPTIONS	ABSXTOL=
Options to Control the Observation Span in Estimation and Forecasting		
specify how many starting response series measurements to exclude during the model estimation phase	ESTIMATE	SKIPFIRST=
specify how many ending response series measurements to exclude during the model estimation phase	ESTIMATE	BACK=
specify how many starting response series measurements to exclude during the forecasting phase	FORECAST	SKIPFIRST=
specify how many ending response series measurements to exclude during the forecasting phase	FORECAST	BACK=
specify how many periods to forecast beyond the forecast span	FORECAST	LEAD=
specify size of forecast confidence limits	FORECAST	ALPHA=
Options to Control the Printing		
suppress printing altogether	PROC UCM	NOPRINT
turn all the print options on	PROC UCM	PRINTALL
suppress the printing of parameter estimates, goodness of fit statistics, and other estimation output	ESTIMATE	PRINT=
suppress printing of forecast output	FORECAST	PRINT=
print filtered or smoothed estimate of the irregular component	IRREGULAR	PRINT=
print filtered or smoothed estimate of the level component	LEVEL	PRINT=
print filtered or smoothed estimate of the slope component	SLOPE	PRINT=
print filtered or smoothed estimate of the autoreg component	AUTOREG	PRINT=
print filtered or smoothed estimate of a cycle component	CYCLE	PRINT=

Description	Statement	Option
print filtered or smoothed estimate of a seasonal component	SEASON	PRINT=
print filtered or smoothed estimate of a block seasonal component	BLOCKSEASON	PRINT=
print parameter estimation related information	ESTIMATE	PRINT=
print forecasts, and smoothed estimates of model decomposition	FORECAST	PRINT=

PROC UCM Statement

PROC UCM *options;*

The following options can be used in the PROC UCM statement:

DATA= *SAS-data-set*
specifies the name of the SAS data set containing the time series. If the DATA= option is not specified in PROC UCM statement, the most recently created SAS data set is used.

NOPRINT
turns off all the printing for the procedure. The subsequent print options in the procedure are ignored.

PRINTALL
turns on all the printing options for the procedure. The subsequent noprint options in the procedure are ignored.

BY Statement

BY *variables;*

A BY statement can be used in the UCM procedure to process a data set in groups of observations defined by the BY variables. The model specified using the MODEL and other component statements is applied to all the groups defined by the BY variables.

ID Statement

ID *variable* **INTERVAL=** *value* **< ALIGN=** *value* **> ;**

The ID statement specifies a variable that identifies observations in the input data set. The variable specified in the ID statement is included in the OUT= data set. Note that the ID *variable* is usually a SAS date, time, or date-time variable. The values of the ID variable are extrapolated for the forecast observations based on the values of the INTERVAL= option.

ALIGN= *value*
controls the alignment of SAS dates used to identify output observations. The

ALIGN= option has the following possible values: BEGINNING | BEG | B, MIDDLE | MID | M, and ENDING | END | E. The default is BEGINNING. The ALIGN= option is used to align the ID variable to the beginning, middle, or end of the time ID interval specified by the INTERVAL= option.

INTERVAL= *value*

specifies the time interval between observations. This option is required in the ID statement. The INTERVAL=*value* is used in conjunction with the ID variable to check that the input data are in order and have no missing periods. The INTERVAL= option is also used to extrapolate the ID values past the end of the input data.

MODEL Statement

MODEL *dependent* < = *regressors* > **;**

The MODEL statement specifies the response variable and, optionally, the predictor variables for the UCM model. This is a required statement in the procedure.

IRREGULAR Statement

IRREGULAR < *options* > **;**

The IRREGULAR statement is used to include an *irregular* component in the model. There can be at most one IRREGULAR statement in the model specification. The irregular component corresponds to the overall random error, ϵ_t, in the model; it is modeled as a sequence of independent, zero mean, Gaussian random variables with variance σ_ϵ^2. The options in this statement enable you to specify the value of σ_ϵ^2 and to output the forecasts of ϵ_t. As a default, σ_ϵ^2 is estimated using the data and the component forecasts are not saved or displayed. A few examples of the IRREGULAR statement are given next. In the first example the statement is in its simplest form, resulting in the inclusion of an *irregular* component with unknown variance.

```
irregular;
```

The following statement provides a starting value for σ_ϵ^2, to be used in the non-linear parameter estimation process. It also requests the printing of smoothed predictions of ϵ_t. The smoothed irregulars are useful in model diagnostics.

```
irregular variance=4 print=smooth;
```

NOEST

This option fixes the value of σ_ϵ^2 to the value specified in the VARIANCE= option.

PRINT= FILTER
PRINT= SMOOTH
PRINT= (FILTER SMOOTH)

This option requests printing of filtered or smoothed estimate of the irregular component.

VARIANCE= *value*

This option is used to supply an initial value for σ_ϵ^2 during the parameter estimation process. Any nonnegative value, including zero, is an acceptable starting value.

LEVEL Statement

LEVEL *< options >* **;**

The LEVEL statement is used to include a *level* component in the model. The level component, either by itself or, together with a *slope* component, form the *trend* component, μ_t, of the model. If the slope component is absent, the resulting trend is a Random Walk (RW) specified by the following equations:

$$\mu_t = \mu_{t-1} + \eta_t, \quad \eta_t \sim i.i.d. \; N(0, \sigma_\eta^2)$$

If the slope component is present, signified by the presence of a SLOPE statement that is explained later, a Locally Linear Trend (LLT) is obtained. The equations of LLT are as follows:

$$\begin{aligned} \mu_t &= \mu_{t-1} + \beta_{t-1} + \eta_t, \quad \eta_t \sim i.i.d. \; N(0, \sigma_\eta^2) \\ \beta_t &= \beta_{t-1} + \xi_t, \qquad \xi_t \sim i.i.d. \; N(0, \sigma_\xi^2) \end{aligned}$$

In either case, the options in the LEVEL statement are used to specify the value of σ_η^2 and to request forecasts of μ_t. The SLOPE statement is used for similar purposes in the case of slope β_t. The following examples illustrate the use of LEVEL statement. Assuming that a SLOPE statement is not added subsequently, a simple Random Walk trend is specified by the following statement:

```
level;
```

The following statements specify a locally linear trend with value of σ_η^2 fixed at 4. It also requests printing of filtered values of μ_t. The value of σ_ξ^2, the disturbance variance in the slope equation, will be estimated from the data.

```
level variance=4 noest print=filter;
slope;
```

NOEST

This option fixes the value of σ_η^2 to the value specified in the VARIANCE= option.

PRINT=FILTER
PRINT= SMOOTH
PRINT= (FILTER SMOOTH)

This option requests printing of filtered or smoothed estimate of the level component.

VARIANCE= *value*

This option is used to supply an initial value for σ_η^2, the disturbance variance in the μ_t equation, at the start of the parameter estimation process. Any nonnegative value, including zero, is an acceptable starting value.

SLOPE Statement

SLOPE *< options >* **;**

The SLOPE statement is used to include a *slope* component in the model. The slope component cannot be used without the level component. The level and slope specifications jointly define the trend component of the model. A SLOPE statement without the accompanying LEVEL statement will be ignored. The equations of the trend, defined jointly by the level μ_t and slope β_t, are as follows:

$$
\begin{aligned}
\mu_t &= \mu_{t-1} + \beta_{t-1} + \eta_t, \quad \eta_t \sim i.i.d.\ N(0, \sigma_\eta^2) \\
\beta_t &= \beta_{t-1} + \xi_t, \quad \xi_t \sim i.i.d.\ N(0, \sigma_\xi^2)
\end{aligned}
$$

The SLOPE statement is used to specify the value of the disturbance variance, σ_ξ^2, in the slope equation, and to request forecasts of β_t. The following examples illustrate this statement:

```
level;
slope;
```

These statements request including a locally linear trend in the model. The disturbance variances σ_η^2 and σ_ξ^2 will be estimated from the data. You can request a locally linear trend with fixed slope using the following statements:

```
level;
slope variance=0 noest;
```

NOEST
This option fixes the value of the disturbance variance, σ_ξ^2, to the value specified in the VARIANCE= option.

PRINT=FILTER
PRINT= SMOOTH
PRINT= (FILTER SMOOTH)
This option requests printing of filtered or smoothed estimate of the slope component β_t.

VARIANCE= *value*
This option is used to supply an initial value for the disturbance variance, σ_ξ^2, in the β_t equation, at the start of the parameter estimation process. Any nonnegative value, including zero, is an acceptable starting value.

SEASON Statement

SEASON LENGTH= *integer* < options > **;**

The SEASON or the SEASONAL statement is used to specify a *seasonal* component, γ_t, in the model. A seasonal can be one of the two types, DUMMY or TRIGONOMETRIC. A DUMMY type seasonal with season length s satisfies the following stochastic equation:

$$\sum_{i=0}^{s-1} \gamma_{t-i} = \omega_t, \qquad \omega_t \sim i.i.d.\ N(0, \sigma_\omega^2)$$

The equations for a TRIGONOMETRIC type seasonal are as follows:

$$\gamma_t = \sum_{j=1}^{[s/2]} \gamma_{j,t}$$

where $[s/2]$ equals $s/2$ if s is even and equals $(s-1)/2$ if it is odd. The sinusoids $\gamma_{j,t}$ have frequencies $\lambda_j = 2\pi j/s$ and are specified by the matrix equation

$$\begin{bmatrix} \gamma_{j,t} \\ \gamma_{j,t}^* \end{bmatrix} = \begin{bmatrix} \cos\lambda_j & \sin\lambda_j \\ -\sin\lambda_j & \cos\lambda_j \end{bmatrix} \begin{bmatrix} \gamma_{j,t-1} \\ \gamma_{j,t-1}^* \end{bmatrix} + \begin{bmatrix} \omega_{j,t} \\ \omega_{j,t}^* \end{bmatrix}$$

where the disturbances $\omega_{j,t}$ and $\omega_{j,t}^*$ are assumed to be independent and, for fixed j, $\omega_{j,t}$ and $\omega_{j,t}^* \sim N(0, \sigma_\omega^2)$. If s is even then the equation for $\gamma_{s/2,t}^*$ is not needed and $\gamma_{s/2,t}$ is given by

$$\gamma_{s/2,t} = -\gamma_{s/2,t-1} + \omega_{s/2,t}$$

Note that, whether the seasonal type is DUMMY or TRIGONOMETRIC, there is only one parameter, the disturbance variance σ_ω^2, in the seasonal model.

There can be more than one seasonal components in the model, necessarily with different season lengths. Each seasonal component is specified using a separate SEASONAL statement. A model with multiple seasonal components can easily become quite complex and may need large amount of data and computing resources for its estimation and forecasting. Currently, at most three seasonals can be included in a model. The following code examples illustrate the use of SEASON statement:

```
season length=4;
```

This statement specifies a DUMMY type (default), seasonal component with season length four, corresponding to the quarterly seasonality. The disturbance variance σ_ω^2 will be estimated from the data. The following statement specifies a trigonometric seasonal with monthly seasonality. It also provides a starting value for σ_ω^2.

```
season length=12 type=trig variance=4;
```

LENGTH= *integer*

This option is used to specify the season length, s. This is a required option in this statement. The season length can be any integer larger than or equal to 2. Typical examples of season lengths are 12, corresponding to the monthly seasonality, or 4, corresponding to the quarterly seasonality.

NOEST

This option fixes the value of the the disturbance variance parameter to the value specified in the VARIANCE= option.

PRINT=FILTER
PRINT= SMOOTH
PRINT= (FILTER SMOOTH)

This option requests printing of filtered or smoothed estimate of the seasonal component γ_t.

TYPE= DUMMY | TRIG

This option specifies the type of the seasonal component. The default type is DUMMY.

VARIANCE= *value*

This option is used to supply an initial value for the disturbance variance, σ^2_ω, in the γ_t equation, at the start of the parameter estimation process. Any nonnegative value, including zero, is an acceptable starting value.

BLOCKSEASON Statement

BLOCKSEASON NBLOCKS= *integer*
BLOCKSIZE= *integer* < *options* > **;**

The BLOCKSEASON or BLOCKSEASONAL statement is used to specify a seasonal γ_t that has a special block structure. The seasonal γ_t is called a *block seasonal* of block size m and number of blocks k if its season length, s, can be factored as $s = m * k$ and its seasonal effects have a block form, that is, the first m seasonal effects are all equal to some number τ_1, the next m effects are all equal to some number τ_2, and so on. This type of seasonal structure can be appropriate in some cases, for example, consider a series that is recorded on an hourly basis. Further assume that, in this particular case, the *hour of the day* effect and the *day of the week* effect are *additive*. In this situation the hour of the week seasonality, having a season length of 168, can be modeled as a sum of two components. The hour of the day effect is modeled using a simple seasonal of season length 24, while the day of the week effect is modeled as a block seasonal that has the days of the week as blocks. This day of the week block seasonal will have seven blocks, each of size 24. A block seasonal specification requires, at the minimum, the block size m and the number of blocks in the seasonal k. These are specified using the BLOCKSIZE= and NBLOCKS= options, respectively. In addition, you may need to specify the position of the first observation of the series using the OFFSET= option, if it is not at the beginning of one of the blocks. In the example just considered, this will correspond to a situation where the first series measurement is not at the start of the day. Suppose that the first measurement of the series corresponds to the hour between 6:00 and 7:00 a.m., which is the seventh hour within that day or at the seventh position within that block. This is specified as OFFSET=7.

The other options of this statement are very similar to the options in the SEASONAL statement, for example, a block seasonal can also be of one of the two types, DUMMY or TRIGONOMETRIC. There can be more than one block seasonal component in the model, each specified using a separate BLOCKSEASON statement. No two block seasonals in the model can have the same NBLOCKS= and BLOCKSIZE= specifications. The following example illustrates the use of the BLOCKSEASON statement to specify the additive, hour of the week seasonal model:

```
season length=24 type=trig;
blockseason nblocks=7 blocksize=24;
```

BLOCKSIZE= *integer*

This option is used to specify the block size, m. This is a required option in this statement. The block size can be any integer larger than or equal to two. Typical examples of block sizes are 24, corresponding to the hours of the day when a day is being used as a block in hourly data, or 60, corresponding to the minutes in an hour when an hour is being used as a block in data recorded by minutes, etc.

NBLOCKS= *integer*

This option is used to specify the number of blocks, k. This is a required option in this statement. The number of blocks can be any integer larger than or equal to two.

NOEST

This option fixes the value of the the disturbance variance parameter to the value specified in the VARIANCE= option.

OFFSET= *integer*

This option is used to specify the position of the first measurement within the block, if the first measurement is not at the start of a block. The OFFSET= value must be between one and the block size. The default value is one. The *first measurement* refers to the start of the *estimation span* and the *forecast span.* If these spans differ, their starting measurements must be separated by an integer multiple of the block size.

PRINT=FILTER
PRINT= SMOOTH
PRINT= (FILTER SMOOTH)

This option requests the printing of filtered or smoothed estimate of the block seasonal component γ_t.

TYPE= DUMMY | TRIG

This option specifies the type of the seasonal component. The default type is DUMMY.

VARIANCE= *value*

This option is used to supply an initial value for the disturbance variance, σ_ω^2, in the

γ_t equation, at the start of the parameter estimation process. Any nonnegative value, including zero, is an acceptable starting value.

CYCLE Statement

CYCLE *< options >* **;**

The CYCLE statement is used to specify a *cycle* component, ψ_t, in the model. The stochastic equation governing a cycle component of period p and damping factor ρ is as follows:

$$\begin{bmatrix} \psi_t \\ \psi_t^* \end{bmatrix} = \rho \begin{bmatrix} \cos\lambda & \sin\lambda \\ -\sin\lambda & \cos\lambda \end{bmatrix} \begin{bmatrix} \psi_{t-1} \\ \psi_{t-1}^* \end{bmatrix} + \begin{bmatrix} \nu_t \\ \nu_t^* \end{bmatrix}$$

where ν_t and ν_t^* are independent, zero mean, Gaussian disturbances with variance σ_ν^2 and $\lambda = 2 * \pi / p$ is the angular frequency of the cycle. Any p strictly larger than two is an admissible value for the period, and the damping factor ρ can be any value in the interval (0, 1), including one but excluding zero. The cycles with frequency zero and π, which correspond to the periods equal to infinity and two respectively, can be specified using the AUTOREG statement. The values of ρ smaller than one give rise to a stationary cycle, while $\rho = 1$ gives rise to a nonstationary cycle. As a default, values of ρ, p, and σ_ν^2 are estimated from the data. However, if necessary, you can fix the values of some, or all, of these parameters.

There can be multiple cycles in a model, each specified using a separate CYCLE statement. Currently, you can specify up to 50 cycles in a model.

The following examples illustrate the use of the CYCLE statement:

```
cycle;
cycle;
```

These statements request including two cycles in the model. The parameters of each of these cycles will be estimated from the data.

```
cycle rho=1 noest=rho;
```

This statement requests inclusion of a nonstationary cycle in the model. The cycle period p and the disturbance variance σ_ν^2 will be estimated from the data. In the following statement a nonstationary cycle with fixed period of 12 is specified. Moreover, a starting value is supplied for σ_ν^2.

```
cycle period=12 rho=1 variance=4 noest=(rho period);
```

NOEST=PERIOD
NOEST=RHO
NOEST=VARIANCE
NOEST= (< RHO > < PERIOD > < VARIANCE >)

This option fixes the values of the component parameters to those specified in RHO=, PERIOD=, and VARIANCE= options. This option enables you to fix any combination of parameter values.

PERIOD= *value*

This option is used to supply an initial value for the cycle period during the parameter estimation process. Period value must be strictly larger than 2.

PRINT=FILTER
PRINT= SMOOTH
PRINT= (FILTER SMOOTH)

This option requests the printing of a filtered or smoothed estimate of the cycle component ψ_t.

RHO= *value*

This option is used to supply an initial value for the damping factor in this component during the parameter estimation process. Any value in the interval (0, 1), including one but excluding zero, is an acceptable initial value for the damping factor.

VARIANCE= *value*

This option is used to supply an initial value for the disturbance variance parameter, σ_ν^2, to be used during the parameter estimation process. Any nonnegative value, including zero, is an acceptable starting value.

AUTOREG Statement

AUTOREG *< options >* **;**

The AUTOREG statement specifies an *autoregressive* component of the model. An autoregressive component is a special case of cycle that corresponds to the frequency of zero or π. It is modeled separately for easier interpretation. A stochastic equation for an autoregressive component r_t can be written as follows:

$$r_t = \rho r_{t-1} + \nu_t, \quad \nu_t \sim i.i.d. \; N(0, \sigma_\nu^2)$$

The damping factor ρ can take any value in the interval (-1, 1), including -1 but excluding 1. If $\rho = 1$ the autoregressive component cannot be distinguished from the random walk level component. If $\rho = -1$ the autoregressive component corresponds to a seasonal component with season length 2, or a nonstationary cycle with period 2. If $|\rho| < 1$ then the autoregressive component is stationary. The following examples illustrate the AUTOREG statement:

```
autoreg;
```

This statement includes an autoregressive component in the model. The damping factor ρ and the disturbance variance σ_ν^2 are estimated from the data.

NOEST=RHO
NOEST= VARIANCE
NOEST= (RHO VARIANCE)

This option fixes the values of ρ and σ_ν^2 to those specified in RHO= and VARIANCE= options.

PRINT=FILTER
PRINT=SMOOTH
PRINT=(FILTER SMOOTH)
This option requests printing of filtered or smoothed estimate of the autoreg component.

RHO= *value*
This option is used to supply an initial value for the damping factor ρ during the parameter estimation process. The value of ρ must be in the interval (-1, 1), including -1 but excluding 1.

VARIANCE= *value*
This option is used to supply an initial value for the disturbance variance σ_ν^2 during the parameter estimation process. Any nonnegative value, including zero, is an acceptable starting value.

DEPLAG Statement

DEPLAG LAGS= *order* **<PHI=** *value ...* **> < NOEST > ;**

The DEPLAG statement is used to specify the lags of the dependent variable to be included as predictors in the model. The following examples illustrate the use of DEPLAG statement:

```
deplag lags=2;
```

If the dependent series is denoted by y_t, this statement specifies the inclusion of $\phi_1 y_{t-1} + \phi_2 y_{t-2}$ in the model. The parameters ϕ_1 and ϕ_2 are estimated from the data. The following statement requests including $\phi_1 y_{t-1} + \phi_2 y_{t-4} - \phi_1 \phi_2 y_{t-5}$ in the model. The values of ϕ_1 and ϕ_2 are fixed at 0.8 and -1.2.

```
deplag lags=(1)(4) phi=0.8 -1.2 noest;
```

The dependent lag parameters are not constrained to lie in any particular region. In particular, this implies that a UCM that contains only an *irregular* component and dependent lags, resulting in a traditional autoregressive model, is not constrained to be a stationary model. In the DEPLAG statement if an initial value is supplied for any one of the parameters, the initial values must be supplied for all other parameters also.

LAGS= *order*
LAGS= **(***lag, ..., lag***)** **...** **(***lag, ..., lag***)**

This is a required option in this statement. LAGS=(l_1, l_2, ..., l_k) defines a model with specified lags of the dependent variable included as predictors. LAGS= *order* is equivalent to LAGS=(1, 2, ..., *order*).

A concatenation of parenthesized lists specifies a factored model. For example, LAGS=(1)(12) specifies that the lag values, 1, 12 and 13, corresponding to the following polynomial in the backward shift operator, be included in the model

$$(1 - \phi_{1,1}B)(1 - \phi_{2,1}B^{12})$$

Note that, in this case, the coefficient of the thirteenth lag is constrained to be the product of the coefficients of the first and twelfth lags.

PHI= *value ...*
lists starting values for the coefficients of the lagged dependent variable.

NOEST
This option fixes the values of the parameters to those specified in PHI= options.

ESTIMATE Statement

ESTIMATE *< options >* **;**

The ESTIMATE statement is an optional statement used to control the overall model-fitting environment. Using this statement, you can control the span of observations used to fit the model using the SKIPFIRST= and BACK= options. This can be useful in model diagnostics. You can request a variety of goodness of fit statistics and other model diagnostic information. Note that this statement is not used to control the nonlinear optimization process itself. That is done using the NLOPTIONS statement where you can control the number of iterations, choose between the different optimization techniques, etc. The estimated parameters and other related information can be stored in a data set using the OUTEST= option. The following example illustrates the use of this statement:

```
estimate skipfirst=12 back=24;
```

This statement requests that the initial 12 measurements and the last 24 measurements be excluded during the model fitting process. The actual observation span used to fit the model is decided as follows: First the observations are scanned and the observation numbers of the first and last non-missing values of the dependent variable are determined. Suppose that the observation numbers of the first and the last non-missing values are n_0 and n_1, respectively. As a result of SKIPFIRST=12 and BACK=24, the measurements between observation numbers $n_0 + 11$ to $n_1 - 24$ form the estimation span. Of course, the model fitting may not take place if there are insufficient data in the resulting span. The model fitting will also not take place if there are regressors in the model that have missing values in the estimation span.

BACK= *integer*
SKIPLAST= *integer*
This option is used if some ending part of the data needs to be ignored during the parameter estimation. This can be useful when one wants to study the forecasting performance of the model on the observed data. SKIPLAST=10 results in skipping

the last 10 measurements of the response series during the parameter estimation. The default is SKIPLAST=0.

OUTEST= *SAS Dataset*

This option is used to specify an output data set for the estimated parameters.

PRINT=NONE

suppresses all the printed output related to the model fitting; for example, the parameter estimates, the goodness of fit statistics, etc.

SKIPFIRST= *integer*

This option is used if some early part of the data needs to be ignored during the parameter estimation. This can be useful if there is a reason to believe that the model being estimated is not appropriate for this portion of the data. SKIPFIRST=10 results in skipping the first 10 measurements of the response series during the parameter estimation. The default is SKIPFIRST=0.

FORECAST Statement

FORECAST *< options >* **;**

The FORECAST statement is an optional statement that is used to specify the overall forecasting environment for the specified model. It can be used to specify the span of observations, the historical period, to use to compute the forecasts of the future observations. This is done using the SKIPFIRST= and BACK= options. The number of periods to forecast beyond the historical period, and the significance level of the forecast confidence interval, are specified using the LEAD= and ALPHA= options. You can request one step ahead series and component forecasts using the PRINT= option. The series forecasts, and the model based decomposition of the series, can be saved in a data set using the OUTFOR= option. The following example illustrates the use of this statement:

```
forecast skipfirst=12 back=24 lead=30;
```

This statement requests that the initial 12 measurements and the last 24 response values be excluded during the forecast computations. The forecast horizon is 30 periods, that is multi step forecasting will begin at the end of the historical period and continue for 30 periods. The actual observation span used to compute the multi step forecasting is decided as follows: First the observations are scanned and the observation numbers of the first and last non-missing values of the response variable are determined. Suppose that the observation numbers of the first and last non-missing values are n_0 and n_1, respectively. As a result of SKIPFIRST=12 and BACK=24, the historical period, or the forecast span, begins at $n_0 + 12$ and ends at $n_1 - 24$. Multi step forecasts are produced for the next 30 periods, that is, for the observation numbers $n_1 - 23$ to $n_1 + 6$. Of course, the forecast computations may fail because of insufficient data in the forecast span. It can also fail if the model has regressor variables that have missing values in the forecast span. If the regressors contain missing values in the forecast horizon, that is between the observations $n_1 - 23$ to $n_1 + 6$, the forecast horizon is reduced accordingly.

ALPHA= *value*

specifies the significance level of the forecast confidence intervals, e.g., ALPHA=0.05 results in a 95% confidence interval.

BACK= *integer*
SKIPLAST= *integer*

This can be useful to specify the holdout sample for the evaluation of the forecasting performance of the model. SKIPLAST=10 results in treating the last 10 observed values of the response series as being unobserved. The default is SKIPLAST=0.

LEAD= *integer*

This option is used to specify the number of periods to forecast beyond the historical period defined by the SKIPFIRST= and SKIPLAST= options, for example, LEAD=10 will result in the forecasting of 10 future values of the response series. The default is LEAD=12.

OUTFOR= *SAS Dataset*

This option is used to specify an output data set for the forecasts. The output data set contains the ID variable (if specified), the response and predictor series, the one step ahead and out of sample response series forecasts, the forecast confidence intervals, the smoothed values of the response series and, the smoothed forecasts produced as a result of the model-based decomposition of the series.

PRINT=DECOMP
PRINT=FORECASTS
PRINT=NONE
PRINT=(FORECASTS DECOMP)

This option can be used to control the printing of the series forecasts and the printing of smoothed model decomposition estimates. By default, the series forecasts are printed only for the forecast horizon specified by the LEAD= option, that is, the one step ahead forecasts during the entire forecast span are not printed. You can request forecasts for the entire forecast span by specifying the PRINT=FORECASTS option. Using the PRINT=DECOMP, you can get smoothed estimates of the following effects: trend, trend plus regression, trend plus regression plus cycle, and sum of all components except the irregular. If some of these effects are absent in the model then they are ignored. You can use PRINT=NONE to suppress the printing of all of the forecast output.

SKIPFIRST= *integer*

This option is used if some early part of the data needs to be ignored during the forecasting calculations. This can be useful if there is a reason to believe that the model being used for forecasting is not appropriate for this portion of the data. SKIPFIRST=10 results in skipping the first 10 measurements of the response series during the forecast calculations. The default is SKIPFIRST=0.

NLOPTIONS Statement

NLOPTIONS *< options >* ;

PROC UCM uses the NonLinear Optimization (NLO) subsystem to perform the nonlinear optimization of the likelihood function during the estimation of model parameters. You can use the NLOPTIONS statement to control different aspects of this optimization process. For most problems the default settings of the optimization process are adequate, however, in some cases it may be useful to change the optimization technique or to change the maximum number of iterations. This can be done by using the TECH= and MAXITER= options in the NLOPTIONS statement as follows

```
nloptions tech=dbldog maxiter=200;
```

This will set the maximum number of iterations to 200 and change the optimization technique to DBLDOG rather than the default technique, TRUREG, used in PROC UCM. A discussion of the full range of options that can be used with the NLOPTIONS statement is given in the chapter on Nonlinear Optimization Methods (Chapter 10, "Nonlinear Optimization Methods."). In PROC UCM all these options are available except the options related to the printing of the optimization history. In this version of PROC UCM all the printed output from the NLO subsystem is suppressed.

Details

Throughout this section, $Diag\,[a, b, \ldots]$ will denote a diagonal matrix with diagonal entries $[a, b, \ldots]$, and the transpose of a matrix T will be denoted as T'.

The UCMs as State Space Models

It is well known that the UCMs considered in PROC UCM can be thought of as special cases of more general models, the (linear) Gaussian State Space Models (GSSM). A GSSM suitable for our purposes can be described as follows:

$$\begin{aligned} y_t &= Z_t\alpha_t \\ \alpha_{t+1} &= T_t\alpha_t + \zeta_{t+1}, \qquad \zeta_t \sim \mathrm{N}(0, Q_t) \\ \alpha_1 &\sim \mathrm{N}(0, P) \end{aligned}$$

The first equation, called the *Observation Equation*, relates the observed series y_t to a state vector α_t that is usually unobserved. The second equation describes the evolution of the state vector in time and is called the *State Equation*. The system matrices Z_t and T_t are of appropriate dimensions and are known, except possibly for some unknown elements that become part of the parameter vector of the model. The noise series ζ_t consists of independent, zero mean, Gaussian vectors with covariance matrices Q_t. For most of the UCMs considered here, the system matrices Z_t and T_t, and the noise covariances Q_t, are time invariant, i.e., they do not depend on time. In a few cases, however, some or all of them may depend on time. The initial state vector

α_1 is assumed to be independent of the noise series, and its covariance matrix P can be partially *diffuse*. A random vector has a partially diffuse covariance matrix if it can be partitioned such that one part of the vector has a properly defined probability distribution, while the covariance matrix of the other part is infinite, i.e., you have no prior information about this part of the vector. The covariance of the initial state α_1 is assumed to have the following form:

$$P = P_* + \kappa P_\infty$$

where P_* and P_∞ are nonnegative definite, symmetric matrices and κ is a constant that is assumed to be close to ∞. In the case of UCMs considered here P_∞ is always a diagonal matrix consisting of zeros and ones, and, if a particular diagonal element of P_∞ is one, then the corresponding row and column in P_* is zero.

The state space formulation of a UCM has many computational advantages. In this formulation there are convenient algorithms for estimating and forecasting the unobserved states $\{\alpha_t\}$ using the observed series $\{y_t\}$. These algorithms also yield the in-sample and out of sample forecasts and the likelihood of $\{y_t\}$. The state space representation of a UCM need not be unique. In the representation used here, the unobserved components in the UCM are taken as elements of the state vector. This makes the elements of the state interpretable and, more importantly, the sample estimates and forecasts of these unobserved components are easily obtained. For additional information on the computational aspects of the state space modeling, see Durbin and Koopman (2001). Next some notation is developed to describe the essential quantities computed during the analysis of the state space models.

Let $\{y_t, t = 1, \ldots, n\}$ be the observed sample from a series satisfying a state space model. Next, for $1 \leq t \leq n$, let the one step ahead forecasts of the series and the states, and their variances, be defined as follows:

$$\begin{aligned}
\hat{\alpha}_t &= E(\alpha_t | y_1, y_2, \ldots, y_{t-1}) \\
\Gamma_t &= Var(\alpha_t | y_1, y_2, \ldots, y_{t-1}) \\
\hat{y}_t &= E(y_t | y_1, y_2, \ldots, y_{t-1}) \\
F_t &= Var(y_t | y_1, y_2, \ldots, y_{t-1})
\end{aligned}$$

using the usual notation to denote the conditional expectations and conditional variances. These are also called the filtered estimates of the series and the states. Similarly, for $t \geq 1$, let

$$\begin{aligned}
\tilde{\alpha}_t &= E(\alpha_t | y_1, y_2, \ldots, y_n) \\
\Delta_t &= Var(\alpha_t | y_1, y_2, \ldots, y_n) \\
\tilde{y}_t &= E(y_t | y_1, y_2, \ldots, y_n) \\
G_t &= Var(y_t | y_1, y_2, \ldots, y_n)
\end{aligned}$$

denote the full-sample estimates of the series and the state values at time t. If the time t is in the historical period, i.e., if $1 \leq t \leq n$, then the full-sample estimates are called the *smoothed* estimates, and if t lies in the future then they are called out of sample forecasts. Note that, if $1 \leq t \leq n$, $\tilde{y}_t = y_t$ and $G_t = 0$, unless y_t is missing.

All the filtered and smoothed estimates $\hat{\alpha}_t, \tilde{\alpha}_t, \ldots, G_t$ are computed using the filtering and smoothing algorithms given in Durbin and Koopman (2001). These algorithms are iterative. If the initial state is diffuse, the effect of the improper prior distribution of α_1 manifests itself in the first few filtering iterations. During these initial filtering iterations the distribution of the filtered quantities remains diffuse, that is, during these iterations the one step ahead series and state forecast variances F_t and Γ_t have the following form

$$\begin{aligned} \Gamma_t &= \Gamma_{*t} + \kappa \Gamma_{\infty t} \\ F_t &= F_{*t} + \kappa F_{\infty t} \end{aligned}$$

The actual number of iterations, say d, affected by this improper prior depends on the nature of the matrix sequence T_t, the rank of P_∞, and the pattern of missing values in the dependent series. After d iterations, $\Gamma_{\infty t}$ and $F_{\infty t}$ become zero and the one step ahead series and state forecasts have proper distributions. In certain missing value patterns it can happen that d exceeds the sample size; that is, the sample information is insufficient to create a proper prior for the filtering process. In these cases no parameter estimation or forecasting is done. The forecasting computations can also fail if the specified model contains components that are essentially multicollinear and the process of computing one step ahead or multi step ahead forecasts is unstable. This condition can also manifest itself as failure to initialize a proper prior for the filtering process.

The log-likelihood of the sample, which takes account of this diffuse initialization steps, is computed using the one step ahead series forecasts as follows

$$\log L_d(y_1, \ldots, y_n) = -\frac{n}{2} \log 2\pi - \frac{1}{2} \sum_{t=1}^{d} w_t - \frac{1}{2} \sum_{t=d+1}^{n} (\log F_t + \frac{\nu_t^2}{F_t})$$

where $\nu_t = y_t - Z_t \hat{\alpha}_t$ are the one step ahead residuals and

$$\begin{aligned} w_t &= \log F_{\infty t} && \text{if } F_{\infty t} > 0 \\ &= \log F_{*t} + \frac{\nu_t^2}{F_{*t}} && \text{if } F_{\infty t} = 0 \end{aligned}$$

If y_t is missing at some time t, then the corresponding summand in the log-likelihood expression is deleted, and the constant term is adjusted suitably.

The portion of the log-likelihood corresponding to the post-initialization period is called the non-diffuse log-likelihood. The non-diffuse log-likelihood is given by

$$\log L(y_1, \ldots, y_n) = -\frac{1}{2} \sum_{t=d+1}^{n} (\log F_t + \frac{\nu_t^2}{F_t})$$

In the case of UCMs considered in PROC UCM, it often happens that the diffuse part of the likelihood, $\sum_{t=1}^{d} w_t$, does not depend on the model parameters, and in these cases the maximization of non-diffuse and diffuse likelihoods is equivalent. However, in some cases, for example, when the model consists of dependent lags, the diffuse part does depend on the model parameters. In these cases the maximization of the diffuse and non-diffuse likelihood can produce different results.

In the remainder of this section the state space formulation of UCMs is further explained using some particular UCMs as examples. The examples will show that the state space formulation of the UCMs depends upon the components in the model in a simple fashion; for example, the system matrix T will usually be a block diagonal matrix with blocks corresponding to the components in the model. The only exception to this pattern is the UCMs consisting of the lags of dependent variable. This case is considered at the end of the section.

Local Level Model

Recall that the dynamics of a local level model are

$$\begin{aligned} y_t &= \mu_t + \epsilon_t \\ \mu_t &= \mu_{t-1} + \beta_{t-1} + \eta_t, \\ \beta_t &= \beta_{t-1} + \xi_t \end{aligned}$$

Here y_t is the response series and ϵ_t, η_t, and ξ_t are independent, mean zero Gaussian disturbance sequences with variances $\sigma_\epsilon^2, \sigma_\eta^2$ and σ_ξ^2 respectively. This model can be formulated as a state space model where the state vector $\alpha_t = [\ \epsilon_t\ \mu_t\ \beta_t\ ]'$ and the state noise $\zeta_t = [\ \epsilon_t\ \eta_t\ \xi_t\ ]'$. Note that the elements of the state vector are precisely the unobserved components in the model. The system matrices T, Z and the noise covariance Q corresponding to this choice of state and state noise vectors can be seen to be time invariant and are given by

$$Z = [\,1\,1\,0\,],\ \ T = \begin{bmatrix} 0\,0\,0 \\ 0\,1\,1 \\ 0\,0\,1 \end{bmatrix} \quad \text{and} \quad Q = Diag\left[\sigma_\epsilon^2, \sigma_\eta^2, \sigma_\xi^2\right]$$

The distribution of the initial state vector α_1 is diffuse with $P_* = Diag\left[\sigma_\epsilon^2, 0, 0\right]$ and $P_\infty = Diag\,[0, 1, 1]$. The parameter vector θ consists of all the disturbance variances, that is, $\theta = (\sigma_\epsilon^2, \sigma_\eta^2, \sigma_\xi^2)$.

Basic Structural Model

Basic Structural Model (BSM) is obtained by adding a seasonal component, γ_t, to the local level model. In order to economize on the space, the state space formulation of a BSM with relatively short season length, season length = 4 (quarterly seasonality), is considered here. The pattern for longer season lengths such as 12 (monthly) and 52 (weekly) is easy to see.

Let us first consider the dummy form of seasonality. In this case the state and the state noise vectors are $\alpha_t = [\ \epsilon_t\ \mu_t\ \beta_t\ \gamma_{1,t}\ \gamma_{2,t}\ \gamma_{3,t}\ ]'$ and $\zeta_t = [\ \epsilon_t\ \eta_t\ \xi_t\ \omega_t\ 0\ 0\ ]'$. The first three elements of the state vector are the irregular, level, and the slope components, respectively. The remaining elements, $\gamma_{i,t}$, are lagged versions of the seasonal component γ_t. $\gamma_{1,t}$ corresponds to lag zero, that is, the same as γ_t, $\gamma_{2,t}$ to lag 1 and $\gamma_{3,t}$ to lag 2. The system matrices can be seen to be

$$Z = [\,1\,1\,0\,1\,0\,0\,], \quad T = \begin{bmatrix} 0 & 0 & 0 & 0 & 0 & 0 \\ 0 & 1 & 1 & 0 & 0 & 0 \\ 0 & 0 & 1 & 0 & 0 & 0 \\ 0 & 0 & 0 & -1 & -1 & -1 \\ 0 & 0 & 0 & 1 & 0 & 0 \\ 0 & 0 & 0 & 0 & 1 & 0 \end{bmatrix}$$

and $Q = Diag\left[\sigma_\epsilon^2, \sigma_\eta^2, \sigma_\xi^2, \sigma_\omega^2, 0, 0\right]$. The distribution of the initial state vector α_1 is diffuse with $P_* = Diag\left[\sigma_\epsilon^2, 0, 0, 0, 0, 0\right]$ and $P_\infty = Diag\,[0, 1, 1, 1, 1, 1]$.

In the case of trigonometric form of seasonality, $\alpha_t = \left[\, \epsilon_t \; \mu_t \; \beta_t \; \gamma_{1,t} \; \gamma_{1,t}^* \; \gamma_{2,t} \,\right]'$ and $\zeta_t = \left[\, \epsilon_t \; \eta_t \; \xi_t \; \omega_{1,t} \; \omega_{1,t}^* \; \omega_{2,t} \,\right]'$. The disturbance sequences, $\omega_{j,t}, 1 \le j \le 2$, and $\omega_{1,t}^*$ are independent, zero mean, Gaussian sequences with variance σ_ω^2.

$$Z = [\,1\,1\,0\,1\,0\,1\,], \quad T = \begin{bmatrix} 0 & 0 & 0 & 0 & 0 & 0 \\ 0 & 1 & 1 & 0 & 0 & 0 \\ 0 & 0 & 1 & 0 & 0 & 0 \\ 0 & 0 & 0 & \cos\lambda_1 & \sin\lambda_1 & 0 \\ 0 & 0 & 0 & -\sin\lambda_1 & \cos\lambda_1 & 0 \\ 0 & 0 & 0 & 0 & 0 & \cos\lambda_2 \end{bmatrix}$$

and $Q = Diag\left[\sigma_\epsilon^2, \sigma_\eta^2, \sigma_\xi^2, \sigma_\omega^2, \sigma_\omega^2, \sigma_\omega^2\right]$. Here $\lambda_j = (2\pi j)/4$. The distribution of the initial state vector α_1 is diffuse with $P_* = Diag\left[\sigma_\epsilon^2, 0, 0, 0, 0, 0\right]$ and $P_\infty = Diag\,[0, 1, 1, 1, 1, 1]$. The parameter vector, in both the cases, is $\theta = (\sigma_\epsilon^2, \sigma_\eta^2, \sigma_\xi^2, \sigma_\omega^2)$.

Seasonals with Blocked Seasonal Values

Block seasonals are special seasonals that impose a special block structure on the seasonal effects. Let us consider a BSM with monthly seasonality that has a quarterly block structure, that is, months within the same quarter are assumed to have identical effects except for some random perturbation. Such a seasonal is a block seasonal with block size m equal to 3 and the number of blocks k equal to 4. The state space structure for such a model with DUMMY type seasonality is as follows: The state and the state noise vectors are $\alpha_t = [\, \epsilon_t \; \mu_t \; \beta_t \; \gamma_{1,t} \; \gamma_{2,t} \; \gamma_{3,t} \,]'$ and $\zeta_t = [\, \epsilon_t \; \eta_t \; \xi_t \; \omega_t \; 0 \; 0 \,]'$. The first three elements of the state vector are the irregular, level, and the slope components, respectively. The remaining elements, $\gamma_{i,t}$, are lagged versions of the seasonal component γ_t. $\gamma_{1,t}$ corresponds to lag zero, that is, the same as γ_t, $\gamma_{2,t}$ to lag

m and $\gamma_{3,t}$ to lag $2m$. All the system matrices are time invariant, except the matrix T. They can be seen to be $Z = [\,1\,1\,0\,1\,0\,0\,]$, $Q = Diag\left[\sigma_\epsilon^2, \sigma_\eta^2, \sigma_\xi^2, \sigma_\omega^2, 0, 0\right]$, and

$$T_t = \begin{bmatrix} 0 & 0 & 0 & 0 & 0 & 0 \\ 0 & 1 & 1 & 0 & 0 & 0 \\ 0 & 0 & 1 & 0 & 0 & 0 \\ 0 & 0 & 0 & -1 & -1 & -1 \\ 0 & 0 & 0 & 1 & 0 & 0 \\ 0 & 0 & 0 & 0 & 1 & 0 \end{bmatrix}$$

when t is a multiple of the block size m, and

$$T_t = \begin{bmatrix} 0 & 0 & 0 & 0 & 0 & 0 \\ 0 & 1 & 1 & 0 & 0 & 0 \\ 0 & 0 & 1 & 0 & 0 & 0 \\ 0 & 0 & 0 & 1 & 0 & 0 \\ 0 & 0 & 0 & 0 & 1 & 0 \\ 0 & 0 & 0 & 0 & 0 & 1 \end{bmatrix}$$

otherwise. Note that when t is not a multiple of m, the portion of the T_t matrix corresponding to the seasonal is identity. The distribution of the initial state vector α_1 is diffuse with $P_* = Diag\left[\sigma_\epsilon^2, 0, 0, 0, 0, 0\right]$ and $P_\infty = Diag\,[0, 1, 1, 1, 1, 1]$.

Similarly in the case of trigonometric form of seasonality, $\alpha_t = \left[\,\epsilon_t\ \mu_t\ \beta_t\ \gamma_{1,t}\ \gamma_{1,t}^*\ \gamma_{2,t}\,\right]'$ and $\zeta_t = \left[\,\epsilon_t\ \eta_t\ \xi_t\ \omega_{1,t}\ \omega_{1,t}^*\ \omega_{2,t}\,\right]'$. The disturbance sequences, $\omega_{j,t}, 1 \le j \le 2$, and $\omega_{1,t}^*$ are independent, zero mean, Gaussian sequences with variance σ_ω^2. $Z = [\,1\,1\,0\,1\,0\,1\,]$, $Q = Diag\left[\sigma_\epsilon^2, \sigma_\eta^2, \sigma_\xi^2, \sigma_\omega^2, \sigma_\omega^2, \sigma_\omega^2\right]$, and

$$T_t = \begin{bmatrix} 0 & 0 & 0 & 0 & 0 & 0 \\ 0 & 1 & 1 & 0 & 0 & 0 \\ 0 & 0 & 1 & 0 & 0 & 0 \\ 0 & 0 & 0 & \cos\lambda_1 & \sin\lambda_1 & 0 \\ 0 & 0 & 0 & -\sin\lambda_1 & \cos\lambda_1 & 0 \\ 0 & 0 & 0 & 0 & 0 & \cos\lambda_2 \end{bmatrix}$$

when t is a multiple of the block size m, and

$$T_t = \begin{bmatrix} 0 & 0 & 0 & 0 & 0 & 0 \\ 0 & 1 & 1 & 0 & 0 & 0 \\ 0 & 0 & 1 & 0 & 0 & 0 \\ 0 & 0 & 0 & 1 & 0 & 0 \\ 0 & 0 & 0 & 0 & 1 & 0 \\ 0 & 0 & 0 & 0 & 0 & 1 \end{bmatrix}$$

otherwise. As before, when t is not a multiple of m, the portion of the T_t matrix corresponding to the seasonal is identity. Here $\lambda_j = (2\pi j)/4$. The distribution of the initial state vector α_1 is diffuse with $P_* = Diag\left[\sigma_\epsilon^2, 0, 0, 0, 0, 0\right]$ and $P_\infty = Diag\left[0, 1, 1, 1, 1, 1\right]$. The parameter vector, in both the cases, is $\theta = (\sigma_\epsilon^2, \sigma_\eta^2, \sigma_\xi^2, \sigma_\omega^2)$.

Cycles and Auto-Regression

The preceding examples have illustrated how to build a state space model corresponding to a UCM that includes components such as irregular, trend, and seasonal. There one can see that the state vector and the system matrices have a simple block structure with blocks corresponding to the components in the model. Therefore, here only a simple model consisting of a single cycle and an irregular component is considered. The state space form for more complex UCMs consisting of multiple cycles and other components can be easily deduced from this example.

Recall that a stochastic cycle ψ_t with frequency λ, $0 < \lambda < \pi$, and damping coefficient ρ can be modeled as

$$\begin{bmatrix} \psi_t \\ \psi_t^* \end{bmatrix} = \rho \begin{bmatrix} \cos\lambda & \sin\lambda \\ -\sin\lambda & \cos\lambda \end{bmatrix} \begin{bmatrix} \psi_{t-1} \\ \psi_{t-1}^* \end{bmatrix} + \begin{bmatrix} \nu_t \\ \nu_t^* \end{bmatrix}$$

where ν_t and ν_t^* are independent, zero mean Gaussian disturbances with variance σ_ν^2. In what follows, a state space form for a model consisting of such a stochastic cycle and an irregular component is given.

The state vector $\alpha_t = \left[\, \epsilon_t \; \psi_t \; \psi_t^* \,\right]'$, state noise vector $\zeta_t = \left[\, \epsilon_t \; \nu_t \; \nu_t^* \,\right]'$. The system matrices are

$$Z = [\,1\;1\;0\,] \quad T = \begin{bmatrix} 0 & 0 & 0 \\ 0 & \rho\cos\lambda & \rho\sin\lambda \\ 0 & -\rho\sin\lambda & \rho\cos\lambda \end{bmatrix} \quad Q = Diag\left[\sigma_\epsilon^2, \sigma_\nu^2, \sigma_\nu^2\right]$$

The distribution of the initial state vector α_1 is proper with $P_* = Diag\left[\sigma_\epsilon^2, \sigma_\psi^2, \sigma_\psi^2\right]$ where $\sigma_\psi^2 = \sigma_\nu^2(1-\rho^2)^{-1}$. The parameter vector $\theta = (\sigma_\epsilon^2, \rho, \lambda, \sigma_\nu^2)$.

An auto-regression r_t can be considered as a special case of cycle with frequency λ equal to 0 or π. In this case the equation for ψ_t^* is not needed. Therefore, for a UCM consisting of an auto-regressive component and an irregular component, the state space model simplifies to the following form:

The state vector $\alpha_t = \left[\, \epsilon_t \; r_t \,\right]'$, state noise vector $\zeta_t = \left[\, \epsilon_t \; \nu_t \,\right]'$. The system matrices are

$$Z = [\,1\;1\,], \quad T = \begin{bmatrix} 0 & 0 \\ 0 & \rho \end{bmatrix} \quad \text{and } Q = Diag\left[\sigma_\epsilon^2, \sigma_\nu^2\right]$$

The distribution of the initial state vector α_1 is proper with $P_* = Diag\left[\sigma_\epsilon^2, \sigma_r^2\right]$ where $\sigma_r^2 = \sigma_\nu^2(1-\rho^2)^{-1}$. The parameter vector $\theta = (\sigma_\epsilon^2, \rho, \sigma_\nu^2)$.

Incorporating the Predictors

As with earlier examples, how to obtain a state space form of a UCM consisting of predictors is illustrated using a simple special case. Consider a random walk model with predictors x_1 and x_2. The dynamics of this model are

$$\begin{aligned} y_t &= \mu_t + \beta_1 x_{1t} + \beta_2 x_{2t} + \epsilon_t \\ \mu_t &= \mu_{t-1} + \eta_t \end{aligned}$$

This dynamics can be captured in the state space form by taking $\alpha_t = [\ \epsilon_t\ \mu_t\ \beta_1\ \beta_2\ ]'$, $\zeta_t = [\ \epsilon_t\ \eta_t\ 0\ 0\ ]'$, and

$$Z_t = [\ 1\ 1\ x_{1t}\ x_{2t}\ ] \quad T = \begin{bmatrix} 0 & 0 & 0 & 0 \\ 0 & 1 & 0 & 0 \\ 0 & 0 & 1 & 0 \\ 0 & 0 & 0 & 1 \end{bmatrix} \quad Q = Diag\left[\sigma_\epsilon^2, \sigma_\eta^2, 0, 0\right]$$

Note that the regression coefficients are elements of the state vector, and that the system matrix Z_t is not time invariant. The distribution of the initial state vector α_1 is diffuse with $P_* = Diag\left[\sigma_\epsilon^2, 0, 0, 0\right]$ and $P_\infty = Diag\,[0, 1, 1, 1]$. The parameters of this model are the disturbance variances, σ_ϵ^2 and σ_η^2, and the regression coefficients, β_1 and β_2. The disturbance variances, being elements of the system matrix Q, are estimated by maximizing the likelihood, while the regression parameters get implicitly estimated during the state estimation (smoothing).

Models with Dependent Lags

The state space form of a UCM consisting of the lags of the dependent variable is quite different from the state space forms considered so far. Let us consider an example to illustrate this situation. Suppose that the preceding random walk with predictors model also includes a few, say k, lags of the dependent variable. That is

$$\begin{aligned} y_t &= \sum_{i=1}^{k} \phi_i y_{t-i} + \mu_t + \beta_1 x_{1t} + \beta_2 x_{2t} + \epsilon_t \\ \mu_t &= \mu_{t-1} + \eta_t \end{aligned}$$

The state space form of this augmented model can be described in terms of the state space form of the preceding random walk with predictors model. A superscript † has been added to distinguish the augmented model state space entities from the corresponding entities of the state space form of the random walk with predictors model. With this notation, the state vector of the augmented model $\alpha_t^\dagger = \left[\ \alpha_t'\ y_t\ y_{t-1}\ \ldots\ y_{t-k+1}\ \right]'$ and the new state noise vector $\zeta_t^\dagger = \left[\ \zeta_t'\ u_t\ 0 \ldots 0\ \right]'$ where u_t is the matrix product $Z_t\zeta_t$. Note that the length of the new state vector is $k + \text{length}(\alpha_t) = k + 4$. The new system matrices, in the block form, are

$$Z_t^\dagger = [\,0\,0\,0\,0\,1\ \ldots\ 0\,], \quad T_t^\dagger = \begin{bmatrix} T_t & 0 & \ldots & 0 \\ Z_{t+1}T_t & \phi_1 & \ldots & \phi_k \\ 0 & I_{k-1,k-1} & & 0 \end{bmatrix}$$

where $I_{k-1,k-1}$ is the $k-1$ dimensional identity matrix and,

$$Q_t^{\dagger} = \begin{bmatrix} Q_t & Q_t Z_t' & 0 \\ Z_t Q_t & Z_t Q_t Z_t' & 0 \\ 0 & 0 & 0 \end{bmatrix}$$

Note that the T and Q matrices of the random walk with predictors model are time invariant, in the expressions above their time indices are kept because it illustrates the pattern for more general models. The initial state vector is diffuse with

$$P_*^{\dagger} = \begin{bmatrix} P_* & 0 \\ 0 & 0 \end{bmatrix} \quad P_\infty^{\dagger} = \begin{bmatrix} P_\infty & 0 \\ 0 & I_{k,k} \end{bmatrix}$$

The parameters of this model are the disturbance variances σ_ϵ^2 and σ_η^2, the lag coefficients $\phi_1, \phi_2, \ldots, \phi_k$, and the regression coefficients β_1 and β_2. As before, the regression coefficients get estimated during the state smoothing, and the other parameters are estimated by maximizing the likelihood.

Missing Values

Embedded missing values in the dependent variable usually cause no problems in UCM modeling; however, no embedded missing values are allowed in the predictor variables. Certain patterns of missing values in the dependent variable can create problems for some models. For example, if in a monthly series all values are missing for a certain month, say May, then a BSM with monthly seasonality cannot be fit to these data. A non-seasonal model such as a local linear model can still be fit to these data.

Parameter Estimation

The parameter vector in a UCM consists of the variances of the disturbance terms of the unobserved components, the damping coefficients and frequencies in the cycles, the damping coefficient in the autoregression, the lag coefficients of the dependent lags, and the regression coefficients in the regression terms. The regression coefficients are always part of the state vector and are estimated by state smoothing. The remaining parameters are estimated by maximizing either the full diffuse likelihood or the non-diffuse likelihood. The decision to use the full diffuse likelihood or the non-diffuse likelihood depends on the presence or absence of the dependent lag coefficients in the parameter vector. If the parameter vector does not contain any dependent lag coefficients, then the full diffuse likelihood is used. If, on the other hand, the parameter vector does contain some dependent lag coefficients, then the parameters are estimated by maximizing the non-diffuse likelihood. The optimization of the full diffuse likelihood is often unstable when the parameter vector contains dependent lag coefficients. In this sense, when the parameter vector contains dependent lag coefficients the parameter estimates are not true maximum likelihood estimates.

The optimization of the likelihood, either the full or the non-diffuse, is carried out using one of several non-linear optimization algorithms. The user can control many aspects of the optimization process using the NLOPTIONS statement and by providing the starting values of the parameters while specifying the corresponding components. However, in most cases the default settings work quite well. The optimization process is not guaranteed to converge to a maximum likelihood estimate. In most cases the difficulties in parameter estimation are associated with the specification of a model that is not appropriate for the series being modeled.

t-values

The *t* values reported in the table of parameter estimates are approximations whose accuracy depends on the validity of the model, the nature of the model, and the length of the observed series. The distributional properties of the maximum likelihood estimates of general unobserved components models have not been explored fully, therefore the probability values corresponding to a *t* distribution should be interpreted carefully as they may be misleading. This is particularly true if the parameters in question are close to the boundary of the parameter space. Harvey (1989, 2001) are good references for information on this topic.

Computer Resource Requirements

The computing resources required for the UCM procedure depend on several factors. The memory requirement for the procedure is largely dependent on the number of observations to be processed and the size of the state vector underlying the specified model. If n denotes the sample size and m denotes the size of the state vector, the memory requirement is of the order of $6 \times 8 \times n \times m^2$ bytes, ignoring the lower order terms. The computing time for the parameter estimation also depends on m and n, as well as on the type of components included in the model. For example, the parameter estimation is usually faster if the model parameter vector consists only of disturbance variances, because in this case there is an efficient way to compute the likelihood gradient.

Printed Output

The default printed output produced by the UCM procedure is described in the following list:

- brief information about the input data set that includes the dataset name and label, and the name of the ID variable specified in the ID statement
- summary statistics for the data in the estimation and forecast spans, which includes the names of the variables in the model, their categorization as the dependent or predictor, the index of the beginning and the ending observations in the spans, the total number of observations and the number of missing observations, the smallest and the largest measurements, and the mean and the standard deviation
- information about the model parameters at the start of the model fitting stage that includes the fixed parameters in the model and the initial estimates of the free parameters in the model

- convergence status of the likelihood optimization process if any parameter estimation is done
- estimates of the free parameters at the end of the model fitting stage that includes the parameter estimates, their approximate standard errors, t-statistics, and the approximate P-value
- the likelihood-based goodness of fit statistics that include the full likelihood, the portion of the likelihood corresponding to the diffuse initialization, the sum of squares of the *innovations* normalized by their standard errors, and the Akike and the Bayesian information criteria AIC and BIC
- the fit statistics that are based on the raw residuals (observed - predicted), that include the mean squared error (MSE), root mean squared error (RMSE), the mean absolute percentage error (MAPE), the maximum percentage error (MAXPE), the R-Square, the adjusted R-Square, the Random Walk R-Square, and the Amemiya's R-Square
- the significance analysis of the components included in the model that is based on the estimation span
- brief information about the cycles, seasonals, and block seasonals present in the model
- the multi step series forecasts

ODS Table Names

The UCM procedure assigns a name to each table it creates. You can use these names to reference the table when using the Output Delivery System (ODS) to select tables and create output data sets. These names are listed in the following table:

Table 29.1. ODS Tables Produced in the UCM Procedure

ODS Table Name	Description	Option
ODS Tables Summarizing the Estimation and Forecast Spans		
EstimationSpan	Estimation span summary information	default
ForecastSpan	Forecast span summary information	default
ODS Tables Related to the Model Parameters		
ConvergenceStatus	Convergence status of the estimation process	default
FixedParameters	Fixed parameters in the model	default
InitialParameters	Initial estimates of the free parameters	default
ParameterEstimates	Final estimates of the free parameters	default
ODS Tables Related to the Model Information and Diagnostics		
BlockSeasonDescription	Information about the block seasonals in the model	default

Table 29.1. (ODS Tables Continued)

ODS Table Name	Description	Option
ComponentSignificance	Significance analysis of the components in the model	default
CycleDescription	Information about the cycles in the model	default
FitStatistics	Fit statistics based on the one step ahead predictions	default
FitSummary	Likelihood based fit statistics	default
SeasonDescription	Information about the seasonals in the model	default
ODS Tables Related to the Component Estimates		
FilteredAutoReg	Filtered Estimate of an Autoreg Component. AUTOREG statement	PRINT=FILTER
FilteredBlockSeason	Filtered Estimate of a Block Seasonal Component. BLOCKSEASON statement	PRINT=FILTER
FilteredCycle	Filtered Estimate of a Cycle Component. CYCLE statement	PRINT=FILTER
FilteredIrregular	Filtered Estimate of the Irregular Component. IRREGULAR statement	PRINT=FILTER
FilteredLevel	Filtered Estimate of the Level Component. LEVEL statement	PRINT=FILTER
FilteredSeason	Filtered Estimate of a Seasonal Component. SEASON statement	PRINT=FILTER
FilteredSlope	Filtered Estimate of the Slope Component. SLOPE statement	PRINT=FILTER
SmoothedAutoReg	Smoothed Estimate of an Autoreg Component. AUTOREG statement	PRINT=SMOOTH
SmoothedBlockSeason	Smoothed Estimate of a Block Seasonal Component. BLOCKSEASON statement	PRINT=SMOOTH
SmoothedCycle	Smoothed Estimate of the Cycle Component. CYCLE statement	PRINT=SMOOTH
SmoothedIrregular	Smoothed Estimate of the Irregular Component. IRREGULAR statement	PRINT=SMOOTH
SmoothedLevel	Smoothed Estimate of the Level Component. LEVEL statement	PRINT=SMOOTH
SmoothedSeason	Smoothed Estimate of a Seasonal Component. SEASON statement	PRINT=SMOOTH
SmoothedSlope	Smoothed Estimate of the Slope Component. SLOPE statement	PRINT=SMOOTH
ODS Tables Related to the FORECAST Statement		

Table 29.1. (ODS Tables Continued)

ODS Table Name	Description	Option
Forecasts	Dependent Series Forecasts	default
SmoothedAllExceptIrreg	Smoothed estimate of sum of all components except the irregular component	PRINT=DECOMP
SmoothedTrend	Smoothed estimate of trend	PRINT= DECOMP
SmoothedTrendReg	Smoothed estimate of trend plus regression	PRINT=DECOMP
SmoothedTrendRegCyc	Smoothed estimate of trend plus regression plus cycles and autoreg	PRINT=DECOMP

NOTE: The tables are related to a single series within a BY group. In the case of models that contain multiple cycles, seasonals, or block seasonals, the corresponding component estimate tables are sequentially numbered. For example, if a model contains two cycles and a seasonal and PRINT=SMOOTH option is used for each of them, the ODS tables containing the smoothed estimates will be named as SmoothedCycle1, SmoothedCycle2, and SmoothedSeason. Note that the seasonal table is not numbered because there is only one seasonal.

ODS Graphics (Experimental)

This section describes the use of ODS for creating graphics with the UCM procedure. These graphics are experimental in this release, meaning that both the graphical results and the syntax for specifying them are subject to change in a future release.

To request these graphs, you must specify the ODS GRAPHICS statement. For more information on the ODS GRAPHICS statement, see Chapter 9, "Statistical Graphics Using ODS."

When the ODS GRAPHICS are in effect, the UCM procedure produces a variety of plots. The main types of plots available are as follows:

- Time series plots of the component estimates, either filtered or smoothed, can be requested using the PLOT= option in the respective component statements. For example, the use of PLOT=SMOOTH option in a CYCLE statement produces a plot of smoothed estimate of that cycle.
- Residual plots for model diagnostics can be obtained using the PLOT= option in the ESTIMATE statement.
- Plots of series forecasts and model decompositions can be obtained using the PLOT= option in the FORECAST statement.

The details of the PLOT= option in different statements are given below.

The PLOT= option in the IRREGULAR, LEVEL, SLOPE, CYCLE, and AUTOREG statements is identical. You can use the FILTER and SMOOTH options to plot the filtered and smoothed estimates of the respective components as follows:

PLOT= FILTER
PLOT= SMOOTH
PLOT= (FILTER SMOOTH)

In the SEASON and BLOCKSEASON statements, the PLOT= option is as follows:

PLOT= FILTER
PLOT= SMOOTH
PLOT= F_ANNUAL
PLOT= S_ANNUAL
PLOT= (<FILTER> <SMOOTH> <F_ANNUAL> <S_ANNUAL>)

You can use the FILTER and SMOOTH options to plot the filtered and smoothed estimates of the seasonal or block seasonal component γ_t. The F_ANNUAL and S_ANNUAL options can be used to get the plots of "annual" variation in the filtered and smoothed estimates of γ_t. The annual plots are useful to see the change in the contribution of a particular month over the span of years. Here the "month" and the "year" are generic terms that change appropriately with the interval type being used to label the observations and the season length. For example, for monthly data with a season length of 12, the usual meaning applies, while for daily data with a season length of 7, the days of the week serve as months and the weeks serve as years.

In the ESTIMATE statement, the PLOT= option is used to obtain different residual diagnostic plots. The different possibilities are as follows:

PLOT= RESIDUAL
PLOT= ACF
PLOT= NORMAL
PLOT= WN
PLOT= (<RESIDUAL> <ACF> <NORMAL> <WN>)

The RESIDUAL option results in the residual plot, the ACF option gives the plot of the auto-correlations of the residuals, the NORMAL option gives the histogram of residuals, and the WN option gives the plot of White Noise test probabilities.

In the FORECAST statement, the PLOT= option can be used to obtain forecast and model decomposition plots. The details are as follows:

PLOT= FORECASTS
PLOT= TREND
PLOT= DECOMP
PLOT= DECOMPVAR
PLOT= FDECOMP
PLOT= FDECOMPVAR
PLOT= (<FORECASTS> <TREND> <DECOMP> <DECOMPVAR> <FDECOMP>

<FDECOMPVAR>)

The FORECASTS option provides the plot of the series forecasts, the TREND and DECOMP options provide the plots of the smoothed trend and other decompositions, the DECOMPVAR option can be used to plot the variance of these components, and the FDECOMP and FDECOMPVAR provide the same plots for the filtered decomposition estimates and their variances.

For an example of how to set up the ODS GRAPHICS environment and use the different PLOT= options, see Example 29.4.

ODS Graph Names

PROC UCM assigns a name to each graph it creates using ODS. You can use these names to reference the graphs when using ODS. The names are listed in Table 29.2.

Table 29.2. ODS Graphics Produced by PROC UCM

ODS Graph Name	Plot Description	PLOT= Option
	ODS Plots Related to the Residual Analysis	
ErrorACFPlot	Prediction Error Autocorrelation Plot. ESTIMATE statement.	PLOT=ACF
ErrorHistogram	Prediction Error Histogram. ESTIMATE statement.	PLOT=NORMAL
ErrorPlot	Plot of Prediction Errors. ESTIMATE statement.	PLOT=RESIDUAL
	ODS Plots Related to the Series Forecasts	
ForecastsOnlyPlot	Series Forecasts Beyond the Historical Period. FORECAST statement.	DEFAULT
ModelForecastsPlot	One-Step-Ahead as well as Multi-Step-Ahead Forecasts. FORECAST statement.	PLOT=FORECASTS
	ODS Plots Related to the Individual Components	
FilteredAutoregPlot	Plot of Filtered Autoreg Component. AUTOREG statement.	PLOT=FILTER
FilteredBlockSeasonPlot	Plot of Filtered Block Season Component. BLOCKSEASON statement.	PLOT=FILTER
FilteredCyclePlot	Plot of Filtered Cycle Component. CYCLE statement.	PLOT=FILTER
FilteredIrregularPlot	Plot of Filtered Irregular Component. IRREGULAR statement.	PLOT=FILTER

Table 29.2. (continued)

ODS Graph Name	Plot Description	Option
FilteredLevelPlot	Plot of Filtered Level Component. LEVEL statement.	PLOT=FILTER
FilteredSeasonPlot	Plot of Filtered Season Component. SEASON statement.	PLOT=FILTER
FilteredSlopePlot	Plot of Filtered Slope Component. SLOPE statement.	PLOT=FILTER
SmoothedAutoregPlot	Plot of Smoothed Autoreg Component. AUTOREG statement.	PLOT=SMOOTH
SmoothedBlockSeasonPlot	Plot of Smoothed Block Season Component. BLOCKSEASON statement.	PLOT=SMOOTH
SmoothedCyclePlot	Plot of Smoothed Cycle Component. CYCLE statement.	PLOT=SMOOTH
SmoothedIrregularPlot	Plot of Smoothed Irregular Component. IRREGULAR statement.	PLOT=SMOOTH
SmoothedLevelPlot	Plot of Smoothed Level Component. LEVEL statement.	PLOT=SMOOTH
SmoothedSeasonPlot	Plot of Smoothed Season Component. SEASON statement.	PLOT=SMOOTH
SmoothedSlopePlot	Plot of Smoothed Slope Component. SLOPE statement.	PLOT=SMOOTH
ODS Plots Related to the Series Decomposition		
FilteredAllExceptIrregPlot	Plot of Sum of All Filtered Components Except the Irregular. FORECAST statement.	PLOT= FDECOMP
FilteredTrendPlot	Plot of Filtered Trend. FORECAST statement.	PLOT= FDECOMP
FilteredTrendRegCycPlot	Plot of Sum of Filtered Trend, Cycles and Regression Effects. FORECAST statement.	PLOT= FDECOMP
FilteredTrendRegPlot	Plot of Filtered Trend Plus Regression Effects. FORECAST statement.	PLOT= FDECOMP
SmoothedAllExceptIrregPlot	Plot of Sum of All Smoothed Components Except the Irregular. FORECAST statement.	PLOT= DECOMP
SmoothedTrendPlot	Plot of Smoothed Trend. FORECAST statement.	PLOT= TREND
SmoothedTrendRegCycPlot	Plot of Sum of Smoothed Trend, Cycles and Regression Effects. FORECAST statement.	PLOT= DECOMP

Table 29.2. (continued)

ODS Graph Name	Plot Description	Option
SmoothedTrendRegPlot	Plot of Smoothed Trend Plus Regression Effects. FORECAST statement.	PLOT= DECOMP

OUTFOR= Data Set

You can use OUTFOR= option in the FORECAST statement to store the series and component forecasts produced by the procedure. This data set contains the following columns:

- the BY variables
- the ID variable. If an ID variable is not specified then a numerical variable, _ID_, is created that contains the observation numbers from the input data set.
- the dependent series and the predictor series
- FORECAST, a numerical variable containing the one step ahead predicted values and the multi step forecasts
- RESIDUAL, a numerical variable containing the difference between the actual and forecast values
- STD, a numerical variable containing the standard error of prediction
- LCL and UCL, numerical variables containing the lower and upper forecast confidence limits
- S_SERIES and VS_SERIES, numerical variables containing the smoothed values of the dependent series and their variances
- S_IRREG and VS_IRREG, numerical variables containing the smoothed values of the IRREGULAR component and their variances. These variables are present only if the model has an IRREGULAR component.
- F_LEVEL, VF_LEVEL, S_LEVEL, and VS_LEVEL, numerical variables containing the filtered and smoothed values of the LEVEL component and the respective variances. These variables are present only if the model has a LEVEL component.
- F_SLOPE, VF_SLOPE, S_SLOPE, and VS_SLOPE, numerical variables containing the filtered and smoothed values of the SLOPE component and the respective variances. These variables are present only if the model has a SLOPE component.
- F_AUTOREG, VF_AUTOREG, S_AUTOREG, and VS_AUTOREG, numerical variables containing the filtered and smoothed values of the AUTOREG component and the respective variances. These variables are present only if the model has an AUTOREG component.
- F_CYCLE, VF_CYCLE, S_CYCLE, and VS_CYCLE, numerical variables containing the filtered and smoothed values of the CYCLE component and the respective variances. If there are multiple cycles in the model, these variables

are sequentially numbered as F_CYCLE1, F_CYCLE2, etc. These variables are present only if the model has at least one CYCLE component.

- F_SEASON, VF_SEASON, S_SEASON, and VS_SEASON, numerical variables containing the filtered and smoothed values of the SEASON component and the respective variances. If there are multiple seasons in the model, these variables are sequentially numbered as F_SEASON1, F_SEASON2, etc. These variables are present only if the model has at least one SEASON component.
- F_BLKSEAS, VF_BLKSEAS, S_BLKSEAS, and VS_BLKSEAS, numerical variables containing the filtered and smoothed values of the BLOCKSEASON component and the respective variances. If there are multiple block seasons in the model, these variables are sequentially numbered as F_BLKSEAS1, F_BLKSEAS2, etc. These variables are present only if the model has at least one BLOCKSEASON component.
- S_TREG and VS_TREG, numerical variables containing the smoothed values of level plus regression component and their variances. These variables are present only if the model has at least one predictor variable or has dependent lags.
- S_TREGCYC and VS_TREGCYC, numerical variables containing the smoothed values of level plus regression plus cycle component and their variances. These variables are present only if the model has at least one cycle or an autoreg component.
- S_NOIRREG and VS_NOIRREG, numerical variables containing the smoothed values of the sum of all components except the irregular component and their variances. These variables are present only if the model has at least one season or block season component.

OUTEST= Data Set

You can use OUTEST= option in the ESTIMATE statement to store the model parameters and the related estimation details. This data set contains the following columns:

- the BY variables
- COMPONENT, a character variable containing the name of the component corresponding to the parameter being described
- PARAMETER, a character variable containing the parameter name
- TYPE, a character variable indicating whether the parameter value was FIXED by the user or it was ESTIMATED
- _STATUS_, a character variable indicating whether the parameter estimation process Converged, Failed, or there was an Error of some other kind.
- ESTIMATE, a numerical variable containing the parameter estimate
- STD, a numerical variable containing the standard error of the parameter estimate. This will have a missing value if the parameter value is fixed.

- TVALUE, a numerical variable containing the t-statistic. This will have a missing value if the parameter value is fixed.
- PVALUE, a numerical variable containing the p-value. This will have a missing value if the parameter value is fixed.

Statistics of Fit

This section explains the goodness-of-fit statistics reported to measure how well the specified model fits the data.

First the various statistics of fit that are computed using the prediction errors, $y_t - \hat{y}_t$, are considered. In these formulae, n is the number of non-missing prediction errors and k is the number of fitted parameters in the model. Moreover, the sum of square errors, $SSE = \sum (y_t - \hat{y}_t)^2$, and the total sum of squares for the series corrected for the mean, $SST = \sum (y_t - \overline{y})^2$, where $\overline{y}$ is the series mean and the sums are over all the non-missing prediction errors.

Mean Square Error
The mean squared prediction error, MSE, calculated from the one step ahead forecasts. $MSE = \frac{1}{n} SSE$.

Root Mean Square Error
The root mean square error (RMSE), $\sqrt{MSE}$.

Mean Absolute Percent Error
The mean absolute percent prediction error (MAPE), $\frac{100}{n} \sum_{t=1}^{n} |(y_t - \hat{y}_t)/y_t|$. The summation ignores observations where $y_t = 0$.

R-Square
The R^2 statistic, $R^2 = 1 - SSE/SST$. If the model fits the series badly, the model error sum of squares, *SSE*, may be larger than *SST* and the R^2 statistic will be negative.

Adjusted R-Square
The adjusted R^2 statistic, $1 - (\frac{n-1}{n-k})(1 - R^2)$.

Amemiya's Adjusted R-Square
Amemiya's adjusted R^2, $1 - (\frac{n+k}{n-k})(1 - R^2)$.

Random Walk R-Square
The random walk R^2 statistic (Harvey's R^2 statistic using the random walk model for comparison), $1 - (\frac{n-1}{n}) SSE/RWSSE$, where $RWSSE = \sum_{t=2}^{n} (y_t - y_{t-1} - \mu)^2$, and $\mu = \frac{1}{n-1} \sum_{t=2}^{n} (y_t - y_{t-1})$.

Maximum Percent Error
The largest percent prediction error, $100 \max((y_t - \hat{y}_t)/y_t)$. In this computation the observations where $y_t = 0$ are ignored.

The likelihood-based fit statistics are reported separately. They include the full log-likelihood, the diffuse part of the log-likelihood (see "Details"), the normalized residual sum of squares, and the Akaike and Bayesian information criteria. Let L denote the log-likelihood, k denote the sum of number of estimated parameters and the number of diffuse elements in the state vector, and n be the number of non-missing measurements in the estimation span. Moreover, let d denote the initialization period, and, ν_t and F_t denote the one step ahead prediction errors and their variances.

Normalized Residual Sum of Squares
Normalized Residual Sum of Squares, $\sum_{t=d+1}^{n} \frac{\nu_t^2}{F_t}$.

Akaike's Information Criterion
Akaike's information criterion (AIC), $-2L + 2k$.

Schwarz Bayesian Information Criterion
Schwarz Bayesian information criterion (SBC or BIC),
$-2L + k\log(n)$.

Examples

Example 29.1. An Example of a BSM

The series in this example, the monthly Airline Passenger series, has already been discussed in an example in the Getting Started section, see "A Seasonal Series with a Linear Trend". Recall that the series consists of monthly numbers of international airline travelers (from January 1949 to December 1960). Here we will examine additional output and use the ESTIMATE and FORECAST statements to limit the span of the data used in parameter estimation and forecasting. The following syntax fits a BSM to the logarithm of the airline passenger numbers. The disturbance variance for the SLOPE component is held fixed at value 0; that is, the trend is locally linear with constant slope. In order to evaluate the performance of the fitted model on observed data, some of the observed data are withheld during parameter estimation and forecast computations. The observations in the last two years, years 1959 and 1960, are not used in parameter estimation while the observations in the last year, year 1960, are not used in the forecasting computations. This is done using the BACK= option in the ESTIMATE and FORECAST statements.

```
   data series_g;
        set sashelp.air;
        logair = log(air);
   run;


proc ucm data = series_g;
     id date interval = month;
     model logair;
     irregular;
```

```
      level;
      slope var = 0 noest;
      season length = 12 type=trig;
      estimate back=24;
      forecast back=12 lead=24 print=forecasts;
run;
```

The following tables display the summary of data used in estimation and forecasting (Output 29.1.1 and Output 29.1.2). These tables provide simple summary statistics for the estimation and forecast spans; they include useful information such as the start and end dates of the span, number of non-missing values, etc.

Output 29.1.1. Observation Span Used in Parameter Estimation (partial output)

Estimation Span Summary

Variable	Type	First	Last	Nobs	Mean
logair	Dependent	JAN1949	DEC1958	120	5.43035

Output 29.1.2. Observation Span Used in Forecasting (partial output)

Forecast Span Summary

Variable	Type	First	Last	Nobs	Mean
logair	Dependent	JAN1949	DEC1959	132	5.48654

The following tables display the fixed parameters in the model, the preliminary estimates of the free parameters, and the final estimates of the free parameters (Output 29.1.3, Output 29.1.4, and Output 29.1.5).

Output 29.1.3. Fixed Parameters in the Model

The UCM Procedure

Fixed Parameters in the Model

Component	Parameter	Value
Slope	Error Variance	0

Output 29.1.4. Starting Values for the Parameters to Be Estimated

Preliminary Estimates of the Free Parameters

Component	Parameter	Estimate
Irregular	Error Variance	6.64120
Level	Error Variance	2.49045
Season	Error Variance	1.26676

Output 29.1.5. Maximum Likelihood Estimates of the Free Parameters

Final Estimates of the Free Parameters

Component	Parameter	Estimate	Approx Std Error	t Value	Approx Pr > |t|
Irregular	Error Variance	0.00018686	0.0001212	1.54	0.1233
Level	Error Variance	0.00040314	0.0001566	2.57	0.0100
Season	Error Variance	0.00000350	1.66319E-6	2.10	0.0354

Two types of goodness of fit statistics are reported after a model is fit to the series (see Output 29.1.6 and Output 29.1.7). The first type is the likelihood-based goodness of fit statistics, which include the full likelihood of the data, the diffuse portion of the likelihood (see "Details"), and the Akike and Bayesian Information criteria. The second type of statistics is based on the raw residuals, residual = observed - predicted. If the model is non-stationary, then one step ahead predictions are not available for some initial observations, and the number of values used in computing these fit statistics will be different from those used in computing the likelihood-based test statistics.

Output 29.1.6. Likelihood Based Fit Statistics for the Airline Data

Likelihood Based Fit Statistics

Full Log-Likelihood	168.67997
Diffuse Part of Log-Likelihood	-13.92861
Normalized Residual Sum of Squares	107.00000
Akaike Information Criterion	-305.35994
Bayesian Information Criterion	-260.76007

Number of non-missing observations used for computing the log-likelihood = 120

Output 29.1.7. Residuals Based Fit Statistics for the Airline Data

Fit Statistics Based on Residuals

Mean Squared Error	0.00156
Root Mean Squared Error	0.03944
Mean Absolute Percentage Error	0.57677
Maximum Percent Error	2.19396
R-Square	0.98705
Adjusted R-Square	0.98680
Random Walk R-Square	0.99315
Amemiya's Adjusted R-Square	0.98630

Number of non-missing residuals used for computing the fit statistics = 107

The forecasts are given in Output 29.1.8. In order to save the space, the upper and lower confidence limit columns are dropped from the output, and only the rows corresponding to the year 1960 are shown. Recall that the actual measurements in the years 1959 and 1960 were withheld during the parameter estimation, and the ones in 1960 were not used in the forecast computations.

Output 29.1.8. Forecasts for the Airline Data

Forecasts for Airline Data (partial output)

Obs	date	Forecast	StdErr	logair	Residual
133	JAN1960	6.049900848	0.0383865	6.033086222	-0.01681463
134	FEB1960	5.996181814	0.043925	5.96870756	-0.02747425
135	MAR1960	6.15571288	0.0492542	6.03787092	-0.11784196
136	APR1960	6.123514784	0.0534002	6.133398043	0.009883259
137	MAY1960	6.168045435	0.0576337	6.156978986	-0.01106645
138	JUN1960	6.302872975	0.0610994	6.282266747	-0.02060623
139	JUL1960	6.434621832	0.0646732	6.432940093	-0.00168174
140	AUG1960	6.449565514	0.0676591	6.406879986	-0.04268553
141	SEP1960	6.265131851	0.0706778	6.230481448	-0.0346504
142	OCT1960	6.138451548	0.0731438	6.133398043	-0.00505351
143	NOV1960	6.015324248	0.0754033	5.966146739	-0.04917751
144	DEC1960	6.121205238	0.0768566	6.068425588	-0.05277965

The figure Output 29.1.9 shows the forecast plot. The forecasts in the year 1960 show that the model predictions were quite good.

Output 29.1.9. Forecast Plot of the Airline Series Using a BSM

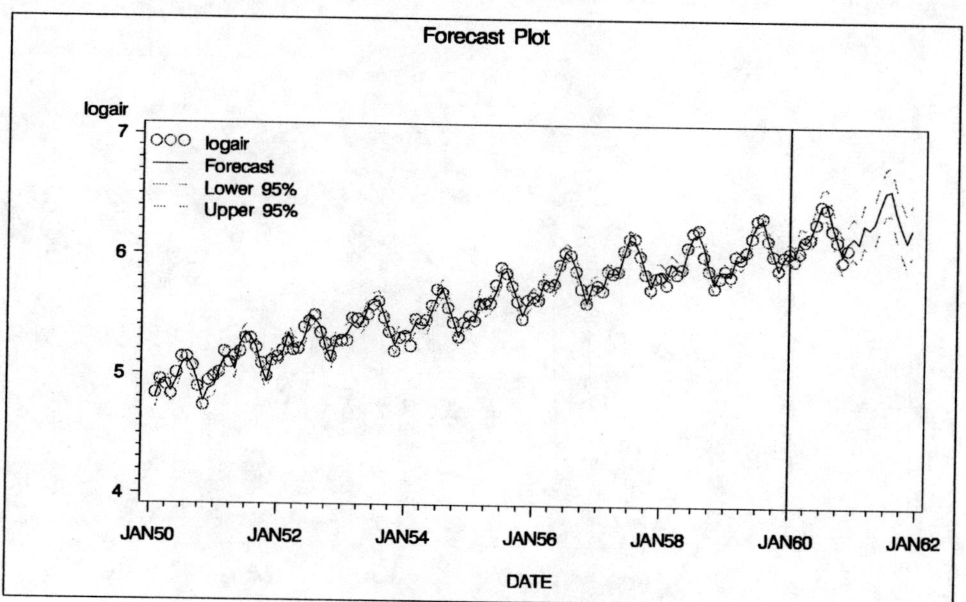

Example 29.2. Variable Star Data

The series in this example is studied in detail in Bloomfield (2000). This series consists of brightness measurements (magnitude) of a variable star taken at midnight for 600 consecutive days. The data can be downloaded from a time series archive maintained by the University of York, England (http://www.york.ac.uk/depts/maths/data/ts/welcome.htm (series number 26)). The following DATA step statements read the data in a SAS data set.

```
data star;
   input magnitude @@;
   datalines;

      25 28 31 32 33 33 32 31 28 25
      22 18 14 10  7  4  2  0  0  0
       2  4  8 11 15 19 23 26 29 32

      /* -- data lines removed - */

      31 33 34 34 33 31 29 26 22 18
      15 11  8  5  3  2  2  2  4  5
   ;
```

The plot of the series is shown in figure Output 29.2.1.

Output 29.2.1. Plot of Star Brightness on Successive Days

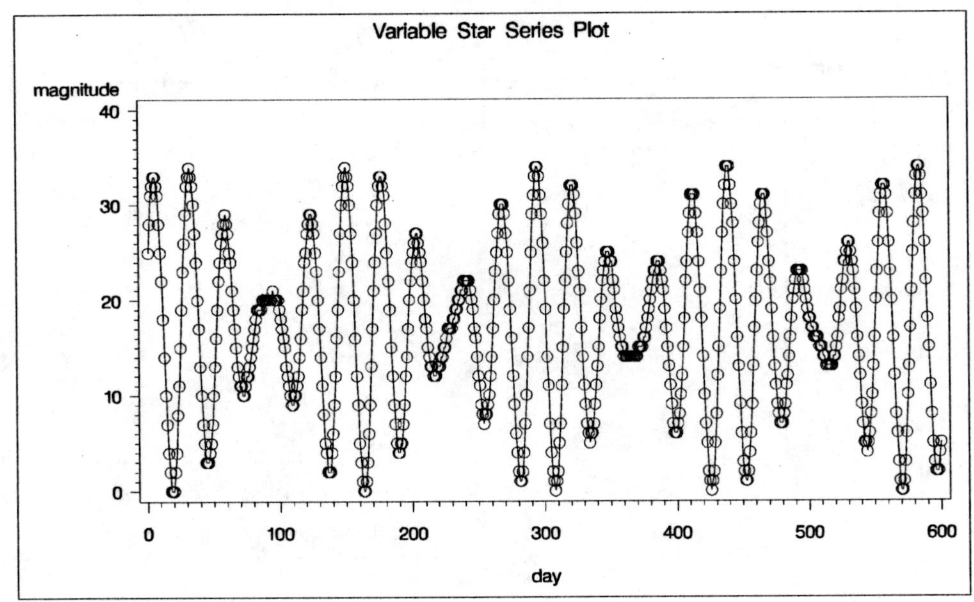

The plot clearly shows the cyclic nature of the series. Bloomfield shows that the series is very well explained by a model that includes two deterministic cycles that have periods 29.0003 and 24.0001 days, a constant term, and a simple error term. He also shows the difficulty involved in estimating the periods from the data (see Bloomfield 2000, Chapter 3). The parameters are estimated by the least squares, and the sum of squares surface has multiple local optima and ridges. In this example we will use the UCM procedure to model this series. We begin with a model that consists of only one stochastic cycle and the level and irregular components. This is because it is quite possible that a single stochastic cycle with time varying amplitude and phase may be adequate to explain the observed series.

```
proc ucm data=star;
    model magnitude;
    irregular;
    level;
    cycle;
    forecast print=forecasts;
run;
```

The final parameter estimates and the goodness of fit statistics are shown below (see Output 29.2.2 and Output 29.2.3).

Output 29.2.2. Parameter Estimates in Single Cycle Model

The UCM Procedure

Final Estimates of the Free Parameters

Component	Parameter	Estimate	Approx Std Error	t Value	Approx Pr > |t|
Irregular	Error Variance	0.02094	0.0076007	2.76	0.0059
Level	Error Variance	3.6126E-10	2.2014E-7	0.00	0.9987
Cycle	Damping Factor	0.99906	0.0007979	1252.18	<.0001
Cycle	Period	27.12640	0.17225	157.48	<.0001
Cycle	Error Variance	0.20111	0.16915	1.19	0.2345

Output 29.2.3. Model Fit of Single Cycle Model

Fit Statistics Based on Residuals

Mean Squared Error	0.31481
Root Mean Squared Error	0.56108
Mean Absolute Percentage Error	4.55372
Maximum Percent Error	60.57167
R-Square	0.99609
Adjusted R-Square	0.99607
Random Walk R-Square	0.94510
Amemiya's Adjusted R-Square	0.99603

Number of non-missing residuals used for computing the fit statistics = 599

A description of the cycle in the model is given below (Output 29.2.4).

Output 29.2.4. Summary of the Cycle in the Single Cycle Model

Cycle description (partial output)

Name	Type	period	Rho	CycleVar	ErrorVar
Cycle	Stationary	27.12640	0.99906	106.68773	0.20111

From the model fit it appears that the single stochastic cycle model with a period of approximately 27 days fits the data reasonably well. However, the residual plot in Output 29.2.5 indicates that the series may contain an additional cycle. The autocorrelation plot of residuals shows this more clearly (this plot is not shown).

Output 29.2.5. Residual Plot for the Single Cycle Model

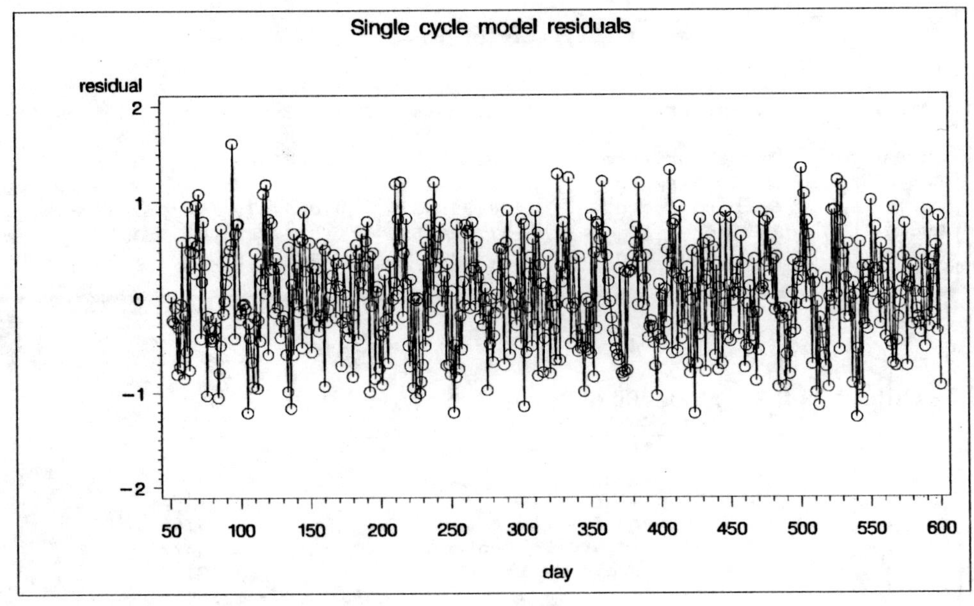

The following statements fit a two-cycle model to the series.

```
proc ucm data=star;
    model magnitude;
    irregular;
    level var=0 noest;
    cycle rho=1 noest=rho;
    cycle rho=1 noest=rho;
    forecast print=forecasts;
run;
```

The model has two cycles, both with damping factors of one, and a constant level component. The final parameter estimates and the goodness of fit statistics are shown below (see Output 29.2.6 and Output 29.2.7).

Output 29.2.6. Parameter Estimates in Two Cycle Model

The UCM Procedure

Final Estimates of the Free Parameters

Component	Parameter	Estimate	Approx Std Error	t Value	Approx Pr > |t|
Irregular	Error Variance	0.09189	0.0053285	17.24	<.0001
Cycle_1	Period	24.00010	0.0013342	17988.2	<.0001
Cycle_1	Error Variance	2.89893E-12	3.08743E-9	0.00	0.9993
Cycle_2	Period	29.00027	0.0013891	20877.1	<.0001
Cycle_2	Error Variance	2.7808E-12	3.00071E-9	0.00	0.9993

Output 29.2.7. Fit of Two Cycle Model

Fit Statistics Based on Residuals	
Mean Squared Error	0.19206
Root Mean Squared Error	0.43825
Mean Absolute Percentage Error	2.72498
Maximum Percent Error	39.03001
R-Square	0.99759
Adjusted R-Square	0.99758
Random Walk R-Square	0.96935
Amemiya's Adjusted R-Square	0.99755

Number of non-missing residuals used for computing the fit statistics = 595

A description of the cycles in the model is given in Output 29.2.8.

Output 29.2.8. Summary of the Cycles in the Two Cycle Model

Cycle description (partial output)

Name	Type	period	Rho	ErrorVar
Cycle_1	Non-Stationary	24.00010	1.00000	2.89893E-12
Cycle_2	Non-Stationary	29.00027	1.00000	2.7808E-12

Note that the estimated periods are the same as Bloomfield's model, and the disturbance variances are very close to zero, implying deterministic cycles. In fact, this model is identical to Bloomfield's model. The residual plot shown below also shows (Output 29.2.9) the improvement in the fit; for easy comparison the scale of the vertical axis is purposely set to be the same as the residual plot of the single-cycle model.

Output 29.2.9. Residual Plot for the Two Cycle Model

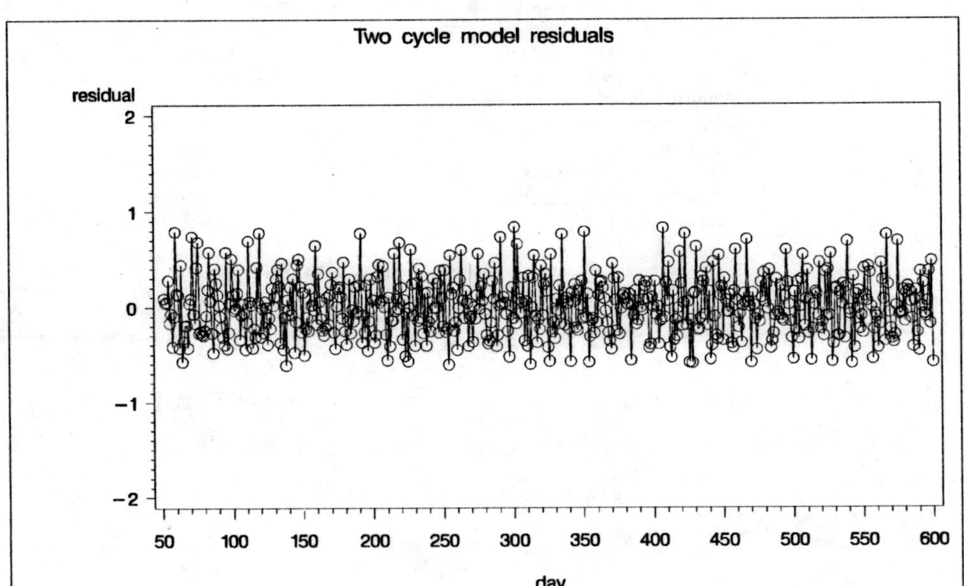

Example 29.3. Modeling Long Seasonal Patterns

In this example the use of the UCM procedure to model complex seasonal patterns is illustrated. Only a broad outline of the analysis is presented. The time series used in this example consists of number of calls received per shift at a call center. Each shift is of a three-hour duration, and the first shift of the day begins at midnight, resulting in eight shifts per day. The observations are available from December 15, 1999, up to April 30, 2000. Initial exploration of the series clearly shows that the time of the day and the day of the week have a significant influence on the number of calls received; however, the series does not show any significant trend. This suggests a simple random walk trend model along with a seasonal component with season length of 56. After fitting this model and examining the residual plots (not shown), the following modified model seems to fit the data quite well.

```
proc ucm data=callcenter;
    id datetime interval=dthour3;
    model calls;
    irregular;
    level;
    season length=56 type=trig;
    deplag lags=2;
    estimate back=112;
    forecast back=112 lead = 112;
run;
```

Along with the seasonal component of length 56 and the level and irregular components, this model also includes two lags of the dependent variable. The last two weeks of the data are withheld to examine the forecasting performance of the model on the observed data. The table in Output 29.3.1 shows the fit statistics for this model, and the plot in Output 29.3.2 shows the fit of the model on the withheld data.

Output 29.3.1. Model Fit for the Saturated Seasonal Model

```
                         The UCM Procedure

                 Fit Statistics Based on Residuals

         Mean Squared Error                          93.91316
         Root Mean Squared Error                      9.69088
         Mean Absolute Percentage Error              19.75413
         Maximum Percent Error                     1102.00394
         R-Square                                     0.98664
         Adjusted R-Square                            0.98666
         Random Walk R-Square                         0.97575
         Amemiya's Adjusted R-Square                  0.98664

           Number of non-missing residuals used for
              computing the fit statistics = 934
```

Output 29.3.2. Forecasts for the Saturated Seasonal Model

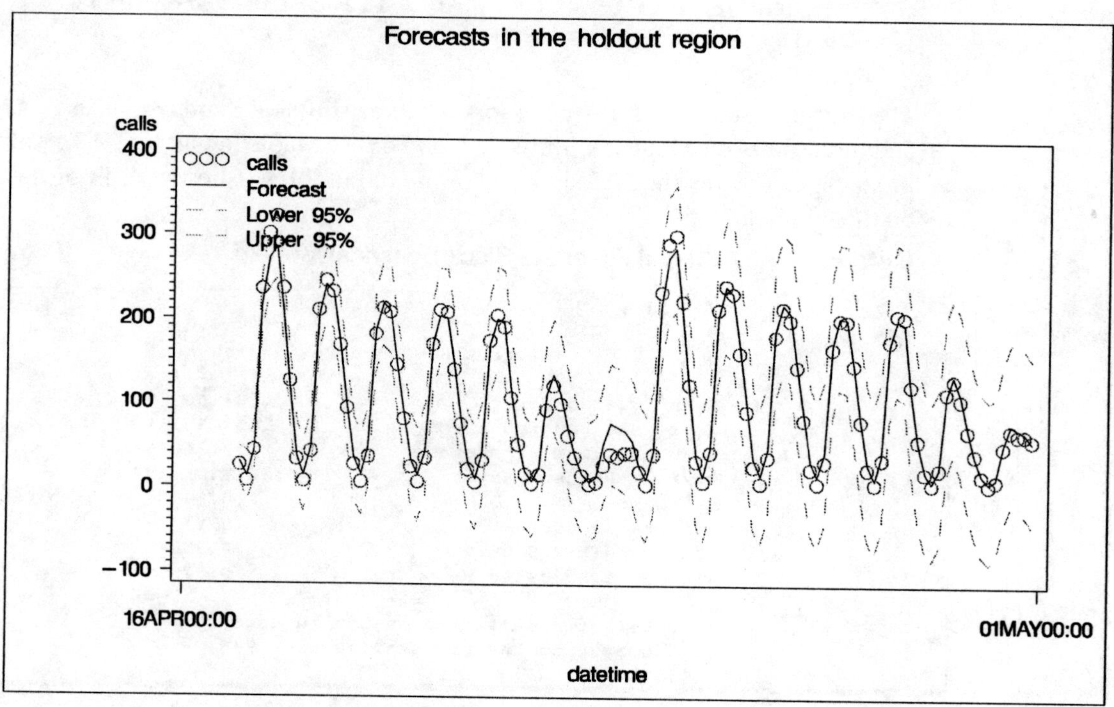

This model fits the data well; however, it takes a considerable amount of time to estimate because the dimension of the state vector in the underlying state space model is large, about 60 (see "Details"). This problem becomes more acute for larger season lengths. More importantly, this model does not offer any insight into the structure of the particular seasonal pattern present at this call center; for example, it may be possible that a similar calling pattern may repeat during each day of the week except for different mean number of calls for different days of the week. Such a pattern is implied by a combination of two components, a simple seasonal of season length 8, for capturing the within day variation, and a block seasonal component of 7 blocks (a block for each day of the week) with block size of 8 that models the day to day variation during the week. The state vector of this model has dimension 17. Examination of the fit of this model reveals that the model fit is poorer than the above saturated seasonal model. The forecasts for Sundays and Mondays are particularly bad. This behavior can be improved somewhat by including dummy variables corresponding to some of the shifts on these days. The following statements specify one such model.

```
proc ucm data=callcenter;
    id datetime interval=dthour3;
    model calls = s_shift3 s_shift4 s_shift6
                  m_shift1 m_shift3 m_shift6;
    irregular;
    level;
    season length=8 type=trig;
    blockseason nblocks=7 blocksize=8 type=trig;
    deplag lags=2;
    estimate back=112;
    forecast back=112 lead = 112 print=forecasts;
run;
```

The model contains dummy regressors for three shifts on Sundays, shifts 3, 4, and 6, and three shifts on Mondays, shifts 1, 3, and 6. The table in Output 29.3.3 shows the fit statistics for this model, and the plot in Output 29.3.4 shows the fit of the model on the withheld data.

Output 29.3.3. Model Fit for the Block Seasonal Model

```
                         The UCM Procedure

                 Fit Statistics Based on Residuals

         Mean Squared Error                          183.66579
         Root Mean Squared Error                      13.55234
         Mean Absolute Percentage Error               38.34285
         Maximum Percent Error                       447.05942
         R-Square                                      0.97387
         Adjusted R-Square                             0.97373
         Random Walk R-Square                          0.95248
         Amemiya's Adjusted R-Square                   0.97354

           Number of non-missing residuals used for
              computing the fit statistics = 936
```

Output 29.3.4. Forecasts for the Block Seasonal Model

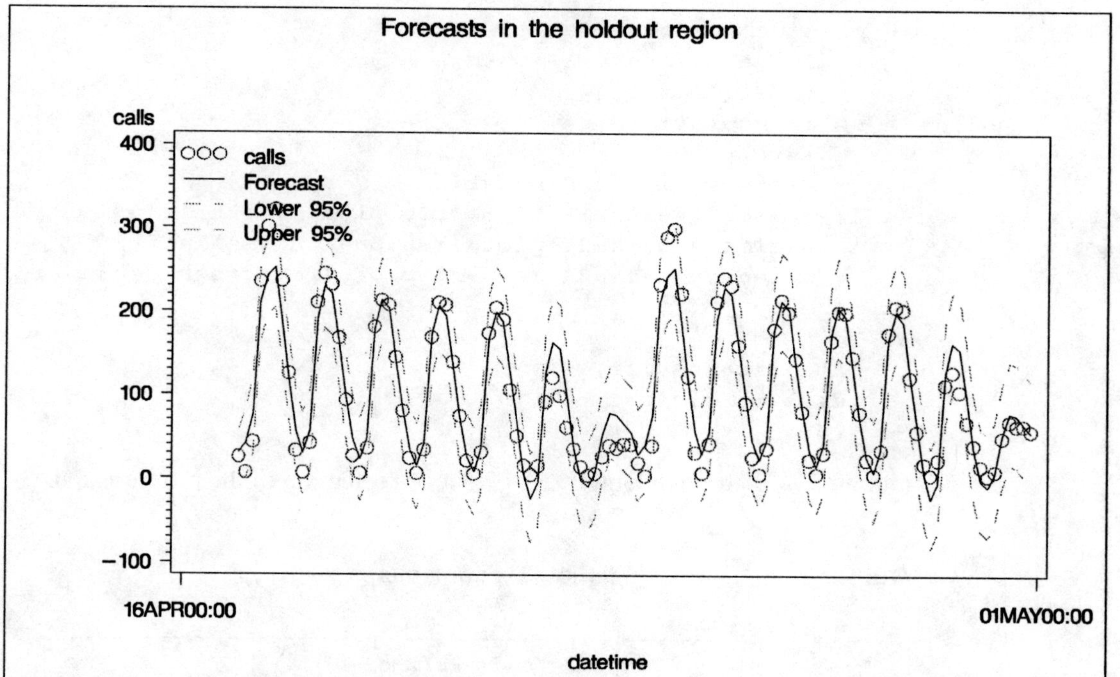

This model can be improved further using similar considerations. The use of block seasonals is only one of several ways to model seasonals with long season lengths. Alternatively, you can also use a smaller set of harmonics than the full set used in the saturated model. This is done by specifying a separate cycle statement for each of the harmonics included in the model.

Example 29.4. Illustration of ODS Graphics (Experimental)

This example illustrates the use of experimental ODS graphics. The graphical displays are requested by specifying the experimental ODS GRAPHICS statement. For general information about ODS graphics, see Chapter 9, "Statistical Graphics Using ODS." For specific information about the graphics available in the UCM procedure, see the "ODS Graphics" section on page 1664.

The following code shows how you can use the PLOT= option in different statements of the UCM procedure to get useful plots for the Airline Passenger example discussed earlier; see Example 29.1. The PLOT=SMOOTH option in the SEASON statement requests plotting of the smoothed estimate of that seasonal component. The use of PLOT=(RESIDUAL NORMAL ACF) in the ESTIMATE statement produces the time series plot of residuals, the histogram of residuals, and the autocorrelation plot of residuals, respectively. Finally, the use of PLOT=(FORECASTS DECOMP) option in the FORECAST statement produces the forecast, the trend, and the trend plus season plots.

```
ods html;
ods graphics on;

proc ucm data=series_g;
   id date interval=month;
   model logair;
   irregular;
   level;
   slope variance=0 noest;
   season length=12 type=trig plot=smooth;
   estimate back=24 plot=(residual normal acf);
   forecast back=24 lead=36 plot=(forecasts decomp);
run;

ods graphics off;
ods html close;
```

Output 29.4.1 through Output 29.4.7 show a selection of the plots created.

Output 29.4.1. Residual Plot (Experimental)

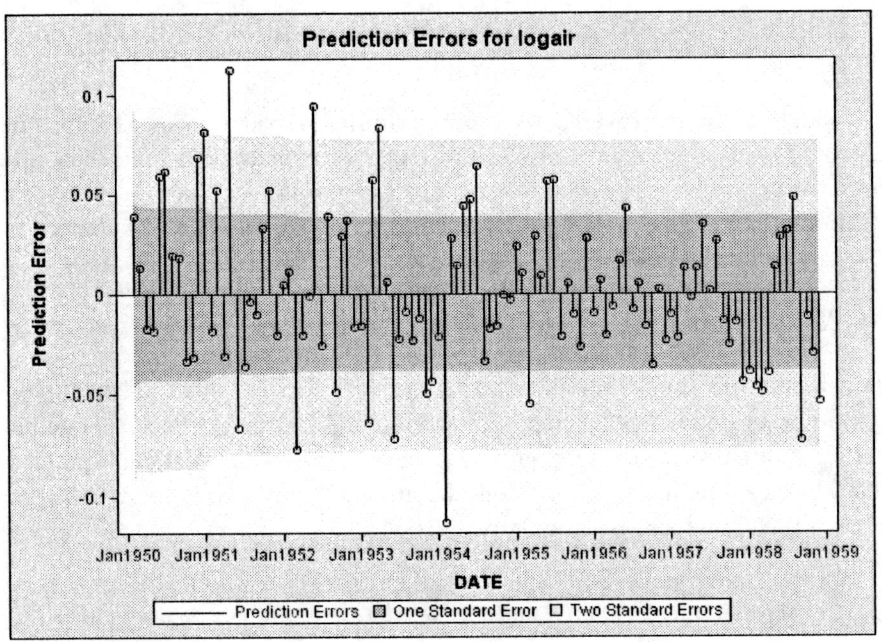

Output 29.4.2. Residual Histogram (Experimental)

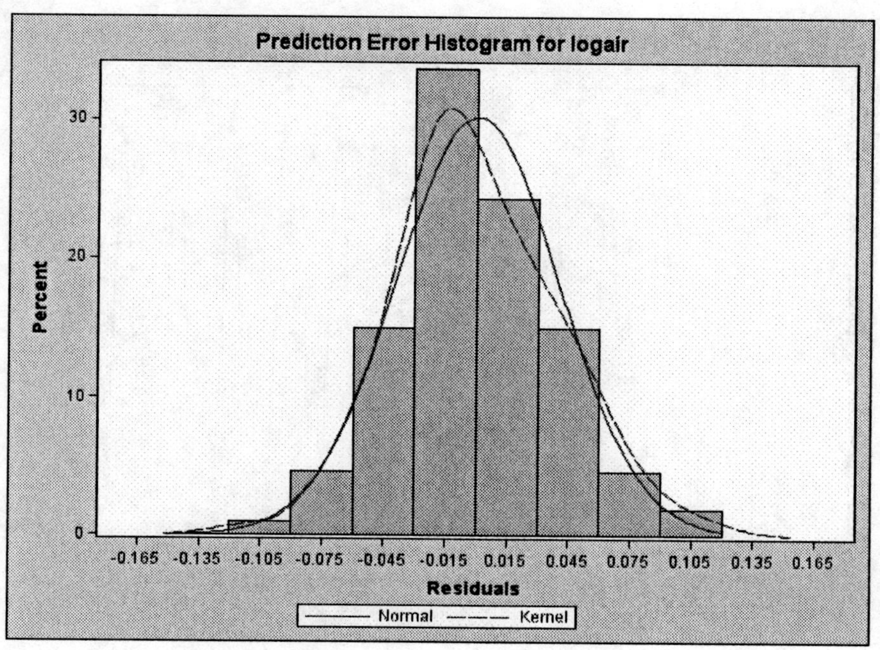

Output 29.4.3. Residual Autocorrelations (Experimental)

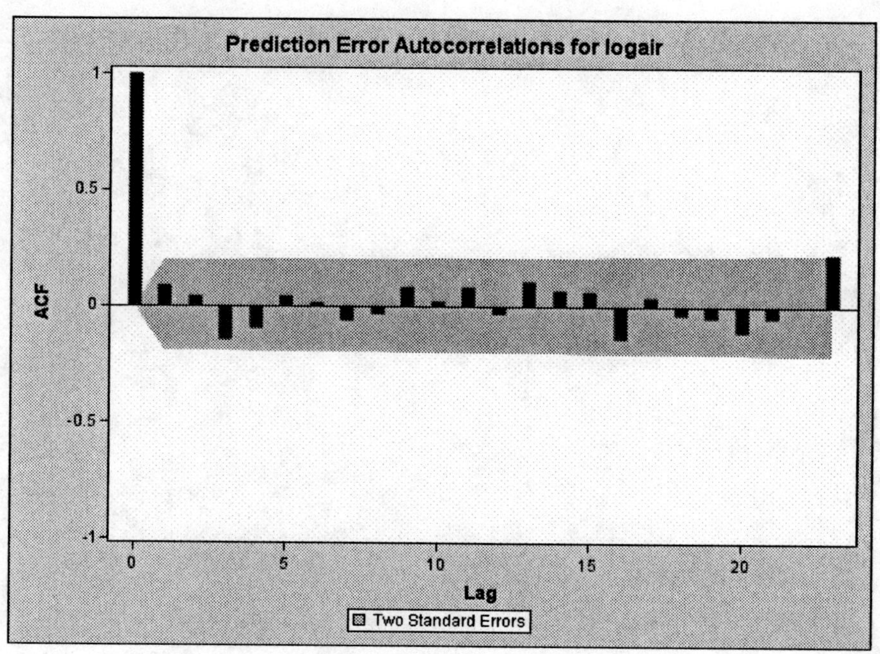

Output 29.4.4. Smoothed Seasonal (Experimental)

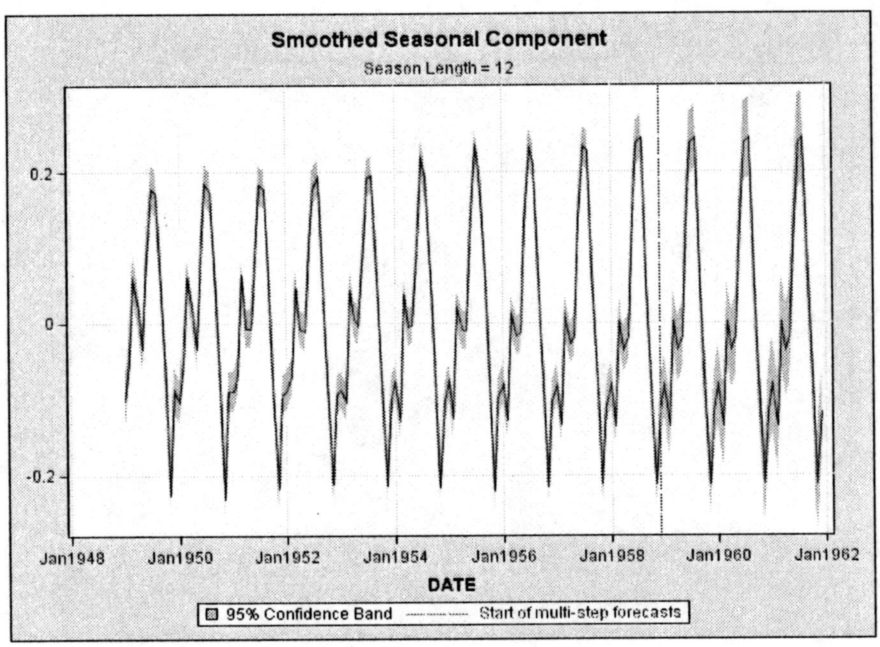

Output 29.4.5. Series Forecasts (Experimental)

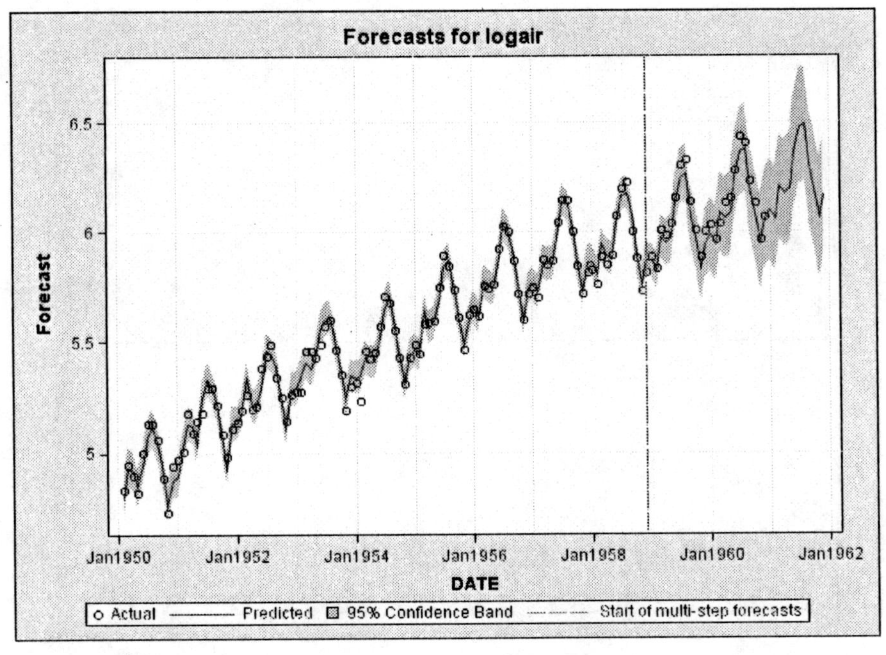

Output 29.4.6. Trend Plot (Experimental)

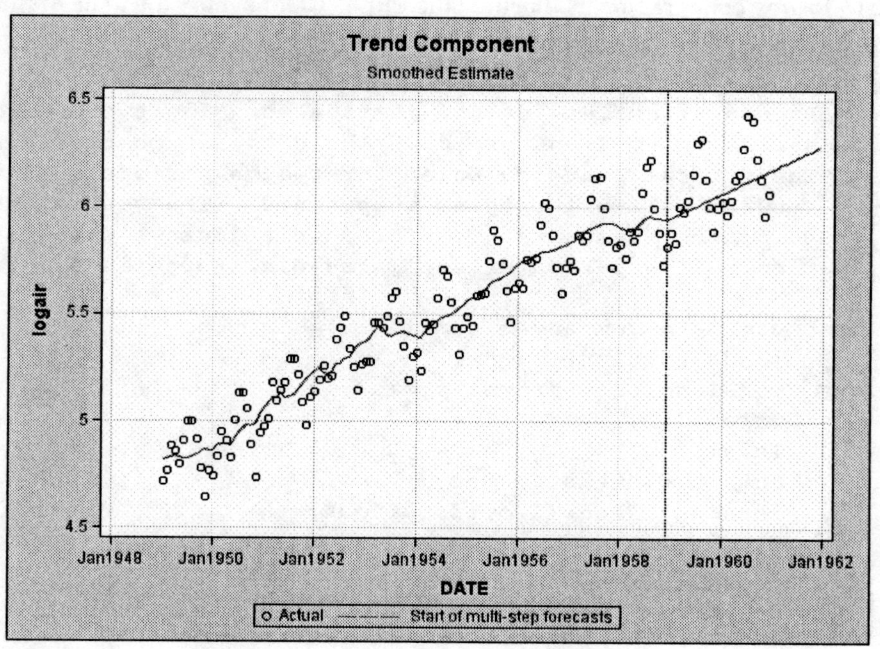

Output 29.4.7. Trend Plus Season (Experimental)

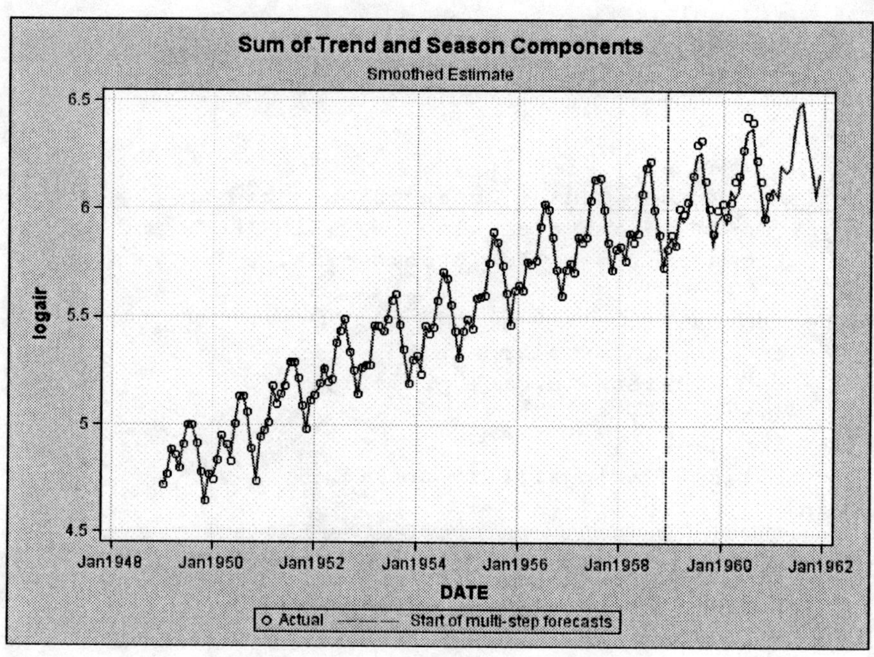

Example 29.5. Many Syntax Illustrations

The following code fragments illustrate the PROC UCM syntax for some of the commonly needed modeling activities.

```
/* Dependent series, sales, is modeled using two predictor
   series, promo1 and promo2.  The data are quarterly.
   The forecasts are computed for twelve periods in the
   future.  All printing is suppressed.  The series and
   component forecasts are stored in an output data set,
   f_out.  The parameter estimates are stored in e_out;
*/
proc ucm data=company_x noprint;
     id date interval=qtr;
     model sales = promo1 promo2;
     irregular;
     level;
     estimate outest=e_out;
     forecast lead=12 outfor=f_out;
run;


/* Request printing of the filtered and smoothed seasonal
   component.
*/
proc ucm data=company_x;
     id date interval=qtr;
     model sales = promo1 promo2;
     irregular;
     level;
     season length=4 print=(filter smooth);
run;


/* Control the span of observations used in the estimation
   of model parameters using the SKIPFIRST= and BACK=
   options in the ESTIMATE statement.
*/
proc ucm data=company_x;
     id date interval=month;
     model sales = promo1 promo2;
     irregular;
     level;
     estimate skipfirst=10 back=12;
run;


/* Supply starting values for parameters. */
proc ucm data=company_x;
     model sales;
     irregular;
     level variance=10.3;
     deplag lags=2 phi=0.2 -1.8;
run;
```

```
/* Fix parameter values */
proc ucm data=company_x;
     model sales;
     irregular;
     level variance=10.3 noest;
     cycle period=4 noest=period;
     deplag lags=2 phi=0.2 -1.8 noest;
run;


/* Using cycles to get an "unsaturated" seasonal model.
   A monthly seasonal model using only the first three
   harmonics.
*/
proc ucm data=company_x;
     model sales;
     irregular;
     level variance=10.3 noest;
     cycle period=12 rho=1 noest=(period rho);
     cycle period=6 rho=1 noest=(period rho);
     cycle period=4 rho=1 noest=(period rho);
run;
```

References

Anderson, T.W. (1971), *The Statistical Analysis of Time Series,* New York: John Wiley & Sons, Inc.

Bloomfield, P. (2000), *Fourier Analysis of Time Series, Second Edition,* New York: John Wiley & Sons, Inc.

Box, G.E.P. and Jenkins, G.M. (1976), *Time Series Analysis: Forecasting and Control,* San Francisco: Holden-Day.

Cobb, G.W. (1978), "The Problem of the Nile: Conditional Solution to a Change Point Problem," *Biometrika,* 65, 243-251.

Durbin, J. and Koopman, S.J. (2001), *Time Series Analysis by State Space Methods,* Oxford: Oxford University Press.

Harvey, A.C. (1989), *Forecasting, Structural Time Series Models and the Kalman Filter,* Cambridge:Cambridge University Press.

Harvey, A.C. (2001), "Testing in Unobserved Components Models," *Journal of Forecasting,* 20, 1-19.

West, M. and Harrison, J. (1999) *Bayesian Forecasting and Dynamic Models,* 2nd ed, New York: Springer-Verlag.

Printed in the United States
18124LVS00004B/22

9 785551 305897

SAS Publishing

SAS/ETS® 9.1 User's Guide

This title serves as a complete reference to SAS/ETS software, which provides the most comprehensive and advanced tools for econometrics, time series analysis, and forecasting for novice and expert users in business, academia, and government. It guides you through the analysis and forecasting of such features as

- **univariate and multivariate time series**
- **cross-sectional time series**
- **seasonal adjustments**
- **multiequational nonlinear models**
- **discrete choice models**
- **limited dependent variable models**
- **portfolio analysis**
- **generation of financial reports.**

Introductory and advanced examples are included for each procedure. New for SAS/ETS 9.1 are procedures for regression based on maximum entropy, for UCM models, and for analyzing and managing transactional data. Several enhancements to existing procedures such as automatic outlier detection for time series and simulated method of moments estimation for multiequational models, with many new examples, are also included.

In addition, you can find complete information about two easy-to-use point-and-click applications: the Time Series Forecasting System, for automatic and interactive time series modeling and forecasting, and the Investment Analysis System, for time-value of money analysis of a variety of investments.

This title is also available online.

Audience

This title serves as a reference for users of SAS/ETS software.

ISBN 1-59047-244-6